# The Miracle Has Landed

*To the Amazin' 1969 Mets, especially those not with us to celebrate the Miracle turning 40:*

*Tommie Agee*
*Don Cardwell*
*Donn Clendenon*
*Danny Frisella*
*Cal Koonce*
*Tug McGraw*
*Rube Walker*
*Eddie Yost*
*Red Murff*
*Bob Murphy*
*Johnny Murphy*
*Lindsey Nelson*
*Joan Payson*
*and none of it would have been possible without Gil Hodges*

*Also in remembrance of those who witnessed the Miracle taking shape and for that big old ballpark where they saw it all come together, a place where black cats emerged, shoe polish smudged at the precise moment, and deficits disappeared in the year that man landed on the moon. No longer with us but forever Amazin'.*

# The Miracle Has Landed

***The Amazin' Story of How the 1969 Mets Shocked the World***


Edited by

Matthew Silverman and Ken Samelson

Copy editors Len Levin and Bill Nowlin



Produced in association with the

Society for American Baseball Research (SABR)

HANOVER, MASSACHUSETTS

Topps® baseball cards that appear at the beginnings of essays are courtesy of the Topps Company, Inc. Reprinted with permission.



Cover design: Garrett Cullen
Front cover photo: Focus on Sport/Getty Images
Back cover: Ernest Sisto/New York Times/Getty Images

Matthew Silverman and Ken Samelson, Editors. *The Miracle Has Landed: The Amazin' Story of How the 1969 Mets Shocked the World*
ISBN: 978-1-934186-17-6
Library of Congress information on file with the publisher



Maple Street Press LLC
155 Webster St, Ste. B
Hanover, MA 02339
*www.maplestreetpress.com*

Printed in the USA
09 7 6 5 4 3 2 First Edition

# Table of Contents

## Manager and Coaches



## Front Office and Announcers



## The Miracle Has Landed



## Perspectives and Conclusions



## Appendix

Photo by Keith Hernandez

# Foreword

by Jerry Koosman

With the count one ball and two strikes on Davey Johnson and the crowd so loud that you could hardly hear yourself think, I threw a fastball with all I had in the hopes it would be in the strike zone, and alas, it was. With the mighty swing of the bat by a second baseman who would one day hit 40 home runs in a season, Davey Johnson hit a fly ball to left field that just about made my heart stop. Because the crowd was so loud, I couldn't judge by the sound of the bat how hard it was hit. I turned around to look at Cleon Jones in left field and he was running back toward the wall. I thought to myself, "Oh, no." With a Baltimore runner on first, a home run would tie Game Five of the World Series.

Just then, Cleon stopped, raised his glove and caught the ball. I was saying to myself, "Squeeze it, squeeze it, don't let it drop out." He went down on one knee as if to say, "Thank you, Lord. The game is over." I turned to look at my catcher, Jerry Grote and he was running toward me on the mound. I jumped up in the air and he caught me and I gave him a big hug. The negative thoughts of possibly losing the game by making a mistake had left my mind and were replaced instantly with "We are world champs. The game is over. We don't need to go back to Baltimore!"

Spring training had started seven months earlier in St. Petersburg, Florida. The spring of 1969 had begun with anticipation of having another personally good year and avoiding the sophmore jinx, as was commonly mentioned by the writers. The spring went well under the guiding hands and great mind of Gil Hodges, our second-year manager, who by the way, had a fun time managing us in 1968 in his first year with the Mets. Some trades had been made and we were anxious to meet our new teamates and see what they could do to improve our second-to-last-place record in the league from the year before.

Spring training is hard and you go through some physically stressful times, but it is something that has to be done to get in shape and besides, it's better than being at home in the cold winter of Minnesota. It was fun seeing your teammates again and certainly under different circumstances from just one year earlier in 1968, when I'd had no idea if I would make the big club or not. This time I was coming to spring training knowing that a job was waiting for me as one of the Mets starting pitchers. All I had to do was get in good shape without hurting my arm.

We left spring training with the feeling that we had a better team, a stricter manager, and we certainly knew our coaches and teamates better. With all the rehearsals of covering first base, pickoff plays, fielding balls hit back at us, rundowns, backing up bases, bunting practice, and everything else that goes into spring training, we felt we were prepared to do much better this season as the plane lifted off the runway on its way to New York. Spring training gets to be long after six or seven weeks of punishing your body in the warm humid air. We were all looking forward to a change of cooler air, a larger ballpark, a nicer locker room, bigger crowds, and hopefully more wins for our team.

It was a fun and relaxing plane ride, but when the suburbs of New York City started to appear out of the plane window during our descent, anticipation of seeing Shea Stadium lingered as we made our way over miles of the great city toward LaGuardia Airport. Finally, there it was, looming outside of the window by my seat, the grass was green, and the colors blue and orange stood out as though it had just been painted. Home at last. This was going to be my home for the next six months and hopefully a happy successful home where all the fans felt like they were your family coming to root you on every night.

This year, 1969, is broken down into minute stories, with detailed biographies of players and coaches and their thoughts from that great season and how it compared with other memorable moments of their careers and lives. This is a book of that remarkable year where the Mets finally made it from last to first place in the National League and went on to win the World Series. Many books have been written about our team that year, but I don't think any have reached the all inclusive, day-to-day happenings as this wonderful time piece displaying the pages of history. I am truly proud to be a part of this 1969 Mets championship team and to have the privilege of writing this foreword. I hope you enjoy the book as I am sure it will be the closest thing to putting you in our place during that exciting year.

— *The Kooz*

# Introduction
## A Magic Summer: Forty Years Later

by Stanley Cohen

Now, 40 years after the fact, the "Miracle" has finally become the property of history. Two generations have quickly slipped by. You need to be in your 50s to have a clear recollection of the Legend of the 1969 Mets and what they meant, banked against the futility of the years that preceded them. Today, most Met fans have heard about the Miracle Mets from their fathers or uncles or from the vast literature that documented that unlikely season, but they were not there when it happened; they have not experienced it first hand; they do not know what it felt like to live through that season day by day, to see the impossible evolve first into the improbable and then, astonishingly, into the inevitable. A distance of 40 years confers any story to the pages of history. Enshrined in the past, it can no longer be treated with the immediacy of current events.

It is now a shade more than 20 years since I began my trek through the 1960s, gathering material for a retrospective on the '69 Mets that became *A Magic Summer*. The project was not an inspiration of my own. If the truth be told, I had been a Yankees fan since the 1940s. I was a native son of the Bronx, growing up a long walk from Yankee Stadium, and I had spent a good part of my youth jeering at the few hapless Dodgers and Giants fans that I ran into. But when our inter-borough rivals left town and the Mets took their place, I was well beyond the age of such adolescent bickering. New York City had educated me at its own cost, right through college, and there was no one, with the possible exception of my father, who embraced the city with greater devotion.

So I had no trouble rooting for the Mets while still investing my principal allegiance with the Yankees. During the 1969 season, with the Yankees flying well below the radar, I followed the fortunes of the Mets closely and with enthusiasm. On that fabled afternoon in mid-October I could be seen dancing a hora on Madison Avenue and 40th Street after watching them win the World Series on TV at the bar of a nearby Italian restaurant.

The project of bringing the '69 Mets back to life came looking for me. I had previously written two well received sports books, and an editor from what was then Harcourt Brace Jovanovich publishers sought me out through my agent. That was early in 1986. Spring training was just getting under way and the Mets, having won 98 games in 1985 and finishing just three games back of the division-winning Cardinals, were deemed a live bet to win the National League pennant. My charge was to reconstruct the championship season, incorporating the views and recollections of members of that team.

Recreating the season would not be a problem. The beat writers for the daily newspapers, particularly the *New York Times*, still described each day's game in full detail back then, instead of filling the space with quotes and ruminations from the clubhouse, as is the fashion today. The challenge was to locate the players and get them to sit for interviews that offered them no profit of any kind. There was no Internet, at least none that had come to my attention, in the '80s, and Google was the last name of a comic character whose first name was Barney.

Playing the percentages, I chose to start with players who were closest to home. A friend of mine was acquainted with Art Shamsky who had an apartment in the East 50s, not far from where I had an office at the time. Shamsky was more than gracious and looking not far removed from playing shape. It was mid-morning and he put up a fresh pot of coffee and leisurely shared his memories of the season with me. He also pointed the way to where I might find some of his former teammates.

If my visit with Shamsky offered the brightest promise of things to come, I soon came upon the first of several bumps in the road. Tommie Agee resided in the New York area and worked in a variety of youth programs for the New York City Police Department. I had both his home and business telephone numbers and called several times but he adamantly refused to speak with me except for financial consideration. Some time later, I interviewed Cleon Jones, up from Alabama and visiting his buddy Agee in New York, but while Cleon spoke freely, Agee kept his silence. In July of 1986, having managed to meet with almost every member of the '69 team, I was in the Mets clubhouse for Old Timers Day, and I took one more shot at Agee. A number of the players near his locker—Wayne Garrett and Ken Boswell among them—greeted me warmly and offered testimony in my behalf, but Agee was determined to let the past stand on its own. He continued to work with youth in the New York area, engaging in many charitable events, until 2001 when he died of a heart attack at the age of 53.

The only other player missing from the book is Donn Clendenon. Clendenon had been practicing law in the Pittsburgh area, but every attempt to reach him went for naught. The Mets public relations office, which helped me to make other contacts, could not locate him either. Years later, I learned that he had been in a rehab center for drug addiction at the time. He eventually kicked the habit and resumed his law practice in South Dakota, where he also worked as a drug counselor. He died of leukemia in 2005 at the age of 70.

I located many of the other players through the good offices of *The Sporting News*, the weekly newspaper based in St. Louis, which was known back then as baseball's bible. The paper routinely provided anyone who asked with the home addresses, but not the phone numbers, of baseball players past and present. My publisher wrote to each of the players advising them of my mission. Most of them had listed telephone numbers, and I followed each letter with a phone call. To my delight and surprise, almost to a man, they seemed pleased to speak with me and eager to help with a person-to-person interview.

The only exception was Ron Swoboda. Swoboda was living in Phoenix and serving as sports director of a local television station. He told me, very politely, that he did not wish to give me an interview. He never offered a reason for turning me down but continued to do so, despite my persistence, as if it was just something he preferred not to do. I tried once more when I came to Phoenix in the brutal heat of an Arizona summer to meet with Gary Gentry, who was working as a real estate developer. Gentry and I had a friendly chat in a downtown Phoenix bar and following the interview he offered to plead my case with Swoboda. When I called later that day, Swoboda agreed to meet with me. "I checked you out with Gentry," he told me. "He said you were harmless." Despite my harmlessness, Swoboda was exceptionally tentative for at least half an hour before loosening up and becoming a touch friendly.

A number of players, even some who clearly welcomed the opportunity to relive their time of glory, seemed to be feeling me out at first meeting, measuring each response against the possibility that I might be starting out slowly on the way to probing areas that best remained untouched. It was the irrepressible Tug McGraw who chose to enlighten me. I met with him in his office in Media, Pennsylvania, a small town not far from Philadelphia. One-to-one, Tug was every bit the engaging, stimulating personality he was in public. He had a television sports show in Philadelphia, but his heart was clearly in an eponymous foundation called Tug McGraw Resources whose objective it was to come to the aid of young people who needed help. Tug defined a "special person" as anyone who needed help or anyone who gave it. He also explained why some players might be hesitant to talk about their playing days.

He told me that writers and reporters sometimes come looking for a story based on rumors they may have heard that one player or another had strayed from the straight-and-narrow while he was on the road—possible drug or alcohol abuse, late-night shenanigans of various types, or perhaps a gambling habit. It would not necessarily be the player you're asking for the interview who is suspect, but perhaps a friend of his that you're looking to get information on. Players tend to be cautious and protective of one another. "As for me," Tug said playfully, "I tried Coke once but I couldn't get the bottle in my nose."

McGraw died of a malignant brain tumor in 2004 at the age of 53; his foundation still exists and continues its charitable work in his name.

The other interviews with the retired players were much like conversations you might have after meeting strangers with whom you find common ground and memories that you both share and treasure. There was Ed Kranepool with whom I spoke at his plant in Jamaica, Queens, where he manufactured marketing displays for stores and exhibit booths; Ed Charles in his apartment in the Washington Heights section of Manhattan; Bud Harrelson, the third-base coach of the Mets, in the team's clubhouse before an afternoon game. On the road I chatted with Jerry Koosman, who met me at the Minneapolis airport after I had flown in from late-night meetings with Al Weis and J.C. Martin in the suburbs of Chicago; Jerry Grote in his real estate office in San Antonio and Ken Boswell at a hotel bar in Austin, Texas; Wayne Garrett, at a luncheon diner in the Sarasota airport; and Dr. Ron Taylor at Exhibition Stadium in Toronto, where he served as team physician for the Toronto Blue Jays. In town for the Mets Old Timers Day, Jim McAndrew and Don Cardwell met with me in the lobby of the Hyatt Hotel on 42nd Street in Manhattan and Cal Koonce in the Mets clubhouse. Koonce died in 1993 of lymphoma; Cardwell passed in 2007 as a result of Pick's disease, a rare neurodegenerative disease.

Photo courtesy metsilverman.com

*Cooperstown holds a place for the 1969 Mets and their artifacts.*

Two players—Tom Seaver and Nolan Ryan—were still active in 1986, and getting to them at the start of the 1986 season presented some logistical problems. I needed to go through the public relations departments of their respective teams and arranging the appointments wasn't easy. Ryan was pitching for the Houston Astros in 1986, and they were coming to New York early in the season. I was to meet with Ryan in the Houston clubhouse at 5 p.m. on the day of the game. We were both there but Ryan seemed to have other priorities. He told me he would not be able to speak with me until after batting practice, which began at 6 p.m. and lasted for about 40 minutes. It was a cold night, with rain on the way, and I waited in the dugout while Ryan shagged balls in the outfield. When he returned to the dugout, other writers were waiting for him.

A few nights earlier, Roger Clemens had struck out 20 batters in a game, breaking by one the record held by Ryan and three others, and newspaper reporters were understandably eager to get his reaction. So Ryan held what amounted to a press conference, each of us taking turns asking a question. I felt out of place pursuing his recollection of 1969 while the focus for everyone else was on the present day. As it turned out, it was not much of an interview, Ryan responding to questions in a clipped, perfunctory manner. He seemed to care little about having won a World Series at age 22 in only his second full season with the Mets. My overall reaction to Ryan reaffirmed how I felt about him as pitcher—more sizzle than substance. For all his strikeouts and no-hitters, Nolan Ryan was never really a winner.

Tom Seaver could not have provided a sharper contrast. He was pitching for the Chicago White Sox in 1986, in what would be the last of his 20 big league seasons, and it was not the best of times for Seaver. His mother had recently passed away and he was impatiently awaiting a trade to Boston that would bring him closer to his home in Greenwich, Connecticut. Throughout my brief stay in Chicago I was expecting a message saying that Tom couldn't make it. But he did. He showed up in the White Sox clubhouse at precisely the appointed time. It was about four hours before a game with the Minnesota Twins and he suggested that we conduct the interview in the Sox dugout. From the outset, it was clear that Seaver was preoccupied. This was not where he wanted to be right now but he had made a commitment and he would keep it. I told him that I understood that conditions were not ideal for him, and I asked him how much time he would offer. "Whatever you need," he said. He answered every question thoughtfully and with typical Seaver precision. The interview lasted about 45 minutes. When I had what I needed, I thanked him and told him I appreciated his following through despite his woes. He wished me luck with the book and gave me his home phone number in the event I needed anything else.

I recently saw Seaver doing a television interview with Tim McCarver. He was discussing his work as a vintner in Calistoga, California. He told McCarver that his day begins at 6 a.m. and he described how he pays strict attention to every detail. He said it was lot like pitching. It required total commitment and you could not cut corners; you had to give it all the time that was necessary. I thought back to our interview. For Seaver it was just another job that you had to perform and you had to do it right. Not for nothing was Tom Seaver known to the Mets as The Franchise.

Stanley Cohen is author of eight books and an award-winning journalist. *A Magic Summer* was re-released by Skyhorse Publishing in 2009.

## 1969: Mets

by Robert L. Harrison

Even cold New Yorkers
turn warm when thoughts
go back to that misty spring
when Flushing lights
were brighter than the stars.

For seven years laughter had held
its grip around the fans' pulse.

Each spring would mock further
any hope of them rising from the ashes.

For errors dig deep as they became
their players last resting stop before retirement.

But the world wobbles, not turns,
and trades and rookies came knocking,
as they were tossed up and grabbed
by hungry management ready for a fix.

And they all fit into the puzzle.
And Hodges taught them well.
And each one caught the fever.

They then took the league for a ride
that shocked and delighted
and pulled off the fairy tale
ending that still lives today.

For those amazing ones
found the world off guard,
when for one shining season
they rode the crest of the wave.

From *Green Fields and White Lines: Baseball Poems* (McFarland & Co., 1995).

# Acknowledgments

While the 1969 Mets seemingly came out of nowhere, *The Miracle Has Landed* is a long time in coming. The last two and a half years proved arduous in getting this book from plan to print. *The Miracle Has Landed* is the result of a concentrated volunteer effort by SABR—the Society of American Baseball Research—and by professionals ranging from diehard Mets fans to Mets haters who still gave their time and energy to this 30-month project. Everyone who contributed, whether it be bios, essays, sidebars, photos, collections, or editing skills, transformed this project from miracle to reality.

The first round of thanks goes to the men who appear in the front portion of the book: Jerry Koosman for writing the foreword, Stanley Cohen for providing an introduction, and Robert L. Harrison for adding a poetic perspective. And an added thanks to Irv Goldfarb who helped get Kooz to write the foreword.

Shannon Forde and Jay Horwitz of the New York Mets responded to numerous requests over the length of the project. The late Jim Plummer, longtime Mets employee and director of corporate services, helped coordinate the Ed Kranepool interview.

In addition to all the authors listed in the Contributors section, a special thanks goes to Doug Feldmann, author of *Miracle Collapse: The 1969 Chicago Cubs* (Lincoln: University of Nebraska Press—available in paperback in October 2009) for allowing us to use an excerpt from his book. And to Rob Taylor and Elaine Maruhn at UNP for handling the details. A special note of appreciation to Talmage Boston, who let us use and update a section of his book *Baseball and the Baby Boomer: A History, Commentary, and Memoir*, published in 2009 by Bright Sky Press. Greg W. Prince gave us leave to use bits of his longer piece on the 1969 Mets from the *Maple Street Press 2009 Mets Annual* to fill holes that sprung up along the way. Mark Armour, who also contributed a bio, served as point man in the early going, putting up the "want-ads" for writers online, and assembling the editors on this project. Appreciation goes to David Raglin and Mark Pattison, editors of *Sock It to 'em Tigers: The Incredible Story of the 1968 Detroit Tigers* (Maple Street Press, 2008) for providing much needed advice.

Of course, this wouldn't be a book without the publisher. As always, Maple Street Press was magnificent in transforming jottings and half-baked ideas from the editors into coherent and attractive pages: their patience and skill was never more evident than in this project. Thanks to publisher Jim Walsh, as well as Ryan Bray, Jon Franke, and the man who has put together more Mets pages since 2008 than anyone outside the club's employ: Bryan Davidson.

Photos are a crucial part of recreating that summer and fall of four decades ago. Great effort was put into compiling a collection of images to illustrates the time and team, including many photos never before seen in print. Since life has certainly gone on since 1969, we included some photos of what some of those legends of yore look like now thanks to opportunities at recent events at Citi Field as well as Shea Stadium, the site of the Miracle that lives in our memory—and in these pages.

Thanks starts with Dan Carubia, whose collection of Mets photos—from the 1970s to the last day at Shea to the salute to the '69 Mets at Citi Field—have been enormously helpful. Also to Gene Caputo, who made the wise choice of a World Series ticket in lieu of a birthday party in October 1969, and who scanned the best part of his 1969 Mets collection for use in this book. Glen Vasey, an Orioles fan who penned a piece from the 1969 Baltimore perspective, offered a treasure trove of signed Mets images from the debut of the world championship highlight film in Baltimore that winter. Lou Longobardi offered his piece of the Shea wall, along with the story and photos to boot. *Cubs by the Numbers* co-author and *bleedcubbieblue.com* maestro Al Yellon generously agreed to write what it felt like watching a dream season burst into flames before a boy's very eyes.

And a special thanks to the company that turned out having more images in the book than any other source: Topps Company, Inc. Clay Luraschi of Topps generously gave us permission to use dozens of images. Jason Fry kindheartedly entrusted us with his collection of Topps cards of every 1969 Met.

On the subject of long-kept photos, special thanks go to *Mets Inside Pitch,* chronicler of the Mets in the printed world for more than a quarter century. Andy Esposito and crew generously lent us the magazine's entire 1969 collection and never said a word as we held onto it for more than a year.

The National Baseball Hall of Fame opened its files up to us and served as host for a day that was more than just file slogging in Cooperstown—it was a day with the '69 Mets in the A. Bartlett Giamatti Library. Thanks to John Horne, Tim Wiles, and Freddy Burowski.

Mike McCann's voice is familiar on WFAN, but his photos were a treasure to stumble onto at Mike McCann's Engaging Images (*mikemccann.blogspot.com*). As a kid in the upper deck on Opening Day 1969, he was wise enough to bring his camera, and wiser still to keep the photos all these years. Dwayne Labakas offered posed shots of most of the 1969 Mets, showing how they looked before destiny arrived. Thanks to Bill Cotter at *worldsfairphotos.com.*

And much appreciation to Keith Hernandez, the Mets great and great person, whose photography of the final day at Shea Stadium helped take us on the field and underneath the stands to catch a glimpse of the stars of 1969 Shea-ing goodbye.

Jacob Kanarek, author of *From First to Worst: The New York Mets, 1973–1977* and founder of *metsintheseventies.com* was not only cajoled into writing about what happened to the club after 1969, but he allowed us use of photos he purchased of that period as well. He arranged for one of the biggest finds of this endeavor, a previously unprocessed roll of film professionally taken at a Mets-Cubs game at Wrigley Field on July 14, 1969, Tom Seaver's first start following his "Imperfect Game." Seaver was great again, but the Cubs scraped together a run to win, 1–0. In the photos from that day scattered throughout this book, you can see the intensity on the faces of these rivals both before and during the game, and see the fun-loving side of players both great and obscure.

Andy Fogel allowed us to enter his home and photograph his Met-ca that is the envy of Citi Field and the memorabilia world. Mere photos do not do justice to the extent of his collection. James Genthner of Dr Pepper Snapple Group gave us permission to use the iconic advertising image of Yogi Berra with a Mets hat, Yoo-Hoo in hand.

Baseball Reference (*baseball-reference.com*) and Retrosheet (*retrosheet.org*) make doing this kind of book far easier and far more enjoyable than it would have been for past anniversaries of the '69 Mets. Thanks for making this information available. Help was provided by Loge 13 (*loge13.com*), Ultimate Mets (*ultimatemets.com*), Mets by the Numbers (*mbtn.net*), and Faith and Fear in Flushing (*faithandfear.blogharbor.com*). Any sites that helped but have been left out here will be mentioned in their entirety in the months and years to come on the web at *metsilverman.com,* where updates and inquiries for this book may be made going forward.

Many people born both before and after the great year of 1969 were helpful in this endeavor. This includes the players and coaches who listened to our questions and gave thoughtful answers, as well as the following: Dave Baldwin, Buzzie Bavasi, Clifford Blau, Craig Burley, Sheridan Gaspar, Bill Gilbert, Kelly McNamee, Rod Nelson, Andrew North, Shawn O'Hare, John Pardon, Robert Pizzella, Blair Rafuse, Tito Rondon, Alan Silverman, Dennis Van Langen, and Craig R. Wright. And a general note of thanks to those contacted yet whose work or ideas or name didn't up in the book. Thanks for your time, effort, interest, and understanding. As a note of information, all uncredited pieces in the book were written by Matthew Silverman.

On a personal note, much thanks to the Samelson family for their patience and enthusiasm. Continued appreciation also goes to the Silverman family for putting up with another Mets project—only this one never seemed to end. And it would be remiss not to mention an unknown black cat that started appearing outside the house soon after work on this project began in earnest. Like the feral cat that suddenly appeared at Shea Stadium and skulked past the on-deck circle and Cubs dugout on September 9, 1969, "Santo"—what else would you call a stray black cat in New York?—never tarried long before heading off on his own business. But a Santo appearance always got the work rolling again. And happy work it was.

# The Players

NEW YORK
Champions
1969

# Tommie Agee

by John Vorperian

| Season | Age | G | AB | R | H | 2B | 3B | HR | RBI | BB | SO | SB | CS | BA | OBP | SLG |
|---|---|---|---|---|---|---|---|---|---|---|---|---|---|---|---|---|
| 1969 Mets | 26 | 149 | 565 | 97 | 153 | 23 | 4 | 26 | 76 | 59 | 137 | 12 | 9 | .271 | .342 | .464 |
| Career 12 Years | – | 1129 | 3912 | 558 | 999 | 170 | 27 | 130 | 433 | 342 | 918 | 167 | 81 | .255 | .320 | .412 |

Tommie Agee was one of the key components to the 1969 Miracle Mets, solidifying the defense and serving as the club's chief power source, albeit from the leadoff spot. His on-field heroics during the '69 season—including socking the only home run to ever reach Shea Stadium's upper deck—helped propel the Mets to their first postseason berth and an unlikely journey to the World Series. Once there, Agee's heroics turned to legend. In Game Three of the Fall Classic he hit a leadoff home run and made two Amazin' catches to ensure a New York victory. He signed a large bonus with Cleveland, was a Rookie of the Year with the White Sox, and spent his last season in Houston and St. Louis, but he will always be remembered as a Met patrolling center field next to his childhood buddy.

Tommie Lee Agee was born August 9, 1942, in Magnolia, Alabama to Carrie and Joseph Agee. He had 10 siblings, nine of them girls. A year after Tommie's birth, the Agees moved to Mobile, Alabama. His father worked for the Aluminum Company of America and Agee grew up in a low income area that had segregated schools and parks. Being on the Gulf of Mexico, Mobile's climate lent itself to year round outdoor sporting activities. The locality also had a rich lode of baseball talent, Hank Aaron and Willie McCovey hail from the area as did legendary Satchel Paige and Agee's Mets teammate Amos Otis. But it was another future teammate in New York that Agee would form a bond with in Mobile.

In junior high, Agee met another youngster, Cleon Jones, who became an immediate school yard teammate and close friend. They were born just five days apart (Cleon was older). Although Carrie Agee wanted her son to become a minister, early on Tommie demonstrated gifted athletic abilities and a desire that placed him on course for a sports career.

Though not yet five years old when Jackie Robinson brought an end to the infamous gentlemen's agreement and opened up major league rosters to men of color, Agee still recalled the excitement it generated. "They had one television set in our part of town and everybody gathered around it one day when Jackie Robinson was playing a game… I knew then that I could be a ballplayer."

Agee attended the local high school, Mobile County Training School. Started in 1880, the facility was the oldest training school in Alabama and for many years was comprised of grades seven through 12. It was reorganized to a middle school in 1970. Agee was a four-sport star at Mobile County, playing football, basketball, and baseball as well as running track. During summer break the teenager played sandlot baseball. In fact he once shagged flies for another Mobile resident, future Hall of Famer Billy Williams.

"There were quite a few playing fields around," said Agee's high school coach, Curtis J. Horton. "The boys had areas in which they could develop.... Fields didn't have to be perfect and smooth. Baseball was played in just about every neighborhood, on every block. If the kids didn't have regulation bats and balls, they played stickball with rubber balls and broomsticks."

On the high school diamond, Tommie batted .390 and also pitched. The team recorded only one loss. Unfortunately, Alabama did not have a state baseball championship while Agee was at Mobile County Training School.

On the gridiron, Agee was an end and his friend Cleon Jones, a halfback. MCTS football had a stellar record—only one loss during Tommie's three years with the squad. He would remember fondly, "We had a play that we called number forty-eight, and it was a halfback option play. The quarterback would hand off to Cleon and he had an option of running or passing to me. During the 1960 season, we made five touchdowns on that play alone."

Agee went on to Grambling State University on a baseball scholarship, a school better known for other sports: NBA star Willis Reed and NFL cornerback Willie Brown, both of whom eventually reached the Hall of Fame in their sports as professionals, attended Grambling the same time as Agee. Dr. Ralph Waldo Emerson Jones who coached the Louisiana school's baseball team remembered Tommie's first game. "We worked on cutting down his swing. You know how it is, all these boys think about is home runs....Well, the first time up, he hits a home run over the left-field fence. The next time he hits one over the center-field fence. The third time he hits one over the right-field fence. Then he hits so far into center that he gets an inside-the-park home run."

Early scouting reports claimed he "lacked coordination" and had poor fundamentals. In fact, Coach Jones initially placed him at first base. The coach moved him to the middle infield and even had him pitch before finally slotting Agee as an outfielder. Hitting was not an obstacle. During his single season at Grambling, Agee batted .533, then the highest average in the Southwestern Athletic Conference's history.

After that colossal college season seemingly every pro birddog scout flocked to Agee's home in Mobile. "I was at his house when he came back after his first year at Grambling," Cleon Jones said. "There were thirty or forty scouts, all of them trying to talk to him, trying to get him signed. That blew me away, man."

Agee inked a contract with the Cleveland Indians with a $65,000 bonus in 1961. He spent parts of two season in Iowa, first at Class D Dubuque, where he hit .261 with 15 home runs in 64 games, and then at Class B Burlington, batting .258 with 25 steals in 500 at-bats. He moved up to Class AAA Jacksonville for two games before being called up to Cleveland. His major league debut occurred in road grays, September 14, 1962 before 25,372 at Metropolitan Stadium. In the top of the ninth, the 5-foot-11, 195-pound Agee flew out against Minnesota southpaw Dick Stigman in an 11–1 Minnesota rout. Agee batted .214 during that initial cup of coffee in 1962. He bounced back and forth from the farm to the parent club through the 1964 season. His cumulative batting average for Cleveland was just .170 with one home run in 53 at-bats.

On January 20, 1965, the 23-year-old Agee was involved in a three-team swap. Pitcher Tommy John, catcher John Romano, and Agee were sent to the Chicago White Sox; the Kansas City Athletics sent Rocky Colavito to Cleveland; Chicago sent Jim Landis and Mike Hershberger to Kansas City; and Chicago sent Cam Carreon to Cleveland. At a later date Chicago sent Fred Talbot to Kansas City. The White Sox wound up the winners in the complicated transaction, though Agee did not pay immediate dividends.

Agee spent almost all of 1965 at Class AAA Indianapolis, batting .226 with 15 steals. He hit even worse in brief duty with the Pale Hose, batting a paltry .158. Agee finally got his chance in 1966.

Agee was tabbed as Chicago's starting center fielder on Opening Day and launched a two-run home run in the seventh inning to tie the game. The White Sox went on to win in 14 innings and Agee, who began the season in the seventh spot in the order, quickly moved up in the lineup—first to leadoff, then moving to the two-hole, before settling into the third spot in the order. He wound up the season batting cleanup.

Agee batted .273 with 22 home runs, 88 RBIs, and scored 98 runs while playing in 160 games.

After attempting just one steal in his past trials in the majors, Agee stole 44 bases for the White Sox (he was caught 18 times). He was named the American League Rookie of the Year and finished eighth in the MVP voting to Triple Crown winner Frank Robinson in Baltimore. Agee earned a Gold Glove and was named to the All-Star team.

Agee was an All-Star again in 1967, but he suffered through a sophomore jinx in the latter stages of the season. He managed through the first half with a split of .247/.317/.401—not bad numbers for that pitching-dominated era on a team where no regular wound up hitting higher than .250—but Agee slumped to .218/.282/.329 in the second half. And while he thrived against lefties, batting .306 and putting together an .844 OPS, he made management wonder if he might be a platoon player by hitting just .199 against righties, though he hit 10 of his 14 home runs against them. His slumping was certainly noticeable as the Chi Sox battled until the final week for the pennant with Boston, Detroit, and Minnesota; the club with scarlet socks nabbed the AL flag on the final day.

Also noticing the outfielder was opposing manager Gil Hodges of the Washington Senators. When the New York Mets traded for Hodges after the season, one of the new manager's first requests was to try to pry Agee from the White Sox. On December 15, 1967, the Mets acquired Agee along with infielder Al Weis. The Mets gave up their best hitter, Tommy Davis, and Jack Fisher, the only Met besides rookie Tom Seaver to make more than 30 starts in 1967. (The Mets also sent Billy Wynne and Buddy Booker to the White Sox in the deal.)

Hodges penciled in Agee as his center fielder, a position where many had tried and failed for the sad-sack Mets to that point. Longtime Mets broadcaster Bob Murphy commented, "The first thing Gil wanted to do was acquire Tommie Agee. He wanted a guy to bat leadoff with speed and that also could hit for power." The deal also re-united Agee with longtime friend and Mets left fielder Cleon Jones.

The '68 Grapefruit League opener was a bleak foreshadowing for Agee's first year as a Met. He was beaned by St. Louis Cardinals ace Bob Gibson on the first pitch of spring training and wound up hospitalized. Agee began the regular season batting third with a 5-for-16 start, good for a .313 average and five runs scored. In the fifth game, however, he endured an 0-for-10 nightmare in a 24-inning loss at the Astrodome, embarking on an 0-for-34 slump that tied Don Zimmer's club record set in 1962. After going hitless for two weeks and seeing his average drop to .102, he finally grounded a single off Philadelphia's Larry Jackson. He did not have his first home run or

Photo courtesy of Mets Inside Pitch Archives

*Tommie Agee led the 1969 Mets in both home runs and RBIs despite batting leadoff.*

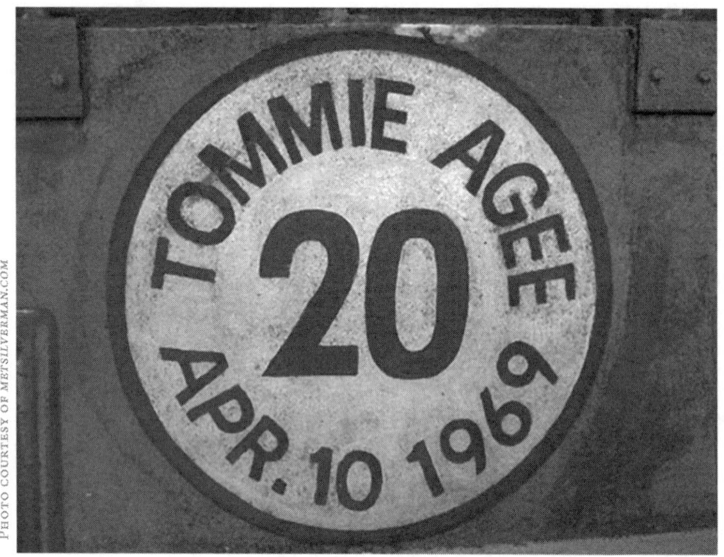


Photo courtesy of *metsilverman.com*

*Tommie Agee's once-in-a-stadium poke was memorialized in left field in the Shea upper deck. No other player ever landed a fair ball in the top deck.*

RBI until May 10. Agee ended the year with a .217 batting average and a mere five home runs and 17 RBIs in 391 at-bats. He walked just 15 times—his lowest total over a full season—while fanning 100 times for the third straight year.

Oddsmakers and baseball pundits tagged the 1969 Mets as a 100-to-1 longshot to win the Fall Classic. Why? Since their inception the hapless club never finished higher than ninth place. The smart money knew only a miracle could turn them around and that wasn't going to happen. Or was it?

Agee, fittingly, was the first Mets batter of 1969. Primed for redemption and rewarding his manager's faith by installing him in the leadoff spot, he knocked in New York's first runs of the season with a three-run double in the second inning on Opening Day. Two days later, on April 10, the 26-year-old launched two home runs. His first of the day was a legendary homer in the second inning that landed in Shea's left-field upper deck.

"I've never seen a ball hit like that," says Rod Gaspar, who had a perfect view of the flight pattern from the on-deck circle. "Just incredible."

Even the pitcher who gave it up was impressed. "It was a low fastball, kind of in, and he hit it almost like a golf ball," recalled Montreal Expos southpaw Larry Jaster. "A lot of times, you don't watch 'em. That one I had to watch because I knew it was hit pretty good." Agee got a hold of another Jaster pitch his next time up for a more garden variety home run.

Agee was the first—and last—to ever land a ball in the rarified air of fair territory in left *or* right field at Shea Stadium. The approximate spot was later memorialized by painting a large circle where he hit his home run with his name, number, and date. Years later, it was estimated at 480 feet.

But long balls were a generally rare event with the Mets. A pitching-first club without a lot of hitting, the 1969 Mets won by scoring just enough runs to win. They went a remarkable 41–23 in one-run games in 1969, often relying on their "lunch pail" everyday center fielder to inspire teammates. Cleon Jones believes Agee did so. Jones, Agee's longtime friend, enjoyed the best season of his career in 1969. "I had a great year because of him," Jones said of Agee. "There weren't many people getting on base, but he was. And he made us a good defensive team. We didn't have a whole lot of offense, but we didn't beat ourselves. He made the difference defensively."

Agee led the 1969 Mets in games (149), at-bats (565), runs (97), and, surprisingly for a leadoff man, he led the club in both home runs (26) and RBIs (76). Though he had a superb season with his glove in center field, Cincinnati Reds right fielder Pete Rose wound up claiming a Gold Glove along with automatics Roberto Clemente and Curt Flood. Rose finished fourth in the MVP voting to Willie McCovey; Agee was sixth.

Agee's offense garnered plenty of notice. After the Mets started slicing off chunks of the 10-game mid-August lead of the Chicago Cubs, he told Larry Merchant of the *New York Post*, "Sometimes a team comes to town and reads in the paper that you've hit a home run leading off."

Indeed, the Cubs must have been perusing the Big Apple tabloids. The first pitch of the September 8 showdown by Cub Bill Hands knocked down Agee.

It was called "a pitch designed to send him and the Mets to their maker." After that game, which New York won with Agee sliding past catcher Randy Hundley in a memorably close call, the outfielder commented, "I don't mind being knocked down. If you're hitting they're going to knock you down. The only thing I don't like is if we don't retaliate." Jerry Koosman took care of that end and the Mets—with a visit from a black cat—took care of the Cubs the next night and took over first place the night after that.

The Mets mowed down the opposition, finishing with a 100–62 record. The Amazin's topped the second place Cubs by eight games and captured the first National League East title in history. The inaugural Championship Series saw New York square off against the West's Atlanta Braves. Agee, who played every day despite Hodges's multiple platoon system, batted leadoff in all three games. After becoming the first Met to ever appear in a postseason game and going hitless in the series opening win, Agee homered in each of the next two games and knocked in four for a .357 average as the Mets swept.

Agee was the first Met to step to the plate in a World Series game and—as he'd done in the NLCS opener—he grounded out. Orioles outfielder Don Buford—a former teammate of Agee's in Chicago—belted a leadoff home run against Tom Seaver as Baltimore took the first game, 4–1. The Mets held on for a 2–1 win the next day to even the Series.

Agee took over Game Three and the Mets shifted into another gear. *Sports Illustrated* labeled Agee's October 14 performance, "The most spectacular World Series game that any center fielder has ever enjoyed." Agee led off the first World Series game played at Shea with a home run against Orioles ace and future Cooperstown entrant Jim Palmer. Agee had been 0-for-8 in the two games in Maryland.

New York was up 3–0 in the fourth inning, but the Orioles threatened with runners on first and third and two outs. Baltimore catcher Elrod Hendricks hit a Gary Gentry pitch to left-center. It looked like a double or even a triple for the Baltimore backstop. As Agee sprinted toward left field, Cleon Jones knew his old friend would make the play. "I saw him pound his fist into his glove," Jones said. "Whenever he got ready to make a catch, he would pound his fist into his glove." Agee reached out and grabbed the ball backhanded as he came to a halt before slamming into the 396-foot sign—with plenty of white showing as the ball lodged in the glove's stretched webbing.

Baltimore loaded the bases in the seventh with two outs. Orioles center fielder Paul Blair represented the tying run as Nolan Ryan came in to replace Gentry. Blair slammed a drive to deep right-center field as Agee again sped in pursuit. At the warning track he dove for the ball as if he were an Olympic swimmer. The ball landed in his glove as he sprawled prone to the ground. Agee later said, "I thought I might get it without diving, but the wind dropped the ball straight down and I had to hit the dirt."

The 56,335 at Shea gave him a standing ovation when he led off in the bottom of the frame. Later on he related, "Words can't describe how that made me feel. I felt like I wanted to hit two home runs in that one time at bat." He walked—the Orioles weren't taking any more chances with Agee.

Press box sports scribes immediately considered Agee's catch that denied Blair of a sure triple or inside-the-park homer with other key Series plays: great grabs like Al Gionfriddo off Joe DiMaggio (1947), Willie Mays off Vic Wertz (1954), or Sandy Amoros off Yogi Berra (1955). After the contest Agee said, "The homer meant only one run. The catches saved more than that."

Agee's leadoff homer accounted for one run and the catches saved at least five runs in the 5–0 win that put the Mets ahead of the overwhelming favorite Orioles in the World Series. Agee had just two more hits in the Series and finished with a .167 average in the five-game victory, but he was still as much a hero as anyone on a team suddenly overflowing with supermen.

Following the World Series, Agee along with a few other Mets appeared in a Las Vegas revue, singing "The Impossible Dream" among other standards. Back in Mobile, Agee and Jones were honored with a parade. Agee later noted somberly, "They never paid any attention to us before. I hate to think it took a World Series, but I guess there wasn't much interest in two black players until something like this happened."

*The Sporting News* named Agee NL Comeback Player of the Year. He continued to be the club's leadoff hitter and starting center fielder for three more seasons. He won his overdue second Gold Glove in 1970 and surpassed his '69 season in several categories. He batted a career-high .286 and had his lone career 30-double season. That year also saw him set team records with 636 at-bats, (broken by Felix Millan in 1973 with 638), 31 stolen bases (topped by Lenny Randle in 1977 with 33), 107 runs (surpassed by one by Darryl Strawberry in 1987), and 298 total bases (erased by Strawberry in '87 with 310). Agee had both a 20-game and a 19-game hitting streak in '70 while his 24 home runs made him the first Met in history to twice lead the club in that category or reach 20 homers in more than one year.

The 1971 and 1972 seasons saw Agee hampered by knee problems. Before the 1972 season, Hodges died suddenly and Yogi Berra was named manager. More change was in store on May 11 when the Mets acquired the greatest center fielder to ever come from Alabama: Willie Mays. Agee still got the majority of starts in center field over the 41-year-old Mays, but he no longer played every day as he had under Hodges. His average stood at .281 the day Mays had his first at-bat as a Met and Agee finished the year at just .227, his lowest average since his first year at Shea.

On November 27, 1972, the Mets dealt Agee to the Houston Astros for outfielder Rich Chiles and right-hander Buddy Harris. Agee appeared in 83 games for Houston and batted .235 with eight home runs. The Astros sent him to the St. Louis Cardinals on August 18, 1973, receiving outfielder Dave Campbell and cash. His last game was September 30, 1973 at Busch Stadium, where he pinch-hit for pitcher Diego Segui in the fifth inning against the Philadelphia Phillies. Agee grounded out to short.

Agee had planned to continue playing and the Los Angeles Dodgers fully expected him to as well. On December 5, 1973, the Cards traded him to Los Angeles for Pete Richert, but the Dodgers released Agee near the end of spring training on March 26, 1974. Agee ended his career, at age 31, with a .255 batting average, 130 home runs, 433 RBIs, and 167 stolen bases. He finished one hit shy of 1,000 for his career.

In retirement, Agee was very active in youth programs in the New York area. He owned a bar near Shea Stadium called The Outfielder's Lounge. He later went into the business sector and was affiliated with Stewart Title Insurance Company. On January 22, 2001, upon leaving a midtown Manhattan office building, Agee was stricken with a fatal heart attack. He was 58 years old. Agee was survived by his wife Maxine and daughter Janelle.

Mets team chairman Nelson Doubleday called Agee "one of the all-time great Mets." On Opening Day 2001 the Mets wore a patch honoring Agee and Brian Cole, a prospect killed in an auto accident shortly before the opener. Agee was inducted into the Mets Hall of Fame in 2002, the last Met so honored at Shea Stadium. Members of his family were invited to take part in the final day at Shea in 2008.

After Agee's death, Cleon Jones still marveled at how his old friend made playing center field at Shea Stadium look easy, despite its poor visibility and swirling winds. "I hated it; every guy before me hated it," recalled Jones, who was the club's center fielder the two years prior to Agee's arrival in New York. "But Tommie never complained. I watched Willie Mays, Curt Flood, Vada Pinson—a lot of guys came into this Shea Stadium outfield. Nobody played it better than Tommie Agee."

**Sources**

*Baseball Digest*
*baseballlibrary.com*
*baseball-reference.com*
*guardonline.com*
Hoch, Bryan, "Agee Earns Rightful Sport in Mets Hall," *The Wave* (Rockaway, New York), August 17, 2002.
National Baseball Hall of Fame
*nytimes.com*
*Retrosheet.org*
Rubin, Adam, "Shea Stadium's Been Raining Long Balls for Years," *http://www.nydailynews.com/sports/baseball/mets/2008/09/06/2008-09-06_shea_stadiums_been_raining_long_balls_fo.html?page=2*
*salisburypost.com*
Spector, Jesse, "Tommie Agee's Upper-Decker Remains Singular Shea Swat" *http://www.nydailynews.com/sports/baseball/mets/2008/09/20/2008-09-20_tommie_agees_upperdecker_remains_singula.html#ixzz0EZQaM9Hs&A*
*Sports Illustrated*
Thorn, John; Palmer, Pete; Gershman, Mike, and Pietrusza, David, *Total Baseball*, sixth edition (New York: Total Sports Publishing, 1999).
Young, A.S. "Doc," *The Mets from Mobile* (New York: Harcourt, Brace & World, 1970).
*108mag.typepad.com*
2008 Mets Media Guide

# Ken Boswell

by Mike Bender

| Season | Age | G | AB | R | H | 2B | 3B | HR | RBI | BB | SO | SB | CS | BA | OBP | SLG |
|---|---|---|---|---|---|---|---|---|---|---|---|---|---|---|---|---|
| 1969 Mets | 23 | 102 | 362 | 48 | 101 | 14 | 7 | 3 | 36 | 47 | 47 | 7 | 3 | .279 | .347 | .381 |
| Career 11 Years | – | 930 | 2517 | 266 | 625 | 91 | 19 | 31 | 244 | 240 | 239 | 27 | 17 | .248 | .313 | .337 |

*"Ken should be of All-Star caliber some day."* —Gil Hodges[1]

*"Everyone raves about Boswell, the hitter. But few rave about Boswell, the fielder"* —New York Times[2]

*"This country had a lot of problems in 1969. There was the war in Vietnam, riots in the cities, protests on college campuses. Plus, the city of New York was close to bankruptcy. When the 1969 Mets came along, people were looking for something they could believe in."* —Ken Boswell[3]

Part of the "New Breed," second baseman Ken Boswell played a key role during the Amazin' Mets' run to the National League championship. And though platooning limited him to just one start in the 1969 World Series, he batted .333, the same robust average as he enjoyed in the NLCS, and celebrated with gusto as a 23-year-old world champion.

A native Texan, Boswell was born in Austin on February 23, 1946, and attended William B. Travis High in Austin. A captain for both the baseball and basketball teams, he led the hoops team in scoring as a senior in 1964, but it was baseball that earned him a scholarship at Sam Houston State University, in Huntsville. Though there was interest from a few teams, he went to school, at the urging of his parents:

> *I probably could have signed with the Yankees out of high school, but my folks wanted me to go to college. So I went to Sam Houston State on a baseball scholarship, but I realized right away that it was a mistake. I was tired of school, and I wasn't your best student in the world anyway. I wanted to play baseball.*[4]

Rules prohibited players that started school from signing a professional contract until their class had graduated. Boswell found a way around the rule—he flunked out of college. After confirming that he was indeed eligible, the Mets selected him in the fourth round of the June 1965 amateur draft, which included fellow 1969 Mets Les Rohr (drafted in the first round), Jim McAndrew (11th round), and Nolan Ryan (12th round).

"I signed for $8,000, which was a lot less than I would have gotten before the draft, but I guess it was more than my dad ever made," Boswell said. "Actually, I was awfully lucky to be drafted by the Mets, because they needed ballplayers and I didn't have to wait very long before being called up."[5]

Boswell was one of five members of the '69 Mets signed by legendary scout Red Murff, along with Ryan, Jerry Grote, Jerry Koosman, and Jesse Hudson. (Murff was also the one who figured out that the flunking-out loophole made Boswell eligible for the first-ever amateur draft.) Boswell made a splash in his debut with Auburn in the New York-Penn League, the club's Class A affiliate, hitting safely in his first 19 games, and winning Rookie of the Year honors. Boswell hit .285 for Auburn, with 20 doubles and seven homers, but he made 14 errors in 72 games at second base.

Boswell continued hitting at his next stop, Williamsport in the double-A Eastern League, batting .299 (second on the team) in 63 games in 1966. Boswell struggled with the glove, however, committing 19 errors in 60 games, carving out a reputation as a "good-hit, no-field" prospect. He was promoted to triple-A Jacksonville in midseason, playing second base and third base for the Suns.

An invitation to spring training with the major league club followed, and in February 1967, Boswell attended his first big league camp with fellow rookies Tom Seaver and Bud Harrelson. The Mets had traded away starting second baseman Ron Hunt after the 1966 season, with the expectation that Boswell would assume the starting job. But Boswell was drafted into the Army, and he spent the spring and most of the season in the military, returning to Jacksonville after his tour. Manager Wes Westrum told *The Sporting News* that "[11] [Boswell] would have had a real shot at the job if he hadn't been drafted."[6]

Boswell was called up to the majors at the close of the 1967 season, and made his Mets debut on the night of September 18, batting sixth and playing third base behind former Jacksonville teammate Tom Seaver. After grounding into a double play against the Dodgers' John Duffie (also making his major league debut) in the first inning, Boswell settled in, notching his first RBI in the fourth inning with a sacrifice fly and then collecting his first hit, an RBI-double in the sixth inning off of Jim Brewer. He also started a 5-4-3 double play to end the top of the seventh inning and help Seaver win his 15th game of the year.

His first major league home run came against Hall of Famer Don Drysdale on September 30. "I didn't have too many at-bats that season, but I remember that same series I got my first home run off Don Drysdale. I was the only Met to hit a home run in Dodger Stadium that year."[7]

Perhaps further cementing his good-hit, no-field reputation, Boswell closed the 1967 season in Los Angeles with a decisive error, booting a groundball in the eighth inning that allowed the tying and winning runs to score in a 2–1 loss to the Dodgers:

*Over in the clubhouse I was a big hero. It was the last game of the season, and a lot of the guys had plane reservations. They were going to Hawaii, Reno, Vegas, and they didn't want to play any more extra innings. They wanted to catch their planes and get out of there. That's how it was over there in '67.*[8]

The attitude in the Mets clubhouse was about to change. In November, the Mets traded a player and cash to the Washington Senators for Gil Hodges. The new Mets manager was impressed by Boswell's play in the Florida Instructional League in the winter of 1967. Although a spring-training battle between Boswell and Bob Heise was anticipated, the search for a regular second baseman in 1968 depended on Boswell's progress, according to the new manager—"the bat will decide who stays and who goes." Farm director Whitey Herzog assessed Boswell's chances in December 1967: "Boswell is ready, I think. But a lot of it is up to him. He's got the talent, but whether he plays up to his ability is something else. Ken is the kind of player you've got to push. You've got to keep after him."[9]

However, a freak injury in early 1968 prevented Boswell from a healthy start to the year. He slipped and fell on icy steps at his Texas home just before the start of spring training, injuring his ribs. Al Weis—acquired at Hodges's request, along with Tommie Agee—received the bulk of the playing time at second base in the spring, with former Yankee Phil Linz seeing plenty of action as well. But Boswell had recovered well enough from the injury to earn the starting position. Most of his playing time came in the first half of the season, though, as a broken finger suffered on June 24 sidelined him until late August.

Boswell's rookie season was a modest success. He hit .261, very respectable in the Year of the Pitcher, in 75 games, and was the runner-up for the 1968 Topps Major League All-Star Rookie Team behind Dave Nelson of the Indians. Boswell was named a Topps All-Star Rookie. He opted out of another season in the Florida Instructional League to take part in scheduled drills with his Army reserve unit.

The Mets were also a modest success in 1968, registering the most wins (73) in club history and passing their expansion partner, the Houston Astros, to finish ninth in the National League. Heading into 1969, *New York Times* predicted better days ahead:

> *This could be the year the Mets will move up another step. But they can't count on it. They have the nucleus for a strong pitching staff, and their catching has improved. But to have a real chance, Manager Gil Hodges must sharply upgrade his infield and outfield. Evidence that the wherewithal for such improvement is in hand is not convincing.*[10]

But no one saw—or could see—a Miracle coming.

As the Mets gathered in St. Petersburg for spring training, Boswell came to camp healthy and able to concentrate fully on the game. Unlike the prior two years, there were no offseason accidents or military obligations to interrupt preparations for the season, and Boswell was entrenched as the second baseman in his manager's left-handed platoon squad.

Boswell started at second base in the Mets historic home opener on April 8 against the expansion Montreal Expos: the first international game in major league history. Batting third, he had two hits and an RBI, but he committed three errors, including a pair in the first inning that led to two unearned runs for Tom Seaver. The Mets lost their eighth consecutive opener, 11–10.

His hot start with the bat carried over for most of April, as Boswell hit .275 over the first 17 games of the 1969 season. Boswell's glove continued to cause some anxious moments, though, such as the April 23 game at Shea Stadium against the Pirates. Boswell's third-inning error on Jim Bunning's groundball forced Jerry Koosman to face Roberto Clemente and Bob Robertson with the bases loaded. The left-hander worked out of trouble to win his first game of the year, a 2–0 shutout. And in the first game of a doubleheader against the Cubs on April 27, Boswell committed a key error in the ninth inning on a Billy Williams grounder (his eighth error of the young season), allowing the Cubs to rally against Cal Koonce and overcome a 6–4 deficit to beat the Mets on Randy Hundley's two-run homer, 8–6.

May opened with the Mets in third place in the new National League East division, two games below .500. Boswell slumped in May, batting .233. But his bat kept appearing in the middle of key rallies and important wins. He had four consecutive multi-hit games early in the month, including five hits in a Sunday doubleheader sweep of the Cubs in Chicago on May 4. Two days later, Boswell followed that performance with a home run off Jim Maloney to help Don Cardwell win his first game of the season. He also tagged a leadoff triple in the seventh inning to break up a Phil Niekro no-hitter in New York on May 14, sparking the team to a 9–3 comeback victory.

But he spent the first two weeks of June serving in the Army reserve, missing most of the club-record 11-game winning streak that started with a late-May win over San Diego. Boswell returned to the lineup in a series at Philadelphia on June 17. Now batting second, he drove in the winning runs with a two-out, two-run, ninth-inning single off of Dick Farrell on June 19 in a 6–5 victory. He also notched two hits against Bob Gibson the following day back at Shea Stadium in front of a league-best crowd of 54,083, including a second-inning triple that drove in Tommie Agee. Boswell hit .261 in June, and the Mets enjoyed their winningest month ever, going 19–9.

Boswell started off well in July. A two-out, 14th-inning single scored Tommie Agee with the go-ahead run in a win at St. Louis on July 2. His ninth-inning, pinch-hit, bloop double on July 8 at Shea against Ferguson Jenkins started the Mets' comeback in their watershed 4–3 win over the Cubs. Because Chicago started left-hander Ken Holtzman the following night, Boswell did not play in Seaver's "Imperfect Game." Boswell did, however, contribute in the return series in Chicago, collecting two hits each at Wrigley in Mets victories on July 15 and 16, including a home run off of Dick Selma that provided the winning margin a day after Seaver had taken a 1–0 loss. But he struggled for most of the month, hitting .222, and found himself on the bench again in late July with a bone bruise in his left thumb. A couple of baserunning errors also contributed to his benching. Boswell was thrown out at second trying to stretch a single in the eighth inning in a 1–0 loss at Wrigley, and he was tagged out at third trying to advance on a groundout in the 12th inning of a 4–3 loss to the Reds just after the All-Star break. Hodges considered the first error "the wrong play.... It was a mistake, but we all make them."[11] After the second error, Hodges said, "His play is hurting. He hasn't been playing well."[12]

As Boswell recalled: "He had such a high level of concentration; he was thinking about the game all the time, and he tried to get the players to think that way.... Gil changed the whole attitude on the club. He was a real disciplinarian, too."[13]

August 1 found the Mets 6½ games out of first place with Boswell on the bench. He returned to the lineup in a series in Houston in the middle of the month. On August 12, however, his error on the relay for a potential double play in the sixth inning contributed to a four-run rally as the Astros came from behind to beat the Mets. The following day, Boswell's failure to cleanly handle a groundball in the first inning extended an Astros rally that culminated in a three-run home run by Denis Menke. The Astros swept the Mets—it was the low point of the season for Boswell and the team. Jack Lang noted in *The Sporting News* on August 30 that Boswell had been "resting a bruised thumb, a weak batting average, and an iron glove for some two weeks."[14] Prior to the benching, Boswell had gone hitless in 20 at-bats.

Photo courtesy of metsilverman.com

*Ken Boswell, in just his second full season in the majors, was third on the '69 Mets in hits, runs, batting, and steals, and the club leader in triples, even though he only had 405 plate appearances.*

After two weeks spent on the bench, Boswell returned to the lineup for good on August 26, as the Mets embarked on a torrid finish to the season. He was moved to the fifth spot in the batting order, occasionally moving to cleanup, as the Mets rolled to a 29–10 record from that on to capture the Eastern Division title. Boswell was locked in at the plate.

He hit .407 over his last 29 games, with 12 multi-hit efforts, including six in a row from September 9 through September 18. And Boswell continued to swing the bat well against some of the league's top pitchers. He had three hits, including a double, against the Giants and Gaylord Perry in a 3–2 win on August 30. He had three more hits, including two off Dodgers ace Don Sutton, in a September 2 win, and two hits and two runs batted in off Ferguson Jenkins and the Cubs in a key win on September 9.

Boswell had arguably the biggest hit in Mets history, up to that time, on September 10. His 12th-inning, two-out single scored the winning run in the first game of a doubleheader against the Expos—a win that put the Mets into first place for the first time in team history.

The day after Pittsburgh's Bob Moose no-hit the Mets, the club's third straight loss, Boswell reached base five times in a September 21 doubleheader sweep of the Pirates. The Mets clinched a few days later. He closed the schedule with a pair of hits against the Cubs in the season-ending game at Chicago, putting him at .279—his best average ever over a full season.

"I think I always hit better when it meant something," Boswell said. "I'll bet I never got a hit with two out and nobody on. I just couldn't concentrate in those situations. I liked to hit when there were men on base and it meant something."[15]

In fact, Boswell did perform better in pressure situations in 1969, hitting .327 with men on base.[16] He also tied for the team lead in game-winning RBIs with 10.[17] Boswell particularly enjoyed tormenting the Cubs, hitting .365 with nine RBIs, his top marks against any team.[18]

The Atlanta Braves, the Mets' opponent in the inaugural National League Championship Series, were scheduled to start three right-handed pitchers in the series. Boswell and the rest of Gil Hodges's left-handed platoon would start each of the games. It was a quick series.

After going hitless and making an error in the first game, Boswell hit two-run homers (his first since mid-July) in Game Two and Game Three, driving in four runs, as the Mets completed an unexpected three-game sweep. He finished the series with a .333 average and a team-high five RBIs. Coach Joe Pignatano dropped Boswell's Game Three home run as it landed in the right-field bullpen, prompting Boswell to tell him after the game, "Hey, Piggy, you've got hands like me."[19]

The NLCS was Boswell's last regular playing time that year. The Orioles had a rotation headed by left-handers Dave McNally and Mike Cuellar, and the right-handed platoon would start most of the World Series contests. He described the Mets' anticipation for the World Series: "They're a real good team. They have big guns at every position. But that doesn't scare me or any of us. We're all looking forward to playing them."[20]

Boswell hosted his father in New York after the teams split the first two games in Baltimore, taking him around the city, and pointing out the sights. "I also pointed out the girls with the no-bras and the see-throughs and things like that," Boswell said. "He couldn't believe those short skirts. Of course, sometimes I can't believe them either."[21]

One of only four bachelors on the 1969 Mets, Boswell attracted considerable attention from female fans as the team started winning. *The New York Times* reported, "The 25-year-old Texan says that girls from Brooklyn are always asking him home to dinner. 'They all offer to cook spaghetti,' he says. 'They'd have a better chance if they fixed spare ribs and chicken.'"[22]

On the field one last time in '69, Boswell started against Jim Palmer at Shea Stadium in Game Three, the first World Series game in New York since 1964 and the first-ever Series game at Shea Stadium. Batting fifth, he had a single and run scored in three at-bats, as the Mets shut out the Orioles in a game best remembered for Tommie Agee's acrobatics in the outfield.

Boswell did not play in either of the final two games of the Series, both wins in the team's final at-bat. He was asked how he would celebrate the Mets' stunning World Series triumph. "When I get home to Austin they are going to have a Welcome Home Ken Boswell Parade. I hope they mean me and not some other Ken Boswell."[23]

The 1969 season was Boswell's finest year. He set career highs in runs (48), triples (7), batting average (.279), and slugging percentage (.381), and tied his career high for stolen bases with seven. However, there was speculation in the offseason that the Mets would find a new position for him. Boswell had the worst fielding percentage of any regular second baseman in the major leagues. His 18 errors in just 96 games also proved to be the worst mark of his career. Second base and third base were considered prime needs in their offseason shopping list. *The Sporting News* surprised no one by stating: "Boswell can hit but must improve in the field."[24] But Boswell proved them wrong.

Boswell made news in 1970 for his glove work—this time good news. As the Mets struggled with injuries and inconsistency while trying to defend their championship, Boswell set a major league record with an 85-game errorless streak at second base, breaking the record of 78 set by Ken Hubbs of the Chicago Cubs in 1962. He gave credit to manager Gil Hodges, who had him working hard on his glovework from the first day of spring training. "He said, 'Look, everybody is saying you can't play second base. I may be the only one who believes you can. We're going to work your butt off down here and you'll be a second baseman when we leave.'... A lot of it is confidence. Gil built up my confidence."[25]

Jerome Holtzman noted in *The Sporting News* that Boswell was not playing second base "on the proverbial dime." Holtzman wrote, "He is ranging well to both sides and making all the plays a good second baseman should. His throwing has been outstanding, too."[26]

Although limited at the end of the season by a groin injury, Boswell set the all-time Mets fielding percentage record (.996) and finished the season with only two errors. He also set a career high in RBIs with 44, although his other offensive numbers dipped, including a 25-point decline in his average to .254.

Speculation in the offseason was that manager Gil Hodges would make Boswell the fulltime second baseman in 1971, playing against both right- and left-handed pitching. And he did play regularly, setting career highs in games played (116), hits (107), and doubles (20) before shoulder tendonitis, a recurring problem that season, finally sidelined him in early September.

The shoulder problem was severe enough to keep him out for the remainder of the season. The pain was so intense that he "couldn't even swing a bat."[27] Medical opinion was that rest and a complete layoff was all that was necessary to bring him back to health. However, in late December, with the pain still lingering, he was flown to New York for another examination.

Although he was given a clean bill of health in January, it remained to be seen whether he could remain pain-free for the season. There was concern in spring training, particularly after he missed the first week of the exhibition schedule. *The Sporting News* offered, "[Mets pitchers] may not feel comfortable with Bozzy at second if he can't make the necessary throws on the double play."[28]

The 1972 season was troubled. With the season beginning with Hodges's tragic death, and Yogi Berra replacing the beloved manager, Boswell struggled mightily. He was benched briefly in June while hitting .173, and he batted .029 in July (1-for-34). He finally cracked the .200 barrier in mid-September, and finished the season batting .211. He also suffered in the field, with the fewest assists of any second baseman starting at least half of his team's games and the second-fewest double plays.

There were some notable moments. Boswell set a career high in home runs (nine). And his error on Roberto Clemente's first-inning ground ball on September 29 temporarily delayed the Clemente's quest for his 3,000th—and sadly, his final—career hit.

But the Mets looked for a long-term answer at second base in the offseason. As a result of Boswell's injuries and overall decline in play, the Mets traded Gary Gentry and Danny Frisella to the Braves for Felix Millan and George Stone. Berra's comment: "We finally got a guy who can play every day."[29]

Boswell assumed a utility role, playing in the fewest games since his rookie year. He was the team's top pinch hitter in 1973, with 12 hits in 51 at-bats, including the only two pinch-hit home runs the Mets had during the season. He also started a handful of games at third base, primarily when Millan was given a day off—Wayne Garrett would start at second because Berra considered him more adept at turning the double play.

After the Mets reprised their stunning '69 finish to grab the division title with just 82 wins, Boswell had one at-bat in the NLCS against the Reds, going hitless as the Mets clinched the National League pennant in five games. He had a far more historic World Series. Boswell tied a Series record with three pinch hits (all singles), plus a run scored, in three at-bats against the Oakland A's.[30] All three hits came off of future Hall of Famers—one off of Catfish Hunter and two off of relief ace Rollie Fingers.[31]

Berra considered trying Boswell in the outfield in the offseason in an effort to shore up the team's offense. "I think Bozzy swings a good bat, and from what I saw of him shagging flies in the outfield, he don't look bad…I want him for his bat, not his fielding."[32]

But the 1974 season found Boswell back in a utility role, splitting time between second base, third base, and the outfield, while serving mostly as a pinch hitter (9-for-42). His two-run home run on August 5, off the Expos' Dennis Blair was the last pinch-hit homer of his major league career.

The 28-year-old Boswell was sent to his home state of Texas shortly after the 1974 season ended. He was traded to the Astros for 26-year-old outfielder Bob Gallagher in a swap of disappointing performers. Gallagher had hit .172 in limited at-bats with Houston and had been strictly a defensive replacement. There was some suspicion that general manager Joe McDonald had made the trade in part due to Boswell's refusal to make a postseason trip to Japan. Two other players that had taken a similar stance—Duffy Dyer and Ray Sadecki—were also traded over the winter. At the time of the trade, Boswell had played the most games at second base in Mets history (506).

"I thought to myself, 'Gee, I don't know that it's such bad news.'" Boswell said at the time. "You see, I've kind of wanted to be traded the last two years. Except I'm not the kind to come out and say, 'Play me or trade me.' I don't know what their plans are for me in Houston, but I'd like a chance to be a starter again."[33]

Boswell competed with Larry Milbourne, Rob Andrews, and Tommy Helms for time at second base in spring training. Andrews secured the starting position, and Boswell resumed his status as his club's number one left-handed pinch-hitter, with occasional starts at second and third.

The Astros had the worst record in the National League in 1975, also the poorest in their 14-year history, and the organization was almost completely overhauled in the offseason. They started a rebuilding program, with the prime goal to develop youth, including Milbourne and Andrews at second base and Enos Cabell and Art Howe at third base. "Boswell would seem to be a victim of that necessity,"[34] *The Sporting News* predicted.

Despite being only 30, Boswell was considered at a disadvantage due to his age and his "extreme value" as a pinch hitter and late-inning defensive replacement at several positions. Milbourne and Cabell won starting roles, with Boswell entrenched as the team's top bat off the bench.[35] It wound up being Boswell's finest season as a pinch hitter. He set an Astros record (since tied by Orlando Palmeiro in 2006) for pinch hits in a season with 20. He went 20-for-65 (.308) off the bench as the team improved by 16 wins.

He closed his major league career with the Astros in 1977, again taking the role as the team's primary left-handed pinch hitter (14-for-53, .264), with occasional starts in the infield. Boswell's final hit was a single off the Dodgers' Dennis Lewallyn at Dodger Stadium on September 30. His final at-bat, against the Dodgers' Charlie Hough, was a fly out to left field that ended the game on October 1. It came 11 seasons after he'd played his first major league game against the Dodgers. Boswell played out his option, and was not selected in the offseason free agent draft.

He remained in Texas with his wife, Toney, in the Austin area. He currently works in antique auto sales in the Austin area and has a large enough spread to call himself a rancher.

**Notes and Sources**

1. *New York Times,* September 24, 1969
2. Ibid
3. *New York Times,* July 18, 1994
4. Cohen, Stanley, A Magic Summer, p.130-131
5. Ibid, p. 131
6. *The Sporting News,* March 11, 1967
7. Cohen, p. 132
8. Ibid, p. 132
9. *The Sporting News,* December 9, 1967
10. *New York Times,* February 16, 1969
11. *New York Times,* July 15, 1969
12. *The Sporting News,* August 9, 1969
13. Ibid, p. 128-129
14. *The Sporting News,* August 30, 1969
15. Cohen, p. 133
16. *www.retrosheet.org*
17. Bock, Duncan & Jordan, John, The Complete Year-by-Year N.Y. Mets Fan's Almanac, p. 77
18. *www.retrosheet.org*
19. Vecsey, George, Joy in Mudville, p. 227
20. *New York Times,* October 8, 1969
21. *New York Times,* October 9, 1969
22. *New York Times,* September 26, 1969
23. *Sports Illustrated,* October 27, 1969
24. *The Sporting News,* November 22, 1969
25. *The Sporting News,* May 23, 1970
26. *The Sporting News,* September 19, 1970
27. *The Sporting News,* February 25, 1972
28. *The Sporting News,* March 25, 1972
29. *The Sporting News,* November 18, 1972
30. Record had been set previously by Bobby Brown (1947 Yankees), Dusty Rhodes (1954 Giants), Carl Warwick (1964 Cardinals) and Gonzalo Marquez (1972 A's)
31. *www.retrosheet.org*
32. *The Sporting News,* December 29, 1973
33. *The Sporting News,* November 23, 1974
34. *The Sporting News,* January 3, 1976
35. *The Sporting News,* March 6, 1976

Bock, Duncan, and Jordan, John, *The Complete Year-by-Year N.Y. Mets Fan's Almanac* (New York: Crown, 1992.

Cohen, Stanley, *A Magic Summer: The 1969 Mets* (New York: Harcourt, Brace Jovanovich, 1988)

*New York Times*

*www.retrosheet.org*

*The Sporting News*

*Sports Illustrated*

Vecsey, Peter, *Joy in Mudville: Being a Complete Account of the Unparalleled History of the New York Mets from Their Most Perturbed Beginnings to Their Amazing Rise to Glory and Renown* (New York: McCall, 1970)

## 1969 Mets Trivia

You know the 1969 Mets as the darlings of New York and they are still beloved by Mets fans 40 years later, but do you know about the competition in 1969? They didn't just wake up one day with a bunch of wins. The Mets beat many good teams and overcame superb performances by numerous players in other uniforms on the way to accumulating 100 wins. Here's a chance to test the memory or at least make a few educated guesses about those who stood in the way of a Miracle. There are a couple of questions about accomplishments by the Mets as well.

1. Who had the most regular-season home runs against the 1969 Mets?

2. Who had the most regular-season RBIs against the 1969 Mets?

3. Who had the highest regular-season batting average against the 1969 Mets (minimum 20 plate appearances)?

4. Only one pitcher beat the 1969 Mets four times. He eventually became a major league manager. Name him.

5. Two future Hall of Fame pitchers went 0-3 against the Mets in the 1969 regular season. Name them.

6. Six times during the season, a Mets player had four or more hits in a game. Name the Met who had four such games.

7. What Mets pitcher had the most strikeouts in a game for them that season, with 15?

8. The most runs the Mets allowed in a game in 1969 was 16. What team scored 16 against the Mets?

9. What future Astros manager had five hits against Tom Seaver in 1969, more than any other player in the regular season?

10. Who was the only player to homer more than once against Tom Seaver in the 1969 regular season?

[Answers on the flip side of the second base platoon—the Al Weis bio, page250.]

# Don Cardwell

by Matthew Silverman

| Season | Age | W | L | Pct | G | GS | SV | IP | H | BB | SO | WHIP | ERA |
|---|---|---|---|---|---|---|---|---|---|---|---|---|---|
| 1969 Mets | 33 | 8 | 10 | .444 | 30 | 21 | 4 | 152.3 | 145 | 47 | 60 | 1.260 | 3.01 |
| Career 14 Years | – | 102 | 138 | .425 | 410 | 301 | 7 | 2112.7 | 2009 | 671 | 1211 | 1.263 | 3.92 |

Don Cardwell seemed the definition of a journeyman pitcher, but his career intertwined with the stuff of legend. He threw a no-hitter two days after being traded, he grabbed love beads off Ron Swoboda's neck at the height of the 1960s culture clash, and Cardwell, who always liked to swing the bat, became the back end of a memorable doubleheader sweep by the '69 Miracle Mets in which the only run in each game was knocked in by the pitcher. It was a long and interesting career for Cardwell that culminated with him being the senior member of a staff that pulled off one of the most unlikely world championships ever.

Donald Eugene Cardwell was born in Winston-Salem, North Carolina, on December 7, 1935. He was the seventh of eight children of Charlie H. and Lillian Denny Cardwell. Obviously, he gravitated toward baseball, but Cardwell also lettered in basketball and football at James A. Gray High School. He later became a near scratch golfer.

After graduation in 1954, he was signed by Phillies scout Wes Livengood and his first stop was Class-D ball in Pulaski, Virginia. He earned Rookie of the Year honors in the Appalachian League. The following year he married his high school sweetheart, Sylvia Greer, who would be his wife for 52 years. They immediately left for Plant City, Florida, for spring training.

He moved up to Class A in Schenectady, New York, and after a year there headed to Miami, the Phillies' top minor league affiliate, in 1956. Cardwell debuted in the major leagues on April 21, 1957 at the Polo Grounds, throwing the last three innings of Philadelphia's 8–5 win over the New York Giants. As a rookie he had a 4.91 ERA and a mark of 4–8. He had a winning record just twice in 14 major league seasons.

In 1959, his first full season in the majors, Cardwell began September with a winning mark (9–7) and a 3.66 ERA, but he was hammered in four of his last five starts and finished at 9–10 with a 4.06 ERA. Cardwell began the 1960 season with six innings of relief to earn the win in 10 innings against the Braves on April 14. He never won again for the Phillies. He started four times after that, losing twice with two no-decisions. On May 6, he allowed just one hit in six innings in Los Angeles, but he walked six Dodgers, hit another, and threw two wild pitches in a game the Phillies eventually won against Sandy Koufax.

A week later, the Phillies and Cubs pulled off a four-player deal, sending Cardwell and first baseman Ed Bouchee to Philadelphia for infielder Tony Taylor and catcher Cal Neeman. Neither team was going anywhere. The two clubs were fighting to see which would stay out of the cellar, a half-hearted battle the Cubs eventually won by one game. Still, the trade created some excitement as it occurred just as the rival Cubs and Cardinals were playing their first series of the year in Chicago.

The Cubs won the first two games against St. Louis before small crowds, but 33,543 filled Wrigley for the Sunday doubleheader. The Cards took the opener and Cardwell took the ball for the Cubs for the first time in the second game. Cardwell walked Alex Grammas with one out in the first inning. That was the closest he would get to trouble.

In the seventh, Cubs manager Lou Boudreau replaced Frank Thomas at third base with Don Zimmer. (Thomas had handled his lone chance cleanly, one of 10 ground balls induced by Cardwell.) Wally Shannon batted for Grammas that inning and flew out. By the time Stan Musial fanned in place of Curt Flood in the eighth, Cardwell had struck out seven and retired 23 in a row. Every play in the field had been routine.

The ninth would not be easy, however, with three left-handed hitters taking turns against Cardwell. Carl Sawatski, batting for catcher Hal Smith, ripped a line drive to deep right that George Altman caught with one hand at the wall. Veteran pinch hitter George Crowe, batting for starting pitcher Lindy McDaniel, hit a long fly to center that was hauled in by Richie Ashburn. Joe Cunningham, who'd made the first out of the game, worked the count to 3-and-1. Cardwell went into his windup—WGN announcer Jack Brickhouse cajoled, "C'mon, Don, get it in there"[1]—and Cunningham watched the fastball before starting toward first base. Umpire Tony Venzon called a strike at the knees and got an earful from Cunningham. The next pitch was lashed to left, but Walt Moryn got a good jump and caught the drive inches off the ground.

"Fans streaming onto the field," shouted Brickhouse over the din. "Don Cardwell has just thrown a no-hitter in the most fabulous break-in for a pitcher in the history of baseball just joining a club."[2]

Cardwell was the first and—to date—last pitcher to throw a no-hitter in his debut with a new team following a trade. He received a bonus of $2,000 to boost his salary to $10,000.[3] Cardwell went just 7–14 the rest of the season, but he had another memorable day against the Cardinals. He homered twice, had three hits, scored three times, and drove in three in a 10–4 win in St. Louis on September 2.

Cardwell was one of the game's top hitting pitchers—he clubbed 15 home runs during his career—but he was also usually among the league leaders in hitting batters. "It took me three years before I learned how to pitch inside without hitting somebody in the head. You just had to hold the ball a certain way. If you hold it one way, the ball tails in. If you grip it across the seams and throw it over the top more, it's straighter."[4]

He won a career-high 15 games for the 1961 Cubs and finished over .500 for the first time despite the Cubs winning just 64 times and finishing seventh for the second straight year. Cardwell led the Cubs in ERA (3.82), complete games (13), and strikeouts (156). His 38 starts were the most in the National League that year and were the most by a Cub since Grover Cleveland Alexander's 40 in 1920. Cardwell's 259 ⅓ innings—third in the NL—were the most by a Cub since Hank Wyse's 278 ⅓ in 1945.

The Cubs suffered the first 100-loss season in franchise history in 1962, kept out of 10th place only by the miserable original Mets. Cardwell fell to 7–16 and his 4.92 ERA was his highest until his final season in the majors. He was taken out of the rotation in mid-September and wound up relieving 12 times for the Cubs. While the Cubs were down on Cardwell, the Cardinals still thought him a valuable commodity. On October 17, 1962, St. Louis shipped Larry Jackson, Jimmie Schaffer, and Lindy McDaniel, the pitcher he'd beaten in his no-hitter, to Chicago for George Altman, Moe Thacker, and Cardwell. A little over a month later, Cardwell was off to Pittsburgh for former MVP Dick Groat in a four-player deal.

Three years removed from a world championship, the Pirates got rid of their championship infield in exchange for younger players. The result was 20 more losses than the year before and a drop to eighth in the National League. Cardwell did his part, however. He was second to Bob Friend in most team pitching categories and put together a 13–15 mark with a 3.07 ERA. He was a full-time starter again, but his lone relief outing of 1963 led to arm problems that dogged him for the next year and a half.

Cardwell tossed five innings and took the loss in the first game of a doubleheader at Wrigley Field on July 21. Manager Danny Murtaugh went through his staff and needed Cardwell to come into the nightcap when the Pirates rallied to force extra innings. He went three innings—allowing only one hit—and wound up getting the win. His two-decision day took a toll, though. "It was too much of a strain on my arm," he said. "Later, when I pitched again, my arm felt heavy. It was like pitching a shot put instead of a baseball."[5]

In his final start of 1963, he threw just one pitch before leaving the game. Cardwell was out until the final month of the 1964 season, starting four games for the Pirates.

He rebounded in 1965 for his second winning season while having his second-highest total for starts (34) and innings (240 ⅓), along with a 3.18 ERA. Despite being a key member of a staff that included Bob Veale, Vern Law, and Friend—and being the youngest of the foursome—Cardwell moved into a bullpen role by midseason 1966 after opening up at 3–6 for new manager Harry Walker. Cardwell did not start after July and pitched just twice after Labor Day. Each of those two outings lasted just two-thirds of an inning.

So it wasn't terribly surprising that on December 6, 1966, the day before his 31st birthday, Cardwell was traded for the third time. The Bucs sent him to the Mets along with outfielder Don Bosch for pitcher Dennis Ribant and light-hitting outfielder Gary Kolb. Mets general manager Bing Devine, who shuttled people in and out of the locker room all year in a flurry of moves, had been eying Bosch to be his center fielder. Bosch turned out to be a bust, but Cardwell remained a Met long enough to see the team scale the unimaginable heights of success in 1969. First, however, there were plenty of rough times ahead for the club.

Cardwell was the second Mets pitcher to make his debut as the Opening Day starter. Though Roger Craig had done so in 1962, that was the first game in franchise history. Yet like Craig, Cardwell started his Mets career with a loss on day one. Cardwell opened the 1967 season with eight solid innings against his former team, but he allowed consecutive doubles to start the ninth and suffered the defeat against the Pirates at Shea Stadium. No other Met made his club debut as the Opening Day starter until Mike Hampton in 2000.[6]

Cardwell went 5–9 with a 3.57 ERA in 26 games (16 starts) for the 1967 Mets. Three of his wins were shutouts—a good idea since the Mets were the worst-hitting club in the league. Hitting was so strenuous for the club that Cardwell got hurt just drawing a walk. "I tried to hold up on a pitch," he said, "and it was like I hit my funny bone. I stepped out of the box and tried to keep working it and working it until finally the trainer came out and asked me what was wrong. The pitch was ball four, and I was left on first base when the inning ended."[7] He allowed three hits and a walk in the bottom of the inning and left the game with an injured elbow and a loss. He did not pitch again for six weeks.

Cardwell started 25 times in 1968 and went 7–13 in his first season under manager Gil Hodges and pitching coach Rube Walker. His ERA in the "Year of the Pitcher" dipped to 2.96, his lowest ever over a full season, which was slightly below the league average of 2.99. It still being the Mets, though, Cardwell managed to lead the club in losses. During one loss, he drop-kicked his glove all the way to the dugout.[8]

He kicked more than just his glove. When Ron Swoboda was given love beads by some young fans in Los Angeles in '68 and wore them on the team flight to Houston, Cardwell, a southern conservative, took offense. "We were on the plane," said Cardwell, "and we had gotten beat the game before. I walked to the back of the plane and saw those love beads and snatched them off and almost got into a fight. I didn't believe in the love beads and all the parades they were having and two of our ballplayers were supporting this. That wasn't me. That just rubbed me the wrong way."[9]

Cardwell was the elder statesman of the pitching staff and second only to Ed Charles age-wise on the club. The 1968 Mets had been the youngest team in the major leagues. The '69 club wasn't much older; they just had much better luck.

Yet the luck was not all good for Cardwell early on. He started off at 0–4 as the Mets scored just twice in his first 28 innings of work. He finally got himself a win by taking matters into his own hands, allowing only a Lee May home run to Cincinnati while breaking the game open with a three-run blast of his own (it turned out be his last major league home run). Cardwell's most famous moment with the bat, however, came in the back end of an extraordinary doubleheader in September.

With the Mets remarkably having taken over first place from the Cubs, the Mets hit Pittsburgh for a Friday night doubleheader. Left fielder Cleon Jones was injured and platoon right fielder Art Shamsky missed the twin bill because it was Rosh Hashanah. The Mets had little offense to begin with and they snuck out a win in the opener with pitcher Jerry Koosman singling in the only run and protecting the lead with a shutout. Cardwell, who'd driven in just one run since his three-run homer against the Reds in May, singled in Bud Harrelson against Dock Ellis in the second inning in the nightcap. Cardwell danced through trouble and the lead held up, with ninth-inning help from Tug McGraw. The twin 1–0 wins with pitchers driving in the only runs of each game—part of 36 consecutive scoreless innings by the club—pushed the Mets to 2 ½ games in front of Chicago. It seemed like further proof that baseball was in the midst of a miracle.

Despite his slow start, Cardwell wound up winning five consecutive decisions as the Mets surged to the division title. Only a poor start in the meaningless season finale pushed his ERA to 3.01 and kept him from having a .500 mark at 8–10.

Cardwell did not get a postseason start. Cardwell recalled having a meeting with Gil Hodges on the subject just before the start of the World Series. "Gil said, 'Cardy, don't feel hurt because you did a great job all year for us and got us into the playoffs and this Series, but here's what we're gonna do. Rube [Walker] and I agreed that we're gonna start Seaver, Koosman, and Gentry in the three games, and then we're gonna come back with them. But you're our seventh game pitcher if it goes seven games.'"

It did not go seven games, but Cardwell, serving as the long reliever, pitched in the opener in Baltimore. Tom Seaver had trouble in the first Mets World Series game ever and Cardwell came in for the sixth inning after warming up several times. He was extremely nervous. "I'd never been there before and I was just keyed up. It's different in football, where you see those guys all worked up and butting helmets. You can't do that in baseball. You just say to yourself, 'Listen, dummy, you've been doing this for how many years? Now is not the time to screw up, pardon the expression.'"[10]

Cardwell retired the Orioles in order in what turned out to be his only career postseason appearance. The Mets won the next four games thanks to excellent starting pitching. They used only two other relievers—Ron Taylor and Nolan Ryan—and hurled complete games in Games Four and Five as the Mets stunned the Orioles.

Cardwell remained in the bullpen in 1970, starting just once in 16 appearances for the Mets. The Braves purchased him around the All-Star break and he finished his career that year in Atlanta's pen. The highlight of his final go-round actually came at Shea Stadium when Cardwell relieved on successive days against the Mets and did not allow a run. He stopped the bleeding on August 26 with the Braves down, 7–1, and Atlanta wound up coming back to win in the ninth. His final career outing didn't go as well. He surrendered a three-run home run in the ninth inning to Houston rookie Cesar Cedeno in Atlanta's home finale.

In 1971 Cardwell began a new career working for Ford. He served as an executive for two North Carolina car dealerships over the next 36 years. He had three children and five grandchildren.

He died at age 72 on January 14, 2008, in the same city in which he was born. The cause was Pick's disease, a rare neurodegenerative disease.

Among the men who fondly remembered Cardwell was Tom Seaver. He made his Mets debut the same week as Cardwell in 1967, only Cardwell had already been in the majors for a decade by the time Seaver threw his first pitch. "He was a tremendous mentor to the young guys on our staff," Seaver said upon Cardwell's passing. "When he said something, you listened. He was the ultimate professional."[11]

**Notes and Sources**

1. Merron, Jeff, "Don Cardwell throws no-hitter in Cubs debut—video of final outs" *http://108mag.typepad.com/the_southpaw/2007/05/don_cardwells_n.html, May 21, 2007.*

2. Ibid.
3. Ibid.
4. Ryczek, Bill, The Amazin' Mets, 1962-1969, McFarland & Company: Jefferson, NC, 2007: 207.
5. Biederman, Les. "Bucs Salvage Two Hill Vets off Junk Heap," The Sporting News, March 20, 1965: 13.
6. Marc Normandin, "Opening Days with New Faces," *http://www.metsgeek.com/articles/2008/04/02/opening-days-with-new-faces/, April 2, 2008.*
7. Ryczek, p. 163
8. Ryczek, p. 228
9. Ryczek, page 241
10. Ryczek, page 254
11. Goldstein, Richard, "Don Cardwell, 72, Pitcher for 1969 Mets, Is Dead," New York Times, January 16, 2008.

Biederman, Les. "Bucs Salvage Two Hill Vets off Junk Heap." The Sporting News , March 20, 1965.

Goldstein, Richard, "Don Cardwell, 72, Pitcher for 1969 Mets, Is Dead." New York Times, January 16, 2008.

Merron, Jeff. "Don Cardwell throws no-hitter in Cubs debut—video of final outs" *http://108mag.typepad.com/the_southpaw/2007/05/don_cardwells_n.html (May 21, 2007 entry).*

Normandin, Marc. "Opening Days with New Faces," *http://www.metsgeek.com/articles/2008/04/02/opening-days-with-new-faces/ (April 2, 2008 entry).*

Ryczek, Bill. The Amazin' Mets, 1962–1969. (Jefferson, NC: McFarland & Company, 2007.)

## A Met Is Born

Twenty-six future Mets were born in 1969, plus former coach Manny Acta and oft-injured Mets pitcher Orlando Hernandez, whose birthdate in Cuba could have been 1959 as far as anyone really knows. Robert Person was born the day the Mets beat the Braves to claim their first pennant (October 6), Jose Valentin arrived the day the Mets won their first World Series game (October 12), and 2008 Met Damion Easley came to life in a New York City that was still in a miraculous euphoria over the unlikely world championship less than a month earlier. Of all those future Mets born in 1969, one was born to a major leaguer... and a Cub, no less.

Todd Randolph Hundley was born on May 27, 1969, in Martinsville, Virginia. His father, Randy, was across the country in San Francisco, going 0-for-4 in a 5–4 loss to the Giants. The day after Todd's birth, a seemingly more relaxed Randy hit a grand slam, knocked in five, and pushed his average over .300 as the Cubs held on for a 9-8 win at Candlestick Park. The Cubs were 30–16 and had a nine-game lead on the fourth-place Mets.

It was a different time. Fathers were not requested—or wanted—in the delivery room and what might today be a two-day birthing sabbatical for the proud papa was just another workday in 1969. Hundley did make plans to hustle back to see the boy before Chicago's ensuing homestand. He also made no bones about what he wanted.

"I've been waiting for a son for seven years," Hundley, whose son was born just a few days shy of his dad's 27th birthday, told a writer shortly after returning to work at Wrigley Field. "I felt like when I saw Todd for the first time, all my dreams had come true. When I went into that waiting room at the hospital when out first daughter was born, I was sure that God didn't make anything but boys. Well, He fooled me twice, but this time I came out a winner. I love my daughters, but wait until you see Todd."

Fortunately, his daughters were too young to read.

Todd grew up to be a catcher like dear old Dad, but a Met of all things. He wasn't the defensive stalwart his father was, but Todd had a lot more power; his 41 home runs in 1996 lasted as the Mets record (tied 10 years later by Carlos Beltran) through the life of Shea Stadium. There were Mets aplenty born the year of Woodstock, the moon landing, Chappaquiddick, and the Miracle at Flushing.

*continued on next page*

*continued*

**Mets born in 1969**

| Met | '69 DOB | Pos. | Year(s) as Met |
|---|---|---|---|
| Manny Acta | January 11 | Coach | 2005–06 |
| Kevin Morgan | March 3 | 3B | 1997 |
| Craig Paquette | March 28 | 3B | 1998 |
| Pete Walker | April 8 | P | 1995, 2001–02) |
| Jeromy Burnitz | April 15 | OF | 1993–94, 2002–03 |
| Ken Takahashi | April 16 | P | 2009 |
| Fernando Vina | April 16 | 2B | 1994 |
| Rick Trlicek | April 26 | P | 1996–97 |
| Pete Schourek | May 10 | P | 1991–93 |
| Todd Hundley | May 27 | C | 1992–98 |
| Mike DiFelice | May 28 | C | 2005–07 |
| Toby Borland | May 29 | P | 1997 |
| Kurt Abbott | June 2 | SS | 2000 |
| Dae-Sung Koo | August 2 | P | 2005 |
| Matt Franco | August 19 | 3B–1B | 1996–2000 |
| Ricky Bottalico | August 26 | P | 2004 |
| Darren Bragg | September 7 | OF | 2001 |
| Jeff Barry | September 22 | OF | 1995 |
| David Weathers | September 25 | P | 2002–04 |
| Robert Person | October 6 | P | 1995–96 |
| Orlando Hernandez | October 11* | P | 2006–07 |
| José Valentin | October 12 | 2B | 2006–07 |
| Shane Halter | November 8 | OF | 1999 |
| Damion Easley | November 11 | 2B | 2007–08 |
| Rigo Beltran | November 13 | P | 1998–99 |
| Pedro Astacio | November 28 | P | 2002–03 |
| Mike Fyhrie | December 9 | P | 1996 |

*True age unsure

# Ed Charles

by Edward Hoyt

| Season | Age | G | AB | R | H | 2B | 3B | HR | RBI | BB | SO | SB | CS | BA | OBP | SLG |
|---|---|---|---|---|---|---|---|---|---|---|---|---|---|---|---|---|
| 1969 Mets | 35 | 61 | 169 | 21 | 35 | 8 | 1 | 3 | 18 | 18 | 31 | 4 | 2 | .207 | .286 | .320 |
| Career 8 Years | – | 1005 | 3482 | 438 | 917 | 147 | 30 | 86 | 421 | 332 | 425 | 86 | 35 | .263 | .330 | .397 |

As a big leaguer, Ed Charles was perhaps the most accomplished player in the brief history of the ill-fated Kansas City Athletics, and he achieved fame as a baseball poet, reciting his poetry on television a few times per year and mailing verse to young fans with requested autographs. But he is best remembered today for the end of his playing career, providing sorely needed veteran presence and perspective on the magically youthful "Miracle Mets" championship squad of 1969. He was known as "The Glider," "Ez," and "The Poet Laureate of Baseball," but the first name that stuck—so to speak—was "Gum," a nickname he inherited from his father.

If Edwin Douglas Charles had never played a day in the big leagues, his story would still be remarkable. Coming of baseball age in the era immediately following the triumphs of Jackie Robinson and Larry Doby, Ed Charles—along with legends such as Hank Aaron and largely forgotten contemporaries such as Percy Miller and Nat Peoples—was part of the generation that repeated Robinson's and Doby's brave stories in dozens of minor leagues on the rosters of the hundreds of teams and that crisscrossed America by bus each summer. These leagues were concentrated in the Deep South—leagues like the Southern Association, the Carolina League, and the Texas League, with roots going back to the 19th century, and still flourishing today.

It was a world that was largely unready to let go of Jim Crow, and a world whose desegregation would not occur with a national press corps watching. And Charles, a son of Daytona Beach, of segregation, lynching, a broken home, and the Great Depression, was an unlikely champion.

His generation of African-American ballplayers would challenge and change the culture of the major leagues, as society at large was undergoing a parallel change. Before all that, Charles arrived in the big leagues—disgracefully late, at almost 29—a veteran of too many racially charged hot southern summers, and a part of that brave generation of minor leaguers that followed Jackie Robinson, who played and lived in the much smaller, but equally dangerous, spotlight. Many of these athletes never made the major leagues. Charles was a survivor of this generation, and he did them proud.

The sensitivity later evident in Ed Charles's poetry made the hypocrisy of the world he grew up in that much more vivid. Born April 29, 1933 in Daytona Beach (three years before the city now so deeply linked with auto racing hosted its first official stock car race), Charles would later recall his school days reciting the pledge of allegiance and reading the United States Constitution, and feeling acutely how those words really didn't apply to him. His home life offered little respite from this paradox. Growing up in a family of nine children in a dilapidated segregated section of town, he recalled his father beating his mother, then getting his in kind from the local police. Food could be as scarce as opportunities, and the boy Ed Charles sought to fend for himself as best as he could. Like too many sons of broken homes, and too many African-American children unable to find meaning in their second-class education, Charles became a dropout.

One incident he would later recall had he and his brothers trying to retrieve a toy that had been stolen by white children. Rather than support them, his grandfather whipped them for confronting the white children—his way of harshly underscoring his warning to his grandchildren that they could get lynched for such confrontations. It was no far-fetched notion. One Lee Snell had been killed in that manner in Daytona Beach when Ed was five.

Charles's story is certainly is one of talent and hard work, but a key X factor that helped change the course of his life is that his hometown was where the Brooklyn Dodgers trained, and young Ed got a front row seat at the story that finally told black America that opportunities could open up for them: the debut of Jack Roosevelt "Jackie" Robinson in a major league training camp in 1946. Robinson, who had faced an army court-martial rather than give up a bus seat as an army lieutenant two years earlier, was twice forced to sacrifice his and his wife's airline seats to white passengers on his way across the country and made the last leg of the journey to spring training exiled to the back of a bus crossing Florida. Embarrassed and bitter, Robinson considered quitting, but he bravely took the field and began his long march into history. Ed Charles never forgot, and would refer to Robinson as a way-shower and redeemer.

"I was just a kid, and I was awed by it all, and I prayed for him," Charles recalled. "I would say, 'Please, God, let him show the whites what we can do so that we can excel like they can.'"[1]

To hear Charles tell it, even at 13, he knew what the moment meant—that to have aspirations, to succeed, to prosper, to merely be accepted as a human being, was suddenly a rational notion, because fulfillment of those aspirations had moved into the realm of the of the possible. If Robinson could succeed in smashing the unstated ban on black ballplayers in the big leagues, all other aspects of Jim Crow were perhaps also giants that could come crashing down.

Charles had already been a Dodgers fan, getting their games on the radio in Daytona and buying into the "Bums" reputation as champions of the downtrodden. But that was before Jackie. Charles described himself as sitting on the left field fence, unable to afford a ticket, and perhaps positioning himself to better fetch home run balls. Charles has told the following account to many writers, and the accounts may differ slightly on small details.

> *Everybody in our part of town wanted to see him. Old people and small children, invalids and town drunks. Some were on crutches, and some people clutched the arms of friends, walking slowly on parade to the ballpark to sit in the segregated section.*
>
> *We watched him play that day and finally believed what we had read in the papers, that one of us was out there on the ball field. When [spring training] was over, we kids followed Jackie as he walked with his teammates down to the train station, and when the train pulled out, we ran down the tracks listening for the sounds as far as we could. And when we finally couldn't hear it any longer, we ran some more and finally stopped and put our ears to the tracks so we could feel the vibrations of that train carrying Jackie Robinson. We wanted to be a part of him as long as we could.*[2]

But the road to fulfill that redemption made possible by Robinson remained long and rocky for the boy left behind in Daytona Beach. Leaving school after eighth grade, he drifted around Florida to live with various relatives—a grandfather, then an older brother, finally an older sister in St. Petersburg. It was there he began to find some stability, finding work as a dishwasher in a restaurant and working his way up to assistant baker, meanwhile receiving local notice starring for a neighborhood softball team, the Harlem Hawks. And a modestly anonymous life as an indifferently educated baker may have been his destiny, if romance hadn't intervened. Bringing home pies from work for his neighbors, Ed found himself smitten with a girl on his street—and she wasn't particularly interested in pursuing a relationship with a dropout, even one with pies. So Charles not only re-entered school, but did so in the 10th grade, not wanting to be a year behind his would-be girlfriend. He told the registrar at his new St. Petersburg school that his previous school in Daytona Beach had burned down, along with their records, and they took him at his word.

Along with the boost for his nascent romance, this proved beneficial for Charles's nascent athletic career at Gibbs High School. His most enduring memory was from the gridiron. He was sent in as a sophomore for his first punt, saw the lineman rushing him, and missed the kick completely. "Don't worry," his coach said. "You'll get another chance to make good."

Two years later, Charles was team captain of the baseball team, gaining the notice of scouts, but also starting quarterback of that same football squad, as Gibbs went undefeated and won the state Class A championship. Charles had made good on his second chance. What became of the girl is unclear.

His initial audition was with the then-Boston Braves—actually with their Class B team. While he was rejected by the team, he was excited to be the first black player to try out. Ed was considering an offer from a Negro League team—the Indianapolis Clowns—but a chance meeting with executive Vern Eckert got him another tryout in 1952 in Myrtle Beach, South Carolina, this time for the Braves' Class C affiliate. He was signed to join the Quebec City Braves.

The Provincial League was a world away from Daytona Beach. Quebec had an established history of welcoming black athletes. And the league, just then transitioning from independence into affiliating with big league teams, was home to many African-Americans, including Negro League veterans and young stars like Charles on their way to the bigs.

There are, indeed, accounts of black players in the league as far back as the 1800s, and they were a constant part of Quebec baseball from the 1920s forward. Of the first six black players signed by big league clubs in 1946, four had played in Quebec and one was Canadian-born. Others in the league at the time included Vic Power, Bob Trice, Carlos Bernier, Silvio Garcia, and longtime Homestead Gray and future Hall of Famer (2006) Ray Brown, who still had enough in the tank to help pitch three Québecois clubs to titles in that era. Charles's manager and occasional first baseman was former big leaguer George McQuinn, a solid first baseman who made seven All-Star teams in his younger days.

It was an uncharacteristically benevolent environment for Charles to start his pro career. The team finished second, 1½ games out, and Ed acquitted himself more than respectably for a rookie, batting .317, slugging .431, and leading the league with 11 triples—probably the outstanding offensive player on the team apart from a juggernaut half season put up by a minor league journeyman named John Werner. The only other teammate from Quebec City who went on to enjoy more than a brief cup of big league coffee was Humberto Robinson, another of Robinson's "disciples." This Robinson, a pitcher, became the first Panamanian-born big leaguer, helping pave the way for the likes of Rod Carew, Manny Sanguillen, and Mariano Rivera and 45 others. Also the first African-American to pitch for the Jacksonville Braves in the South Atlantic League, Robinson would set a Sally League record with 23 wins in 1954. He was additionally notable for reporting a $1,500 offer to throw a game in 1959.

Having never been out of Florida, Charles was simply used to being called "nigger" in white environments. But though he braced himself for that sort of attack, it never came. His landlords were white schoolteachers and surprised him with their tolerance. At worst, the black players were treated as a novelty, and Charles recalled being followed by a pack of small children as they walked to the ballpark, maybe reminiscent of young Ed and his friends following Jackie Robinson and the Dodgers to the train station.

It was perhaps important to go through Quebec and show himself and his organization that he could play professional baseball, because the next eight years would lead him through a breadth of Dixie locales—Corpus Christi, Louisville, Jacksonville, Fort Lauderdale among them—that would challenge him more than any fastball. For all Robinson's heroism, Jackie merely touched down in the

South before rising also to Quebec—famously starring for the Montreal Royals—and then on to the major leagues, which was still centered in the industrial belt. Charles spent the better part of a decade eating on the bus while his teammates went into restaurants, relieving himself in the shrubs, bunking with local black families while his teammates stayed in hotels, a quota system leading to the release of black players over less talented whites, and of course enduring the abuses and obstructions of fans—knowing all the while how disposable he was if he let these second-rate conditions affect his game. Some white teammates were supportive, but certainly not all, and the black players knew that if they complained to management of racial harassment from a white player, the team would likely deal with it based on who had the higher batting average. Getting justice was about continuing to hit.

PHOTO COURTESY OF METSILVERMAN.COM

*Ed Charles*

The 1953 season saw Charles assigned to the Fort Lauderdale affiliate of the Milwaukee Braves. He would describe the season as his favorite of his tour of the southern states. One of four black players on the team, his status as a native Floridian helped him garner the support of local newspapers as well as African-American fans. The familiarity of the environment also played to his favor. While the eating/lodging/travelling restrictions of segregation were firmly in place, the circuit hit larger cities like Tampa-St. Petersburg, West Palm Beach, and Miami, thus avoiding (at least to Charles's mind), the harsher sting of racial strife that he saw as present in the smaller Floridian towns. His manager in Fort Lauderdale was the old St. Louis Cardinal All-Star Pepper Martin. Charles enjoyed playing for "The Wild Horse of the Osage" and felt that all Martin judged their players by was how well they played.

After spending 1954 and a chunk of 1955 in the military, Charles found himself at spring training in 1956 in a competition for a big league job with future Met Felix Mantilla, and veteran Danny O'Connell. Unfortunately for Charles, who had mostly played shortstop in the minors, the available job was at second base. The Braves ended the competition by trading for veteran Red Schoendienst and making Mantilla the utility infielder. Ed was left on the outside looking in and sent to join the Wichita Braves.

It was in Wichita that an incident almost led Charles to quit. Juan Pizarro, an Afro-Puerto Rican, had an injured leg but his coaches insisted he go through the running workout. Seeing Pizarro running at a depressed speed, the coach told him that if he didn't want to run he could go back to Africa. Abuse from fans, opponents, even teammates was one thing, but being undercut by coaches was another. A discouraged Charles recounted the incident by phone to his grandfather, a Baptist minister in Daytona Beach. The advice he got was to simply sleep on it before making a decision. Ed thought that night of what Robinson endured without quitting, and he recommitted himself the next day. Charles would remember this as his low point, and he never again entertained the thought of quitting. Pizarro went on to an 18-year big-league career.

Ed would remember his South Atlantic League years as the most abusive circuit he played in—describing the racial taunts in Knoxville and Macon as so harsh as to make him appreciate the relative tolerance of Corpus Christi, Daytona Beach, and St. Petersburg. It was in Knoxville, playing for the Jacksonville Braves, that Charles recalled one of the best games of his life—diving stops on defense and spraying the ball all over the place on offense—only to be stopped by a spectator on the way out of the stadium.

"This southern gentleman was standing there," Charles said. "And he said to me, 'By golly, nigger, you are one hell of a ballplayer.'"

Charles looked back at the man. "I just shook my head and walked on by him."[3]

In one account, Charles recalls that story with frustration, but in a later recollection, he sees a minor victory in winning as much respect as the heckler could muster, suggesting the man's racism would have been that much more acute had he not watched Charles play (and play well) that Sunday. "Any forum of integration can lift the cloud of ignorance from us."[4] The most challenging situations also provided some of the more satisfying victories. The integration of the team forced the integration of other aspects of society when black and white players were asked to go together to represent the team at functions and charity events.

> *You had a chance to interact with whites in various fields. It gave us a chance to know each other better. Once you get to know someone, you're not going to feel as threatened. You probably tend to be more compassionate toward that person. You reach a higher level of a relationship when you interact together.*[5]

The turmoil reflected itself perhaps in the win column. That 1957 Jacksonville team, a perennial contender prior to that season, finished sixth, eventually needing two managerial changes to finish the season.

The next three seasons were a period of intense frustration for Charles. Stuck at the AAA level in Wichita, Louisville, and finally Vancouver, as he put together three batting years that would suggest to any observer that he was big league material, hitting .284, .270, and .305, respectively. While Charles would in later years cite a quota system keeping him on the farm, one reality was that the Braves had star slugger Eddie Mathews at third base (Charles had moved to the hot corner in 1959). The Braves nonetheless tried many players at second base—a position Charles apparently also considered himself a candidate for—during this period, including aging vets like the white Red Schoendienst and the Mexican Bobby Avila. Charles saw himself and his talents as deliberately overlooked. "Baby," Charles would recall, "that was a hurtin' thing."[6]

It was winter ball in Puerto Rico in 1961 when Ed Charles first took up his hand at poetry. In truth, that which survives doesn't indicate a special ability in the craft of verse—often evincing the novice poet's practice of reversed phrasings and twisting of meter to resolve a rhyme scheme. What makes it compelling is the honest peek into the soul of a witness to such a brutal but important era in African-American history. A line about Jackie Robinson, "He ripped up the sod along the baselines," initially seems quite prosaic, until you read on and slowly realize the sod was also the firmament of the American racial divide, and Jackie's cleats were tearing it apart.

After several good seasons at the top of the minor league ladder, Charles was nearing the end of his twenties without so much as a day on a big league bench. But 1962 would be the second straight season of expansion in the big leagues, leaving teams with four more rosters to fill, and that offseason saw players regularly shuffled around to fill in gaps after the Mets and Houston Colt 45s (later Astros) established their initial rosters with the October expansion draft. Finally, on December 15, 1961, Ed Charles's big break came: He was traded to the Kansas City Athletics with Joe Azcue and Manny Jimenez in exchange for Bob Shaw and Lou Klimchock (two future Mets, incidentally).

Having waited so long for his break, Charles disappointed neither himself nor his new employers. Given the third base job over Wayne Causey, Ed posted a .288 batting average, reached base at .356 clip, and slugged .454—his 17 homers that season would remain his career high. He made the league's all-rookie team as the perennial sad-sack franchise increased its win total from 61 to 72.

But enigmatic A's owner Charlie Finley lived up to his reputation. According to Charles, as he excelled throughout his rookie season while making the major league minimum of $7,000, Finley made a point of tearing up his contract and substituting a $10,000 contract in its place. After the season, however, Charles was never given the $5,000 raise to $15,000 that he had been promised. He was instead given a $12,000 salary—$5,000 over his original contract. The experience affected the third baseman's enthusiasm through his tenure in Kansas City.

Charles nonetheless capitalized on his chance and became a consistent performer on these Athletics teams. He offered no standout skill, but usefully adequate levels of contact, power, speed, and defense. He found a home in Kansas City—formerly the base of so many great Negro League teams—and married. The former dropout began taking college courses and eagerly awaited the birth of his first child. But when that son, Eric, came and was diagnosed with cerebral palsy, his career took on a new seriousness. He began to worry about the lifelong care his son would need. He would initially be shy about bringing his son to the ballpark as other players would with their children, fearing the negative attention the child's condition might attract.

Ironically, Charles has Finley to thank for perhaps becoming the most accomplished player in the short history of the Athletics tenure in Kansas City—in between their Philadelphia and Oakland addresses. The fickle Finley effectively operated as his own general manager, and made changes on a whim, firing his managers and strangely trying to imitate the Yankees' success by ordering a renovation of his stadium's outfield walls to match the dimensions of Yankee Stadium—a plan that was stopped by the league.

But Charles was a steady player who never quite rose to the level of "star." This sort of quiet success would eventually (and forever, presumably) make him the Kansas City Athletics' all-time leader in games played (726) and total bases (1,065). He is second in runs scored (344), hits (703), and runs batted in (319). Yet he never made the All-Star team as one of the top players on a club that never won more than 74 games in his five full seasons with the club.

The 1967 season was largely a struggle for Ed Charles. He came out of the gate slowly, managing just 15 hits in his first 61 at-bats, and only one of those for extra bases. The A's were looking to bring a rookie named Sal Bando at third. They turned the position over to Bando and traded Charles to the New York Mets for Larry Elliot and $50,000. While Bando would go on to anchor third for championship clubs after the A's moved to Oakland, he wasn't yet ready, and contributed little in what would be the club's final season in Kansas City. Charles, meanwhile, had a championship of his own ahead of him.

"I had no bad feelings about New York," Charles later recalled, "but I had been in Kansas City since 1962, and I thought I would finish up there. I was thirty-four years old at the time and I had talked with Mr. Finley, and he said they were thinking of making me a coach, so I was a little discouraged when they traded me. Any trade hits you hard, especially when it comes near the end of your career."[7] His main regret was leaving his wife and the son he worried about so much. His wife Betty was from Kansas City and wouldn't be initially joining him in New York.

The 1967 season was a most unusual one for the Mets. It was their lone year under famed executive Vaughan P. "Bing" Devine, and the season was run more or less as a tryout camp, with Devine constantly bringing in new blood and dealing off the players who didn't make an impression. Fifty-four men would take the field for the team that season, the largest National League team ever. A 55th (Nolan Ryan) would suit up but not appear. They would also have two different managers (Wes Westrum and Salty Parker). It was a seemingly crazy way to run a franchise—the Mets fell backwards in the standings to 61 wins—but by the end, when Devine returned to the St. Louis team he had come from, he would leave behind almost every eventual contributor to the Mets' championship two years later.

The incumbent third baseman for the Mets at the time of the deal was Ken Boyer, and Charles wasn't looking like much of an upgrade, but Boyer was two years older, and Devine was looking to move him while he still had some trade value. By midseason Boyer was gone, and third base was Charles's alone, the latest (number 32) in an already long line of Met third basemen.

But the .238 average and a .319 slugging percentage Charles posted in 1967 were no guarantees that he would remain in New York. Had Devine remained, he may well have found another address for Charles. Under replacement GM Johnny Murphy and new manager Gil Hodges, Charles was removed from the roster after the season, and came to camp in 1968 on a minor league contract.

But 1968 was a new year in more ways than a turn of a calendar page. Under Hodges, the Mets took the field with a renewed purpose and a seriousness absent in previous Mets seasons. Charles responded well to Hodges's regime, won back his job, and had a remarkable season. Though a .276 batting average, .328 on-base percentage, and .434 slugging percentage may not make the eyes pop at first glance, it has to be remembered that 1968 was to become known as "The Year of the Pitcher," with the entire National League hitting only .243. The Mets, as usual, took up the rear at .228, despite Charles's efforts.

A lot of things have to go right for a team to win a championship, a lot of players staying healthy, and a confluence of players having good or outstanding years at the same time. It's hard to imagine the Mets sniffing their eventual success of 1969 if Art Shamsky or Tommie Agee played as poorly as they did in 1968. Tug McGraw split 1968 between the minors and the military. But 1968 was actually Ed Charles's best year for the Mets. He even led the team in home runs, despite getting into only 117 games. What's more, his senior status helped define the Mets culture. Accounts have rookie Jerry Koosman nicknaming him "The Glider." It has largely been understood as a complimentary moniker, alluding perhaps to the fluid motion of the athlete in action, but there was a teasing element implied also, suggesting that the veteran Charles had learned to play with a certain degree of economy, never running faster than he had to make a play, never throwing the ball any harder than he had to beat the runner. Like the aircraft of the same name, The Glider could fly certainly, but never seemed to be providing any extra propulsion. "Pops" and "Old Man" were also names he heard in the clubhouse.

Charles took it in stride and became something of a field commander for Hodges and the attitudes he tried to instill.

> *Guys gravitated to me because I was older, both the black and the white players. Being in the minors so long was something a lot of them couldn't understand. They had made the bigs after a year or two. When I first got there in 1967, they would laugh after losing games. That changed with Hodges. I wanted to make sure the guys didn't slip back into that frame of mind after the 1968 season. Nobody laughed when we lost. We were playing serious baseball."*

Charles sensed divisions in the clubhouse that he sought to help heal. The longtimers—Ed Kranepool and Ron Swoboda, specifically—seemed to clash with some of the younger players, primarily Tom Seaver. Charles also tried to keep Cleon Jones from getting down on himself, as he endured whispers that he wasn't hustling on the field.

But Charles's field leadership and clubhouse diplomacy in 1968 provided no more job security than his productive bat did. He was exposed to that year's expansion draft and asked owner Joan Payson (he called her "Mama Payson"[9]) if he could return to the team the following spring as a non-roster player. When Montreal and San Diego each passed on him, that's what he did, and he ended up making the squad, even though he wasn't exactly clear how he fit into the team's plans. The Mets had a talented young outfielder in Amos Otis, but the club considered itself set at all three outfield positions. Having a reputation for being unable to establish more than a passing occupant at third, they envisioned a future for Otis at the hot corner, and Charles's duty was to help prepare Otis for the position and then bow out gracefully when Otis was ready. But Otis brashly considered himself the team's best outfielder, resisted the internship, and ended up playing few games at third base, to Charles's surprise as much as anybody's.

> *I wanted to help him (Otis) and I didn't worry about my job. I thought they would keep me as a pinch hitter anyway. He just didn't want to learn that position. He just hated third base. He was afraid of the ball down there and he wasn't going to learn."*[10]

The season opened with Ed playing the first seven games at third. Perhaps unready for regular duty, he got untracked slowly, hitting .154 over those first seven games. He yielded the position to Otis, then to utility player Kevin Collins, and finally to Wayne Garrett, a rookie acquired that offseason in the Rule V Draft.

By mid-May, Gil Hodges would settle on a platoon of Charles and Garrett. It was a jerry-rigged solution to be sure, but the team was already surprising the league by regularly playing competitive ball. Charles, easily the oldest player on a team that had borne the nickname of "The Youth of America" was fully aware that his days as a big leaguer were waning. He cherished the team's run of success, and began to take more seriously his role as a calming veteran presence on the squad. Charles was a regular among the team's contingent when they made charity visits, and he would counsel Jones and Tommie Agee—both from the Mobile, Alabama area (as was Otis)—about the ongoing adjustments to life in the majors as African-Americans. Charles also began bringing his son Eric to the park that summer, delighting in the boy giving his all with the other children on Family Day, and perhaps offering some perspective to his newly contending teammates. Charles's role as field general became more formal as well, so entrenched was he in the Gil Hodges command structure that actual orders no longer became necessary. "After a while I had these vibes with Gil," Charles recalled. "I wouldn't say anything and he wouldn't say anything, but I always knew what he wanted. I think I acted as his emissary on the field."[11]

The only problem was that Charles wasn't hitting. And with the team in the hunt for this new prize called a "division championship," they needed him to.

There were many key markers the Mets needed to pass before achieving their miracle of 1969. For many teams, reaching—and then surpassing—a .500 record, at least after the first week of the season, is part of that journey. The Mets briefly reached that point at 18–18 on May 21 as Tom Seaver beat Phil Niekro and the Braves, but a mini-slump followed.

Charles's bat woke up in a big way on May 31. With second baseman Ken Boswell serving army reservist duty, Wayne Garrett was shifted to second, and Charles saw some time against right-handed pitchers, including that day's draw, future Hall of Famer Gaylord Perry. Down 2–0 at Shea, Charles slugged a three-run homer to put the Mets ahead in the fourth. He added an RBI single in the eighth to tally all of the Mets offense that day as they won, 4–2, the third victory of what would be an 11-game winning streak.

Two days later, on June 2, the Mets reached the .500 mark never to look back, as Jerry Koosman outdueled Claude Osteen of the Dodgers, 2–1. Charles, who entered the day hitting .147, scored the go-ahead run and added a double. As the media gathered around Koosman looking for a quote, he gave them a poetic salute to his poetic teammate that probably wasn't original, but it became seared that night into Mets history: "Never throw a slider to the Glider."

Charles's bat started heating up that June—to the tune of a .295 batting average and a .360 on-base percentage. And team was making their move as well, entering the month at 21–23, going 19–9 and ending the month eight games over .500. The first-place Cubs were hot also, and the Mets merely improved from nine games back to 7 ½, but the two teams would soon be meeting head-to-head.

Charles credits Gil Hodges platooning strategy with helping the team catch the Cubs that summer. (Three other positions besides third were shared on the Mets once Donn Clendenon joined the team in a mid-June trade.) "It wasn't just going against left-handers and right-handers. It also helped rest our guys. One of the reasons we caught the Cubs was that we were stronger in July and August. They were older and more tired than the rest of us."

Older, perhaps, then most of the Mets. If the platoon strategy kept other players strong deep into the summer, Charles's bat was cooling again. He batted .176 in July and .188 in August. The .207 batting average he would have at the end of the year was the mark of a borderline major leaguer, but this was a team where everybody's contribution was needed—and not just in the clubhouse. On September 24, as the Mets stood a game away from their division title, Shea Stadium was packed. There were six games left, but this would be their last chance to clinch the title at home. Their opponent was the Cardinals and emerging superstar southpaw Steve Carlton, who had struck out 19 Mets a week before. Now the Mets opened with a rally. Bud Harrelson led off with a single and Tommie Agee followed with a walk. After Cleon Jones fanned, Donn Clendenon stepped to the plate and slugged a three-run homer.

But the Mets and their righty platoon weren't done. After Ron Swoboda walked, Ed Charles took Carlton the other way, homering to right. It was the last of the 86 home runs in his late-starting career, and probably the biggest. He rounded third exuberantly clapping. The Mets cruised to a 6–0 win in their clincher, the only season in Charles's major league career that he played for a winning team.

Charles got into only 61 games that storied season, and the clincher was his last. He also sat out the three-game sweep of the Atlanta Braves in the inaugural National League Championship Series, as the Braves started three right-handed pitchers. Yet with the Baltimore Orioles throwing two lefties in their three-man World Series rotation, Charles looked to be back in action. "The worst feeling is not to be part of things" he said, "not to feel you've made a contribution." He had already told his friends of his intention to retire.

Batting sixth in Game One, Charles went 0-for-4 as the Mets dropped the first game with Mike Cuellar besting Tom Seaver. Game Two featured a matchup of two lefthanders—Koosman and Dave McNally—and the two teams locked up in a 1–1 tie heading to the ninth. The Mets were in danger of dropping the first two games as their first two batters made outs and Charles stepped to the plate. McNally had struck out seven Mets that day and yielded only three hits, but one of these was a seventh-inning double by Charles, deep down the line in left. Charles was getting around, and he did so again, singling through the left side of the infield. Getting the steal sign a few pitches later, he took off for second with a 2–2 count on Jerry Grote, hustled into third on Grote's single to left, and scored the go-ahead run on the next pitch on a single by Al Weis.

But his day was not done. When Koosman couldn't finish the Orioles off in the ninth and walked two straight batters, Ron Taylor came in to face Brooks Robinson. The Orioles star worked the count full and Gil Hodges had the option of playing Charles straight away, to guard against the game-tying single, or on the line, to prevent the game-winning double. Perhaps sensing Hodges's "vibes" as he claimed he could, he cheated a step or so toward the line. When Robinson pulled the ball toward the third base bag, Charles was able to slide over and make a nifty stop. But the play was only half over. His initial instinct was to get the force at third, but after starting in that direction, he realized pinch runner Merv Rettenmund had him beat. With little time to spare, he rushed the throw across the diamond, on line but low. Clendenon dug the ball out of the dirt and the Series was even.

Charles played in Games Four and Five as the Mets rallied in each contest to claim the world championship. He handled his chances cleanly but had no further hits. He had asked merely to make a contribution, and in Game Two he had. In the memorable photos of Jerry Koosman and Jerry Grote embracing after the final out of Game Five, one of

Photo courtesy of *Mets Inside Pitch* Archives

*As the club's elder statesman, Ed Charles provided leadership on a young team and helped show the likes of Bud Harrelson the ropes in the major leagues.*

the most identifiable faces is that of Ed Charles running in from third, the veteran's face beaming like a child's. "This is the summit," Charles said later in the locker room celebration. "We're number one in the world and you just can't get any bigger than this."

That same joy animated the love affair America would have with the unlikely heroes over the next few weeks, with Ed's smile beaming through the ticker tape parade. When the parade stopped at Bryant Park, and the Mets were greeted by singer/actress/Mets fan Pearl Bailey, Edwin Charles was invited to recite a poem he had written back in 1962, when he had finally gotten his call to the majors. It began:

*Author of my talents, only You have I praised,*
*To Thee only shall my hands be raised.*
*For when I'm burdened with the weight of my team,*
*To my rescue You come, it will always seem.*
*For outstanding is my play on any given day*
*When You intervene and help lead the way.*
*Grateful to You I'll always be*
*For exploiting my talents for the world to see.*

The parade was followed by the team's appearance singing on *The Ed Sullivan Show.* Like the club's comical attempt to cut a musical album, Charles enthusiastically participated. When he returned to Kansas City, his flight was greeted by a welcoming delegation of civic leaders. Then, a little over a month after the end of the championship season, on December 1, 1969, Charles was released. He retired from baseball on top, part of perhaps the unlikeliest championship team ever.

While the press took his side, sensing an injustice to the spirit behind that back-page smile, Charles was ready to go. He had a job offer from the Mets' promotion department and was ready to move on. But he and Mets GM Johnny Murphy had a falling out over moving expenses. Charles instead went to work in promotions for Buddha Records—a label known mostly for "bubblegum" acts like the Lemon Pipers and the 1910 Fruitgum Company, but also the home of novelty recordings, including the recent LP release, *The Amazing Mets,* that the team had recorded. (Buddha owner Art Kass would later marry Carol Kranepool, ex-wife of the Mets' Ed.) As some Mets were offered $10,000 each to form a Las Vegas lounge act that winter, Ed followed through on a commitment to join a baseball tour of US military bases in Asia, particularly Vietnam. Johnny Murphy would suffer two heart attacks that winter, the second one fatal. Murphy died just weeks after trading Amos Otis, the center fielder who wouldn't play third, for Joe Foy, the third baseman the Mets erroneously thought could take Charles's place.

The Charleses' second son, Eddie, was born in the spring of 1970, and Ed started his new career in promotion. He also tried some entrepreneurial enterprises, but found little success—neither in the novelty business, nor in furniture. But entrepreneurship brought Ed, in 1972, to the Small Business Administration in lower Manhattan, where happenstance introduced him to his idol. Putting together a line of baseball novelties, he was at the offices when he crossed paths with Jackie Robinson. Robinson, prematurely breaking down from diabetes exacerbated by the tireless schedule he kept as a civil rights advocate, was getting into the construction business. Charles found himself initially unable to speak, finally thanking Robinson for everything he endured on behalf of others.

"You're welcome. That means a lot to me," Robinson replied.[12] Robinson would be dead before the year was done.

Charles stayed around baseball in retirement, but he also applied the lessons he learned in baseball to other parts of life. As the Mets' fortunes faded in the 1970s, he was invited to return to the team as a minor league instructor and scout. He lasted nine years, scouting the heartland states from his Kansas City base. His greatest contribution during this era was perhaps his scouting and signing of Neil Allen, the Mets' 1976 draftee out of Kansas City's Bishop Ward High School. A top closer during the Joe Torre era, Allen is also remembered as one of two players traded by the Mets for Keith Hernandez, a key player on their 1986 squad. This connection allows one to argue that Charles contributed to both Mets world championships.

It was Charles's understanding was that he was being groomed to take over as director of community relations when Tommy Holmes retired. But he again had a falling out—this time with colleague Ken Berry—and director of minor league operations Steve Schryver took Berry's side. Charles saw a racial element in the dynamic, and left. He had studied law enforcement at Rockford College in Illinois, and, having endured racial roadblocks throughout his playing career, he saw no reason continue. He had other options.

Charles has since lived out much of his post-baseball life in New York City's Washington Heights, spending decades working with children in the city's Department of Juvenile Justice, and with Youth Options Unlimited in the Morrisania section of the Bronx. Supervising juvenile offenders in a low security environment, Charles was able to pass on lessons going back to his troubled and disadvantaged youth, trying to impart lessons that could steer his charges on a path to perseverance, as Jackie Robinson had done for him.

"I never tell them I played baseball," he said. "But most of them find out and the question they ask most is, 'Why are you here?' I tell them, 'I'm here because you're here.'"[13]

For his signature lesson, he would reach all the way back to his football coach at Gibbs High in St. Petersburg, reminding them that, like him with his failed punt, they'll get "another chance to make good."[14]

The late 1980s featured a new growth industry that was perfect for Charles—the baseball fantasy camp, and he became a regular guest at Florida sessions, instructing middle-agers in the finer points of the game and thrilling them with the same enthusiasm that captivated them two decades earlier. He would occasionally return to the baseball stage—often bringing the juveniles in his care to Shea Stadium—but sometimes at a higher profile, such as in 1997, when he participated in many of the festivities celebrating the 50th anniversary of Jackie Robinson breaking baseball's color line. Among other things, he was part of three-day symposium at Long Island University reading a poem he had written decades earlier after Robinson's death.

*Yes, he made his mark for all to see*
*As he struggled determinately for dignity.*
*And the world is grateful for the legacy*
*That he left for all humanity.*

So might the world be grateful for the legacy of Charles and those like him, who hammered out the promise Jackie Robinson initiated, and so turned the path Robinson carved into a highway.

Charles returned to Shea Stadium on several occasions, notably for celebration of the careers of longtime broadcasters Bob Murphy and Ralph Kiner, offering ballads in their honor. Murphy delighted in the appearance of Charles as one of the treats of Bob Murphy Night that he most appreciated. Of Kiner, Charles took the time to allude to the legend's famous malapropisms—suggesting that they tended to occur when he was most scripted, but that Kiner was at his best when he was off-script.

On September 28, 2008, the Mets played their final game at Shea Stadium, their longtime home. After a crushing loss that cost the team a playoff berth, the Mets held a ceremony honoring the history of the team and the stadium. Forty-three players were introduced to represent that history. Ed Charles played less than three seasons with the Mets, amassing merely 279 games and 214 hits. But there was a fondly recalled 75-year-old Ed among superstars like Tom Seaver and Mike Piazza. It was a day for honoring excellence, but also for honoring something deeper that defined the team and their relationship with the fans through the years.

In his perseverance in the face of racial obstacles and his enthusiastic leadership for a miracle squad, Ed Charles could always be counted on to represent something deeper.

**Notes and Sources**

1 Lamb, Chris. *Blackout: The Untold Story of Jackie Robinson's First Spring Training.* University of Nebraska Press (Lincoln, Nebraska), 2004.

2 Ibid 1.

3 Coffey, Wayne. "The Inspiration of a Lifetime Seeing Jackie in '46 Helped Shape Ed Charles Forever." *New York News.* April 6, 1997.

4 Adelson, Bruce. *Brushing Back Jim Crow: The Integration of Minor-League Baseball in the American South.* University of Virginia Press (Charlottesville), 1999.

5 Ibid 4

6 Vecsey, George. *Joy in Mudville.* McCall (New York), 1970.

7 Cohen, Stanley. *A Magic Summer: The '69 Mets.* Skyhorse Publishing (New York), 2008.
8 Ibid 7.
9 Ibid 7.
10 bid 7.
11 Allen, Maury. *After the Miracle: The 1969 Mets Twenty Years Later.* Franklin Watts (New York), 1989.
12 Ibid 7.
13 Bell, Bill. "A Whole New Ballgame." *New York News.* May 6, 2000.
14 Ibid 13.

Adelson, Bruce. *Brushing Back Jim Crow: The Integration of Minor-League Baseball in the American South.* (Charlottesville: University of Virginia Press, 1999.)

Allen, Maury. *After the Miracle: The 1969 Mets Twenty Years Later.* (New York: Franklin Watts, 1989.)

Bell, Bill. "A Whole New Ballgame." *New York News.* May 6, 2000.

Coffey, Wayne. "The Inspiration of a Lifetime Seeing Jackie in '46 Helped Shape Ed Charles Forever." *New York News.* April 6, 1997.

Cohen, Stanley. *A Magic Summer: The '69 Mets.* (New York: Skyhorse Publishing, 2008.)

Durso, Joseph. *Amazing: The Miracle of the Mets.* (Boston: Houghton Mifflin Company, 1970.)

Halberstam, David. October 1964. (New York: Villard, 1994.)

James, Bill. The New Bill James Historical Baseball Abstract. (New York: The Free Press, 2001.)

Lamb, Chris. *Blackout: The Untold Story of Jackie Robinson's First Spring Training.* (Lincoln: University of Nebraska Press, 2004.)

Moffi, Larry, and Jonathan Kronstadt. *Crossing the Line : Black Major Leaguers, 1947-1959.* (Lincoln: University of Nebraska Press, 2006.)

Springer, Jon. "Bing Devine's Tenure as General Manager of the Mets." Lecture presented to the Society of American Baseball Research, 2005 Casey Stengel Chapter Annual Meeting. January 28, 2005.

Tygiel, Jules. Baseball's Great Experiment: Jackie Robinson and His Legacy. (New York: Random House, 1983.)

## Their Bats Weren't Miraculous—No Offense

The '69 Mets were not a potent club offensively. They were built on pitching and defense while scoring just enough runs to win consistently. It was a model that worked well, based on the club's 41–23 mark in one-run games.

Only one Mets regular, Cleon Jones, hit over .300 in 1969 (.340). Outfielder Art Shamsky hit .300 in a reserve role. Two other regulars hit over .270: Ken Boswell (.279) and Tommie Agee (.271). And only one Met, the leadoff hitter Agee, exceeded 20 home runs. He homered 26 times and scored 97 runs—impressive totals yet still not near the NL's top 10. No Met drove in over 80 runs, though Agee came closest, with 76. Jones, who that year had become the first Mets outfielder to start an All-Star Game, led the team in hits (164), steals (16), doubles (25), on-base-percentage (.422), and OPS (.904). Shamsky, though batting 180 fewer times than Jones, had a .488 slugging percentage—.006 higher than Cleon's career-best mark.

–Joseph Wancho

# Donn Clendenon

by Edward Hoyt

| Season | Age | G | AB | R | H | 2B | 3B | HR | RBI | BB | SO | SB | CS | BA | OBP | SLG |
|---|---|---|---|---|---|---|---|---|---|---|---|---|---|---|---|---|
| 1969 Mets | 33 | 72 | 202 | 31 | 51 | 5 | 0 | 12 | 37 | 19 | 62 | 4 | 1 | .288 | .348 | .515 |
| Career 12 Years | – | 1362 | 4684 | 594 | 1273 | 192 | 57 | 159 | 682 | 379 | 1140 | 90 | 57 | .274 | .328 | .442 |

His big brother in college was Martin Luther King, Jr.

Somehow, it's appropriate to begin with that fact when discussing Donn Clendenon. During his years at Morehouse College, one of the most pivotal players in Mets history was mentored by the greatest and most pivotal African-American of the 20th century. The big brother tradition for "Morehouse men" typically assigned juniors and seniors to incoming freshmen, but the King family knew the Clendenons well, and the future legend Martin Jr.—though he had already graduated from "The 'House," continued his studies at Crozer Theological Seminary, and received his ordination—volunteered for the duty.

If Ed Charles's remarkable baseball life was set in motion by being present as history was made by Jackie Robinson, you'd figure it would be hard for a teammate to have a bigger claim at being touched by greatness, but there you have it. As the Nobel laureate King would go on to almost define the civil-rights movement which culminated in many of the cultural upheavals of the 1960s, his protégé's modest contribution to that era would be as the final piece of the puzzle of the storied championship baseball team that capped the decade and captured the nation's imagination, a year after the murder of his mentor threatened to tear the nation apart.

It's just too good a story when it's told that way. But, while that's all true, it's too easy to paint King as the figure who set Donn Clendenon's remarkable baseball life in motion, but Donn would have told you that such an honor could only belong to Nish Williams.

Donn Alvin Clendenon never knew his father, a double PhD who taught mathematics and philosophy at Langston University, an all-black state university in Oklahoma. Claude Wendell Clendenon was just 32 when he died of leukemia, and his son only six months old. Growing up in a strictly segregated Atlanta, Donn had the fortune to be born into a comfortable middle-class family, and a mother strong and wise enough to step out of her mourning and go to work for the Scripto Pen Company (a huge employer of Atlanta blacks at the time) and to raise him with his father's intellectual ambition. (Donn graduated from high school at 15, a lone B-plus robbing him of a valedictorian status in his high-school class.)

But Donn also had a hero. He was six when his mother remarried, to Nish Williams, a successful restaurateur in black Atlanta and a 13-year veteran of the baseball's Negro Leagues, playing for several teams, primarily the Nashville/Columbus/Washington Elite Giants. Spending much of his career as a catcher noted for his arm, Williams moved around the diamond a lot, and was knocked into the outfield when the legendary Biz Mackey joined the Elites and became their backstop.

Nish raised his stepson with the all the attention and pride one could hope for out of any biological father, and brought a baseball knowledge comparable to Claude Clendenon's academic prowess. A player-manager with the Atlanta Black Crackers, Williams continued to play and coach semipro ball after his retirement, and worked for many years as an unpaid assistant coach with his alma mater, Morehouse. No less than Satchel Paige once credited Williams with being the only man who get around on the famed "hummer"—Paige's legendary fastball. It was Williams, too, who fine-tuned young Roy Campanella's catching skills.

It was an environment a boy with baseball ambitions could only dream of. Baseball was the "language" spoken by the denizens of the family restaurant, many retired and active ballplayers among them. Clendenon lists them all in his biography: Paige, Campanella, Jackie Robinson, Joe Black, Don Newcomb, Dan Bankhead, Sad Sam Jones, and more. When a 10-year-old Donn was exhibiting an aversion to getting hit by a thrown ball, his stepfather took him one evening to a local high school field where no less than Paige and Jones were assembling a wooden cage. The plan was for Donn to stand in the cage without a bat while the legends pitched and Nish caught, assigning Donn to identify the pitches as they crossed the plate. The caveat was that the cage was open only on the side facing the pitcher, leaving Donn vulnerable on that side, but unable to bail to any of the other three.

The experiment worked initially, as Paige's legendary control kept the ball over the plate. Donn wasn't so fortunate with Jones, however, receiving a welt on his backside from Sad Sam's first offering. But the greater humiliation was when Jones released his curveball—starting behind Donn's head, sweeping across the plate, and triggering the child to wet his pants somewhere in between.

Decades later, an outstanding 1970 season by Clendenon triggered an unexpected congratulatory phone call from James "Cool Papa" Bell. Bell, just scraping by at this time in his life, followed with a tearful apology for missing Williams's 1968 funeral, and Clendenon reciprocated the honor of the call with an invitation for Bell to visit the Mets clubhouse—regaling Mets both black and white with stories of the old times and the players to whom they were all indebted, transfixing them in the sort of major league locker room he himself had been barred from in his playing days.

But despite the environment of his upbringing, it wasn't baseball ambitions that drove Clendenon, and he resisted his stepfather's vision of stepping into Nish's spikes even as he grew into an athletic frame out of proportion with that of the son of an academic. Like many young men, Donn sought to define himself on his own terms rather than his parents', preferring UCLA to Morehouse, and basketball and football as better suited than baseball for his powerful body. But a conspiracy was afoot. With his bags packed for California, his family received a visit from a pair of Morehouse professors/coaches, who told his mother the 16-year-old freshman was too young to head across the country to UCLA. She bought the argument, went upstairs, unpacked Donn's bags, and he was headed to Morehouse, where the best and brightest of black Atlanta typically went. Clendenon's initial plan was to rebel by refusing to go out for any sports (he was attending on an academic scholarship), but his stepfather persuaded him to join the football team merely as the substitute punter when the regular punter was hurt, and Clendenon's competitive instincts did the rest. On his first play, he faked his kick, ran 55 yards for a touchdown, and his athletic career was restarted in earnest.

It can't be understated what it meant to be a "Morehouse man" at that time in history. "It was well known," Clendenon states in his biography, "that 80 to 85 percent of the African-American medical doctors and lawyers in the United States were graduates of Morehouse College." One may suspect that figure is disputable (certainly a Howard University man might), but even if it is, Clendenon's faith in it speaks of the stature the school held for black Atlantans, as well as African-Americans across the country. Be it his mother's dream of his becoming a doctor, or his stepfather's dream of his becoming a professional athlete, he was at a place that they both trusted of their own dreams for him. The advocacy of the coaches and professors and their high-pressure recruiting ploy, and his adoption by the King family could only underscore this point. King fulfilled the big brother's job—helping Clendenon adjust to the school over occasional dinners in the King home. Clendenon had an open invitation to drop by, and if Martin Jr. wasn't there, he had the ear of Martin Sr. (Class of 1926 and future trustee of the school); Martin Jr.'s wife, Coretta Scott King; or Martin's influential sister Christine King (a 1948 graduate of Spelman, Morehouse's sister school, and the alma mater of Clendenon's and King's mothers). And if not that, the young athlete could appreciate the home-cooked meals.

Greatness was all around and simply expected of Morehouse men. Clendenon wasn't the youngest person in his freshman class. That honor belonged to 15-year-old Maynard Jackson, who went on to become Atlanta's first black mayor. Donn starred in sports, but he was careful to think of sports as an avocation rather than a vocation. He considered a possible career as a high school teacher and coach, and his first job after graduation was teaching fourth grade and coaching. His education taught him not only to view the slim long-term prospects for a career in sports, but the narrow realities of the nominally integrated baseball scene of the '50s. Yes, black stars could find work, but how many marginal bench players of color would a team carry? Yes, an African-American player could get a chance in uniform, but would any team allow that player a chance to be a manager or executive when his playing days ended?

Nish Williams wasn't ready to give up on Donn. He had coached him on the semipro Atlanta Black Crackers during his summers, but the colder weather months concentrated Donn's thinking on the cold reality that his mind and education were his best assets in pursuing a success in life, and helping his family, his community, and his society—as he was raised and taught at "The 'House" to do. (And Clendenon was acutely aware that there were no guarantees there either—his postman had a PhD in physics!) Williams convinced Donn that he could have a true vocation, but that perhaps a career of a dozen or so years in his avocation as an athlete would help establish his name as a professional asset. The competitor in Clendenon again could not resist the argument. But Williams's job was only half-done. The 6-foot-4, 215-pounder graduated with 9.6 speed in the 100-yard dash, and that and the dexterous hands had the Cleveland Browns interested. And football players weren't asked to apprentice in the minors. But as at so many crossroads in Clendenon's life, he found legends to help steer him. In 1956, the oddly named 100 Percent Wrong Club, made up of black civic leaders of Atlanta, named Donn the College Athlete of the Year and Jackie Robinson the Man of the Year. Stuck at the banquet next to Robinson and keynote speaker Branch Rickey, Clendenon found his resistance futile as Rickey's silver tongue worked its magic and the stately Robinson—who himself was more highly celebrated on the gridiron in his own college days—provided the model of what he could become. Clendenon may have wondered if Rickey, Robinson, and his stepfather had planned it all out beforehand.

Convinced by Rickey that baseball would spare him football's high risk of a career-ending injury, he accepted an invitation to attend a Pittsburgh Pirates tryout camp in 1957—no contract in hand. Clendenon received 10 days of leave from his teaching assignment, got some last-minute advice from Nish ("be yourself; relax"), arrived in Jacksonville, and was assigned the cap and number 317. Over 500 hopefuls spread out over the six-diamond complex and were assigned to games. While Donn knew several players from his amateur and semipro experience, his own reputation hadn't preceded him. Pitchers sized him up, went with the notion that big men can't handle the curve, and fed him a steady diet of benders. His lessons with Sad Sam and Satchel paid off, and he clobbered the ball. He went through throwing drills and 60-yard dashes, running future All-Star Julian Javier to a draw. At the end of the day, the black players were sent to bunk with local black families. The next day, the names of players who were to report to management for a bus ticket home were posted, and for nine days, Clendenon's name didn't appear. His leave of absence being up, however, with no word on his status, he grew miffed, caught a plane back to Atlanta, and went home.

Donn returned home to several messages from the Cleveland Browns and a contract in the

Photo courtesy of metsilverman.com

*Even before he was a Met, Donn Clendenon sought out Gil Hodges, then manager of the Washington Senators, to help him with his fielding.*

bination of bad weather, low attendance, and a local ordinance prohibiting ballpark beer sales. The players went their separate ways with different assignments, and Donn was told to stay at the local YMCA and await instructions. Three weeks later, he was assigned to Salem, Virginia, in the Class D Appalachian League.

Minor league ball in the South was still quite a burden for a black player in 1957, and playing for a team called the Rebels can really put things in context.

mail from the Harlem Globetrotters. He brooded over the weekend and considered his options. Reporting to school the next morning, he found two new students in the back of his class, Pirates general manager Joe L. Brown and minor league director Branch Rickey Jr. They apologized for the misunderstanding, stating that they had intended to offer him a contract on his final day in camp. (Javier was the only other survivor of the 500.) Showing all of the flair and tightfistedness of Rickey Sr., they offered him a contract right there in the school—for $500 (nearly $5,000 in 2009 dollars). He went home, considered the challenges of the minors, the limited opportunities for blacks, and the reality that the only two black Pirates—Roberto Clemente and Roman Mejias—were Afro-Caribbean. He knew he could play at the top level immediately in basketball and football. He talked with his parents, and let his heart cross up his head. He signed.

It was back to training in Jacksonville for his first season with the Jamestown Falcons (Class D), and a long bus ride between Florida and upstate New York. Clendenon counted six other black players, but all Dominican (including Javier) plus a Virgin Islander (Elmo Plaskett). In 180 at-bats at Jamestown, Donn posted a .239 batting with six doubles, three triples, and only one home run before the team ceased operations in midseason due to some com-

Black and Hispanic players were again assigned to stay with black families rather than lodging with the white players. But Donn relaxed a little, put up a .275 average, with nine doubles, three triples, five homers, and a hundred calls to his stepfather.

His avocation in gear, his vocational work was mostly limited to substitute teaching in the offseason. But Clendenon's entrepreneurial spirit kicked in during his next season in Grand Forks, North Dakota, of the Class C Northern League. He asked for and got the clubhouse duties and was paid $5 by each player for laundry and shoe-shining service. No bootblack, he subcontracted the work to high schoolers, both at home and on the road, supervising them for quality assurance.

The season was another cultural jolt for Clendenon. There was one black family within about 100 miles, and he found himself fixed up with their daughter for the sole purpose of keeping him away from white women. The matchmaker was the team's general manager.

His play continued to progress, however, particularly his power stroke. Getting 453 at-bats, he hit .265 with 21 doubles, 12 triples, and 10 home runs while driving in 70 runs. His season ended a week early with a draft notice. With the intervention of the parent Pirates, Clendenon was placed in the Army Reserve and assigned to basic training at

Fort Jackson in Columbia, South Carolina. Despite his athletic prowess and zeal, he found himself prohibited from playing for the base basketball team, which was the province of the regular Army, and not reservists. Again, greatness intervened, as the base commander, the World War II hero General Mark Clark, did some fancy footwork. Clendenon remained a reservist, but his dog tags said Regular Army. Clark wanted a basketball championship for his base, and Clendenon starred for the team over the next four months, and lived the privileged life of a base jock, with Clark himself intervening if a superior tried to dress Clendenon down. For his part, Donn led the base team to the championship, and was discharged in time for spring training in 1959 in the best shape of his life.

He led the Pirates in every offensive category that spring , but when minor-league camp opened in Jacksonville (where the black players were housed above a black nightclub, and were kept up at night by the music and prostitutes), he was reassigned. When the season opened, it was the Class B Wilson Togs of the Carolina League for him. His torrid spring continued into April, and several weeks into the season he was hitting .370 when reality struck him square in the face. It was only the second integrated season for the team, and Wilson had nine African Americans in uniform. When the team was referred to as "the Black Togs" in the local press, the parent club demoted the team's offensive leader—Clendenon—to Idaho Falls in the Class C Pioneer League. The same pride that led him to head home from Jacksonville tryouts two seasons earlier was again stirred, and he packed his bags for home.

Nish Williams, whose color denied him a chance even at C ball, would have none of it, and told his stepson so. Clendenon contacted the Cleveland Browns, but Branch Rickey Jr. had learned from his father just how powerful the reserve clause is, and the Pirates' refusal to give Donn his release kept him out of the NFL. With Clendenon ready to sign with a Canadian baseball team, Rickey Jr. for the second time made a trip to Atlanta to smooth some feathers. Satisfied that the organization was paying attention to him, Clendenon reported to Idaho Falls determined to prove himself.

He clobbered the ball. He hit .356 and had a slugging average of .599 in 105 games, hitting 15 homers and knocking in 96 runs. Rickey Jr. sent him a $5,600 bonus—$100 for every point of batting average over .300.

The 1960 season opened for Clendenon with the Class A Savannah Pirates of the South Atlantic League. With Atlanta only 250 miles away, the Sally League was home stamping grounds for Clendenon. Playing mostly in the outfield, he repeated his success of 1959, only this time earning the league MVP, hitting .335 and slugging an eye-opening .606. His 28 homers and 109 RBIs led the league. The season was also notable for some transaction drama. Clendenon received word that he was to report to New York, having been traded to the perennial champion Yankees. He pointed his car north with visions of joining Roger Maris and Mickey Mantle in the outfield, only to be pulled over in Virginia and informed by a state trooper that the trade was off.

Donn headed home hoping for a September promotion to the bigs. But the pennant-bound Pirates were conservative with their call-ups in order to preserve team chemistry. With a stunning swing from second baseman Bill Mazeroski, the Pirates defeated the Clendenon-less Yankees in the World Series. But there would be a New York championship in Clendenon's future yet.

Clendenon started the 1961 season at a crossroads. He was 25, and had come off a remarkable minor league season. The double-A and triple-A levels, then more than now, were for retreads and emergency replacements, and a star player could expect to skip one or both of those levels on the way to the majors. Meanwhile, the world champion Pirates were loaded with batsmen, sporting Dick Stuart at first and Bob Skinner, Bill Virdon, and Roberto Clemente (already a legend though less than a year older than Clendenon) in the outfield. Though his life away from the game during his offseasons in Atlanta mostly consisted of substitute teaching and being a letter carrier, he remained convinced that a quota system was retarding his baseball prospects. He was farmed out to the triple-A Columbus Jets and fumed. Perhaps that fueled his bat, however, because he put up his third straight MVP-caliber season, finishing second in the voting, but hitting

.290, slugging for a .507 average, and adding 82 RBIs and 25 stolen bases. The Jets won their first pennant in more than 20 years, and when the season ended, Clendenon got the call.

He called his parents, and reported to the Pirates on September 9, 1961. He had spent five years in the minors, often asked to sleep, dine, and relieve himself in substandard facilities. At the age of 26, Nish Williams' stepson put on a big-league uniform, and promptly sat for 13 days.

The pride didn't get the best of him this time, however, and perhaps we can see greatness intervening again. After Donn's call-up, Roberto Clemente came to his locker and invited him to a big party. After the party, he went home with Clemente, and lived with him for the rest of the season. Clemente, who had refused to identify himself as black in the minor leagues even as he was subjected to the same Jim Crow segregation as Clendenon, was establishing himself as the leader of the black players on the Pirates. It was a decade away—and Clendenon likely couldn't have imagined it—but Clemente's Pirates would grow into the first team to ever field an all-African American and Afro-Latin lineup. What Clendenon perhaps knew was that he had another legend in the making for a big brother. Another future martyr, as it turned out.

Clendenon waited his turn and again made the best of it, getting into only nine games after his call-up but batting .314. His future seemed secure. When Joe Brown asked him to join the squad of Pirates third baseman Don Hoak, who would be managing in the Dominican Republic, he took what looked like a good career opportunity, having previously played two winters in Puerto Rico. The highlight of this winter, however, was helping to bail Hoak out of a barroom brawl, and fleeing the country when the assassination of dictator Rafael Trujillo led to anarchy. The assignment lasted all of three days, followed by three weeks holed up with other Americans in a resort hotel, before completing the winter season in Nicaragua, with no further uprising-related interruptions.

The next key figure to emerge was Dick Stuart, a legend mostly in the ironic sense of the word. Ralph Kiner, Frank Thomas, Stuart, and Clendenon form an interesting quartet as a succession of Pirates right-handed sluggers who would go on to make their marks in Mets history, and most of them notably, having clashed with the Rickeys while with Pittsburgh. When the Pirates let go of Rocky Nelson after the 1961 season, that left Clendenon as Stuart's backup at first. But backing up Stuart was a pretty secure position, for Dick, despite a shocking amount of power (he once hit 66 homers in the minors), was a disaster defensively. He was nicknamed Dr. Strangeglove and was booed regularly. Donn started the season platooning in left field with Bob Skinner and subbed for Stuart on defense. In the middle of the season, he was told that he would be the first baseman, was sent down to Columbus for a few weeks to get this timing, and tore the cover off the ball. He returned at the end of July and took his full-time role. With a.302 batting average, .477 slugging mark, and a .376 on-base percentage in 80 games, it was fair to say that he had arrived. When Chicago Cubs second baseman Ken Hubbs received 19 of 20 Rookie of the Year votes, the lone dissenting vote went to Clendenon. The end of the season also saw future star Willie Stargell called up, and Stuart was shipped away to Boston in November.

After he was called up to the Pirates in 1961, Donn was hired by the Mellon National Bank and Trust Company, training during the offseason and continued the following season during Pirates homestands. The tradition of players having off-season jobs (and the most loyal fans knowing where their favorites plied their trade) is a delightful part of baseball lore, but the thought of a young star continuing a second job during the season is potentially jaw-dropping to anyone used to seeing the impressively compensated athletes of today.

Also notable during the 1962 season was the birth of Donn's son, Val Eric. Donn and Val's mother risked scandal by electing not to get married, but both families were supportive and Donn proudly owned up to his fatherhood. Though the couple didn't stay together, the boy was raised with the name Clendenon, and went on to follow in the family tradition as a Morehouse man.

A player on the rise, Clendenon received no shortage of advice from fellow African-American players, to hustle, keep his drinking moderate, stay in shape—and avoid white women. His first season as a full-timer was a modest success; he hit .275 but his slugging average was only .430. He also struck out 136 times, leading the league in that category.

Incredibly, Clendenon's parallel career at Mellon Bank morphed when one of the Mellons persuaded him to go to work for Robert Duggan, the Pittsburgh area's ambitious district attorney. While continuing to star with the Pirates, Clendenon became an Allegheny County detective working with juvenile delinquents, but with full arrest authority, bringing pride to Pittsburgh with his bat, and helping the community as best he could when the game ended. The job also exposed him to the courtroom for the first time.

In 1964, not wanting to be another Dick Stuart, Clendenon sought out Gil Hodges, his future manager with the Mets, to work on his play at first base. Hodges came up as catcher before converting to first and becoming a famed defender, the best ever to some judges. Jackie Robinson had always praised his former teammate's character to Donn. Hodges had just started his managing career with the Senators, but when their teams' paths crossed during that spring, he took the time to meet with Clendenon and help him work on his defense. The two got along and talked hitting as well. Clendenon had a similar season at the plate—hitting .282 with .446 slugging. His defense improved and he cut his strikeout rate. Meanwhile, Stargell broke through and excelled for the team, despite not having a position; Stargell, who hit the first home run ever at Shea Stadium that year, saw time in left, right, and center, as well as a few games at first.

The other great Pittsburgh corporate giant besides Mellon Bank was US Steel, and Clendenon left the DA's office to work for the steel giant, training in its personnel department. But his experience suggested that it would take a law degree to get the kind of business success he was looking for. In August 1964, he applied to law school at both Harvard and Boston University, and was accepted at both. He elected for Harvard, and attempted to commute to Boston during the season. The experiment failed, and he dropped out, but remained determined. He would try again with Pittsburgh's Duquesne University in 1965. Duquesne was not immediately open to his attempting to juggle his baseball career with law school, but the young ballplayer was able to make enough connections to not only help him gain admission, but to win a full senatorial scholarship and serve as a deputy clerk for a federal judge. Clendenon later said there were three blacks in the school, his constitutional law professor, the janitor, and himself.

The 1965 season was also Clendenon's most productive to that point. Hitting .301 and slugging .467, he played in all 162 games. He finished second to Ernie Banks in fan voting for the All-Star Game, but Clendenon was left off the squad nonetheless. Danny Murtaugh retired as Pittsburgh's manager that season, replaced by Harry "The Hat" Walker—a minor star of the postwar years. A slap hitter and 1947 batting champ, Walker wasn't shy about giving hitting advice, even to sluggers. Though Clendenon and Walker clashed, the first two seasons under "The Hat" were nonetheless productive. Having Stargell in the lineup with him and Clemente certainly didn't hurt.

Pirates general manager Joe Brown, who initially encouraged Clendenon's pursuit of his law degree, changed his tune in the 1965–1966 offseason, wondering out loud if his big first baseman was overdoing it. Clendenon bristled, but it was true that Clendenon, who had hit .300 and slugged .573 in August 1965, dropped to .255 and .363 when the fall semester started in September—and the Bucs dropped from 4½ to seven games out.

The 1966 Pirates earned their Lumber Company nickname, posting a team batting average 16 points higher than any other team in the league. Clendenon had the most productive year of his career, batting .299 with .520 slugging in 155 games, hitting 28 homers and driving in 98 runs. New Pirates center fielder Matty Alou joined the party, winning the batting championship at .342 (up from .231 the year before in San Francisco).

The Lumber Company was nonetheless pitching-poor, and finished third in 1966. The highlights of the season for Clendenon were his marriage to Deanne Marriott and the birth of his second son, Donn Jr. The family bought a home in the Pittsburgh suburb of Monroeville, becoming the first family of color in the neighborhood. The choice was more poignant in the light of his near-arrest with Roberto Clemente when the Pirates visited Houston that year. The sluggers' crime was attempting to buy tickets to a movie. Two years after the Civil Rights Act, certain businesses in Houston still reserved their goods and services for white clientele only. Even in the splashy new Astrodome, black Pirates found themselves barred from the stadium's nightclub, hours after they were the attraction on the field.

The 1967 season was a fallback year for Clendenon: He lost 50 points off his batting average and 150 off his slugging percentage. The Pirates were hard-pressed to match their numbers from the previous year (though Clemente had perhaps his finest season), and the team fell to .500. The players had grown increasingly frustrated with the volatile management of Walker, and the conflict came to a head, according to Clendenon, when he failed to get a bunt down against Bob Gibson. Walker called a mandatory bunting clinic for the next morning and received a brushback pitch from Clendenon's roommate, Bob Veale. With the team ready to mutiny against Walker, Joe Brown brought back Danny Murtaugh to finish the season for the Bucs. Whatever reconciliation it brought, it couldn't help Clendenon, who turned 32 on July 15 and was seemingly on the downside of his career. Brown couldn't have been happy to see Clendenon post an even more flaccid September, hitting .197 and slugging .289 as the Pirates staggered home 20½ games back.

The 1968 season was Clendenon's last in Pittsburgh. It was a tough year all around as his beloved stepfather, Nish Williams, was diagnosed with colon cancer. Clendenon dropped out of law school, sold his home in Monroeville, and returned to Atlanta to be close to his family. The restaurant had fallen out of date, and Williams and Clendenon both saw that Donn's management and now-famous name were needed if Williams was to leave a profitable legacy to his family. Willams was honored at the Atlanta Braves Old-Timers' Day that spring. But his cancer surgery was unable to help him. In the end, neither was the morphine, and when Nish Williams died on Labor Day 1968, his stepson saw it as a relief.

The ordeal contributed to another disappointing statistical season for Clendenon, and he was forced to more seriously shape his nonathletic aspirations. Apart from the family restaurant, he had taken a job in the personnel department at the Scripto Pen Company, where his mother had worked years before, after his father died. Placed between the mostly white management and the mostly black workers, he sought to improve working conditions, hired black foremen and forewomen, and actually encouraged unionization. When labor and management were at an impasse, he called local ministers, including his old big brother Martin Luther King Jr., and told them to preach to the workers to stand firm. When he encouraged the more volatile Stokely Carmichael to visit the factory, the company's president dissented. Fortunately for Clendenon, that president was soon replaced.

King was assassinated in April 1968, and the loss of his now world-famous big brother combined with the death of Nish Williams to weigh on Clendenon. Donn was also elected player representative for the Pirates, and the end of the season was a continual grind as he worked with his fellow reps to hammer out a new contract and avert a work stoppage.

A last key change in 1968 was Clendenon's old mentor Gil Hodges taking over as manager of the long-struggling New York Mets. Under general manager Bing Devine the year before, the Mets had held a yearlong tryout camp, acquiring players, playing them for a few months, dealing them off, and getting a good look at their replacements, before perhaps dealing them as well. As Hodges assumed the manager's position, Devine returned to the Cardinals having left Gil a solid nucleus to build on, led by pitchers Tom Seaver, Jerry Koosman, Gary Gentry, and Nolan Ryan. Hitting was where the Mets fell short. Hodges opened the storied season of 1969 platooning at three positions, and moving men around when he had to.

Clendenon moved around as well. He was surprised to find himself not only exposed in the expansion draft, but claimed by the new Montreal Expos franchise. Saddened that his dreams of winning a championship with the Lumber Company were not to be, Clendenon's fortunes seemingly changed when, with Jesus Alou, he was flipped in a trade to Houston, bringing Rusty Staub to Montreal. While the Astros had much better prospects for success, they also had a new manager, one Harry Walker. Though he tried to come to terms with another season under The Hat, whom Clendenon had long given up on as an unreformed racist, Clendenon could not come to terms with Houston's front office. Considering the groundwork for his civilian life laid, Clendenon announced his retirement on March 1.

While the Astros tried to void the trade, the Expos had already begun marketing their team around "Le Grande Orange"—the Expos weren't sending Staub back. Unable to unscramble the eggs, new commissioner Bowie Kuhn ruled that the trade stood, but that the Astros would be owed additional compensation from Montreal. Kuhn then asked Clendenon to meet with him, and he was accompanied by Scripto's new president, Arthur Harris. Clendenon found himself surrounded by several owners—including Judge Roy Hofheinz of Houston and Charles Bronfman of Montreal. Harris was quickly told by the Lords of Baseball that he was unwelcome to speak. Clendenon was accused of being paid by a third party to retire. Harris later told Clendenon that after the meeting Astros general manager Spec Richardson passed on a threat from Hofheinz to buy Scripto and have Harris and Clendenon fired. The rational solution prevailed, however, and on April 8, Montreal sent Houston "additional compensation"—two players (including future All-Star Jack Billingham) and $100,000. Harris, somewhat shaken by the meeting and the threat, began encouraging Clendenon to return to the game. When baseball legend Monte Irvin appeared at the family restaurant with a generous three-year deal for Clendenon to report to Montreal, Clendenon at last agreed. The issue for management in the end didn't appear to be the money (as it was to Clendenon), but that a player had asserted his rights.

Having skipped spring training, Clendenon was out of shape when he reported to Jarry Park in Montreal. Coming off two subpar years and dropping from a powerful lineup to an expansion team was a struggle. He opened the season with an 0-for-5 game against the Cubs, and despite a three-run home run in his second start, he struggled to catch up. With the security of a three-year contract and a lack of alternatives for expansion manager Gene Mauch, Clendenon used the next six weeks as his spring training. After 38 games, he was hitting only .240 with four home runs when the June 15 trade deadline rolled around. Donn received a call in his hotel room. "I want Clendenon," the caller firmly stated.

"You can have him," Clendenon jokingly replied. "He has a history of slavery and can be bought, but not cheaply."

Who the joke was on is unclear. Mets general manager Johnny Murphy had asked the operator for his Montreal counterpart John McHale, but instead got Clendenon's room. Realizing the mistake, and knowing Clendenon's history, Murphy (in a move that would surely lead to a tampering complaint today) asked Donn if he would like to play for the

PHOTO COURTESY OF METSILVERMAN.COM

*Donn Clendenon*

Mets. Donn's old mentor Gil Hodges, recognizing his team's need for more offense, wanted Clendenon in his lineup, and Murphy completed the deal by sending Steve Renko, Kevin Collins, and two minor leaguers to the Expos. Though Murphy's predecessor, Bing Devine, had turned over to him a more or less complete team, the deal that night was perhaps the only one of consequence Murphy made in building his championship squad.

When Clendenon arrived, Hodges privately told him that (1) he had watched his progress since they had worked together; (2) they were hoping to acquire him in the offseason before the Montreal claim; and (3) while Clendenon wasn't keen on being platooned with Ed Kranepool, Hodges intended to use him thusly and gradually expand his role. Clubhouse manager Nick Torman assigned him the uniform number 22 and told him that he was "double deuce." In baseball jargon, "number one" was a white person and "number two" was a black person. He noted that numbers 20 and 21 also went to star African-Americans—Tommie Agee and Cleon Jones, respectively. Tom Seaver made a point to remind Clendenon that Donn was his first strikeout in the big leagues.

Always a serious ballplayer, the soon-to-be 34-year-old Clendenon knew that part of what he was expected to bring to the young team was leadership. And to him, that meant loosening up in order to help break the tension among a group of players in their first pennant race. Clendenon became the clubhouse jokester. When Wayne Garrett was in a batting slump, Clendenon took the time to praise his fielding, and then speculated that the rookie developed his dexterity through frequent masturbation. When Cleon Jones received a death threat, Clendenon suggested that his backside would make a better target for a gunman than his head. Later on, he told Cleon of the funeral speech he had prepared for him: "There lies a no-good mother-fucker who couldn't pull a fastball to left field if his life depended on it."

Jones, safely in the clubhouse, responded, "Clendenon, you probably sent the goddamn letter because you're jealous I'm batting close to .360."

None of that leadership would have worked as well, though, if Clendenon hadn't brought his bat. And about two weeks into his tenure in New York, his lumber caught fire. From the second game of a doubleheader on July 1 through July 8, Clendenon appeared in six games and collected 10 hits in 26 at-bats. New York won the last five of those games, all on the road. Donn provided the crucial edge in the last two games, including a three-run go-ahead homer against his old mates in Pittsburgh and a ninth-inning pinch-hit double against the front-running Cubs—after which he scored the tying run on a Cleon Jones double. In the postgame stories, Cubs manager Leo Durocher and captain Ron Santo both made a point of ripping their center fielder Don Young, who failed to catch up with another double that inning as well as Clendenon's.

Maybe Clendenon's most notable icebreaker came the next day, in perhaps the greatest game ever pitched by a Met. On July 9, with the Mets 4½ games behind Chicago, Tom Seaver was giving the visiting Cubs a performance that would not only gain the Mets a game, but also a dispiriting psychological edge. With eight innings gone, Seaver had retired all 24 Cubs to come to the plate, striking out 11 of them. With the Mets up 4-0, Cubs catcher Randy Hundley led off with a bunt, which Seaver crisply fielded. Coming up next was a little-used rookie backup center fielder named Jimmy Qualls, of whom the Mets' scouting reports said little. When Qualls singled cleanly, Seaver's perfect game and no-hitter were lost. (And the historically pitching-rich Mets never recorded such a gem in Shea Stadium or anywhere else.)

From his position at first, Clendenon saw Seaver's shoulders deflate and his head go down. Knowing that the team still needed a focused Seaver to finish off the win, he walked over to the mound and looked at Seaver. "All right, Tom," he said, "you fucked up."

Seaver, with a serious on-field manner hardened in the Marines, took such a challenge seriously: "I fucked up?" he responded.

"Yeah, Tom," finished Clendenon. "You pitched a great game and I'm proud of you. We still have to finish the inning though, so don't let down now."

Seaver, refocused on the job at hand, recorded the last two outs without incident and walked off the field to a standing ovation.

Clendenon hit as he hadn't for 2½ years. In a pitcher's league, playing in a pitcher's park, he batted .252 and slugged .455 for the Mets, with 12 homers and 37 RBIs in just 202 at-bats. Though he was particularly effective against lefties, batting .281 and slugging .474, he saw more time against righties as the season progressed, though Gil Hodges was careful never to completely abandon Ed Kranepool. When the Mets at last clinched the division and were faced with the first-ever National League Championship Series, the opposing Atlanta Braves started three right-handed pitchers. Not only did Clendenon get passed over in favor of Ed Kranepool in all three starts, he didn't see a single at-bat as the Mets swept. Clendenon's time was to come.

The 1969 World Series is known in part for the verbal sparring that occurred, and the new jocular Clendenon played his part. When Frank Robinson stated on the field, "No hard feelings, but you guys can't beat us," Clendenon replied that the Mets would "kick your ass, maybe in four straight games!" Clendenon's confidence was boosted by the fact that Baltimore had two left-handers in their powerful four-man rotation, and were in fact cutting to a three-man rotation for the Series with southpaws scheduled to throw four of the first five games. Clendenon knew his at-bats were coming and was happy with how he was hitting lefties, but Game One didn't work out so well. Tom Seaver scuffled, lasting only five innings, and lefty Mike Cuellar dominated the all-right-handed-hitting Mets lineup, to the tune of a 4–1 win. Clendenon, for his part, got two hits and scored the first World Series run in Mets history.

His confidence undiminished by the loss, Clendenon found the Mets clubhouse after the game otherwise. He asked Hodges if he could address the beleaguered team. Hodges agreed, and Donn started by letting Seaver off the hook. They had chased the team's (and league's) best pitcher, but the Orioles still didn't dominate the game. "Gentlemen, trust me!" he shouted. "We have much better pitching than they do. Our pitchers are better and they throw a hell of a lot harder than [Baltimore's] pitchers. Let's not get down, and let's look at what we can do if we just play our game." He even mocked Cuellar, who hadn't succeeded earlier with St. Louis and Houston, as taking refuge in the American League in order to succeed. Recounting his oration later, he sounded as chipper as a Shirley Temple character, finishing, "Trust me fellows! We will win!"

Game Two opened with a prediction more typical in its saltiness when Clendenon completed a batting-practice exchange with Paul Blair, telling the Baltimore center fielder, "We are going to send you home with your fucking heads between your legs." Jerry Koosman no-hit the Birds through six innings and Clendenon opened the scoring with a fourth-inning home run, ending 23 straight scoreless postseason innings for southpaw Dave McNally. With the score tied 1–1 in the ninth, Al Weis singled in Ed Charles to put the Mets ahead. An Orioles rally in the home ninth brought on Ron Taylor for the save, and when Brooks Robinson grounded to Ed Charles, Clendenon was forced to dig Charles's throw out of the dirt to record the final out.

Game Three at Shea was packed with celebrities as right-handers Jim Palmer and Gary Gentry matched up. Clendenon yielded first base to Ed Kranepool as the Mets won behind two spectacular Tommie Agee catches in center, 5–0. With the Mets up by a game now, Game Four was to feature a rematch of the opener: Cuellar vs. Seaver. Getting through the first inning scoreless this time, Seaver pitched like the ace he was, and Clendenon once again came through, turning on a full-count Cuellar fastball in the second and knocking it into the Baltimore bullpen for a 1–0 lead.

The Mets had been playing crisp defense the whole Series, and in the third, Clendenon took his turn. With two on and nobody out and Don Buford batting, Clendenon was positioned in for the bunt when Buford smacked a hard one-hopper his way. Reaching behind him for the ball as it shot past, Clendenon made the snag and got the out at second. A deft play by Seaver on a bunt and a Frank Robinson foul pop to Clendenon and the Mets escaped with their lead.

The score stood at 1–0 to the ninth, and Gil Hodges stuck with Seaver, even as the Orioles put runners at first and third with one out. When Brooks Robinson drove a ball to right-center, Ron Swoboda made a full-extension dive for one of the truly greatest catches in World Series history. Frank

Robinson tagged and scored the tying run. Clendenon always maintained that Swoboda should have played the ball on a hop, that it was the go-ahead runner on first (who may have come around to score had the ball gotten by Swoboda). He made a point of spelling out his thinking to Swoboda when they got to the dugout. The Mets were fired up, however, and they won the game with a 10th-inning run as Rod Gaspar scored from second on a bunt play when the throw hit J.C. Martin on the wrist.

Game Five returned Koosman and McNally to the mound. For the first time since Game One, the Orioles took the early lead, on a two-run homer by McNally. Frank Robinson's blast made it 3–0. It was still that score when the Mets batted in the bottom of the sixth, when Cleon Jones was apparently hit by a curve in the dirt, and the ball rolled into the Mets dugout. Clendenon asked umpire Lou DiMuro to check the ball for shoe polish, and when Hodges produced a smudged ball from the dugout, Jones was awarded first base.

With the Orioles angered by the call—Frank Robinson had been denied a similar call on an inside pitch from Koosman in the top of the inning—Clendenon waited out McNally. He hit McNally's 2–2 pitch off the auxiliary scoreboard in left for his third homer of the Series, pulling the Mets within a run.

A seventh-inning homer by the light-hitting Weis tied the game. When a two-run rally in the eighth put the Mets up, Koosman closed out the side in the ninth. When Cleon Jones squeezed the last out, the Mets completed the most unlikely championship run in anybody's memory.

As pandemonium broke out on the Shea infield, Clendenon made his way to the clubhouse to be told he had been named the Most Valuable Player of the World Series—despite strong cases for Tommie Agee, Jerry Koosman, and Al Weis (that winter, the second baseman would receive the Babe Ruth Award from New York sportswriters as the top player in the Series). Clendenon's three homers tipped the scale in his favor for the prestigious MVP award. The last man to join the 1969 Mets stood the tallest at their hour of victory.

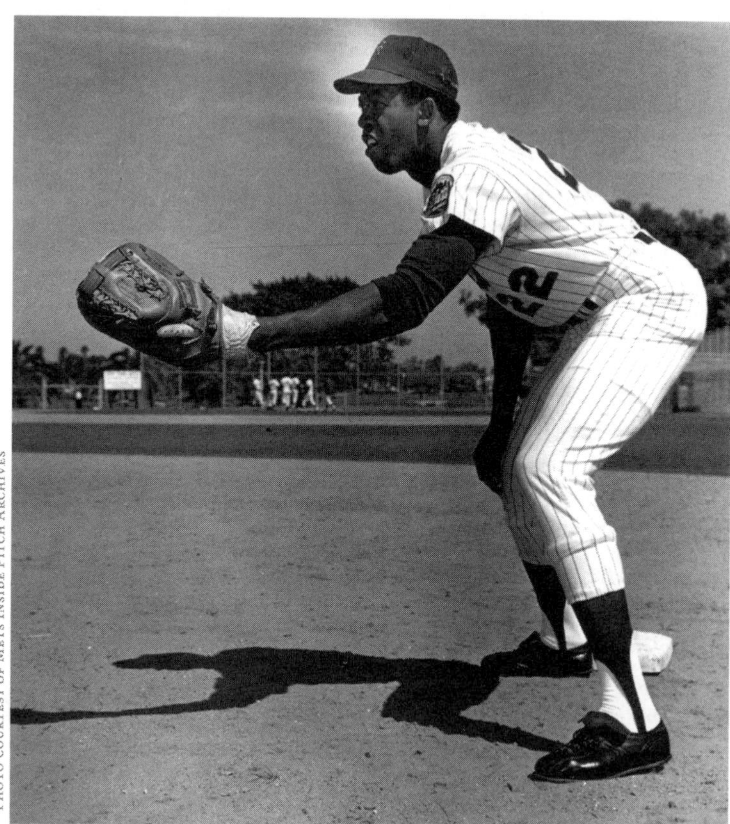


PHOTO COURTESY OF METS INSIDE PITCH ARCHIVES

*Donn Clendenon quickly became a leader on a young Mets team bound for glory.*

His MVP award came with a 1969 Dodge Challenger and he was immortalized in a painting by famed sports artist LeRoy Nieman (oddly enough, batting left-handed). Victory is fleeting, and Clendenon received a call at the stadium informing him that nothing of value was left in his apartment. "Fans" had broken in and taken almost everything—clothes, dishes, even wallpaper. Clendenon was given a penthouse suite at the Essex House while the place was restored, and enjoyed the pandemonium and tickertape parade in the World Series afterglow, but exhaustion led him to bail out partway through the route, and he absorbed a $500 fine from Gil Hodges—the same figure as his original signing bonus. He appeared with teammates on *The Ed Sullivan Show,* and in Las Vegas as part of a singing act with six other Mets. His celebrity, like that of his teammates but only enhanced by his MVP, was in full flower.

The story of Donn Clendenon and the Mets too often ends in 1969. In fact, he had quite a year in 1970. The Mets shocked Ed Kranepool, the last player from their inaugural 1962 season, by farming him out that season, nine years into his career, leaving first base the exclusive province of Clendenon. Donn responded with his best full season since 1966, one of his best ever, in fact, as he batted .288, slugged .515, clubbed 22 homers, and drove in 97 runs—a Mets record for RBIs at the time. But not enough magic was left, and the Mets fell to third place, six games behind his old Pittsburgh club. Clendenon was again overlooked at All-Star time, despite his manager's picking the squad's reserves (Donn never made an All-Star team), but he did finish 13th in league MVP voting. No Mets hitter would get that much consideration again until the mid-1980s.

But the third year of his unusual three-year contract showed age to be finally catching up with Donn. His numbers fell off, and, with Kranepool returned and resurgent, Clendenon again saw the majority of his time against left-handers, but he no longer showed an increased ability in those situations. Appearing in 88 games, he batted .247, slugged .411, hit 11 homers, and drove in 37 runs. Shortly after the season, he got his release from the Mets. He caught on with the St. Louis Cardinals for one final unproductive season (.191 in 136 at-bats), and retired.

Growing unhappy at Scripto Pen, Clendenon resigned shortly before the corporation was sold to the Wilkinson Sword company. In the summer of 1971, he joined General Electric as a management personnel consultant. He swept through training and hit the ground running that winter. Eventually, he was put in charge of recruiting minority candidates. When he attended a strategy session and heard a high-ranking officer lament the lack of qualified black candidates, Donn put his job on the line. Challenging the executive to produce 50 job descriptions with a salary range of $45,000 to $75,000, Clendenon promised to fill every one with a qualified black candidate or resign. Clendenon reached out to his Atlanta connections, including Vernon Jordan, a high-school classmate and future advisor to President Bill Clinton, developed a network, and filled each of the positions. His success rankled his rival, who vowed to get even, and Clendenon moved to the Mead Corporation as a management personnel consultant.

Clendenon eventually returned to Duquesne University and completed his law degree in 1978. He worked with Mead's legal department before becoming a founding partner in Bostick, Gerren & Clendenon, practicing criminal law.

Like too many successful people in the 1980s—athletes and businessmen alike—Clendenon allowed himself to be seduced by cocaine. He went through rehab, and withdrew to the quieter lifestyle of Sioux Falls, South Dakota, where he became a certified addictions counselor. Even his sobriety was ambitious. He continued to practice law with the Minnesota firm of Clendenon, Henney & Hoy, and regularly attended Mets reunion events when his work and health permitted.

After a long struggle, Clendenon succumbed to leukemia on September 17, 2005, in Sioux Falls. He left behind his wife, two sons, his daughter, Donna, and a grandson, Alex.

**Sources**

Allen, Maury. *After the Miracle: The 1969 Mets Twenty Years Later* (New York Franklin Watts, 1989).

Amoruso, Marino. *Gil Hodges: The Quiet Man.* (Middlebury, Vermont: Paul S. Erickson Publisher, 1991).

Clendenon, Donn. *Miracle in New York: The Story of the 1969 Mets... Through the Eyes of Donn Clendenon, World Series MVP.* (Sioux Falls: Penmark Publishing, 1999).

Durso, Joseph. *Amazing: The Miracle of the Mets.* (Boston: Houghton Mifflin Company, 1970).

Durso, Joseph. "Clendenon Is in Series Driver's Seat." *New York Times,* October 22, 1969.

Goldstein, Richard. "Donn Clendenon, 70, M.V.P For the 1969 'Miracle Mets,' Dies." *New York Times,,* September 19, 2005.

Robinson, Tom. "Right Place, Right Time Fate Led Donn Clendenon to the New York Mets at a Propitious Moment. Some 25 years Later, He Revels in His Place in History." *Virginian-Pilot,* July 8, 1994.

Zimmerman, Paul D. and Schaap, Dick. *The Year the Mets Lost Last Place* (New York: The World Publishing Company, 1969).

## Musical Mets

Rock music had a legendary year in 1969. Woodstock. The Jimi Hendrix version of "The Spangled Banner." *Abbey Road.* The Who's *Tommy.* The Band. Creedence Clearwater Revival. The Rolling Stones concert at Altamont. The interminable "In-A-Gadda-Da-Vida" by Iron Butterfly. Plus lighter, toe-tapping fare: the Fifth Dimension, Henry Mancini, the Archies… and the New York Mets?

Yes, the world champion New York Mets tried their chops at singing as well. Their album *The Amazing Mets* wasn't earth shaking—at least not to the degree of their World Series win—but the LP gave fans something different from heroes they were used to seeing throw and hit and run. Its well-timed release in November 1969 from New York label Buddha Records took advantage of the team at the height of its popularity. Buddha also hired Ed Charles in the promotions department after the third baseman was released by the Mets after the '69 season.

Like rock acts of the time, the Mets even backed up the album with a few notable appearances. They sang in the sudsy locker room after their unlikely championship. The team then appeared on the most popular variety show of the day, *The Ed Sullivan Show,* on Sunday, October 19, just three days after slaying the Orioles in the World Series. Not to be confused with the Beatles' groundbreaking stint with Sullivan five years earlier, the Mets sang "You've Got to Have Heart" from the musical *Damn Yankees.* Heart was something the Mets had certainly showed plenty of over the previous six months and some of them seemed to universally enjoy their newfound fame as pop stars. The camera panned each of the 27 Mets in three rows, only proper names were used: Don Dyer, Frank McGraw, Darrell (not the correct name, Derrel) Harrelson, Gerald Grote, Joseph Martin… it's surprising they didn't call the album *The Amazing Metropolitan Baseball Club, Inc.*

Tom Seaver got a pie in the face during a TV special in which he sang to his wife, Nancy. Tom Terrific—so dubbed for his pitching not his singing—led a select group of Mets to Las Vegas in November. Elvis Presley was enjoying his own revival in Sin City, so why not the Mets? It wasn't a complete team, featuring two pitchers (Jerry Koosman and Seaver) and two first baseman (Donn Clendenon and Ed Kranepool), though they did bring a full complement of outfielders (Cleon Jones, Tommie Agee, and Art Shamsky). Decked out in black tuxes with numbers in white on the back and accompanied by comedian Phil Foster and singer Jimmie Rodgers, the Mets were booked for two weeks at Caesar's Palace. *Variety* opined, "Unfortunately, the seven Mets don't have an act."

Turns out, the best music involving the Mets was still before games and between innings…from Shea Stadium organist extraordinaire Jane Jarvis. And nothing has ever been able to top the 1963 Mets-centric hit written by Ruth Roberts and Bill Katz called "Meet the Mets."

# Kevin Collins

by Jon Springer

| Season | Age | G | AB | R | H | 2B | 3B | HR | RBI | BB | SO | SB | CS | BA | OBP | SLG |
|---|---|---|---|---|---|---|---|---|---|---|---|---|---|---|---|---|
| 1969 Mets | 22 | 16 | 40 | 1 | 6 | 3 | 0 | 1 | 2 | 3 | 10 | 0 | 0 | .150 | .209 | .300 |
| Career 6 Years | – | 201 | 388 | 30 | 81 | 17 | 4 | 6 | 34 | 20 | 97 | 1 | 2 | .209 | .245 | .320 |

Kevin Collins was a hard-nosed infielder who stood up for his teammates and whose teammates stood up for him. He rose through the ranks with the Miracle Mets of 1969 only to be traded for the final piece of that championship puzzle.

"When people say I wasn't an important part of the 1969 Mets, I tell them, 'Are you kidding? They wouldn't have gotten Donn Clendenon without me,'" says Collins with a laugh. "I was very important!"

Kevin Michael Collins was born in Springfield, Massachusetts on August 4, 1946, the middle child and only son of Mike and Virginia Collins. Athletics came easily to Collins, who, though young for his grade in school, often played an age-level ahead in sports. His father, an insurance salesman, was his biggest influence. "He encouraged me, but he never pushed me," Kevin said in a 2008 interview. "We had a great relationship."

At Springfield High School of Science and Technology, Collins was an All-City selection in basketball and also played halfback in football, but he excelled most in baseball, where the left-handed hitting shortstop led Springfield Tech to two Western Massachusetts championships. While Massachusetts wasn't exactly a hotbed of baseball talent, Collins nevertheless competed against future big leaguers Mark Belanger of Pittsfield High, and Fran Healy, from nearby Holyoke, during his high school years.

Pro scouts took notice of Collins as early as his freshman year in high school. Shortly after graduating in 1964, and still just 17 years old, Collins signed with scout Red Fazio and the Mets for $25,000. The Yankees—as well as the University of Massachusetts and a few other colleges—had also pursued Collins.

"My mother wanted me to go to college, but I didn't want to be looking back when I was 50 years old, wondering if I was going to make it. So I had my mind made up, much to the chagrin of my mother," he recalled. "My dad didn't lead me any way. He told me just to follow my conscience and follow your heart. With him it was, 'If you want it, go for it.'"

Collins was shortly off to Cocoa Beach, Florida, and the Rookie League Mets squad. In 44 games he batted a modest .220 but nevertheless earned a promotion to the 40-man roster, joining fellow freshmen Ron Swoboda and Collins's roommate, Tug McGraw, as first-time additions to the big league roster.

For these players—the "Youth of America" as Casey Stengel often referred to them—the Mets truly represented a world of opportunity. With the team still overcoming the aftereffects of a preposterous expansion draft that populated the major league team with rejects and longshots, young players like Collins could and did advance quickly. Collins saw his generation of prospects as having an outlook and an identity distinct from that of the major league club.

"The Mets in their embryonic stage were very interesting for me, because when I got to the minors we didn't have the same mindset that the big league team did. They had some good ballplayers like Ronny Hunt, but basically, the talent was down in the minors," he said. "They ended up with some good players in the expansion draft but they had people that nobody else wanted. We didn't have that mindset in the minor leagues. Most of us came from winning organizations in high school and college, and we didn't have the world-against-us mentality."

The velocity with which prospects could advance in this atmosphere—and the absurdity of draft rules that encouraged teams to carry first-year players, often in their teens, on their roster rather than risk losing them on waiver claims—was reflected the following spring, when Collins made the Mets Opening Day roster as an 18-year-old reserve infielder. McGraw (20), Swoboda (21), outfielder Danny Napoleon (23), and pitcher Jim Bethke (18) were other first-year players who came north with that team.

On April 25, 1965, Collins was to have made his big league debut, but fate intervened. Stengel had Collins's name penciled in the lineup of the second game of a Sunday doubleheader at Candlestick Park. But while tossing warm-up throws between games, Collins felt a tear in his shoulder soon diagnosed as a ruptured latissimus muscle requiring surgery.

The injury would delay his major league debut by more than four months. Collins resurfaced in September without having gotten a single at-bat that year in the minors. He debuted as a pinch hitter for pitcher Rob Gardner, who was also making his major league debut, on September 1 in the second game of a doubleheader at Shea Stadium. Little surprise that the unprepared teen struck out looking against Houston's Turk Farrell. Collins's first hit—a single off Pittsburgh's Bob Friend at Forbes Field—came three weeks later.

Collins, who had just turned 19, was in over his head. "I never should have been there. It was probably the worst thing for my development but those were the rules at that time," he said. The amateur draft, which went into effect for the first time that summer, helped bring an end to such arcane first-year player rules.

Collins summarily returned to the developmental pipeline, although his instructional league season in 1965 was cut short when he was hit by a thrown ball and hospitalized with a concussion. The following spring the Mets had Collins bat right-handed in an attempt to refashion him as a switch-hitter, but the experiment was eventually abandoned. Collins was assigned to Class AA Williamsport, where he spent the entire season as a shortstop under manager Bill Virdon, hitting .251 with six home runs and 32 RBIs.

In 1967, Collins was assigned to Class AAA Jacksonville, managed again by Virdon. By then it was becoming clear that Collins's road back to New York could be blocked for a long time to come. Bud Harrelson—then a Mets rookie—was just beginning what would be a decade-long run as an everyday shortstop. Jacksonville also employed Sandy Alomar, who failed to stick with the Mets but had a long career ahead of him as an everyday infielder in the American League; and Amos Otis, whose hitting ability guaranteed he'd get a job somewhere on the diamond—third base being one of those spots. And so Collins began preparation for a utility role that he saw as his best chance to break back in. He played 40 games at shortstop in 1967, 50 at second base, and 24 at third. When the Mets recalled Collins in September he got two starts, both as a second baseman alongside Harrelson at short.

"Somewhere along the line you accept that there may be people who do it a little better than you," he said. "You don't like it, you don't really believe it, but you have to accept it. I knew I was going to go to third base eventually because Buddy was ahead of everybody else and there wasn't room for both of us."

Maintaining motivation in a reserve role was never an issue for Collins. But it was a difficult mental adjustment, he admits. "I believed that the more often you play, the better you get," he said. "If you're in there every day, it makes a lot of difference. Familiarity breeds success. Knowing it's not one game and out, it takes a lot of mental heat off you. Otherwise you say, 'Oh, I better go 2-for-4 today or I'm going to sit for 10 days'. If you go 0-for-4 and know you have another shot at them tomorrow, it tends to come back to you in confidence."

Collins began 1968 in Jacksonville but was recalled in May when Harrelson reported for military duty. Though the Mets had initially planned to send Collins back to AAA when Harrelson returned from the Army, Collins's play in part-time duty impressed manager Gil Hodges enough to change those plans. Greg Goossen was sent down instead. On June 15, Collins collected three doubles in three at-bats against Giants ace Juan Marichal.

Collins by this time was a married man. He wed Linda Laflamme, a South Hadley, Massachusetts girl whom he'd met shortly before leaving for his first professional assignment in Cocoa Beach. A photograph from their wedding, published in *The Sporting News* in March of 1968, shows Collins receiving a handshake from Tug McGraw, an usher, while another usher, their former teammate Bill Denehy, kisses the bride.

Two of the most notable achievements in Collins's Mets career came during an August road trip in Houston. On August 6 he hit a two-out, three-run home run off Dave Giusti in the top of the ninth inning, to break a 1–1 tie. It was his first major league home run and Collins drove in all four runs in the 4–1 win.

The next night, Collins was manning third base for the Mets when Doug Rader tripled, arriving at third base with a hard pop-up slide and an elbow into Collins's jaw. The Mets infielder collapsed onto his back in a daze.

"I'm waiting for the throw and here comes Rader. I remember catching the ball but never even coming down to make a tag," Collins said. "He came in with a pop-up slide and a forearm right in my face that broke my jaw. All I remember then was looking up and seeing the roof of the Astrodome. I'm not sure if I was knocked out, but I was dazed. I was like, 'Wow.'"

Collins's teammates jumped to attention. Mets coach Joe Pignatano briefly scuffled with Astros manager Harry Walker, and Mets pitcher Don Cardwell socked Rader above the eye. A bench-clearing brawl was on.

COURTESY OF DWAYNE LABAKAS COLLECTION

*Kevin Collins*

"The funny thing is, while all this is going on, here's the Irishman, the kind of guy who would get into anything, and he can't get off the ground," Collins said. "I might not win the fight, but I will be there with you. And I can't even get off the ground. And I remember everybody—Cardwell, [Tommie] Agee, Joe Pignatano...everybody just going at it. Unfortunately I couldn't participate because I was on my back, staring up the roof of the Astrodome."

Though Collins, who missed a week of play as the result of his broken jaw in the collision, held no ill will toward Rader ("it was just hard baseball"), writers speculated the brawl was the culmination of hostilities between the clubs dating as far back to a hard slide by Agee that injured the Astros' Joe Morgan in the first week of the season. Houston would be the 1969 Mets' most ornery opponent, winning 10 of 12 meetings against New York that year, the only club with a wining record versus the Mets (Cincinnati was 6–6).

In 1969, Collins made the Opening Day roster for the first time since 1965—and this time he didn't get hurt before getting in a game. Collins was one of three candidates to play third base along with the veteran incumbent, Ed Charles. Otis got the first crack, but he didn't take to the position and got on the wrong side of manager Gil Hodges. Collins got the next shot but struggled offensively. He hit .150 over 16 games (11 starts) and was dispatched to the new Class AAA affiliate in Tidewater in early May. The Mets turned to rookie Wayne Garrett, who wound up sharing the job with Charles.

Collins took his demotion with a "touch of class," *The Sporting News* reported. "He placed a note in the locker of Ken Boswell, his roommate, saying, 'Keep hitting, Roomie.' And in the locker inherited by [Art] Shamsky, the man who also inherited his job, Collins left one that read, 'Good luck, Kid.'"

It turned out to be his last goodbye, at least to his Mets teammates. In June, he was one of four minor leaguers traded to Montreal in the deal for Clendenon (along with Steve Renko, Dave Colon, and Bill Carden). The trade brought Collins back to the major leagues as he played second base and spotted right-handed-hitting Coco Laboy at third base. Collins etched his name in the Montreal record books by providing the franchise's first pinch-hit home run, a three-run shot off Jim Bunning of Pittsburgh on July 17.

Collins described parting with the Mets as "bittersweet," but said he learned a lot from Gene Mauch, the Montreal manager. At a 30-year reunion of the 1969 Mets at Shea Stadium, Collins recalled an encounter with Jack Lang, the beat reporter who covered that team for the *Long Island Press*. "He told me, 'The Mets wanted Clendenon, but Gene Mauch wanted you.' That was a very nice thing to hear. It made me feel good."

Montreal assigned Collins to AAA Winnipeg to begin the 1970 season, and sold his contract to Detroit later that summer. Collins played the remainder of the 1970 season and all of 1971 with the Tigers as a pinch hitter, hitting .208 in 1970 under Mayo Smith and .268 in 1971 under Billy Martin. Collins roomed with outfielder Gates Brown in '71. The then-rare pairing of white and black players captured the attention of the news media but Collins raised no eyebrows. "I don't consider this a breakthrough of any kind," he told *The Sporting News*. "People are people. That's the way I was brought up."

Collins said Brown, as a veteran, could have chosen to live alone but preferred a roommate, in part, to help him with his neckties. Collins remarked that the only challenge of rooming with Brown was enduring his roommate's snoring. "The key with Gates was I wanted to fall asleep earlier than he did," said Collins, who remained close to Brown long after their careers. "And you hoped to hell you'd fall asleep before he started honking. It was like the Burlington Northern coming down the track."

Collins was assigned to Toledo following the 1971 season and played there through June of 1973 when he was traded to Cleveland, which assigned him to its Oklahoma City franchise. Collins played first base for the 89ers through May of 1974 when he decided to retire.

"I decided I had enough. My daughter was going into school the next September. I had a job offer in Michigan, and I said, 'I'm gonna take it.' I'm not going to be Crash Davis. I don't need Susan Sarandon, I have a nice wife."

The job was with Mexican Industries, the auto parts supplier founded in Detroit by former Tigers pitcher Hank Aguirre. Collins, who during baseball offseasons had attended North Adams State College, not far from where he grew up, and completed a degree at American International College in his native Springfield. Collins stayed with the company until retiring to Sand Point, Michigan. Still married to Linda, Collins says he enjoys golf and spending time with his three grandchildren. His daughter is an attorney and his son is a restaurateur.

Reflecting on his baseball career, Collins said he has few regrets. "I was a guy who played the game the right way," said Collins. "I didn't have a lot of power but I could hit the fastball, and left-handed pitching didn't bother me too much. I could field my position and I had a good arm. I could run a little. Nobody ever had to tell me how to compete. I was the kind of guy who gave you all I had, whether or not that was enough."

**Sources**

Author interviews with Kevin Collins, 2008

*New York Times*

*New York Herald Tribune*

*The Sporting News*

The Ultimate Mets Database (*www.ultimatemets.com*)

# Jack DiLauro

by Sam Bernstein

| Season | Age | W | L | Pct | G | GS | SV | IP | H | BB | SO | WHIP | ERA |
|---|---|---|---|---|---|---|---|---|---|---|---|---|---|
| 1969 Mets | 26 | 1 | 4 | .200 | 23 | 4 | 1 | 63.7 | 50 | 18 | 27 | 1.068 | 2.40 |
| Career 2 Years | – | 2 | 7 | .222 | 65 | 4 | 4 | 97.3 | 84 | 35 | 50 | 1.223 | 3.05 |

Jack DiLauro, a left-handed pitcher from Akron, Ohio who appeared in 23 games for the New York Mets in 1969, played a small but valuable role in the Mets' march to the National League pennant that season.

Jack Edward DiLauro was born on March 3, 1943 in Akron. He starred in football, basketball, and baseball at Akron North High School and earned a football scholarship to the University of Akron, which he declined in favor of signing a professional baseball contract.[1] DiLauro also pitched in the Greater Akron AA Baseball League for competitive players 18 years old and over. Joining the Tramonte Black Labels in 1961, DiLauro had an 8–1 record in 1962 and led that team to the Greater Akron AA championship that season.[2]

In 1963 DiLauro signed a contract with the Detroit Tigers for a $15,000 bonus[3] that sent the 19 year-old prospect to Jamestown of the New York-Penn League. Following a 14–10 , 3.54 ERA season, the Tigers moved him to the Class A Duluth in the Northern League where DiLauro posted a 14–8 record and a 2.81 ERA. Next came Rocky Mount (Class A Carolina League) and then a promotion in 1966 to Syracuse, Detroit's triple-A International League team and the last hurdle for DiLauro to make the majors.

DiLauro showed some promise in Class AAA, especially after the Tigers moved the Syracuse team to Toledo for the 1967 season. "Akron was about a two-hour drive from Toledo, so I could come home once in a while," DiLauro told Bruce Winkworth of the *New York Mets Inside Pitch.* "My parents and my brother and my old buddies used to come up and watch me pitch. I'd been playing long enough so that it didn't bother me at all to pitch in front of friends and family."[4]

Getting some home cooking didn't hurt DiLauro on the mound either. In 1967 he was 6–5 with a 4.88 ERA and helped the Mud Hens to victory over Columbus in the 1967 International League playoffs.[5] In 1968 he improved to 11–6 and a 3.65 ERA. DiLauro felt he had nothing left to prove in the minors and he itched to get a chance to join Detroit, but the Tigers were in pretty good shape just then. The 1968 Tigers rolled to their first pennant since 1945 and, after losing three of the first four World Series games, reeled off three straight wins to shock the Cardinals and claim the world championship. Detroit's rotation seemed pretty much set for the '69 season with staff that included reigning AL MVP and Cy Young winner Denny McLain (31–6), World Series hero Mickey Lolich (17–9), Earl Wilson (13–12), Joe Sparma (10–10), and John Hiller (9–6). DiLauro thought there were plenty of teams that needed pitching. The Mets, who had a lot of good young talent, were not on that list.

Nevertheless, the Tigers shipped DiLauro to New York for minor league catcher Hector Valle prior to the 1969 season. "It was a surprise when I got traded to the Mets. I had pitched against Seaver and McGraw and Gentry and some of those guys when the Mets were in Jacksonville. When I got traded, I looked at the pitching staff. I didn't know much about Koosman, but I knew about Seaver, that he had a great arm and a good head, and I knew Ryan could throw a million miles an hour, but didn't know where it was going. Gentry and McAndrew were both up there.[6]

"I'm thinking, 'Jeez, I get traded to the Mets, of all places to go. I'm going to be back in the minors and might never get called up.' They were just so young, and at 26 years old, I was the oldest rookie that the Mets had at the time."[7]

DiLauro began the season in Tidewater under the watchful eye of farm director Whitey Herzog, who had scouted the southpaw and had recommended him to the Mets even though DiLauro's reputation lacked a power game. According to DiLauro, Herzog "seemed to know that a guy could win without throwing a ball through a wall. I owe him a lot for that chance."[8]

After four very good minor league starts, DiLauro was called up after Nolan Ryan, who had missed some playing time with blisters and military reserve training, was placed on the disabled list on May 11 with a pulled a groin muscle. Ryan would return in June but DiLauro's performance kept him with the Mets for the rest of the season.

In his major league debut on May 15, 1969 at Shea Stadium, DiLauro was called in to relieve Don Cardwell in the fourth inning as manager Gil Hodges went with a pinch hitter for Cardwell in the third inning with the Mets down, 4–1. Leading off for the Atlanta Braves was the eighth-place hitter, shortstop Sonny Jackson. He greeted DiLauro with a double to left. Pitcher Pat Jarvis unsuccessfully tried to bunt Jackson to third and struck out. Jackson was caught stealing third and Felipe Alou flied out to end the inning. DiLauro retired Atlanta one-two-three in the fifth and his first outing in the big leagues was a success, even though the Mets still wound up losing the weekday matinee.

On June 4, DiLauro may have made his greatest contribution to the team and its pennant chances. It was his first start and, according to writer Maury Allen, "May have been the game that convinced the Mets they were a contending team."[9]

On Monday June 2, Jerry Koosman led the Mets to a 2–1 victory over the Dodgers that put them back to .500 (23–23 ) and one game behind second place Pittsburgh and 8 ½ behind the Cubs. On Tuesday, Tom Seaver and Tug McGraw combined on a three-hitter to push them past the Pirates in the standings. The Wednesday afternoon game preceded a long, 12-game, four-city road trip that would begin in San Diego.

DiLauro told writer Stanley Cohen, "Gil told me I'd be starting two or three days in advance but it felt more like a month. I was really nervous, and it took me a couple of innings to settle down."[10]

Both DiLauro and Dodgers starter Bill Singer were on top of their games. DiLauro gave up a double to Bill Russell in the first and a double to Ted Sizemore in the second but he extricated himself with the help of Bud Harrelson's glove and some effective pitching. During one stretch in the game, DiLauro retired 19 consecutive batters. Unfortunately, the Mets had been unable to put up any runs against Singer and the game remained scoreless when DiLauro was lifted for a pinch hitter in the ninth. *The New York Times* reported that DiLauro was "accorded a standing ovation" for his "variety of curveballs" that stymied the Dodgers.[11] The Mets went on to take the game in the 15th inning, stretching their win streak to a club record-tying seven games. They had won two consecutive series at home and would win the next four on the road. By the time they returned to Shea on June 20 they were in second place, six games behind the Cubs.

DiLauro called that game the "biggest thrill of my career." He told Cohen, "I had been pitching in the minors for six years, trying to make it to the big club; and now, after my first start, to get an ovation like that from a New York crowd…it's a moment I'll never forget. Of course it would have been even better if I'd have gotten the win, but still…"[12]

After a gap of 11 days, DiLauro was tapped to start against in Los Angeles on Sunday afternoon, June 15. He would be pitching against future Hall of Famer Don Drysdale. DiLauro allowed his first runs in the major leagues—on a home run by Andy Kosco—and Jack suffered his first loss in the majors, 3–2 . In his first 22 ⅔ innings as a Met, however, he had an ERA of 1.19.

Six days later he threw another good game against St. Louis at Shea but lost again. A two-run home run by opposing pitcher Nelson Briles pushed the only runs against him across the plate. His next outing, other Cardinals hit the ball hard off him as well and he dropped to 0–3. After that DiLauro was relegated to the bullpen. He picked up his first major league win in relief at Montreal's Jarry Park in the second game of a doubleheader on July 20.

"I was no green rookie," DiLauro told Allen. "I had been around baseball six or seven years by then. I felt if I pitched well I would get a chance to make a career. I pitched well (a 2.40 ERA in 63 ⅔ innings) but it didn't matter. I wasn't very comfortable with Gil Hodges there. He just never talked to me. I don't think he talked to anybody other than his coaches. I don't think there was a single player on that team who had a one-to-one with Gil."[13]

"I hung out with the other rinky-dinks on the team, [Rod] Gaspar, Bobby Pfeil after he came up from Tidewater, a couple of the scrubs. I got close to Nolan Ryan. He was very unhappy there. He never got along with Hodges. He was not used properly. Anybody could see the greatness in him. Somehow or other he was never used in turn, something would come up, a rainout, an injury, anything to disrupt his schedule. They never explained anything to him. Nolan never talked negatively about anybody, but you could see he was unhappy. He grumbled once in a while about being stuck on that team. But he could throw smoke. Wow. I think he was lucky to be traded away when he was. He might not have achieved all those things if he stayed in New York."[14]

Regardless of Jack DiLauro's sentiments, the Mets went on to overtake the Cubs, defeat the Braves in the first National League Championship Series and emerge as World Series champions. After that last start in St. Louis on July 1, Jack appeared in another 16 games for New York, all in relief but he never appeared in the Mets sweep of Atlanta or their four-games-to-one triumph over the Baltimore Orioles. In fact the Mets used only six pitchers in the World Series and the three relievers (Don Cardwell, Ron Taylor, and Ryan) combined for only 5 ⅔ innings of work.

Still, DiLauro was very proud of the Mets' accomplishments that season. "That was the year of dreams, really," he told Winkworth. "It was like the words Casey coined, 'It was amazin.'"[15] DiLauro usually wears his championship ring and is pleased to show it to all who ask. Unfortunately, that magic carpet ride ended quickly after the Series. DiLauro and Ed Charles were dropped from the 40-man roster to protect younger players like Jon Matlack, Les Rohr, John Milner, Tim Foli, Fred Reahm, and Dave Schneck.[16] DiLauro hoped he could earn an invitation to spring training, the first in his career.

Instead, the Houston Astros took DiLauro in the Rule V draft. The Astros were in need of a left-handed relief pitcher for the 1970 season so Houston personnel director Tal Smith fed scouting reports on 300 lefties available in the draft to a computer in their business office. DiLauro came out on top. Smith told *The Sporting News* that "the value to the scouting department is in getting a 30-second answer in summary to evaluations that, done manually, used to take all winter. Last winter was the first time we used it, and we used it for all positions and angles for ready references on trades and deals."[17]

While the New York management said it hated to move him to the Tidewater (International League) roster and expose him to the draft at the season's end, the club had too many young pitchers who had to be protected.[18] Initially, DiLauro saw it as another opportunity.

"I was a victim of the Mets' outstanding pitching staff," DiLauro told Cohen. By going to Houston, DiLauro could continue his progress on a team that really needed him. "For two months [in 1970], I was the best reliever in the majors, but from August 28 [actually, August 25] until the end of the season I never threw a pitch."[19] Beginning on April 21 through July 6, Jack appeared in 22 games without yielding an earned run. He finished the season with a 4.28 ERA in 33 ⅔ innings pitched and a 1–3 record. A falling out with manager Harry Walker and GM Spec Richardson, due in part to a misunderstanding,[20] ended his career with Houston. DiLauro was sold to Hawaii of the Pacific Coast League after spring training in 1971.

Eight games into the season Hawaii sold DiLauro to the Atlanta Braves, who put him in AAA again with Richmond. DiLauro gave up 26 earned runs in 38 innings (0–5 , 6.16 ERA). The Braves released him and DiLauro signed with the Class AAA club of the Montreal Expos in the International League, the Peninsula Whips. A good season with the Whips (4–2 , 3.30 ERA in 60 innings) did not earn Jack a call-up to the majors. He engineered a trade to Texas for 1973, but that fell through. "I never did go to spring training with the Rangers," DiLauro told Winkworth. "I had contract problems with them. I was supposed to go to spring training with the big league club and have a chance of making it. In the offseason they picked up a couple more left-handers, so they didn't take me to camp. I couldn't come to terms with a minor league contract, so I more or less retired at the old age of 29."[21]

After retirement, DiLauro returned to Akron and joined the Koenig Sporting Goods Company. Eventually he became district manager of the chain of 31 stores. He also continued to pitch in the Greater Akron AA League leading the Easton Sports Pride to two league championships. When he retired in 1975, Jack became the AA League President for two years.[22] He resides in Malvern, Ohio with his wife Jane.

In 1974 Jack DiLauro was inducted into the Summit County (Ohio) Sports Hall of Fame[23] and in 1984 he was inducted into the Greater Akron Sports Hall of Fame.[24]

DiLauro told Maury Allen, "I left baseball with a bitter taste. I guess I think about those days too much. I was used. They needed me at the end of the season. I was only 29 when I was finished with baseball. I didn't have anything to do, anyplace to go, any training for anything else. I never made any money in baseball so it was all very hard for me. I got this job [Koenig Sporting Goods] and became the manager a few years back. We are all right now. I have a nice house on a lakefront site. We're comfortable.[25]

"I wanted more of the game. I didn't want to leave so early. I wished I could have gotten along better with the managers and the front-office people…hardly a day goes by that I don't think about something relating to the Mets of 1969. I guess I always will." [26]

**Notes and Sources**

1 Butler, Jason, Akron Beacon Journal, December 24, 1999, p. D6

2 Greater Akron Baseball Hall of Fame, *http://www.acorn.net/gabhof/inductees/1984.html*

3 Allen, Maury, *After the Miracle: The 1969 Mets Twenty Years Later*, p. 227

4 Winkworth, Bruce, "Unsung Hero", *New York Mets Inside Pitch*, V.12 No. 5, May 1994, p. 42

5 *The Sporting News*, September 30, 1967

6 Winkworth, p. 42

7 Winkworth, p. 42

8 Allen, p. 228

9 Allen, p. 224

10 Cohen, Stanley, *A Magic Summer: The '69 Mets*, p. 73

11 Anderson, Dave, *New York Times*, June 5, 1969, p. 58

12 Cohen, p. 73

13 Allen, p. 226

14 Allen, p. 226

15 Winkworth, p. 42

16 Lang, Jack, *The Sporting News*, November 8, 1969, p. 35

17 Wilson, John, *The Sporting News*, March 14, 1970, p. 26

18 Wilson, p. 26

19 Cohen, p. 74

20 Allen, p. 225

21 Winkworth, p. 42

22 Greater Akron Baseball Hall of Fame

23 Summit County (OH) Sports Hall of Fame *http://www.summitcountysportshalloffame.com/Inductees/1974.htm*

24 Greater Akron Baseball Hall of Fame

25 Allen, p. 226.

26 Allen, p. 229

*The Akron Beacon Journal*
*The New York Times*
*The New York Mets Inside Pitch*
*The Sporting News*
*Baseball-Reference.com*
*Retrosheet.org*
*Summitcountysportshalloffame.com*
*Spot.acorn.net/gabhof*
Allen, Maury, *After The Miracle: The 1969 Mets Twenty Years Later* (New York: Franklin Watts, 1989)
Cohen, Stanley, *A Magic Summer: The '69 Mets* (New York: Harcourt Brace Jovanovich, 1988)

# Duffy Dyer

by Adam Ulrey

| Season | Age | G | AB | R | H | 2B | 3B | HR | RBI | B | SO | SB | CS | BA | OBP | SLG |
|---|---|---|---|---|---|---|---|---|---|---|---|---|---|---|---|---|
| 1969 Mets | 23 | 29 | 74 | 5 | 19 | 3 | 1 | 3 | 12 | 4 | 22 | 0 | 0 | .257 | .295 | .446 |
| Career 14 Years | – | 772 | 1993 | 151 | 441 | 74 | 11 | 30 | 173 | 228 | 415 | 10 | 4 | .221 | .306 | .315 |

In the sitcom *Cheers*, guys came in to have a cold one, talk about whatever was going on, and—most emphatically—defend Sam Malone. Malone, played by Ted Danson, was a washed up pitcher for the Boston Red Sox turned owner and bartender of Cheers. Judging by the stories patrons would tell about his mediocre career, you would have thought he was Walter Johnson. If a stranger walked in off the streets and said anything negative about Malone's career, the customers would unite to defend him.

Back in 1969 there was such a place—Donovan's, an Irish Pub in Woodside-Jackson Heights area of Queens. This was Duffy Dyer country. Duffy was a light-hitting, good-fielding catcher who played with the New York Mets for half of his major league career. He became a fan favorite on Opening Day of the 1969 season by belting a pinch-hit, three-run homer. Donovan's became the home for Dyer fans to gather.

"We haven't had a fight in here in a long, long time," the bartender at Donovan's said. "But if somebody puts the knock on Duffy in here, look out."

Don Robert Dyer, nicknamed Duffy, was born in Dayton, Ohio, August 15, 1945. His family was of Irish-English-Dutch stock. There was an old radio show called *Duffy's Tavern* and the family would sit around and listen to it every week. Duffy's mom was quite pregnant and laughing very hard at a joke on *Duffy's Tavern*. Suddenly, she fainted. When she came to, she was in the recovery room of the maternity ward, and still in the twilight zone.

"How's Duffy?" said Mrs. Dyer faintly.

"Oh, he's doing just fine," said one of the nurses, who was, of course, accustomed to such mutterings. The nurses started calling the infant boy "Duffy," and so did Mrs. Dyer.

"Honest," says Duffy Dyer. "That's how my mother told me it happened."

His father, William E. Dyer, moved the family to Arizona and Duffy blossomed as one of the state's top ballplayers. He played baseball, basketball, and football at Cortez High School in Phoenix. He helped lead his team to the state Class AA championship in his senior year in 1963. He was named to All-City and All-State teams. He also received honorable mention on the All-Arizona prep football team at quarterback. It was then on to Arizona State to play for the Sun Devils.

The 1965 season was one to remember for Dyer and his Arizona State teammates. It was also the start of a continuous trek for the Sun Devils to the NCAA Tournament. Dyer batted .325, four home runs, 38 RBIs, and 15 stolen bases in leading the Arizona State to the Western Athletic Conference championship. Also on that team were Rick Monday, Sal Bando, and a freshman not yet eligible to play on the varsity named Reggie Jackson.

Arizona State won the NCAA District Seven in two games over Colorado State and Dyer was named to the All-Conference team. The Sun Devils steamrolled to their first NCAA title in 1965, beating Ohio State in the championship game, 2–1. In the first three games of the College World Series, the Sun Devils won by a combined score of 36–8. Dyer went 3-for-6 with a two-run homer in their 13–3 rout of St. Louis. He played mostly in the outfield and it wasn't until 1966 that he became full-time catcher.

At the end of season he was drafted by the Milwaukee Braves, but Dyer decided to stay in school and play in a summer league called the Basin League. The Basin League was established in 1953 with seven teams from South Dakota (Mitchell, Watertown, Winner, Chamberlain, Yankton, Huron, and Pierre) and one from Nebraska (Valentine). It was a league using former professional players with a mix of amateurs. The name "Basin" came from the geographical fact that a number of teams were situated in cities along the Missouri River Basin. It was a league where players could retain their amateur status yet scouts would still come to have a look. In later years when the Basin League became just a summer college league, it was touted as the finest in America. Dyer played for the Valentine Hearts in the summer of 1965, before returning for his junior season at Arizona State. He batted .237 in 50 games for Valentine.

In 1966 at ASU, he hit .326 with 10 triples and batted in 32 runs. He was named to the All-Conference First Team and *The Sporting News* College All-American Second Team. He tied for second on the all-time Sun Devils consecutive hits list with eight. He would later be inducted into the ASU Hall of Fame.

The New York Mets drafted him with their first pick in the January 1966 secondary phase of the free agent draft. Signed by Bob Scheffing and Dee Fondy, Dyer was sent to Williamsport of the Eastern League. There in 22 games he hit a sparse .173 with only two extra-base hits. He was then moved down to Greenville in the Western Carolinas League. He was able to get back on track a little, hitting .246 in 19 games.

Dyer was back at Williamsport in 1967, playing in 106 games. He still was having a hard time adjusting to the league, batting only .194. On June 22, 1967, he "almost" hit his first home run as a pro. With the bases loaded he hit a pitch by York's Rupe Toppin over the left-field wall, but the runner on first base held up until the ball cleared the fence and Dyer passed him and was called out. As a result he got credit for a single, but did get three RBIs in Williamsport's 4–2 victory.

He moved on to Jacksonville of the International league for the 1968 season. There he found his power with 16 home runs and 43 RBIs for the season. His batting average was still just .230, but his defense and his power earned him a spot in the International League All-Star Game. He was called up to New York with three weeks left in the season. He played in just one game, starting and catching Dick Selma in a 3–1 loss to the Phillies. Dyer was 1-for-3 with a single off Chris Short.

While, of course, 1969 was a very special season for the Mets and for Dyer, the rookie almost didn't get a chance to be a member of that world championship team. On March 29, 1969, a report in *The Sporting News* claimed that Paul Richards, vice president of the Braves sought a package of pitcher Nolan Ryan, infielder Bob Heise, first baseman Ed Kranepool, and either catcher J.C. Martin or Duffy Dyer, for Joe Torre and Bob Aspromonte. Instead Richards traded Torre to the Cardinals. Dyer made the Mets out of spring training as the third-string catcher to Jerry Grote (Martin was the backup).

"Dyer proved himself a good defensive catcher at Jacksonville last year and capable of hitting home runs," Mets manager Gil Hodges said. "Found him to be a good, steady receiver in intersquad and exhibition games, and decided to keep him."

Dyer had a flair for the dramatic right from the start. On Opening Day he got a call from Hodges to come out of the bullpen and pinch hit in the bottom of the ninth with the Mets trailing Montreal, 11–7.

"I remember walking up to bat in front of a full house, sold-out Shea Stadium and my knees were shaking. This is my first at-bat in New York and I just wanted to hit hard. I hit the ball and right away I knew it was gone. I sprinted to first base. By the time I got to second base I realized that I just hit a home run in the big leagues. I was flying around those bases. I was 10 miles high. That was one of my biggest individual thrills in the big leagues."

His pinch-hit single on May 30 gave the Mets a 4–3 win over the Giants. He was optioned to Tidewater on July 3 because the minor league club was out of catchers. He compiled a .313 average with five homers and 26 RBIs in 35 games for Tidewater. A little more than a month later he was back in the fold in New York and providing late-game heroics again. In the first game of a doubleheader on August 17, he hit a three-run homer off Joe Niekro to spark a 3–2 win.

In the World Series he only had one pinch-hitting opportunity and grounded out to shortstop Mark Belanger. Dyer ended the year hitting .257 with three homers and 12 RBIs in 29 games for the '69 Mets, but he got a world championship ring as a rookie. It turned out to be the only one in 14 seasons in the majors.

He remained behind Jerry Grote in New York, but the durable, hardy, and aggressive Dyer gave the Mets assurance at that vital position when Grote needed a rest or was injured. After J.C. Martin was traded in spring training in 1970, Dyer moved up to second string and wound up getting into 59 games, hitting .209 with two homers. In 1971 he again played in 59 games and hit a little higher at .231. Perhaps his best game that year happened on May 29, when he hit two doubles and a triple while calling signals for the young Nolan Ryan in a 2–1 victory over San Diego. Ryan fanned 16 Padres as the Mets swept a doubleheader.

The 1972 season was arguably Dyer's best as a pro. Grote's continuing health problems allowed Dyer to take full advantage of his opportunity. He played in a career-high 94 games—starting 91 behind the plate—and also reached career bests with eight homers and 36 RBIs. He led National League catchers with 12 double plays and threw out the majority of runners that tried to steal (40 of 79). He won National League Player of the Week June 12–18 and was playing so well that even after Grote came back, manager Yogi Berra decided to stay with Dyer. His improvement with the bat can be traced back to his fall session in Florida with the former home run champ and Mets broadcaster Ralph Kiner.

"I'd like to think I helped him," said Kiner modestly, "but he's the guy doing the job."

Dyer began the season on fire and after a four-hit game on

PHOTO COURTESY OF DWAYNE LABAKAS COLLECTION

*Duffy Dyer*

May 17, he was hitting at .533. He batted .300 until the final week of June.

Dyer almost caught his first no-hitter in the opening game of a July 4 doubleheader against San Diego. Tom Seaver was pitching and had one out in the ninth when Leron Lee broke his bat on a low inside pitch and looped into center field. Duffy was more upset by the hit than Seaver. He picked up Lee's bat after the hit and threw it aside in disgust. Later in the dugout, he angrily ripped off his catching gear and threw it around.

"I was all psyched up for a no-hitter," the usually quiet receiver admitted. "I wouldn't have been so mad if he hit a home run. But it was the right pitch and Tom threw it in the right spot."

Yogi explained it all very simply why Dyer, who labored in Grote's shadow for three years was playing instead of Grote. "He worked hard to improve himself and he did," Berra declared. "And he gives us more of a threat with the long ball."

Dyer's offseason hobby was somewhat unusual for a ballplayer. He made flower arrangements at a show called "Artistry in Flowers" at the Mall at Roosevelt Field. In a demonstration, Dyer created a little bouquet of white and red carnations. Dyer first became entranced with bouquets as a boy in Phoenix. "I used to watch florists and marvel at how they put together such intricate designs," he explained.

Over the next two years he went back to his role as the second-string catcher behind Grote, who was finally healthy and had won his job back. Dyer was almost traded, as there was interest from the California Angels with his former coach at Arizona State, Bobby Winkles, as the manager in Anaheim. Over those two years (1973–74), Duffy only hit one homer and barely kept his average above the .200 mark.

Still, Dyer made key contributions. The biggest came on the night of September 20, 1973. The Mets, who had been in last place a month earlier, found themselves 1 ½ games behind the Pirates at Shea Stadium, but they were down to their last out. Dyer's pinch-hit double off lefty Ramon Hernandez tied the game in the ninth inning. The eventual NL champion Mets went on to win in 13 innings thanks to a wild ricochet in what became known as the "Ball on the Wall Game." That was, however, Dyer's last at-bat of the year and he finished with his lowest batting average as a Met at .185.

After hitting .211 in 63 games the following year, he was traded to the Pirates for outfielder Gene Clines on October 22, 1974. Dyer served as the primary backup for Manny Sanguillen, but in spring training he found himself playing some games at first and third base along with his catching duties. Pirates manager Danny Murtaugh had plans for Dyer.

"I'm looking for Dyer to give Sanguillen some relief behind the plate," Murtaugh said. "Manny was in 151 games last year and I think it would be better for him and the team if he got some more time off. I've seen enough of Dyer to think he can hit better than he did last year."

Ex-Met Dyer came back to haunt his former teammates with a game-winning homer off Bob Apodaca leading off the 15th inning on August 3. The doubleheader sweep, with Dyer playing in both games, helped the Pirates retain their lead in the NL East. He walked with the bases loaded to bring in a run in his only postseason appearance that fall, as the Bucs were swept by the Reds in the NLCS.

Over the 1975 and '76 seasons, Dyer served as more than adequate in his backup role. The highlight of the 1976 season was catching a no-hitter by John Candelaria. "He didn't have his real good velocity," said Dyer, "but his fastball was moving well. The big thing was that he was keeping the ball down. He's usually a high-ball pitcher. But tonight he kept it down." Dyer's got almost as much a kick out of the no-hitter as Candelaria. "You always dream of catching a no-hitter," he said. "This is one of my biggest thrills."

The trade of Sanguillen to the A's for manager Chuck Tanner would open the door for Dyer to claim the starting spot in 1977. Tanner praised Duffy's handling of the pitchers. "He is a good example of a player who shouldn't be judged by statistics. He is a plus man on any club." Coming out of spring training, Tanner was stressing defense and gave the starting job to Dyer over Ed Ott.

Dyer had his second-best season hitting the ball. In 270 at-bats, he hit 11 doubles, three homers, and 19 RBIs to go with a .241 average. Dyer was like a coach on the field and was frequently asked for his thoughts when it came to the pitchers. Dyer had a knack of being able to tell when a pitcher was losing his stuff. In one game, Dyer told Tanner that left-hander Terry Forster had outstanding stuff. Forster appeared to be a stopgap reliever, brought in to face a few left-handed hitters against the Mets. When it came time for Mike Vail, Dave Kingman, and Joe Torre, all righty hitters, Tanner figured to go with a right-handed ace reliever, Rich Gossage. He stuck with Forster, who struck out Vail and Kingman and nailed Torre on a soft comebacker.

Dyer was sometimes compared to the old Indians catcher, Jim Hegan, for his defensive ability. In 545 total chances during the 1977 season, Dyer made only two errors. He wound up with a .992 career fielding percentage and made only 30 errors during 14 years in the big leagues. The 1978 season, in which he slumped to .211 in 58 games, was his last for the Pirates. Pittsburgh released him in November. He signed a three-year deal with the Montreal Expos to be the backup to Gary Carter. He served as a quality role player, hitting .243 in just 74 at-bats. He was traded during spring training in 1980 to the Detroit Tigers for future Mets manager Jerry Manuel. This was Dyer's last stop as a player; 1980 was his last year as a productive backup catcher with four homers and 11 RBIs. He ended his playing career with 30 home runs, 173 RBIs, and a .221 average. This would not be the end of his baseball career. Not by a long shot.

Dyer was back in baseball in 1983 as the bullpen coach for the Chicago Cubs. The following two years he would be the manager of Kenosha of the Midwest League, an affiliate of the Minnesota Twins. His first year the team went 70–68. His club went 79–60 and won the league championship in 1985. Dyer was named Manager of the Year. Then it was onto double-A El Paso in the Brewers organization and another championship in 1986. El Paso also had its league's best record, going 85–50. Looking to repeat in 1987, Dyer led his team to a 75–59 record and another playoff appearance. He was also named for the second time in three years Manager of the Year. The Brewers moved him up to manage triple-A affiliate Denver. They would go 72–69.

The Brewers were very impressed with Dyer's ability to manage, but decided they wanted him up on the major league club to be the third base coach. He held that position in Milwaukee for the next seven years. He moved over to the Oakland A's as a coach from 1996 to 1998. Dyer really wanted to manage again and got that opportunity for the Orioles to take over Bluefield in the Rookie League. He experienced his first losing season, going 25–43. The next year his team of mostly first-year players posted a 31–32 record. Dyer was a very hands-on manager and considered by many to be a good teacher.

The independent Bridgeport Bluefish of the Atlantic League hired him for the 2001 and 2002 seasons. He led the Bluefish to a playoff appearance in his second season. After almost three decades, Dyer returned to the Mets as a scout in 2003 and 2004. He went back to the field as manager of the Erie SeaWolves in 2005 and 2006. Dyer was named minor league catching coordinator of the San Diego Padres in 2008.

Dyer and his wife, Lynn, have four children: Cami, Megan, Brian, and Kevin. They reside in Phoenix during the offseason.

Dyer's managers during his career were some of the best in the game: Gil Hodges, Yogi Berra, Danny Murtaugh, Chuck Tanner, Dick Williams, and Sparky Anderson. He was a player that every club needs: a quality person willing to accept his place on the team and work hard at all times. He was the prototypical bench player and could be counted on for contributions off the bench and when called on to start. So if you ever go into Donovan's, remember to have a beverage for old Duffy.

**Sources**

New York Daily News. *Amazin' Mets: The Miracle of 69 (Daily News Legends Series)*. Sports Publishing 1969

*The Sporting News*, 1966-1982

*Sports Collectors Digest*, January 23, 1998

*www.baseball-reference.com*

*www.retrosheet.com*

*www.easternleague.com*

*www.mwlguide.com/managers*

*www.baseballchronology.com/baseball*

*http://minors.sabrwebs.com*

*www.attheplate.com/wcbl/basin_league*

Duffy Dyer player file; National Baseball Library (various clippings)

Arizona State Sun Devils Media Guide

## Another Opening, Another "L"

The 1969 Mets seemed assured of finally winning on Opening Day after opening their first seven seasons with defeats. The team was coming off its best season to date, fresh off a solid spring training, playing at Shea Stadium in front of 44,541, and—*la pièce de résistance*—the Mets were playing an expansion team, the Montreal Expos to open the 1969 season. The Expos, managed by Gene Mauch, featured a squad of castoffs and misfits, and if they were anything like the Mets in their inaugural year in 1962, the Expos would be easy pickings.

The Mets were once again disappointed. With their best pitcher on the mound, the Mets tied the dubious franchise mark set in the inaugural game in '62 by allowing 11 runs to start a season.

Bob Bailey had the first hit in Montreal history, a two-run double that followed a Ken Boswell error and two-out walk by Tom Seaver. Tommie Agee's bases-clearing double knocked out Expos starter Mudcat Grant in the second and put the Mets in front where they seemingly belonged. Montreal tied it in the third on a Rusty Staub single and took the lead in the fourth on a the first home run in Expos history…off the bat of relief pitcher Don McGinn. The Mets rallied back in the home fourth on a game-tying single by Rod Gaspar, and RBI-hits by Boswell and Cleon Jones, with Boswell nailed at the plate on Jones's double to end the inning. Though he did not have his best stuff, Seaver did leave after five innings with a 6–4 lead. Cal Koonce quickly blew the save—the first certified save opportunity in Mets history (the save became an official stat in 1969)—as Mack Jones doubled in two runs to tie the game in the sixth.

Things only got worse. Koonce gave up the lead in the seventh on a single by Maury Wills. Staub homered off an original Met—'62 alum Al Jackson—and the immortal Coco Laboy blasted a three-run home run off Canadian Met Ron Taylor. The Expos took their 11–6 lead into the ninth, when the Mets put together a rally. Jerry Grote singled in a run and Duffy Dyer followed with his first career home run, a three-run bomb against pitcher of record Don Shaw to make it an 11–10 game. Carroll Sembera came in and allowed a single to Amos Otis and a walk to Agee, putting the tying and go-ahead runs on base. He fanned Gaspar for the first save in the first Expos win.

The 10 runs scored by the Mets remains unsurpassed by the club in 48 Opening Days—and they lost to a team playing its first game ever. The Mets won the next two against Montreal and throttled the Expos when it mattered later in the year, but the Mets would have to wait until 1970 to win their first Opening Day. They beat the Pirates in 11 innings, 5–3, with Donn Clendenon snapping the tie and Taylor getting the win in the last opener at venerable Forbes Field. The mood was even brighter a week later when the Mets and Pirates played again—this time at Shea. It marked the day the Mets raised their '69 world championship flag.

# Danny Frisella

by Greg Spira

| Season | Age | W | L | Pct | G | GS | SV | IP | H | BB | SO | WHIP | ERA |
|---|---|---|---|---|---|---|---|---|---|---|---|---|---|
| 1969 Mets | 23 | 0 | 0 | – | 3 | 0 | 0 | 4.7 | 8 | 3 | 5 | 2.357 | 7.71 |
| Career 10 Years | – | 34 | 40 | .459 | 351 | 17 | 57 | 609.3 | 529 | 286 | 471 | 1.338 | 3.32 |

Danny Frisella's 11-year career in professional baseball is often overshadowed by his unusual death, but the right-handed pitcher spent at least part of 10 different seasons in the majors. The big, beefy hurler with the nickname "Bear" saw his greatest success in his stint as the top right-handed reliever with the Mets from 1970 to 1972.

Frisella grew up in San Francisco as the son of an Italian-American firefighter and an Irish-American mother. He was a star baseball player at Serra High School in San Mateo before pursuing a college education, first at the College of San Mateo in his freshman year, and then at Washington State University in his sophomore and junior years. In both of his years at Washington State, he led his college team to a division title and was named to the All-Conference team. Frisella was the first baseball player from WSU to play in the major leagues, a group that later included Dodgers stalwart Ron Cey and future Mets Doug Sisk, John Olerud, Mike Kinkade, and Aaron Sele.

Frisella was first drafted in 1965 by the Braves, but the young pitcher opted to continue his education for another year instead of signing with Milwaukee. In the summer of 1965, the right-hander played baseball in Fairbanks, Alaska, for the Goldpanners, along with another pitcher who would not sign with the Braves after being drafted: Tom Seaver. The two future Mets right-handers helped lead the Goldpanners to the state championship. In 1966, after his junior year in college, Frisella was again drafted by a major-league team. This time the team was the Mets, and Frisella quickly signed and started his professional career with Auburn in the New York-Penn League.

Frisella spent the following three seasons shuttling between the majors, the minors, and the Air National Guard. The right-hander was not a particularly hard thrower, but his excellent curveball allowed Frisella to quickly sail through the lower minors. While he reached Triple-A Jacksonville after just 24 starts in Class A, and debuted in the majors in Los Angeles on July 27, 1967—just his second year as a pro—Frisella's stuff proved to be inadequate for a major-league starter. He was never able to establish himself in that role as a major leaguer. His 11 starts as a Met in 1967 were more than he made the rest of his career combined (he made six starts in 1968 and one each in '70 and '74). The interruptions to his seasons that came about as part of his military training probably didn't help matters, but he was far from the only major leaguer dealing with that obstacle, and of course it was nothing compared with being drafted to serve in Vietnam.

Frisella's wife, the onetime Pamela Marshall, played an important role not only in his personal life but in his athletic career. She was quite athletic herself. Before their marriage she had spent a year as an offensive end and safety in a women's professional football league. In her, Danny Frisella had not only a life partner but a motivator and an active participant in his training.

After spending significant periods of time in the majors in 1967 and 1968, Frisella pitched only 4 ⅔ major-league innings during the Mets' miraculous 1969 season, making three appearances during a July call-up. But the pitcher's career took a positive turn in the winter of 1969 when Diego Segui taught him the forkball in Venezuela. The forkball proved to be the out pitch Frisella needed, and in 1970 Frisella came up to the majors to stay. Serving as Tug McGraw's right-handed counterpart in the Mets bullpen, Frisella enjoyed the best season of his career in 1971. The season began on a positive note for Frisella, as he picked up a win on the season's first weekend when the Mets edged the Reds 3–2 in 11 innings. On April 27, Frisella picked up his first save of the year by pitching the ninth inning of a 2–1 victory over the Cardinals. On May 21, after Nolan Ryan put a 6–2 Mets lead over the Braves in jeopardy in the top of the ninth inning by plunking Eddie Williams and Ralph Garr and walking Hank Aaron, Frisella came into the bases-loaded situation and induced Orlando Cepeda to ground out to end the game. This stint earned the right-hander his club-leading fifth save.

Frisella continued to pitch spectacularly through the first half of the season. At the All-Star break, Frisella had thrown 47 innings and had allowed only 10 runs on 38 hits, 12 bases on balls, and 3 home runs while striking out 51 batters. Frisella's second half wasn't nearly as strong as a result of soreness in his shoulder that started in July, but he did pitch effectively in September and ended the '71 season with 42 games finished and 12 saves while posting a 1.99 ERA in 90 ⅔ innings. In 1972, Frisella picked up nine saves, but as a result of further arm problems his overall numbers were down and he was dealt to the Atlanta Braves along on the offseason with roommate Gary Gentry for Felix Millan and George Stone in what turned out to be a great trade for the Mets. It did not work out so well for Frisella.

After two poor seasons in the Braves bullpen—his 4.67 ERA over 78 games proved to be the highest he would have for any of the five major league clubs he pitched for—Frisella was traded to the Padres for Cito Gaston. He bounced back in his one season in San Diego with a 3.13 ERA in a career-high 97 ⅔ innings (1–6 record notwithstanding), but Frisella was traded again just before Opening Day in 1976 to the St. Louis Cardinals. He spent just two months there before he was moved to the Milwaukee Brewers. Despite the multiple stops, 1976 was another successful season for Frisella as he closed for the Brewers and picked up 10 saves, his most since leaving the Mets.

Unfortunately, 1976 was to be Danny Frisella's last season. On New Year's Day, 1977, Frisella was killed in a tragic accident. He and a friend were riding at a relatively slow speed in a dune buggy less than 100 feet from the Frisella's Phoenix home when the pitcher, reacting to the vehicle tipping in the sand, pulled the hand brake and tried to jump off. In his attempt to escape the vehicle, however, his foot got stuck and his head was crushed by the rollbar. Frisella left behind his wife, Pamela, and two sons, Jason and Daniel, the latter of whom had yet to be born when his father died, along with a jewelry business the couple had started to prepare them for life after baseball.

**Sources**

The National Baseball Hall of Fame Library Player Archive

Allen, Maury, "Danny Frisella: A Kid With A Lot of Guts," *New York Post*, January 4, 1977

Draper, Dick, "For Pam Frisella, Memories of Danny Linger," *San Mateo County Times*, no date

Lang, Jack "Ex-Alaska Goldpanners Seaver, Frisella Hit Pay Dirt With Mets," *Long Island Press*, no date

Lang, Jack, "McGraw and Frisella—Supreme Game-Savers," *Long Island Press*, July 1, 1972.

Russo, Neal, "Danny Has Early Success Thanks to Pam's Fat Hand," *St. Louis Post-Dispatch*, May 9, 1976

"The Adventures of Dan and Pam," *New York Sunday News*, July 25, 1971

"Dan Frisella Making Hay With New Fork Ball," *New York Post*, May 16, 1970

"Danny Frisella Dead in Car Mishap At 30," *New York Times*, January 4, 1977

# Wayne Garrett

by Les Masterson

| Season | Age | G | AB | R | H | 2B | 3B | HR | RBI | BB | SO | SB | CS | BA | OBP | SLG |
|---|---|---|---|---|---|---|---|---|---|---|---|---|---|---|---|---|
| 1969 Mets | 21 | 124 | 400 | 38 | 87 | 11 | 3 | 1 | 39 | 40 | 75 | 4 | 2 | .218 | .290 | .268 |
| Career 10 Years | – | 1092 | 3285 | 438 | 786 | 107 | 22 | 61 | 340 | 561 | 529 | 38 | 30 | .239 | .350 | .341 |

If the New York Mets only had confidence in Wayne Garrett as their starting third baseman, the franchise might have never traded Nolan Ryan and Amos Otis. Instead, New York's National League team spent nearly every offseason during Garrett's 7½-year Mets tenure searching for someone else to take over the third-base job. Considered a good glove man who could play three positions, Garrett was initially seen as a utility infielder, but he ultimately played an offensive role for two legendary Mets teams.

Ronald Wayne Garrett was born on December 3, 1947, in Brooksville, Florida. He played baseball at Sarasota High School, and was drafted by the Milwaukee Braves in the sixth round of baseball's first amateur draft, in 1965. The Braves were well aware of the Garrett family as Wayne's brothers both were already in the Braves minor league system. Like their younger brother, Henry Adrian Garrett and Charles James Garrett were called by their middle name.

As an 18-year-old, Wayne played for his hometown Sarasota team in the Florida State League. In his professional debut, he collected four hits in his first four at-bats. He hit .269 in 43 games for the year. It was his highest batting average during his four years in the Braves farm system, including stops in West Palm Beach, Kinston, and double-A Shreveport. After the Atlanta Braves left him unprotected in the 1968 Rule V draft, the Mets paid $25,000 for the 21-year-old infielder. Garrett turned out to be the club's only move before the 1969 season.

Mets scout Bob Scheffing had watched Garrett in the Arizona Instructional League in 1968 and was impressed with the young infielder. Mets general manager Johnny Murphy was looking for a utility infielder in case Bud Harrelson was not ready following knee surgery. Joe McDonald, who led the Mets farm system, said, "We really didn't have him listed as a prospect. But we found out later that six clubs that saw Wayne in Arizona also had him on their draft lists. We just were fortunate enough to have an early pick."[1]

In Garrett's first major-league training camp, the Mets didn't wait long before giving the fresh-faced, red-headed kid a look. The team kicked off its 1969 spring-training schedule with four rookies starting against St. Louis, including Garrett, who played shortstop. Of the four new faces, Garrett was the only one to play a role for the 1969 world champions.

With the Mets required under the draft rules to keep Garrett on the team or send him back to Atlanta, Wayne was added to the 25-man roster out of spring training as a utility player. He watched from the bench as the Mets got off to a sluggish start.

He started at second base in his first major-league game on April 12, 1969. As an example of the lack of Mets firepower, the rookie, who hit below .250 in his minor league career, batted third in the order. Garrett went 1-for-3 in a 1–0 loss to Dave Giusti and the St. Louis Cardinals.

"I was so scared. It was just like at the World Series. I wasn't nervous at all at the plate, but in the field...God, I was so tense, my hands were like iron," Garrett recalled several years later.[2] He had never been to a city the size of New York before Opening Day 1969. It took getting used to both on the field and away from it.

Manager Gil Hodges penciled the skinny redhead into the lineup the next day, April 13, against future Hall of Famer Bob Gibson. Garrett doubled off Gibson, but the Cardinals hurler beat Mets ace Tom Seaver, 3–1.

The rookie, nicknamed Red and Huckleberry Finn (a name he never liked) for his youthful appearance and golden features, used his flexibility to play a key role in 1969. He filled in for starters serving in the military reserve. Garrett played three infield positions. He played nine games in place of Bud Harrelson at shortstop. He split time with Al Weis filling in for second baseman Ken Boswell. Garrett even played the last two innings as a defensive replacement at second base in Seaver's "Imperfect Game" on July 9. (Chicago's Jimmy Qualls broke up Seaver's bid for a perfect game with a single in the ninth inning.)

Most of Garrett's starts, however, were at third base. He was the 40th third baseman in the Mets' eight-year history and one of six that season. In his first start at third base—at Wrigley Field on May 4—he had his first multi-hit game as the Mets stunned the red-hot Cubs with a doubleheader sweep. In his second start at third, two days later, Garrett crushed his first and only regular-season home run that year in an 8–1 win over Gary Nolan and the Cincinnati Reds at Shea Stadium. Garrett's power display had *The Sporting News* wondering if the revolving door at third base was over for the Mets. Under a photo of the Mets' rookie third baseman was the line: "Red Garrett...End of Disaster Era?"

Garrett continued to impress in 1969 in a third base platoon with veteran Ed Charles. The accolades rolled in. Hodges pointed to Garrett as one of five players who transformed the Mets from mediocrity to a championship-caliber club (the others were Tommie Agee, Cleon Jones, Harrelson, and Tug McGraw). Hodges called Garrett "the surprise of the year." Tom Seaver suggested Garrett, Gary Gentry, and Hodges as the reason for the team's success.

Dick Young of the *New York Daily News* called the Mets' $25,000 payment to draft Garrett "the bargain of the year."[3] Another New York sportswriting fixture, Jack Lang, wrote that the Garrett deal was the best deal since "some Indians sold Manhattan for $24."[4]

Garrett's heroics continued throughout the season, including a 15th-inning single against the Los Angeles Dodgers on June 4. His drive skipped under outfielder Willie Davis's glove and scored Agee with the winning run.

Garrett also played a key role in one of the biggest moments of 1969. During the sixth inning of the September 8 showdown against the Cubs, Garrett stepped to the plate with Agee on second. He hit a single to right off Bill Hands. Right fielder Jim Hickman gobbled up the ball and unleashed a strong throw to Randy Hundley; the catcher tagged Agee but not before the runner reached the plate. Umpire Satch Davidson's call sparked a heated argument with Hundley and Cubs manager Leo Durocher. The Mets won, 3–2, and crept to within 1½ games of the Cubs for the NL East lead.

Garrett hit only .218 in his rookie season while playing in 124 games and collecting 400 at-bats, but he was a star in the first-ever National League Championship Series. He batted .385 while starting all three playoff games and batting second against the right-handed Braves starting staff.

Garrett doubled and scored the tying run during the Mets' five run eighth inning in Game One, had two hits and knocked in a run in Game Two, and stroked an 0–1 pitch over the right-field wall in Shea's first postseason game in Game Three. His homer off Pat Jarvis with Nolan Ryan aboard put the Mets up 5–4; they ultimately won the game, 7–4, and swept the series with Garrett throwing to Ed Kranepool to retire Tony Gonzalez for the final out.

Garrett sat out the first two World Series games, but started Game Three against Baltimore's Jim Palmer, collecting two walks in four plate appearances.

After their shocking World Series win, the Miracle Mets were the toast of New York. Garrett was a bachelor and enjoyed the Miracle Mets gravy train that offseason. He even appeared on *The Dating Game* with Rod Gaspar and Ken Boswell.

"That 1969 year I had a good time. I was just discovering everything, New York, nightlife, being a big-league ballplayer, having fun at all times. It was terrific," Garrett said.[5]

His platoon partner, Ed Charles, retired after the 1969 season, but the Mets were not content with Garrett as their lone third sacker. In what became a theme over the next few seasons, the Mets looked to add another third baseman. Echoing similar statements by Mets brass in future years, Murphy said after the 1969 season, "I think that kid Garrett is going to make a heck of a third baseman, but we need someone to take Ed Charles's place."[6]

The Mets' "solution" was trading one of their top hitting prospects, Amos Otis, to the Kansas City Royals for third baseman Joe Foy. Otis went on to a solid career in which he stroked more than 2,000 hits. Foy, on the other hand, struggled in New York, and the Mets cut loose the troubled player after one season.

Splitting time between third and second, Garrett hit 12 home runs in 1970, third best on the team, while leading the club with a .390 on-base percentage and batting .254. A highlight of his season was a game on July 26 in which he stroked two homers against the Dodgers, but as an example of how the team brass remained unsold on the slightly built youngster, Hodges pinch-hit Agee for Garrett later in the game. The move backfired as Agee grounded into a double play in the 5–3 loss to the Dodgers.

Though he didn't have faith in Garrett that day, Hodges considered him his starting third baseman for 1971. Alas, another issue blocked Red's path to the starting third baseman's job—military service.

Garrett joined the Bayside National Guard Unit after the 1970 season. Draft-exempt his first two years with the Mets because of a back ailment, Garrett was reclassified 1-A and considered ready for duty. With Garrett slated to spend at least four months on active duty, the Mets traded pitcher Ron Herbel to Atlanta for former Brooklyn Dodger Bob Aspromonte.

Garrett entered the service as his teammates traveled to start spring training in St. Petersburg. He spent the next five months in the reserve in Army communications school while his team sputtered through mediocrity. His military training completed, Garrett was optioned to Tidewater in July before returning to the Mets.

Garrett's time away from major league ball wasn't evident in his season debut as his three singles, two runs batted in, and three runs scored helped the Mets beat the Houston Astros at Shea Stadium, 9–3, on July 24. Despite that great start, Garrett struggled through much of 1971, with a 0-for-29 drought near the end of the season relegating him to a .213 average.

While Wayne struggled in 1971, his older brother, Adrian, who spent 11 years in professional baseball and collected only six at-bats in the majors (including five strikeouts), finally got the call. Adrian tore up the Pacific Coast League with the Chicago Cubs' Tacoma farm team that year, stroking 43 home runs and 119 RBIs. The Oakland A's, who were on the cusp of a three-year dynasty, were impressed with the numbers and traded for the slugger. He played with the club during the final month of the season. Topps named Adrian a Triple-A All-Star at the end of the season.

Things were looking up for Adrian, but Wayne received more sobering news during the offseason. The Mets made what is still considered the worst trade in franchise history by dealing future Hall of Famer Nolan Ryan and three other players to the California Angels for Jim Fregosi. The former All-Star shortstop was seen as the answer to the team's third-base puzzle, and again that solution did not include Garrett.

But Fregosi's body was well beyond his 30 years. While Ryan went on to greatness he only hinted at in Flushing, the Mets bounced Fregosi's achy body and weak hitting by the middle of 1973.

During spring training in 1972, Fregosi broke his right thumb while taking ground balls from Hodges. The Mets skipper moved to Plan B and planned to split time between Garrett and Tim

Foli. Garrett, however, strained his shoulder lunging for a grounder and pulled a hamstring. The injuries cut short a spring training in which he was hitting .276. Plans changed as a strike shortened the end of spring training, Foli was traded to Montreal in the Rusty Staub deal, and one of the great shocks in franchise history occurred on April 2 when Hodges died of a heart attack.

A hamstring injury kept Garrett from joining new manager Yogi Berra's club until April 30. He reinjured the muscle running out a double in his first start, on May 3 in San Francisco, and sat out another two weeks. Garrett ultimately played 82 games at third and 22 at second base in his injury-marred 1972 season, hitting .232 with four game-winning RBIs in 298 at-bats.

PHOTO COURTESY OF DWAYNE LABAKAS COLLECTION

*Wayne Garrett wore number 17 to win a spot in spring training 1969, but he switched to 11 in New York.*

Entering the 1973 campaign, the Mets saw Garrett as a 25-year-old utility infielder and Fregosi as their third baseman. Fregosi, who had come to spring training overweight the previous year, was both in shape and enthusiastic in '73, but a sore arm impeded his throws to first base. The injury created an opening for Garrett, who in 1973 became the third baseman the Mets had sought since the team's founding. The Fregosi era, on the other hand, ended on July 11 when the Texas Rangers picked him up off waivers.

Garrett had a career year for the "Ya Gotta Believe" Mets. Inserted into the leadoff spot in May, he was second on the club with a career-high 16 home runs, and also topped the team in triples and walks; he was third in RBIs, doubles, runs, and hits. He led the team in stolen bases with six (the team did not believe in speed; the 27 stolen bases by the club are the lowest in franchise history in a nonstrike year). On the defensive side, Garrett was second among NL third basemen with 36 double plays.

While he played a complementary role for the 1969 Miracle Mets, Garrett was a leader for the 1973 squad. He played a key part in one of the biggest moments in Mets history—"The Ball on the Wall Play." Just three weeks after being in last place, the Mets found themselves battling for first place against the Pittsburgh Pirates. Facing Pittsburgh on September 20, the Mets rallied to tie the game in the ninth. With the Pirates' Richie Zisk at first in the 13th inning, Dave Augustine crushed a Ray Sadecki pitch to left. The ball carried over Cleon Jones's head and appeared headed to the Whitestone Bridge, but the ball landed on top of the wall. Rather than ricochet over the fence for a home run, the ball bounced back on an arc directly to Jones.

The left fielder spun around and fired the ball to the cutoff man Garrett, who had moved to shortstop in extra innings. Standing in short left field, Garrett took the throw and fired to catcher Ron Hodges, who tagged Zisk before he reached the plate. The play came to symbolize the never-say-die, miracle-redux nature of the 1973 season. The Mets won the game in the bottom of the inning and took over first place the next night.

Garrett was clutch in 1973, leading the team with 11 game-winning hits, including four in September: a leadoff homer against Montreal's Steve Renko in a 1-0 Mets win; a pinch-hit single that beat the Phillies 4-2 in 12 innings; a two-run homer on September 22 that provided the only runs in a shutout of the Cardinals; and a two-run triple that broke up a 2-2 tie and carried the Mets to a 5–2 win over the Cards the following day. Garrett hit .323 with 6 home runs and 17 RBIs during the final month of the season and his .393 average with two homers and six RBIs earned him NL Player of the Week (September 17–23).

The 1973 postseason was not nearly as strong for Garrett. He hit .087 against the Cincinnati Reds in the National League Championship Series and .167 in the World Series against the Oakland A's, including 11 strikeouts, which tied a World Series record (since broken). His only two hits in the World Series were home runs, including his leadoff blast in Game Three at Shea. His popup while representing the tying run against Darold Knowles was the final out of the series, the only one of Garrett's four career postseason series that didn't end with a frenzied celebration at Shea Stadium.

After a great year in which he helped his team to the World Series, the future looked bright for the young man. But during the offseason, Garrett injured his shoulder while horseback riding in Tennessee. He struggled with throwing the ball during spring training in 1974, but he played through the pain during the season.

Garrett reached career highs in games (151) and at-bats (522), led the team with 89 walks, stroked 13 home runs and had 53 RBIs in 1974, but his average dropped to .224 for the first Mets team to not achieve a winning record since 1968. His playing time decreased in 1975 after the Mets acquired former All-Star Joe Torre. (Ironically, the Mets had tried to acquire Torre during Garrett's first Mets training camp in 1969, but the team had passed because the Braves had wanted the team's best prospects in return.) Garrett hit .266 with six home runs and had 34 RBIs in 274 at-bats in '75. He was a successful pinch-hitter, batting .545 in 11 at-bats, including two home runs.

In 1976, Garrett split time at third with youngster Roy Staiger. With many of the Miracle Mets either already retired or playing elsewhere, Garrett's days with the team also came to an end. He was traded with outfielder Del Unser to the last-place Montreal Expos for Pepe Mangual and Jim Dwyer on July 21. At the time of the trade, Garrett was hitting .223 with four home runs and 26 RBIs. "I am surprised, certainly, but it hasn't been a good year for me, and I guess that was the reason," he said at the time.[7]

Garrett finished his Mets career with a .237 batting average, 667 hits, 55 home runs, and 295 RBIs . His 709 games at third base were the most for any Met at that time. As for the trade: It wasn't the Ryan or Otis deal, but the Mets traded two starters for two players who never played a game for the team after 1976.

Garrett took over second-base duties in Montreal, and hit .243 in 59 games. He made his former team pay in their last home game of the season as his grand slam helped propel the Expos past Seaver and the Mets, 7–2, at Shea. His first career grand slam was also his sixth home run of the season and second with Montreal.

During the offseason, the Expos acquired Dave Cash and planned to play Garrett more at third along with Larry Parrish and Pete Mackanin at new Olympic Stadium, but Garrett's right shoulder continued to bother him. Expos manager Dick Williams initially gave Parrish the third-base job and Garrett was once again spending most of his time on the bench. He was hitting only .133 after 45 at-bats after the first game of a doubleheader on June 26, but Williams began platooning him against right-handers and a hot streak helped push Garrett's final average to .270. His season ended early after he suffered ligament damage in his right knee while sliding into second on a steal.

Once again in 1978, Garrett fought for playing time along with Stan Papi, Sam Mejias, and Unser. Garrett was hitting .174 in 69 at-bats when he was sold to the Cardinals on July 21.

For the Cardinals, Garrett hit .333 in 33 games, including .389 with runners in scoring position. The Cardinals saw him as a utility infielder and pinch hitter for 1979, but the two sides could not agree on a contract, so Garrett left the US and got a job with the Chunichi Dragons in Japan.

"I just couldn't run anymore. The Cards could see that. I got an offer to go to Japan for two years and I accepted it. They paid me $125,000 for the two seasons, about twice as much as I was making in the big leagues," Garrett said.[8]

"I had so many injuries. I was so discouraged. I was just burned out. I wish it had lasted a few more years, but I probably would have just been hanging on. If I could have played well, run, and thrown normally, that would have been different. I went to Japan, took the money, and did as well as I could. I earned my salary there. It wasn't the same. It was just to make a few bucks. It wasn't a lot of fun," he added.[9]

Forty years after the Miracle Mets, Garrett remained a regular part of 1969 Mets reunions and fantasy camps. He has worked in the courier business along with other ventures in Sarasota. He was one of 40-plus Mets invited to Shea Stadium's closing ceremonies at the end of the 2008 season. The team's brass may have overlooked his ability during his playing days, but Garrett's invitation to the Shea Goodbye ceremonies showed the team understood his stature in Mets history. For the millions who cheered for him at Shea, Red Garrett was the finest Mets third baseman in the team's first two decades. And despite many bigger names who manned the hot corner at Shea, Garrett remains the only one to play on two Mets pennant winners.

**Notes and Sources**

1 *The Sporting News*, October 25, 1969
2 Kathryn Parker, *We Won Today: My Season with the Mets*, 1977
3 *The Sporting News*, July 19, 1969
4 *The Sporting News*, October 25, 1969
5 Maury Allen, *After the Miracle: The 1969 Mets Twenty Years Later*, 1989
6 *The Sporting News*, December 6, 1969
7 *The New York Times*, July 21, 1976
8 Maury Allen, *After the Miracle: The 1969 Mets Twenty Years Later*, 1989
9 Ibid

New York Mets Media Guides: 1969, 1973, 1975, 1976, 1977
Stanley Cohen, *A Magic Summer: The 1969 Mets.*
William J. Ryczek, *The Amazing Mets: 1962-1969*, 2008
Joseph Durso, *Amazing: The Miracle of the Mets*, 1970
Peter Golenbock, *Amazin': The Miraculous History of New York's Beloved Baseball Team*, 2002
Dennis D'Agostino, *This Date in Mets History*, 1981
Duncan Bock and John Jordan, *The Complete Year-by-Year NY Mets Fan's Almanac*, 1992
Leonard Koppett, *The New York Mets: The Whole Story*, 1974
*The Sporting News*
*The New York Times*
Art Shamsky with Barry Zeman, *The Magnificent Seasons*, 2004
Maury Allen, *After the Miracle: The 1969 Mets Twenty Years Later*, 1989
"Total Mets," From *Total Baseball: The Official Encyclopedia of Major League Baseball*, 1997
Kathryn Parker, *We Won Today: My Season with the Mets*, 1977
*Baseball-reference.com*

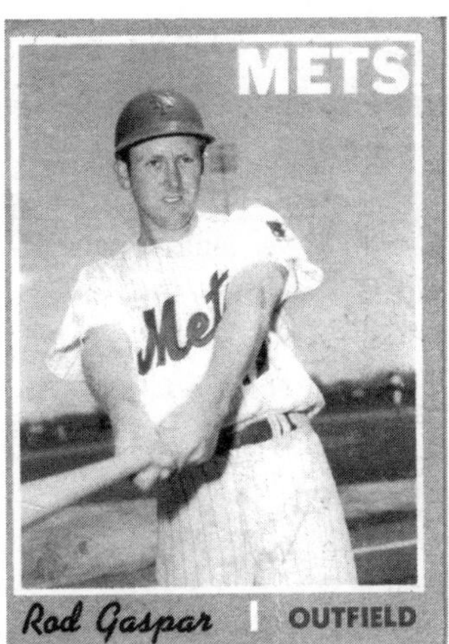


# Rod Gaspar

by Maxwell Kates

| Season | Age | G | AB | R | H | 2B | 3B | HR | RBI | BB | SO | SB | CS | BA | OBP | SLG |
|---|---|---|---|---|---|---|---|---|---|---|---|---|---|---|---|---|
| 1969 Mets | 23 | 118 | 215 | 26 | 49 | 6 | 1 | 1 | 14 | 25 | 19 | 7 | 3 | .228 | .313 | .279 |
| Career 4 Years | – | 178 | 260 | 35 | 54 | 6 | 1 | 1 | 17 | 33 | 29 | 8 | 4 | .208 | .301 | .250 |

Though his major-league career was limited to parts of only four seasons, Rod Gaspar was anything but a footnote player. While he played in only one full year in the majors, it was as a world champion. Gaspar led National League outfielders in double plays while scoring a pivotal run in the 1969 World Series. Six years later, he witnessed a second baseball "miracle" in Honolulu. Wherever he played, Gaspar was known for his spectacular outfield defense and his late-inning heroics.

Rodney Earl Gaspar was born on April 3, 1946, in Long Beach, California.[1] The son of an iron-worker and a homemaker, he and his two brothers were raised in a working-class environment.[2] Gaspar was initially noted as a good athlete at Lakewood High School. Playing baseball and basketball, he was an All-City athlete in 1964, his senior year.[3] On the diamond, he was particularly adept at hitting for average, baserunning, and defense in the outfield. His baseball acumen earned him a scholarship to Long Beach State University.[4] The New York Mets thought enough of Gaspar to draft him in 1966 after he batted .393.[5] He decided to remain in school, hitting .342 in his junior year.[6] The Mets drafted Gaspar once again in June 1967. This time, he signed with scouts Nelson Burbrink and Dee Fondy.[7] His first team was Williamsport in the Eastern League. Although Gaspar hit only .260 at the Mets' double-A affiliate, it was enough to place him as one of the top ten hitters in the league.

"We played in a pitchers' league," he recalled. "The air was heavy and the lights in most of the ballparks were not good. In Pawtucket, the sun would set in center field. There was only one guy who hit .300 and that was my teammate, Bernie Smith. He hit exactly .300. [actually, .306]." The Mets moved their double-A affiliate to Memphis in 1968, where Gaspar proceeded to tear up the opposition, leading the league with 160 hits and batting .309 with 25 stolen bases to earn a Texas League All-Star berth. [8] Gaspar then reported to the Mexican Winter League, again batting better than .300.[9] The young outfielder continued his meteoric rise through the Mets farm system, receiving an invitation to training camp at St. Petersburg in 1969. But could the switch-hitter who stood six feet tall and weighed 160 pounds crack a roster already boasting Tommie Agee, Cleon Jones, and Ron Swoboda in the outfield?

"I was just up from Memphis and they didn't know who I was. [Gil] Hodges didn't know who I was, the coaches didn't know...no one did," Gaspar told author Stanley Cohen.[10] He appeared destined for triple-A Tidewater when fourth outfielder Art Shamsky hurt his back. "Gil started me in the outfield and I went on a hitting streak. I think I hit in 13 straight games and they ended up keeping me." [11]

Gaspar learned on his 23rd birthday that he had made the team. He told sportswriter Ferd Borsch, "I was at the right place at the right time."[12] His greatest thrill at that time in his career was being told he was the Mets' starting right fielder against the expansion Montreal Expos on Opening Day, April 8, 1969. [13] Going 2-for-5 with a stolen base and an RBI, he remarked that "the thrill of being out there will always be with me."[14] With the tying run on second base, he was struck out by Carroll Sembera to end the game, an 11–10 victory for the Expos in their first-ever game.[15] Having lost their previous seven National League openers, the Mets continued their tradition of beginning each season below .500. This season, however, would end very differently than the first seven.

Although relegated to a supporting role when Shamsky returned from the disabled list, Gaspar was often called on in clutch situations, rarely disappointing his manager or his fans. He credited Hodges with understanding and using the talents of all his players to field a formidable club.

"[Gil] really knew how to utilize his personnel. I always felt a part of the club. I know I wasn't a star but I knew I was a contributor." Gaspar added that Hodges "made every player feel a part of that unit and vitally important to the team's success."[16] Deep into retirement, he remained enthusiastic when describing the symbiosis he shared with Mets fans, calling them "the best, the most energetic, and among the most passionate in baseball."

Gaspar saved his most monumental efforts for games against teams from his native California. On May 30 before a crowd of 52,272, he hit a home run off the San Francisco Giants' Mike McCormick. His teammates rallied to overcome a 3–0 deficit, tying the game and ultimately winning, 4–3. It was the second victory in what became an 11-game winning streak. A week later, on June 7 in San Diego, Gaspar rapped a triple off Jack Baldschun in a 4–0 victory over the Padres.[17] Perhaps the most unusual game of Gaspar's rookie season occurred on August 30 at Candlestick Park in San Francisco. As the Mets and Giants were deadlocked in the bottom of the ninth, Gaspar was in left field as Willie McCovey strode to the plate.

"McCovey was the league MVP that year and I think they intentionally walked him more than any other player," he said.[18] With one away and Bob Burda representing the go-ahead run on first base, Gil Hodges had Tug McGraw pitch to McCovey. The Mets decided to play the percentages by invoking "the McCovey shift." Donn Clendenon stood "on the line" at first, Tommie Agee played in right-center field, and Gaspar shifted to left-center.[19] This is how Gaspar remembered the play:

> *As soon as McCovey hits the ball, [Burda] takes off. We were playing in Candlestick Park, and if you're familiar with the weather in San Francisco, you'd know that the field was wet. He hits "a high fly ball down the left-field line" as our announcer Bob Murphy describes it and it lands fair [by a foot], near the warning track. There was no way I could catch the ball. My only thought was, Burda was the winning run and I had to throw him out at home plate. As I approached the ball it was stuck in the ground. I grabbed it bare-handed, pivoted off my left foot and threw blindly toward home plate. Thankfully it was a strike to catcher Jerry Grote.*[20]

As Gaspar remembered the play, Grote must have been so shocked by the long throw that he forget that Burda was only the second out. The catcher rolled the ball to the pitcher's mound as if the inning was over. Donn Clendenon, one of impeccable mental alertness, raced to the mound to field the ball and threw it to Bobby Pfeil to nab McCovey at third base.[21] Just your average 7-2-3-5 double play—on a hit no less—for those keeping score. The Mets went on to win the game, 3–2, when Clendenon hit a solo home run off Gaylord Perry the following inning.[22]

When the dust cleared on the 1969 pennant race, the Mets sat atop the National League East, finishing ahead of the Cubs by eight games. Amid a surplus of talented outfielders, Rod Gaspar led the senior circuit with six double plays in just 91 games in the field.[23] He also led the Mets with a dozen assists and stole seven bases in ten tries.[24] At the plate, he batted .228 with 14 RBIs and drew 25 walks while fanning just 19 times. However, despite their 100 victories and a sweep of the favored Atlanta Braves in the National League Championship Series, not everyone took the Mets seriously on the eve of the World Series—least of all, Frank Robinson of the American League champion Baltimore Orioles.

After the Orioles had swept the Minnesota Twins in the American League Championship Series, Robinson heard that Rod Gaspar had predicted that the Mets would win the World Series in four games. Robinson said, "Who in the hell is Ron Gaspar?" Fellow Baltimore outfielder Paul Blair eavesdropped on Robinson's sarcasm, correcting him, "That's not Ron. It's Rod, stupid!" In a retort worthy of an Abbott and Costello routine, Robinson said, "All right, bring on Rod Stupid."[25]

Notwithstanding Robinson's overconfidence, the Mets and Rod Gaspar enjoyed the last laugh in Game Four of the World Series. With the score deadlocked 1–1 in the 10th inning, the Mets summoned Gaspar to run for Jerry Grote, who had led off with a sun-aided double. After an intentional walk, J.C. Martin came to bat for Tom Seaver. Martin put a perfect bunt down the first-base line. Orioles southpaw Pete Richert fielded the ball and threw toward first baseman Boog Powell, but the ball glanced off Martin's wrist. Meanwhile, Gaspar steamed home with the winning run.[26]

As he remembered the play, "I could see it hit and I just took off. Eddie Yost, our third base coach, [who stood only two feet away] was screaming for me to go home, but I never heard him. There were over 55,000 people there and the noise was incredible. Only after I turned and saw the ball rolling toward second base that I took off for home and scored. The first person to greet me was the winning pitcher, Tom Seaver. It was his only World Series victory in his career."[27]

It also turned out to be the last time Gaspar got into a postseason game in his career. Manager Gil Hodges did not resort to his bench in Game Five, a 5–3 triumph to win the Mets the first world championship by an expansion team. Quite literally, the Miracle Mets were the toast of the town, appearing on the *Ed Sullivan Show*.[28] New York was an exciting city to be young and famous in, and Rod Gaspar enjoyed every minute of the 1969 season and its aftermath.[29] Gary Gentry, also a '69 rookie, was his roommate and Gaspar developed close friendships with other young teammates including Wayne Garrett, Ken Boswell, Art Shamsky, Bob Pfeil, and Danny Frisella. Frisella grew to serve an important role in Gaspar's personal life when in April 1970, the relief pitcher introduced him to Sheridan Poulton.[30] Rod and Sheridan married three months later, on July 7, 1970.

Despite the personal milestone, 1970 was a bittersweet season for Gaspar. On the heels of winning a World Series in his rookie year, he spent most of the year in triple-A Tidewater.[31] Looking back on the season, Gaspar blamed only his "nickel-brained attitude" for failing to make the big club.

"For the first time in my life, I didn't work out after the 1969 season. Gil wanted me to play in Venezuela. I said, 'Heck, why do I have to go down there?' So I didn't play any ball over the winter and I reported to spring training out of shape." He added that "if I hadn't been sent down to the minors, there was something wrong with *them*. I *should* have been sent down."[32] Playing for Tidewater, Gaspar found his swing, batting .318 and knocking in 37 runs.[33] When he was recalled, the Mets found themselves embroiled in a pennant race with the Cubs and the Pirates. Seeking a right arm as bullpen insurance, the Mets acquired pitcher Ron Herbel from the Padres on September 1.[34] While Herbel pitched well, compiling a 1.38 ERA in 13 innings, the Mets fell short of a second consecutive division title. Meanwhile, as the Mets still owed the Padres one player, and Gaspar was dispatched to San Diego on October 20.[35] Watching Gaspar as a Met, Padres president Buzzie Bavasi remarked that he "made you like him because he hustled and played hard all the time."

Gaspar attended San Diego's 1971 spring training camp in Yuma, Arizona, one of eight candidates vying for a starting outfield role.[36] Though considered by many to be the leading contender to play left field, Gaspar again had a poor spring training. Manager Preston Gomez optioned him once to the Hawaii Islanders of the Pacific Coast League.[37] Hawaii enjoyed an unusual arrangement as the Padres' top farm club. In an attempt to bring major league baseball to Honolulu, general manager Jack Quinn signed his own players, operated his own farm system, and even participated in the amateur draft independent from any big-league organization.[38] Gaspar joined a roster loaded with well-traveled veterans including Merritt Ranew, Tom Satriano, Leon Wagner, and Steve Whitaker. Quinn added to his club's credentials on June 16 when he signed free-agent third baseman Clete Boyer.[39]

Photo courtesy of *Mets Inside Pitch* Archives.

*Rod Gaspar*

Dave Baldwin, who'd been a reliever for Gil Hodges and later Ted Williams in Washington, also wound up in Hawaii and lived in the same apartment complex as Gaspar. Acquired in a cash deal with the Milwaukee Brewers prior to the 1971 season, Baldwin remembered Gaspar's "great range" and his ability to "go get 'em in the outfield." Baldwin saw Gaspar as an ideal complement to the older players in the Islanders lineup. Extra-inning heroics remained a specialty of Gaspar's. Hosting Tacoma on April 12, the Islanders were tied, 2–2, in the 10th inning when Gaspar delivered a two-out single to score Rafael Robles as the go-ahead run.[40] Two nights later, Gaspar hit his only home run of the season as Hawaii shut out Tacoma, 6–0.[41]

As Dave Baldwin remembered, they brought a unique brand of fandom to the baseball diamond. "They always had a great time whether we won or lost. In addition, the weather was always perfect for baseball. Many of the women dressed in leis and muumuus. Honolulu Stadium was ideal for the fans—they felt close to the action, a part of the game. They would yell out advice to us about putting on the hit-and-run or shading the outfield to the left for a particular hitter. The fans helped the players play better, something I never saw on the mainland." One year earlier, Hawaii fans had supported the team in droves, nearly outdrawing the Chicago White Sox as the Islanders decimated the Pacific Coast League with a record of 98–48.[42] Vendors at Honolulu Stadium offered concession items including sashimi, poi, and boiled peanuts. Jim Bouton, who pitched for the Vancouver Mounties in 1969, remembered sampling siamin soup—a concoction of shredded pork, noodles, and native herbs—while awaiting his turn to pitch from the bullpen.[43]

By the end of May 1971, Gaspar was batting .326, including an astonishing .500 in 120 at-bats as a leadoff hitter.[44] Only once in the first two months did he fail to reach base.[45] For the season, Gaspar set an Islanders record with 107 walks while batting .274 and stealing 26 bases.[46] In September, he was promoted to San Diego, where he went 2-for-17 off the bench for the Padres.[47]

Gaspar remained under contract with the Padres organization throughout his tenure in Honolulu, and this status would play a pivotal role as his baseball career evolved. In 1970, Mets general manager Bob Scheffing offered Gaspar a raise from the minimum $10,000 to $19,000, a salary he earned again in 1971. When demoted to Hawaii once again in 1972, Gaspar was removed from the Padres 40-man roster. Accordingly, general manager Edwin Leishman restructured his contract to a minor league deal paying $2,000 a month. Under the reserve clause, their actions were standard procedure among baseball executives.[48] Gaspar felt differently.

"Knowing me at the time, I probably said, 'I'm not going to sign that,'" Gaspar said. "Leishman basically told me that if I wouldn't sign, I could stay in Hawaii. We had a relief pitcher named Al Severinsen who felt strongly about what other players were offered in their contracts. He felt badly for my situation and encouraged me to negotiate for my 1971 salary." Gaspar filed a grievance with Major League Baseball, which he won; thus, he was entitled to receive the $7,000 differential at the end of the season.

Regardless, Gaspar batted only .234 in 111 at-bats for the Islanders in 1972.[49] Manager Rocky Bridges did not play him regularly and on July 1, the Padres loaned his contract to the Cincinnati Reds.[50] Reporting to the Indianapolis Indians, Gaspar made his presence known immediately when on July 4, he scored the winning run on a bases loaded 12th-inning single.[51] His highlight with the Indians came on July 26 when Gaspar homered off Don Shaw in the bottom of the ninth to win the game.[52]

Though opening the 1973 campaign on the Islanders' bench, Gaspar earned a spot in the starting lineup by the end of April. What transpired was another .300 season in which he drove 48 runs. Gaspar attributed his regained success partly to new manager Roy Hartsfield. Replacing Bridges on May 21, Hartsfield extolled Gaspar as "a consistent hitter" whose "fielding speaks for itself," adding that "he deserves another chance in the majors."[53] Gaspar proved his manager's fielding report when he executed more than a dozen spectacular catches in the span of just two days. He caught a 430-foot moonshot at the center-field gate on June 23 to rob Eugene's Bob Spence. The next day, Gaspar rapped a triple with the bases loaded before his leaping catch deprived Dick Wissel of a home run.[54]

Gaspar began the 1974 season yet again in Hawaii, but the Padres recalled him in May.[55] However, after a disappointing 3-for-14 stay, he was demoted to Hawaii after the All-Star break.[56] By now, it was apparent that without a modern playing facility, Jack Quinn could never succeed at bringing a major league franchise to Hawaii. While the promising Aloha Stadium was under construction, it would not be ready for baseball until 1976.[57] In the meantime, the Islanders were relegated to the now-derelict Honolulu Stadium, a place that neither the American nor National League could endorse, what with its miniscule grandstand, paltry 81 parking spaces, and decaying infrastructure. It was called the Termite Palace, according to future systems engineer Dave Baldwin: "The well-known joke was that all the termites were holding hands, but if they ever let go, the whole thing would fall apart."[58]

What followed was nothing short of a miracle. Although the Islanders consistently fielded talented teams, exhaustive road trips usually relegated the club to a .500 record. In 1975, the Islanders took first place on May 7 and never looked back.[59] Amid freezing rain in Salt Lake City on May 19, Gaspar scored three of the Islanders' 19 runs as Gary Ross pitched a bizarre five-inning perfect game against the Gulls.[60] In a Ross victory over Tacoma on June 22, Gaspar had three hits.[61] He scored the go-ahead run against Phoenix on July 8.[62] After his teammates were no-hit in the first game of a July 17 doubleheader, Gaspar homered in the nightcap in a 10–2 revenge victory.[63] At the end of the regular season, Gaspar had 58 RBIs and a .264 batting average as the Islanders cruised to an 88–56 record and a first-place finish in the West Division.[64] Only months after facing removal from the league, the Islanders triumphed over the rival Gulls to win the Pacific Coast League championship in six games.[65]

The Islanders were finally allowed to move to the cavernous Aloha Stadium in 1976, celebrating with another Pacific Coast League championship. Gaspar set a personal record with five home runs, including two off David Clyde in a 19–1 decimation of the Sacramento Solons on May 5.[66] He enjoyed a 21-game hitting streak in May, lifting his batting average from .259 to .328.[67] On August 18, Gaspar thrilled the Honolulu fans with another tiebreaking single as the threat of postponing the game by curfew was only minutes away.[68] He ended the year batting .298.[69]

Although Gaspar earned a place on the Pacific Coast League All-Star team, the outfielder was disappointed when the Padres did not recall him. Meanwhile, Roy Hartsfield was hired to manage the expansion franchise in Toronto. Although several Islanders, including Chuck Hartenstein, were invited to train with the 1977 Blue Jays in Dunedin, Florida, Gaspar was not among them. Disappointed, he decided to retire from baseball. Years later, he asked Hartsfield why he was not drafted. Replied the manager, "I would have loved to draft you. You would have been my Opening Day center fielder. Trouble was you were a National League player and I could only draft from the American League." Hartsfield had control over only the expansion draft and not over other trades and purchases. Although Padres farmhands John Scott, Dave Roberts, and Dave Hilton joined the Blue Jays from Hawaii, their contracts were purchased in separate transactions.[70]

"I was 30 years old and had enough of the minor leagues," Gaspar said. "I was tired of the travel and fed up with the time away from my family. We had two kids under the age of five. I decided to retire and get a real job." The Gaspars returned to California, settling in Mission Viejo with their children, Heather and Cade, and would later welcome sons Corte and David and daughter Taylor to the family. Yet it is one child in particular who occupied the forefront of Gaspar's thoughts.

"I would like to talk about our fourth child, David Matthew Gaspar, a very talented and wonderful boy. He died of leukemia at the age of nine in 1992. Obviously, it affected our family as well as many other people. For years, our other children would not talk about David in my presence. All the pictures of him were put away. They grew up in a state of fear, having seen death firsthand. Obviously I was wrong in how I handled David's death. My wife, Sheridan, is much tougher than I concerning this situation. She learned how to grieve, I didn't. Over the last couple of years I have opened up my feelings concerning our boy. The pictures have returned, but even as I write this today I get sad. Hopefully I am coming across as a father who mishandled the death of his son, and not merely looking for sympathy. I wouldn't want anybody to feel sorry for my situation."

Two years after the family tragedy, Cade followed in his father's footsteps by signing a professional contract with the Detroit Tigers. An excellent pitcher and shortstop at Pepperdine University, he was previously drafted by the Astros and the Yankees. In June 1994, the Tigers selected him as their first draft choice, signing him for $825,000. After posting a record of 1–3 with a 5.58 earned run average at Lakeland, he was assigned by the Tigers to a weight training program. Cade's rapid muscle development forced him to change his delivery. Consequently, he hurt his arm. He was traded to the Padres in March 1996 and retired after one season at Rancho Cucamonga. The elder Gaspar remembered numerology playing a significant role in his son's baseball career:

"Throughout his career, Cade always chose to wear one of two numbers. Number 17 was his dad's number with the Mets, and number three was the Little League number worn by David Matthew Gaspar."

Rodney Earl Gaspar went to work in the financial services industry after retiring as a player, specializing in asset management, insurance, and business planning. His children provided him and Sheridan with seven grandchildren. Gaspar won several national titles in handball—"the technique is the same as baseball." Despite his numerous talents and complexities, Gaspar will always be remembered as a member of the Miracle Mets.

Twenty years after the first championship at Shea Stadium, Gaspar told Maury Allen that "there was something so special, so exciting about the 1969 team."[71] Two decades beyond, Gaspar continued to be reminded of the millions of fans who were enthralled by the accomplishments of his club.

"As I'm sure all my teammates still get fan mail about that year, I do also. You can easily imagine that when people find out that I played for the 1969 world champions and they see 'the ring,' the atmosphere changes. What a wonderful baseball year. What a great group of guys. We were the best."

**Acknowlegements**

Dave Baldwin, Buzzie Bavasi, Clifford Blau, Craig Burley, Rod Gaspar, Sheridan Gaspar, Bill Gilbert, Paul Hirsch, Bruce Markusen, Kelly McNamee, Rod Nelson, Andrew North, John Pardon, Tito Rondon, Dennis Van Langen

**Notes and Sources**

1. "Rod Gaspar," (Brooklyn: Topps Chewing Gum Inc., 1971), 383.
2. Allen, Maury. *After the Miracle: The Amazin' Mets – Two Decades Later*. New York: St. Martin's Press, 1989., 208.
3. Weissman, Harold, ed. *New York Mets 1969 Official Year Book*. (Flushing, New York: The Metropolitan Baseball Club, Inc., 1969), 38.
4. Allen, 208.
5. Weissman (1969), 38.
6. Weissman (1969), 38.
7. Weissman (1969), 38.
8. Weissman (1969), 38.
9. Weissman (1969), 38.
10. Cohen, Stanley. *A Magic Summer*. (New York: Harcourt Brace Jovanovich, 1988), 142.
11. Cohen, 142.
12. Borsch, Ferd. "Hawaii Favorite Gaspar Reaching Bat Potential." in *The Sporting News*, August 11, 1973, 33.
13. Allen, 209.
14. Allen, 209.
15. Allen, 86.
16. Allen, 210.
17. *www.retrosheet.org*

18. Markusen, Bruce. *Tales From the Mets Dugout.* (Champaign, Illinois: Sports Publishing Inc., 2005), 40-41.
19. Markusen, 41.
20. Markusen, 41.
21. Markusen, 41.
22. *www.retrosheet.org.*
23. Weissman, Harold, ed., *New York Mets 1970 Official Year Book.* (Flushing, New York: The Metropolitan Baseball Club, Inc., 1970), 40.
24. Weissman (1970), 40.
25. Schoor, Gene. *Seaver.* (Chicago: Contemporary Books Inc., 1986), 139.
26. Allen, 120.
27. Allen, 211.
28. Allen, 211.
29. Allen, 207.
30. Markusen, 87.
31. Cohen, 142.
32. Cohen, 142-143.
33. *www.baseball-almanac.com/minor-league/index.html*
34. *www.baseball-reference.com*
35. *www.baseball-reference.com*
36. Cour, Paul. "Ollie, Going the Other Way, Finds Bright Path as Padre," in *The Sporting News*, April 17, 1971, 16.
37. Cour, 16.
38. Weiss, Bill, and Wright, Marshall. "Team 38: 1970 Hawaii Islanders," on Minor League Baseball History: Top 100 Teams, 29 pars, [journal online]; available from *http://web.minorleaguebaseball.com/milb/history/top100.jsp?idx=38; accessed 25 October 2007.*
39. Borsch, Ferd. "A New Lease on Life—Boyer in Hawaii," in *The Sporting News*, July 3, 1971, 42.
40. "Pacific Coast League" in *The Sporting News*, May 1, 1971, 37.
41. "Pacific Coast League," May 1, 1971, 37.
42. Johnson, Lloyd: *The Encyclopedia of Minor League Baseball* (Durham, North Carolina: Baseball America, 1997), 510.
43. Bouton, Jim. *Ball Four: The Final Pitch.* (North Egremont, Massachusetts: Bulldog Publishing, 2000), 135.
44. "Pacific Coast League" in *The Sporting News*, May 29, 1971, 40.
45. "Pacific Coast League," May 29, 1971, 40.
46. Borsch, (August 11, 1973), 33.
47. "Giants Face Some Tough Challengers," *The Sporting News*, February 26, 1972, 25.
48. Elliott, Bob. *The Northern Game: Baseball the Canadian Way.* (Toronto: Sport Classic Books, 2005), 139.
49. Weiss, Bill. "Pacific Coast League Batting and Pitching Records," *The Sporting News*, July 8, 1972, 32.
50. "American Association" in *The Sporting News*, August 12, 1972, 34.
51. "American Association" in *The Sporting News*, July 22, 1972, 38.
52. "American Association," August 12, 1972, 34.
53. Borsch, August 11, 1973, 33.
54. Borsch, August 11, 1973, 34.
55. "Collier, Phil. "McCovey Finding Home Run Range" in *The Sporting News*, August 10, 1974. 33.
56. Eger, Bob. "Islanders to Wear PCL Crown in New Ballpark" in *The Sporting News*, October 11, 1975, 35.
57. Eger, 35.
58. Eger, 35.
59. Herbat, Ray. "Ross Has Short Perfecto in Weirdo at Salt Lake" in *The Sporting News*, June 7, 1975, 40.
60. "Pacific Coast League" in *The Sporting News*, July 12, 1975, 33.
61. "Pacific Coast League" in *The Sporting News*, July 26, 1975, 32.
62. "Pacific Coast League" in *The Sporting News*, August 2, 1975, 34.
63. Weiss, Bill. "Pacific Coast League Batting and Pitching Records" in *The Sporting News*, September 20, 1975, 33.
64. Johnson, 532.
65. "Pacific Coast League" in *The Sporting News*, May 22, 1976, 38.
66. "Pacific Coast League" in *The Sporting News*, June 12, 1976, 46.
67. "Pacific Coast League" in *The Sporting News*, September 4, 1976, 28.
68. Weiss, Bill. "Pacific Coast League Batting and Pitching Records" in *The Sporting News*, September 25, 1976, 35.
69. Cauz, Louis: *Baseball's Back in Town: From the Don to the Blue Jays, A History of Baseball in Toronto* (Toronto: Controlled Media Corporation, 1977), 190.
70. *www.minors.baseball-reference.com*
71. Allen, 211-212.

*www.baseball-almanac.com/minor-league/index.html*
*www.baseball-reference.com*
*www.minors.baseball-reference.com*
*www.retrosheet.org*
"American Association" in *The Sporting News*. St. Louis: July 22, 1972: 38.
"American Association" in *The Sporting News*. St. Louis: August 12, 1972: 34.
"Deals of the Week" in *The Sporting News*. St. Louis: May 25, 1974: 40.
"Giants Face Some Tough Challengers" in *The Sporting News*. St. Louis:
February 26, 1972: 25
"Pacific Coast League" in *The Sporting News*. St. Louis: May 1, 1971: 37-38.
"Pacific Coast League" in *The Sporting News*. St. Louis: May 29, 1971: 40.
"Pacific Coast League" in *The Sporting News*. St. Louis: September 4, 1971: 40.
"Pacific Coast League" in *The Sporting News*. St. Louis: July 12, 1975: 33.
"Pacific Coast League" in *The Sporting News*. St. Louis: July 26, 1975: 32.
"Pacific Coast League" in *The Sporting News*. St. Louis: August 2, 1975: 34.
"Pacific Coast League" in *The Sporting News*. St. Louis: May 22, 1976: 38.
"Pacific Coast League" in *The Sporting News*: St. Louis: June 12, 1976: 46.

"Pacific Coast League" in *The Sporting News*. St. Louis: September 4, 1976: 28.

"Rod Gaspar." Brooklyn: Topps Chewing Gum Inc., 1971: 383.

Allen, Maury. *After the Miracle: The Amazin' Mets—Two Decades Later*. New York: St. Martin's Press, 1989.

Armour, Mark. "The Revolution Started Here—The Story Behind *Ball Four*" in *Rain Check: Baseball in the Pacific Northwest*. Cleveland: The Society for American Baseball Research, 2006.

Borsch, Ferd. "A New Lease on Life—Boyer in Hawaii" in *The Sporting News*. St. Louis: July 3, 1971: 42.

Borsch, Ferd. "Hawaii Favorite Gaspar Reaching Bat Potential" in *The Sporting News*. St. Louis: August 11, 1973: 33-34.

Bouton, Jim. *Ball Four: The Final Pitch*. North Egremont, MA: Bulldog Publishing, 2000.

Cauz, Louis. *Baseball's Back in Town: From the Don to the Blue Jays, A History of Baseball in Toronto*. Toronto: Controlled Media Corporation, 1977.

Cohen, Stanley. *A Magic Summer*. New York: Harcourt Brace Jovanovich, 1988.

Collier, Phil. "McCovey Finding Home Run Range," *The Sporting News*. St. Louis: August 10, 1974: 12, 33.

Cour, Paul. "Ollie, Going the Other Way, Finds Bright Path as Padre" in *The Sporting News*. St. Louis: April 17, 1971: 16.

Eger, Bob. "Islanders to Wear PCL Crown in New Ballpark," *The Sporting News*. St. Louis: October 11, 1975: 35.

Elliott, Bob. *The Northern Game: Baseball the Canadian Way*. Toronto: Sport Classic Books, 2005.

Herbat, Ray. "Ross Has Short Perfecto in Weirdo at Salt Lake" in *The Sporting News*. St. Louis: June 7, 1975: 40.

Johnson, Lloyd. *The Encyclopedia of Minor League Baseball*. Durham, NC: Baseball America, 1997.

Markusen, Bruce. *Tales From the Mets Dugout*. Champaign, IL: Sports Publishing Inc., 2005.

Schoor, Gene. *Seaver*. Chicago: Contemporary Books Inc., 1986.

Weiss, Bill. "Pacific Coast League Batting and Pitching Records," *The Sporting News*. St. Louis: July 8, 1972: 32.

Weiss, Bill. "Pacific Coast League Batting and Pitching Records," *The Sporting News*. St. Louis: September 20, 1975: 33.

Weiss, Bill. "Pacific Coast League Batting and Pitching Records," *The Sporting News*. St. Louis: September 25, 1976: 35.

Weiss, Bill, and Marshall Wright. "Team 38: 1970 Hawaii Islanders" on Minor League Baseball History: Top 100 Teams: 29 pars. [Journal Online]. Available from *http://web.minorleaguebaseball.com/milb/history/top100.jsp?idx=38*. *Accessed* 25 October 2007.

Weissman, Harold, ed. New York Mets 1969 Official Year Book. Flushing, NY: The Metropolitan Baseball Club, Inc., 1969.

Weissman, Harold, ed. New York Mets 1970 Official Year Book. Flushing, New York: The Metropolitan Baseball Club, Inc., 1970.

## What's the *Frequency*, Kenneth (Boswell)?

As time passes, tales of past exploits grow larger in the retelling. As the Miracle Mets glided past the 30th anniversary of their unlikely world championship, one of the more bizarre tributes was a 2000 film called *Frequency*.

It could take another three decades to explain everything that happens in the film—there's a ham radio that enables a father and son séance, sun spots that can alter time and space, plus plenty of fire rescue and mystery solving. There's also the '69 Mets. A two-generational love of the Mets by a Queens family helps reunite departed Frank Sullivan and his son John. The film stars Dennis Quaid, who would later show he could pitch in *The Rookie*, and James Caviezel, better known for his title role in Mel Gibson's *The Passion of the Christ*. Not to give away *Frequency*'s plot, which would be almost impossible, but the "Shoe Polish Incident" serves as a crucial moment in the film for Andre Braugher, who plays a detective in the film—as he had in the TV show *Homicide*.

Dana Brand, English professor at Hofstra University, Mets-crazed teen in 1969, and among the wisest commentators on the Mets psyche, aptly described the Metsian meaning of the implausible film in his seminal book, *Mets Fan*.

> *If the people who made* Frequency *just needed some way for John to prove that he was really in the future, they could have chosen anything. They could have set the film in July of 1969, during the moon landing and have John tell the father what Neil Armstrong would say when he stepped on the moon. But that wouldn't have been the same. The story of the 1969 Mets works as an emotional core of the film because it suggests that it might be possible to have what you know perfectly well you can't have.*

The film, which cost New Line Productions $31 million to make, grossed almost $69 million—a good luck figure surely. Maybe those sunspots helped the 2000 Mets, who would go on to take the pennant. They also won on *Frequency* Night at Shea Stadium in April while wearing '69 throwback uniforms.

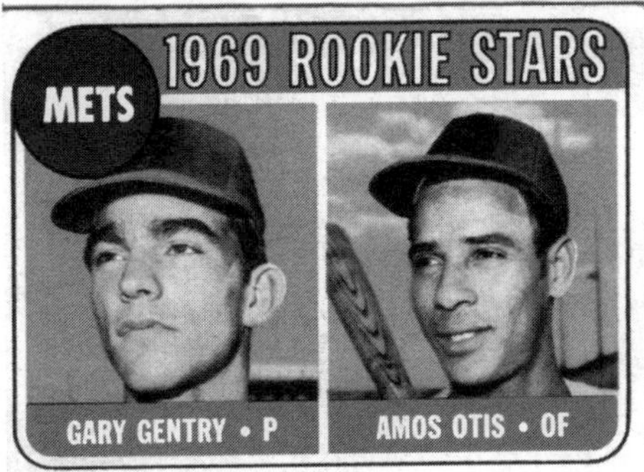


# Gary Gentry

by Andrew Schiff and Matthew Silverman

| Season | Age | W | L | Pct | G | GS | SV | IP | H | BB | SO | WHIP | ERA |
|---|---|---|---|---|---|---|---|---|---|---|---|---|---|
| 1969 Mets | 22 | 13 | 12 | .520 | 35 | 35 | 0 | 233.7 | 192 | 81 | 154 | 1.168 | 3.43 |
| Career 7 Years | – | 46 | 49 | .484 | 157 | 138 | 2 | 902.7 | 770 | 369 | 615 | 1.262 | 3.56 |

The 1969 Miracle New York Mets will always have a special place in baseball lore. Not only are the *Amazin'* Mets remembered for their stunning upset over the heavily favored Baltimore Orioles, but also in the way in which they won, with some of most remarkable defense and pitching ever displayed in World Series history. The Mets staff, which stifled the dominant hitting Orioles, led by the likes of two-time Most Valuable Player Frank Robinson and Boog Powell, featured eventual 1969 Cy Young Award winner Tom Seaver, stellar second-year southpaw Jerry Koosman, and a raw, but talented, Nolan Ryan (who was used out of the bullpen). These three—along with reliever Tug McGraw, who didn't pitch against the Orioles—are the most famous names associated with that championship team. Overlooked, however, was a 22-year-old rookie—a young right-handed pitcher from Phoenix, Arizona—named Gary Gentry.

Gentry only played parts of seven seasons of big league ball, but his role in helping the Mets win their first world championship has forever cemented him a special place in New York's baseball history. First, the Arizona native pitched the clincher for the National League East Division title against the Cardinals in September (with future Mets and Yankees manager Joe Torre bouncing into a game-ending double play that sent the delirious crowd swarming on the field). After matching Seaver and Koosman with lukewarm performances in the first NLCS—New York's bats yielded enough offense for the Mets to still sweep the Braves—Gentry started Game Three of the World Series. He held the Orioles scoreless into the seventh inning, until Ryan came in relief and Tommie Agee saved the day, for the second time that afternoon.

Born in Phoenix on October 6, 1946, Gary Edward Gentry was a supremely gifted athlete and a hard worker. He recalled in the *New York Times*, "When I played American Legion ball, I worked at a freight line from six to two, then went home for a nap, and pitched that night." Gentry didn't pitch that much growing up, however. His father, Ed Gentry, whom Gary credited with giving him his "first boost in baseball," advised his son not to pitch. Gary heeded that advice early when he played second base for Camelback High in Phoenix.

When it became clear that his strong right arm was his ticket to a professional career, he chose Phoenix Junior College "because it played 35–40 games a season," and "I thought I'd get more experience than if I played freshman ball at a larger university." When he completed his first two years at Phoenix JC, he chose baseball power Arizona State "as a stepping stone." The 6-foot, 180-pound

Gentry had already led Phoenix JC to a national junior college championship and then helped Arizona State claim the NCAA title in the College World Series.

Gentry went 17–1 as a junior at ASU and set a collegiate record with 229 strikeouts in 174 innings. In the CWS semifinal in Omaha, Gentry threw a 14-inning, 15-strikeout masterpiece against Stamford—he did not allow a runner past first base after the sixth inning and wound up scoring the winning run. He was named Pitcher on the All-College World Series team to go along with being named All-American and the National College Player of the Year.

Gentry had three opportunities to play professional baseball before the Mets selected him in the third round of the 1967 amateur draft, in the secondary phase. Gentry had previously been selected in the 11th round by the Houston Astros in 1965, in the first round by the Baltimore Orioles in the early winter of 1966, and six months later in the third round by the San Francisco Giants. He waited, though, and went with the fourth organization that chose him. He signed with New York four days after the Sun Devils won the '67 College World Series. Some said he got what he deserved after spurring the other suitors and winding up with the worst team in baseball. Little could most people imagine that two years after winning a title at Arizona State, he would do it again in New York. Gentry didn't expect anything less.

"I never played on a team that didn't expect to win," Gentry told Stanley Cohen years later in *A Magic Summer*. "So what happened in 1969 was a natural transition for me. I was accustomed to winning. In 1965, in junior college, we won the national championship; in '66, we got there again but lost in the finals; in '67, at Arizona State, we won the NCAA championship; that same year I spent the last two months of the season with Williamsport and we won the league title; in '68, when I was with Jacksonville, we won the championship there, too. So when I came up to the Mets in '69, I never thought about anything except winning. I didn't know much about the team's history. I just knew that I was going to pitch in the big leagues, and I expected to win."

With Williamsport in the Eastern League, Gentry amassed an earned run average of 1.59 with a 4–4 record in 10 starts (eight complete games). In 1968, Gentry went 12–8 for Jacksonville, compiling an ERA of 2.91 in 30 starts. After 198 innings with the triple-A Suns, Gentry then pitched in Florida Instructional League and dominated the competition. The Mets had considered leaving Gentry exposed in the expansion draft when the Montreal Expos and San Diego Padres came into existence. Instead, the Mets left veteran Dick Selma exposed, to be selected eventually by the Padres.

Mets beat writer Jack Lang described the rookie trying to make the team out of spring training in 1969, "[He] wears cowboy boots, blue jeans, and looks more like a ranch hand than a player, [but he] could be this year's Tom Seaver or Jerry Koosman." Lang said that the young pitcher "was just what the manager expected. A good pitcher beyond what his experience showed."

Gentry was the third man in the rotation from the beginning, making as many starts in 1969 as Seaver (35) and winning two games in his first week in the majors, even though the club got off to a sluggish start. He then lost three in a row before winning again. He tossed a two-hitter for his first major league shutout on June 17 in Philadelphia, beating another ballyhooed rookie, Billy Champion, 1–0, and striking out a season-high nine. Gentry pitched into the ninth inning 13 times as a rookie, completing six, throwing three shutouts, and blanking the Giants for 10 innings on August 19 and getting no decision. The Mets eventually beat San Francisco, 1–0, during what turned out to be the early stages of the miraculous run that saw the Amazin's overtake the first-place Chicago Cubs by winning 37 of their last 48 games. The Mets finished with a 100–62 record, the first time the Mets had ever approached a winning record. Gentry finished the year with a 13–12 mark, a 3.43 ERA and 154 strikeouts in 233 ⅔ innings. On a team like the Mets had that year, it's surprising his record wasn't better. He was right around .500 all season with run support of 3.66 per game that wasn't much above his ERA (though his support was more than Koosman's 3.38 and less than Seaver's 4.37).

Gentry started the first postseason game ever at Shea Stadium—and on his 23rd birthday, no less. The Mets had a two-games-to-none lead in the best-of-five National League Championship Series against Atlanta, but things didn't start out well when Hank Aaron hit a two-run home run off Gentry in the first inning. He navigated through the rest of the order, but Aaron collected a double his second time up to put two runners in scoring position with nobody out. Manager Gil Hodges removed the rookie with the Mets still down, 2–0. Nolan Ryan came in, got out of the inning, and remained in the rest of the game as the Mets rallied to take the pennant with Ryan pitching the last seven innings for the win.

Gentry was called on to start Game Three against the Orioles, the first World Series game ever played at Shea Stadium. The Mets had split the first two games in Baltimore and back at Shea, Gentry shut out the Orioles for the first 6 ⅔ innings. Center fielder Tommie Agee, who'd already helped Gentry with a leadoff home run, saved the 3–0 lead in fourth inning by running down an Elrod Hendricks blast to left-center with two outs and two on. He made a sprinting backhand catch, the ball showing in the webbing of his glove as he came to a rest at the 396-foot mark.

*Gary Gentry all smiles in his Mets uniform.*

PHOTO COURTESY OF *METS INSIDE PITCH* ARCHIVES.

The Mets managed four runs in all against Baltimore's ace Jim Palmer, but when Gentry struggled in the seventh, loading the bases, Ryan entered from the bullpen. Again Agee came to the team's aid, this time with a sprawling catch of a Paul Blair liner in right-center to leave the sacks full. Ryan blanked the O's for the final 2 ⅓ innings to get the save for Gentry. New York went on to win the next two games to capture the World Series.

In a 1969 interview with *The Sporting News*, Gentry credited three people for his meteoric rise: Gil Hodges, Arizona State coach Bobby Winkles, and his father Ed Gentry. He also explained his pitching philosophy, saying that he tried "to learn something about the hitters every time I go to the mound and have a 'good time' out there. I guard against getting upset at myself or my teammates when things go wrong."

That proved easier to say than do. Gentry's outspokenness and temper aggravated opponents, umpires, teammates, and even fans. "New York is a dirty, dirty town. I can't leave soon enough when the year's out," he told Maury Allen in 1971. That was a tumultuous year for Gentry. Coming off a sophomore slump in '70—though he threw a one-hitter in Chicago the year after the championship, he went 9–9 with a 3.68 ERA for a team that slipped to third place—things seemed off kilter for Gentry in 1971.

With his wife in Phoenix trying to rent their home, three-year-old son Chris nearly drowned in the family's pool. Janet Gentry thought the boy was following her, but when she turned around he had disappeared. She ran outside and found him at the bottom of the pool. Janet jumped in and gave the boy mouth-to-mouth resuscitation. Manager Gil Hodges told Gentry to go to Phoenix to be with his family and rejoin the team in Pittsburgh in time for his next start. In that game, Gentry was ejected when umpire Shag Crawford said his bunt attempt ticked his bat for a strike when Gentry thought there was no contact and it should have been a ball. Gentry pushed the ump slightly during their nose-to-nose argument at Three Rivers Stadium and was subsequently suspended three days and fined $150. In July, he missed a start and needed 15 stitches above his right eye when he and Jim McAndrew collided shagging flies at the Astrodome.

More alarming were Gentry's noncontact incidents with teammates. He claimed the Mets gave Seaver preferential treatment because he always made his starts while other pitchers were skipped when there were rainouts and offdays. This came during a year where Seaver would go 20–10 with a 1.76 ERA and 289 strikeouts while Gentry—in four fewer starts—went 12–11 with a 3.23 ERA and 155 strikeouts. Twice Gentry showed up his outfielders—throwing his glove in the air after a perceived lackadaisical throw from Cleon Jones and in another game standing with hands on hips, shaking his head, and looking out toward center field after Tommie Agee misjudged a fly ball that went for a three-run triple in a loss to the Reds. Gentry later said, "All my anger was directed at the umpire because he missed the pitch before the hit that should have been the third strike." The pitcher received several nasty letters from fans after the Agee incident.

"The temper goes back to when I was born," Gentry told Murray Chass of the *New York Times* as all those incidents came to a boil in August 1971.

PHOTO COURTESY OF DWAYNE LABAKAS COLLECTION

*Gary Gentry*

"I've never had any trouble releasing my temper. I just have to learn to cope with it. Hodges says when you do something on the field—if you throw your glove, or stomp off the mound—thousands of people see it. I'll just have to cut down on showing my outward emotions. I think I can still get teed off but not show it—take a deep breath and keep it in."

Gentry, still just 24 when the 1971 season ended, remained a hot commodity with the club and with other teams. Jack Lang noted that the Padres and Angels both asked for Gentry in deals that winter and were rebuffed by Mets general manager Bob Scheffing.

"The Angels wanted Gentry in the Jim Fregosi deal. The answer was, 'No,'" Lang wrote. "Instead, the Angels had to settle for Nolan Ryan, who has only become the talk of the American League with his blazing fastball." Gentry-for-Fregosi would have involved players who turned out to be on the down end of their careers. Dealing Ryan—whose inconsistency had frustrated the Mets for years—wound up being as bad a trade as any in team history. But no one, least of all Gentry, knew how things would turn out.

At the end of 1971, Mets pitching coach Rube Walker said of Gentry, "He's still just a kid. He has great ability. With the stuff he's got he's not going to be a .500 pitcher."

A year later, after falling to 41–42 for his career, Scheffing deemed Gentry "my biggest disappointment of the season." A 7–10 mark and his worst ERA as a Met (4.01), not to mention his temper and arm problems—which had caused him pain since he joined the Mets and was originally misdiagnosed by the team—made the GM bite this time when teams asked about the 25-year-old hurler. On November 1, 1972, he was sent to the Braves along with Danny Frisella, for Felix Millan and George Stone. Steady play from Millan at second base and a career year from the southpaw Stone helped the Mets steal a pennant the following year, but the change of scene did not help Gentry at all.

He spent three season with the Braves, but he was injured most of that time. Gentry was standing in the Atlanta bullpen trying to catch Hank Aaron's 715th home run on the historic night of April 15, 1974. Tom House wound up catching the ball and presenting it to Aaron...Gentry wound up having surgery. After having bone chips removed the previous year, he left his only start of 1974 and soon underwent tendon surgery.

When the Braves wanted to cut his $50,000 salary by 20 percent in 1975, he refused to sign a contract. Though other players were testing the reserve clause that year—pitchers Dave McNally and Andy Messersmith were part of the case that brought an end to the clause and the start of free agency—Gentry was not concerned with history but rather about the size of the cut. "I would feel belittled," he said in spring camp with the Braves. "It's not my intent to test the reserve clause... it's just that I've always told myself that I wouldn't sign for the kind of pay cut they wanted me to take."

The Braves released Gentry in May after seven appearances. He blew a lead in Cincinnati and then picked up his final career win when the Braves rallied. The Giants—the team he'd had his best outing against in April—pounded him for five runs in the ninth inning of his final major league game on May 6. Gentry had a career mark of 46–49 and a solid 3.56 ERA in 157 career games when he was released by Atlanta.

As it turned out, Gentry's performance in the World Series was his greatest accomplishment as a major league player. Even though he never lived up to his promise as a top prospect or as the next great Mets ace, fans still missed him when he was traded. Jack Lang wrote, "It was a blow to many New Yorkers to lose Gentry, who had been the surprise pitcher of 1969, as Seaver had been in 1967 and Koosman had been in 1968." The Mets, in fact, tried to get Gentry back. He signed with the Mets a few weeks after he was released by Atlanta, although he did not keep in shape during the interval. Upon Mets pitching coach Rube Walker's advice, Gentry went down to Class AA Jackson to try to show that he could still pitch. Despite a triumvirate of Seaver, Koosman, and Jon Matlack, the '75 Mets were remarkably thin at the back end of the rotation, so the 28-year-old Gentry had a real chance of making it back to Shea. He tore the flexor muscle in his right elbow after three pitches in Jackson, went home to his wife and two children in Phoenix, and as he told Cohen in *A Magic Summer*, "started learning the real estate business from the bottom up."

Gentry, who pitched just one year of Division I baseball and became the third straight Sun Devil to be named National Player of the year (Rick Monday and Reggie Jackson were the first two), was named to the Arizona State Hall of Fame in 1976.

Still residing in Arizona, where he runs a nursing home, Gentry returned to New York for the 1969 team's 40th anniversary celebration at Citi Field in August 2009.

**Sources**


Allen, Maury, *Sports Today*, June 1971.

Chass, Murray, "Gentry Hopes Curbing Temper Will Aid His Won-Lost Mark," *New York Times*, August 15, 1971.

Cohen, Stanley, *A Magic Summer: The '69 Mets* (New York: Harcourt Brace Jovanovich, 1988).

Gergen, Joe, "Ex-Met Star Gentry a Has-Been at 28?" *Newsday*, June 29, 1975.

Lang, Jack, "Five New Men Elbow Way Into Mets Jobs," *The Sporting News*, April 12, 1969.

Lang, Jack, "Accidents Keeping Mets in Stitches," *The Sporting News*, July 31, 1971.

Lang, Jack, "Gentry Is Met Flop of Year, McAndrew the No. 1 Hero," *The Sporting News*, September 2, 1972.

Lang, Jack, and Simon, Peter, The New York Mets: Twenty-Five Years of baseball Magic (New York: Henry Holt, 1986).

Lipsyte, Robert, "Sports of *the Times*; Before the Game," *New York Times*, September 25, 1969.

Minshew, Wayne, "'Won't Be Belittled,' Says Gentry, Nixing Brave Pact, *The Sporting News*, March 15, 1975.

Pepe, Phil, "Gentry's Wife Gets a Save," *New York Daily News*, May 13, 1971.

Young, Dick, "Fine, Ban Gentry," *New York Daily News*, May 17, 1971.

"ASU's Major-Leaguers," *http://graphics.fansonly.com/photos/schools/asu/sports/m-basebl/mediaguide/History_2.pdf*

## Let's Play Two. Again

The doubleheader was a major part of baseball life four decades ago. No Mets club since 1969 has matched the 22 twinbills the team played that year. The 1962 Mets endured a club-record 30 doubleheaders… and lost 17. The '69 Mets went 11–3–8 in doubleheaders, more than twice as many sweeps as any Mets club before or since. The '69 club earned six sweeps in their last nine doubleheaders starting on August 16—the day the Mets began the 38-11 finish that finished off the Cubs and captured in the NL East title.

When the schedule came out before the seaso n, the Mets were on tap for 13 doubleheaders, including five during the week. Due to rainouts, the Mets wound up adding nine twinbills to the schedule—a single game was also moved from St. Louis to New York and played on an off day on September 22.

Unlike modern day-night doubleheaders with separate admissions and several hours between contests, 1960s twinbills were played one after the other, with a half hour in between. An exception on the Mets calendar was Banner Day on August 17, as players cooled their heels for a while longer as fans paraded around the field with homemade signs declaring their love for the Mets. As happened the previous day, the Mets swept the Padres when the twin bill resumed.

Here's how the '69 Mets fared in double duty. Results for splits list individual wins and losses in the order occurred. Sweep means the Mets won both; Lost means the opposite; @ designates a road twinbill—otherwise it took place at Shea Stadium. An * means the doubleheader was on the original schedule.

| Doubleheader | Opponent | Result |
|---|---|---|
| *Sunday, April 27 | CHI | Split: L, W |
| *Sunday, May 4 | @CHI | Sweep |
| Sunday, May 11 | HOU | Split: L, W |
| *Tuesday, June 17 | @PHI | Split: W, L |
| *Sunday, June 22 | STL | Sweep |
| *Tuesday, June 24 | PHI | Sweep |
| Tuesday, July 1 | @STL | Lost |
| *Friday, July 4 | @PIT | Sweep |
| *Sunday, July 13 | MON | Sweep |
| *Sunday, July 20 | @MON | Split: L, W |
| Wednesday, July 30 | HOU | Lost |
| Tuesday, August 5 | @CIN | Split: L, W |
| *Friday, August 8 | @ATL | Split: W, L |
| Saturday, August 16 | SD | Sweep |
| *Sunday, August 17 | SD | Sweep |
| *Tuesday, August 26 | @SD | Sweep |
| *Sunday, August 31 | @SF | Split: W, L |
| Friday, September 5 | PHI | Split: W, L |
| Wednesday, September 10 | MON | Sweep |
| Friday, September 12 | @PIT | Sweep |
| Friday, September 19 | PIT | Lost |
| *Sunday, September 21 | PIT | Sweep |

# Jim Gosger

by Mark Armour

| Season | Age | G | AB | R | H | 2B | 3B | HR | RBI | BB | SO | SB | CS | BA | OBP | SLUG |
|---|---|---|---|---|---|---|---|---|---|---|---|---|---|---|---|---|
| 1969 Mets | 26 | 10 | 15 | 0 | 0 | 2 | 0 | 0 | 1 | 1 | 6 | 1 | 0 | .133 | .188 | .267 |
| Career 10 Years | – | 705 | 1815 | 197 | 411 | 67 | 16 | 30 | 177 | 217 | 316 | 25 | 18 | .226 | .309 | .331 |

Jim Gosger was a hustling, hard-working ballplayer for 13 professional seasons, years that took him all over the baseball map, and to the majors for parts of 10 seasons with five different teams. He played a good center field but never really established himself as a good enough hitter to stay in a lineup long. Gosger spent a lot of time in triple-A baseball, but he kept playing well enough to earn numerous shots at major league ball. At his best, the left-handed Gosger was a solid fourth outfielder who could play defense and pinch hit when needed.

James Charles Gosger began life on November 6, 1942 in Port Huron, Michigan. The city rests at the base of Lake Huron and along the St. Clair River that separates Michigan with Ontario, Canada. He loved the town so much he never moved away—67 years after his birth he was still living in the house he grew up in. He lived the life of a boy in small-town America after the war, playing sports night and day, including Little League, Babe Ruth League, and American Legion baseball.

Most major league players were former high school star athletes, and Gosger was no exception, lettering in baseball, football, basketball, and track at Port Huron's St. Stephen High School, from which he graduated in 1960. In his senior year, he was an All-State guard in basketball and an All-State halfback in football. His size (5-feet-10, 180 pounds) might have kept him from going on to play at a higher level in either of those sports. He attended Port Huron Junior College (now St. Clair County Community College) for a year and a half.

During his second year of college, he was signed by Boston Red Sox scout Maurice De Loof and assigned to their Winston-Salem affiliate in the Carolina League. Though this might have been a culture shock for the Northerner, he did not take long to establish his professional credentials. After garnering just one hit in nine at-bats in his first two games, on April 21 he set a league record by driving in 10 runs in a 15–3 victory over Rocky Mount. His day began with a three-run home run in the first, followed by a grand slam in the second, a run-scoring single in the third, and a two-run single in the sixth. Gosger hit .283 with 19 home runs and 83 RBIs in his first pro season and was named to the postseason league all-star team, along with such players as Rusty Staub, Tony Perez, Mel Stottlemyre, and teammate Rico Petrocelli. "Those 19 home runs were the worst thing that ever happened to me," recalled Jim a few years later. "All of a sudden I began to think of myself as a slugger. I guess I went a little home run crazy for a while after that, but I got over it."

In one of baseball's many attempts to curb signing bonuses in the years before the amateur draft, the Red Sox had to put Gosger (who had received a bonus to sign the previous year) on their 40-man roster after the season, and keep him on the team for the entire 1963 season. In reality he was not a major leaguer and rarely played, but had he been optioned he could have been drafted by another team. His only hit for manager Johnny Pesky was a pinch-single off Detroit's Frank Lary on August 6 with the Red Sox trailing by six runs. He did not start a game until September 21. On the season he accumulated 16 at-bats in 19 games, getting just the one single, for an .063 batting average. He needed development, but he did not get it in 1963. "I sat on the bench and didn't like it," recalled Jim. "I wanted to play. I watched guys go to the plate and strike out and I'd brood and tell myself I couldn't do any worse."

For the 1964 season the Red Sox were free to demote Gosger, and they did so—sending him to Reading, Pennsylvania to play for their club in the Eastern League. Jim had a fine year there, hitting .274 in 133 games, with 22 stolen bases. He led the league in both triples (13) and outfield assists (6) playing for Eddie Popowski's strong second place ballclub.

The next season Jim began the year with the Toronto Maple Leafs, who were led by Dick Williams making his managerial debut. By mid-summer Jim was hitting .299 with 14 home runs as the club's center fielder, before he again got the call to Boston. The Red Sox were in ninth place, already 20 games out of first in early July when Jim got there. Unlike his 1963 stint, this time the Red Sox wanted him to play, and play he did. Jim immediately became the starting center fielder, replacing Lenny Green. Gosger moved to right field for a few weeks when Tony Conigliaro got hurt in late July, then finished the season back in center. Often batting leadoff, Jim hit .256 with nine home runs in half a season, a year in which the league batting average was .242. Gosger always played great defensively, causing first-year manager Billy Herman to keep him in the lineup. Gosger had one of the thrills of his career when he homered off future Hall of Famer Whitey Ford on the last day of the 1965 season, though it came in Boston's 100th loss of the season.

By this stage of his career Gosger already had a reputation as a hustler. One writer compared him to Enos Slaughter, a legendary player from the 1940s and 1950s who, it was said, never walked on a baseball field. Slaughter ran everywhere. "Every minute [Gosger]'s in the ball park, he runs and hustles," said Herman. "I like that in him and in anyone else." His reputation as a hustler stayed with him for the rest of his career.

The Red Sox lost 100 games in 1965, their most since 1932. Though the club obviously had a lot of building to do, during the offseason Red Sox owner Tom Yawkey labeled the 23-year-old Gosger untouchable in trade talks. The club did acquire outfielder George Thomas from the Tigers in the fall, and to start the 1966 season the right-handed hitting Thomas and lefty-swinging Gosger platooned in center field. Through June 12, Gosger was hitting about as he had in 1965: .254 with five home runs in 126 at-bats, including the only two-homer game of his career—both against Detroit's Denny McLain at Tiger Stadium on June 8. Nevertheless, on June 13, two days before the trading deadline, the last-place Red Sox decided Gosger was "touchable." They dealt him to the eighth-place Kansas City Athletics in a six-player trade. Boston also included pitchers Guido Grilli and Ken Sanders, and acquired pitchers Rollie Sheldon and John Wyatt and outfielder Jose Tartabull. The trade worked out well for the Red Sox, as Wyatt and Tartabull both played big roles on their surprise pennant-winning club in 1967.

Gosger played almost every day for the Athletics, splitting his appearances between left and right field. He hit just .224 with five home runs in Kansas City, a less favorable hitting environment than Boston's Fenway Park. The next season the Athletics brought up Rick Monday to be their center fielder, but Gosger saw a lot of action in all three outfield spots—at least 27 starts at each position, a total of 89 outfield starts and 134 total games. He hit .242 on the season, with five home runs. His defense continued to impress.

"The thing about Gosger is he never lets his troubles at the plate hurt his fielding," said manager Alvin Dark. "I like his arm—he gets the ball away quickly and it's accurate. He has good speed, too. And we need speed on this type of club." Gosger returned the compliment, saying that Dark was the best manager he had ever played for.

In 1968, the Athletics relocated to Oakland, California, and began their gradual ascent to the top of the American League. Unfortunately for Gosger, the club now had Reggie Jackson in right field, severely impacting Gosger's playing time. For the 1968 season Jim started just 37 games in the field, but between pinch hitting and mid-game defensive replacements, he played in 88 games and gathered 150 at-bats. He hit just .180 and rarely played the last several weeks of the season. His meager offensive accomplishments that year can be chocked up somewhat to it being the "Year of the Pitcher." Despite a rough year, Gosger was still wanted somewhere.

The Seattle Pilots, who would begin play the next season, selected Gosger in the expansion draft on October 15. Once again, Gosger opened the season as a club's center fielder. He batted sixth in the first Pilots lineup and walked during the four-run first inning in the season-opening win that proved no harbinger of good things to come for the Seattle club. He also squeezed the first out ever recorded by the franchise when he caught a ball hit by Bill Voss in the bottom of the first in Anaheim. Things went downhill for Gosger—and the Pilots—after that first inning.

He started the season 0-for-17, broke out with a home run and two doubles on April 16, and then stopped hitting again. When he lost his regular job at the end of April he was hitting .139, and over the next six weeks he singled just once in 23 at-bats. Batting just .109 in mid-June, Gosger was demoted to Vancouver. It was his first time in the minor leagues in four years.

Gosger's time in Seattle is immortalized along with his teammates in the book *Ball Four*, Jim Bouton's irreverent diary of his 1969 season largely spent with the Pilots. Bouton recounts a memorable scene on a road trip when Gosger was hiding in the closet while his roommate was "entertaining" a woman in the adjoining bedroom. At one point the woman exclaimed, "Oh darling, I have never done it *that* way before" at which point Gosger opened the closet door and said, "Yeah, surrre." The phrase became a staple the rest of the season whenever a Pilot wanted to express exaggerated skepticism. When Gosger was sent to Vancouver, he told Bouton, "You know, I didn't think I was that bad a ballplayer, but they're making a believer out of me."

In his first 12 Pacific Coast League games Jim hit .462 with five extra-base hits. The Pilots then sent Gosger to Tidewater, the New York Mets triple-A affiliate in the International League, as payment for their earlier acquisition of Greg Goossen. Gosger continued crushing the ball, batting .341 with 10 home runs and 14 doubles in just 58 games. He hit in 35 of his first 36 games with the Tides. He was named the league's player of the month by Topps. "For the last two years, I've just been sitting around. All I've been doing is a little pinch hitting and playing the outfield in the late innings. Right now I'm happy to be playing. I'm just having fun." Along with all that fun, Jim played a big role in Tidewater winning the International League title in 1969. On September 5, after the conclusion of their season, Gosger was promoted to the New York Mets.

On the day Gosger joined the club the Mets were 4½ games behind the Chicago Cubs, but in the midst of an historic stretch drive. After two pinch-hitting appearances and one as a defensive replacement, Jim got his first starting action on September 12, by which time the club had soared past the Cubs and held a two game lead. With Cleon Jones ailing and Art Shamsky not playing because of Yom Kippur, Gosger played left field in both games of the doubleheader that night at Forbes Field. It was a memorable night for the Mets. Each game ended with a 1-0 Mets victory with the starting pitchers—Jerry Koosman and Don Cardwell—driving in the only run in each game. Gosger led off the nightcap with a double (his first hit as a Met), but as no pitcher batted that inning, he was stranded. New York's lead increased to 2½ games over the Cubs.

Gosger was not needed much again by the Mets. His next start was on September 28, after the Mets had long since clinched the division title. Overall, Gosger had just two hits, both doubles, in 15 at-bats. His role with the Miracle Mets was very small, yet he was on hand for one of the most remarkable nights of the season and got to celebrate the clinching of the first National League East division title. Though he was ineligible to take part in what would have been the only postseason of his major league career, Gosger's efforts were rewarded with $100 as part of the Mets' World Series share.

Gosger was on the move again that winter, heading to the San Francisco Giants this time. The Mets dealt Gosger with infielder Bob Heise for pitcher Ray Sadecki and outfielder Dave Marshall. Gosger might have wondered where he would play in San Francisco, as the club already had Willie Mays, Bobby Bonds, Ken Henderson, and Jim Ray Hart in the outfield, and he would have been right to wonder. After spending the spring with the team, he was assigned to Phoenix in the Pacific Coast League. Eight games later, including just three hits in 16 at-bats, he was sold to the Montreal Expos and assigned to Buffalo of the International League. The deal reunited him with manager Clyde McCullough, who had also skippered Gosger in 1969 during his great half-season in Tidewater.

Soon after joining Buffalo, Gosger hit home runs on consecutive days (April 25 and 26). This was the start of a great month of hitting: .327 and eight home runs in just 30 games. He had a 15-game hitting streak at the time of his recall to Montreal on June 2. Once again, the itinerant Gosger was back in the big leagues.

In his debut with the Expos on June 3, Gosger doubled as a pinch hitter. His hot hitting continued for several weeks, including home runs on successive days in June against the Braves in Montreal. His homer against future Hall of Famer Phil Niekro helped spark an Expos comeback victory from a 7–2 deficit on June 18.

"I have never felt so relaxed, confident and happy in major leagues," Gosger said that summer. At the end of June, he was hitting .364 in 66 at-bats. His average slowly drifted downward until it reached .263 at the end of the season. Overall, he played 91 games for the Expos, 50 of them in center field, while also playing left field and at first base. After the season he stuck around Montreal to work in the public relations department, talking to groups about buying tickets and holding local clinics for youngsters. He also played with several teammates on an Expos basketball team in the area.

Jim started the 1971 season on the disabled list after spraining his wrist making a tumbling dive for a ball in spring training. When he finally returned, on May 5, he had lost his spot in the outfield rotation. By the end of June he was hitting just .164 in limited time and was demoted to Winnipeg, where the Expos' Buffalo affiliate had moved. After a month in the minors he got back to the Montreal to finish out the season. His hitting did not improve after his recall—he ended at .157 in 102 at-bats. In December he was traded to the Mets for four minor leaguers, only one of whom—Curtis Brown—ever appeared in a major league game.

Jim spent the entire 1972 season with Tidewater, the Mets affiliate in Virginia he had last played for in 1969. He appeared in 142 games, the most he had ever played for a team in a single season, but he only batted .244. He began the next season back in Tidewater, but was called up to New York early in May. He played two months in the majors, hitting .239 with no home runs, before heading back down to Tidewater. On the season for the Tides he hit just .236 in 67 games. As was the case in 1969, Gosger did not get to experience the postseason for the '73 pennant-winning Mets.

In 1974 he again played for Tidewater, appearing in 95 games and hitting .268. In early August he got called to New York once again, and stayed with the Mets for the rest of the season. He hit just .091 (3-for-33) in limited time. In October, the Mets gave him his unconditional release. Gosger chose to retire rather than continue his odyssey around the baseball map. He played parts of 10 seasons in the major leagues, hitting .226 with 30 home runs in 705 games.

Gosger says he was promised a minor league hitting instructor's job with the Mets, but they never contacted him. So Gosger went back home to his beloved Port Huron, a place he'd always called home, even when he was drifting around the country for 15 years playing baseball. He worked in the utlities division for his native city and was also a respected high school and junior college football and basketball referee for three decades.

Gosger married early in his baseball career to Mary Carol Draper and the couple raised four children. Later divorced, Jim remarried in the late 1980s to Kathleen and they had a daughter of their own, Kellie, who graduated from high school in Port Huron in 2008.

**Notes and Sources**

Jim Gosger file at the National Baseball Hall of Fame.
*Sporting News* articles accessed via PaperOfRecord.com.
*The Sporting News*. January 15, 1966
*The Sporting News*. July 8, 1967.
*The Sporting News*. August 30, 1969.
*The Sporting News*. September 27, 1969.
*The Sporting News*. July 4, 1970.
Bouton, Jim and Leonard Schecter. *Ball Four*. World, 1970.
Buckley, Steve. *Boston Red Sox—Where Have You Gone?* Sports Publishing, 2005.
Jackaki, Rick. "Gosger Fulfills a Dream," (Port Huron) *Times Herald*, April 19, 2009., found at *http://www.thetimesherald.com/article/20090419/SPORTS/904190317/1006/NEWS17*.

## Can't Tell the Miracle Without a Scorecard

Below is a numerical roster of every Met who appeared in uniform during the 1969 season, and the dates they wore their numbers during their Mets careers. This includes future All-Stars who sat the bench but did not play in a game (marked with *), coaches (marked with a "C"), and manager Gil Hodges (marked "M"). Note that three of the four numbers the Mets eventually retired were in use in 1969: #14 for Hodges, #41 for Tom Seaver, and #42 for Ron Taylor (that number was eventually retired throughout baseball in honor of Brooklyn Dodgers trailblazer Jackie Robinson at a Shea Stadium ceremony in 1997). First manager Casey Stengel's #37 was retired in 1965.

| Number | Player | Start | End |
|---|---|---|---|
| 1 | Kevin Collins | 7-Apr-69 | 10-May-69 |
| 1 | Bobby Pfeil | 24-Jun-69 | 15-Oct-69 |
| 3 | Bud Harrelson | 31-Aug-65 | 2-Oct-77 |
| 4 | Ron Swoboda | 15-Apr-66 | 1-Oct-70 |
| 5 | Ed Charles | 23-May-67 | 15-Oct-69 |
| 6 | Al Weis | 10-Apr-68 | 25-Jun-71 |
| 7 | Ed Kranepool | 10-Apr-65 | 30-Sep-79 |
| 8 (C) | Yogi Berra | 11-Apr-65 | 30-Sep-71 |
| 9 | J.C. Martin | 9-Apr-68 | 15-Oct-69 |
| 10 | Duffy Dyer | 7-Apr-69 | 2-Oct-74 |
| 11 | Wayne Garrett | 7-Apr-69 | 21-Jul-76 |
| 12 | Ken Boswell | 9-Apr-68 | 2-Oct-74 |
| 14 (M) | Gil Hodges | 9-Apr-68 | 30-Sep-71 |
| 15 | Jerry Grote | 14-Apr-66 | 31-Aug-77 |
| 16* | Mike Jorgensen | 5-Sep-69 | 12-Jun-71 |

*continued on next page*

continued

| Number | Player | Start | End |
|---|---|---|---|
| 17 | Rod Gaspar | 7-Apr-69 | 1-Oct-70 |
| 18 | Jim Gosger | 5-Sep-69 | 1-Oct-69 |
| 20 | Tommie Agee | 8-Apr-68 | 4-Oct-72 |
| 21 | Cleon Jones | 14-Apr-66 | 27-Jul-75 |
| 22 | Donn Clendenon | 14-Jun-69 | 30-Sep-71 |
| 24 | Art Shamsky | 10-Apr-68 | 30-Sep-71 |
| 25 | Amos Otis | 6-Apr-69 | 30-Sep-69 |
| 27 | Don Cardwell | 10-Apr-67 | 12-Jul-70 |
| 29 | Danny Frisella | 23-Jun-67 | 19-Jul-69 |
| 29 | Bob D. Johnson | 5-Sep-69 | 1-Oct-69 |
| 30 | Nolan Ryan | 10-Apr-68 | 1-Oct-70 |
| 31 | Jack DiLauro | 13-May-69 | 15-Oct-69 |
| 33 | Les Rohr | 6-Sep-69 | 2-Oct-69 |
| 34 | Cal Koonce | 1-Aug-67 | 8-Jun-71 |
| 36 | Jerry Koosman | 10-Apr-67 | 1-Oct-78 |
| 38 | Al Jackson | 9-Apr-68 | 12-Jun-69 |
| 38 | Jesse Hudson | 5-Sep-69 | 1-Oct-69 |
| 39 | Gary Gentry | 7-Apr-69 | 4-Oct-72 |
| 41 | Tom Seaver | 11-Apr-67 | 15-Jun-77 |
| 42 | Ron Taylor | 11-Apr-67 | 30-Sep-71 |
| 43 | Jim McAndrew | 18-Jul-68 | 21-Oct-73 |
| 44* | Jim Bibby | 8-Sep-69 | 2-Oct-69 |
| 45 | Tug McGraw | 7-Apr-69 | 2-Oct-74 |
| 52 (C) | Joe Pignatano | 9-Apr-68 | 4-Oct-81 |
| 53 (C) | Ed Yost | 10-Apr-68 | 3-Oct-76 |
| 54 (C ) | Rube Walker | 10-Apr-68 | 4-Oct-81 |

# Jerry Grote

by Joseph Wancho

| Season | Age | G | AB | R | H | 2B | 3B | HR | RBI | BB | SO | SB | CS | BA | OBP | SLG |
|---|---|---|---|---|---|---|---|---|---|---|---|---|---|---|---|---|
| 1969 Mets | 26 | 113 | 365 | 38 | 92 | 12 | 3 | 6 | 40 | 32 | 59 | 2 | 1 | .252 | .313 | .351 |
| Career 16 Years | – | 1421 | 4339 | 352 | 1092 | 160 | 22 | 39 | 404 | 399 | 600 | 15 | 23 | .252 | .316 | .326 |

In the summer of 1985, Birmingham Barons manager Jerry Grote realized he had a problem. Between games of a twin bill in Columbus, Georgia, the supply of healthy players with catching experience was nil. His two catchers were beset with injuries (Papo Rosado had a bad shoulder and Steve Eagar had aggravated a thumb injury while playing in the first game). The only other player with catching experience on Birmingham's roster was nursing an ailing leg. Since it had rained the day before, making the field unplayable, Grote saw no need to risk further injury. Grote placed a call to general manager Al Clarkson to discuss the situation and ask that he be activated for the second game. The request was granted and the 42-year-old first-year manager, who hadn't played in a game in four years, became the starting catcher for the nightcap.

"To me it was no big deal," said Grote. "In the minor leagues, you never have enough help. You end up doing a lot of the work yourself." Grote, who had become accustomed to warming up pitchers in the bullpen or catching batting practice, did not get a hit in the game. But he walked once and laid down a successful sacrifice bunt. After the game, he was promptly deactivated. Grote understood that his age was against him as far as playing at the major-league level was concerned, commenting that "everybody's got their mind made up. You're that old, you can't do the job anymore."

Gerald Wayne Grote was born on October 6, 1942 in San Antonio, Texas. Jerry was the oldest of three children, with sisters Iris and Debbie, born to Mr. and Mrs. Clarence Grote. Jerry attended MacArthur High school and was a three-sport, star excelling in cross-country, track and field, and, of course, baseball. Grote caught, pitched, and played third base during his high school days. Grote threw a one-hitter and a no-hitter while at MacArthur. (He lost the no-hitter because of two errors by the second baseman.)

After graduating from high school in 1961, Grote was offered a contract to play for the expansion Houston Colt 45s. Grote turned down the offer and instead enrolled at nearby Trinity University. At Trinity, Grote both pitched and caught, leading the team in batting average (.413), home runs (5) and triples (5). He was tutored in the finer points of catching by Trinity coach Del Baker, who had caught for Detroit from 1914 to 1916. Baker was a manager and coach for more than 25 years in the major leagues, taking Detroit to the World Series in 1940. "One person I owe a lot to as far as baseball is concerned is Del Baker," said Grote. "He helped me a lot, both in hitting and catching."

Houston scouts Red Murff and Andy Andrews again made an offer for Grote's services in 1962, and this time he accepted their offer over five other teams bidding for the young catcher. "I feel that I have a better opportunity of getting up there [to the major-league level]," he explained of his decision to sign with expansion Houston.

Grote reported to the San Antonio Missions of the Texas League in 1963. Just before the season began, the Missions, keeping to the beat of the parent club in Houston, changed their name to the Bullets. The Bullets won the Alamo City's first Texas League pennant since 1908. Grote contributed with a .268 batting average, .300 in his last 200 at-bats for the season, while hitting 14 home runs. Grote was honored by the Houston Chapter of the Baseball Writers Association of America as the minor leaguer from Texas who is considered to be the best major-league prospect.

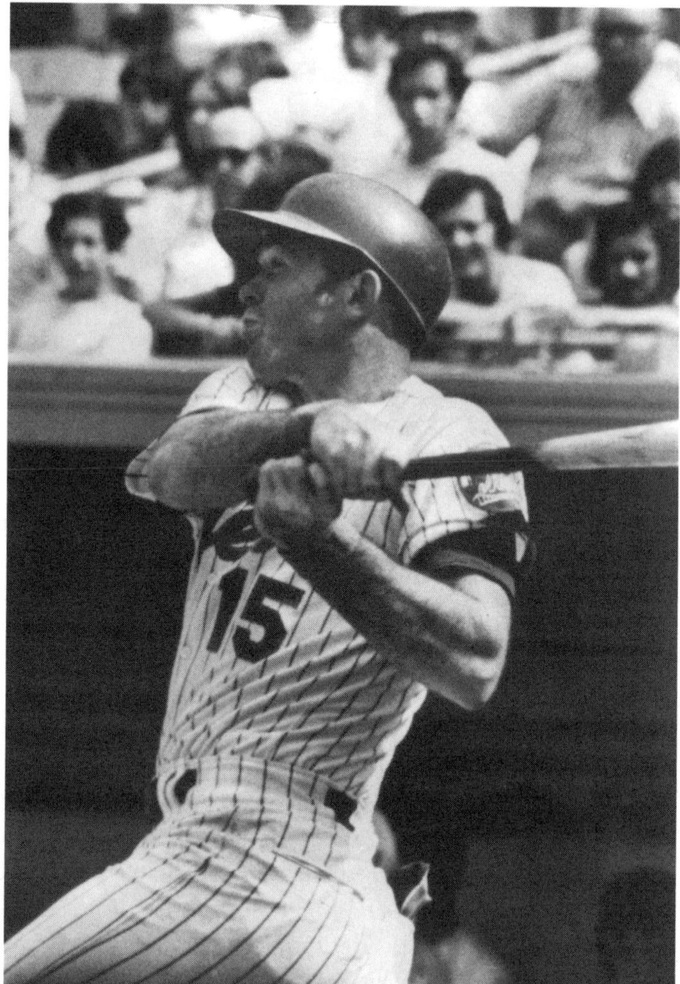

Photo courtesy of *Mets Inside Pitch* Archives

*Jerry Grote said that manager Gil Hodges "got me to shorten my stride and showed me how to be quicker with the bat."*

Grote was called up to the parent club at the end of the 1963 season. In his debut, on September 21, Grote replaced John Bateman as the catcher in the fifth inning, and got his first big league run batted in by way of a sacrifice fly off Dallas Green. On the 27th, Grote singled in the sixth inning against Met Al Jackson for his first major league hit.

In an effort to improve his hitting, Grote constructed a batting cage on his parents' farm in San Antonio. The cage, made of chicken wire and reinforced by carpeting, took some beating as Grote pounded every pitch thrown by "Iron Mike," the pitching machine he and his friend Larry Fulbright, who played college ball at Southwest Texas State, rigged up in the 60-foot batting cage.

Jerry split time behind the plate with John Bateman in 1964 and started 88 games for Houston. He hit only .181, but was superb behind the plate; throwing out the first seven of eight would-be basestealers. During the offseason, Houston changed its name from the Colt 45s to the Astros, and moved its home games into the nation's first indoor baseball park, the Astrodome. As the season began, Ron Brand, a Rule V draftee, and Bateman handled the caching duties for the Astros and Grote was sent to Oklahoma City of the Pacific Coast League. Eventually Bateman was also sent down to the 89ers to hone his catching abilities. Grote moved to third base for the rest of the season as the 89ers won the PCL pennant.

Although 1965 may have seemed like a setback in Grote's professional career, his biggest break was yet to come. On October 19, he was shipped to the New York Mets for pitchers Tom Parsons and Gary Kroll. Red Murff, the scout who signed him for Houston, had moved on to the Mets and recommended picking up the catcher. For his part, Grote was eager to be back behind home plate for the Mets, commenting that the team drew big crowds "and the fans were behind you."

Over the next three years, the fans really got behind the man in the mask. From 1966 to 1968, Grote threw out 44 percent of attempted basestealers, and averaged more than 620 putouts and 59 assists per year. Grote's defensive mastery prompted St. Louis stolen base legend Lou Brock to remark, "For quickness in getting rid of the ball and accuracy, I have to pick Grote." Brock said that when Grote was behind the plate, he tried to take bigger leads off first base and take advantage of the pitcher to give himself an edge on the bases.

All was not so rosy for Grote and the Mets during these years. Despite the promising pitching staff and some pieces of the puzzle falling into place, New York still found itself battling with Houston for last place in the National League. Grote, who was often characterized as cantankerous and ill-tempered to sports writers, snappish to teammates, and argumentative to umpires, demonstrated this attitude in a game at Los Angeles on July 27, 1967. The situation arose when Mets manager Wes Westrum had only 21 players available for the game. Grote entered the game as a pinch runner in the top of the seventh inning and went behind the plate in the bottom of the inning. Irritated with home-plate umpire Bill Jackowski's calls, Grote shouted uncomplimentary remarks at Jackowski after returning to the dugout, and threw a towel onto the field from the dugout. Jackowski ejected Grote. Outfielder Tommy Reynolds was pressed into service behind the plate even though he had never caught before. Leading 5–3 when Grote was ejected, the Mets went on to lose to the Dodgers, 7–6 in 11 innings. Westrum fined Grote $100 for his umpire baiting and general manager Bing Devine chewed out Grote for his irresponsibility in getting tossed from the game with no suitable replacement at catcher. The fact that he was hitting .194 at the time—an average that increased only one point the rest of the year—made him sit there and take the deserved berating from a GM known for making trades.

In 1968, Grote rebounded with his finest offensive season to that point. He batted .282 in 124 games and was the National League's starting catcher in the All Star Game. New manager Gil Hodges worked with Grote on his hitting. "Gil got me to shorten my stride and showed me how to be quicker with the bat. It has helped me to no end," Grote said later.

As spring training broke in 1969, Grote predicted big things for the Mets. "We're a young team. We're just coming," insisted Grote. "We all played together last year and we're together again this year. When you play together a few years, you get to know each other and things improve. Yes sir, there's a different feeling on the team this year. There's more togetherness. There's more pride. We're a close-knit team." His words proved to be prophetic.

One difference in 1969 for Major League Baseball was the realignment of the American and National Leagues. Each league gained two new expansion teams with San Diego and Montreal in the National League, and Kansas City and Seattle in the American League. Each league split into two divisions, East and West. At the conclusion of the season, a Championship Series between the division winners determined the pennant winners. The Mets were in the National League East Division along with the Cubs, Cardinals, Pirates, Phillies, and Expos.

The Cubs led the NL East for most of the summer, enjoying a 10-game lead over the Mets as late as August 15, but New York kept chipping away and after a two-game sweep of Chicago at Shea Stadium on September 9, the gap was closed to a half-game. The Mets went 18–5 the rest of the campaign, while the Cubs went 8–12 to finish the year and the Mets won the division title by eight games, clinching on September 24 with a 6–0 win over the St. Louis Cardinals at home.

Pitching and defense steered the Mets to the title. Hodges platooned at first base, second base, third base, and right field, but Grote caught 112 games, even with capable backups J.C. Martin and rookie Duffy Dyer on the squad.

Grote's batting average dipped 30 points, to .252 in 365 at-bats, but he had career bests with six home runs and 40 RBIs. His defense was sparkling: a superb .991 fielding percentage, 718 putouts, and 40 of 71 runners thrown out trying to steal. Grote was given as much credit for the pitching staff's success as the pitchers themselves. "He's the best catcher a pitcher could want to throw to," said ace Tom Seaver (25–7, 2.21 ERA).

Grote caught every inning of the team's fabled postseason run in 1969. He hit just .167 in the NLCS victory over Atlanta, but the rest of the club's bats and a solid bullpen effort carried the club to a sweep of the Braves in three games. Awaiting them in the fall classic were the heavily favored Orioles. Baltimore, which swept Minnesota in the ALCS, was a formidable team with two 20-game winners, Mike Cuellar and Dave McNally, and 16-game winner Jim Palmer. The team hit for power and average and was superb defensively.

Game One featured a pitching matchup of the ages as Seaver opposed Cuellar. Each received the Cy Young Award for their work that season (Cuellar as co-winner with Denny McLain in the AL). Cuellar won, 4–1, and the oddsmakers appeared to be right. But then the Mets reeled off four wins in a row—allowing just five runs in those games—to claim the world championship, with Koosman winning twice. Grote hit .211 for the Series, with two doubles, a run scored, and one driven in. Two of Grote's four hits helped set up winning rallies. His single in Game Two kept the ninth inning alive and Al Weis followed with the tiebreaking hit. With Game Four tied, Grote doubled to start the 10th inning when Orioles left fielder Don Buford had trouble with the ball in the sun. Pinch runner Rod Gaspar scored the winning run when an errant throw hit J.C. Martin on the wrist. A day later, Grote and Gaspar combined to douse New York Mayor John Lindsay with champagne in the jubilant Mets clubouse.

Grote led the league in putouts the next two years, with 855 and 892 respectively. On April 22, 1970, he set a major league record with 20 putouts in a game. Tom Seaver notched 19 strikeouts against San Diego that day, and set his own major-league mark with 10 consecutive strikeouts. Grote commented that he didn't even bother to call pitches after the eighth inning that day, and just held out his glove to catch Seaver's unhittable fastball.

Following the death of Gil Hodges just before the 1972 season, new manager Yogi Berra wasted little time in replacing Grote with Duffy Dyer. The young Dyer gave the team more of a threat with the long ball, but it was a mystery to many of the Mets faithful as to what had happened to Grote. Had the Mets given up on him? Was he on the trading block? The mystery was solved when Grote had surgery to remove bone chips from his right elbow in late September. Berra had been saying that he wanted to take a look at Dyer, keeping under wraps the secret of Grote's injury.

In May 1973, Grote was hit on the right forearm with a pitch from Pittsburgh's Ramon Hernandez, breaking a bone and sending Grote to the disabled list. He missed two months, but he returned in mid-July. His batting suffered after his return, dipping to .178 by August 2. Yet three weeks later he was up to .256 as the Mets made their move from last place to claim the lead in the National League East. The Mets were in fifth place on September 11 and 10 days later were in first place. They took the title in a makeup game the Monday after the season ended, with Grote's two-run single opening up a 1–0 contest.

The Mets disposed of the Cincinnati Reds in five games to claim the pennant. The highlight was a fight in Game Three between the Reds' Pete Rose and Mets shortstop Bud Harrelson at second base. The bench-clearing brawl took several minutes to clear, with neither combatant getting thrown our. Grote wound up hitting .211 the upset of Cincinnati.

The World Series pitted the Mets against the Oakland A's, who like Baltimore in 1969, were heavy favorites. Grote hit .267 for the Series, but his passed ball in the 11th inning of Game Three put the winning run in position for the A's. With Ted Kubiak at first base, a fastball from Mets pitcher Harry Parker glanced off of Grote's mitt and sailed to the backstop. Bert Campaneris singled home Kubiak for the winning run. The A's won the Series in seven games, the second of three straight world championships for Oakland.

As is custom for the home team, five dozen baseballs were provided to the umpiring crew so that they could be rubbed in mud to take the shine off the balls. According to an article in the *New York Daily News* in 1974, Mets officials had made complaints to the league office that an inordinate amount of baseballs given to the umpires before the game, were missing after each game. The Mets placed a team official in the stands to account for every ball, fair or foul or a ball that was tossed out of the game. The Mets officials suggested that the umpires were pocketing baseballs.

On May 20, 1974, in a home game against Chicago, home plate umpire Bruce Froemming sent some baseballs to the Met clubhouse with a note: "Here's your five dozen baseballs. Count them." In the eighth inning, a pitch from Parker got by Grote and hit Froemming. Froemming later charged that Grote had deliberately let the pitch get by him. "It was a bush league stunt, strictly out of Class D," the umpire said. While Berra and Grote insisted that Grote was crossed up on the pitch, Froemming replied that Grote had not moved his glove and did not go out to the mound to talk to Parker, which often happens when a catcher is crossed up. "All I consider is where the accusations came from," said Grote. "That article about the missing baseballs really must have hit home."

Grote was named to the National League All-Star team in 1974, but he wound up splitting time with Dyer due to continued injuries, and appeared in only 97 games. Grote missed the final month after a foul ball off his hand left him unable to catch. The Mets stumbled to fifth place.

PHOTOS COURTESY OF METSILVERMAN.COM

*Jerry Grote was one of the few people on record before the 1969 season as saying that he thought the Mets could win. He was the everyday catcher that year and for most of his 12-season Mets tenure. Forty years later he still holds the franchise record for most games caught in a career.*

The Mets brought six catchers to camp in 1975. Dyer was traded to Pittsburgh and Jerry Moses was brought in for some veteran experience and added depth. John Stearns became Grote's backup and the heir-apparent to the catcher's position. Despite more back problems and a strained shoulder, Grote hit .295 and led the league with a .995 fielding average and six pickoffs, playing in 111 games behind the plate, his most since 1971. Manager Berra was fired that season and replaced on an interim basis by Roy McMillan as the Mets finished in third place, 10 games behind the Pirates.

Joe Frazier took the reins for the Mets in 1976, and again New York finished in third place. Playing in 95 games, Grote had a .993 fielding percentage while hitting .272. He started just four games in the final month of the season because of his now chronic back problems.

With Stearns nine years younger and a better hitter than the 34-year-old Grote, the veteran catcher considered his future with the club and in the game. At first he said he planned to retire but soon reconsidered.

In 1977 spring training, Grote, for the first time in his Mets tenure, was clearly not the first option behind the plate. "I am here to help [Stearns] and fill in for him on the days he needs a rest," Grote said. Though the Mets had two capable catchers—along with third-stringer Ron Hodges—they were thin in other places as the club struggled in 1977. Grote played third base 11 times that season, making only two errors at the hot corner. A third baseman in high school, he had played the position in only seven games during his dozen years in the majors.

Joe Torre, who took over for Frazier at the end of May, switched recently-acquired Lenny Randle from second to third base and returned Grote behind the plate, though Stearns still caught the majority of the games. "Grote is a catcher who hits," said Torre, "while Johnny Bench and Ted Simmons are hitters who catch."

Grote did not catch much longer with the Mets. With Tom Seaver traded and the team sinking, the Mets dealt Grote to the Dodgers for two minor leaguers. Los Angeles had a firm grasp on first place in the National League West. Grote played in 18 games for the Dodgers and batted .259. He appeared in both the NLCS against the Phillies and the World Series against the Yankees, his third Series played in New York. The Dodgers lost the fall classic in six games.

Grote returned to Los Angeles in 1978, playing in a minimal role for the Dodgers after suffering a fractured left wrist. The Dodgers bested the Phillies in the League Championship Series once more, but in the World Series L.A. again lost to the Yankees in six games.

Yankees president Al Rosen made an offer to Grote for 1979, with an option for the following year. He would play in no more than 40 games a year as a backup to Thurman Munson. But Jerry refused, opting to stay home in San Antonio and spend more time with his family. He stayed retired until 1981, when a recommendation from Kansas City Royals pitching coach Billy Connors, a former Mets teammate, got him back in the game with Kansas City, the defending AL champions.

"I'd retired to be with my wife and kids. Last November, she filed for divorce, so I decided to get it back together again," Grote said at spring training. With John Wathan and Jamie Quirk nursing injuries, manager Jim Frey looked for Grote to make contributions to the team beyond being a third-string backup. "I'm thinking of a guy who can pinch hit and fill in in other ways," said Frey.

On July 3, 1981, Grote drove in seven runs in a game, a team record that has been tied but never surpassed through 2008. In a 12–9 win over Seattle, Grote went 3-for-4 with a home run, a double, a stolen base, and a run scored. The big blast was a grand slam in the fifth inning off Ken Clay. "The older the violin, the sweeter the music," said Grote. "It just happened to be there tonight."

The grand slam was his only home run of the year and he knocked in just two more runs in his other 21 games as a Royal. Though Grote was hitting .304—his highest mark of any season—he was released on September 1. He was picked up by the Dodgers, played in one game, and was released at the end of the season.

Through 2008, Grote ranked among the career leaders for catchers in games played (1,348), putouts (8,081), and fielding percentage (.991). Three decades after his final game as a Met, he had still caught more games than anyone else in club history (1,176), and his 1,235 games overall as a Met stood third all-time behind former teammates Ed Kranepool and Bud Harrelson. Grote finished just shy of 1,000 hits as a Met (994). Grote has been honored for not only his major league accomplishments, but also his amateur career. He has been inducted into the New York Mets Hall of Fame (1992), the Texas Baseball Hall of Fame (1991), and the San Antonio Sports Hall of Fame (1998).

In retirement, Grote spent his time owning and operating many businesses near San Antonio, including a stint as sales manager at a real-estate company, and running a meat market and a cattle ranch. Grote and his wife, Cheryl, took up residence in San Antonio. Jerry had three children from his first marriage, daughters Sandra and Jennifer and son Jeffrey. He has been a favorite instructor in Mets fantasy camps, reporting few physical problems despite the countless squats he endured behind the plate.

**Sources**
The *New York Times.*
*The Sporting News.*
The *San Antonio Light.*
The *San Antonio Express.*
*www.retrosheet.com*
*www.sabr.org*
*www.jerrygrote.com*
*http://newyork.mets.mlb.com/*

# Bud Harrelson

by Eric Aron

| Season | Age | G | AB | R | H | 2B | 3B | HR | RBI | BB | SO | SB | CS | BA | OBP | SLG |
|---|---|---|---|---|---|---|---|---|---|---|---|---|---|---|---|---|
| 1969 Mets | 25 | 123 | 395 | 42 | 98 | 11 | 6 | 0 | 24 | 54 | 54 | 1 | 3 | .248 | .341 | .306 |
| Career 16 Years | – | 1533 | 4744 | 539 | 1120 | 136 | 45 | 7 | 267 | 633 | 653 | 127 | 60 | .236 | .327 | .288 |

For a player who endured nicknames such as Twiggy, Mini-Hawk, and Mighty Mouse forgetting his light weight and short stature, Bud Harrelson is perhaps best known to the casual baseball fan getting into a fight. There's no doubt that Pete Rose got the better of him in their brawl at second base during Game Three of the 1973 National League Championship Series, but Harrelson's Mets got in the last punch: They won the pennant. And this came just four years after Bud had helped the Mets pull off the ultimate David vs. Goliath upset of the vaunted Baltimore Orioles in the 1969 World Series.

Bud was not known as much of a hitter—as his 16-year career average of .236 with only seven home runs attests—but his defense at shortstop was outstanding. His lifetime fielding percentage was .969 and he won a National League Gold Glove Award in 1971. In addition to appearing in two All-Star Games, Harrelson set a since-broken major-league mark with 54 consecutive errorless games at shortstop in 1970. After his playing career ended, he was a coach, a scout, a special instructor, a broadcaster, and a manager in both the minor leagues and major leagues, all in the Mets organization. Said friend and teammate Tom Seaver, "We simply don't win two pennants without him."

Derrel McKinley Harrelson was born on June 6, 1944 (the same day as the D-Day invasion), in Niles, California, on the Oakland side of San Francisco Bay. After the second grade, his family moved to nearby Hayward. It was a working-class family. Bud's father, Glenn, was an auto mechanic and a foreman for a used-car agency. The Harrelsons were an athletic household; Glenn was a former football player who dropped out of high school to support his family. Bud's older brother, Dwayne was a running back in football and a shortstop and catcher in baseball. His mother, Rena, ran track in high school and supported her children's pursuit of athletics.

Dwayne unintentionally gave his kid brother the nickname Bud. Dwayne couldn't pronounce Derrel, so he called him Brother, which morphed into Bud. Dwayne was offered a professional contract by the Washington Senators after his senior year of high school, but he chose to go to college instead. An ankle injury dashed any hopes of a career in baseball.

Bud was a natural athlete. Despite his small size and weight, he made his high school football, basketball, and baseball teams. He weighed only 97 pounds when he played football. "I was all helmet and pads," he said, "but I played both ways—halfback and safety." Through sheer toughness, he led his league in receptions and made all-star honors. In basketball, he was a great outside shooter, averaging 11 points per game, and an outstanding defender.

He captained Sunset High in all three sports and was voted East Bay Athlete of the Year. His first love, of course, was baseball.

Bud played for his high school team in the spring, American Legion ball in the summer, and weekend semipro games in the fall. He had a great arm and played all positions in Little League. In Babe Ruth League he played mostly third base; he didn't move to shortstop until his sophomore year. He cited coach Don Curley at Sunset High as the biggest mentor in his entire career. "With his help, I really worked at it," Harrelson said. "He taught me a lot and hit grounders to me for hours on end so I could practice. I worked and worked and worked, but I enjoyed it. I learned fast. Shortstop was always for me."

After high school graduation, no scouts would offer him much because of his size. He was turned down flat by his hometown team, the San Francisco Giants. Bud decided to go to college and improve his chances and mature as a ballplayer. Ironically, he won a basketball scholarship to San Francisco State, but played only baseball. He batted .430 in 30 games to help lead his team to a Far Western Conference Championship. "I was a physical-education major, but I had no intention of staying in school," Harrelson told a biographer. "I had already agreed to go to Alaska to play summer ball, which a lot of the college kids do, but when the scouts made serious pitches of bonuses at me I decided to sign."

Bud spoke to several scouts, notably from the Yankees, the Cubs, and the Cardinals. The Yankees offered him the most, but he didn't think he would get much playing time. The Mets, coming off their 40–120 inaugural season, offered a much better opportunity for advancement. Scout Roy Partee signed Harrelson on June 7, 1963, the day after the shortstop turned 19, for a little more than $10,000. "I figured I could make that club fast," Bud said. He was right.

Harrelson's professional career began with the Salinas Mets of the Class A California League. Playing not far from where he grew up, Harrelson was familiar with the area, but not with professional pitching. A right-handed hitter, Bud had no power and was taught how to just make contact and not be a free swinger. His season ended after only 136 at-bats when he was hit by a pitch that broke his left arm. He batted .221 with one homer, two triples, and knocked in nine. He made 18 errors in just 36 games.

That winter, Harrelson began a five-year hitch in the National Guard. In February 1964, he was invited to an early spring training session at St. Petersburg, Florida. He did his best to make the big league team that spring, with eating as big a part of it as hitting or fielding. Throughout his career he would lose weight off his meager frame as the season progressed. Even a dozen bananas a day didn't do much. In the end, he spent another summer in Salinas, where he showed he could stand up to the rigors of a full season. His fielding also improved; he made 34 errors in 596 chances to lead the league with a .943 fielding percentage. He batted .231 with three homers and 48 RBIs in 135 games.

In 1965, Harrelson moved up to Triple A with the Buffalo Bisons of the International League. He played in 131 games and batted .251 with 15 doubles, two home runs, and 36 RBIs. His fielding was erratic, as it would be early in his career. He led the league in errors with 31 and had a .950 fielding percentage. He was a September call-up for the Mets and made his major league debut on September 2, 1965. He was inserted as a pinch runner in the eighth inning of a game against the Houston Astros at Shea Stadium, and played shortstop in the ninth.

Harrelson's first plate appearance came on September 5 in St. Louis. Taking over for Roy McMillan in the second game of a doubleheader, He grounded back to pitcher Ray Washburn. Harrelson's first hit was a single off Cubs pitcher Bob Hendley in the first inning of a game at Wrigley Field on September 19. He appeared in 19 games in all and had a meager 4-for-37 account (.108) in his first taste of the big leagues.

After the season, on December 17, Bud married his first wife, Yvonne. He started the 1966 season playing for the Jacksonville Suns, the franchise's new International League farm team. There he met future teammate Tom Seaver. The two Northern Californians—Seaver from Fresno and Harrelson from Hayward—became instant friends. They roomed together on the road with the Mets from 1968 until Seaver's departure from the club in 1977.

At Jacksonville, Harrelson taught himself to become a switch-hitter. One day he tried batting left-handed in the batting cage, and impressed manager Solly Hemus and the director of player development, Bob Scheffing. They suggested that he try it during an exhibition game. Harrelson played a game later that day and bunted left-handed against White Sox knuckleballer Hoyt Wilhelm.

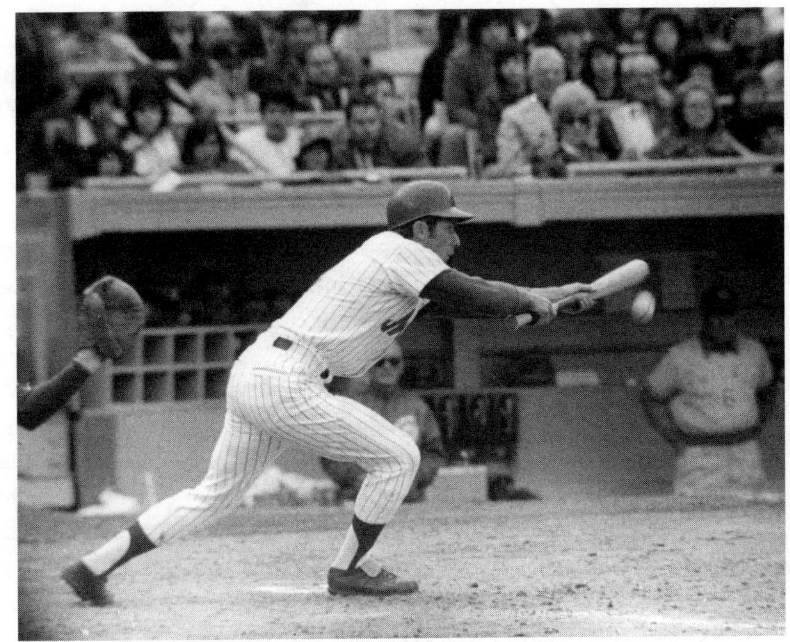


*Bud Harrelson laid down more sacrifices than any position player in Mets history. His 77 sacrifices were as many as roommate and friend Tom Seaver and are tied for third behind the 85 by Dwight Gooden and Jerry Koosman.*

Appearing in 117 games for Jacksonville, Harrelson hit .221 with five triples and 26 RBIs. He made 28 errors in 601 chances for a .953 fielding percentage. Called up to the Mets on August 12, 1966, he played in 33 games, hit .222, stole six bases including home against the Giants, and made just one error in 144 chances (.993 fielding percentage).

Harrelson became the Mets starting shortstop in 1967, already the 18th in the team's brief history. That happened after his predecessor and mentor Roy McMillan felt a pop in his shoulder during spring training. McMillan's playing career was over. The Mets had acquired Sandy Alomar during that spring to help with the infield, but he contributed little offensively or defensively (Alomar went 0-for-22 as a Met). That left Harrelson, who did not start the season well. He committed 21 errors in his first month, but made only 11 the rest of the season. (In a career that lasted another decade in New York, his 144 starts at shortstop were more than every year except 1970.) McMillan helped Bud work on his fielding, while coach Yogi Berra taught him how to make better contact and use a heavier bat. Skipper Wes Westrum was pleased with the results, even Harrelson's .254 batting average (only his 1973 average of .258 would surpass it in his Mets tenure). Harrelson's speed was also a tremendous asset, as he was successful in his first seven major league steal attempts, though he was eventually caught 13 times in 25 tries).

Bud hit first major league home run on August 17, 1967. It was an inside-the-park job in the eighth inning while batting right-handed at Pittsburgh's Forbes Field. "Juan Pizarro was the pitcher," he recalled. "I hit it right down the line in right field and Al Luplow tried to make a shoestring catch and missed. It rolled all the way to the wall and then it rolled away from him after it hit the wall. I kept running and I had an inside-the-parker. It won the game for us, too."

Harrelson's offense fell precipitously in 1968, but that wasn't uncommon in the Year of the Pitcher. The Mets now had Gil Hodges running the team—Westrum had resigned in the next-to last week of New York's 101-loss 1967 season—and Harrelson spent much of '68 fulfilling his military obligation, dealing with knee problems, and fighting to keep his batting average out of the low .200s. He finished with a .219 average and then had cartilage removed from his knee, which he had first injured with Jacksonville in 1966 during a takeout slide. With an expansion draft coming and each team required to make players available, Harrelson wasn't worried about being taken by either Montreal or San Diego. He joked that the Mets' owner, thoroughbred enthusiast Joan Payson, wouldn't allow him to be left unprotected. "She figures if I can't play ball, I can ride one of her horses."

Harrelson arrived in St. Petersburg in 1969 having spent the winter lifting weights and quitting smoking. He came in weighing 165 pounds and ceded the lightest-Met prize to 157-pound Amos Otis. Gil Hodges favored platoons for his club at the corners in the outfield and infield, plus second base. Catcher, center field, and shortstop were too important to Hodges to tinker with, even though Jerry Grote was no great shakes with the bat and Tommie Agee in center had a lower 1968 batting average than Harrelson (.217).

Harrelson was sorely missed when he had to serve his military obligation starting in July. Al Weis filled in at shortstop and—true to form for the Mets that year—hit both of his home runs for the season in a huge series at Wrigley Field. Harrelson started just one game in a five-week span because of his obligation, and his batting average, which had surpassed .290 at the beginning of June, got over .250 only a couple of times the rest of the season; he finished at .248. His .341 on-base percentage was crucial since he usually batted second against right-handers and slid down to eighth against southpaws. But on a team with the pitching the '69 Mets had, his glove was more important than what he generated with his bat. Harrelson committed just 19 errors in 119 games at shortstop; his best remembered play of that season was grabbing Joe Torre's grounder and starting the double play that clinched the first Eastern Division title in National League history and set off a riot at Shea Stadium on September 24. Harrelson's game-winning single the night before against Bob Gibson had set the party in motion by assuring the Mets of at least a tie for the division title.

Harrelson was practically flawless in the field in the miraculous postseason. His only error in 44 chances came with two outs and no one on in the seventh inning of New York's 11–6 win over the Braves in Game Two of the National League Championship Series. Though he was only 2 for 11 in the NLCS, he drove in three runs and both his hits went for extra bases—giving Harrelson, who would have a lifetime .288 slugging percentage, a stunning .455 slugging mark in the Mets' three-game sweep. He batted .176 in the World Series against the Orioles, but he had three singles and three walks to give him a .300 on-base percentage.

Harrelson played 157 games for the Mets in 1970 and appeared in his first All-Star Game. He went 2-for-3 and scored twice in the game that ended with Pete Rose barreling over Ray Fosse to win the game in the 12th inning. Bud started the All-Star Game the next year at Tiger Stadium as part of a National League lineup that included Hank Aaron, Willie Mays, Willie McCovey, Willie Stargell, and Johnny Bench—Roberto Clemente didn't even start! The game is best remembered for Reggie Jackson's home run off a light tower. Bud told a sportswriter he was intimidated. "I didn't even want to take batting practice with those guys. They were

PHOTO COURTESY OF JACOB KANAREK/METSINTHESEVENTIES.COM

*Bud Harrelson was the first Met to steal 100 bases; he was also the first to be thrown out 50 times.*

hitting balls on the roof and beyond. I know the fans didn't want to see me hit. I think I took two swings and let the other guys get a few more cuts."

Harrelson at least had an out-of-the-park home run under his belt by that time. It came on April 17, 1970, off Phillies lefty Grant Jackson: "I was sort of stunned," Harrelson said of the moment. "As I saw it go out, I considered sliding into second, third, and home on my way around, but decided I better not...As I ran around the bases I got some looks from the Phils standing there. You know, the who-you-kidding kind of looks. If I smiled, I'd be agreeing with them that it was an accident. I wasn't going to give them the satisfaction, so I didn't smile. As I rounded third, coach Eddie Yost yelled, 'Smile,' but I didn't dare."

The 1970 season was arguably Harrelson's best. To go along with his fence-clearing blast, he knocked in 42 runs and drew 95 walks, by far the most in either category in his career. He also had career highs in games (157), at-bats (564), runs (72), and doubles (18); he flexed as much power as he would ever conjure, with eight triples and eight sacrifice flies. He stole 23 bases in 27 tries after stealing just once successfully in '69. He had a good follow-up season in 1971, winning his only Gold Glove, batting .252, and collecting a career-best 138 hits and 28 steals, but after that season Harrelson's frail frame was seemingly banged up more often than not. He missed 300 games with injuries to his hands, sternum, back, and knee over the next four seasons.

In 1973, the Mets almost pulled off another miracle. They spent most of the year in last place in the National League East and ended the season near the bottom of the league in virtually all offensive categories: 11th in batting (.246), home runs (85), runs (608), and stolen bases (27). Yet they won the pennant.

The Mets were devastated by injuries as they staggered through much of the first five months of the '73 season. Harrelson himself went on the DL twice. He was out of commission with a fractured wrist from June 5 to July 8, and with a fractured sternum in August. When he returned August 18, the Mets were in last place, 13 games under .500, and were still in the cellar on August 28. But propelled by their pitching, the Mets went 19–8 in September to win the division at just three games over .500 (82–79). Harrelson started every game during the stretch run and batted .280 while scoring 12 times and drawing 13 walks in September.

The Mets clinched the NL East on October 1. It was the 161st game of the '73 campaign, played the day after the season ended because the Mets and Cubs had waited out two days of rain at Wrigley Field. The Cincinnati Reds, the West Division winners, were the odds-on favorites to win the best-of-five NLCS. The five games were slated to be played on successive days with the first two games in Cincinnati. The Mets managed a split at Riverfront Stadium, with Tom Seaver losing a 2–1 game and Jon Matlack following with a two-hit shutout.

Back at Shea, the Mets trounced Cincinnati, 9–2, backed by a complete-game, nine-strikeout performance by Jerry Koosman and two home runs by outfielder Rusty Staub. In the fifth inning, already leading by seven runs, the Mets turned a far-from-routine 3-6-3 double play.

The day before, asked by reporters about the way the Reds had hit in the game, Harrelson said, "They all look like me hitting." During pregame warmups for Game Three, Reds second baseman Joe Morgan grabbed Bud by his uniform shirt and said, "If you ever say something like that about me again, I'll punch you out!" Morgan told Harrelson, "Pete [Rose] is going to use this to get the club fired up. If he has a chance, he is going to come and get you at second."

The game was so far gone that Reds relief pitcher Roger Nelson batted for himself and fanned to start the fifth against Koosman. Batting second was Rose, who singled to center. The next hitter was Morgan, who hit a ground ball to Milner at first base. Milner scooped up the ball and threw to Harrelson at second, who fired back to Milner to complete the double play. In the process, Rose had slid hard into second, hitting Bud with his elbow. The 160-pound shortstop then said to the man 40 pounds heavier, "That was a cheap [bleeping] shot." Rose said, "What did you say?" and Harrelson repeated the words, after which Rose grabbed Bud and pinned him to the ground. The first to come out to join the fracas was Mets third baseman Wayne Garrett. Next came the Reds coaches and then seconds later both benches cleared and the bullpens charged in.

Immediately after the dust had seemed to settle, there was another brief altercation between a Red and a Met. Mets reliever Buzz Capra was struck by Reds reliever Pedro Borbon. After that fight was broken up, players from both sides put on their caps. Borbon put on what another teammate told him was a Mets cap. Borbon, who earned the nickname Dracula after another incident in 1974, took off the cap and bit a hole in it with his teeth.

Harrelson was left with a bruise over his eye, which he said came from having his sunglasses broken. Neither Rose nor Harrelson was ejected and that was a mistake. The game was nearly called after the Reds took the field in the bottom of the inning. Rose had taken left field when an array of objects were thrown his way, including a whiskey bottle. Manager Sparky Anderson took his team off the field as the game was delayed for 20 minutes. National League president Chub Feeney, who after conferring with the six umpires, the commissioner, and both teams, decided to send out players from the Mets dugout to restore order. It was only after Willie Mays, Seaver, Staub, Cleon Jones, and Yogi Berra came out to the field to try to calm the fans that play was resumed.

"Being a little guy, I always wore a Superman t-shirt under my jersey," Harrelson said. "When the reporters came over after the game, I taped [an X] over the Superman logo and said, 'It looks like Pete had a load of kryptonite today.'"

With Game Three finally in the books, the Mets had an unlikely lead in the series. But not for long. Rose came back to homer in the 12th inning of Game Four and even the series. Game Five was a lot like Game Three, except the riot took place after the game. The Mets had a comfortable lead and after Tug McGraw squelched a Reds rally in the ninth, the Shea field was instantly filled with people and the players had to run for their lives.

The Mets nearly knocked off another Goliath in the Oakland A's. Harrelson batted .250 against the A's in the World Series, but his most memorable moment came while running the bases. With Game Two tied in the 10th inning, Harrelson tried to score from third on a short fly by Felix Millan. Joe Rudi's throw to the plate was gloved by catcher Ray Fosse, who "tagged" out Bud...according to umpire Augie Donatelli. Willie Mays, in the on-deck circle, got down on his hands and knees and questioned how Donatelli could make the call. Manager Yogi Berra and Harrelson were more demonstrative in their arguments. The call stood but Harrelson did come around to score the go-ahead run in the 12th inning when he led off with a double and Mays singled him home. The Mets scored three more times and won the game, thanks to two errors that inning by Mike Andrews.

The Mets dropped the World Series after heading to Oakland leading three games to two. It was a sour ending to a great run, but it had been so unexpected that it was hard to say it was heartbreaking. Yet the 13 years that would follow without a pennant would be heartbreaking indeed.

Though Harrelson was injured for much of the four seasons that followed, there was still a core group of the 10 Mets who'd appeared in the 1969 and 1973 World Series. Tug McGraw, Ken Boswell, and Duffy Dyer had been traded after the 1974 season, Cleon Jones was released after an ugly episode in 1975, and Garrett had been dealt during the 1976 season. These Mets had been together through Gil Hodges, Yogi Berra, interim skipper Roy McMillan, Joe Frazier, and now Joe Torre, who'd been elevated from the roster to became manager.

The night before the trade deadline of June 15, 1977, Harrelson, Jerry Grote, Jerry Koosman, and Tom Seaver all went out together. "We were in Atlanta and we went out to dinner, kind of like the Four Musketeers," Harrelson recalled. "Seaver said, 'Come on, we're going out tonight. I will be gone tomorrow.'" Sure enough, a deal went down right before the deadline. The Franchise was dealt to the Cincinnati Reds for pitcher Pat Zachry, infielder Doug Flynn, outfielder Steve Henderson, and outfielder Dan Norman. The Miracle was a distant memory.

"You know you grow close to a guy after playing with him for 10 years," Harrelson told a reporter after the trade. "You're with him 172 days a year—having hundreds of dinners together, exchanging hundreds of bad jokes. We were perfect roommates. Tom did all the reading and I did all the talking."

PHOTO COURTESY OF JACOB KANAREK/METSINTHESEVENTIES.COM

*A contact hitter, Bud Harrelson batted at the top or bottom of the order for almost every start he made as a Met.*

*News* beat man Jack Lang, "Harrelson just sat and twiddled his thumbs in spring training. The Mets weren't going to use him, and Bud was unhappy with a bench role."

So at the end of spring training, the Mets sent Harrelson to the Phillies for cash and Fred Andrews, an infielder whose .174 average had been even lower than Harrelson's anemic .178 in 1977. Andrews didn't even make the lowly Mets club and spent a year playing at triple-A Tidewater. Harrelson, reunited with old friend Tug McGraw, played second base for the first time in his career. He played all three games of Philadelphia's first trip to Shea Stadium. It was far from the packed homecoming Seaver received and though Harrelson had a hit and scored a run, the Mets came away with the win when they roughed up McGraw and won in the ninth. Harrelson had only one more hit the rest of the weekend, including an 0-fer against Koosman. Harrelson wound up hitting .125 at Shea and .214 overall as a Phillie in 1978. He did not appear in the postseason as the Phillies lost to the Los Angeles Dodgers.

In 1979, Harrelson was joined in Philadelphia by Pete Rose. The former combatants now played on the same side of the infield, though Rose was in the lineup far more frequently than Harrelson. They had patched up the ill feelings about their fabled fight years before. Harrelson told Met Lee Mazzilli about his first trip to Cincinnati after the fight on May 27, 1974. "After Pete was booed in New York, the Reds fans had to boo me," Mazzilli recalled Harrelson telling him. "In my first at-bat [actually his third] I hit a home run to left field over Pete Rose's head. Between innings Rose waited for me at shortstop and told me, 'You got to be [bleeping] kidding me' shaking his head."

Harrelson wound up hitting .282 for the Phillies with a .395 on-base percentage. Those were the highest numbers of his career, though the 71 at-bats were his fewest since he debuted in 1965. He became a free agent after the season and had

Harrelson finished out the year on the Seaverless Mets. He played against his old friend when Seaver returned to Shea on August 21. Seaver struck out Harrelson the first two times the old roommates faced each other. Harrelson singled his third time up and scored the only run against Seaver that day on a sacrifice fly by Ed Kranepool, who was also a holdover from '69 and '73. Koosman had the tough assignment of starting against Seaver and—of course—taking the loss.

Infielder Tim Foli, a one-time Mets prospect sent to Montreal in the Rusty Staub deal in 1972, was purchased from San Francisco in the 1977 offseason. The Mets felt Harrelson was done and they handed the job to Foli, and in the words of *Daily* one more reunion, with ex-Mets Matlack and Staub in Texas. Harrelson returned to shortstop and started 77 games there for the Rangers. He hit his final career home run on June 18, giving him seven for his career—all of them coming batting right-handed, his natural side. In his final game, on October 5, 1980, Harrelson started at shortstop and spent the last five innings at second. He committed an error in the ninth inning, but handled the last ball hit to him cleanly. Seattle's Mike Parrott retired him on a grounder back to the mound to give him a .272 average for the year and a .236 career mark. He played in 1,533 games, 1,322 as a Met. That is still second in franchise history to Ed Kranepool; Harrelson also remains second in at-bats (4,390). He retired as one of just three Mets to have reached the four-digit mark in hits (1,029), and while he dropped a few places on the list, it seems ironic to see the diminutive shortstop's name a few hits ahead of Mike Piazza and Darryl Strawberry on the team rolls. Bud's 45 triples, 115 steals, and 573 walks were all tops in Mets history when he retired. He has since been surpassed in those categories, but Harrelson and Rusty Staub will always share the distinction of being the first Mets players inducted into the club's Hall of Fame, in 1986.

On November 2, 1981, Harrelson was named first base coach for the Mets under manager George Bamberger for the 1982 season. In 1983, he broadcast games for the SportsChannel cable network with Tim McCarver and Ralph Kiner. He became a manager of the first time in 1984, when he skippered the Class A Little Falls Mets to a 44–31 record and a New York-Pennsylvania League championship. His other minor league assignment came the following year, 1985, with the Columbia Mets of the Class A South Atlantic League. He managed for 35 games, going 22–13, before being promoted to New York to take over for Bobby Valentine as third-base coach after Valentine left to manage the Texas Rangers.

Under manager Davey Johnson, the Mets were suddenly a formidable club again. Johnson, whose flyout to Cleon Jones as a member of the Orioles had clinched the 1969 world championship at Shea, managed the team to its second world championship. The 1986 team was the most dominant in Mets history. While the Mets had rallied past the Cubs to take the NL East in 1969, the 1986 Mets had the division wrapped up all summer. They won 108 games, winning the division by 21½ games, beat the Houston Astros in a thrilling six-game NLCS, and defeated the Boston Red Sox in a World Series that will forever be known for Bill Buckner's error at first base in the 10th inning of Game Six. Harrelson, coaching at third, had one of the happiest responsibilities in franchise history, waving Ray Knight home with the winning run and running with him across home plate and into the waiting arms of the entire team. "They've got pictures of me racing home with Ray Knight," Harrelson said. "I tell everybody, 'Yeah, actually, I was leading.' I got so excited I was running until I figured out he had to be the one to touch home plate."

Harrelson was the only Met to be in uniform for both the 1969 and 1986 world championships, but his old roommate was in uniform in the other dugout: Tom Seaver, who had been traded to the Red Sox during the season but was injured and unable to pitch (he would never pitch again in the majors, though he have an aborted comeback with the Mets in '87). When it seemed the Red Sox were going to win the Series in the bottom of the 10th, Seaver had caught Harrelson's eye, held his thumb to his ear, and his pinky to his mouth to indicate "I'll call you." When the Mets won Game Seven, Harrelson made the same gesture to his old friend in the Red Sox dugout.

Harrelson remained a coach for the Mets throughout Davey Johnson's tenure. He even had a very brief comeback as a player, appearing for the St. Lucie Legends of the short-lived Senior Professional Baseball Association. Harrelson played just one game and went into the books with a .333 average.

One of his dreams was to manage the Mets and on May 29, 1990, he got that chance when Johnson was fired. Under Harrelson, the Mets won 10 of 17 games before reeling off 11 straight victories to put them three percentage points ahead of the eventual division champion Pirates. The Mets slumped in September, but the club stayed in contention until the last week despite a slew of injuries and new players inserted into a ragtag lineup

But in 1991, with Darryl Strawberry gone to the Dodgers, the remnants of the contending clubs of the 1980s and the replacement parts the Mets had gotten when they'd sent those players away made for a poor mix. Harrelson's managing instincts were sometimes questioned by the media and players. Bench coach Doc Edwards was accused by players of running the team. During a game, Edwards called a pitchout for David Cone to throw while he was facing the Reds pitcher Kip Gross. The June 4, 1991, TV broadcast from Cincinnati captured a finger-pointing exchange between Cone and Harrelson over the call. One player commented, "Buddy has spent the whole season managing like he was everyone's pal, and that doesn't work."

Although the Mets put together a 10-game winning streak to start July of 1991, when the streak was over, the team's season soon followed. The Mets were 2½ games behind the Pirates with a 49–34 record, but New York dropped 50 of its last 78 games. The Mets finished in fifth place, 20½ games out of first place; it was the team's worst finish since 1983, the year before Davey Johnson arrived.

Bud was replaced by as manager by coach Mike Cubbage in the final week of the '91 season. After his firing, Bud said, "If the public wanted a manager with vast experience, I wasn't it. ... If they wanted somebody who would grow with the organization, I think that was me."

At the time of his dismissal, he held the second-best winning percentage among Mets managers (.529), behind Davey Johnson (.588) and even ahead of mentor Gil Hodges (.523).

In the late 1990s, Bud was instrumental in bringing minor league baseball to Long Island. The Long Island Ducks began play in 2000 as part of the independent Atlantic League, with Harrelson as co-owner, first-base coach, and senior vice president for baseball operations. "It might sound crazy, but this is the best thing I've done in baseball," said Harrelson. He managed the Central Islip-based team during their inaugural season and led the Ducks to a tie for first place, at 82–58. In 2004, under manager Don McCormack, the Ducks won the Atlantic League championship.

Harrelson was one of the 43 former Mets on hand for the final game at Shea Stadium in 2008. When they cued up to touch home plate for the last time, Harrelson jumped on it to a big ovation.

Years after it happened, the 1973 playoff fight between Harrelson and Pete Rose became a marketing tool. They appeared together signing photos of the famous incident. "Pete and I got along fine when we played on the Phillies, and I still see him today," Bud said.

After his divorce from his first wife, Harrelson married Kim Battaglia in 1975. He became the father of five: Kimberly, Tim, Alexandra, Kassandra, and Troy Joseph. He moved permanently to Long Island on Opening Day 1969, and never left. "I'm not from New York," Bud said, "but I always say I grew up in New York."

**Sources**

"That Championship Season: 1973." Mets official Yearbook, 1983.

Associated Press. "Just a Melody Lingers for Harrelson." June 18, 1977. Clipping in Harrelson's file, Baseball Hall of Fame, Cooperstown, New York.

Blatt, Howard. *Amazin' Met Memories: Four Decades of Unforgettable Moments* (Atlanta: Albion Press, 2002).

Borgi, Augie. "Bud Impressed Braves, but Winning's the Thing." *New York Daily News.* May 13, 1976.

Centerfield Maz blog, June 5, 2008, *http://centerfieldmaz.blogspot.com/2008/06/bud-harrelson-met-of-day-born-june-6th.html)*

Daley, Arthur. "The Big Switch." *New York Times,* March 24, 1968.

Doyle, Al. "The Game I'll Never Forget: Former Mets shortstop recalls 1969 World Series When New York Upset the Baltimore Orioles." *Baseball Digest,* August 2005.

Elliot, Rich. "Harrelson a Good Luck Charm for Mets." *Connecticut Post,* September 29, 2006. *http://www.connpost.com/richelliott/ci_4415977*

Gergen, Joe. "Managers Have Star-Studded Resumes," *Newsday.com,* July 11, 2002, *http:www.newsday.com/sports/columnists/ny-gerg112780900jul11.column*

Herrmann, Mark. "Buddy: The Mets Long-Haul shortstop," *Newsday.com.*

Lang, Jack, and Peter Simon. *The New York Mets: Twenty-Five Years of Baseball Magic* (New York: Henry Holt, 1986).

Libby, Bill. *Bud Harrelson: Super Shortstop. New York:* (New York: G.P. Putnam's Sons, 1975).

Ryczek, William. *The Amazin' Mets 1962-1969.* (Jefferson, North Carolina: McFarland & Company, Inc. 2008).

Sexton, Joe. "Two Out: Harrelson Joins Cashen," *New York Times,* September 30, 1991.

Young, Dick. *New York Daily News,* February 5, 1970.

## Tripling Your Pleasure

The 1969 Mets were the first team in club history to amass 41 triples, including a still-standing mark of tripling in five straight games, May 16-23. Several later Mets clubs, starting with the 1970 edition, wound up surpassing the Miracle Mets in the overall triples department.

The 41 triples by the Mets were only good for sixth in the National League. That was the club's highest-ranking offensive category—unless you count strikeouts (1,089, third) or sacrifices (82, tied for fourth). In every other offensive category the Mets were below average and often near the bottom of the pile in the 12-team league. New York finished 11th in doubles (184), ninth in home runs (109), 10th in on-base percentage (.311), 11th in slugging (.351), and—not surprisingly—11th in OPS (.662). Their batting average of .242 tied for eighth with the Giants.

So, you ask, they must have scored enough runs somehow? Well, yes, the '69 Mets won 100 games, but the club was just ninth in scoring; the Cardinals were the only non-expansion NL team to cross the plate fewer times than the 632 by the Mets. Of course, when you're only allowing 541 runs (487 earned), your pitching—and just enough timely-hitting magic (a .217 average after the seventh inning in tight games)—can take you a long way.

**1969 NL Team & League Standard Batting**

| Tm | #Bat | BatAge | R/G | G | PA | AB | R | H | 2B | 3B | HR | RBI | SB | CS | BB | SO | BA | OBP | SLG |
|---|---|---|---|---|---|---|---|---|---|---|---|---|---|---|---|---|---|---|---|
| ATL | 33 | 29.1 | 4.27 | 162 | 6098 | 5460 | 691 | 1411 | 195 | 22 | 141 | 640 | 59 | 48 | 485 | 665 | .258 | .321 | .380 |
| CHC | 39 | 29.2 | 4.42 | 163 | 6243 | 5530 | 720 | 1400 | 215 | 40 | 142 | 671 | 30 | 32 | 559 | 928 | .253 | .323 | .384 |
| CIN | 32 | 26.3 | 4.9 | 163 | 6301 | 5634 | 798 | 1558 | 224 | 42 | 171 | 750 | 79 | 56 | 474 | 1042 | .277 | .335 | .422 |
| HOU | 34 | 26.5 | 4.17 | 162 | 6196 | 5348 | 676 | 1284 | 208 | 40 | 104 | 618 | 101 | 58 | 699 | 972 | .240 | .330 | .352 |
| LAD | 35 | 27.4 | 3.96 | 162 | 6166 | 5532 | 641 | 1405 | 185 | 52 | 97 | 584 | 80 | 51 | 484 | 823 | .254 | .315 | .359 |
| MON | 40 | 27.7 | 3.59 | 162 | 6073 | 5419 | 582 | 1300 | 202 | 33 | 125 | 542 | 52 | 52 | 529 | 962 | .240 | .310 | .359 |
| NYM | 32 | 25.9 | 3.9 | 162 | 6102 | 5427 | 632 | 1311 | 184 | 41 | 109 | 598 | 66 | 43 | 527 | 1089 | .242 | .311 | .351 |
| PHI | 34 | 27.2 | 3.98 | 162 | 6080 | 5408 | 645 | 1304 | 227 | 35 | 137 | 593 | 73 | 49 | 549 | 1130 | .241 | .312 | .372 |
| PIT | 33 | 27.2 | 4.48 | 162 | 6235 | 5626 | 725 | 1557 | 220 | 52 | 119 | 651 | 74 | 34 | 454 | 944 | .277 | .334 | .398 |
| SDP | 42 | 26.2 | 2.89 | 162 | 5891 | 5357 | 468 | 1203 | 180 | 42 | 99 | 431 | 45 | 44 | 423 | 1143 | .225 | .285 | .329 |
| SFG | 35 | 27.9 | 4.4 | 162 | 6375 | 5474 | 713 | 1325 | 187 | 28 | 136 | 657 | 71 | 32 | 711 | 1054 | .242 | .334 | .361 |
| STL | 39 | 29.1 | 3.67 | 162 | 6152 | 5536 | 595 | 1403 | 228 | 44 | 90 | 561 | 87 | 49 | 503 | 876 | .253 | .316 | .359 |
| LgAvg | 34 | 27.5 | 4.05 | 162 | 6159 | 5479 | 657 | 1372 | 205 | 39 | 123 | 608 | 68 | 46 | 533 | 969 | .250 | .319 | .369 |
| | 407 | 27.5 | 4.05 | 1946 | 73912 | 65751 | 7886 | 16461 | 2455 | 471 | 1470 | 7296 | 817 | 548 | 6397 | 11628 | .250 | .319 | .369 |

Statistics courtesy of Baseball-Reference.com

# Bob Heise

by Bill Nowlin

| Season | Age | G | AB | R | H | 2B | 3B | HR | RBI | BB | SO | SB | CS | BA | OBP | SLG |
|---|---|---|---|---|---|---|---|---|---|---|---|---|---|---|---|---|
| 1969 Mets | 22 | 4 | 10 | 1 | 3 | 1 | 0 | 0 | 0 | 3 | 2 | 0 | 0 | .300 | .462 | .400 |
| Career 11 Years | – | 499 | 1144 | 104 | 283 | 43 | 3 | 1 | 86 | 47 | 77 | 3 | 7 | .247 | .280 | .293 |

Robert Lowell Heise was born in San Antonio, but doesn't remember a thing about the place. His father, William Heise, was an officer in the military and was moved around quite often. Bob remembers more of Lompoc and Vacaville, in California. His father had a degree in sociology and criminology and, after his military career, served in corrections work, ending up at the California Medical Facility in Vacaville. Bob's mother stayed at home to look after Bob, his younger brother Ben, and their sister. After Bob graduated from high school, she got her master's degree and became a schoolteacher. Ben Heise played in the Cleveland Indians organization, making it as high as Triple A; his team won a gold medal in the Pan Am Games. Ben was an infielder, too, but he wasn't able to climb the final rung of the ladder.

Baseball appealed to Bob early on. William Heise played fast-pitch softball and had played football in college. It was in Lompoc that Bob first remembers becoming interested in baseball at the age of five. "I knew that's what I wanted to do. It was imbedded with me. And I just took it very serious. I wanted to play ball, all my life."

His dad was supportive, but the drive came from within: "He played catch with me and encouraged me to, but most of the encouragement came that I wanted to do it on my own. It was my love. That's what I wanted to do." When the family moved to Vacaville, Bob was nine and Little League was starting up, fielding four teams. Bob, batting and throwing right-handed, was a natural infielder. After Little League, it was American Legion, Babe Ruth, and high school ball. At Vacaville High, he helped spark the Bulldogs to the 1964 Golden Empire League championship. Bob's American Legion Post 165 team, coached by his father, won the league championship in 1965. "Bob was a very intense ballplayer, but that was one of the things that was so great about him," remarked Vacaville High's athletic director Tom Zunino. Heise graduated from high school in 1965.

Following Bobby Heise's development was scout Roy Partee, who signed him for the Mets at age 18 in February 1966. In the winter of 1965, Heise had played in the Peninsula League just for fun—it wasn't semipro—and Bud Harrelson of the Mets, like Heise, an infielder from California, was at one of the games, keeping an eye out on behalf of Partee. "You would play a doubleheader on Saturday and a single game on Sunday. I was playing second base, and Buddy Harrelson, I think, told Roy Partee, 'This kid has a little talent.'" Partee offered Heise a contract. There was a bonus, but it was, in Heise's words, "Very little. Very little. I'll leave it at that."

Heise was assigned to Jacksonville, Florida, for extended spring training in 1966 and then was sent by the Mets to Greenville, South Carolina. With the Single-A Greenville team in the Western Carolinas League, Heise played in 122 games, batting .283 with six homers, 50 RBIs, and 90 runs scored. He was named to the league's all-star team. In 1967, he played in Durham, another single-A team in the Carolina League. He hit for a higher average, .298, but with just one home run and 37 RBIs. In 1967, Heise joined the Mets after a stretch in the United States Marine Reserve, getting into his first game on September 12 as the starting second baseman against the Atlanta Braves. Heise was 1-for-4 that day, singling with two outs in the ninth. He was caught stealing to end the inning, and the Braves scored twice in the bottom of the ninth to win the game, 4–3. By season's end, Heise played in 16 games and hit for a .323 average. It was his first of 11 major league seasons.

Heise saw only limited action each of the next two years, as a September call-up both in 1968 and 1969. In 1968, he was a regular for Jacksonville in the International League, as he was in 1969 for Tidewater. Both seasons were solid, if not spectacular. He played in four games and batted .300 in 10 at-bats (plus three walks) for the historic 1969 Mets. He started all three games at shortstop during a weekend series in Philadelphia after the Mets had clinched the NL East. All three games were shutouts—part of a club-record 42 consecutive scoreless innings by Mets pitching. Heise was not on the postseason roster.

In 1970, Heise made the big league club out of spring training—but it was for the San Francisco Giants. The Mets had traded him and Jim Gosger to the Giants for Ray Sadecki and Dave Marshall on December 12, 1969. With San Francisco, Heise more or less split his time between backup roles at shortstop and second base, getting into 67 games, but batting only .234. Before his time in the majors was up, Heise accumulated 1,144 at-bats but he hit his one and only major league home run on June 30, 1970, off Danny Combs. The Giants were hosting the San Diego Padres at Candlestick Park.

Does Heise remember it? "Yeah! They made a [phonograph] record of it, and I played it for my grandson just recently. He found it in a drawer. So we played it for him." It's not the sort of thing one forgets. He had some good people around him in the lineup that day: Bobby Bonds led off, Heise batted second, Willie Mays was in the three hole, and Willie McCovey hit cleanup. In the third inning, Coombs made a mistake and Heise hit one out. The Padres won the game nevertheless, 3–2.

Heise had flashes of real success. He was traded to the Brewers on the first day of June in 1971 and during one stretch of 10 games for Milwaukee, there were three separate games in which Heise had 3-for-4 days. They were the exceptions, though. Heise batted .234 in 1970, and didn't have a hit in his first 11 at-bats for San Francisco in 1971 prior to the trade to Milwaukee. He hit .254 for the Brewers that year, improving to .266 in 1972, when he had a career-high 271 at-bats. In 1973, he hit just .204 and was traded to the Cardinals for Tom Murphy in December. In mid-1974, St. Louis traded him to the Angels on July 31 for a player to be named later. After the season was over, the Cardinals got Doug Howard.

"I loved the Angels," Heise says now. "They gave me the opportunity to play. I was having a great year with Tulsa, hitting .340 or something like that, playing for Kenny Boyer." Heise improved while playing more regularly for California, hitting .267 in the second half of the 1974 season.

In one of the first trades after the season ended, Boston sent Tommy Harper to the Angels in December 1974 and Heise became a member of the Red Sox, just in time to be on the pennant-winning 1975 Red Sox team. Heise batted just .214, but he knocked in 21 runs and made several key contributions. His best day was during a July 6 doubleheader in Cleveland, where he went 4-for-7 with five RBIs. He pretty much won the first game, driving in three runs in a 5–3 Red Sox win. After a three-hit game in an 11–8 win over Texas on July 11, his average stood at .262, but he had just one hit over the next month and dipped down to .194 in late August. He was able to pull it up to .214 by the final day of the season, after the Red Sox had clinched the AL East title.

Come the playoffs and the World Series, though, all the regular infielders were healthy—Carl Yastrzemski, Denny Doyle, Rick Burleson, and Rico Petrocelli. "I was there, and my whole family was there. All the regulars played. The regulars played and hit .300. You got to realize the position

Photo courtesy of Dwayne Labakas Collection

*Bob Heise*

that you're in, and what your job is. And you don't bitch about it. I did not bitch about it. The Red Sox treated me great. Tom Yawkey treated me really well. I really didn't expect to be treated that well. I had always been treated like Frank Lane would treat you in Milwaukee: 'If you're not under contract...or I'll bury your ass in the minor leagues.' That's how I got treated in my time."

Heise was with Boston for the full 1976 season, but he saw much more limited action: just 56 at-bats (though he hit .268). After the season, the Sox sold Heise to the Kansas City Royals in early December. He put in a full year playing under Whitey Herzog with the Royals, typically a late-inning sub in 54 games and accumulating only 62 at-bats. Kansas City made it into the playoffs, losing in five games to the New York Yankees. Once again, Bob hugged the bench as the regulars saw all the action. Again, he doesn't voice dissent. "I think the baseball person I had the most respect for of this whole game while I was playing, was Whitey Herzog... They let me go, then I knew it was over. Maybe I'd been losing a step here, a step there. If it was Whitey Herzog who let me go, I knew it was over. I didn't bitch about it and complain. So I guess that was it."

Bob Heise took retirement philosophically. "I sort of did. I wanted to raise my kids. I wanted to be at home. And that's what I did. I became a police officer, and I did that for 26 years until a couple of years ago. I retired, and I got cancer. I had cancer for about two and one-half years and right now I've beat the cancer. At my last checkup, I was cancer-free." Heise's work in corrections saw him work at Vacaville himself, as well as San Quentin and a couple of other facilities. He also worked fighting fires for 16 years.

Heise has two children and two stepkids. One son was, in Heise's words, "very good in baseball, but he did not have the drive I had." He served in the Army instead, and graduated from police academy, going on to get a college degree. Heise himself gets offers to join some of the card and memorabilia shows, but he hasn't taken up the offers, recognizing that there, too, he'd be playing the role of a utilityman. He's content to stay home in his small two-stoplight town and play golf several times each week.

Did he feel happy when the Red Sox finally won it all in 2004? "I did. I did, for one person—Tom Yawkey. He treated everybody really great. He ripped up my contract twice in that '75 [season]. Before I came over for Tommy Harper, I kind of wrote a letter and said that I, you know, I signed this for California and the Angels. Going to Boston will cost a little more. They ripped it up. One time after I drove in some big important RBIs and we were going to get into the playoffs, he ripped [it] up again. And then after that, he gave me another raise. We're talking about little [amounts], but back in those times, they were big," he says, laughing.

Tom Yawkey was "one of the best owners in baseball, ever," Heise reflects. So wherever he's at, you know, you know, in his grave or whatever, that was really great to see Boston win it.

"You know, I have an American League championship ring, and it says Boston Red Sox on it. And it's a thing that I'll get to pass down to my son, Bobby Jr. And now he just had a son, that's Robert Lowell Heise III, and he'll pass it down to his kid."

**Sources**

Personal interview, August 23, 2005
*www.retrosheet.org*
*www.thebaseballcube.com*
*The Reporter*, Vacaville CA

## One-Run Wonders

The New York Mets went 41–23 in one-run games in 1969. That number didn't just lead the major leagues that year, it tied for the most all-time since the two league format was adopted in 1901. The 1940 Cincinnati Reds, another surprise 100-game winner that won the World Series, were the first team to win 41 times by a single run.

The team vanquished by the Mets in the '69 World Series, the Baltimore Orioles, figured if you can't beat 'em, join 'em. The 1970 Orioles won 40 one-run games and took the World Series. The O's tied their American League record in 1974, winning their fifth division title in six years.

The 1978 San Francisco Giants established the current mark by winning 42 times by one-run, but the Giants are the only team on this list not to reach the postseason. The Giants finished third with 89 wins overall.

—Mark Simon

**Most One-Run Wins**

| Team | Wins |
|---|---|
| 1978 Giants | 42 |
| 1969 Mets | 41* |
| 1940 Reds | 41* |
| 1974 Orioles | 40 |
| 1970 Orioles | 40* |

*Denotes won World Series.

# Jesse Hudson

by William H. Johnson

| Season | Age | W | L | Pct | G | GS | SV | IP | H | BB | SO | WHIP | ERA |
|---|---|---|---|---|---|---|---|---|---|---|---|---|---|
| 1969 Mets | 20 | 0 | 0 | – | 1 | 0 | 0 | 2 | 2 | 2 | 3 | 2.000 | 4.50 |
| Career 1 Season | – | 0 | 0 | – | 1 | 0 | 0 | 2 | 2 | 2 | 3 | 2.000 | 4.50 |

Jesse James Hudson was a southpaw with an outlaw's name and a mix of luck. He had the good fortune to not only play professional baseball, but to be the youngest member of the 1969 Miracle Mets. Less than two months past his 21st birthday, he debuted for the Mets a week before they wrapped up their unlikely division title—and he never pitched again in the major leagues.

He was born on July 22, 1948, in Mansfield, Louisiana. The son of a farmer, he attended DeSoto High School and teamed with future American League MVP Vida Blue to form a left-handed pitching tandem unequaled in the region. In the fall, on the football field, Hudson also served as quarterback Blue's favorite receiver, catching 17 touchdown passes in their senior year of 1966. Hudson told Roy Blount, in a July 12, 1971 article for *Sports Illustrated*, that Blue didn't want to carry the ball, and didn't want to tackle, but he certainly could throw the ball.

Hudson graduated from DeSoto in the spring of 1967, and he was drafted by the Mets in the 11th round of the 1967 amateur draft. (Blue was taken in the second round by the Kansas City A's.) At 6-foot-2 and 165 pounds, Hudson was well beyond "wiry" and was more accurately termed "skinny." He pitched the remainder of 1967 for the Marion Mets of the rookie Appalachian League, going 7–1 with a 2.07 ERA. He opened 1968 with the Mankato Mets of the low A Northern League. After posting a 9–4 record with a 1.83 ERA, he was called up to the high A California League, joining Visalia for the rest of the season.

That time in central California proved to be, statistically, Hudson's least successful stretch as a professional pitcher. He won only two games (against nine losses), and recorded a 4.71 ERA. That was the only stint—with the exception of his single appearance for New York—in which his ERA with any team was higher than 4.00. He was left unprotected in the 1968 Rule V draft, and was selected by the Cincinnati Reds in the third round. Eventually, however, he was returned to the Mets organization.

Back with the club that originally drafted him, Hudson was promoted to Pompano Beach (Florida State League) to begin 1969. Appearing in seven games, starting one, he notched three wins in three decisions over 26 innings, and posted a microscopic and year-appropriate 0.69 ERA. Success brought yet another move, as he was told to pack his bags and report to the Memphis Blues of the Class AA Texas League.

Hudson appeared in 20 games with the Blues, even tying the Memphis single-game record with 13 strikeouts. After he helped pitch the Blues to the Texas League championship, his 1.38 ERA (to go with a 3–2 record) earned him a cup of coffee in New York. He would need to make that cup last.

Wearing uniform number 38, the September call-up sat in the bullpen with the Mets in the midst of one of the great final pushes in the game's history. Even these Mets were bound to cool off and when they lost the first game of a doubleheader with Pittsburgh on September 19, the Mets were on their first slight downturn in a month. They had just ended a 10-game winning streak before coming home and dropping the opener against the Pirates. When starter Jim McAndrew was hit hard in the second game that night, and reliever Ron Taylor's spot came up with two men on in the seventh—forcing manager Gil Hodges to send up pinch hitter Bob Heise—that's when Hudson's spot was punched in the *Baseball Enyclopedia*, published that year by Macmillan for the first time.

Hudson took over for Taylor with Pittsburgh leading after seven innings, 7–0. The first batter, Pirates catcher Jerry May, grounded back to Hudson. Shortstop Freddie Patek walked, but Hudson took care of the lead runner by fielding pitcher Luke Walker's bunt and forcing Patek at second.

Matty Alou, playing center field that day, broke up the party with a single to right, moving Walker to second. Second baseman Dave Cash followed with a double to left field, driving in Walker and moving Alou to third. In what was Hudson's career highlight, he then struck out future Hall of Fame slugger Willie Stargell to end the rally.

The Mets did not score in the bottom of the eighth, and Hudson opened the ninth inning by striking out fellow Louisianan John Jeter. Al Oliver then flied out to left. Richie Hebner walked, but Hudson fanned May looking to end the inning. Without his knowing it, that also ended Hudson's career in the major leagues.

The Mets still owned a 91–60 record at the end of the day, good for a four-game lead in the division. They even trimmed a game off their magic number—from eight to seven—because the Cubs had split their doubleheader that day with St. Louis.

And Jesse Hudson had had his 15 minutes of fame. His line on the day, and for his major league career: two innings, two hits, one earned run, three strikeouts, and two walks. Hudson never batted, and didn't factor in the decision, but he did earn his tiny share of immortality by appearing in the majors. Due to his late call-up, Hudson was ineligible for postseason play, but even had he been able to be on the October roster, the Mets won the World Series that fall with a small cadre of extraordinary pitchers, and did not often need to use their available depth.

Spring training in 1970 was difficult. One week after a particularly bad outing in Florida, in which he gave up nine runs in only three innings to the Phillies, he was assigned to the minor league camp in St. Petersburg. From there he was eventually slotted to the triple-A Tidewater Tides in Norfolk, Virginia. That season he won six games in the International League, but he lost seven despite keeping his ERA at 2.86. In late June, after Nolan Ryan was activated for Army Reserve duty, the Mets reportedly considered bringing up Hudson to fill the gap, but opted instead for right-hander Danny Frisella.

The Mets did recall Hudson for the final week of September 1970, and added him to the 40-man roster in the offseason, but he was generally regarded as a midgrade reliever at best, with little chance of cracking the rotation. Hudson did not pitch during at all in his second big league visit, and there were unsubstantiated whispers of arm trouble after the season ended.

In February 1971, *The Sporting News* reported that the pitcher had agreed to terms with the Mets for the '71 campaign, but that spring Hudson was one of the first pitchers cut and returned to minor league camp. Even more abruptly than it began, his professional baseball career ended and he returned to Louisiana. That same year, his old high school buddy Vida Blue burst onto to the major league scene, winning both the American League MVP and the Cy Young Award with a 24–8 record and a 1.82 ERA for the Oakland A's.

As of 2008, Jesse and his wife, Lillie, still lived in Louisiana, in a modest house in the village of South Mansfield, across the road from the local water treatment facility.

**Sources**


Baseball Reference. Available online *http://www.baseball-reference.com/h/hudsoje01.shtml*

Roy Blount, "Humming a Rhapsody in Blue." *Sports Illustrated*, July 12, 1971. Available online *http://vault.sportsillustrated.cnn.com/vault/article/magazine/MAG1085062/index.htm*

Interview with Jesse Hudson, April 23, 2008, by William H. Johnson

SABR Minor League Database. Available online *http://minors.sabrwebs.com/cgi-bin/player.php?milbID=hudson001jes*

Various editions of *The Sporting News*; St Louis, Missouri (1968–1971)

# Al Jackson

by Greg W. Prince

| Season | Age | W | L | Pct | G | GS | SV | IP | H | BB | SO | WHIP | ERA |
|---|---|---|---|---|---|---|---|---|---|---|---|---|---|
| 1969 Mets | 33 | 0 | 0 | – | 9 | 0 | 0 | 11 | 18 | 4 | 10 | 2.000 | 10.64 |
| Career 10 Years | – | 67 | 99 | .404 | 302 | 184 | 10 | 1389.3 | 1449 | 407 | 738 | 1.336 | 3.98 |

In George Vecsey's modestly titled *Joy In Mudville: Being a Complete Account of the Unparalleled History of the New York Mets from Their Most Perturbed Beginnings to Their Amazing Rise to Glory And Renown,* a moment illustrating the time-flies transformation of the Mets franchise from bottom feeders to top dogs in eight short seasons is captured as poignantly as it transpired.

The episode occurred in the jubilant Mets clubhouse on September 24, 1969 in the minutes after the Miracle Mets clinched their first *positive* title of any kind, the National League Eastern Division championship. Into the champagne-soaked celebratory scrum walked Original Met Hot Rod Kanehl. Kanehl was an icon of the 1962 Mets, a scrappy utility-playing avatar of those most perturbed beginnings—he legendarily accepted manager Casey Stengel's offer of $50 to get himself hit by a pitch with the bases loaded—and, having involuntarily retired from the majors in 1964, ventured into the clubhouse as no more than a suitably dazzled and slightly grizzled spectator of the team's amazing rise to glory.

Kanehl, 35, visiting the party alongside fellow long-gone Original Met Craig Anderson, then 31, sought out center fielder Tommie Agee, 27, and introduced himself. After Hot Rod moved on, Agee, according to Vecsey, turned to a friend and asked, "Who is that?"

Hot Rod Kanehl was a stranger in a strange land that Wednesday night, underscoring the incongruity of an Original Met wandering among the Miracle Mets. Vecsey's anecdote showed how far the Mets had traveled to shed their family resemblances and how little they were tangibly related to the foibles and foundering of their very first forebears, even if the Original Mets presaged the Miracle Mets by a mere seven years.

All of which makes the presence of a vintage April 1962 New York Met among those who would become October 1969 world champion New York Mets—not as a well-wisher but as a peer—somewhat startling. If you scour the complete roster of those '69 Mets, one name jumps out as amazin'ly anachronistic: Al Jackson.

It's not that Jackson was chronologically, even for the era, out of code. The diminutive southpaw reliever—forever "Little Al Jackson" to Mets announcer Bob Murphy—was 33 during the 1969 baseball season. Hoyt Wilhelm, albeit with the aid of a knuckleball, helped pitch the Atlanta Braves toward the same inaugural National League Championship Series as the Mets at age 47. Bob Gibson was born not seven weeks earlier than Jackson and won 20 games for the fourth-place St. Louis Cardinals. Even in an era when management was hesitant to trust the skills of anyone over 30, Jackson's left arm was not hopelessly dated. But it and he were something out of another age for the 1969 Mets. He was, within the context of the youth and emerging success of that club, in the right place at the wrong time.

It was not an unfamiliar circumstance for Jackson, a man with an uncanny knack for being on teams that reached October around him but never with him square in the middle of the hoopla. He appeared as a Pittsburgh Pirate in 1959 and 1961, but managed to miss 1960, the year of Bill Mazeroski's World Series heroics. He was in Cincinnati as the gears of the Big Red Machine were tightened for the dynasty that lay ahead but was released one week into Cincy's 1970 pennant romp. He was a part of the 1967 world champion Cardinals, going 9–4 starting and relieving, but of the 10 pitchers—including three lefties—skipper Red Schoendienst utilized in defeat of the Boston Red Sox in seven games, none of them was named Al Jackson.

So it was that the 1969 Mets, remembered for pitchers like Tom Seaver, Jerry Koosman, Nolan Ryan, and Tug McGraw, rendered Al Jackson's participation in baseball's miracle of miracles into a footnote. The Mets, needing to clear roster space (Ryan was coming off the disabled list as second baseman Ken Boswell returned from military reserve duty), sold Jackson to the Reds on June 13. The deal severed the last active link the Mets would ever have to their most humble beginnings. (Though Ed Kranepool was a '69 Met—and would stay with the team for another decade—he was a late arriver to the '62 team, receiving a few token at-bats at the Polo Grounds after being signed out of high school earlier in the year.)

Whatever sentimentality might have lingered over the transaction was ultimately obscured by Jackson's undistinguished 1969 Mets line: no decisions; 13 earned runs allowed over 11 innings; the team's record a most unmiraculous 1–8 when Al Jackson took the mound.

Jackson's final outing as a 1969 Met, on May 22, was straight out of 1962: with the Braves up 10–0, he replaced Cal Koonce to pitch the bottom of the seventh at Atlanta-Fulton County Stadium. With a runner on first when he entered, Jackson surrendered a single, a walk, a sacrifice fly, a fielder's choice, an RBI single, and a two-run double. When he gave way to Ron Taylor, the Mets trailed 14–0. The loss lowered the Mets' record to 18–19, noteworthy in Mets lore because it dropped the Mets below .500 one night after the players claimed to disbelieving reporters that they didn't consider a break-even mark any kind of milestone, that they had loftier goals in their immediate sights.

PHOTO COURTESY OF DWAYNE LABAKAS COLLECTION

*Al Jackson*

The Mets would sag to 18–23 before forever burying the ghosts of 1962 by reeling off 11 consecutive wins. But by then, Al Jackson—1969 ERA of 10.64—was all but bound for Ohio, relegated to the role of observer of a miracle as much as Kanehl and Anderson and any Original Met. (His wallet missed the action as well; by completing '69 as third-place Red in the NL West, Jackson earned an also-ran World Series share of $203.97, while a full winner's share with the Mets was worth $18,338.18.)

The thickest of ironies here is Al Jackson, one of the least consequential Mets of 1969, was perhaps the 1962 Met who soared the highest above his team's sorry morass. Granted, no individual on a team that accumulated 120 losses could be said to stand completely apart from the muck of historic futility, but Jackson, despite his surroundings, showed honest promise and progress to the fans who populated the Polo Grounds at its end and Shea Stadium at its beginnings.

A native of Waco, Texas, born on Christmas Day 1935 as the lucky 13th of 13 children, Alvin Neill Jackson attended Wiley College in Marshall, Texas prior to signing with Pittsburgh in 1955. He led the Western League in 1958 with a 2.07 ERA while winning 18 and logging 230 innings in Lincoln, Nebraska, and followed that with a 15–4 season in Columbus that ended with Jackson in the big leagues for the first time. Yet the Bucs bypassed him in their championship year of '60 and (after only three appearances in '61) exposed him to the National League expansion draft. Jackson was chosen by the Mets as one of its $75,000 choices and started the third game ever in the franchise's existence.

It was a loss.

Al Jackson was not alone among Mets pitchers in defeat. The 1962 Mets lost their first nine games, but Jackson would do what he could to turn things around, no matter how much like spitting into the ocean those efforts amounted to. He notched the club's first shutout, in the opener of a doubleheader against Philadelphia on April 29, thereby forging the Mets' first-ever winning streak (it pushed them to 3–12). His second shutout, over fellow NL newcomers the Houston Colt 45s, represented the Mets' first-ever one-hitter, the only Colt safety coming off the bat of Joey Amalfitano in the first (he came within five outs of a no-no at Pittsburgh's Forbes Field on July 21, 1965, seeing it broken up by Willie Stargell in the eighth and settling for a two-hit, 1–0 win). On those 40–120 freshman Mets, Al Jackson threw a team-leading four shutouts—their only four shutouts in '62. All of them, strangely enough, were pitched in the first games of doubleheaders. It was enough to earn him recognition on the Topps 1962 All-Rookie team.

Nevertheless, the most famous game those '62 Mets played, also a twin bill opener, may tell Al Jackson's story of being a bit of a bystander to history. It was Sunday, June 17, 1962, Father's Day against the Cubs at the Polo Grounds. Jackson started and fell behind 4–0 immediately in a top of the first, capped by Lou Brock's two-run homer into the distant center-field bleachers and set up when first baseman Marv Throneberry didn't execute a rundown. His teammates, in a rare display of timely support for one of its pitchers, came to his rescue... in their unique way.

With one run in and two men on, Throneberry hit what everybody at the Polo Grounds assumed was a triple. Except "Marvelous Marv" neglected to touch various combinations of first and second bases. Though the two runners scored, Throneberry was ruled out on appeal. Jimmy Breslin in *Can't Anybody Here Play This Game?* chiseled what happened next into Mets mythology, reporting that after Charlie Neal homered, Stengel bolted from the dugout to point to each base to make sure every bag was touched.

Little remarked upon in that comedy of errors that exemplified the 1962 Mets was that Al Jackson acquitted himself pretty well the rest of the day, pitching into the ninth and giving up only an Ernie Banks home run in the third and a Brock RBI double in the eighth and allowing the Mets a chance to come back on the Cubs. (Naturally for Jackson and those beleaguered Mets, Throneberry struck out as the potential winning run with two out in the bottom of the ninth; they lost the nightcap by a run as well.)

With outings like those too often the norm and a final record that reflected that reality at 8–20 (not even the most losses among Mets starters; Roger Craig suffered 24 Ls), it is little wonder Jackson uttered and Breslin inimitably scribbled the southpaw's assessment of the 1962 Mets after a particularly frustrating defeat: "Everybody here crazy."

Seriously speaking, Jackson shone as the best of a fey lot on those first Mets staffs. Nobody struck out more hitters in the Mets' first four grisly campaigns; nobody posted more victories in a single season than the 13 he put up in '63 for a 51–111 outfit; he earned Opening Day starts in '64 and '65; and the 10 shutouts he spun between 1962 and 1965 are still good for sixth all-time (tied with Ron Darling) on the all-time Mets career list. Al Jackson trails only Seaver, Koosman, Jon Matlack, Dwight Gooden, and David Cone in that category.

It's little wonder that as the Mets moved into Shea Stadium in 1964, Little Al Jackson stood tallest on a roster that was otherwise easily overlooked. *The Sporting News* hailed him as the likeliest candidate to become "Shea Stadium's first 20-game winner," a proposition that seemed that much more realistic on April 19 when Jackson's 6–0 whitewashing of the Pirates went down as the club's first win in their new home. "I thought it was heaven," Jackson said of Shea Stadium in *Newsday* in 2008, particularly in comparison to the doomed Polo Grounds.

It was the left-hander's final start of 1964, however, that remains his signature Mets moment. With the Cardinals trying to take advantage of the Phillies' epic collapse, St. Louis saw the NL flag as theirs for the taking by dint of the schedule maker's kindness: the Redbirds' final three games came at home against the 51–108 Mets...and they had ace Bob Gibson going against the perennial cellar dwellers.

But the Mets had Al Jackson going against the first-place Cardinals and on Friday, October 2, Jackson got the best of Gibson, beating the future Hall of Famer, 1–0 when he scattered five hits and clinched the best-ever win total by the franchise to date. One might also argue that beating a team like St. Louis in such a situation might have been the franchise's best-ever win to date, but that point is moot because the next day they beat the Cardinals again. The Cards, with Gibson coming out of the bullpen on one day's rest, righted the ship on Sunday by coming from behind to finally defeat the Mets and win their first pennant since 1946.

In 2008, Jackson recalled for *Newsday* the Cardinals' reception for him as he walked through their clubhouse on that last Friday night to appear on Harry Caray's postgame show. "Oh, did they call me a bunch of names. They said, 'You guys are 59 games out of first place and you've got to pitch a game like this?' Man, did they rip me."

The 10th-place Mets actually trailed the first place Cardinals by only 41 games entering play on October 2, but the stakes were too high for statistical niceties in St. Louis.

That was as close as Al Jackson ever came to a pennant race as a New York Met. One year and one day after making the Cardinals sweat, Jackson completed his first term in Flushing. Though the prescient might have seen the seeds of a miraculous future—the home team lineup on October 3, 1965 included 1969 mainstays Ron Swoboda, Bud Harrelson, and Ed Kranepool—to Jackson, it had to look like the same old same old. He lost the first game of a season-ending doubleheader to the Phillies, 3–1, leaving his bottom line for '65 at 8–20...identical to the 8–20 of '62. His respective ERAs (4.40 in '62, 4.34 in '65) were eerily similar, too, while the team's record of 50–112 was their worst since their first. Jackson remains the only Met to ever lose 20 games in a season more than once, but he was certainly not alone in piling up the L's; in both '62 and '65 Jackson wasn't even the team leader in that category (Roger Craig and Jack Fisher, respectively, each lost 24).

In the 1965 offseason, Jackson was granted a professional reprieve and traded with Charley Smith to the Cardinals for former NL MVP Ken Boyer. Come 1967, Jackson was part of team that glided to a National League championship but, despite going 9-4 as a spot starter, he wasn't considered enough of an essential ingredient by the Cards to be used in the World Series or retained for their repeat run in '68. *The Sporting News* lumped him in among the "dead wood" St. Louis cleared away after winning the fall classic without him.

Jackson returned to the Mets as payment for reliever Jack Lamabe the day after the '67 Series ended. Though fellow Original Met Gil Hodges was back in New York to manage the 1968 club, the Polo Grounds reunion in Queens didn't result in a renaissance for Jackson, who pitched only 25 times (nine starts) for his old teammate and new skipper. His appearance in the Opening Day slugfest against the brand-new Montreal Expos on April 8, 1969, wherein he surrendered an immediate home run to Rusty Staub and allowed two more baserunners who would score, did not augur well for Jackson's longevity in his encore Mets tenure.

A little more than two weeks after Jackson's June sale to the Reds, Tom Seaver (en route to becoming Shea Stadium's first 20-game winner) won the 44th game of his young career and, in doing so, broke Little Al's franchise mark for most wins. Their Mets circumstances couldn't have been more different. After beating Pittsburgh on June 29, Seaver's lifetime mark was 44–28 and his club was in second place, seven games over .500. Al Jackson's body of yeoman work as a New York Met netted him no better than a record of 43–80, providing the bulk of his career 67–99 won-loss ledger—a very respectable 24–19 when not a Met.

When he was a Met between 1962 and 1965, Al Jackson's team's winning percentage was .300. Even Tom Seaver would have had a tough time being terrific with the odds stacked so solidly against him. Seaver eventually took away Jackson's club loss record as well, though it took him until 1974. (Jerry Koosman now holds the record for Mets losses with 137.)

Since retiring as a player, Jackson served as pitching coach with the Red Sox (1977–79) and Orioles (1989–91) but otherwise has instructed Mets pitchers on an ongoing basis these past few decades. Jackson tried his hand at managing with Kingsport in 1981 (21–49), but he served the organization best by working exclusively with pitchers.

Ron Darling credited Jackson, then pitching coach under Davey Johnson at triple-A Tidewater, with staying on him relentlessly in 1982 and designing special workouts to prepare the 22-year-old pitcher to make the final step to the major leagues. "I was young and single, living on the beach in Norfolk, Virginia. I was content," Darling wrote in *The Complete Game*. "But Al kept on me. He'd say, 'What do you have to be content about? You haven't done anything. You haven't struggled.'"

Darling said of Jackson's pitching philosophy, "According to Al, starting the game is a process, but once the game begins there's no easing into it. It's full-on, right from the first pitch."

Jackson was the bullpen coach for the 1999 Wild Card and 2000 National League champion Mets under Bobby Valentine. Those squads' left-handed ace, Al Leiter, credited Jackson for lifting his game, an echo, perhaps, of the advice Jackson told *Newsday* he gave young Seaver and Koosman in 1968 and '69 when he was a Mets' elder statesman and they were the league's unmatched young guns. Jackson, part of the final ceremonies at Shea Stadium in 2008 and the '69 celebration in '09 at Citi Field, remains employed by the Mets as a pitching consultant (a "lifer," he told *Newsday*) and his wisdom has literally reached far and wide. In 2007, he was part of a delegation of Major League Baseball officials who traveled to West Africa to teach and promote America's National Pastime and, presumably, answer lingering questions regarding the day Marvelous Marv Throneberry didn't touch second.

Or first.

**Sources**

Breslin, Jimmy. *Can't Anybody Here Play This Game?* (New York: Viking, 1963).

Darling, Ron with Paisner, Daniel. *The Complete Game: Reflections on Baseball, Pitching, and Life on the Mound* (New York: Alfred E. Knopf, 2009).

Hermann, Mark. "Al Jackson Knows How Bad the Mets Can Be." *Newsday*, June 29, 2008.

Vecsey, George. *Joy In Mudville: Being a Complete Account of the Unparalleled History of the New York Mets from Their Most Perturbed Beginnings to Their Amazing Rise to Glory And Renown* (New York: The McCall Publishing Company, 1970).

## Expanding Horizons

The Mets improved by 27 games in the standings between 1968 and 1969, winning 24 games in '69 against teams that didn't exist in '68. The Montreal Expos and San Diego Padres joined the National League and the Mets took advantage like a senior remembering his own hazing and eager to punish the incoming freshmen. The 'spos and Pods lost 110 games each—not enough to threaten the expansion record of 120 set by the 1962 Mets, but a nice round number.

The Expos beat the Mets to open the '69 season, but New York won 13 of the remaining 17 games with Montreal. A doubleheader sweep on September 10 against the Expos put the Mets in first place for the first time. Ever.

The Cubs, meanwhile, were just 10–8 against Montreal, including a 2–2 mark in September. The Cubs were playing the Expos the day the Mets clinched the division.

Both the Mets and Cubs dutifully beat up on San Diego, each going 11–1. The Padres won their first game ever against the Mets, but New York won every remaining game—including a perfect mark in San Diego and a 5–1 mark at Shea despite averaging just 2.2 runs per game at home against the Padres.

An expansion draft on October 14, 1968 cost the Mets six players, only one of which had an immediate impact: reliever Dick Selma, who wound up with the '69 Cubs in the bullpen following a trade with San Diego. Outfielder Jerry Morales, who would be an All-Star in 1977 and a Met in 1980, was also picked by the Pads in the expansion draft and traded to the Cubs—though that Windy City deal wasn't until 1973. The most important personnel move involving the Mets and an expansion club was the June 15 deadline deal with the Expos that delivered slugger Donn Clendenon in exchange for Kevin Collins, Steve Renko, Bill Carden, and Dave Colon.

A list of the Mets taken in the expansion draft:

| Pick/Pos. | Player | New Team |
|---|---|---|
| 5. Pitcher | Dick Selma | Padres |
| 16. Outfielder | Jerry Morales | Padres |
| 26. Outfielder | Larry Stahl | Padres |
| 40. Pitcher | Don Shaw | Expos |
| 49. Pitcher | Ernie McAnally | Expos |
| 60. Pitcher | John Glass | Expos |

# Bob Johnson

by Bruce Markusen

| Season | Age | W | L | Pct | G | GS | SV | IP | H | BB | SO | WHIP | ERA |
|---|---|---|---|---|---|---|---|---|---|---|---|---|---|
| 1969 Mets | 26 | 0 | 0 | – | 2 | 0 | 1 | 1.7 | 1 | 1 | 1 | 1.200 | 0.00 |
| Career 7 Years | – | 28 | 34 | .452 | 183 | 76 | 12 | 692.3 | 644 | 269 | 507 | 1.319 | 3.48 |

Those fans who don't remember Bob Johnson as a member of the 1969 Mets can certainly be excused. Johnson, 26, pitched in all of two September games that season—notching one save in the team's 100th win of the year and allowing no runs—before being rendered ineligible for postseason play. Still, those brief Mets appearances represented a significant pit stop in what turned out to be a fascinating career for the journeyman righthander.

Robert Dale Johnson was born in Aurora, Illinois, on April 25, 1943. He attended Bradley University and pitched there for two years before signing with the Mets in 1964. As a green rookie he pitched 37 times for 172 innings—both highs for his minor league career—for Auburn in the New York-Penn League that year. The 6-foot-4, 220-pound Johnson was a hard thrower who racked up plenty of strikeouts in the minors, but he did not show appreciable results... and he nearly lost his leg. In 1967, while pitching for the Mets' Williamsport farm team in the Eastern League, Johnson suffered a badly broken leg in a terrifying motorcycle accident.

"I was going along pretty good when the bike skidded on about three feet of gravel on the road," Johnson told *The Sporting News*. "My left leg was mangled." How badly? Two doctors recommended amputation of at least part of the limb.

Fortunately, a third doctor believed that the injured leg could be saved. The decision—and the operation—was a turning point in Johnson's life and saved his career. It also left him with a resolution. Johnson promised himself that he would never drive another motorcycle for the duration of his professional career.

Fully recovered in 1969, he had a breakout season, going 13–4 with a 1.48 ERA at Double-A Memphis. He was moved up to triple-A Tidewater, pitching mostly in relief, before being promoted to New York in September.

Johnson's career as a Met would not last long. After the 1969 season, the Mets traded him, along with a young outfielder-third baseman named Amos Otis, to the Kansas City Royals for veteran third baseman Joe Foy. After Foy muddled through an unproductive season in New York, the Mets dumped him on the lowly Washington Senators. In the meantime, Otis became a five-time All-Star with Kansas City. Through no fault of his own, Johnson had been involved in one of the most one-sided trades in franchise history. The inclusion of the promising Johnson—as if a center fielder who'd reach 2,000 hits and claim three Gold Gloves for a five-time division champ wasn't enough—made the deal even worse in the eyes of the Mets.

The Royals benefited directly from Johnson's promise in 1970. Johnson finished second to Bert Blyleven in *The Sporting News'* Rookie Pitcher of the Year voting. Johnson displayed a live arm, striking out 206 batters. His high strikeout total was the most of any American League right-hander, surpassing even Hall of Famer Jim Palmer. Lefties Sam McDowell of Cleveland and Mickey Lolich of Detroit were the only AL pitchers with more K's in 1970. Johnson was also durable, completing 10 starts and logging 214 innings.

Johnson's performance caught the eye of Joe Brown, the astute general manager of the Pittsburgh Pirates, who was not deceived by his misleading 8–13 won-loss record for the Royals, a 97-loss team in just their second year of existence. Captivated by the tall right-hander who threw better than 90 miles an hour, possessed an above-average breaking ball, and exhibited the versatility to start or relieve, Brown targeted Johnson in wintertime conversations with the Royals.

As he talked trade during the offseason of 1970–71, Brown insisted that the Royals include Johnson as part of a package for touted shortstop Freddie Patek. The Pirates gave up Patek, catcher Jerry May, and right-hander Bruce Dal Canton for Johnson, shortstop Jackie Hernandez, and catcher Jim Campanis.

Pitching mostly out of the back end of Pittsburgh's rotation, Johnson endured a disappointing first year as a Pirate. He finished the 1971 regular season with an unspectacular earned run average of 3.45 and a middling record of 9–10. Several major league scouts noted that Johnson was trying to finesse opposing hitters, in contrast to the power-pitching style he had shown with the Royals. As one scout told sportswriter Dick Young, "You can look at [Johnson's] face and tell he can't finesse anybody."

Thankfully, the Pirates' ascendancy to the National League East title gave Johnson a chance for redemption in the postseason. With the National League Championship Series tied at a game apiece, the Pirates prepared to host the San Francisco Giants in Game Three. Moments before game time, scheduled starter Nellie Briles told manager Danny Murtaugh that his injured groin would prevent him from pitching. Thinking quickly, Murtaugh decided to tap the shoulder of Johnson.

Game Three provided the stage for Johnson's most impressive work as a member of the Pirates. On short notice, he pitched brilliantly. He overcame several rough spots, including a key situation in the second inning. Willie McCovey and Bobby Bonds reached on back-to-back singles with no one out. Johnson responded by fanning Dick Dietz, retiring Dirty Al Gallagher on a groundout, and striking out Chris Speier.

Buttressed by a Bob Robertson home run, Johnson nursed a 1–0 lead into the top of the sixth inning. A throwing error by Richie Hebner produced a tainted run for the Giants, but Johnson prevented further damage by wading through the middle of San Francisco's formidable lineup, which included Willie Mays, McCovey, and Bonds.

In the top of the eighth inning, Johnson encountered another critical situation. With two out and two runners on, he faced Dietz, a dangerous right-handed hitter with power. Johnson ran the count to two balls and no strikes, prompting a visit from pitching coach Don Osborn. "Listen, you big ape," Osborn told Johnson bluntly. "I don't have an SOB in the bullpen that's got the stuff you got out here today, so get this guy out." Johnson responded to Osborn's diatribe by retiring Dietz on a harmless groundball, ending the threat.

In the bottom of the eighth inning, Johnson left the game for a pinch hitter. Two batters later, Richie Hebner lofted a home run into the right-field stands at Three Rivers Stadium. Dave Giusti replaced the departed Johnson in the ninth, preserving the 2–1 win for the talented right-hander. After the game, Johnson attributed his success against the Giants to an improved fastball. "I think I threw harder today than I did all year," he told the *New York Daily News*.

Johnson started and lost Game Two of the World Series against Baltimore. He later came on in relief in the sixth inning of Game Six in a one-run game with two on and no one out. He retired three straight batters to quell the threat. He batted in the top of the seventh and came out to pitch the bottom half. He got two outs but put two men on before being replaced by Dave Giusti, who allowed a game-tying hit to Davey Johnson. The Pirates lost the game to even the Series, but the Bucs won the world championship the next day.

Now the owner of a World Series ring, Johnson followed up by posting one of his best seasons in 1972, forging an earned run average of 2.96 as a long reliever and spot starter. He came on in Game Two of the NLCS in the first inning after Bob Moose was yanked after allowing hits to the first five Cincinnati Reds. Johnson threw five innings of one-hit ball, though Cincinnati held on to win, 5–3. Johnson appeared once more in the NLCS, though the Pirates lost on a Moose wild pitch in ninth inning of deciding Game Five.

Johnson returned to mediocrity in 1973, pitching almost exclusively in relief. He appeared in a career-high 50 games and chalked up his worst ERA to that point: 3.62. After the season, the Bucs traded him to the Cleveland Indians for an obscure minor leaguer named Burnel Flowers. Once a prized acquisition, Johnson had seen his Pirates career come to an end after three seasons, two of them mostly disappointing.

Injuries played a part in hurting Johnson's career. So did an off-the-field obstacle. Later in his career, Johnson announced publicly that he had struggled with a severe drinking problem. Johnson said he had begun drinking with the Royals in 1970, and only increased his alcohol habit during his three-year stay with the Pirates. "It was affecting my behavior. I was saying things I shouldn't have been saying. I was hung over in the clubhouse most of the time," Johnson revealed in a 1977 interview with Phil Pepe. In May of 1974, Johnson's heavy drinking led to an episode of erratic behavior aboard the Indians' team flight from Detroit to Dallas. Johnson became angered when the flight's departure was delayed. He also argued with stewardesses about a mix-up in seating assignments. "I was snockered," Johnson admitted to Pepe. Johnson abruptly walked off the plane during a stopover in Indianapolis. The Indians fined him a reported $500. They waived him later that season.

In October 1975, Johnson vowed to never again to take another drink. Two years later, after failed attempts to make the rosters of the Texas Rangers and New York Yankees and an aborted return to the Royals, he attempted a comeback with the Atlanta Braves. Johnson pitched briefly—and unsuccessfully—for Atlanta. "I knew that it was time for me to call it quits," Johnson told *Sports Collectors Digest* in 1997. "I didn't just want to hang on."

For Johnson, a career that had begun with so much promise ended with a lifetime record of just 28–34, with two shutouts, 12 saves, and 692⅓ innings pitched in 183 career games (76 starts). The highlights of his career had come early—as a member of two world championship teams, the '69 Mets and the '71 Pirates. In between those seasons he had his career year as a rookie for a second-year expansion team that finished 33 games out of first place.

Out of the major leagues since 1977, Johnson has owned and operated a construction company, while staying active in the game as an American Legion coach and umpire in southern Oregon. "I am staying in baseball at a lower level, but I am still in baseball," Johnson told *Sports Collectors Digest*. "I really love the game."

A resident of Cave Junction, Oregon, Johnson continued to maintain a low profile in his post-playing days. Somehow that seems like a fitting legacy for one of the least known—but most promising—pitchers on the 1969 Miracle Mets.

**Sources**

*The Sporting News*
*Sports Collectors Digest*
*New York Daily News*
Bruce Markusen *The Team That Changed Baseball.* (Yardley, Pennsylvania: Westholme, 2006).

## Ten Is the Loneliest Number

At the close of August 14, 1969, the Mets were 10 games out—their deepest deficit of the year before their fateful and successful assault on first place. Many sources today claim that 9½ games behind the Cubs was as bad as things got for the Mets that year, but a closer look at the day by day standings—courtesy of *www.baseball-reference.com*—shows an even 10 back midway through August.

July ended with a four-game Mets losing streak, including a doubleheader sweep by the Astros at Shea in which the Mets were outscored by a margin 27–8—featuring Gil Hodges's fabled walk out to left field to remove Cleon Jones in mid-inning. The Mets began August by sweeping the Braves to salvage the long homestand (5–5) that followed the All-Star break; that was a decent homestand for any Mets team during the franchise's first seven seasons, but these contending Mets had stumbled from five games back at the break to 6½ behind Chicago. And the Cubs had played five more games than the Mets.

The Mets then dropped three of four to the Reds, with Jerry Koosman and Tom Seaver losing the first two games at Crosley Field. The Mets won three of four in Atlanta, but the next stop on the trip was a three-game sweep by the Astros, the third straight time they'd been swept by Houston in '69. The Mets ended the season series against their '62 expansion mates with a 2–10 mark. Other than the Reds, against whom the Mets split the season series, the '69 Mets had a winning record against every other team they played.

The only bright side following the 4–7 trip was that the Mets didn't have any more games with either the Reds or the Astros. They left Houston at 11 games over .500 (62–51), and in third place, 10 games behind the Cubs and one behind the Cardinals.

The standings remained unchanged with the Cubs, Cardinals, and Mets having off the next day. The Mets were rained out on Friday, August 15—a day bettered remembered by history as the start of the Woodstock Music and Art Fair at Max Yazgur's 600-acre farm in Bethel, New York. The Mets stood at the now familiar 9½-game deficit only after the Cubs lost that night in San Francisco, starting Chicago's infamous 18–27 slide. The Mets roared to a 38–11 finish, beginning their fabled run with consecutive doubleheader sweeps of the expansion Padres while scoring a total of just 10 runs in the four games at Shea Stadium. The '69 Mets made every run count.

By September 10, after winning both games of a two-game set with the Cubs—highlighted by a black cat walking in front of the Cubs dugout at Shea—and then sweeping a doubleheader from the Expos, it was the Mets who held a lead of one. For Leo Durocher's Cubs, that number must have seemed—as in the Three Dog Night song "One" of that year—"the loneliest number." The Cubs finished eight back while the Cardinals fell to fourth, 13 games back. The Pirates claimed third place at 12 games behind the first-ever NL East champions. The Mets had engineered an 18-game reversal in 49 games, overcoming a 10-game deficit in four weeks and then adding on an eight-game bulge to win going away. Amazin' indeed.

# Cleon Jones

by Fred Worth

| Season | Age | G | AB | R | H | 2B | 3B | HR | RBI | BB | SO | SB | CS | BA | OBP | SLG |
|---|---|---|---|---|---|---|---|---|---|---|---|---|---|---|---|---|
| 1969 Mets | 26 | 137 | 483 | 92 | 164 | 25 | 4 | 12 | 75 | 64 | 60 | 16 | 8 | .340 | .422 | .482 |
| Career 13 Years | – | 1213 | 4263 | 565 | 1196 | 183 | 33 | 93 | 524 | 360 | 702 | 91 | 48 | .281 | .339 | .404 |

The Last Out Of The 1969 World Series. The Carom. The Shoe Polish Incident.

There are other great moments in Mets history, like The Buckner Ball and The Grand Slam Single, but surely any listing of the most significant moments in Mets history, particularly of the Mets' first two decades, would have to include these three. The common thread for these three incidents is Cleon Jones, the first consistent, legitimate offensive threat ever to play for the Mets.

October 16, 1969—Game Five of the World Series. The Mets led three games to one. The powerful Orioles jumped out to a 3–0 lead and the Mets needed to do something to turn the game around. In the bottom of the sixth inning, Dave McNally's pitch to Cleon Jones hit the dirt and bounced into the Mets dugout. Umpire Lou DiMuro called it a ball. Jones had started toward first believing he was hit by the pitch. DiMuro disagreed until manager Gil Hodges came slowly out of the dugout, showed DiMuro the ball, and pointed at a small smudge of shoe polish. DiMuro sent Jones to first. Donn Clendenon followed with a home run that tightened the game and began the comeback that won the game and the World Series.

October 16, 1969—"Come on down, baby. Come on down." Those were the words of Cleon Jones as he spoke to Davey Johnson's fly ball with two outs in the ninth inning of Game Five of the 1969 World Series. No Mets fan will ever forget watching that ball settle into his glove and seeing Jones almost kneel upon catching it. No Mets fan will ever forget the elation showed by Jones as he then raced toward center field to celebrate with lifelong friend Tommie Agee.

September 20, 1973—Going into this game against Pittsburgh, the Mets were in third place, just 1½ games back of the Pirates. The Mets had scored a run in the bottom of the eighth to tie the game, 2–2. The Pirates scored again in the ninth. The Mets answered in the bottom of the inning to force extra innings. In the 13th inning, with the game still tied, Dave Augustine hit a long fly to left. It was well over Jones's head and would clearly score Richie Zisk from first, if it wasn't a home run. But the ball hit the corner of the top edge of the wall, bouncing directly to Cleon Jones. He turned and threw to Wayne Garrett, who relayed it to Ron Hodges to nail Zisk at the plate. The Mets went on to win in the bottom of the inning, starting the final surge that led the Mets to the division title, the World Series, and almost another world championship.

Cleon Jones was the linchpin to all these moments, even though he is somewhat overlooked in the pantheon of great Mets today.

Cleon Joseph Jones was born on August 4, 1942 in Plateau, a section of Mobile, Alabama, whose most notable characteristic was the ever-present smell from the local paper mills. According to Jones's autobiography, race didn't really seem to matter much during daily life in the pre-integration South. There were surely some problems but most of the time blacks and whites simply behaved as local custom prescribed. Jones downplayed one aspect of this, however: Race problems caused Jones to grow up without his father in the home. One day in 1945, his parents, Joseph and Carrie Jones, were waiting to take a bus back home. Carrie Jones was standing in front of a white woman in line. That apparently offended a white man who grabbed Carrie by the hair. Joseph responded by beating the man rather severely. Rather than risk trial in the Alabama courts, Joseph quickly relocated to Chicago, leaving Cleon, and older brother Tommie Lee, to be raised by their mother and their grandmother, who was affectionately known as Mama Myrt.

Two years later, Carrie Jones moved to Philadelphia to find work. That was the family arrangement for about five years. Life changed dramatically for Cleon when his mother died in Philadelphia. In his autobiography, Jones relates the emotion the family experienced on hearing the news, but also the stability and love provided by his grandmother. "I guess Tommie Lee and I started crying, too. But when my grandmother looked at us and sobbed, 'My poor babies, you have no one now,' we knew she was wrong. We had Mama Myrt."

Cleon Jones's life always involved sports. There were baseball and football games in the streets and vacant lots of Mobile. The odd arrangement of some of those street games led to Cleon batting right-handed while throwing left-handed. He told Maury Allen how it happened:

> *There was this one field that we put some old shirts down for bases. Behind right field there was this little creek and behind left field, well, man, it just went on and on for miles. We played our games there and after a couple of games I had lost four or five balls when I hit them left-handed into the water. We didn't have too many real baseballs so when the other guys came to me and said, "You better stop doing that or we ain't got no more baseballs here," I just turned around. That's how I became a right-handed hitter. I just wanted to save those balls.*

Athletic success at County High followed, where Cleon teamed with Tommie Agee in both baseball and football. Success there led to playing college football for Alabama A&M. After one year there, Clyde Gray, a man from Mobile, tried to get the Kansas City Athletics and New York Mets to look at Jones. Tommie Agee had signed with the Cleveland Indians and Gray thought Jones had a future in baseball as well. Gray regularly worked to try to help young blacks from Mobile. Some help was needed. After all, this was still only 15 years after Jackie Robinson integrated the major leagues. The Athletics showed no interest in Jones, but the Mets did and he signed with them

Photo courtesy of metsilverman.com

*Cleon Jones takes a cut during one of the many Mets-Cubs showdowns in 1969. He knocked in 11 and scored 11 against the Cubs that season.*

*Cleon Jones was a veteran of three major league campaigns when 1969 began. He hit 73 points above his career mark of .267 and was an All-Star.*

on July 5, 1962. Because of how late in the season the signing took place, Jones went back to college for a while.

Jones's professional career started in 1963; he hit a combined .317 with Raleigh in the Carolina League and Auburn in the New York-Penn League. He also made his major league debut that year, coming in as a defensive replacement for center fielder Duke Carmel on September 14. The abysmal Mets were eager to find young stars but Jones was not ready. He finished 1963 with just two singles in 15 at-bats. In 1964, the Mets kept Jones in Buffalo in the International League for the entire season. He turned in a solid year, batting .278, slugging .442, and hitting 16 homers in 500 at-bats.

In 1965, Jones found himself in New York on Opening Day. He appeared as a pinch hitter for Tom Parsons in the Mets' 6–1 loss to the Dodgers. Two days later, on April 14, Jones made his first start. With no hits and two strikeouts in his first four at-bats, the debut was less than inspiring. But the Mets saw a hint of what was to come when Jones singled in the 11th, scoring Joe Christopher and Dan Napoleon to bring the Mets to within one run of the Astros, though they still lost the game.

By May 2, with Jones hitting .156, it was obvious he was still not quite ready, so it was back to Buffalo. He played 123 games for the Bisons. For a while, Jones really struggled in Buffalo. One reason for that, according to Jones, was Buffalo manager Sheriff Robinson's insistence that Jones try to pull the ball and hit home runs. When Robinson went up to the majors to be a coach for Wes Westrum, Kerby Farrell, a former major league manager who had befriended Jones during training camp in 1963, became the Buffalo manager. He encouraged Jones to ignore the pressure to pull and resume hitting to all fields. Though his numbers were still a little lower than in 1964, he began to get his swing back and was establishing himself as a solid ballplayer.

Jones was a September call-up for the Mets, appearing in 17 games from September 3 until the end of the season. Though he never got his batting average higher than .169, Jones had seen his last days in the minor leagues.

On Opening Day 1966, Cleon Jones batted leadoff as right fielder for manager Wes Westrum.

In the bottom of the eighth, Jones hit a home run off Braves starter Denny Lemaster, giving the Mets a 2–1 lead. Unfortunately, Jones committed an error in the ninth that led to a run as the Mets fell, 3–2. By the end of the season, Jones had batted .275 with eight home runs and 16 stolen bases. He finished tied for fourth in the Rookie of the Year voting, with Randy Hundley and Larry Jaster, behind winner Tommy Helms (Sonny Jackson and Tito Fuentes were second and third, respectively).

Jones's strong 1966 was followed by a very trying 1967. He started the season 0-for-18 before finally getting a hit. Before long, Westrum was giving Jones a lot of time on the bench. He didn't get his batting average above .150 until June 3. After one game, Westrum blasted Jones in the press, further discouraging the young outfielder. Veteran Ken Boyer encouraged Jones to not let the treatment get to him. Things did finally start to turn around. Beginning with the second game of a June 18 doubleheader, Jones had a 10-game stretch during which he hit .341. He batted .277 for the remainder of the season, leaving him at .246. On a 101-loss Mets team, that wasn't terrible, and it was almost an achievement given how long he'd struggled.

A big change, not just for Jones, but for the entire team occurred on November 27, 1967. Gil Hodges came to the Mets as manager in exchange for $100,000 and pitcher Bill Denehy. Hodges, a star with the 1950s Brooklyn Dodgers and an Original Met in the last years of his playing career, brought a quiet strength and a winning attitude to the perennially losing Mets. Jones called Hodges the best manager for whom he ever played. Hodges treated his players like men, expecting much, but also supporting and encouraging them.

Another big change, of a particularly personal nature for Jones, occurred on December 15. Tommie Agee, Jones's high school friend from Mobile, was traded to the Mets by the Chicago White Sox along with Al Weis for Tommy Davis, Jack Fisher, Billy Wynne, and Buddy Booker. Having a poised, supportive manager and having his good friend on the Mets gave Jones a much-needed confidence boost.

Jones started slowly in 1968. At the start of June he was hitting in the .220s, but he then hit in 11 straight starts. By the last day of the season, his average was up to .298. A 1-for-5 finish against Chris Short dropped him to .297, but it was clear that Jones had established himself as a solid major leaguer. Agee, however, had a dismal 1968, featuring a beaning and several long hitless streaks. But in 1969, the friends from Mobile, along with the rest of the Mets, shocked the baseball world.

Casey Stengel was once quoted as saying that man would walk on the moon before the Mets would win the pennant. On July 20, 1969, Neil Armstrong walked on the moon. Less than three months later, on October 16, 1969, the Mets became world champions.

Cleon Jones was as big a part of the Mets championship as anyone. He batted .340 with an on-base percentage of .422. He led the team in batting average, on-base percentage, slugging, hits, doubles, stolen bases, walks, and even hit by pitches. He was second on the team in RBIs, one behind Agee. He started in the All-Star Game (two singles, reached on an error, and scored twice) and finished seventh in the league Most Valuable Player voting, behind winner Willie McCovey and teammates Tom Seaver and Tommie Agee.

During the first National League Championship Series in history, Jones batted .429 with a homer, two doubles, and four RBIs. The Mets hit .327 overall in the three-game sweep of Atlanta.

In the World Series win over Baltimore, Jones hit only .158, but he was in the thick of things. His foot and his knee live in Mets immortality. He was hit by Dave McNally's "shoe polish" pitch and scored on Donn Clendenon's homer, getting the Mets back in the game. And then, in the top of the ninth, he gently coaxed Davey Johnson's fly ball into his glove, making the Mets the world champions.

In 1970, Jones had another solid year, hitting .277. He followed that with his second .300 season, hitting .319 in 1971. After that, injuries hindered him considerably. In 1972, he was limited to 106 games and hit only .245. In 1973, he helped the Mets to the seventh game of the World Series by hitting .260 but played only 92 regular season games. The carom found him in the famous "Ball on the Wall" game that helped the Mets turn the corner and he batted .300 in the NLCS victory over the favored Reds. He hit .286 in the World Series loss to the A's and homered during New York's 12-inning win in Game Two.

Jones had a resurgence in 1974, hitting .282 with 13 home runs, but he only played in 124 games. His Mets career came to an unexpected end in 1975, batting .240 with only one extra base hit and two RBIs in 21 games. It was an abrupt and bitter finish to what was the greatest offensive career by any Met to that time.

In addition to the wonderful moments mentioned earlier, Cleon Jones is also remembered for some less pleasant moments.

On July 30, 1969, Cleon was in a battle with Matty Alou for the league lead in batting and the Mets a factor in a pennant race for the first time in their history. In the second game of a soggy doubleheader in Shea Stadium, the Astros' Johnny Edwards hit a ball to left field. Jones did not go after the ball particularly quickly due to the rain and some hamstring problems. Gil Hodges liked neither the slow run to the ball nor the weak throw that allowed Edwards to get a double. Hodges started walking out of the dugout. He went past the mound, past shortstop Bud Harrelson, and out into left field. Jones tells the story: "He said, 'If you're not running good, why don't you just come out of the ball game?' Then he turned around and headed toward the dugout. I knew he had something more than my leg in mind, and I followed him in."

The manager pulling a league-leading hitter for not hustling made it clear that the Mets were no longer league doormats. Interestingly, years later, Hodges' widow, Joan, said that the incident was less intentional than it seemed. Regarding going out to get Jones, she quoted Gil as saying, "I never realized it until I passed the mound and I couldn't turn back."

The end of Cleon's Mets career came in 1975 following a couple of unpleasant incidents.

Jones was left in Florida at the end of spring training in order to rehabilitate his knee following surgery. On May 4, police found him in the back of a van with a woman. He and the woman were charged with indecent exposure. Though he was never prosecuted, the Mets made sure to punish him. They ordered him back to New York to attend a press conference where he was made to apologize, with his wife, Angela, at his side. The public humiliation caused by the way M. Donald Grant handled the situation seemed to really hurt Jones.

Two months later, on July 18 in New York, manager Yogi Berra had Jones pinch-hit for Ed Kranepool. He lined out to shortstop. At the beginning of the next inning, Jones refused to go out to play the field. According to *The Sporting News*, "There was a shouting match between [Jones and Berra] on the bench and ended with Jones flinging his glove down, pulling towels off the rack and storming up the runway to the clubhouse." Berra called it "the most embarrassing thing that's happened to me since I became a manager." Berra told the Mets it was "him or me" and the Mets immediately started trying to trade Jones. Finally, on July 27, after a trade to the Angels fell through, Jones was released. There were no winners in this situation. Berra, who'd been with the Mets since he'd been hired as a player-coach in 1965, was fired shortly thereafter. Jones and Berra had been in Mets uniforms longer than anyone other than Ed Kranepool.

PHOTO COURTESY OF METSILVERMAN.COM

*Cleon Jones, swinging, Gil Hodges, smiling, and the celebrating '69 Mets are a welcome sight for anyone arriving at Citi Field.*

Photo courtesy of Dwayne Labakas Collection

*Cleon Jones*

No offensive player was more important to the Mets in their first dozen years than Cleon Jones. When Jones left the Mets, he ranked as the leader in many career statistical categories. He was first in extra base hits, hits, RBIs, times reaching base, runs, singles, total bases, and home runs. He was second in at-bats, average (for rate statistics, minimum 1,500 plate appearances), doubles, games, hit by pitches, plate appearances, sacrifice flies and triples. He was third in OPS and stolen bases, fourth in intentional walks, on-base percentage, slugging average, and walks, and sixth in home run percentage.

Even the passage of a third of a century has not erased Jones's influence on Mets history. He still ranks second in hit by pitches, hits and singles, third in at-bats, plate appearances and sacrifice flies, fourth in games and triples, fifth in times reaching base and runs, sixth in RBIs and total bases, seventh in doubles and extra base hits, and tenth in batting average and intentional walks. His 1969 production still ranks high on the all-time season highs. His .340 batting average remained unchallenged for 30 seasons until John Olerud topped it at .354 in 1998.

Jones signed with the White Sox in 1976. His tenure there was less than four weeks. He got into a dozen games, batting just .200 before he was released again. His major league career was over.

While in the minor leagues, Jones married his wife, Angela, who is a second cousin to Hall of Famer Billy Williams. They have two children, Anja and Cleon, Jr. Jones did a bit of big league coaching, and he worked with the young Darryl Strawberry. But major league coaching jobs were not as available as Jones would have liked. He coached for a time at Bishop State Community College in Mobile, working with both the women's softball team and the men's baseball team. He ran a fast-food business for a while, though it was not successful. He worked for a maintenance company and then spent a number of years doing community service work in Mobile. "I work for the city, work with kids, work with the elderly. I enjoy it," he told Maury Allen.

It is unlikely anyone will argue Cleon Jones is the best player in New York Mets history. But there is little doubt that he is one of the most important. He was inducted into the Mets Hall of Fame in 1991, the sixth player inducted. He took part in the 2008 closing ceremonies at Shea Stadium, the place he brought to bedlam with his bow in left field in 1969.

**Sources**

*108 Magazine*

Allen, Maury. *After the Miracle* (New York: St. Martin's Paperbacks, 1991).

Jones, Cleon with Hershey, Ed. *The Life Story of the One and Only Cleon* (New York: Coward-McCann, Inc., 1970).

*http://www.ultimatemets.com*

*minors.sabrwebs.com*

*The New York Times*

*The Sporting News*

*www.baseball-reference.com*

*www.retrosheet.org*

*Lee Sinins' Complete Baseball Encyclopedia*

# Cal Koonce

by Matthew Silverman

| Season | Age | W | L | Pct | G | GS | SV | IP | H | BB | SO | WHIP | ERA |
|---|---|---|---|---|---|---|---|---|---|---|---|---|---|
| 1969 Mets | 28 | 6 | 3 | .667 | 40 | 0 | 7 | 83 | 85 | 42 | 48 | 1.530 | 4.99 |
| Career 10 Years | – | 47 | 49 | .490 | 334 | 90 | 24 | 971.3 | 972 | 368 | 504 | 1.380 | 3.78 |

Cal Koonce was a valuable and reliable member of the Mets bullpen under Gil Hodges. A starter early in his career, he became a reliever who won six games and saved seven for the 1969 Mets. His alliterative name and easygoing manner made him a memorable member of the Miracle Mets; his skill as a coach made him a treasured citizen in his native North Carolina.

Koonce was born on November 18, 1940, in Fayetteville, North Carolina. He grew up in Hope Mills and was a star athlete in the area. He played baseball and basketball for Campbell College (then a two-year school but later a four-year university). His freshman year he had 19- and 17-strikeout games while compiling a 4–3 record. As a sophomore, Koonce pitched in 17 games, starting 14, with a 10–4 record. He was a junior college All-American at Campbell in 1961 and played with his brother Charles, a freshman. The elder Koonce signed with the Cubs that year.

For his first taste of professional baseball, the Cubs sent Cal Koonce across the country to Wenatchee, Washington. He pitched 22 times for the Wenatchee Chiefs of the Class B Northwest League, getting hit pretty hard to the tune of 6–10 with a 4.81 ERA. The next year he spent in Chicago.

For a franchise that had played its first professional game as a founding member of the National Association in 1871, the Cubs established a new low in 1962. The Cubs lost 100 games for the first time ever. Finishing 42½ games out of first place were also a new standard. The Cubs were in the midst of being mismanaged—or more accurately, not managed at all—by the "College of Coaches." Owner Philip K. Wrigley's idea of letting a revolving door of coaches run the team instead of one set manager changed the way the professional game had been run since, well, the franchise played their first game some 91 years earlier. It was a management scheme ridiculed by all and never tried by another club, but the Cubs kept at it for five long seasons. The 103-loss Cubs were protected from the basement only by the 120-loss expansion Mets in 1962.

The 21-year-old Koonce was the most successful Cubs starter that rookie season, going 10–10 for a team that had one 20-game loser in Dick Ellsworth and two others (Glen Hobbie and Koonce's future Mets teammate Don Cardwell) who were each nine games under .500. Koonce had a 3.97 ERA while tossing 191 innings, though his 84–86 strikeout-to-walk ratio left something to be desired. He nearly had a no-hitter as well.

Koonce was 7–2 with a 4.12 ERA coming into a game at Wrigley Field against Cincinnati on July 13, 1962. He retired the first 10 Reds before allowing a clean single to center by Don Blasingame. The game was scoreless until the sixth inning when the Cubs' Ernie Banks reached on an infield hit and took second on a throwing error. He went to third on a groundout and scored on a Ron Santo sacrifice fly. It was the only run that Cincinnati's Bob Purkey—or any pitcher—would allow on the day.

After Blasingame's hit, Koonce allowed only a walk to Gordy Coleman and immediately took care of it by getting Vada Pinson to bounce into a double play. The Reds got a baserunner with two outs in the ninth when Santo mishandled a grounder by Wally Post. Blasingame, whose hit was all that stood between Koonce and a no-hit bid, came up with the tying run on base. He rapped a grounder to Banks at first to end the game and give Koonce his first career shutout.

Koonce lost his next decision before beating the Astros to improve to 9–3 with a 3.60 ERA. He lost his next six decisions before finally getting his 10th win on September 20 in Philadelphia. He was hit hard by the same Phillies team in his final start at Wrigley to even his record in Chicago's 102nd loss of the year.

The Cubs were better in 1963, but Koonce was not. He was sent down to Salt Lake City of the Pacific Coast League in June with his ERA hovering around 6.00. He went 5–3 with a 3.00 ERA in Triple-A before being recalled in August, and the beatings continued. Koonce finally got his first win as a Cub since May 5 in Milwaukee, beating the Braves on the road in his final start of the year. At County Stadium he was 2–0 with a 1.26 ERA in 1963; everywhere else that year he was 0–6 with a 5.40 ERA. The Cubs kept the 23-year-old righty in Salt Lake City for most of 1964. He won 11 and lost 15, logging 238 innings with a 3.48 ERA in 36 starts for the Bees.

Koonce's hard work in Utah paid off with a promotion to Chicago, where he went 3–0 with a 2.03 ERA to finish the season. He was a regular in Chicago's rotation in 1965, spending the whole season in the majors and going 7–9 with a 3.69 ERA in 173 innings.

The Cubs finally ditched the College of Coaches after the 1965 season and brought in legendary Leo "The Lip" Durocher to take over as manager. Koonce had the distinction of again having a .500 record (5–5) on a 100-loss Cubs team. Durocher was looking at what he had to work with and tried a lot of different players. Koonce started only five times and relieved in 40 games—not surprising given that future Hall of Famer Fergie Jenkins pitched 48 times in relief that year—but Koonce also spent several weeks in the minors after a poor start. He started eight games for Chicago's triple-A affiliate in Tacoma and, after going 5–3 in eight starts there, he was back in Chicago. The Durocher regime took some getting used to and it wasn't something Koonce recalled fondly.

"With the Cubs, Leo would use the same reliever game after game until he ran out of gas," Koonce told Stanley Cohen in *A Magic Summer*. "If you were on a hot streak, you knew that you'd be the first one to be called every day until your streak ended. During one period, I warmed up in the bullpen 14 days in a row, and it takes something out of you. That was Leo's style of managing. He did the same thing in 1969, not only with his pitchers but with his infielders too."

Koonce's ERA kept dropping until he ended the season with a poor relief outing against the pennant-winning Dodgers; his 3.81 ERA at the time was his best of any season in which he'd gone more than 40 innings in the majors. Only Jenkins exceeded Koonce's 45 appearances for Chicago.

Koonce again started poorly in 1967. Though he was able to overcome his bad start, Durocher had run out of patience. In a three-game span against San Francisco's powerful lineup in late July, Koonce threw two scoreless innings and picked up the win in 12 innings on Friday at Wrigley Field; he blew a lead on Saturday by allowing three hits without retiring a batter in a game the Cubs again won in their last at-bat; and he threw two scoreless innings the next afternoon in a game the Cubs lost. He did not appear again for a week, throwing a scoreless inning in a close loss in Cincinnati. It was his last game as a Cub. Koonce was sold to the Mets on August 2.

The Mets, in the midst of a season in which they went through a club-record 54 players, tried Koonce as a starter. It worked. After retiring the only batter he faced in his Mets debut against a Giants club he knew quite well, Koonce got the start six days later against Pittsburgh and went the distance for the win. He won his next start as well and threw another complete game on September 2 in St. Louis. He got a chance at redemption in his next start at

Wrigley Field, but former teammate Joe Niekro stymied Koonce and the Mets. Former batterymate Randy Hundley knocked in two runs in Niekro's 5–0 shutout. Koonce lost again in his next start and then he headed back to the bullpen.

Things were changing in New York. Manager Wes Westrum knew he would be fired and resigned with a week left in the season. Coach Salty Parker took the helm. The Mets were a laughingstock for their first six seasons—the only time they hadn't finished 10th was during the second 103-loss season by the Cubs—and now they had both a new manager (Gil Hodges) and general manager (Johnny Murphy). They carefully evaluated who should stay and who was just passing through. They kept Koonce and he thrived under Hodges.

Other than a couple of starts late in the 1968 season, Koonce made 53 relief appearances to place second on the team to Ron Taylor, another reclamation project who paid dividends. If not for a horrible ninth inning in the last game of the year—a 10–3 loss to the Phillies after the Mets had been assured of not finishing in the basement—Koonce would have finished with an ERA under 2.00. As it was, his 2.41 ERA was still his career lowest for a full season. His ERA and 6–4 record topped the Mets bullpen.

Koonce later said one of the main differences between the Cubs and Mets was that New York had a staff of former catchers: Rube Walker, Joe Pignatano, Yogi Berra, and Gil Hodges, who'd started his career as a catcher. What's more, on a young team like the Mets, Koonce—though just 28 coming into the 1969 season—was a respected veteran. With the conversion of Tug McGraw to reliever that year, the Mets had a bullpen that could come to the rescue of its young staff. With Taylor, McGraw, Koonce, and a few others, Hodges didn't have to worry about burning out the arms from overuse—as wound up happening that summer in Chicago.

"With the Mets it was different; we took turns," Koonce said of the disparity between the management style of the two NL East clubs. "If you were brought in one day, you knew you would have a day or two to get ready before you were called on again. That's why we were fresh at the end of the season."

His pitches also had the occasional movement indicative of a wet ball. Koonce had, after all, gone to the same college as Gaylord Perry. Koonce's secret was perspiration from his hand or wrist—aka "the sweatball." The difference is that he admitted it while still pitching.

"I threw a half-dozen every game," he said of his mound transgression. "A lot of pitchers did, but nobody would admit it because the spitball has been illegal since 1920. It was getting ridiculous, so I admitted it."

A journeyman pitcher needed every advantage just to begin to keep up with the Mets pitching staff in 1969. The deep starting staff included Tom Seaver, Jerry Koosman, Don Cardwell, and rookie Gary Gentry, plus as talented a swingman as anyone in team history: Nolan Ryan.

So it was little surprise that for the first time in his career, Koonce did not start a game. He again, however, started the season poorly, taking the loss on Opening Day against the brand-new Montreal Expos at Shea Stadium. Koonce did manage to pick up three saves in April, which counted in his statistics now that the save had become official (it had unofficially been counted for several years, with Koonce picking up 11 for the Mets in 1968). Yet Koonce was hit hard. He wound up allowing as many home runs in 1969 as he had in the previous two seasons combined.

Even as the previously moribund Mets rallied and shocked the world, Koonce's ERA never recovered from the early pounding. Though the mounds had been lowered in response to the "Year of the Pitcher" in 1968, Koonce still had an ERA of 6.00 as the Mets went on a tear in June. Like most members of that '69 team, though, Koonce had his moments of glory.

He picked up three wins in a span of five appearances in July, beginning with a four-inning stint on July 13 at Shea against the Expos as the Mets earned a doubleheader sweep to match the twin bill taken that same day by the first-place Cubs. Three days later, Koonce threw five innings of shutout relief in a win at Wrigley Field, allowing the Mets to pull within four games of Chicago. And following a disastrous sweep by the Astros later that month, Koonce took over for Don Cardwell in the first inning the next day against Atlanta and threw 6⅓ innings as the Mets went on to a 5–4 win over the NL West leaders.

PHOTO COURTESY OF DWAYNE LABAKAS COLLECTION

*Cal Koonce*

In all, Koonce had nine appearances in which he threw three or more innings. He had one of the two wins by a Met against the Astros (New York was 2–10 against Houston in '69). Not all his outings were brilliant, though. Hodges brought him in to take one for the team on occasion, such as when he threw five innings and absorbed five runs and 10 hits in a game the Mets lost 10–6 at Dodger Stadium on September 1. He pitched only twice more that year, both games the Mets lost. He did not appear in the postseason, but the starters were so sharp in the World Series that the bullpen logged fewer than six innings in the five-game victory over the Orioles.

Koonce began the 1970 season in New York, a place he had come to like after initially being repelled by it. "I had always told my wife, Peggy, that if I ever got traded or sold, New York was the one place I did not want to live," he told Stanley Cohen in *A Magic Summer*. "Of course, when we visited New York we were always downtown. I never got to see the residential areas, but once we moved there and settled down, I fell in love with it. We lived in Roslyn Heights, out on Long Island, and out there it was just like it was back home."

He hadn't counted on being sent farther north. With Koonce having appeared in just 13 games in early June 1970, the Mets sold him to the Red Sox. He wound up seeing more action in Boston, even starting eight games and throwing what turned out to be his final career complete game. He went 3–4 with a 3.57 ERA for the Red Sox after going 0–2 as a Met with a 3.27 ERA in 1970.

The next year Koonce fell into the same pattern of infrequent use in Boston that he'd experienced with the Mets. The Red Sox released him in August, three months shy of his 30th birthday. He did not pitch in the major leagues again.

Koonce had worked as a stockbroker in the offseason during his career and had spoken about becoming a golf professional, but after leaving the majors, he soon found his way back to baseball. The father of four, living in the same area where he'd grown up and made a name for himself, went into coaching. He began as a coach and physical education teacher at Fayetteville Academy in 1974, and then moved on to South View High School in his hometown of Hope Mills from 1974 to 1979.

Koonce returned to his alma mater, Campbell University, and took over the baseball program. During his tenure as head coach from 1980 to 1986, the Fighting Camels won 20 or more games six times and achieved 30 wins in a season for the first time in school history. He retired in 1986 after being named the Big South Coach of the Year, the only Campbell coach so honored.

Koonce was inducted into the Campbell Sports Hall of Fame in 1987, the first Campbell baseball player inducted besides Gaylord Perry and older brother Jim Perry, the first brothers to each win Cy Young Awards. Koonce's younger brother, Charles, who played for Campbell when it was transitioning from a two-year to a four-year college in the mid-1960s—hitting .400 at both levels—was inducted into the school's Hall of Fame in 1992.

Cal Koonce was Campbell University's all-time winningest coach when he retired, compiling a record of 174–123. Chip Smith passed Koonce's mark for wins in 2002, but Koonce's .586 career winning percentage is still almost 100 points higher than that of any other baseball coach in the university's history. Koonce was succeeded as baseball coach at the school by Mike Caldwell, another successful former major league pitcher from North Carolina.

In 1987, Koonce became general manager of the Fayetteville Generals, the first minor league team in that city in more than three decades. The Generals, the Class A farm team of the Detroit Tigers, were a member of the South Atlantic League. (The club was later known as the Cape Fear Crocs before moving to New Jersey to become the Lakewood BlueClaws.)

"I was looking for an opportunity to get back into professional baseball," he said shortly after taking the job. "And I wanted to see how things looked from the other side, the administrative view. But I suspect that winning feels good, no matter what your role is."

Koonce stayed with the Generals for two years before returning to coaching, this time at Terry Sanford High School in Fayetteville from 1989 to 1991. He also worked as a scout for the Texas Rangers in 1991 and 1992. But by then he was gravely ill. In addition, he served as a town commissioner in Hope Mills, North Carolina, from 1987 to 1992 before illness forced him to resign the post.

Koonce had lymphoma, a form of cancer that attacks the lymph nodes and glands. He battled the disease for four years before dying at Baptist Hospital in Winston-Salem at the age of 52 on October 29, 1993.

Art Shamsky, a teammate of Koonce's on the 1969 Mets team, said, "I never heard him say a bad word about anybody. He was just a down-to-earth person. He had a quiet dignity about him. All the players respected him and looked up to him. People respected what he had to say."

Chris Koonce, Cal's son, said of his father, "Even though he played in some of the biggest cities in America, he never lost track of who he was and where he came from. His family always maintained a house in Hope Mills during his entire career."

Cal Koonce was the kind of person who took a middle-of-the-road approach to life. He never got too high or too low. He was the kind of coach who could always find a mistake to correct even in victory, yet always found a positive to take away from a loss. He successfully conveyed these lessons to hundreds of students at various levels of education.

He played in a time when player salaries probably averaged only about $20,000 to $40,000 per year, yet he and his wife helped put four children through college. Koonce was also very generous with his time in serving his community. He was elected to the Hope Mills Town Board and served many roles with the Administrative Board at Hope Mills United Methodist Church.

Koonce's multiple careers packed into a short life, combined with the number of young people he touched in his native state, resulted in one final honor. On August 12, 1997, coincidentally 30 years to the day from his first start—and win—with the Mets, the North Carolina General Assembly passed a resolution to honor the man and his family.

*GENERAL ASSEMBLY OF NORTH CAROLINA*

*1997 SESSION*

*RATIFIED BILL*

*RESOLUTION 30*

*HOUSE JOINT RESOLUTION 1236*

*A JOINT RESOLUTION HONORING THE LIFE AND MEMORY OF CALVIN LEE KOONCE, JR.*

*Whereas, Calvin Lee Koonce, Jr. was born in Cumberland County, North Carolina on November 18, 1940, and was a native of the Town of Hope Mills; and*

*Whereas, Calvin Lee Koonce, Jr. graduated from Hope Mills High School in 1959 and attended Campbell College where he earned Junior College All-American Honors in 1961; and*

*Whereas, because of his outstanding baseball talent, Calvin Lee Koonce, Jr. was signed by the Chicago Cubs in 1961; and*

*Whereas, Calvin Lee Koonce, Jr. played the position of pitcher and won 10 games in his Rookie Season with the Cubs in 1962; and*

*Whereas, in 1967, Calvin Lee Koonce, Jr. joined the New York Mets and played on the 1969 Mets World Championship Team; and*

*Whereas, in 1971, his last year playing professional baseball, Calvin Lee Koonce, Jr. played for the Boston Red Sox; and*

*Whereas, after his professional career, Calvin Lee Koonce, Jr. returned to North Carolina where he coached baseball at Fayetteville Academy in 1974, South View High School from 1974 to 1979, Campbell University from 1979 to 1986, and Terry Sanford High School from 1989 to 1991; and*

*Whereas, Calvin Lee Koonce, Jr. served as general manager of the Fayetteville Generals from 1986 to 1988, and as a scout for the Texas Rangers from 1991 to 1992; and*

*Whereas, Calvin Lee Koonce, Jr. was inducted into the Campbell University Sports Hall of Fame in 1987; and*

*Whereas, Calvin Lee Koonce, Jr. was devoted to public service, having served as the Hope Mills Town Manager from 1992 to 1993, as an elected member of the Hope Mills Board of Commissioners, and as Mayor-Pro Tempore; and*

*Whereas, Calvin Lee Koonce, Jr. was an active member of the Hope Mills Methodist Church, where he served on the Administrative Board; and*

*Whereas, Calvin Lee Koonce, Jr. died on October 18, 1993; and*

*Whereas, Calvin Lee Koonce, Jr. is survived by his wife, Peggy Koonce; a son, Chris Koonce; three daughters, Kelly Taylor, Kim Owen, and Kerry Gowan; three grandchildren, Garrett Gowan, John Calvin Owen, and Lynnsey Taylor; his mother, Mary Koonce; a sister, Marilyn Koonce; and two brothers, Charles Koonce and Don Koonce;*

*Now, therefore, be it resolved by the House of Representatives, the Senate concurring:*

*Section 1. The General Assembly expresses its high regard for the life and service of Calvin Lee Koonce, Jr. and mourns the loss of this distinguished citizen.*

*Section 2. The Secretary of State shall transmit a certified copy of this resolution to the family of Calvin Lee Koonce, Jr.*

*Section 3. This resolution is effective upon ratification.*

*In the General Assembly read three times and ratified this the 12th day of August, 1997.*

*Marc Basnight*
*President Pro Tempore of the Senate*
*Harold J. Brubaker*
*Speaker of the House of Representatives*

**Sources**

Cohen, Stanley. *A Magic Summer: The 1969 Mets* (New York, Skyhorse Publishing, 2009).

E-mail from Chris Koonce (sent to and generously shared by Craig Hardee), April 16, 2008.

*Fayetteville* (NC) *Observer-Times*, October 30, 1993.

Joint Resolution Honoring The Life And Memory Of Calvin Lee Koonce, Jr. General Assembly Of North Carolina, 1997 Session, Ratified Bill. Resolution 30. House Joint Resolution 1236. *http://www.ncga.state.nc.us/sessions/1997/bills/house/html/h1236v2.html*

New York Mets, *Official 1969 Yearbook.*

Zumsteg, Derek. *The Cheater's Guide to Baseball.* New York: Houghton Mifflin, 2007 (page 149).

# Jerry Koosman

by Irv Goldfarb

| Season | Age | W | L | Pct | G | GS | SV | IP | H | BB | SO | WHIP | ERA |
|---|---|---|---|---|---|---|---|---|---|---|---|---|---|
| 1969 Mets | 26 | 17 | 9 | .654 | 32 | 32 | 0 | 241 | 187 | 68 | 180 | 1.058 | 2.28 |
| Career 19 Years | – | 222 | 209 | .515 | 612 | 527 | 17 | 3839.3 | 3635 | 1198 | 2556 | 1.259 | 3.36 |

It has become almost legend, though in reality there are a few different versions of the story: In March of 1966, three New York Mets farmhands, all going by the name of Jerry, set out from Atlanta on their way to minor league training camp in Homestead, Florida. Jerry Johnson sat between the driver, Jerry Wild, and the car's owner, who was fast asleep in the passenger seat. While motoring through Athens, Georgia, they were blind-sided by a woman rushing back from her lunch break. The Jerrys' car was ruined. Suddenly stranded far from their destination, the three pitchers needed a ride. The owner of the car first called his father, who promised to wire him some money for a new one; then a call went out to Mets farm director Joe McDonald, requesting an additional $50. When the cash arrived, a used car was located and the players continued on toward their baseball careers.

Frankly, the player who had called McDonald wasn't performing all that well; a left-hander, he had combined for a 5–13 record at two different stops in 1965. "We didn't think he was much of a prospect," McDonald admitted later. "He threw hard, but he didn't have a breaking ball." However, just as the Mets were on the verge of releasing him, McDonald remembered the $50 loan. He decided he'd take the money out of the player's paycheck, then let the lefty go once the debt was paid. But thanks to a new pitch learned that winter, and markedly better results on the mound, the Mets decided they'd let him stay.

And on a crisp fall afternoon in October 1969, when a Davey Johnson fly ball landed softly in the glove of Cleon Jones, the lefty on the mound turned in delight and jumped into the arms of catcher Jerry Grote. The Mets' decision to keep him had paid off, and in return, Jerry Koosman had helped lead the New York Mets to one of the biggest upsets in World Series history.

Jerome Martin Koosman was born on December 23, 1942, in Appleton, Minnesota. Though some contemporary baseball records listed his birth year as '43, Koosman later admitted he had fudged his age the first time he lined up on the field after being signed by the Mets. "When the guy next to me said he was 22, they told him he was too old. So I said I was 21."

Koosman's father, Martin, was a farmer, raising livestock and growing crops. His mother, Lydia, raised four children. Along with Jerome were his two brothers, Elton and Orville, and a sister, Violet. There were farm duties: cleaning barns, repairing fences, and even driving the huge tractor, but Jerry and Orville found time to balance their chores and schoolwork with their other interests: ice fishing on the lake and playing baseball in the hayloft, where they alternated between pitching and catching.

Soon, the younger Koosman's talent became known around the area and by the time he was 13, Jerome began the local tour, pitching in beer leagues, for semipro teams, and in American Legion ball, sometimes facing batters twice his age. After high school, he attended the Morris branch of the University of Minnesota, but the school had no baseball team. He transferred to the State School of Science in Wahpeton, North Dakota, but he was ineligible to play there, as he was a transfer student. While debating whether to go to school for engineering, Jerome was drafted into the Army in 1962.

After basic training, Koosman was stationed at Pere Marquette State National Park in Grafton, Illinois, but with no baseball facilities to speak of there either, he became disillusioned. His dentist, however, happened to be a commanding major general of the Minnesota National Guard (and also the guy who first started calling him Jerry instead of Jerome), and Koosman asked for help in getting transferred to a place where he could play ball.

Figuring that transfer would never come through, Jerry took the officer's candidate test; he had always wanted to fly and hoped he could train in helicopters. He passed the test, but while he awaited his new orders, Jerry's transfer came through and he was ordered to Fort Bliss in El Paso, Texas, to play baseball. Upon his arrival, he was sent to see the commanding officer, who immediately chewed him out for not getting there through the proper chain of command.

He was then handed off to PFC Pete Peters, who grabbed a catcher's mitt and had Koosman throw to him. After just a dozen pitches, Peters had seen enough. "You're starting," he said. In later years, Koosman said that if not for his dentist, he might have become a helicopter pilot and could have found himself flying a chopper in Vietnam. "Most of those guys didn't come back. I was two weeks from having my destiny changed."

At 6-foot-2 and 210 pounds, Jerry was already throwing hard. While he was at Fort Bliss, his catcher was Queens native John Luchese, whose father was an usher at Shea Stadium, the brand-new facility of the New York Mets. Luchese wrote home about the left-hander and his father passed it on to Joe McDonald. Acting on the tip, McDonald sent Mets scout Red Murff to see Koosman in person. Murff waited three days for Jerry to start. When he finally pitched, the southpaw fanned a dozen and Murff offered him a $2,000 bonus. But a few ex-players who had seen Jerry pitch in camp told the young lefty that his arm was worth much more than that, so Koosman turned down the contract. Murff returned to watch him again, then offered him only $1,900. When it got down to $1,600, Koosman signed, on August 27, 1964. "I figured I'd better take it or I'd owe them money!" he joked later.

Koosman's 1965 season was far from memorable: Along with a 5–11 record at Greenville in the Western Carolinas League, he had a 4.71 ERA (though he did pile up 128 strikeouts), then lost both his starts after being promoted to Williamsport, Pennsylvania, of the double-A Eastern League. It was at this point that the Mets considered releasing him—until McDonald remembered his $50, and it was here that fate intervened once more. Following in the wake of his dentist, and a well-connected usher at Shea Stadium, and then Red Murff, Koosman crossed paths with ex-major leaguer Frank Lary, who'd become a pitching instructor in the Mets system. Lary cemented Koosman's future in baseball with a simple step: He taught the lefty the slider.

"I caught on to it right away," said Koosman, and Lary believed his protégé's command of the new pitch to be so proficient that he suggested the Mets give Koosman another chance. Clyde McCullough, manager at Class A Auburn of the New York-Penn League, took on Koosman, but once again the young lefty made a bad first impression. Oversleeping the night before he was to report, Koosman missed his plane and showed up late the first day. He was immediately in McCullough's doghouse, sitting on the bench and participating in strenuous workouts for almost a month before finally getting into a game. Once he stepped on the field, however, impressions changed. Koosman led the league in 1966 with a 1.38 ERA, collecting 174 strikeouts. The following spring, he joined the Mets.

Koosman's first appearance in a big league uniform was in Philadelphia on April 14, 1967. He relieved starter Jack Fisher and threw 2⅔ innings, striking out two, walking two, and not allowing a hit. But after the season's first 30 days, the Mets had to cut three players, and Jerry was sent to Jacksonville, along with Greg Goossen and former World Series headliner Ralph Terry.

Though his record was just 11–10 in triple-A Jacksonville, Koosman led the International League with 183 strikeouts, allowing just 137 hits in 178 innings. He was called back to the Mets on September 1. In nine total appearances, including three starts, Koosman ended his first stint in the majors at 0–2, with a 6.04 ERA over 22⅓ innings.

Despite those numbers, Koosman made the starting rotation in New York the following spring under a new manager. Gil Hodges had been hired after Wes Westrum's departure in the final week and a half of the '67 season. Westrum had been "very kind to me," Koosman said of his previous manager, "so I was pretty downhearted when he got released." Anticipating a strong disciplinarian in Hodges, Koosman and many of his teammates were pleasantly surprised to find that the former Dodgers star was, at first, happy-go-lucky. "We had a lot of fun... but once he had his own club put together and knew the personalities, he became strict...[but] I doubt we would have won it with another manager. He was perfect for us."

Koosman was slated to make the first start of what became a brilliant rookie season in San Francisco, but Martin Luther King, Jr. had been assassinated the week before and the date had been designated as a national day of mourning; the major leagues canceled the entire day's schedule. Koosman was pushed back to open a series in Los Angeles on April 11, and he responded by beating the Dodgers on four hits in a 4–0 shutout.

Six days later, he started the home opener against San Francisco and began by loading the bases with nobody out. He then struck out Willie Mays looking, got left fielder Jim Ray Hart to foul out, and fanned catcher Jack Hiatt, on his way to another shutout.

Right fielder Ron Swoboda remembered the bases loaded sequence vividly. "What a display....I was thinking, 'Oh [expletive], we're in trouble.' Four, five, six were up...and Koosman retired all three of them, and in a hurry it became, 'Oh, [expletive], *they're* in trouble.'" The seven-hit, 3–0 masterpiece against the Cubs was the first home opening victory in the seven-year history of the New York Mets.

With back-to-back shutouts under his belt, Koosman cemented himself as the Mets' number two starter behind future Hall of Famer Tom Seaver. Swoboda said this arrangement made the lefty's job even harder. "Koosman got a lot of the tough matchups....Why would you burn your number one guy against the other team's number one? Koosman was number two, and he got some of the tougher matchups." Swoboda also marveled at the lefty's dominance. "He could get that fastball in on right-handers....Boy, you talk about eat them up!...His stuff was every bit as good as Seaver's."

Meanwhile, the Mets were learning about Koosman's makeup on the mound. Jerry Grote was a gritty catcher whose reputation had already been established. "If you didn't throw the ball where you were supposed to...Jerry had such a great arm that from a squatting position he could throw the

PHOTO COURTESY OF DWAYNE LABAKAS COLLECTION

*Jerry Koosman*

ball back at you as hard as you threw it up there," Koosman recalled. "He could handcuff you right in front of your belt buckle. He used to do this to [Mets right-hander] Jim McAndrew a lot. McAndrew would never challenge the hitters...so Grote kept firing it back and handcuffing him in front of his belt buckle, and we would kind of laugh about it." During a game in New York, however, Grote fired one back at Koosman; utilizing the calm demeanor he had already learned from his manager Hodges, the big lefty called his catcher out to the mound.

"I told him, 'Grotes, if you throw the ball back at me once more time like that I'm going to break your [freakin'] neck.'...He never threw it back at me [hard] again. We always had respect for each other after that."

At midseason of '68, Koosman—along with Grote and Seaver—made the NL All-Star team. Koosman struck out Carl Yastrzemksi for the final out in the 1–0 win. He was used to pitching with a razor-thin margin since he and the rest of the Mets pitching staff had to deal with their team's offense, or, to be more precise, their lack of it, on a daily basis. "Our feeling was this," Koosman said. "If you got four runs, it was a laugher. If you got three runs, you'd win. If you got two runs, you had to win half your games, and some of them you should win one to nothing. We just knew we'd have to win with one, two, or three runs."

By year's end, Koosman had met the challenge. Even in what was known as "The Year of the Pitcher" because of the dominance of pitching, Koosman's year could compare with that of almost anyone in the National League. He completed his first full major-league season at 19–12 with a dazzling 2.08 ERA and 178 Ks; the wins, ERA, and his seven shutouts broke club records set by Seaver the previous year. Koosman defeated every team in the league at least once and came up just short of the NL Rookie of the Year Award, losing out to Reds catcher Johnny Bench by a single vote, the closest tally to that time.

The Mets had reason to hope for the first time after seven seasons of existence. They had their staff of the future with Seaver, Koosman, and young fireballer Nolan Ryan. Highly touted Gary Gentry was ready to start the year in the rotation. Still, no one could have expected what was to come.

The Mets entered '69 amid a player boycott, offensive personnel who hadn't changed much, and a manager experiencing health problems. (Hodges had to give up smoking and drop 24 pounds before doctors would allow him to manage again following a heart attack at the end of the '68 season.) And even with the National League having split into divisions, the Mets were saddled with the two-time defending league champion Cardinals, a powerful Pirates team, and a Cubs squad with enough talent to run away with the division. "The Cubs had an excellent ballclub, just top-notch," said Koosman. "Leo Durocher was a manager who tried to intimidate umpires, and it became a great rivalry."

The Cub who annoyed the Mets the most was third baseman Ron Santo, who would jump and click his heels after every victory. "The fans in Chicago loved that act but it wasn't professional," said Mets coach Joe Pignatano. "You don't show up the other team."

Games between the clubs became instant classics, including one at Shea on July 9, when Durocher started outfielder Jimmy Qualls, appearing in only his 18th major league contest. Qualls broke up Tom Seaver's perfect game with one out in the ninth inning, the closest any Mete ever came at Shea Stadium—or anywhere else—of throwing a no-hitter.

By the time the Cubs returned to New York in early September, a Chicago lead that had been as large as 10 games in August had dwindled to 2½, and Koosman found himself matched up against righty Bill Hands on a cold night at Shea. In the bottom of the first, Durocher called for a knockdown pitch of Mets leadoff hitter Tommie Agee; Hands complied, throwing his first delivery right at Agee's head. Koosman's teammates, however, knew their starter had their backs. "Hands was a sinker/slider pitcher," remembered Swoboda. "Jerry Koosman threw a 90-plus fastball, and when he hit you, you stayed hit...And Koosie would *hit* ya." "When the Cubs came to bat in the second inning, Santo came up and Koosman drilled him. "No one moved," said Swoboda. "I think it scared the living (expletive) out of them."

Nobody had to tell Koosman what to do. "Hodges didn't say a word. It's just something you learn. It's how the game is played....I was telling them, 'Here's what happens if you throw at my hitters." But when Jerry came up for his second at-bat, Hands threw at *his* head. Koosman cursed at him. "You don't throw the ball hard enough to hurt anybody," he shouted. "And he threw at me three more times!"

The Mets won the game and the series, which included a controversial Agee slide under Randy Hundley's tag at the plate, a handkerchief-waving throng at Shea chanting, "Goodbye, Leo," and a black cat that cut in front of the Chicago dugout on its dash around the field.

By the time the Cubs left New York, they led the Mets by a mere half-game. But it was the pitch that hit Santo that most of the Mets remembered. "After that nobody would intimidate us," recalled Pignatano. "I don't think Santo clicked his heels after that."

And after a doubleheader sweep of the Montreal Expos on September 10, the Mets took control of first place, never to relinquish it. The startling accomplishments continued. On September 12, Koosman and righty Don Cardwell were the starters in a doubleheader in Pittsburgh; both games ended 1–0 with each pitcher driving in the only run of his win. (It was Koosman's only RBI of the season.) Three nights later in St. Louis, Steve Carlton struck out 19 Mets, but Swoboda hit two two-run homers in a 4–3 win. And finally, at Shea Stadium on September 24, rookie Gary Gentry threw a four-hitter against Carlton and the Mets beat the Cardinals, 6–0, to clinch the first NL East Division championship in history.

The Mets finished the '69 season with a record of 100–62. The pitching staff threw 28 shutouts, including six by Koosman, who ended the season at 17–9 with a 2.28 ERA, 180 strikeouts, and a second All-Star appearance. He struck out 15 San Diego Padres in 10 innings on May 28 and piled up 23 consecutive scoreless innings in June. He won eight of his final nine decisions.

In the inaugural NLCS, however, Mets pitching wasn't nearly as effective. This time the hitting picked them up. Koosman had an 9–1 lead in the fifth inning of Game Two, but he gave up six runs on seven hits in 4 ⅔ innings before Hodges removed him. "The worst beating I ever took," he declared in an interview in 2008. Nonetheless, the Mets won the game, 11–6, and went on to sweep the Atlanta Braves and advance to their first World Series. "We were so elated," said Koosman. "I just wish it had happened later in my career, so I'd remember it more."

As it turned out, the 1969 World Series provided a lifetime of memories. The Mets were heavy underdogs to the Orioles, Seaver lost the opener in Baltimore, 4–1, and it was up to Koosman to even the Series against lefty Dave McNally. "My goal from when I was 16 years old was to pitch a perfect game in the World Series," remembered Koosman. He came close, entering the seventh inning up 1–0, having not allowed a baserunner. Paul Blair finally got the first Baltimore hit ("I shook off Grote and Blair hit a curveball"), stole second, and scored on a Brooks Robinson single to tie the game.

But light-hitting infielder Al Weis singled in the go-ahead run for the Mets in the ninth with Koosman waiting on deck. Kooz got the first two outs in the bottom of the inning, before walking Frank Robinson and Boog Powell. Hodges brought in righty reliever Ron Taylor to get the last out and the Mets had tied the Series.

Back at Shea, they won Games Three and Four behind Seaver and Gentry (along with Nolan Ryan in relief). There were remarkable plays from Agee and Swoboda, plus an errant throw that hit baserunner J.C. Martin's wrist to bring in the winning run in Game Four and set up the potential clincher. Jerry Koosman was set to start Game Five.

He paced the bullpen, afraid to overwork before the game started. When it did, he gave up a two-run home run to his opposite number, McNally, then a solo shot to Frank Robinson. Both came in the third inning, but Koosman wasn't fazed. "Let's score some runs, boys," he declared in the dugout. "They will not get another run off of me." They didn't. The Mets scored five of their own, with home runs from Weis and Donn Clendenon keying the offense, along with a little help from shoe polish on a ball that started an unlikely rally.

In the sixth inning, McNally ostensibly hit Cleon Jones in the foot with a pitch. When home-plate umpire Lou DiMuro called a ball, Gil Hodges brought the baseball back out to the plate and showed a streak of shoe polish to DiMuro, who

*Jerry Koosman went 2–0 against the Cubs in 1969, and had the same record against the Orioles in the World Series.*

awarded Cleon first base.

But even *that* incredible "stroke of luck" can be credited to the Mets ace left-hander.

In a 2008 interview, Koosman went into detail: "[The ball] came to me. I wasn't sitting but a couple of yards from Gil and he says, 'Slide it on your shoe and throw it here,' and I did it. And he took it and he walked out to the umpire with it. And there was shoe polish on the ball. Whether it was mine or Cleon's is debatable. I didn't have time to look [to see if there was shoe polish on it], it all happened so fast. Hodges was way ahead of me. He was a genius."

When questioned about dispelling this Mets myth four decades after the fact, the crafty Koosman confirmed the tale. "Yes, it was me."

Tom Seaver, for one, doesn't sound as sure about it. Shortly before the closing of Shea Stadium—an event both Koosman and Seaver attended—Koosman's old friend and teammate simply said, "Koozy loves to tell stories." So, four decades later, this touchstone moment in Mets history remains a mystical event. What will never change is what happened next.

Donn Clendenon homered to left field on a McNally offspeed pitch to make it a 3–2 game and get the Mets offense rolling. An inning later, Al Weis hit his first-ever home run at Shea to tie the game. Ron Swoboda broke the tie with a double in the eighth and an insurance run scored on an error.

The Mets led 5–3 in the ninth. Koosman remembers it as the toughest inning he ever pitched, thanks to the noise at Shea and his own nervousness. "You couldn't hear yourself think," he said. "I couldn't control the ball anymore....I was *so* nervous and excited....I was just trying to throw it down the middle."

Relying exclusively on his fastball, Koosman walked Frank Robinson, but he got Boog Powell to ground into a force play. After Brooks Robinson flied out, second baseman Davey Johnson, who 17 years later would manage the Mets to their only other World Series title, lofted a fly to left. "You couldn't hear the crack of the bat," said Koosman. "I thought it was going to be a home run, but when I turned around at looked at Cleon, I knew right away....I thought, 'Oh, my God, whatever you do, just don't drop this ball.'" Jones didn't. Koosman jumped into Grote's arms, then fought his way through jubilant Mets fans on his way to the dugout. "I remember stepping on the side of one guy's leg and just tore his leg up with my spikes."

Once the Mets were inside the clubhouse, emotions were different. Koosman and Grote sat in front of the catcher's locker with a few other teammates, just looking at each other. "We were so choked up with emotion we couldn't talk." Koosman had posted a 2–0 record in the World Series, with a 2.04 ERA and just seven hits allowed in 17⅔ innings. It capped off a remarkable season.

Coach Joe Pignatano assessed the situation as others would not: "I think Koosman was a better big-game pitcher for us that year than Seaver."

But what no one talked about was how the star southpaw had pitched much of the season in pain. There was an accident with a pan of boiling butter while making popcorn during a team baby-sitting night at his apartment; he had burned the skin off the index and middle fingers of his pitching hand. And in April, while facing the Expos on a cold night in Montreal, Koosman felt his arm go numb in the fifth inning. "Grote came out to see what was wrong and I told him I had no feeling in my arm," recalled

Koosman. Hodges took him out of the game, then sent him back to New York. X-rays were negative, but while being examined, the doctor put some pressure on Koosman's teres minor muscle, part of the rotator cuff, that sent him flying off the table. It turned out to be a major knot in the muscle, requiring long, painful massages to work it out. He missed almost a month. Additionally, Koosman had almost as much trouble with his feet as with his left arm—bone spurs in his heel forced him to wear shoe cushions and subsequently he began to favor one leg over the other.

"People didn't realize the physical problems the guy had," said Swoboda. "He was a wreck. His arm hurt all the time, and he pitched the entire season in pain. I would see all that and he never complained, and I just admired the hell out of him."

Entering the 1970 season, the historically cellar-dwelling Mets were now defending world champs. It became obvious, however, that they were no match for the Pittsburgh Lumber Company, or the Big Red Machine in Cincinnati. The Mets ended the season (along with the next two) with a third-place finish.

The 1970 season was another painful year for Koosman as well: While running in the outfield in Cincinnati during batting practice on June 7, and despite Ron Taylor's warning shouts, Koosman was hit in the mouth with a line drive off the bat of Gentry. The shot broke Koosman's upper left jaw and drove at least five teeth back into his mouth. Unconscious for a few seconds, Koosman woke up on his hands and knees, "bleeding like a stuck hog." He had to push the teeth back into position. His jaw was wired shut for six weeks and he was ordered by Hodges to keep his weight up with caloric liquids for the duration. "Milkshakes," says Koosman, "*and* he made me drink a beer every game while I was on the bench. In six weeks, I only lost three pounds!"

Despite missing additional starts with tightness in his forearm, he ended his injury-plagued season at 12–7, his 3.14 ERA good for fifth in the NL. In 1971, his ERA dropped to 3.04, despite his being five games under .500. But it was another season of missed time for Koosman. Pitching in the cold, he felt a rhomboid muscle, in his upper back, tear during a 10-inning start in windy San Francisco. He spent time on the disabled list once again, but he observed that this particular injury made him a control pitcher, forcing him to pitch more carefully while waiting for the adhesions to tear.

Spring 1972 saw the untimely death of Gil Hodges. It was April 2 and Koosman was the only Met who had stayed behind at training camp while the rest of the team flew north, wondering if the start of the season would be lost to a player strike. Having no one to throw with, Koosman happened to meet Mick Tingelhoff at the hotel pool and the Minnesota Vikings center, a catcher in high school, offered to help. Afterward, while Koosman was showering, he heard sirens; when he rushed to the lobby, New York sportswriter Red Foley told him Hodges had been taken away in an ambulance and the two hurried to the hospital, where various Mets personnel were standing over the bed. "How's Gil?" he asked. "Gil's dead," pitching coach Rube Walker told him. Two days before his 48th birthday, Hodges had died from a massive heart attack after playing golf with his coaches.

"It was like a stone fell and hit your heart," said Koosman. "I don't even remember what happened after that. I don't remember too much about the funeral. We were all still in shock." Along with much of his team, Koosman worried that no one would be able to replace their beloved manager. "Oh, man, it was a huge void. Everybody went through the motions, trying to do what we thought Gil wanted us to do."

The Mets tried their best, naming coach and Yankees legend Yogi Berra to take over as manager. "Those shoes would have been impossible to fill," Koosman said.

Koosman had a rough start to the '72 season. "I literally forgot how to wind up," he remembered. "I used to use a cadence count when I pitched: it was 'one-two-three-four, then pitch,' but I had picked up a lot of bad habits." He had lost his rhythm. After three straight April defeats, Berra sent him to the bullpen, both to work out his problems and to utilize the veteran's ability to get warm quickly. Being in the bullpen "was very beneficial," said Koosman. He made 10 relief appearances and picked up his first regular-season save. After returning to the rotation, he won four straight to end at 11-12.

By the middle of the 1973 season, there were

rumors that Yogi would be canned. Reliever Tug McGraw succinctly described some of the players' feelings about the differences between the old manager and his replacement. "By the third inning, Gil [Hodges] was thinking about what he was going to do in the sixth; in the sixth, Yogi was thinking about what he *should* have done in the third." Twice during the season, Berra put in a relief pitcher, then tried to remove him before facing a batter, which is, of course, against the rules.

But despite the questions about leadership, the Mets stunned baseball again by coming from last place and 11½ games out on August 5 to capture the division with an 82–79 record, the lowest winning percentage to claim a league title since the founding of the National League in 1876. Koosman, who got the win that clinched at least a tie, remembers the celebration that occurred the next day at Wrigley Field when the Mets won the division. "We couldn't believe we had won it and that nobody else wanted to win it," he said.

Koosman had epitomized his team's up-and-down season, first being named NL Player of the Month for April with a 4–0 record and a 1.06 ERA, then losing 14 of his next 18 decisions including eight of nine; much of it due to a woeful offense. The Mets were shut out three times in those eight losses, and scored three runs or less in seven of them. The lefty's season turned again, however, on August 19, when he began a streak of 31⅔ scoreless innings, not allowing a run through September 7, a club record set by number 36 that remained 36 years later. The streak included a 10-inning complete-game victory over Juan Marichal. Koosman won six of his last seven decisions, ending the season at 14–15 with a 2.84 ERA and 12 complete games.

The Mets' opponents in the best-of-five National League Championship Series were the Cincinnati Reds, and Koosman faced Ross Grimsley with the series tied in what would become infamous Game Three. "I started it," said Koosman of the fireworks to follow. After getting Pete Rose to pop up on a slow curve, Rose began to curse Koosman from the dugout for throwing off-speed pitches. "I could hear him holler out to me, 'Throw the ball, you big, dumb [freakin'] donkey.'" In Rose's next at-bat, Koosman tried to hit him, but Rose singled. Though trailing in the fifth inning, 9–2, Rose barreled into shortstop Bud Harrelson while trying to break up a double play, starting one of the most famous brawls in postseason history.

"You're not going to let them intimidate you," said Koosman. "We were David going against Goliath...and maybe we didn't have the strength that Cincinnati had, but we weren't going to back down..." Koosman ended the day with a complete game and the Mets led the series, two games to one, en route to a five-game victory.

In the World Series, the Mets faced the defending world champion Oakland A's and they entered their second fall classic as heavy underdogs. After the Mets lost the opener, Koosman started Game Two in Oakland, but he allowed three runs on six hits in just 2⅓ innings; the Mets rallied, however, for a 12-inning victory. After the teams split Games Three and Four at Shea, Koosman pitched 6⅓ innings in Game Five, allowing just three hits. The 2–0 victory put the Mets one win away from their second world championship in five seasons.

At this point, Berra's managing came into question again. Left-hander George Stone had had a great first season for the Mets, going 12–3, but Berra, perhaps reluctant to use his fourth starter on the road in Game Six, instead chose Seaver on three days' rest. The future Hall of Famer pitched well, but the Mets lost, 3–1. Berra then passed over Stone again for Game Seven, going with Jon Matlack, also on short rest.

Koosman was warming up during the final game and felt good. "I had a great fastball. I could hit the corner of a cigarette pack," he recalled. When Matlack got into trouble in the third inning, Koosman asked Rube Walker to tell Yogi he was ready. Berra didn't call. "I never got into that ballgame," said Koosman. "That's the game I remember most, being in the bullpen and just so ready to come in." Home runs by Bert Campaneris and Reggie Jackson spurred the A's to a 5–2 victory and their second of three consecutive world championships.

The Mets were miserable in 1974, posting their worst record in seven seasons, though Koosman went 15–11 with a 3.36 ERA and 188 strikeouts. The next year started slowly as well. The organization had lost many of the executives and coaches who had built two NL champs and Berra was feeling the heat. "Yogi was making moves that didn't sit well with the team," said Koosman. "Gil always said, 'We have one set of rules here.'...Those were Hodges's rules." But under Berra, "If somebody made a mental error...Yogi would say, 'Next time it's gonna cost ya.' And it became a saying, 'Next time it's gonna cost ya.' And you'd get away with it over and over." Berra didn't get away with losing much longer. He was fired in August, replaced first by ex-Met Roy McMillan, then at the start of '76 by career minor league manager Joe Frazier.

The Mets ended 1975 in third place, Koosman going 14–13 with a 3.42 ERA. The impressive ERA on a team barely over .500 was a precursor to his '76 season, an emotional one for Koosman, whose father died on March 30. "I felt the spirit of my dad was on my shoulder the whole year," Koosman said of his intense focus that season. "My cadence count was in perfect rhythm the entire year. I was never, ever able to reach that level of concentration again."

He also appreciated his new manager. "[Frazier] handed me the ball and said, 'Take care of it.' He put more responsibilities on the starters than Yogi did." Koosman rewarded that trust, finishing 1976 with a 21–10 record, a 2.69 ERA, and 200 Ks. It was the most wins he accrued over 19 major league seasons, and he finished second to San Diego's Randy Jones in the Cy Young Award voting. "That was my greatest year," he said. The following season, however, was probably his worst.

The 1977 campaign was filled with turbulence, underscored by the infamous "Midnight Massacre" on June 15 when Mets management dealt Seaver to the Reds. "It was a tough thing to see happen," said Koosman of his comrade-in-arms. "We were in Atlanta, and there were a lot of tears shed." It was also the start of the biggest downturn in Mets history since Koosman's arrival. The team's penny-pinching had stripped it of most of its talent. Koosman felt that general manager Joe McDonald, who also traded slugger Dave Kingman the same night as Seaver, was making senseless deals. "We were not getting better. We were getting worse....Every general manager in the league was taking advantage of us. We were competing in the National League with double-A and triple-A ballplayers."

The Mets ended the year 34 games under .500, with Koosman a miserable 8–20. It was the most losses he ever endured in a season and made him the last pitcher in major league history to lose 20 after winning 20 the previous season. As was his habit, however, he finished with a decent 3.49 ERA, again highlighting the lack of support from his offense. The 1978 season saw more of the same: 3–15 with a 3.75 ERA, and an ironic meeting on September 29, when Koosman once again found himself facing the same Davey Johnson who had made the final out of the 1969 World Series. Pitching in relief, Koosman got him to fly out again—this time, however, it was to right field—and it was Johnson's final at-bat in the major leagues.

But the Mets finished the season in last place. "We had *no* offense, and *terrible* defense," said Koosman. And though they were friends, he even had issues with his latest skipper, Joe Torre, whom he called a hitter's manager: "I can remember a few occasions when the score was 0–0 in the fifth, two outs and a runner on second, and I'm coming up to hit, and Torre pinch-hit for me. I said, 'Let me throw a shutout. Maybe we'll score one in the ninth.' He just would not allow me to stay in there long enough."

His disillusionment with the team's sorry state started him thinking seriously about life after baseball. Issuing an ultimatum to the man whose $50 loan had inadvertently started Koosman on the path to stardom, Kooz gave GM Joe McDonald a list of 10 teams, telling him that if he wasn't traded he'd retire. When nothing happened, he tightened the list to five, then to one: "Either trade me to the Twins or I'm out of here," said Koosman. And on December 8, 1978, the Mets traded Jerry Koosman to Minnesota for Greg Field and a player to be named later: left-hander Jesse Orosco, the reliever who went on to become a vital cog in future Mets successes. And who, in 1986, would join Koosman as the only Mets to ever be on the mound the moment the franchise won a World Series.

"I hated to leave," said Koosman, but he figured if he was going to play for a losing club, it might as well be closer to home. "The front office of the Mets did not want to win, and I just couldn't stomach that." Koosman, however, acknowledged in 2008 that he was just bluffing. "I told them I was going into the air freight business." When asked what he would have done the next season had the Mets not agreed to trade him, he laughs. "I would have been with the Mets!"

Nevertheless, Koosman left New York after 12 seasons, with a deceptive 140–137 record, a 3.09 ERA, 108 complete games, and 26 shutouts. Thanks to the miserable teams at the end of his Mets tenure, Koosman passed Seaver for most losses in franchise history. However, he also ended his Mets career second to the Hall of Famer in team annals in starts, complete games, shutouts, innings pitched, wins, and strikeouts (Dwight Gooden later passed him for second in Ws and Ks).

"It was sad," he said of leaving the team he had grown up with. "I had my heart and soul and blood in the Mets, and I wanted to do everything I could to make them succeed. But our top form was so short-lived. Only five years, from '69 through '73....Where did it all go? How could it happen so fast?"

Jerry Koosman began the 1979 season for a team other than the New York Mets for the first time in his career. Koosman's first year with the Twins was by far his best post-Met campaign; he went 20–13 with a 3.38 ERA. Over the next season and a half, Koosman went 19–22, but the Twins had begun to use him in relief and he picked up seven saves. The White Sox, looking for a reliever for their playoff push, inquired about him and Koosman, though he had veto power, agreed to a trade with Chicago in August of 1981. The price was three minor leaguers and cash.

The White Sox employed Koosman as a spot starter/reliever and he rang up identical 11–7 records in 1982 and '83, making the playoffs with Chicago the latter season, but in the postseason, he pitched only a third of an inning and was touched for two earned runs on a hit and two walks.

The White Sox re-signed him as a free agent in December 1983, but they sent him to the Phillies two months later as the player to be named later in a trade for pitcher Ron Reed. While the deal wound up keeping him from reuniting with Seaver—who had been picked up by the White Sox after he briefly reunited with the Mets—greeting Kooz in Philadelphia was Tug McGraw, who'd been Kooz's teammate in both the minors and majors, and had been instrumental in both Mets pennants.

Koosman returned to the Shea Stadium mound for the first time in a visitor's uniform on April 29, 1984. The homecoming was not a happy one, as Koosman allowed four runs over 5⅔ innings, losing to the Mets, 6–2. The save that day went to Jesse Orosco, the young lefty the Mets got back from the Twins in the 1979 deal for Koosman.

Also during the 1984 season, 11 years after the infamous brawl with the Reds, Koosman found himself facing Pete Rose, now with Montreal. "I had him 0–2 and threw him a fastball high and away," he remembered. The pitch broke Rose's bat, but the ball found its way to the outfield, where it landed on the foul line and rolled for a double. It was Rose's 4,000th career hit.

At the age of 41, Koosman was the workhorse on the staff of the defending NL champion Phillies. His 34 starts, 14 wins, and 15 losses were the most by anyone in Philadelphia's rotation. The Phillies brought him back in 1985, but an old injury flared up during the season, and Koosman's knee filled with fluid and bone chips. After having the knee drained, he tried to come back too quickly; while pitching the first inning in a game against the Dodgers on August 21, the knee filled up again and Jerry felt his leg buckle. Tossing a bloop toward the direction of the plate while falling to the ground, he regained his balance, got back up, and walked off the field for the last time.

Jerry Koosman retired after 19 games in 1985 with a career record of 222–209, 140 complete games, 33 shutouts, and more than 2,500 strikeouts. His career ERA for 19 seasons was 3.36.

Koosman settled in Chaska, Minnesota, where he got together other professional players and coaches, to promote America's Best, a program designed to showcase the finest young baseball talent in the country. After finding an interested sponsor, Major League Baseball would not provide the necessary financial support and the program floundered. A few years later, the Mets brought Koosman back as a minor-league pitching instructor, and he spent 1991 at Pittsfield, Massachusetts, and '92 in Columbia, South Carolina.

Photo courtesy of Jacob Kanarek/metsintheseventies.com

*Thirty-plus years after he threw his last pitch as a Met, Jerry Koosman remains the leader among all southpaws in nearly every pitching category in club history.*

In 2009, failure to pay past income tax resulted in a six-month jail sentence in Wisconsin, where he had his own machine design business. Koosman was divorced from his wife, LaVonne, in 2003; they had three children: Danielle, Shawn, and Michael, the first "Met baby," born at rookie camp in St. Petersburg.

Koosman said the best compliment he ever got from another player came from the late Pirates star Roberto Clemente, who once said that Koosman's fastball was the only one he ever saw "that never moved the same way twice." Seaver said he believed that if his teammate "hadn't gotten hurt, he'd have been in the Hall of Fame." Koosman received scant support for Cooperstown, getting just four votes in 1991, his lone year on the ballot. He was elected to the Mets Hall of Fame in 1989 as the fourth player inducted after former teammates Bud Harrelson, Rusty Staub, and Seaver.

Said Koosman in a 2008 interview of his major league career: "I could have had more shutouts and more strikeouts. But I always believed in throwing the least amount of pitches possible and letting them hit it." This efficiency, along with endless determination, led Jerry Koosman to become one of the most popular New York Mets of all time and, some say, the most valuable Met of the miracle 1969 season. And though no one who watched the Mets could deny his obvious talent, few were aware of the pain and difficulties he so often had to pitch through.

And it also makes Mets fans shudder to think what might have been had Jerry Koosman not had to borrow money so he could to buy himself another car.

**Sources**

Two interviews with Jerry Koosman: July 2008.

Allen, Maury. *After The Miracle: The 1969 Mets Twenty Years Later.* New York: Franklin Watts, 1989.

Barrow, Ed: "Just Terrific: Tom Seaver Gives Mets an Identity & a Title." *New York Daily News* Special Section entitled "Memories of Shea: An Amazin' History, 1964-2008," September 21, 2008.

Golenbock, Peter. *Amazin': The Miraculous History of New York's Most Beloved Baseball Team.* New York: St. Martin's Press, 2002.

New York Mets Yearbooks: 1965-73.

New York Mets Media Guides: 2005, 2008.

New York Mets Scorecard: 2003, Volume 42, Issue 5

Wikipedia listing for Jerry Koosman

## Walking on the Moon

The Mets took their second series from the Cubs in July and found themselves in foreign territory in more ways than one. New York, four games behind Chicago, could forge a first-place tie at the All-Star break with a sweep in Montreal and a Phillies sweep of the Cubs at Connie Mack Stadium. There was a better chance of a man landing on the moon.

Shortly after the Mets navigated the 750 miles through the air between Chicago and Montreal, astronauts Neil Armstrong, Buzz Aldrin, and Michael Collins started their 240,000 mile journey from the earth to the moon. On Sunday, July 20, a last-minute improvisation to avoid a boulder field left Apollo 11 with just 30 seconds of fuel. With alarms sounding, the craft touched down on the moon at 4:18 p.m. EDT. "Houston, Tranquility Base here. The Eagle has landed," Armstrong told the world. It would be more than six hours before he took his famous steps on the moon's surface.

Back on earth—at Jarry Park, to be precise—the Mets lost the first game of a doubleheader in Montreal when Gary Gentry allowed three home runs in the fourth inning. The Mets blew leads in the eighth and ninth in the nightcap before Bobby Pfeil's two-out bunt brought home the go-ahead run and Jack DiLauro picked up his first major league win. The Mets were lucky to get a split of the day and the series, considering Cleon Jones got in a fight after a play at the plate and Tom Seaver, winner of 13 of 14 starts—plus a no-decision that the Mets won, anyway—lost his second straight game after getting knocked out in the third inning Saturday; he left that game in Montreal complaining of a sore right shoulder. The Cubs took three of four in Philly and headed into the break up by five games, the biggest lead in any of the three competitive divisions (the Orioles had wrapped up the American League East with an 11-game lead over Boston).

While Armstrong and Co. prepared to walk on another planet, the Mets could not get out of Canada. A defect in their 727's oil system kept the team grounded in Montreal and they watched the historic moon walk of Armstrong and Aldrin from a small television in an empty terminal. The Mets finally made it to New York, a 90-minute flight that didn't return to New York until 2:45 a.m.

"That's one small step for man…one giant leap for mankind."

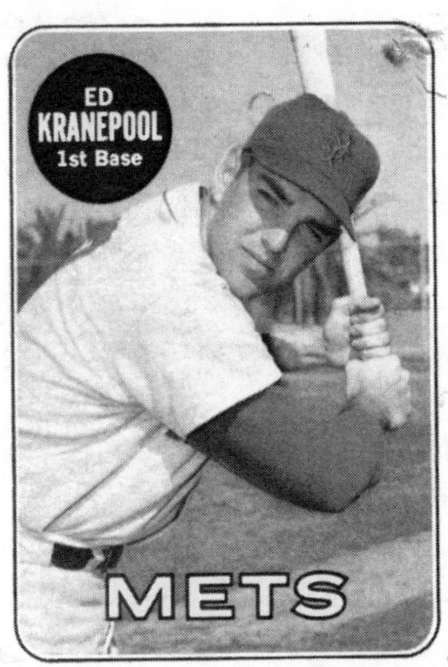


# Ed Kranepool

by Tara Krieger

| Season | Age | G | AB | R | H | 2B | 3B | HR | RBI | BB | SO | SB | CS | BA | OBP | SLG |
|---|---|---|---|---|---|---|---|---|---|---|---|---|---|---|---|---|
| 1969 Mets | 23 | 112 | 353 | 36 | 84 | 9 | 2 | 11 | 49 | 37 | 32 | 3 | 2 | .238 | .307 | .368 |
| Career 18 Years | – | 1853 | 5436 | 536 | 1418 | 225 | 25 | 118 | 614 | 454 | 581 | 15 | 27 | .261 | .316 | .377 |

It was a damp night at Shea Stadium in early August 1977. The last-place Mets, toiling through extra innings against the Los Angeles Dodgers, looked done for after the would-be National League champions took a 7–6 lead in the top of the 11th. But they managed to put runners at first and second with one out in the bottom of the inning. With light-hitting shortstop Doug Flynn due up next, manager Joe Torre signaled for the pinch hitter.

Fans sensed what was coming, and what started as a low buzz of speculation among the stragglers of the crowd of just above 9,000 crescendoed into an all-too-familiar chant:

"Ed-die! Ed-die! Ed-die! Ed-die!"

Sure enough, the big lefty with the number 7 on his back started taking practice cuts in the on-deck circle. Time for Steady Eddie Kranepool, pinch hitter extraordinaire, to play hero once again.

And once again, he came through, rapping out an RBI single to tie the score. The Mets would eventually win the game, 8–7, in the 12th on a single by Joel Youngblood, Kranepool's clutch hitting reduced to a footnote. Business as usual in the life of a role player—and Kranepool was about as good a role player as they came. In 1974, he had set the all-time season record for pinch-hit batting average (over 30 at-bats) by compiling a mark of .486 (17-for-35) in those situations In his career, he had 90 hits—including six home runs—off the bench.

Half a lifetime ago, though, Ed Kranepool was thought by some to be the next Lou Gehrig: a powerful left-handed slugging first baseman signed with much fanfare to a team just a borough away from where he was born and raised. When he fell far short of those weighty expectations, he might have disappeared, like so many other bonus babies who had failed to meet their potential.

But if Kranepool had one thing in common with the Iron Horse it was resilience. He refused to quit, and wouldn't go away. Years later, he'd seen it all—from the Amazin'ly awful '62 Mets to the Miracle of '69, to the '73 squad that would only "believe," to the teams of the late '70s that maybe didn't so much believe. When he retired in 1979 after 18 seasons with the organization, he held just about every franchise record, and still holds some to this day. For better or for worse, he was the one constant for almost the entire first two decades of Mets history, and the fans in Flushing showered the last original Met with respect.

On July 28, 1944, 31-year-old Sgt. Edward Kranepool was machine-gunned down in Saint-Lô, France, leaving behind a three-year-old daughter, Marilyn, and a wife, Ethel, six months pregnant. The son, Edward Emil III, was born on November 8 of that year, in the Castle Hill section of the Bronx.

Faced with having to raise two small children herself, Ethel Kranepool survived on a military widow's pension, and worked odd jobs to supplement her income.

"We were not an affluent family, obviously on a military pension, and I guess that's why my days were spent in a playground as an athlete," Ed Kranepool recalled. "When I was 10 years of age, I joined Little League, and that was the start of my baseball career."

His neighbor and Little League coach, Jim Schiaffo, was about as close to a father as young Ed had.

"He was a good, good friend," Kranepool said. "I thought when his wife died he and my mother would get married and they never did. He had two sons and he considered me the third son he never had. He loved baseball; he loved working with the kids."

Schiaffo tirelessly worked with young Ed from an early age to improve his play. When he developed a habit of "stepping in the bucket"—bailing out the front foot on a pitch—Schiaffo placed a trough of water in the offending spot, so that every time his protégé stepped the wrong way, he'd end up with a wet foot. This literal interpretation of stepping in the bucket eventually worked.

"He would teach ways of how to hit and how not to hit and if you didn't do it right, you paid the penalty," Kranepool said. "He went to every one of my games after I graduated from Little League. He took a real interest."

Kranepool, who grew up with images of the Yankees and Mickey Mantle's heroics gracing the television, said that he never wanted to be anything but a baseball player. And he realized his talent early on. "I played every day of my life some kind of sport, preferably baseball or basketball," he said. "We played stickball in those days in the street—I used to beat the big kids in stickball." In Little League, he added, "I led the league in hitting three years in a row—I hit .700 every year. That's gotta tell you you're better than the average kid. Not to brag or anything."

Most of the best players as children start off pitchers or catchers, and Kranepool starred on the mound; he still has the news clippings of those early feats. But when he was 11, he broke his left elbow rounding the bases.

"A guy on the opposing team stuck his leg out and I tripped over it on the concrete," he said. "Medically, they didn't set it properly and it just never healed properly. I performed well afterwards, but I never pitched as well as I did."

He adjusted, instead, teaching himself to throw right-handed until the left arm was at full strength. When his velocity didn't quite come back, he focused on playing first base and the outfield, positions where a powerful throwing arm isn't necessarily top priority. And he never really had much trouble walloping the ball.

It also helped to live in the right school district: James Monroe High School, then, as now, a perennial city baseball powerhouse. A growth spurt his sophomore year helped him become a star basketball player, too, and as a 6-foot-3, over-200-pound senior he scored a then-school record 385 points (24 points per game) and was named to the All-New York City team. Several colleges, including St. John's and North Carolina, offered him scholarships.

But basketball was more, for him, just a means to get in shape for the spring, and the baseball scouts were after Kranepool early. In three years with the Monroe varsity, he hit 19 home runs. Nine of them came his senior year, breaking a 1929 school record set by Hank Greenberg, who didn't do so badly in the majors himself. Students nicknamed a large oak in right-center field "Eddie's Tree," after the long balls he hit in that direction. In 1962, Monroe made the Public School Athletic League (PSAL) finals, but lost, 6–5, to defending champion Curtis, a Staten Island school, in part because Kranepool, showing extreme hustle after a popup, had tripped over a garden hose someone had left out in right field and dropped the ball, allowing two runs to score. Kranepool had also come on to pitch in the seventh inning in that game, and recorded a scoreless eighth and ninth. Within weeks, he'd signed a major league contract.

Nearly all the big league clubs had sent scouts to see Kranepool at some point or another. The Yankees would have been his first choice, naturally, and in the years before the First-Year Player Draft, prospects were free to sign with the highest bidder. There was more money to be had elsewhere. His physical education director had connections to the White Sox, and Greenberg, then the team vice president, had expressed some interest. But the expansion Mets, in search of its first home-grown star, recruited Kranepool relentlessly—they'd even invited him to cut classes and sit in the owner's box at the team's inaugural game at the Polo Grounds on April 13—and the lure of playing close to home was also an enticement.

On June 27, Mets scout Bubber Jonnard and vice president Johnny Murphy personally came to Kranepool's home at 847 Castle Hill Avenue to work out the details. Ethel Kranepool, who was fully supportive of her son doing what he wanted to do, told the *New York Mirror* that she'd had a figure in her head about what she thought would be a fair offer when Murphy asked her son what he thought he should get. "When he came out with the identical figure I had in mind, I was stunned," she said.[1]

"We hashed it out; it was a numbers game," Ed Kranepool said. "Did I get the best contract? Probably not. Money wasn't the only thing—I just wanted to play somewhere. There was an incentive clause; I get a bonus to get to the major leagues; if I had an agent, they would've not reduced it a bit." But, he added, "It was more money than I ever expected in my life." He signed the contract on the kitchen table.

For any 17-year-old kid nowadays, the number would have been somewhat staggering; in 1962 (before inflation and multimillion-dollar free agency), it was flat-out overwhelming: an $80,000 bonus, another $1,000 if he reached Double-A, another $3,000 for Triple-A, another $7,500 for the major leagues. He would hit them all by the end of the season. After the government swallowed half the contract, Kranepool invested the rest in a white T-bird convertible and an eight-room split-level in White Plains he shared with his mother.

Kranepool immediately flew out to Los Angeles—his first plane ride—to join the Mets, who were facing the Dodgers on June 30. His first day in a Mets uniform was only a harbinger of what his experiences would be in those early years with the team, as he watched Sandy Koufax no-hit his new teammates. Kranepool, who would eventually play on the losing end of four no-hitters in his career, might have made it five had he gotten in the game that day, as manager Casey Stengel went to the bench late in the game, but passed over the rookie in favor of Gene Woodling.

"I remember saying 'thank God,' to myself," he recounted in his 1977 instructional, *Baseball*, written with Ed Kirkman. Kranepool had "wanted no part of the Dodgers lefty."

After one week of riding the bench as a uniformed spectator, Kranepool was farmed out to triple-A Syracuse for seasoning. But after struggling at the plate there, he was demoted to Class A Knoxville (a Tigers farm club the Mets had an agreement with) in mid-July, and Class D Auburn a week later. With Kranepool batting somewhere better than .340 at Auburn and, the Mets, on their way to shattering all kinds of records for futility with a 120-loss season, decided to recall him to New York on September 12. Kranepool's first major league appearance came on September 22 (loss 116) against the Cubs, relieving Gil Hodges at first base in the seventh inning, and grounding out in his only at-bat in the eighth. A day later, in the Mets' final home game (a win), he started at first base, and sliced a double down the left-field line in the eighth for his first major league hit.

As the 1963 season dawned, Kranepool, who had played winter ball in Florida in the months between, had reason to be hopeful he would be on the roster to stay. The New York writers were certainly hot on the Mets' boy wonder, and manager Casey Stengel was spouting comparisons to Mel Ott, the Giants' Hall of Famer who had also started at the Polo Grounds as a teenager. Young women from all over the country would flood his locker in those early years with love letters and marriage proposals. And Kranepool, who started at first base and the outfield early in the season and hit his first home run on April 19, could certainly be cocky about reports of his apparent maturity at such a young age. When Duke Snider, in the twilight of a Cooperstown-bound career, happened upon Kranepool slapping balls up the middle and to left field during batting practice, he reprimanded him to pull the ball to right, like a proper left-handed hitter should. Kranepool, who'd been specifically instructed by Stengel to spray the ball to the opposite field that day as a way of working on his timing, snapped back at his elder teammate, "You're not going so good yourself."

Part of Kranepool's problem was that, in the days before all big league teams regularly employed hitting coaches, he never learned how to hit properly. "I was aggressive, very competitive. I would swing at balls I couldn't hit, being young and anxious, and I would get out," he said, adding that even though he always had good hand-eye coordination, "My eyes probably went against me...When I swung the bat at a ball, I hit it; I didn't strike out. When a pitcher throws the ball that's not in the hitting area, I'd hit a ground ball to second base, first base, and get out. Better hitters swing and miss at good pitches, so when they do make contact, it goes."

Kranepool continued to slump, and, with his average down to .190 by early July, he was sent to triple-A Buffalo, where he batted .310 with five home runs. He was recalled in early September, and started out at a 9-for-20 clip. He finished the year batting .274 (17-for-62) to lift his season average to .209. He reported to spring training in 1964 again confident he would remain in the majors, but again, things soured fairly quickly.

On his third day in Florida, he pulled his left hamstring running out a grounder to first. "Who ever heard of a 19-year-old kid pulling a muscle?"[2] Stengel barked angrily to the media, intoning that if Kranepool had reported to camp in better shape, he wouldn't have gotten hurt. Kranepool also took criticism, mainly from the press, for not running fast enough, and not hustling on the basepaths.

But Kranepool never had anything bad to say about Stengel. "In the baseball world, he gave me as much guidance as he could," he recalled. "If I messed up, he didn't expose me, he tried to help me."

On May 13, batting .139, Kranepool was sent back to Buffalo. He cried. But after two weeks of batting .352 with three home runs, he was recalled to the parent club. Following a doubleheader at Syracuse on May 30, he hopped an early-morning flight to Newark Airport and cabbed it to Shea Stadium, the Mets' brand new ballpark, to start both ends of a sold-out 1 p.m. doubleheader against the Giants that day. The second game of the May 31 twin bill went 23 innings and finished a half-hour before midnight (the Mets lost both games). Kranepool was on the field for every out, marking a total of 50 innings of baseball played in two different cities, in two days.

"I wanted it to go a little longer," he was often quoted afterwards. "That way, I could always say that I played in a game that started in May and ended in June."[2]

Kranepool started nearly every inning of every game at first base the rest of the season—with the exception of a three-week stretch in July when he sprained his ankle backing away from a pitch thrown by the Cardinals' Ray Sadecki—batting .257 with 10 home runs and 45 RBIs in 420 at-bats. Even though the Mets lost 100 games for the third straight season, they found themselves playing a role in the hotly-contested pennant race in a season-ending series with St. Louis. With the Cardinals leading the Cincinnati Reds by a half-game, the Mets miraculously took the first two games of the series to move the first-place teams into a tie on the last day of the season. New York led in the fifth inning of the final game before St. Louis mounted a sizeable comeback; Kranepool's foul popup in the ninth inning was the final out that clinched the Cardinals the National League pennant.

Banners unfurled at Shea that summer read, "IS ED KRANEPOOL OVER THE HILL?" and "SUPERSTIFF." He hadn't even hit his 20th birthday, and already he was being written off as a failure.

Kranepool had signed with the Mets partially because their situation seemed to promise an accelerated path to the Show (the Yankees, for one, had several prospects at first base who might have gotten in his way), but as the years went by, he slowly began to realize that may have been a grave mistake.

"It might not have been to my best advantage to get to the major leagues so fast," said Kranepool. On an expansion team like the Mets, "you have [more] inexperience than on a better ballclub; a kid of 17 isn't equipped to handle that pressure. If I was on a good ballclub, the pressure to handle that wouldn't be so great. With the Mets, we were a bad ballclub. They said, 'Ed's going to lead them from a bad ballclub to the pennant.' One player, even a Hall of Famer, can't do that."

History, in some ways, has overglamorized the Mets' propensity for ineptitude before 1969—it wasn't something they passively accepted in the way the fans unconditionally loved them for it. Ron Swoboda remembered Kranepool telling him of those early years, "We used to celebrate rainouts."[3] When asked once on a survey what his

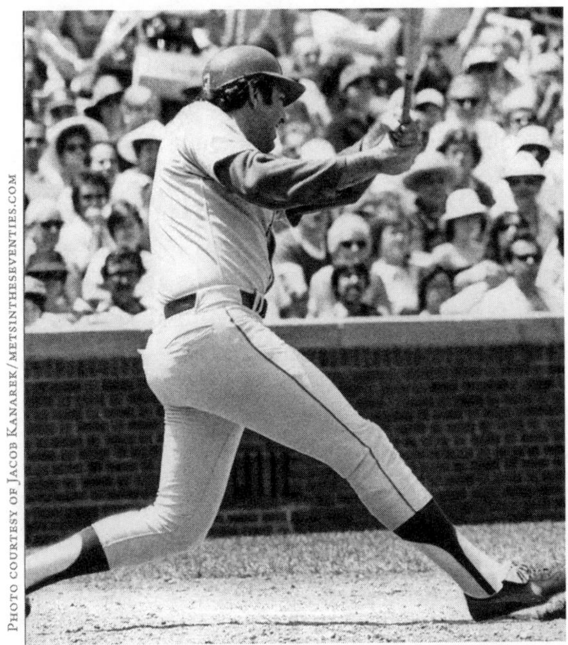
PHOTO COURTESY OF JACOB KANAREK/METSINTHESEVENTIES.COM

*During his 18 seasons as a Met, Ed Kranepool at one point held nearly every significant Mets offensive record. Thirty years later he still holds club records for total bases, games, at-bats, hits, doubles, pinch hits, multi-hit games, and sacrifice flies.*

"greatest memory" of the 1962 season was, Kranepool wrote, "NONE."[4]

"I still hit .255, .265, against Koufax or whoever, but everyone expected me to hit .350 ... I was always scrutinized by the fans in New York," Kranepool said. "If you struggled in the minors, you struggled down in Podunk. They didn't read about it in the papers every day."

And there were social obstacles Kranepool hadn't even considered. "My first roommate was Frank Thomas. He was 34; I was 17," Kranepool said. "You tell me—what can you have in common with a 34-year-old? They used to go out, I couldn't even drink!"

After the 1964 season, Stengel let go Tim Harkness, who had often started at first base the two previous years when Kranepool hadn't, a further indication that Kranepool would finally be given chance to shine. When Warren Spahn joined the team that spring, Kranepool voluntarily handed over his number 21 jersey out of respect for the great pitcher who'd worn it his entire career. "I didn't get a Rolex for it or a car; I just gave it to Warren," he said. Kranepool picked up number 7.

With a new number and a guaranteed roster spot, Kranepool came out swinging in 1965, leading the league in batting at the end of April. He was hitting .288 with seven home runs and 36 RBIs on July 7 when he found out he'd been selected to the National League All-Star team as the Mets' lone representative. He ended up not playing in the game in Minnesota, but just making the squad at such a young age alongside a cast of future Hall of Famers was a thrill.

"I was looking to the right of me, and there was Willie Mays; to the left, Henry Aaron," Kranepool said of what would end up being his lone All-Star experience. "I was the only [Met], I made the 'Hall of Shame,' I guess."

Upon his return from the Twin Cities, Kranepool fell into a second-half slump, and ended up batting .253 with 10 home runs and 53 RBIs. As the season came to a close, he was regularly platooning with Jim Hickman, too.

In 1966, he was again promised by new manager Wes Westrum (Stengel retired in the middle of the previous season due to a broken hip) that he would be the starting first baseman, but the Mets acquired righty Dick Stuart; Kranepool ended up platooning again, with Stuart (who batted .218 and was released in June), and a cast of characters including Hickman, Hawk Taylor, and Ed Bressoud. Kranepool finished the season with similar numbers to the previous year: .254, 16 home runs (which turned out to be his career high), and 57 RBIs.

In the winters of 1964 and 1965, Kranepool had taken courses at the Institute of Finance. He successfully passed the exam for his stockbroker's license on his 21st birthday, the first day he was eligible. By early 1967, he had built up a steady clientele of around 160 accounts at the brokerage firm of Brand, Grumet & Seigel. He married a secretary from the firm, the former Carole Henson, just before spring training.

As one of only two licensed brokers in the National League at the time (pitcher and future US Senator Jim Bunning being the other), Kranepool would often discuss the Mets' ups and downs in terms of the boom and bust of the stock market. He would read *The Wall Street Journal* every day, and carry paperwork from the office with him on road trips. Sometimes, players would ask him for financial advice.

"During the World Series, the Dow-Jones wire carries the score every inning, plus the home runs and pitchers," he mused at the time. "Wouldn't it be great if the Mets got into the Series and I hit a home run that was flashed over the ticker along with the quotations? Boy, the office would go wild."[5] Kranepool had no idea just how prophetic those words would be.

The Mets still were finishing towards the bottom of the league in 1967 and 1968 (as Kranepool continued to platoon with a laundry list of names), but the hiring of manager (and ex-'62 Met) Gil Hodges in the latter season, and the infusion of new, young talent at the major league level showed signs that fortunes were about to turn around. Kranepool was maturing, as well—he and Carole had moved out to South Farmingdale, Long Island, and he became a father to Edward Keith Kranepool on March 2, 1969—and he was suddenly finding himself surrounded by teammates his own age. As the only player left who'd been part of the '62 team, he had, oddly, become the seasoned veteran, in terms of service. (Al Jackson, an original Met, had been reacquired in 1968, but was traded away in the middle of the 1969 season.)

"Spring Training, Gil Hodges wanted you to lead by example," Kranepool said of early 1969. "He built the ballclub around leadership. First, we had to get over .500—we never got to the .500 level before—it's the only way to win the game. The team that makes the fewest mental mistakes does. We didn't beat ourselves; we had good pitching and defense; we started to play well. We did get to .500, beat L.A. and San Diego, and went on a 10-game winning streak."

The first-place Cubs swaggered into New York for a three-game series, holding a 5½-game lead in the newly created National League East division. In the opening game on July 8, Kranepool's solo home run in the fifth had been Mets' only hit off starter Fergie Jenkins until the ninth inning. After the Mets had rallied from a 3–1 deficit to tie the score in the bottom of the ninth—with Cubs center fielder Don Young having trouble with two consecutive fly balls—Kranepool singled to left field to drive in Cleon Jones for the winning run in front of a crowd of 55,000. The Mets would go on to win the series with Tom Seaver taking a perfect game into the ninth the following night. The Cubs, who had dismissed the Mets as an inferior team—third baseman Ron Santo said of the infield that day of Kranepool, Wayne Garrett, Al Weis, and Bobby Pfeil, "I wouldn't let that infield play in Tacoma"—soon found that New York's young team had the talent to overtake Chicago.

"That was like the turning point of the season," Kranepool said. "When you sweep them"—the Mets actually lost the third game of the series, but went 5–2 against the Cubs the rest of the season—"you pick up a lot of ground in a hurry. We built up our confidence. That was probably my biggest hit."

The Mets finished the year with a league-best 100–62 record and swept the Braves in the three-game divisional playoff to win their first pennant and face the 109-win American League champion Baltimore Orioles in the World Series. Though Kranepool played all three NLCS games against Atlanta—and batted .250—Kranepool was benched in favor of the right-handed-hitting Donn Clendenon for all but one of the Series' five games (the only game started by a right pitcher). Kranepool made it count, hitting a home run off Dave Leonhard in the eighth inning of Game Three. After 800 defeats—most of which Kranepool had witnessed himself—the Mets were crowned world champions.

With the Mets the toast of the town, Kranepool and Ron Swoboda partnered up to do publicity for a resort in the Poconos. They also opened a restaurant called "The Dugout" in North Amityville, Long Island, in the offseason.

"We did it for a couple of years," Kranepool said. "It was a tough business—a lot of hours, very time-consuming. It's a business you have to be there for. We wanted to be at the restaurant for the people."

Kranepool also took his place as the face of the Mets as their player representative at meetings for the burgeoning Players' Association that fall. He was outspoken, never hesitant to call out superstars he felt were undermining the union's goals. (Carl Yastrzemski, for example, was "nothing more than a yo-yo for American League president Joe Cronin," he told the media.)

"I wasn't afraid to protect the players and attend the meetings and the associations," he said of why the Mets chose him. "And the players, themselves, that doesn't bode well for you, sometimes, when you're speaking on behalf of the group, owners can take it as a bone of contention. I wasn't afraid of getting traded, nor was I afraid of speaking out against others' interests."

When he negotiated his contract for 1970, despite having hit .238 and platooning with Clendenon at first base the previous season, Kranepool was one of the last holdouts (along with Swoboda), arguing for a raise on the grounds the he helped the team win the World Series. He got one, signing for $32,000 (up from $24,500 in 1969) in late February.

*Where* he would play was another story, though. The Mets retained four first basemen out of spring training, and three of them—Kranepool, Art Shamsky, and Mike Jorgensen—were left-handed. With Shamsky starting against right-handed pitching and Jorgensen going in as a defensive replacement—not to mention Kranepool and Hodges often butting heads—the writing on the wall was more than obvious.

Over the years, Kranepool's name had often surfaced in trade talks. (A deal had almost been made to include him in a package to acquire Braves catcher Joe Torre before the 1969 season, for instance, and another potential transaction had him going to Philadelphia for Richie Allen.) But even later in the 1970s, when the Mets began dismantling the team that had won two pennants and a World Series, nothing ever materialized regarding Kranepool.

Part of it might have been favoritism. Team owner Joan Whitney Payson had taken a special liking to Kranepool, and he thought of her "like a grandmother."

"If a trade came up—unless it was for Henry Aaron or something—she was not just going to give Ed Kranepool away. Donald Grant liked me also," Kranepool said, referring to the team chairman. "I was very straight—I didn't create any problems. If you talk to me, you may not like me, because I'm going to tell you exactly how it is. I don't sugar-coat it."

Nevertheless, Kranepool's dwindling playing time and productivity nearly forced the Mets to give up on their once-prized investment. Through June 23, Kranepool had gone to bat a mere 34 times, with four hits (.118), none of which came in his 18 appearances as a pinch hitter. The Mets, looking to bring up outfield prospect Ken Singleton, asked for waivers on Kranepool; when no team claimed him, he was optioned to triple-A Tidewater.

Thus, a mere eight months after winning the World Series, Kranepool began to consider walking away from the game forever. He still had his stockbrokerage business, after all, and his restaurant business, and other financial investments to get by just fine without baseball. But he wasn't ready. Not to mention M. Donald Grant had promised him that he would return to the big league club if he performed well in the minors. "He was from the old school where a handshake meant something," Kranepool said.

So Kranepool tore up Tidewater, batting .310 with seven home runs in 47 games, and returned to the Mets on August 14. He finished with a .170 average (almost always as a pinch hitter) as the Mets finished third at 83–79.

Spring training 1971 seemed for Kranepool—in the words of coach and future Mets manager Yogi Berra—to be déjà vu all over again. He managed to secure a contract for the exact same salary as the previous season; he still was competing with at least four first basemen; he still doubted Hodges had much confidence in his abilities. Writers who'd called his demotion the previous season the end of an era were now forecasting this might be Kranepool's final spring. The one difference was that this year, Kranepool felt he had nothing to lose; if he made the team, so much the better, but if not, perhaps he could play well enough that one of the other 23 teams would want him. Being sent down to the minors had been a humbling experience, and had caused Kranepool to shed much of the bitter conceit that had marked his earlier years.

"Gil Hodges and I had a different relationship after that," Kranepool said. "I didn't like him. I didn't like Gil Hodges when I first played. When you're on a bad ballclub, you get negative vibes around you. Certain things, he didn't like what I did; I didn't like how he handled me. When I got sent down and came back—I could've quit at that point—I did very well, and he learned to respect me, and I learned to respect him."

Hitting seems to cure all ills, too, and in 1971, Kranepool put together perhaps his best season in the majors. His name hadn't even been on the All-Star ballot because he hadn't been expected to start before the season began, but he received numerous write-in votes from fans. He wasn't selected, but he did finish the season tied for the club lead in home runs (14), and with a career high in RBIs (58), and what was then his highest batting average (.280). A bizarre brief dugout scuffle on May 26 with rookie Tim Foli—in which the hot-tempered infielder had taken offense at Kranepool's refusal to throw to him during pregame warmups, and wound up with a black eye—seemed like his season's only blemish. Kranepool received a $10,500 raise the next season.

The Mets were stunned in spring training 1972 when Gil Hodges died suddenly of a heart attack. Many members of the team, Kranepool included, regarded him as the best manager they ever played for. "Strategically, fundamentally, he was a sound manager, knew the game, taught you how to win," Kranepool said. "If he would've continued and not passed away, we would've won more pennants."

About new manager Yogi Berra, Kranepool mused, "Yogi was a great guy, fun-loving, well-liked by the players. Very easygoing, but not the leadership Gil Hodges had. The inmates can't run the asylum."

Kranepool homered and knocked in three against the world champion Pittsburgh Pirates on April 15, the strike-delayed Opening Day of 1972, but by midseason, he was struggling (and platooning) again. He finished batting .269 with New York again in third place. With the Mets floundering around midseason of 1973, M. Donald Grant came into the clubhouse one day for a rare inspirational pep talk. Toward the end of his speech was when struggling pitcher Tug McGraw stood up and animatedly began yelling, "Ya gotta believe." Grant left the room, thinking McGraw was mocking him. Kranepool was McGraw's roommate at the time, and realized the potential for trouble.

"I said to Tug, as the player rep, 'You better tell Donald Grant you didn't mean anything, that you were endorsing what he was saying,'" Kranepool said. "We went outside the locker, Donald was there, and Tug stopped him and he apologized and everything was fine. It cleared the air. It was not a negative rant. And it became the rally cry of the team that year, 'Ya gotta believe.'

"Mr. Grant, you have to realize, he was a pinstripe dresser: black-tie, pinstripe, Wall Street executive. He was very prim and proper like Mrs. Payson was. So when someone starts ranting and raving, he's going to take offense. Tug, as my roommate, I was protecting him, because I didn't want him to end up in the doghouse."

The Mets—and McGraw—did turn it around that season, of course, taking the league championship with the lowest winning percentage of any team in history (.509), and narrowly losing the World Series in seven games to an Oakland A's team on its way to three consecutive titles. Kranepool's average dipped to .239 (sharing time with John Milner and starting some games in the outfield), and he started the decisive Game Five of the NL Championship Series in place of the injured Rusty Staub, driving in two runs with a first-inning single. In his appearances in the World Series, he was 0-for-3 pinch-hitting, though his groundball to first for an error in the ninth inning of Game Seven scored the Mets' final run of the Series.

It might have been foreshadowing. Kranepool's role as a starter was diminishing, as younger prospects were tried out at first base. In 1974, Kranepool was used frequently as a pinch hitter. For many players, transitioning from starting to pinch-hitting can be a warning sign that one's days in baseball—or

PHOTO COURTESY OF DWAYNE LABAKAS COLLECTION

*Ed Kranepool was the last Met from the franchise's inaugural 1962 season and the 1969 world championship season still in uniform.*

with a particular team—are numbered, but Kranepool seemed to fit right in.

"I was able to motivate myself to pinch-hit and perform," Kranepool said. "I was trying to prove the managers wrong by not playing me, and I wound up very successful."

Between 1974 and 1978, Kranepool batted .396 as a pinch hitter. He hit the .300 mark in a season twice in his part-time playing role in those years that included the occasional start at first base, in 1974 and 1975, the latter when he batted a career-high .323 (in 325 at-bats). Always willing to help the younger players coming up through the system, he even co-authored a book on baseball fundamentals in 1977, drawing from his own experiences from Little League all the way through the professional level; naturally, there was a chapter devoted to pinch-hitting.

His relationship with Mets front office, however, slowly headed downhill. It started in 1975, with the death of Mrs. Payson. Kranepool was the only player at her funeral, and her death hit him hard. "She was the sweetest person you'd ever meet," Kranepool said. "You had a lot of respect for her for who she was, not because she owned the ballclub."

The new management fell to her daughter, Lorinda de Roulet, with whom Kranepool said he should have gotten along, but didn't. Mrs. de Roulet wasn't quite equipped to go from running social parties to running a corporation, and she preferred to rely on Joe McDonald, who'd become general manager in 1974, to make business decisions, instead of Donald Grant.

"I didn't have a good relationship with Joe McDonald. I didn't respect him. I didn't like him; he didn't know anything about baseball," Kranepool said. "There were termites who ate away at the organization, and he was part of the termites. Donald Grant got blamed for it, but Joe McDonald was the one who made the trades."

The sticking point in Kranepool's disdain for McDonald arose from contract squabbles before the 1977 season. With the advent of free agency, players had more bargaining power and the ability to negotiate multiyear deals, and Kranepool said he needed some time to think over the figure McDonald had offered him.

"I live 30 minutes from Shea Stadium; as soon as I got home, the phone rang—he'd taken back the contract," Kranepool said. "I said, 'Joe how could you rescind the contract? I just got home!' But that's what he did. I cursed him out and used a lot of not-nice words I probably shouldn't've been saying. And hung up."

Kranepool alerted Grant of the situation, and the two met at Fahnestock & Company, Grant's firm on Wall Street, where a phone call to McDonald confirmed Kranepool's story. "Donald Grant said, 'You got the contract, and you got an additional $10,000,'" Kranepool recalled. "It was with a handshake that I signed the contract in his office. A three-year contract. When it was up in '79, I knew Joe McDonald was not going to offer me a contract."

As the Mets continued to tailspin back into their form of the early 1960s, Kranepool began hinting that 1979 would be his last year; the rift between him and Mets management was too deep, and he wasn't getting very many opportunities to play—even as a pinch hitter—so his performance off the bench declined. And the fact that manager Joe Torre—at one time Kranepool's roommate when the two were players—said little on his behalf, hurt even more.

"Joe Torre knew what my plans were and didn't protect me at the end, and I never talked to him again," Kranepool said. "Joe Torre knew the situation. Sometimes, you have to be a man and stick up for your friends. I was the one that was his right-hand man in the three years as a manager, and he knew he had to protect his own job: 'Let Ed fend for himself.' To me, that's being a turncoat."

Torre would say years later that letting Kranepool go was one of the hardest things he ever had to do.[6]

The final nail in Kranepool's coffin came during the Mets' final homestand, when the Mets chose to honor retiring Lou Brock of the Cardinals and did not even acknowledge that Kranepool was probably suiting up for the final time at Shea. He received a short notice in the mail that offseason detailing his release, but not even the original: a carbon copy of the note sent to his agent, Dick Moss. Kranepool filed for free agency, but it seemed more of a formality. After 18 seasons, 1,853 games, 5,436 at-bats, 1,418 hits (for a .261 average), and 118 home runs, he was through.

"I never knew I retired," he said. "I went from one thing to another." Kranepool had given thought to what he might do after his career was over; he had little interest in managing, but he felt he might be suited to work in the front office. Earlier that year, he had gotten wind from Charles Payson, Mrs. Payson's widower, that the Mets might be up for sale, and Kranepool put together a group to buy the team, the package which he presented to Lorinda de Roulet that September.

"And then she put together her friends, her social group, and they bought the ballclub," Kranepool said. New owners Fred Wilpon and Nelson Doubleday brought in Frank Cashen as the new general manager, and Kranepool left baseball for good.

"I left the Mets when I should've been on top, and ended out at the bottom," Kranepool said. "I can't have any harsh feelings for the Wilpons and the team."

He unintentionally stirred up some minor controversy in 1986 when he appeared in a campaign commercial for friend and former US Senator Al D'Amato in a Mets uniform, causing the team to release an adamant statement that it did not take political sides.

For six years, Kranepool was also a spokesperson for Pfizer, traveling the country promoting diabetes awareness—a disease he learned he had developed the year he retired.

"That was the most fun I had working for a company, and they were a great company," said Kranepool, whose activities included penning a cooking booklet, "Ed Kranepool's Favorite Recipes for Diabetes Control," in 1990. "It was not up for me to sell drugs; I just had to get awareness to the doctors and awareness to the public: 'people can get checked,' 'be aware of the symptoms,' 'go to your doctor,' 'do what can be done for it.'

"Then, when I was taken off the medication, I had to give up the position at the company. The way they are, you give up the medication, you can't be part of their team. I had to go back on insulin for a few years. The drug I was on wasn't as effective anymore; I couldn't endorse that pill."

In 2004, he launched The Memorabilia Road Show, a traveling and online auction that collected pieces of memorabilia personally from players and or from their family members who needed a place to sell it, in turn giving the items a degree of authentic integrity that couldn't otherwise be provided by a third-party dealer. Kranepool sold the company shortly after it opened, and it didn't last long afterwards without him.

Kranepool currently has an office at IRN Payment Systems in Westbury, Long Island, soliciting businesses and retailers who need credit card processing. "This is a business, knowing stores and establishments," he said. "Being who I am gets the visibility to the decision-makers. It's something that has to be done; it's all who's doing it."

He does frequent charity work, of which much of the money gets directed toward diabetes and autism research. In 2008 he was honored by the Hagedorn Little Village School, for special needs children, in Seaford, Long Island.

Kranepool and his second wife, Monica, a real estate agent at Sotheby's, live in Nassau County. His son, Keith, developed into a decent athlete—he's 6-foot-7—but he never settled on one sport, and chose to pursue other interests. He works in electronics, and has two preschool-age sons.

"They both seem to like baseball," Kranepool said of his grandchildren. "I was playing over the weekend trying to help them; they both can hit—they probably have more talent than their father. So maybe, one day, who knows? But it's a long way away."

**Notes and Sources**

1. Janowicz, Irene. "Woman In The Family." *New York Mirror*, April 28, 1963.
2. Daley, Arthur. "Sports of The Times: The Boy Wonder." *New York Times*, March 22, 1965.
3. Golenbock, Peter. *Amazin': The Miraculous History of New York's Most Beloved Team* (New York: St. Martin's Griffin, 2002) p. 169.
4. National Baseball Hall of Fame Archives
5. *www.baseballlibrary.com.*
6. Barmakian, Ed. "Cone doesn't help bid for playoff spot; Indians make it an unhappy return." *Star-Ledger*, September 16, 2000.

All quotes from Ed Kranepool, unless otherwise noted, come from telephone conversations with the author on May 13 and 14, 2008. Statistics, unless otherwise noted, are from *www.baseball-reference.com*, *www.retrosheet.org*, and *minors.sabrwebs.com*. Special thanks to Gabriel Schechter of the National Baseball Hall of Fame Archives, from where much of this information was taken. Special thanks to the late Jim Plummer for his assistance in contacting Ed Kranepool.

# J.C. Martin

by Neal Poloncarz

| Season | Age | G | AB | R | H | 2B | 3B | HR | RBI | BB | SO | SB | CS | BA | OBP | SLG |
|---|---|---|---|---|---|---|---|---|---|---|---|---|---|---|---|---|
| 1969 Mets | 32 | 66 | 177 | 12 | 37 | 5 | 1 | 4 | 21 | 12 | 32 | 0 | 0 | .209 | .257 | .316 |
| Career 14 Years | – | 908 | 2189 | 189 | 487 | 82 | 12 | 32 | 230 | 201 | 299 | 9 | 8 | .222 | .291 | .315 |

Despite a lifetime batting average of only .222, J.C. Martin is remembered by baseball historians mostly for an offensive play, though it took place on the baselines, not at the plate. That it happened in the World Series gives it continuing life. At baseball card shows or conventions, most of the questions are about the play. "I kid around with the fans and show them how I swelled up," Martin told an interviewer. "I just stick my arms out. I don't care what some people say about the play or what I did. The umpire said I was safe so I must have been safe. They show my old play again at first base and I could see that ball bouncing off my wrist. It didn't hurt a bit then and it doesn't hurt now. I just get a kick out of seeing that ball roll away and old Rodney [Gaspar] running around those bases; and getting in for that winning run. That's a satisfying scene, yes sir, it certainly is."

After nine years with the Chicago White Sox, J.C. had spent two seasons as a backup catcher with the New York Mets. In the second of those two seasons, 1969, he was a key contributor to the Mets' playoff run. In Game One of the National League Championship Series against the Atlanta Braves, Martin drove in two runs with a pinch-hit single off Phil Niekro (a third run scored on an error) as the Mets rallied with five runs in the eighth inning for a 9–5 victory. The Mets swept the series in three games and went on the face Baltimore in the World Series.

But Game Four was J.C.'s time to shine. The Mets led Baltimore two games to one. With the score tied, 1–1, in the bottom of the 10th inning, catcher Jerry Grote hit a sun-aided leadoff double against the Orioles' Dick Hall. Rod Gaspar ran for Grote, and Al Weis was given an intentional walk. Manager Gil Hodges sent up Martin to bat for pitcher Tom Seaver. Baltimore manager Earl Weaver had been ejected earlier, and pitching coach George Bamberger brought in southpaw Pete Richert to face the left-handed hitter. With runners at first and second and no one out, Martin bunted perfectly on the first base side near the foul line. Richert sprang off the mound, grabbed the ball in his bare hand, and threw to first base. The throw appeared to have Martin beat, but it struck him on the left wrist and bounded across the infield dirt between first and second base. Gaspar sprinted home from second base and the Mets were winners. Martin was mobbed by his teammates.

The next morning, controversy swirled around the play. Under the playing rules, if Martin strayed from the three-foot line that parallels the basepath for 45 feet, and in the umpire's opinion interfered with the play, he was out. First base umpire Lou DiMuro did not call interference. Press box observers clearly believed Martin was out of the base-

PHOTO COURTESY OF METSILVERMAN.COM

*J.C. Martin*

line, in fair territory when the throw hit him. Later photos indicated conclusively that that was the case. When asked after the game how the throw managed to hit him, Martin smiled and said, "I swelled up."

"You try to do everything you possibly can," Martin said years later. "You know from experience that if you run close to the first-base line, the throwing angle is very narrow, particularly if the pitcher is left-handed and has to turn to make the throw. So you run as close as you can. I wasn't thinking about getting hit or anything. I was just looking to shield the ball from the man covering first. As it turned out, the ball happened to hit me on the left wrist. But there was no argument at the time. All the controversy was in the media the next day." Even Seaver admitted years later that the films showed J.C. ran out of the baseline. But history showed that Seaver got the win in Game Four and the Mets won the Series the following day.

But New York and the World Series was a long way off when Joseph Clifton Martin was born on December 13, 1936, in Axton, Virginia, 60 miles south of Roanoke and close to the border of North Carolina. Both of his grandfathers were named Joseph, so his family called him by his initials.

In his youth, J.C. was an active outdoorsman. He and his younger brother Melvin would hunt coon, possum, and fished in a river along the family farm. His parents told him if he wanted to fulfill his dream of becoming a major league ballplayer, he could not drink or smoke. Martin, from a devout Christian upbringing, saw firsthand where other paths could lead. His father was a county deputy and J.C. would often stop off at the county jail after school to visit his dad and witness the men incarcerated there.

At Ridgeway High School, J.C. lettered in baseball, football, basketball, and track. In 1956, as a basketball player, he was selected to All-State. Several colleges offered him scholarships. Eight baseball clubs extended offers. White Sox scout Harry Postove, assured Martin that he would rapidly advance through Chicago's minor league system as a first baseman. As a result, J.C. signed with the White Sox, for $4,000. (This was still nearly a decade before the first free-agent draft for amateur players.)

After working out with the White Sox in Chicago for three days, Martin was assigned to Holdrege of the Nebraska State League, a Class D circuit that used only players without pro experience. Life in the minor leagues, even a rookie league, was an awakening for the 19-year-old Martin. His teammates drank, smoked, and met women. This was not J.C.'s lifestyle.

Holdrege finished in sixth place with a 33–30 record, eight games behind the Lexington Red Sox. Martin hit .276 in 64 games, smacked 10 home runs, had 51 RBIs, and scored 64 runs. After the season, he persuaded high school sweetheart Barbara Cox to leave college and get married.

In 1957, Martin was moved up to Davenport of the Class B Three-I League, where his manager was Frank "Skeeter" Scalzi, his manager at Holdrege the year before. In the faster competition, J.C. batted only .208 in 19 games before being sent down to the Dubuque Packers of the Class D Midwest League. There, he rebounded, batting .286 in 103 games and earning a promotion for 1958 to Duluth-Superior of the Class A Northern League. In mid-July, Martin was leading the league in batting, with a .358

average; in that month, he had an 18-game hitting streak. Then he cooled off somewhat, and finished the season with a .330 average, 10 home runs, and 86 RBIs.

His performance at Duluth-Superior earned J.C. a promotion to Class AAA for 1959. At Indianapolis, the top farm team of the White Sox, Martin batted .287 in 133 games, with 13 home runs and 57 RBIs, earning a "cup-of-coffee" look by the pennant-winning White Sox at the end of the season. White Sox manager Al Lopez impressed Martin, who said of him, "Al was the kind of manager who let you play. He wouldn't run you down by playing you day after day after day. He knew the game. He got me into the big leagues and I have nothing but respect for him. We all did."

The 22-year-old made his major-league debut at Comiskey Park on September 10 against the Washington Senators. In the top of the eighth inning, the White Sox trailed, 8–2. J.C. pinch hit for pitcher Turk Lown, and struck out against the Senators' Camilo Pascual.

The White Sox clinched their first American League pennant in 40 years in Cleveland on September 22. Martin recalled, "It was a real thrill. I still remember Gerry Staley coming in to pitch to Vic Power. Staley threw one pitch, Power hit into a double play and that was it. It was pandemonium in the locker room. Then we flew right back to Chicago to Midway Airport. I don't know how many people were there but it was a lot. [The *Chicago Sun Times* estimated the crowd at 125,000.] I know we had to get on a bus and drive out to where our cars were parked."

Martin collected his first major league hit and RBI on the last day of the season, at Detroit. He replaced Bubba Phillips at third base in the sixth inning, and singled to center field with Jim McAnany on second base three innings later. As a September call-up, J.C. was ineligible for the postseason. The Los Angeles Dodgers defeated Chicago four games to two in the World Series.

After his cup of coffee, Martin returned to the minors. In 1960, with the Class AAA San Diego Padres, he played first and third, and batted .285 with 13 home runs and 73 RBIs, and had another cup of coffee with the White Sox.

Spring training of 1961 was not good for Martin. He was learning to play third base, made a slew of errors, and his hitting was poor. Manager Al Lopez, ever patient with rookies, had Luis Aparicio work with Martin. Luis let Martin use his glove, and the difference in his fielding was remarkable. The White Sox ordered an Aparicio model glove for Martin. In the season opener, at Washington, Lopez started Martin at third base, batting fifth. The White Sox won but Martin was hitless. Al Smith played the majority of games at third for the White Sox, with Martin getting 36 games at third and 60 at first base. He hit .230.

During the White Sox organizational meetings in the offseason, team officials agreed that Martin's bat was too weak for third base, and decided to make him a catcher. He was sent to Savannah of the South Atlantic League to learn the position. The Savannah manager was Les Moss, a former White Sox catcher. Martin had a strong fielding percentage (.986), but also set a league record with 32 passed balls. In the fall, Martin returned to the White Sox and was installed as the third-string catcher, behind Cam Carreon and Sherm Lollar.

On September 7, after pinch-hitting in the seventh inning, Martin went behind the plate for the first time in the major leagues, calling signals for Dave DeBusschere, better known as a future New York Knick and Basketball Hall of Famer. Martin made his first start on September 10, catching for Ray Herbert.

Martin was Opening Day catcher for the White Sox in 1963. He caught 98 games that season and batted just .205. He caught 122 games the following year, but his average plunged even deeper to .197. Early in the season, he platooned with Cam Carreon, but Martin eventually won the first-string job.

The 1965 season represented the best offensive year in the majors for J.C. He hit .261 in 112 games, though he did commit 33 passed balls. In '66, he had another decent season at the plate (.255), but lost his starting job to Johnny Romano and caught only 63 games.

The White Sox started the 1967 season with three catchers. Martin and rookie Duane Josephson handled the majority of the catching. After Josephson jammed his thumb in a collision, Martin platooned with Jerry McNertney. On July 25, J.C. homered in both games of a doubleheader against Cleveland. The first was a walk-off shot against hard-throwing lefty Sam McDowell. The second was hit off Sonny Siebert in the fifth inning of the nightcap, which the White Sox won in the 16th inning on a homer by Ken Berry. (It was only the second time in major league history that both games of a doubleheader ended with walk-off home runs.) Martin hit .234 in 101 games as the White Sox engaged in a tight race with Boston, Minnesota, and Detroit for the pennant, eventually won by the "Impossible Dream" Red Sox.

On September 10, Martin was behind the plate as Joe Horlen pitched a no-hitter against the Tigers. "In the ninth inning," Martin recalled, "we got the first two guys out. I called time and went out to the mound. I asked Joe what he wanted to throw to the next hitter, Dick McAuliffe. Joe paid me a great compliment because he said, 'You've called the first $8\frac{2}{3}$ innings, you finish it up.'" Martin called for a pitch away to Dick McAuliffe, who grounded out to shortstop.

In the offseason, Martin went to the Mets to complete an earlier deal between the two clubs. New Mets manager Gil Hodges planned to platoon him behind the plate with Jerry Grote. Martin was the starter on Opening Day, catching Tom Seaver. In the ninth inning, San Francisco's Jim Ray Hart hit a foul ball that struck Martin on the right hand and fractured a finger. He was on the disabled list until May 2. He wound up catching in 53 games, playing first base in 14, and batting .225. Grote wound up making the All-Star team and remained the team's top catcher for nearly a decade.

Spring training in 1969 was briefly delayed by a dispute over the distribution of television revenue. When the season got going, the Mets had three catchers as rookie Duffy Dyer took the third spot.

As the season advanced, Martin often drove to Shea Stadium with his good friend Al Weis, and pitchers Don Cardwell and Cal Koonce. In the clubhouse, J.C.'s locker was one of four which belonged to Koonce, Cardwell, and Ron Taylor. Martin, Koonce, and Cardwell were southerners. Taylor was from Canada. Someone walked up to the four and asked Taylor what he was doing there. He replied, "I'm from South Canada."

Martin caught 48 games and batted a weak .209, going hitless in the regular season after September 1 (an 0-for-15 finish). Yet like most Mets in 1969, Martin still managed to contribute as the Amazin's overtook the Cubs for the division title:

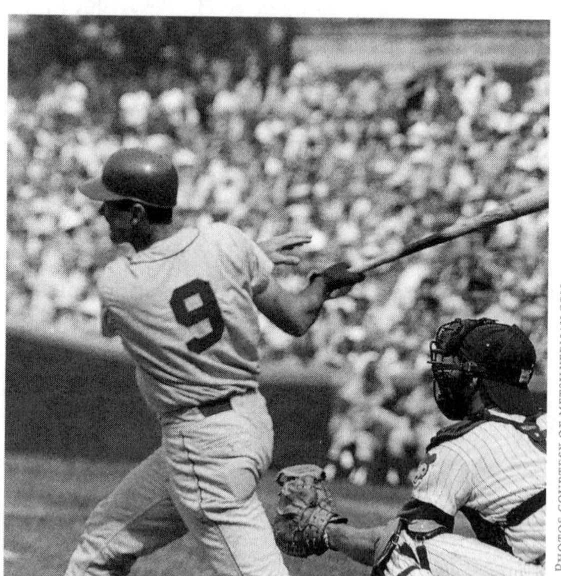

PHOTOS COURTESY OF METSILVERMAN.COM

*Dueling Nines: Opposite numbers J.C. Martin of the Mets and Randy Hundley of the Cubs trade places around home plate at Wrigley Field on July 14, 1969. While the lefty-swinging Martin had two of the Mets' six hits, Cubs catcher Randy Hundley went hitless, though he did call a shutout. (Martin and Hundley would be Cubs teammates in 1970.) Umpire Bob Engel stands as witness and judge.*

PHOTO COURTESY OF METSILVERMAN.COM

*J.C. Martin, who became a broadcaster after he retired, gets some practice in front of the microphone as a Met.*

- Martin doubled in a run to collect his first hit of the season on April 16 against Pittsburgh's Bob Moose, who would no-hit the Mets on September 20 (with Martin taking an 0-for-3 collar that day).
- He had his first multi-hit game with an RBI at Wrigley Field on May 3.
- He had two hits and knocked in two against Houston in a May 11 victory (one of just two wins the Mets had against the Astros in 1969).
- His 2-for-5 performance helped the Mets to a *Game of the Week* victory over the Reds at Crosley Field on May 17.
- On June 17, Martin singled in the only run of Gary Gentry's two-hit shutout in Philadelphia.
- Two days later, his leadoff walk in the ninth sparked a come-from-behind victory in Philly.
- After losing the first game after the All-Star break in 12 innings to the Reds, J.C. was the hero the next night, July 25: his two-out, two-run home run off Clay Carroll in the eighth inning provided the Mets with a 4–3 victory.
- Martin's last multi-hit game of the year resulted in the first and last RBIs of the night in a 4–1 win in Atlanta on August 8; his average stood at .227

His bat remained mostly dormant the last two months of the season as Duffy Dyer got more and more of the backup catching assignments down the stretch. Fate would intervene on Martin's behalf during the Amazin' postseason. But World Series hero or not, Martin was on the move again the next season, traded to the Chicago Cubs for catcher Randy Bobb, a dozen years his junior. Playing behind Chicago's iron man backstop Randy Hundley, Martin caught just 36 games and hit a paltry .156.

In the winter of 1971, Cubs pitching coach Verlon Walker (brother of Mets pitching coach Rube Walker) was hospitalized for a persistent fever. As a result, Cubs general manager John Holland named Martin the interim pitching coach. When the season began, Mel Wright, a pitcher, a scout, and coach for 11 years in the Cubs organization, was named pitching coach. Martin's .264 batting average in 47 games was the best of his career. He played his final season in 1972. At the age of 35 he batted mostly against right-handers, hitting .240 in 25 games. Defensively, his throwing arm had diminished—throwing out 1 of 15 basestealers—and he caught sparingly.

Martin was released as a player before the 1973 season. By 1974, he was the bullpen coach on the staff of Cubs manager Whitey Lockman. The following year Martin worked alongside the legendary Harry Caray on WSNS-TV for the White Sox, an assignment he didn't enjoy. "I didn't really fit in with Harry," he said.

Despite his anemic career batting average of .222, J.C.'s memories of his time in the major leagues are sweet: "I wouldn't trade it for anything. I spent 14 years in the big leagues seeing the best players ever, guys like Bob Gibson, Willie Mays, Carl Yastrzemski. Players like that just aren't around anymore. Baseball was better back then....They didn't have the DH, which has killed all the suspense in the American League, and the ballparks were fair. You didn't have this emphasis on hitting home runs all the time. It was great."

**Sources**

Allen, Maury. *After the Miracle: The 1969 Mets Twenty Years Later* (New York: Franklin Watts, 1989).

Cohen, Stanley. *A Magic Summer: The '69 Mets* (New York: Harcourt Brace Jonavich Publishers, 1988).

Goldstein, Richard. "Shag Crawford, 90, Longtime Baseball Umpire, Dies." *New York Times*, July 14, 2007.

Helfey, James C. *The Will to Win- Faith In Action In The Lives of Athletes.* (Grand Rapids, Michigan: Zondervan Publishing House, 1968).

Holtzman, Jerome. *The Sporting News.* March 3, 1971, p.36.

Honig, Donald. *Great World Series Remembered by the Men Who Played Them* (New York: Simon & Schuster, 1979).

*http://www.whitesoxinteractive.com;*

Liptak, Mark. Flashing back with J.C. Martin. WSI: White Sox Interactive News.

Marazzi, Rich. "Baseball Rules Corner: Batter-Runner Interference Calls Can Create Disputes." *Baseball Digest*, February 2002.

Metro, Charlie and Altherr, Tom. *Safe by a Mile.* Lincoln: University of Nebraska Press, 2002).

Nemec, David. *The Rules of Baseball—An Anecdotal Look at the Rules of Baseball and How They Came to Be* (New York: Lyons & Bufoerd, Publishers, 1994).

Pasculli, Len. SABR Bioproj—The Baseball Biography Project; Bobby Richardson. *http://bioproj.sabr.org/bioproj.cfm?a=v&v=l&bid=1172&pid=11891*

Rosciam, Chuck. "Catchers Who Caught The Most Hall Of Fame Pitchers (Their Starts)." *http://batteries.sabr.org/caught-most.htm*

1969 World Series, Game #4 Baltimore vs. New York; The Paley Center for Media; 25 West 52 Street, New York, NY 10019.

## No Streaking

"The Year of the Pitcher" in 1968 saw Denny McLain win 31 games, Bob Gibson pitch to a microscopic 1.12 ERA in 300-plus innings, and Carl Yastrzemski claim the American League batting title at .301. The Mets had a team batting average that year of .228, lower even than the NL-low .230 average against that was doled out by the club's stingy and talented pitching staff. Not surprisingly, no '68 Met had a hitting streak longer than Tommie Agee's 12-gamer. This streak was a big deal because, as it came in September, it set the tone for Agee's great 1969 season. Agee was hitting .189 entering the streak, then batted .422 over the dozen games it spanned to help finish at .217 in his first year as a Met.

The 1969 Mets—like everyone else—benefitted from the lowering of the mound and the tightening of the strike zone. The Mets offense improved all the way to a .242 average in '69. Mets pitchers, by contrast were even better than the previous year, permitting just a .227 batting average that led the league by 10 points. The longest hitting streak by a Met in 1969 was 11 games (Agee and Cleon Jones). Yes, that's right. The longest Mets hitting streak in their championship season was shorter than their longest hitting streak in the Year of the Pitcher.

—*metswalkoffs.blogspot.com*

# Jim McAndrew

by C. Paul Rogers III

| Season | Age | W | L | Pct | G | GS | SV | IP | H | BB | SO | WHIP | ERA |
|---|---|---|---|---|---|---|---|---|---|---|---|---|---|
| 1969 Mets | 24 | 6 | 7 | .462 | 27 | 21 | 0 | 135 | 112 | 44 | 90 | 1.156 | 3.47 |
| Career 7 Years | – | 37 | 53 | .411 | 161 | 110 | 4 | 771.3 | 712 | 213 | 424 | 1.199 | 3.65 |

Twenty-five-year-old Jim McAndrew emerged from spring training 1969 to start the second game of the year for a New York Mets team that boasted one of the game's top young rotations. Yet due to a series of misfortunes, injuries, and bad luck—a continuation from the previous year where the Mets were shut out in his first four major league starts—McAndrew did not record his first victory until June 24. Finally healthy in August, McAndrew pitched six inning or better in nine straight starts, including back to back shutouts and tying the club record with 23 straight scoreless innings. A skinny and unheralded prospect from Iowa farm country, McAndrew provided Mets management with more than they expected, though he never quite rose to the ranks of heralded teammates Tom Seaver, Jerry Koosman, and Nolan Ryan.

James Clement McAndrew was born on January 11, 1944 in Lost Nation, Iowa, a farming community of less than 600 residents about 50 miles west of Davenport. His father, C.J., farmed 750 acres and Jim grew up with three sisters. He began playing Little League at age nine and by his freshman year in high school stood only 5 feet tall and weighed a mere 95 pounds. He was 17 when he graduated from high school and had grown to 5-feet-11, although he still weighed only 135 pounds. McAndrew played varsity basketball and baseball well enough to draw the attention of the University of Iowa, where future NCAA executive director Dick Schultz was the baseball coach. St. Louis Cardinals scout Kenny Blackman also came for a look and they discussed signing a contract, but Blackman told him that with his size he would be better off going to college and developing his game there.

McAndrew wanted a college education and matriculated to the University of Iowa. He played baseball and basketball until he hurt his knee during the basketball season in his sophomore year. The injury convinced him that he should stick with baseball. He had pitched and played shortstop in high school but was never a great hitter and so decided his best shot would be as a pitcher. But he favored his bad knee and hurt his arm in the spring before his junior year. He missed the season and that summer tried unsuccessfully to pitch for Rapid City in the Basin League, a summer college circuit.

Although McAndrew could not fully straighten his arm, he found that he could pitch without pain for his senior year at Iowa. He pitched well but finished 4–4 for the Hawkeyes. One of his starts was against Ohio State's top prospect Steve Arlin in Iowa City. McAndrew lost to Arlin and the Buckeyes, 2–0, on two unearned runs. He did, however, spark interest of scouts from the Cubs and Mets, who were at the game to watch Arlin (the Ohio State right-hander would be drafted in the first round by the Phillies the following year).

Upon the recommendation of scout Charley Frey, the Mets drafted McAndrew in the 11th round of baseball's inaugural draft in 1965. Nolan Ryan was chosen by the Mets one round earlier and both he and McAndrew were assigned to Marion, Virginia in the rookie-level Appalachian League. After two solid starts, McAndrew was promoted to Auburn, New York, in the Class A New York-Penn League. There in 11 starts he finished 5–5 but with an unpromising 5.37 earned run average. McAndrew was sent to the fall instructional league, where Bob Scheffing, Mets director of baseball operations, took him under his wing. McAndrew credited Scheffing with straightening him out and teaching him how to pitch.

After finishing his psychology degree at Iowa in the offseason, McAndrew was back with Auburn in 1966. He improved to 11–7 with a respectable 3.61 ERA. McAndrew and future Mets teammate Jerry Koosman led the club to an 80–49 mark that took the pennant by eight games. McAndrew's performance with Auburn earned him a promotion to the Eastern League and the Double-A Williamsport Mets for 1967. He continued his advancement by posting a 10–8 mark and a minuscule 1.47 ERA that led the league and was almost four full runs less than his first year as a pro. In 153 innings he allowed only 119 hits. He also started against a future Hall of Famer. Robin Roberts, who at 40 was trying to make a comeback with the Reading Phillies, beat McAndrew that day, 5–3, but he retired from baseball after that outing.

Even with his strong showing in 1967, the Mets did not protect McAndrew from the minor league draft that winter. No other organization selected him and McAndrew gave serious thought to retiring from baseball. He had married his college sweetheart, Lyn, right after his graduation from Iowa and now had a son. It was difficult supporting a family on a minor league salary so Jim thought it was time to stop bouncing around and put his college degree to use. Lyn, however, persuaded her husband to give baseball another try.

The Mets assigned McAndrew to the triple-A Jacksonville Suns of the International League for 1968. In spring training one day, he felt tearing in his elbow and feared that he had reinjured his arm. It turned out that lesions from the old injury had finally broken loose, enabling him to straighten his right arm for the first time in years. It added about a foot to his fastball and also enabled him to improve his breaking pitch.

Jacksonville manager Clyde McCullough still was not impressed and McAndrew began the International League season in the bullpen with a very sporadic workload. Whitey Herzog, the director of player personnel for the Mets, thought McAndrew had major league potential. When he learned that McAndrew was languishing in the bullpen, he ordered McCullough to put him in the starting rotation. When the manager did not follow instructions,

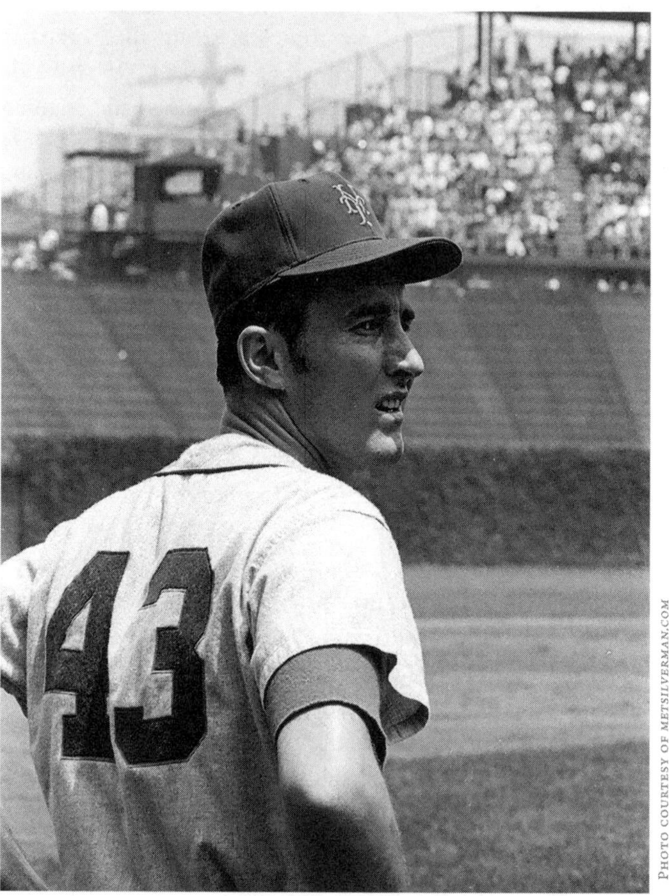


PHOTO COURTESY OF METSILVERMAN.COM

*Jim McAndrew*

Herzog nearly fired him for insubordination. McAndrew finally got his start and flourished, becoming the team's ace. After just six starts, McAndrew earned an emergency start for the Mets on July 21.

Unfortunately, McAndrew's debut drew Bob Gibson and the defending world champion Cardinals; in St. Louis, no less. Gibson was in the middle of a remarkable season in which he won the Cy Young Award with a 22–9 record and put together a 1.12 ERA, the lowest in the National League since 1906. In six innings on a sweltering afternoon, McAndrew allowed only an inside-the-park home run by Bobby Tolan, helped by some shaky fielding in the Mets outfield. He left the game having allowed only that run and the Mets were eventually blanked by Gibson, 2–0. It was one of 13 shutouts Gibson tossed that year, the most in the NL since 1916.

The following day, McAndrew was headed back to Jacksonville as planned. In what would be his last start for the Suns, he had a perfect game after five innings when McCullough pulled him. McAndrew soon learned, however, that he was headed back to the Mets and was scheduled to start two days later when Nolan Ryan left the club for his two-week active military duty. McAndrew finished in Jacksonville with an 8–3 record and a 2.54 ERA. He never pitched another minor league inning for the Mets.

His second major league start was in Dodger Stadium against Mike Kekich, who picked that evening to pitch a one-hit shutout. McAndrew again lost, 2–0. Next, against the Giants in Candlestick Park in San Francisco, he ran into Bob Bolin, who tossed a four-hit shutout at the Mets, this time a 1–0 defeat. It got no better in McAndrew's fourth start, his Shea Stadium debut. This time the Astros beat him, 1–0, as Don Wilson and John Buzhardt combined on a four-hitter. Four starts and the Mets had yet to score a run. McAndrew was 0–4 with an earned run average of 1.82. Welcome to "Year of the Pitcher."

The luckless McAndrew drew Juan Marichal for start number five. The Mets finally scored some runs behind him and he actually held an early 2–1 lead, but San Francisco roughed up the rookie and he wound up losing his fifth straight game, 13–3.

For his sixth start, on August 26, McAndrew drew young Cardinals left-hander Steve Carlton. He tossed a five-hit shutout as the Mets scraped together a run in the eighth inning on a single to left by Tommie Agee, a sacrifice bunt by Phil Linz, a steal of third, and a sacrifice fly to right by Cleon Jones. McAndrew made the game's lone run hold up and finally had a victory. In his third start against a future Hall of Famer—and 300-game winner to boot—McAndrew was finally in the winner's circle.

McAndrew continued to pitch well after his hard luck 1–5 beginning and won three more games while losing two for the rest of the year. His totals for the ninth-place Mets in 1968 were 4–7 in 12 starts with a sparkling 2.28 earned run average. In five of those losses, the Mets did not score and he did the same to the opposition twice.

McAndrew went into 1969 spring training with high hopes, but his bad luck continued and he caught the flu late in spring training after getting a flu shot. Then, when he flew to New York to join the team, he was picked up at the airport by a friend who drove him to a restaurant for dinner. Jim's luggage was in the back seat of the car and was stolen while he was eating dinner. The theft wiped out his wardrobe.

His bad luck still wasn't over. In his first start in the second game of the year, he was knocked out in the second inning by a batted ball up the middle that struck the middle finger of his pitching hand. He spent so much time with his finger in the whirlpool that he softened the skin. As a result, the next time he pitched he developed a blister on the finger. McAndrew then spent the month of May soaking the finger in pickle brine to toughen the skin (a remedy that Nolan Ryan also tried that made for a better story than it did a medication). McAndrew was anxious to get back on the mound, but he hurt his shoulder while pitching batting practice and trying to relieve pressure on his finger.

At the time, McAndrew developed something of an inferiority complex because he didn't throw particularly hard or have great stuff, especially compared with Seaver, Koosman, Ryan, or touted rookie Gary Gentry. McAndrew, who had taught in Job Corps, also had doubts whether throwing a baseball had any value to society in the tumultuous '60s. Manager Gil Hodges told McAndrew that what mattered were results and that the best pitcher he had ever seen was Whitey Ford, who didn't throw as hard as McAndrew. A visit with an uncle who was an executive at Pfizer convinced Jim that ballplayers were entertainers who provided real value to society.

Still, by late June, McAndrew had a 0–2 record for the year. He pronounced that he was sound and won two straight starts to even his record. On July 6 he didn't make it out of the first inning at Pittsburgh. Afterward Gil Hodges had a heart-to-heart talk with the pitcher, telling him that he was being selfish and hurting the team by trying to pitch when his arm was still sore.

McAndrew learned his lesson and did not start again until early August, when he threw seven shutout innings against the Atlanta Braves. Now healthy, he reeled off nine starts covering 73 innings and pitching to a 1.60 ERA. He threw three straight complete games, including the 23 consecutive shutout innings.

Still, the Mets had such depth in starting pitching that most of McAndrew's starts down the stretch came in doubleheaders where the Mets needed an extra starter. One of those games came on September 10 against the Montreal Expos at Shea Stadium with the Mets tied with the swooning Cubs. McAndrew pitched 11 crisp innings before being lifted with the score tied, 2–2. The Mets won in the 12th on an RBI single by Ken Boswell. With the Cubs losing their seventh straight that afternoon to the Phillies, the Mets were in first place. His last start of the year was another no-decision that went extra innings, a win over the Cardinals that put the Mets one game from capturing the NL East title.

McAndrew did not appear in the playoffs or World Series. His record in his first full major league season was 6–7 with 21 starts and 27 appearances. He had a 3.47 ERA in 135 innings, above the team's league-leading 2.99 ERA but below the league's average.

McAndrew started the 1970 season as the club's number three starter behind Seaver and Koosman and ahead of Gentry, who had pitched the third game in both the NLCS and World Series for the 1969 Mets. McAndrew continued to be plagued by poor run support and his own inconsistency. By early July, he was only 3–6 in 13 appearances—nine starts—with two complete games. He was relegated to the back of the rotation, but in the dog days of August and then September, McAndrew pitched consistently well, as he had in his first two seasons. McAndrew finished with a 10–14 mark and 3.57 ERA in 27 starts and five relief appearances, covering 184 innings. Five of his losses were by one run, further cementing his reputation as a hard-luck pitcher.

McAndrew's luck only worsened in 1971. In early May, he collided in the outfield with Gentry while shagging fly balls in pregame warmups. He woke up in the hospital with 38 stitches in the side of his head and top of his ear. Although he was not placed on the disabled list, McAndrew was inconsistent as a starter and by early June was out of the rotation and in the bullpen. Two starts in August still left him winless for the year against five losses. He again pitched well late in the year and picked up wins in both of his September starts to finish 2–5 with an unwieldy (for the times) earned run average of 4.40. He threw just 90 innings for the season but surrendered only 78 hits, indicating that he still had good stuff.

McAndrew finally reversed his history of slow starts in 1972 after beginning the season in the bullpen under new manager Yogi Berra, who had taken over following the shocking death of Gil Hodges. McAndrew got his first start in May against the Montreal Expos and won, 2–1, the first of four wins in a row. Even though he was having the best year of his career, he still had to endure a 21-day stretch in July when he did not take the mound at all. It was not because of injury or his performance but rather due to outstanding starting pitching during that stretch by Tom Seaver, Jerry Koosman, Jon Matlack, and Gary Gentry. He started the year 9–3 and faded a little down the stretch, though he still had a sharp 2.80 ERA for the third-place Mets. In 28 appearances and 23 starts he threw 161 innings and allowed just 133 hits.

McAndrew began the 1973 season as the number four starter behind Seaver, Koosman, and Matlack—Gentry had been traded to Atlanta. Because of a light early-season schedule, McAndrew did not get his first start until the season was a week old and then never could get untracked. Although the Mets squeaked to the National League East with only an 82–79 record, McAndrew was never a factor, finishing with a 3–8 record and a 5.38 ERA in just 80 innings. George Stone, who came from the

Braves with Felix Millan in the Gentry deal, had been the anchor on the back end of the rotation. McAndrew did not make an appearance in the postseason as the Mets defeated the Cincinnati Reds in the NLCS before losing to the Oakland A's in seven games in the World Series.

It was clear that McAndrew no longer fit in the Mets plans and shortly before Christmas of 1973 the club traded him to the San Diego Padres for Steve Simpson, a minor league who had one season in double A with the Mets before calling it a career.

McAndrew's career was also drawing to a close. Although he reported to spring training with high hopes, more bad luck awaited with the Padres. Pitching coach Bill Posedel expected the pitchers to take part in "rundown" or "hotbox" drills in which the infielders practiced getting runners out in rundowns between the bases. Because of his chronically bad knee, McAndrew tried to beg off and just run in the outfield, but Posedel would have none of it. Sure enough, he reinjured his knee in a hotbox situation, with a pop that could be heard all over the infield.

PHOTO COURTESY OF METSILVERMAN.COM

*Jim McAndrew had one of the best spans of his career late in the 1969 season, throwing three complete games, 23 straight shutout innings, and starting the game that put the Mets in first place for the first time on September 10.*

Although the club physician recommended surgery, Jim opted to ice the knee for several days, which had generally worked before. He then strained his ribs while trying to pitch and was never able to get healthy. McAndrew struggled to a 1–4 record in 15 appearances and five starts when the Padres released him on June 1. Although just 30 years old, his baseball career was over.

He made 161 major league appearances, including 110 starts, 20 complete games, and six shutouts. He pitched 771 innings and gave up less than a hit per inning, with 712 hits allowed. His seven-year career totals were 37 wins, 53 losses, and a 3.65 ERA.

McAndrew had a growing family to support and didn't look back after his release by the Padres. He began a career in sales and management in the coal industry, first in Chicago for five years, then in Denver for 15 years, and St. Louis for eight years. He and his wife, Lyn, raised four children, Jamie, Jeff, Jon, and Jana. Jamie, the oldest, was a first-round draft choice in 1989 out of the University of Florida and pitched for the Milwaukee Brewers for two years in the 1990s.

After more than 25 years in the coal industry, Jim was able to retire at the age of 56 and settle in the Phoenix area with Lyn.

**Sources**

Durso, Joseph. *Amazing—The Miracle of the Mets.* (Boston: Houghton Mifflin Co., 1970).

Fox, Larry. *Last to First—The Story of the Mets.* (New York: Harper & Row, 1970).

Golenbock, Peter. *Amazin'—The Miraculous History of New York's Most Beloved Baseball Team.* (New York: St. Martin's Press, 2002).

Koppett, Leonard. *The New York Mets—The Whole Story.* (New York: The Macmillan Co., 1970).

McAndrew, Jim. Clippings file, National Baseball Library, Cooperstown, New York.

Oppenheimer, Joel. *The Wrong Season.* (Indianapolis: Bobbs-Merrill, 1973).

Ryczek, William, *The Amazin' Mets—1962-1969.* (Jefferson, North Carolina: McFarland & Co., Inc., 2008).

Shatzkin, Michael, ed. *The Ballplayers.* (New York: William Morrow and Co., Inc. 1990).

Telephone Interview with Jim McAndrew, December 18, 2008.

Vecsey, George. *Joy in Mudville.* (New York: McCall Publishing, 1970).

Zimmerman, Paul, and Dick Schaap. *The Year the Mets Lost Last Place.*(New York: World Publishing, 1969).

## All American (Almost)

In contrast to baseball in the 21st century, 33 of the 35 players who appeared for the 1969 Mets were born in the United States. Canadian Ron Taylor, a Toronto native, whose 59 appearances were the most of any '69 Mets hurler, and Les Rohr, born in Lowestoft, England, who appeared in just one game, were the exceptions and Rohr was raised in Montana. Sorted by birthplace, the '69 Mets represented 18 states—make it 19 if you count manager Gil Hodges, a native of Princeton, Indiana. Although these Mets represented every time zone in the continental US, the majority of the players came from warm weather states, with five apiece coming from California and Texas. For the record, seven Mets who took the field that year were African American.

Below is a breakdown of where the Miracle Mets came from (native town or city in parentheses).

**Alabama:** Tommie Agee (Magnolia), Cleon Jones (Plateau), Amos Otis (Mobile)

**Arizona:** Duffy Dyer (Phoenix), Gary Gentry (Phoenix)

**California:** Danny Frisella (San Mateo), Rod Gaspar (Long Beach), Bud Harrelson (Niles), Tug McGraw (Vallejo), Tom Seaver (Fresno)

**Florida:** Ed Charles (Daytona Beach), Wayne Garrett (Brookville)

**Illinois:** Bob Johnson (Aurora)

**Iowa:** Jim McAndrew (Lost Nation)

**Louisiana:** Jesse Hudson (Mansfield)

**Maryland:** Ron Swoboda (Baltimore)

**Massachusetts:** Kevin Collins (Springfield)

**Michigan:** Jim Gosger (Port Huron)

**Minnesota:** Jerry Koosman (Appleton)

**Missouri:** Donn Clendenon (Neosho), Art Shamsky (St. Louis)

**New Jersey:** Bobby Pfeil (Passaic)

**New York:** Ed Kranepool (Bronx), Al Weis (Franklin Square)

**North Carolina:** Don Cardwell (Winston-Salem), Cal Koonce (Fayetteville)

**Ohio:** Jack DiLauro (Akron)

**Texas:** Ken Boswell (Austin), Jerry Grote (San Antonio), Bob Heise (San Antonio), Al Jackson (Waco), Nolan Ryan (Alvin)

**Virginia:** J.C. Martin (Axton)

# Tug McGraw

by Matthew Silverman

| Season | Age | W | L | Pct | G | GS | SV | IP | H | BB | SO | WHIP | ERA |
|---|---|---|---|---|---|---|---|---|---|---|---|---|---|
| 1969 Mets | 24 | 9 | 3 | .750 | 42 | 4 | 12 | 100.3 | 89 | 47 | 92 | 1.355 | 2.24 |
| Career 19 Years | – | 96 | 92 | .511 | 824 | 39 | 180 | 1514.7 | 1318 | 582 | 1109 | 1.254 | 3.14 |

Back when being a character could keep you locked in the minor leagues and being a reliever was considered a career demotion, Tug McGraw excelled in both roles like few before or since. As a rookie starter for Casey Stengel, McGraw ended the Mets' long losing streak against Sandy Koufax; converted to a reliever by Gil Hodges, he was outstanding as the Mets pushed past the Cubs on their way to a Miracle in 1969; and he was as dominant as any reliever in the game in the early 1970s. Just as he was experiencing his worst year, he turned it around and lived his mantra of "Ya Gotta Believe" to help the Mets claim another unlikely pennant. Traded by the Mets, who foolishly thought him damaged goods, McGraw achieved the impossible again: helping the Phillies win their first world championship nearly a century into their existence. His enthusiasm never wavered as his playing career drew to a close and he tried other pursuits.

Even people not in the least interested in baseball recall Tug as the father of country star Tim McGraw, who embraced Tug after years of estrangement. Tim cared for Tug as brain cancer eventually took his dad too soon. Tug McGraw's 59 years were certainly packed with living.

Frank Edwin McGraw was rarely quiet, even as an infant. He was born in Martinez, California, on August 30, 1944, the second of three sons of Frank and Mabel McGraw (a fourth child died shortly after birth). He was never called by his given name.

"I never answered to another name," he told author Stanley Cohen in *A Magic Summer*. "My mother started calling me Tug when I was an infant because of the way I nursed. 'He's a real Tugger,' she said.

"On my first day of kindergarten, the teacher called the roll and when she finished she said, 'Is there anyone whose name I didn't call?' I raised my hand. 'My name is Tug McGraw,' I said. She looked at the roll and said, 'I have a Frank McGraw.' I said, 'No, that's my dad. He already went to kindergarten.'"

Mabel McGraw was, in Tug's words, "bipolar—the latest term for someone who is manic-depressive—not that we knew about that then." She was physically and verbally abusive. She spent time at a mental health facility and abandoned the family while on a weekend pass from Napa State Mental Hospital. The parents divorced and the three boys grew up under the father's care. It was a sports household.

Although Tug's athletic father, known as Big Mac, never played baseball, he made sure that his boys had the opportunity. His occupations included butcher, trucker, and fireman before studying to be a water treatment plant operator and engineer in Vallejo, California. He sent his sons—Hank, Tug, and Dennis—to a Catholic school, St.

Vincent Ferrer, close to the family's Vallejo home. Tug followed his older brother's lead and played baseball despite being just 4-feet-11 and 98 pounds as a high school freshman. Hank, who'd stood a foot taller at that same age, had scouts drooling over his talent as a catcher. He signed with the Mets in 1961. Tug graduated two years later and went to junior college in his hometown. Hank asked Roy Partee, the Mets scout who'd signed him, to take a look at Tug after every other team stopped looking at the young southpaw following a terrible outing in a junior college tournament. Hank was convincing. "He said, 'If there isn't room in this game for my brother, then I don't want to play either,'" Tug told Cohen. "He threatened to quit. The Mets weren't really pleased about it, but Hank was a good prospect, so they offered me a $7,000 bonus and sent me to their rookie league."

Tug was summoned to attend what would be Casey Stengel's last major league spring training camp in 1965. The left-hander made his major league debut a few weeks later at the age of 20. That was partly to protect Tug from being drafted by another organization. A rule at the time required bonus babies—players who'd received more than $4,000 to sign with a club—to stay with the major league club for their first full season or risk being taken by someone else. And the sad sack Mets could ill afford to let any pitcher slip through their fingers.

After just 11 appearances in two stops in the minors in 1964—all starts, including a no-hitter in his professional debut at Cocoa Beach—McGraw appeared in his first major league game against the Giants in relief at Shea Stadium on April 18, 1965. He was so excited about striking out Orlando Cepeda in his debut that he was given a tranquilizer to calm down in case the Mets needed him in the second game of that day's doubleheader. Tug appeared in 37 games with a 3.31 ERA and a 2–7 record as a rookie. The second of those wins, however, stands out as the most memorable start of his career.

Dodgers legend Sandy Koufax had won his first 13 decisions against the Mets, including his first no-hitter and the first thrown against the franchise, in 1962. In 14 starts against the Mets, Koufax had missed earning the "W" only once—and the Dodgers later won that game. Koufax was 4–0 against the Mets in 1965 and had 21 wins already for the season when he pitched at Shea on August 26. Los Angeles even gave Koufax a lead before he took the mound when Lou Johnson doubled in a run against McGraw in the top of the first. The Mets jumped ahead in the bottom of the inning and McGraw did not allow another run until the eighth. With the score 3–1, Maury Wills tried to stretch a single and was thrown out at second. That was critical because Wes Parker followed with an RBI triple. Jack Fisher took over for McGraw and saved what turned out to be a 5–2 victory that broke the Koufax hex (though he still finished his career with a 17–2 mark against the Mets). The victory over Koufax was McGraw's final win of the year as he dropped his last five decisions.

He struggled at the major league level the next two years. After he hurt his arm "muscling up" with weights in the offseason while serving in the Marine Reserve, the Mets sent Tug all the way to the Instructional League following the 1966 season. Instructor Sheriff Robinson was an old-fashioned guy who didn't want young kids monkeying around with new pitches—it was, after all, only the Instructional League—and Robinson made sure things like that didn't happen on his watch. So Tug McGraw learned the pitch that enabled him to last almost two decades in the big leagues from fellow pitcher Ralph Terry… on the golf course.

Terry had thrown the last pitch in two World Series: 1960 (Bill Mazeroski's famous home run) and 1962 (Willie McCovey's searing Series-ending lineout). By 1966, Terry was relegated to the minor leagues for a franchise that had just made history by *not* losing 100 games for the first time. Terry was in Florida trying to learn a knuckleball in an attempt to save his career at 31. (Unlike youngsters, apparently, washed-up pitchers could try anything they wanted.)

Typical of those early Mets, Terry had come to the franchise when he didn't have much left. Yet he did have something to show Tug and it changed the young lefty forever: the screwball. That pitch would transform his career, but neither Tug nor his screwball arrived overnight.

McGraw threw his version of the pitch by holding the ball parallel to the seams, while Hall of Famer Carl Hubbell, who talked to Tug about the pitch at Shea Stadium on Old-Timer's Day in 1969, held it differently. The pitch acted the same in both cases, darting in on right-handed batters and away from lefties. The screwball required practice and tinkering, and coaches had to let a pitcher throw it frequently to get it right. Getting the chance to practice was almost as hard as learning the new pitch.

Photo courtesy of Dwayne Labakas Collection

*Tug McGraw*

Despite the success many major leaguers had with the screwball, there was always trepidation regarding the pitch. Hubbell had been spurned by Tigers player-manager Ty Cobb in the 1920s because he thought the screwball would ruin the kid's arm. (It did, but not before he'd won 253 games.) John McGraw, whose New York Giants had been dominant behind Christy Mathewson's "fadeaway"—a successful right-handed version of the pitch—signed Hubbell in 1928. John McGraw was long dead by the time Tug McGraw (no relation) was making his way back to the big leagues. And innovative thinking was in short supply in the minor leagues with those moribund Mets.

Not content to spit on Tug's screwball, Sheriff Robinson also tried to change the way Tug threw his curveball. Tug couldn't make it work so he went back to doing it his own way. He earned praise from the salty Sheriff, who thought he'd gotten the young pitcher to see things his way. Tug's brother Hank, who would later famously be suspended for not cutting his hair, set the Sheriff straight. "You dumb high school coach," Hank shouted, "that just goes to show that you don't know what you're talking about. He tried to throw it your way and he couldn't, so he went back to throwing it his way and you like it. Why don't you just leave him alone and let him do his own thing." Hank never reached the big leagues after putting in a dozen years in the minors.

Despite winning the International League ERA title (1.99) for Jacksonville in 1967, Tug McGraw did not pitch in the majors at all the following year—going 9–9 with a 3.42 ERA in 23 starts at Jacksonville—and was available in that fall's expansion draft for the first three rounds. Luckily for the Mets, there were no takers in Montreal or San Diego. After an excellent spring training and a solid start to the 1969 season for Tug—among other April feats, he earned the Mets' first win of the season while handing the Montreal franchise its first-ever defeat—manager Gil Hodges made a decision that would change McGraw's career.

"The only other pitcher with a screwball was Jim Brewer of the Dodgers, so the hitters weren't used to seeing it," McGraw said. "By June, I was still pitching well and Gil called me into his office again. He said, 'Tug, I have three pieces of advice for you. One, I think you should think about staying in the bullpen permanently. You could be a great reliever and at best an average starter. Two, this team needs a late-inning stopper, and I want you to be my stopper. Three, I think you'll make a lot more money as a reliever than as a starter. Now it's up to you.' I said, 'Gil, if you think that's the way for me to go, I'm there already.' The rest is history."

McGraw and veteran righty reliever Ron Taylor were vital instruments in New York's overcoming a 10-game deficit to the Cubs on August 13. While Mets starters were completing 21 of their last 48 starts, the bullpen was nearly flawless when called into service. In his last 19 appearances, McGraw allowed two earned runs over 38 innings for a 0.47 ERA. Together McGraw and Taylor went 7–2 in the final push with 11 saves and an ERA of 1.00. For the year, McGraw had 12 saves and Taylor 13 in the first year in which the save was an official statistic.

McGraw made four early starts, including a complete-game victory in Chicago in May, while relieving 38 times to surpass 100 innings for the first time. And after coming into the year with a 4–19 career record, McGraw went 9–3 with a 2.42 ERA. During the club's pivotal stretch in August and September, McGraw had a decision or a save in eight straight appearances. McGraw was the winner on September 15 in St. Louis, the night Steve Carlton set a record with 19 strikeouts yet lost on two home runs by Ron Swoboda. McGraw went the final four innings as the Mets beat the Cardinals in 11 at Shea on September 23, putting the Mets a game from clinching the first National League East title.

A reliever like McGraw would be an October workhorse in today's game, but he made just one appearance in the 1969 postseason. That appearance, however, was crucial for both the Mets and McGraw. Jerry Koosman couldn't make it out of the fifth after being spotted a big early lead in Game Two of the inaugural National League Championship Series, and McGraw took over for Taylor to start the seventh inning in Atlanta. He threw three shutout innings for the save in the 11–6 victory. It was that outing that made McGraw finally feel that he belonged in the major leagues. Although McGraw didn't get to pitch in the World Series—Mets starters recorded all but eight outs in Games Two through Five—that postseason was the turning point of Tug's career.

"Thanks to that NLCS appearance, I was convinced that I was not only a viable major leaguer, but one who could excel in the future," he wrote years later with Don Yaeger in *Ya Gotta Believe!* "Everything changed for me in 1969, the year we turned out to be goddamned amazing, all right."

McGraw became known as a nonconformist who took life as it came. He went to Vietnam with several major leaguers on a goodwill tour, where he was slapped by bullpen mate Ron Taylor for smoking marijuana. Back in New York, Tug sprained his ankle on a toboggan run with teammate and fellow free spirit Ron Swoboda; McGraw came up with the excuse that he hurt his leg slipping on ice while taking out the trash.

And he loved giving haircuts. He cut the hair of transients in the Bowery and Mets icons alike. "I had him on *Kiner's Korner* after a ballgame that he was instrumental in," Ralph Kiner recalled. "He was in the service, he was in the Marines, and he cut hair, so he cut my hair on the show. It took me about four months for me to grow my hair back."

McGraw's barber skills remained questionable, but his pitching continued to improve. He began 1970 by saving Opening Day, the first season opener ever won by the franchise. While his ERA increased to 3.28, he appeared in 15 more games than in the world championship year because the young starting staff was not quite the same invincible group as the previous season. In 1971, McGraw had the best season to that point by a Mets reliever. Sharing fireman duties with Danny Frisella limited McGraw to eight saves, but he went 11–4 while holding batters to a .189 average and .266 slugging. His screwball made him especially tough against righties, who hit just .155 in 306 at-bats.

McGraw had a 1.70 ERA for the second straight year in 1972, and now he was getting more recognition. Manager Yogi Berra, who took over after the death of Gil Hodges that April, used McGraw nearly twice as often as Frisella, which made sense since McGraw's ERA was about half the righty's. McGraw racked up 27 saves, a club record he would hold until another Mets lefty, Jesse Orosco, broke it 12 years later (Orosco also broke McGraw's Mets career saves mark of 86).

McGraw appeared in his only All-Star Game in 1972 (he was named to the NL squad in 1975 but not pitch). He picked up the '72 win when Joe

Morgan singled home Nate Colbert in the 10th inning in Atlanta. McGraw struck out four in two innings, including the side in the ninth inning: Reggie Jackson, Norm Cash, and Bobby Grich.

In mid-July, McGraw's ERA rose above 2.00 for the only time all year. It stayed above that mark—though never getting higher than 2.06—until August 1, when McGraw threw 6⅓ shutout innings of relief in a game the Mets eventually won in 18 innings over the Phillies at Shea. It went down steadily and capped off at 1.70 with six outings without an earned run to end the season (covering nine innings), though he did lose an 11-inning game against the Phillies on an error. He allowed just three home runs in 106 innings in relief while facing 419 batters. After the season, Cincinnati's pennant-winning manager Sparky Anderson dubbed McGraw, "The Seaver of saves."

McGraw experienced both fame and failure at astonishing levels in 1973. He started out brilliantly, pitching to a 1.32 ERA the first month. He had five saves through May 3, but then came the kind of ERA-inflating, ego-deflating outing that can ruin the back of a reliever's baseball card for a year.

With the Mets leading the Astros with two on and two out in the sixth inning at Shea, McGraw came in to face Cesar Cedeno. He allowed a run-scoring double and then a three-run homer to Bob Watson to tie the game. McGraw stayed in the next inning and walked in the go-ahead run before being removed. To make things worse, three more runs were charged to him after he left. He got stuck with the loss and a 5.14 ERA that went even higher in his next outing. On May 19 against the Pirates, he allowed a game-tying home run to Bob Robertson in the ninth and a three-run shot to Willie Stargell the next inning. He had already equaled the home run total he allowed in '72. He had just one save over a six-week span. When McGraw finally broke that string in the first game of a doubleheader at Wrigley Field on July 1, he gave up a three-run, game-ending home run to Randy Hundley in the nightcap. Two days at Jarry Park, later he faced 11 Expos and seven scored.

"I'd been playing professional baseball for ten years and I'd been playing ball since I was seven," he commented after the '73 season. "And standing on the mound up in Montreal, I didn't have any feel for the baseball at all. I didn't have any idea how to throw the baseball. It was as though I'd never played before in my entire life."

The Mets were in last place at 33–42 and would've qualified for the basement in any division in baseball. They stood 11½ games behind the Cubs in the NL East. The three-time defending division champion Pirates were just two games ahead of the Mets in fifth place. The division eventually was turned around completely, but not before Tug McGraw turned around his season.

When McGraw blew a save against the Braves on July 7, it upped his ERA to 6.20 and dropped his record to 0–4. Berra started him twice at the end of the month to try to get him to snap out of it. Tug pitched horribly in a game the Mets won with seven in the ninth in Atlanta and pitched decently in a game the Mets wound up losing to Montreal. He returned to the bullpen and showed improvement.

He also had a better outlook because of talks he had with Joe Badamano, a motivational speaker who had been close to Gil Hodges. After lunch with Badamano one day that summer, "Joe kept saying, 'You've got to believe in yourself,'" McGraw said. "If I didn't *believe*, I could never do it. I had to stop worrying, start thinking positively. 'You gotta *believe*, Tug,' he said. 'That's it, I guess, you gotta *believe*.'"

McGraw started repeating that saying to fans, teammates, and even the team chairman. M. Donald Grant held a team meeting to talk about the disappointing season. There had been rumors about a managerial change, but Grant's purpose at the clubhouse meeting was to try to calm the team. "Relax, we love you guys," McGraw recalled the tiresome Grant saying, "We understand there have been a lot of injuries, you wouldn't be here if we didn't. We still believe in you."

The reliever could only contain himself so long when he heard the saying. He later admitted that Grant "took 20 minutes for him to say what should have taken five," and McGraw started shouting his new mantra. He "stopped the speech in its tracks. I jumped and ran around to a couple of lockers, grabbing guys and yelling, 'Do you believe? Ya gotta believe!'" While some of his teammates were laughing, Grant wasn't. He marched out of the Shea locker room "with his entourage of suits behind him."

McGraw's roommate, Ed Kranepool, came over and told him that Grant wasn't happy and he should go straighten it out. McGraw did. Immediately.

In the chairman's office, Grant said that he was offended by the outburst and "the only thing that will keep you here is if we start winning some ballgames." One could say, the rest was history, but the Mets—and McGraw—continued to perform poorly in the weeks immediately after the midsummer summit.

McGraw had some encouraging outings in August—including four scoreless innings before losing in the 13th inning in San Francisco—and then finally won his first game of the season on August 22, this time at the expense of another reliever, Jim Brewer, the right-handed screwball pitcher. The Dodgers held a 3–2 lead in the ninth at Shea when Felix Millan singled in the tying run off Brewer. After a Rusty Staub single, Brewer was lifted for Pete Richert, who promptly allowed the game-winning single to John Milner. McGraw was now 1–6 and the Mets were 57–67 and still in last place, though only six games behind the first-place Cardinals.

Photo courtesy of metsilverman.com

*Number 45, Tug McGraw, lives on at Citi Field as one of the Mets featured—along with old friends Tom Seaver and Rusty Staub—on the wall outside the left-field entrance.*

Despite losing three of their next four to fall 12 games under .500 and 6½ games back, the Mets turned out to have the division right where they wanted it. By then, several Mets were finally healthy and the team took off. The offense started scoring runs and the triumvirate of Tom Seaver, Jerry Koosman, and Jon Matlack pitched brilliantly—as did George Stone—to help the Mets push from the basement to the top floor in the NL East in the last five weeks. And leading the way was the believer himself, Tug McGraw.

Starting with McGraw's 14th save in 21 chances on August 27, the Mets reeled off a 24–9 mark to finish the season. The Mets won or at least split each of the 11 remaining series. McGraw saved 12 games, won four more, and put together an ERA of 0.88 over his last 41 innings. As if there wasn't enough going on those final weeks of the season, Tug's wife, Phyllis, gave birth to the family's second child, Cari Lynn, on September 1 (they already had a son, Mark).

McGraw had four saves in five days in mid-September as the Mets climbed to 3½ games behind Pittsburgh. He picked up the win in Chicago to shave another game off that lead and the Mets headed into a five-game home-and-home showdown with the Pirates. The Mets lost the opener at Three Rivers Stadium and were down 4–1 headed into the ninth inning in the second game. On the verge of falling 4½ behind with less than two weeks remaining in the season, the Mets rallied for five runs in the ninth. McGraw got the win when Don Hahn notched the deciding hit. The scene shifted to Shea and Tug earned the save against the Pirates the next night.

Thursday, September 20, was a touchstone game in Mets history: a night when the unbelievers truly started believing. Again, the Mets were down in the ninth inning; this time it was Duffy Dyer coming through with the big hit that tied the game. In the top of the 13th inning, a ball caromed off the top of the left-field wall and instead of landing in the bullpen for a home run, came right back to Cleon Jones, whose throw to Wayne Garrett and relay home nailed Richie Zisk.

Rookie catcher Ron Hodges applied the crucial tag and then singled in the winning run in the bottom of the inning. When the Mets won the next night, they were at .500 for the first time since May 29. And they were in first place.

A perfectly-timed seven-game winning streak enabled the Mets to push past the feeble competition in the NL East, but they weren't that far removed from the rabble. The Mets lost the last home game on the schedule at Shea before heading to Chicago for the season-ending four-game set. They waited out three days of rain while the other NL East competitors clumsily tried to make up ground. The Mets finally played a doubleheader on Sunday. The Cubs won the opener, 1–0, bringing hope to the second-place Cardinals and third-place Pirates, both on their way to winning the last game on their schedules. Jerry Koosman won the nightcap at Wrigley to clinch at least a tie.

A doubleheader was scheduled again on Monday. Tom Seaver started and held the lead through six innings, but his last pitch was whacked into the empty bleacher seats—the rain-soaked Wrigley crowd numbered just 1,913—and McGraw was summoned by Berra. He retired the first six batters he faced before allowing a Ken Rudolph single to start the ninth. He struck out Dave Rosello, Tug's fourth K since coming in, to bring up Glenn Beckert, a remnant of the Cubs club that the Mets had rallied past in 1969. Beckert hit a soft pop to Milner, who stepped on first base for the double play and the lowest winning percentage for a postseason berth at that point in history. The second game was scratched and the Mets celebrated in the cramped clubhouse at Wrigley Field.

Mets beat writer Jack Lang wrote, "McGraw kept yelling, 'You gotta believe!' and even Grant, who was also in the clubhouse, did not mind it now."

With the NLCS games starting in the afternoon the following weekend—to accommodate the NFL on television—relievers weren't needed as the squinting Cincinnati hitters flailed at Seaver and Jon Matlack and the Mets emerged with a split against the 99-win Reds. Koosman also went the distance as the Mets took Game Three at Shea, though Bud Harrelson took the loss in his famous scuffle with Pete Rose. A rested McGraw was needed in Game Four, throwing 4⅓ scoreless innings as the game remained tied through 11. Rose exacted some revenge for the fans' ire with a home run the inning after Tug was removed for a pinch hitter.

It looked as though McGraw's work for the NLCS was done as Seaver cruised into the ninth inning of Game Five with a 7–2 lead. But the Reds loaded the bases to chase Seaver and bring in McGraw to face Joe Morgan with the tying run on deck. He got Morgan to pop up and Dan Driessen followed by pulling a ball to Milner, who flipped to McGraw. The stands, crammed with young fans who had crowded down to the field level, burst forth when McGraw stepped on first. Shea was instantly awash with people tearing up everything in sight and McGraw, who had earned his 12th save since the end of August, dashed off the field to save himself.

"When we flew to San Francisco two days later to open the World Series, we still felt punchy because so many hellish things had happened to us in the last six months," McGraw said via Joseph Durso in *Screwball*, published after the '73 season. "We'd been denounced, damned, cheered, mobbed, written off, written up, screwed up, and we were bombed out of our minds."

McGraw, one of several Mets from the Bay Area, was disappointed that A's owner Charlie Finley had not put up bunting at Oakland Coliseum, which was not sold out for the Series. McGraw relieved Matlack in the seventh inning of the opener and did not allow a run, but the Mets lost anyway, 2–1. The next day, McGraw took over in the sixth inning, already the fourth Mets pitcher of the game. Although he allowed a pair of two-out hits to tie the game in the bottom of the ninth, he stayed on the hill until the 12th inning after the Mets scored four times in the top of the frame with McGraw getting a hit and scoring a run in the rally. McGraw couldn't get through his seventh inning of relief, allowing a triple to Reggie Jackson after Willie Mays lost a ball in the sun. Following a walk to Gene Tenace, McGraw was replaced by George Stone, who allowed Jackson to score but saved the 10–7 win for McGraw.

For someone who hadn't pitched at all in the 1969 World Series, McGraw logged eight innings in the first two days of the '73 Series. He tossed two more innings in Game Three in frigid Flushing—the first postseason night game in New York City history—but as had happened eight days earlier against the Reds, the inning McGraw came out, Harry Parker allowed the deciding run. McGraw was exhausted but he had the hearts and minds of the city. When he returned to the house he was renting in Manhasset, Long Island, late at night following the cross-country flight after lengthy Game Two, the whole neighborhood had greeted him, complete with a homemade banner on a bedsheet that simply said, "We Believe."

McGraw was given Game Four off, with Ray Sadecki retiring the side in the ninth. McGraw made up for it the next night, throwing 2⅔ innings to save the 2–0 win in Game Five that put the Mets one win away from a world championship. They never got that win. The Mets lost the last two in Oakland, with McGraw throwing an inning in Game Six to give him a 2.63 ERA over five games and 13⅔ innings in the Series, more work than any Met except for Matlack, who started three times, and Seaver, who started twice. McGraw worked more than twice the number of innings thrown by Oakland lefty reliever Darold Knowles, who became the first pitcher to work in all seven games of a World Series. Rollie Fingers, who tossed in six games for the A's, threw the same number of innings as McGraw. Jackson, the only Oakland regular to bat .300 and whose homer chased Matlack in Game Seven, was the Series MVP.

The whirlwind '73 season proved impossible to follow. For both McGraw and the Mets. The team had nearly the same mark in mid-August 1974 that they'd had a year earlier. After consecutive wins in relief by McGraw, the Mets stood in fifth place and 8½ games behind first-place Pittsburgh on August 14—just one game further out and one less team to climb over than on the same date in '73. Only this time there was no miraculous turnaround.

McGraw was one of several Mets injured during the season, suffering through shoulder pain all season. He started giving up grand slams—a major league record four slams amid a career-worst 12 homers allowed in just 88⅔ innings—and he was taking painkillers to deal with his shoulder. The team's response to McGraw's pain was to start him. He started three times in a row at the end of August, going 2–1 with a complete-game shutout against Atlanta, the only shutout of his 824-game career. He went eight innings in a loss to Montreal on September 10, so when the Mets played 25 innings the next night against St. Louis, the team's top reliever was not available. They lost to the Cardinals on an error by recently called up right-hander Hank Webb. Not surprisingly, McGraw was brought in the next night when the exhausted bullpen got shelled by St. Louis. He finished the season at 6–11 with a 4.16 ERA and just three saves—the most losses, fewest saves, and highest ERA since Gil Hodges had converted him to a reliever.

McGraw started once more on the last Saturday of the year. He was hit hard by the Pirates, who were still in a tight race for the division title with St. Louis—the Mets were 16 games back and suffered their first 90-loss season since 1967. McGraw exited the game in the fifth inning after allowing a two-run home run to Richie Zisk. It was the last game he would ever pitch as a Met.

"They just put me on display," McGraw wrote in *Ya Gotta Believe!* "By starting, it made me look like I was healthy, which was important because the word had started to spread around the league that I wasn't. So they put me on display as a starter after being a reliever all those years."

The Mets had a new general manager in the waning days of the '74 season. With Joe McDonald taking over for Bob Scheffing, the Mets made a splash at the winter meetings by trading McGraw, Don Hahn, and Dave Schneck to the Phillies for Del Unser, John Stearns, and Mac Scarce. It was the first in a long line of deals that would send away every star player from the '73 team. It also turned out to be the only trade of McGraw's career.

The Phillies knew nothing about McGraw's shoulder problems until he arrived for spring training. He had surgery to remove what turned out to be "a benign mass of gristle that had built up over the years. Removing it was a simple procedure," he said. "I was able to throw freely after that."

Despite not making his Phillies debut until the end of April because of the surgery, he put together an excellent first campaign with the Phillies, going 9–6 with a 2.98 ERA. The first day he ever pitched at Shea wearing a road uniform came on June 29. He wound up throwing seven innings in a twin bill, saving the first game and winning the second. McGraw retired 21 of the 22 Mets he faced in the doubleheader sweep.

In a decade as a Phillie, he was especially overpowering against his former club. His 22 saves against the Mets were more than he had against any team, quite a feat given that his first nine seasons were spent with New York. His 2.39 ERA against the Mets was also his best mark against any team as a Phillie—McGraw had enjoyed a 1.61 ERA against the Phillies as a Met. The Phillies hadn't been to the postseason since 1950; Philadelphia went six times with Tug on the team.

The Phillies won 101 games in both 1976 and 1977. Their solid starting staff included future Hall of Famer Steve Carlton, along with Jim Kaat, Jim Lonborg, and McGraw's close friend Larry Christenson. They also had a strong bullpen that shared the load. Manager Danny Ozark used Ron Reed, Gene Garber, and McGraw equally in save situations. Even lefty starter Tom Underwood picked up a couple of saves as the Phillies ran away with the division in 1976. McGraw pitched poorly twice in the NLCS as the Reds swept in three games.

The Phillies took the NL East again in 1977, although McGraw was fourth on the team in appearances and had just nine saves. Against the Dodgers in the NLCS, McGraw saved the Phillies' first postseason win since 1915, spotting Philadelphia a series lead on the road. The Dodgers won Game Two, but the Phillies had a two-run lead in the ninth with Gene Garber pitching his third inning of relief. A succession of bloops, bunts, and bad plays pushed across three runs for L.A. as McGraw sat in the bullpen. He came in the next night in a steady rain with the Phillies trailing and threw two scoreless innings as the Dodgers took the pennant.

The Dodgers were the foe again as the Phillies won the division for the third straight time in 1978. McGraw had taken a larger share of the load since Garber was traded to Atlanta during the season for starter Dick Ruthven. Tug pitched three times against Los Angeles and threw the final pitch of the NLCS, a single by Bill Russell that plated Dusty Baker with the pennant-winning run in the bottom of the 10th inning of Game Four.

McGraw had said he felt the Phillies had brought him in to help loosen up the team as well as provide a top-notch reliever. He did just that. Among other things, he had names for all his pitches: "Cutty Sark … because it would sail," "Bo Derek, which had a nice little tail to it," "the John Jameson was hard and straight, just like the Irish whiskey," and even gopher balls had a name—"Frank Sinatra" because the result was "Fly Me to the Moon." The Phillies felt they needed other changes, replacing Richie Hebner at first base with Pete Rose and—after the injury-riddled club tumbled in the standings in 1979—firing Ozark and elevating farm director Dallas Green to manager.

McGraw, like many Phillies, had a poor '79, but for the first time since his trade from the Mets, he led the team in appearances (65), games finished (43), and saves (16), even if his 5.16 ERA was a full run higher than the team average. It all came together in 1980.

Philadelphia's slogan in spring training was "We, not I," which made some players initially roll their eyes, but it sounded a lot better than the "Philadelphia Pillies," a name picked up after the double-A farm team's doctor in nearby Reading was caught prescribing diet pills to Phillies wives, who passed them along to their husbands. The team was still barely over .500 in August when Green held a meeting in which he got in many players' faces, including reliever Ron Reed, who had to be restrained. The Phillies won 21 of their last 28.

McGraw was magnificent. He did not allow a run in July (8⅔ innings) and then doubled his workload the following month, posting a 1.04 ERA. After allowing runs in consecutive outings in Pittsburgh in mid-August, McGraw permitted just one more earned run all season, covering 40⅓ innings. For those 24 appearances, he had an ERA of 0.22 with nine saves to go with five wins, including the division-clinching victory. The Phillies, one out away from being tied with the Expos on the next to last day of the season at packed Olympic Stadium, evened the score in the ninth on a hit by Bob Boone. McGraw came in and allowed just one hit in three innings. After Mike Schmidt's homer in the top of the 11th made it 6–4, McGraw retired Gary Carter, Warren Cromartie, and Larry Parrish for Philadelphia's fourth division title in five years.

Just as in 1973, McGraw was winless until August and then didn't lose again—though he did not have a volatile start as he did in his "Ya Gotta Believe" season. His final 1980 numbers were 5–4 with a 1.46 ERA in 57 games with 20 saves, the most he'd had since '73. He finished fifth in that year's Cy Young Award balloting to fellow Philly southpaw Steve Carlton and 16th in the National League MVP voting to teammate Mike Schmidt (McGraw had placed 15th in the MVP vote in 1973).

So in the tightest five-game NLCS ever played, it only made sense that McGraw pitch in every game. He threw two innings for the save against the Astros in the opener at Veterans Stadium, a 3–1 win that turned out to be the only game that didn't go extra innings.

He allowed the go-ahead run in the eighth inning in Game Two, only to have the Phillies tie it in the bottom of the inning. Ron Reed took the loss in 10 innings. McGraw suffered the loss the next night when, in his fourth inning of relief, he allowed the only run of the game on a Denny Walling sacrifice fly in the 11th inning. Green brought in Warren Brusstar to save Game Four, but when he allowed the tying run in the ninth and the Phillies scored two runs in the top of the 10th, McGraw took the ball. He was perfect and the series was tied.

With the pennant on the line in the Astrodome, the Phillies rallied for five runs in the eighth inning to knock out Nolan Ryan and take a 7–5 lead. McGraw entered and nearly got out of a jam, striking out both Gary Woods and Enos Cabell looking, but he surrendered run-scoring hits to Rafael Landestoy and Jose Cruz to tie it. Green sent up a pinch hitter to bat for McGraw with two on and two outs in the ninth. The Phils didn't score but Dick Ruthven got the 8–7 win when Garry Maddox knocked in the run that wound up clinching the pennant in the 10th inning.

The World Series seemed a breeze by comparison. Philadelphia faced a Kansas City club that—like the Phillies—had spent the latter half of the 1970s winning division titles repeatedly only to lose in crushing fashion in the League Championship Series. The Phillies added to Kansas City's heartbreak. After the Royals took an early 4–0 lead in the opener, the Phillies scored five in the third and went on to win by a run. McGraw pitched the last two innings, allowing just one hit and earning the save. He was not as sharp in his next outing, surrendering the game-winning hit to Willie Mays Aikens in the bottom of the 10th inning in Game Three. With the Series tied and the Royals leading by a run, the Phillies scored twice off Dan Quisenberry in the ninth inning of Game Five to take the lead. McGraw, who'd been on the mound since the sixth inning, walked the bases full. He struck out Jose Cardenal to end it and put the Phillies a game away from their first-ever World Series title.

"By the time Game Six of the World Series came around," McGraw later admitted, "whenever I threw certain pitches, especially the screwball, I felt like I was banging my elbow on the corner of a table. I had to be careful because I knew I had only a limited amount of pitches left, especially the screwball. And I knew I wouldn't be there if I didn't have the screwball."

McGraw took over for Carlton in the eighth inning of Game Six with two men on and a four-run lead. He allowed a run on a sacrifice fly, and—after being asked by Green if he was okay—he went out for the ninth inning. A single by Cardenal loaded the bases with one out. "I was close to calling Dallas and having him come and get me," McGraw later said.

Ninth-place hitter Frank White—the Series still operated under an every-other-year DH rule regardless of which team was home—popped up in foul ground. Catcher Bob Boone couldn't hear Pete Rose call for the ball. Boone stuck out his glove near the dugout, it popped out...and Rose snagged it out of the air.

With the Phillies an out away from the first world championship in their 97-year history, and with recent sackings of fields by riotous fans in other cities—including Shea Stadium with McGraw on the field in 1973—Philadelphia police entered the playing field with officers on horseback and dogs. Two innings earlier, McGraw had had to ask a policeman to coerce the German shepard stationed in the bullpen to get off his glove so he could warm up. Now as he stood on the mound ready to pitch to Willie Wilson, McGraw caught sight of a horse relieving itself on the Astroturf at the Vet.

"I just thought, 'Hmmm, if I don't get out of this inning, that's what I'm going to be in this city,'" McGraw said.

He got ahead of Wilson and came with the fastball. Wilson waved at it—for his record 12th strikeout of the Series—and McGraw leaped in the air as the 66,000 fans cheered in the stands. McGraw called it "the high point of my career."

Just as happened after his exceptional workhorse effort in 1973, McGraw had injury problems the following year. He had signed a four-year contract that would keep him in the major leagues until he was 40, but his days as the team's primary reliever were drawing to a close. He led the Phillies with 10 saves in strike-shortened 1981, posting a 2.62 ERA in 34 appearances. Tug had one last superb effort in the postseason as well. With the Phillies playing Montreal in the Division Series created by crowning pre- and post-strike champions, McGraw threw the last three innings of Game Four at the Vet. He allowed just one baserunner and erased him on a double play he started. George Vukovich batted for McGraw in the 10th inning and homered to force a deciding game. The Expos topped the Phillies the next day to advance to the next round. In 1982, for the only time in McGraw's career, he had more blown saves (six) than saves (five).

The gray-haired bullpen of Reed and McGraw remained together as they had been since 1975, but others took more prominent role. Al Holland assumed the ninth-inning responsibility and Willie Hernandez was becoming an elite reliever as well. Even the "Wheeze Kids" didn't have room for the 39-year-old McGraw. He had no saves for the first time since they had become an official statistic in 1969 and he was left off the active roster as the Phillies reached the postseason for the fifth time in six years. Philadelphia took the pennant but lost to the Orioles in the World Series in five games.

McGraw pitched in just 25 games in 1984; old Mets buddy Jerry Koosman, a year older than Tug, pitched 11 more times than that as a starter for the Phillies. McGraw's final big league appearance was at a familiar location yet with an unaccustomed result. He trotted in from the Shea Stadium bullpen in the eighth inning on September 25, the tying run at the plate. In the last couple of years of his career, with his screwball not what it once was, McGraw had actually become more difficult for lefties to hit (.243 by right-handed hitters and .250 by lefties in 1984, compared with .226/.268 for his career). He retired tough lefty swingers Keith Hernandez and Darryl Strawberry to end the eighth. With a chance to get his first save since 1982 and both the Mets

Photo courtesy of *Mets Inside Pitch* Archives

*Tug McGraw split his career between New York and Philly, yet even the demanding fans in those two cities never held his shared allegience against him. He was always revered at Shea Stadium when he visited for Old-Timers' Day.*

and Phillies eliminated from the race, manager Paul Owens sent McGraw out for the ninth.

Hubie Brooks doubled and Mookie Wilson tripled, putting the tying run on third with no one out. McGraw left the field at Shea for the last time. Former '73 Mets heroes came through that inning against reliever Larry Andersen: Ron Hodges, who had won the "Ball on the Wall" game as a rookie just over 11 years earlier, got the tying hit against Andersen, and Rusty Staub, who had hit .423 against the A's in the World Series with an injured shoulder, put a capper on the proceedings with a home run against Andersen.

McGraw officially announced his retirement on February 14, 1985. His record was 96–92 with 180 saves and a 3.14 ERA, numbers that don't begin to measure his value to teams that depended on him to come in with the game in jeopardy, get out of the jam, and throw multiple innings as needed.

One of the great personalities in the game could not simply disappear, however. A syndicated cartoon, *Scroogie*, about a major league relief pitcher, had appeared in newspapers and in book form during his career. McGraw moved into TV as a reporter and was a sought-after speaker. His wife, Phyllis, tired of years of being a baseball widow and frustrated by his new time-consuming pursuits, continued life without Tug. They eventually divorced in 1987.

Though he spent seven years at Philadelphia's Channel 6, handling colorful features, he struggled with the sports assignments he was asked to do. "I hated going down to the clubhouse and having all the ballplayers look at me in a suit with a microphone in my hand," he later wrote. "We used to heckle reporters—calling them green flies—and now I was one of the annoying flies being swatted at by my former teammates."

He moved to Orlando, California, and later back to Philadelphia with Diane Hovenkamp and her two children from a previous marriage. They married in 1995, shortly after they learned she was pregnant. Matthew was born when Tug was 51; he was McGraw's fourth child and 28 years younger than his first.

Tim McGraw had been born in 1967 to Betty D'Agostino, who had met Tug when he pitched at triple-A Jacksonville in 1966. He did not acknowledge Tim as his son and met him only twice—reluctantly—during his playing career. A lawsuit finally forced him to accept responsibility and the two became close. Tug helped Tim sign his first recording contract.

Tug thought Tim didn't have the talent to be a professional singer, but his son had determination. While meeting Tug at Mardi Gras in New Orleans, Tim announced to his father that he was selling everything he had—including the car and other items Tug had given him—dropping out of Northeastern Louisiana State University, and moving to Nashville to try it in country music. "That crazy stunt—taking off with no plan like that—made him even more of a McGraw in my eyes," Tug said.

It was during the 10th anniversary of the 1980 world championship that Tug found himself seated next to a record company executive named Bruce Wendell of Curb Records. Tug offered him a ride back to the hotel and he happened to slide Tim's demo tape into the stereo. A few days later a meeting was set up and Tim McGraw was signed to his first recording contract. Another save set up by Tug.

Tug bought Tim a van and a trailer for his new eight-man band to hit the road. His first two albums weren't successful and an executive at Curb suggested he consider going back to Louisiana. Tim said that since his career was on the line that he should be allowed to produce his next album and pick his songs. *Not a Moment Too Soon* came out in 1994 and sold six million copies. Faith Hill was a singer on the tour. They married in 1996 and had three daughters.

"I'd have to say that while I tried for so many years to deny that I fathered Betty's child, deep inside I must have known that he was mine. That is my only explanation for my confession to Phyllis that I may have a son, my never throwing out his pictures that Betty sent me, and my reluctance to do a paternity test until the day I met him, all grown up, face to face," he wrote in *Ya Gotta Believe!*, which was published just after his death.

On March 12, 2003, while at spring training as a Phillies instructor in Clearwater, Florida, Tug was hospitalized with a brain tumor. Surgery revealed that the brain cancer was malignant and inoperable.

Though he was given three weeks to live, chemotherapy and a cocktail of cancer drugs helped shrink his tumors. But less than three weeks later the cancer had spread again. The end was coming fast. Tim, who had paid for the costly experimental medicine in Tug's treatment and had been involved in all the decisions, spent the last days with his father at the country star's cabin in Brentwood, Tennessee. Tug died there on January 4, 2004, at 4:45 p.m.

In his final year, with the public knowing full well the situation, Tug, Tim, and a cadre of friends toured places he wanted to see for the last time—or the first time. A member of the Mets Hall of Fame since 1993 and the Phillies Wall of Fame since 1999, Tug was able to take part in celebrations at the places he called home and where the fans loved him. He was at Shea Stadium—against the Phillies, it so happened—for the 30th anniversary of his 1973 "Ya Gotta Believe" club. He was in Philadelphia in September for the closing ceremonies at Veterans Stadium.

Both teams honored him posthumously in 2004. The Phillies wore a green shamrock on their sleeve that read "Tug," fitting because he so loved his Irish roots and was responsible for bringing green uniforms to St. Patrick's Day in spring training—even though a genealogical study of his family revealed that his true background was mostly Czech. The 2004 Mets honored him on their sleeve with his name and three simple words: "Ya Gotta Believe."

Even in death, Tug was still represented in these disparate cities at major occasions for each franchise in 2008. Sons Matthew and Mark represented him at Shea Stadium for the final game at the park where their dad debuted in 1965 and where he helped the Mets win two pennants, something that only Tug and nine teammates achieved in the stadium's 44-year history. And when the Phillies reached the 2008 World Series, Tim McGraw took the mound to throw the ceremonial first pitch in Game Four. He sprinkled some of Tug's ashes. Tug had died three months before Citizens Bank Ballpark opened. Part of him would always be on a pitcher's mound.

**Sources**

Bock, Duncan, and John Jordan. *The Complete Year by Year N.Y. Mets Fan's Almanac.* New York: Crown, 1992.

Cohen, Stanley. *A Magic Summer: The '69 Mets.* New York: Skyhorse Publishing, 2009.

Ralph Kiner, personal interview, June 21, 2007.

Lang, Jack, and Peter Simon. *The New York Mets: Twenty-Five Years of Baseball Magic.* New York: Henry Holt and Company, 1986.

Mandel, Ken. "Tim McGraw Finds Way to Honor Tug," mlb.com, October 26, 2008.

McGraw, Tug, and Joseph Durso, *Screwball.* Boston: Houghton Mifflin, 1974.

McGraw, Tug, with Don Yaeger. *Ya Gotta Believe! My Roller Coaster Life As a Screwball Pitcher and Part-Time Father, and My Hope-Filled Fight Against Brain Cancer.* New York: New American Library, 2004.

*www.nndb.com/people/402/000026324/*

*www.ultimatemets.com*

## Broadway Joe & Co.

On the surface, the result of the 1969 World Series is one of the most stunning upsets in sports history. In actuality, it was the second time in that calendar year that a Shea Stadium-based team had knocked off a heavily-favored foe from Baltimore.

On January 12, 1969, the New York Jets became the first American League Football club to beat a club from the established National Football League. Though Super Bowl III is remembered for Joe Namath making good on his "guarantee" and beating the 20-point favorite Baltimore Colts by a score of 16-7, the ground game controlled the clock and put the upstart Jets in a position to win. Matt Snell, who ran for 121 yards at Miami's Orange Bowl, scored New York's only touchdown in the second quarter. The Jets capitalized on three Jim Turner field goals and a defensive effort for the ages. The Colts finally scored with 3:19 left in the game, but the defense held even after Baltimore recovered the ensuing onsides kick. Broadway Joe threw for 206 yards against the Colts and was named MVP.

Namath's feared arm opened up the running game—and it's also what got the Jets to the big game. Because the Mets were the primary tenant at Shea and changing the stadium configuration to football hampered the field, the Jets did not play at home until the Mets finished their schedule. In the 1968 season, the Jets played three straight road games to open the season and were 2–1 before beginning the home portion of the schedule. They wound up winning eight of their last nine, yet the most famous game that season was the one loss in that span.

With 1:05 left on the clock in Oakland on November 17, the Jets held a 32–29 lead over the Raiders. That was when NBC switched over to the film, Heidi, and the eastern and central time zones missed the Raiders' two touchdowns in the final minute to win. "The *Heidi* Game" became part of legend—and the volume of furious calls and letters resulted in networks no longer switching away in participating markets while the game was still undecided. "The *Heidi* Game" was also a precursor of the AFL title game. This time it was the Jets scoring late and Ralph Baker scooping up a lateral to thwart any visions of Daryle Lamonica leading the Raiders to a comeback victory as he'd done in November while the world watched Heidi. Lamonica's 401 yards at Shea set an AFL Championship Game record; Namath threw for 266 yards and three touchdowns.

In 1969, the Mets' newfound postseason success meant the Jets had to wait even longer to play at Shea. They spent the first five weeks on the road (winning three times), and then hosted seven games in a row. Like the Mets, the Jets couldn't lose in October and reeled off a six-game winning streak en route to the AFL East title. Miracles, though, seemed frozen at Shea as the year drew to a close. On an icy, wind-swept field, the Kansas City Chiefs stopped the Jets three times from the one-yard-line in the playoffs and came away from Shea with a 13–6 win. The Chiefs wound up as the final AFL Super Bowl participant, beating the NFL Vikings in the last game before the two leagues officially merged.

# Amos Otis

by William Lamberty

| Season | Age | G | AB | R | H | 2B | 3B | HR | RBI | BB | SO | SB | CS | BA | OBP | SLG |
|---|---|---|---|---|---|---|---|---|---|---|---|---|---|---|---|---|
| 1969 Mets | 22 | 48 | 93 | 6 | 14 | 3 | 1 | 0 | 4 | 6 | 27 | 1 | 0 | .151 | .202 | .204 |
| Career 17 Years | – | 1998 | 7299 | 1092 | 2020 | 374 | 66 | 193 | 1007 | 757 | 1008 | 341 | 93 | .277 | .343 | .425 |

Late in the evening of May 15, 1973, Amos Otis lifted a Nolan Ryan fastball to Royals Stadium's spacious right-center-field gap that was hauled in by Angels right fielder Ken Berry. Some 35 years later, Otis still remembered the moment, the pitch, and who caught it. "Right there on the warning track," he told the *Kansas City Star*, recalling that Berry had come in for defense. "If Bob Oliver had been out there, I'd have had it, I'd have broken it up."

Instead, with Otis's help, Ryan took a major step on the path that led him to immortality. The no-hitter was the first of seven fired by the famed Ryan Express, and it resurfaced from the annals of baseball history in 2008 when Kansas City was no-hit for a second time (by Boston's Jon Lester). Ryan's career led him to the Hall of Fame, while Otis played for another decade and was one of the most productive and popular players in Royals history.

While no one could have known it in 1973, Otis and Ryan would remain linked for another reason. They came to symbolize the two worst trades the New York Mets have ever made. While the 1973 Mets were a shocking pennant winner in the National League, they soon endured seven straight seasons finishing fifth or sixth and fading to obscurity in the largest media market, where baseball is king. In 1980, *Sports Illustrated*'s Henry Hecht referred to Otis as New York's WT 1 (worst trade number 1), with Ryan checking in as Hecht's WT 2. Ryan—and three other prospects—brought former All-Star shortstop Jim Fregosi to the Mets, but Otis brought much less in return to New York. The fledgling Royals received Otis and pitcher Bob Johnson for third baseman Joe Foy, who played only 140 more games in the majors, while Johnson was later shipped from Kansas City in a package of players that brought the Royals Freddie Patek. It was Foy's failure at third base that set the wheels in motion for the eventual trade of Ryan for Fregosi, whom the Mets unsuccessfully attempted to make into a third baseman.

Otis, however, was stellar—but not with the Mets. Outside of short stints with the Mets at the beginning of his career and a season in Pittsburgh at the end, Otis became a Royals legend. The five-time All-Star finished in the top 10 in the American League batting race four times, and in the top 10 in steals (six times), runs (six times), hits (four times), and total bases (three times). He twice paced the AL in doubles. In terms of numbers that became more recognized after he retired in 1984, Otis was among the best 10 players in the junior circuit in runs created four times and in OPS (on-base percentage plus slugging percentage) twice.

Otis left the Royals in 1983 as the team's all-time leader in many categories. Even after more than a quarter-century, Otis remained in the top five in team history in games played (third, 1,891), runs (second, 1,074), RBIs (third, 992), walks (second, 739), and stolen bases (second, 340). In fact, he ranked in KC's top five in just about every offensive career category except batting average. (And his .280 batting average for Kansas City was sixth all-time among Royals who played at least 1,000 games for the franchise.) A.O., as he was called, helped lead the Royals from the futility of their early expansion era to one of baseball's most successful franchises in less than a decade, and inspired the chants of "Aaaay-Oh! Aaaay-Oh!" which reverberated across the shimmering turf of sparkling Royals Stadium.

And while every Mets fan knows that the organization let Amos Otis slip through its hands, many don't know that in reality he got away from the Amazin's twice. In 1964, the year before Major League Baseball instituted the amateur player draft system, Otis was among 35 players flown to Shea Stadium for a workout during a Mets road trip. Sent. home to Mobile, he was told the Mets would contact him.

Otis heard from a major league team several months later, but it wasn't the Mets. The Boston Red Sox drafted him with the 95th selection of MLB's first draft. Like his hometown hero Hank Aaron, Otis was drafted as a shortstop. Mobile produced Hall of Famers Aaron and Billy Williams and major league regulars like Tommie Agee and Cleon Jones, Otis's future Mets teammates. Otis, however, was the only player ever drafted out of Mobile's Williamson High School. He was also the kicking specialist for his high-school team that was undefeated for three straight years. But Amos Joseph Otis—born April 26, 1947, in Mobile—used his feet to glide across outfields and steal bases at a clip that made him one of the game's best outfielders.

Success did not come easily and acceptance for the Alabaman in the 1960s South was far from given. While Otis hit .329 with nine home runs and 10 stolen bases for the Harlan (Kentucky) farm team in the Appalachian League in 1965, and led third basemen in fielding (.910), chances accepted (122), and double plays (13), his assimilation into the life of a professional ballplayer masked a tumultuous summer away from the diamond. One of two African Americans on the squad, Otis recalled in a 1969 *New York Times* feature that he received an anonymous phone call several weeks into his rookie season in Harlan admonishing him to leave town in strongly worded, racially inflamed language. Red Sox management chose not to heed Otis's pleas for reassignment, and he and teammate Bobby Mitchell endured sporadic threats and harassment not uncommon for the time and place.

A change in scenery arrived the next season. Otis advanced to Oneonta of the New York-Penn League, and he responded by earning All-Star honors. He hit .270 that summer with three homers, drawing 39 walks while stealing 14 bases. After the season ended, though, Otis received a jolt. The Mets, two years after working him out at Shea Stadium, drafted Otis from Boston's farm system.

Taking the move in stride, Otis hit .268 with 36 walks for triple-A Jacksonville in 1967, with 11 doubles, seven triples, and three home runs. He stole 29 bases, and earned a September call-up to Shea Stadium. Otis indicated in a 1996 article in *Sports Collectors Digest* that he arrived in the majors with a clear sense of his defensive role, although New York manager Wes Westrum initially played him at third base. "I was a jack-of-all-trades in high school, I could play all nine positions," he told an interviewer. "I started out my pro career at shortstop, kind of lost interest at shortstop, and moved over to third base for a while. Then I was the fastest guy in the outfield for the Mets and then I wanted to be an outfielder."

Returning to Jacksonville in 1968, Otis hit .286 with 15 home runs, matching his previous career total as a professional, and stole 21 bases. He walked 50 times and played in the triple-A All-Star Game.

His 1968 record landed Otis in an awkward position entering spring training in 1969. The 22-year-old was lauded as "the best piece of property we've got" by Mets farm director Whitey Herzog, who later was instrumental in Otis's career in Kansas City. General manager Johnny Murphy tagged Otis as "untouchable" in trade negotiation with Atlanta for Joe Torre before the 1969 campaign. The Mets drew scorn from Braves GM Paul Richards (who asked—prematurely, it seems—"If they got so many 'untouchables' on that club, how come they haven't won any pennants?"). New York sportswriters also wondered about an untouchable list that included Tom Seaver, Jerry Koosman, and Bud Harrelson. Broadcaster Howard Cosell even asked Otis in a spring training interview if he expected to win Rookie of the Year honors.

If trying to break into a lineup for a New York major league team wasn't pressure enough, the label of untouchable was. "That untouchable label was a terrible burden," Otis told sportswriter Arthur Daley in 1971. He broke camp in 1969 as a third baseman. Veteran Ed Charles worked with him at third at spring training, but Otis never seemed comfortable; Charles got first crack at the position. He later told the *St. Petersburg Independent* that when the 1969 season started, "I didn't play for three weeks. After they had a losing streak I finally got to play and we broke the streak. Then [the press] started coming out with all this 'phenom Otis breaks streak' and all that stuff. I played three games in a row." Otis returned to spot duty, playing primarily in the outfield and his bat went cold.

On June 15, with only nine hits in 66 at-bats, Otis was farmed out to make way for Donn Clendenon, who had been acquired in a trading deadline deal with Montreal. Recalled on September 2, Otis saw some action, but being brought up after the rosters expanded eliminated him from consideration for the postseason roster. He was Steve Carlton's 19th strikeout victim on September 15, putting the Cardinals lefty in the record books as the first pitcher to ever fan that many in a nine-inning game. In the next-to-last regular-season series, in Philadelphia, Otis went 3-for-9, and GM Murphy, in an article in *The Sporting News,* said manager Gil Hodges thought Otis "looked like the player we always said he was." That series was Otis's last appearance as a Met.

Otis also opened the eyes of Cedric Tallis, Kansas City's "flim-flam man," as Bill James once referred to the architect of the great Royals teams of the 1970s. Tallis built those teams by acquiring other teams' talented young players, and the Mets were Tallis's first victim. Sent with Bob Johnson to the Royals on December 3 for the infamous Joe Foy, Otis was installed in Municipal Stadium's spacious outfield. Royals manager Charlie Metro told Kansas City Star writer Joe McGuff that the Otis acquisition was made to plug Kansas City's hole in center field.

Tallis correctly read New York's displeasure with their third-base platoon of 35-year-old Ed Charles and rookie Wayne Garrett. The organization's desperation to fill a hole at the hot corner dated back to the first days of the Mets in 1962. Tallis hawked the Mets through the summer and fall with the idea of moving Foy, who had been a regular in Boston's "Impossible Dream" ballclub that captured the 1967 AL pennant.

"During the World Series, we sent a lot of people to Baltimore and New York," Tallis said. "I assigned two men to each of the other 23 clubs to sound out their needs and what they would give in a trade." Tallis told sportswriter Joe Trimble that the Mets had tried to acquire a young third baseman from Cleveland, but that the teams didn't match up. Negotiations began between the Mets and Kansas City at the World Series, according to Tallis, with talks heating up at the general managers meetings at Colorado Springs after the season. "That was a kind of four-day outing, mostly golfing," Tallis recalled. "Murphy didn't play golf but we got together at night. We couldn't agree at that time, but promised to talk again at the winter meetings in Miami. Bob Scheffing [who would succeed Murphy after his untimely death that winter] and Whitey Herzog [the Mets farm director] were there, too. We finally made the deal with Foy going to New York and Otis and Johnson coming here."

Evaluating the opportunity facing him, Otis celebrated in ironic fashion. "December third was the happiest day of my life. I didn't get to drink any of that World Series champagne, but on the day I was traded my wife and I went out and bought our only bottle," he told sportswriter Joe Trimble in 1970. Otis, who had been voted a World Series share by his teammates (though he didn't receive a championship ring), was heading from a team that had become the talk of the baseball world to a club that had been in existence for one year. He later told *Sports Collectors Digest*: "The disappointment came from being traded from a World Series champ to an expansion team; it had only been around one year. The best thing about that was there were no superstars over there; the only name I recognized there was Lou Piniella. He was Rookie of the Year that year. So it was like I went from being on top of the water barrel to being under the water barrel. That was probably my biggest thrill in baseball, getting a chance to play more in Kansas City, and I stayed there for 14 years."

Otis expressed mixed emotions about his opportunity in New York when he visited with *Newsday*'s Paul Ballot in August of 1970. "I didn't want to play third with the Mets, but I think I could have played it if I'd really gotten a shot at it. But three games? That's no test. I never got an explanation from anyone why I was benched." Hodges showed little remorse in letting Otis go, commenting after the deal that it may have been "unfair to the boy to ask him to play third. He didn't like the position and he didn't play well there." Comments by Hodges in the spring of 1969 offer further clues to the uneven career and limited opportunity Otis experienced in New York. "Lackadaisical is the word people in our organization use" to describe Otis, Hodges told Jack Lang in the March 22, 1969 issue of *The Sporting News*. "Seems like I play my best ball when they're pushing me," Otis offered in that same article.

Otis's impact in Kansas City was immediate and unquestionable. In his first spring training with the Royals, he told the *New York Times* in 1971, "I was standing in the outfield not far from the right-field foul line when I saw Charlie Metro walking toward me. I didn't even know what to say to him and so

PHOTO COURTESY OF NATIONAL BASEBALL HALL OF FAME LIBRARY, COOPERSTOWN, NY

*Amos Otis, right, worked with Ed Charles throughout 1969 spring training to help the center fielder learn to play third base. Though Charles did his best to instruct the man the Mets wanted to take his job, Otis didn't stick and only played third base three times in 1969. A year later he was an All-Star center fielder in Kansas City.*

I headed toward center field. I looked again and he was coming my way. Finally he pinned me against the left-field fence. 'Amos,' he said, 'you're my center fielder for as long as you can hold the job.'"

On his way to hitting .284 in 1970 with 36 doubles, tied for the league lead, Otis reached base by hit or walk in 136 of his 159 games. He became the first Royal to play in an All-Star Game—catcher Ellie Rodriguez had been named a reserve for the 1969 game but saw no action—and Otis was involved in one of the best-known plays in midsummer classic history. Otis made the throw to the plate on which Pete Rose collided with Ray Fosse in the 12th inning to end the game. That throw, Otis recalled in *Sports Collectors Digest,* spawned the nickname Famous Amos "because I made that great throw from center field. It was a one-hop throw.... That's the way baseball's supposed to be played."

If 1970 announced Otis's arrival, the next year marked his coming-out party. Playing in 147 games, Otis stole a league-leading 52 bases in 60 attempts to set a stolen base percentage record (since surpassed), and hammered 15 home runs with 26 doubles. He hit .301 and won the first of his three Gold Glove Awards. His 1971 honors included the Kansas City Sports Personality of the Year Award from the city's Jewish Community Center. The Royals continued to improve, adding Patek, Cookie Rojas, and John Mayberry to the infield mix through trades, and matriculating George Brett and Paul Splittorff through the farm system. They battled through Oakland's five-year run of division crowns (1971–75), finishing second to the A's three times. Otis played well through this period, earning renown for his speed and glove. He led AL outfielders in putouts (404) and total chances (418) in 1971, and on September 7 of that season stole five bases in a nine-inning game against Milwaukee, one short of the major league record. He became only the fifth player since 1900—and the first since 1927—with five swipes in a game. Otis and Patek stole 101 bases between them that season, the highest total by two American League players on the same team since 1917.

In 1973, Otis finished third in the American League's MVP voting, behind Reggie Jackson and Jim Palmer. He made his only All-Star start that year; it came at his home stadium and he had two hits while batting fifth in the AL order. (Royals first baseman John Mayberry batted third.)

Otis's production slipped some in 1974, a season in which some hard feelings emerged on both sides in his relationship with Royals fans. "I can't help it if I make things look easy," Otis told Joe McGuff early in 1975 about the perception that he occasionally coasted. "Even in 1973, when I had my best year, people said I could do better. Last year I didn't have the year I wanted to have. I got to pressing. It was just something I couldn't overcome. Everything I do on this team, I'm first or second. I can't do much more than that. I know I didn't have the year I wanted, but you can't always do it. I got so I hated to come to the park. It was embarrassing.... As soon as you came out of the dugout, they were on you. After a while, you just hated to play."

Otis tied an AL record for most steals in two consecutive games with seven (April 30-May 1, 1975), but he struggled with injuries. A midseason tonsillectomy limited him to 132 games—his lowest total in the 1970s—and he finished with a .247 average. His walk total, however, spiked to 66; his on-base percentage held at .342, and his 39 steals were third in the league. Otis rebounded in 1976, and Kansas City—in its first full season with Herzog as manager—finally outraced Oakland to the American League's West Division title. The American League Championship Series brought heartache, however. In his first career postseason at-bat, leading off the bottom of the first inning in Game One at Royals Stadium, Otis severely sprained his ankle running out a grounder. He missed the remainder of the series. Kansas City was locked in a 6–6 tie with the Yankees in the deciding Game Five when Chris Chambliss homered off Mark Littell, setting off an insane celebration on the field in the Bronx and starting a string of three straight ALCS in which New York beat the Royals for the pennant.

Otis nearly made another career move following Kansas City's first divisional crown. After the season, the Royals completed a deal sending him and Cookie Rojas to Pittsburgh for Al Oliver. Rojas voided the transaction by using his 10-and-5 veto rights (10 years in the majors and five with one team). Otis remained a fixture in Kansas City's outfield. He was credited with popularizing the one-handed catch, a move he said helped him get rid of the ball faster. He won Gold Glove Awards in 1971, '73, and '74, and led AL outfielders in fielding average in 1978 and '79.

In 1980, the Royals finally beat the Yankees to advance to the World Series. Otis belted three home runs, knocked in seven, and hit .478 in a losing effort against the Phillies in six games. It was his only career World Series action. (He played in the ALCS four times for the Royals, batting .279; he went hitless in 12 at-bats in a sweep against the A's during the Divisional Series created by the strike in 1981.)

Otis's last season with the Royals was 1983. The club declined to exercise its option after he played the two guaranteed seasons on a $1.27 million contract. The Royals wanted to move Willie Wilson to center field. A free agent, Otis signed with the Pirates—the team he hadn't wanted to go to seven seasons earlier—and filled a reserve role for a struggling Pittsburgh club. After batting only .165 in 97 at-bats, Otis, 37 years old, was released in August, ending his career as a player.

Otis remained sporadically active in baseball after his playing days, working in the Rockies organization as a hitting instructor for a time in the late 1990s. He became a somewhat forgotten ballplayer everywhere except in Kansas City. Otis and former teammate Steve Busby were the first players inducted into the Royals Hall of Fame, in 1986. Voters for the National Baseball Hall of Fame in Cooperstown, however, did not cast a single vote for Otis in his first year of eligibility, and he was thus barred from the baseball writers' ballot.

Bill James, the renowned baseball writer, statistician, Kansas native, and staunch Amos Otis supporter, wrote a testament to the swift center fielder's legacy the year he left the Royals. In the *Bill James Baseball Abstract 1984,* James wrote:

> *Amos Otis was an intensely private man leading an intensely public life. He disdained showmanship—probably he hated showmanship—of any type and to any extent. He could never quite deal with the fact that his business was putting on a show. This is what is called 'moodiness' by the media. Yet there was a rare, deep honesty about him that was the defining characteristic of him both as a man and as a ballplayer. He could not stand to do anything for show. He could not charge into walls (and risk his continued existence as a ballplayer) after balls that he could not catch. He could not rouse the fans (and risk his continued existence as a baserunner) with a stirring drive for a base too far. He never in his career stood at home plate and watched a ball clear the fence. McRae and Brett, they did that sort of thing; Otis would sometimes turn away interview requests with a sardonic comment, 'Talk to Brett and McRae. They're the team leaders.'*
>
> *It went further than that. Amos could not quite walk down the line when he hit a popup (that, too, would be dishonest) but he could not bring himself to run, either. Because it was false, you see? He wouldn't have been running for himself or for the team or for the base; he would have been running for the fans, or for the principle that one always ran.*

It was to the neverending consternation of Mets fans that Otis did almost all his running and hitting and catching as a Royal.

**Sources**

Bordman, Joe. "Royals' Otis En Route to Super Star Status," *Kansas City Star*, August 14, 1971.

Fimrite, Ron, "It's A Game of Pinches," *Sports Illustrated*, June 30, 1975.

Fimrite, Ron, "The West," *Sports Illustrated*, April 12, 1976.

Herron, Gary. "Another Famous Amos (Otis) Offers Some Pretty Startling Revelations…for the Record," *Sports Collectors Digest*, February 9, 1996.

Kansas City Royals 1980 Media Guide.

Keith, Larry, "Noble Mobile From Mobile," *Sports Illustrated*, June 21, 1971.

Leggett, William, "A Jam-up Of Talent At Third," Sports Illustrated, April 28, 1969.

Leggett, William. "Now Comes the Big Blue Machine," *Sports Illustrated*, April 23, 1973.

LeNoir, Bob. "Royal Thank You for Otis' Trade," *St. Petersburg Independent*, March 18, 1971.

Matthews, Denny, Fred White, and Matt Fulks, *Play by Play: 25 Years of Royals on Radio*, (Kansas City: Addax Publishing Group, 2002).

McGuff, Joe. "Otis Loosens Up—He's One of the Royals' Elite," *Kansas City Star*, March 27, 1971.

Mellinger, Sam. "Amos Otis Remembers the Last No-hitter Thrown against the Royals," *Kansas City Star*, May 20, 2008.

O'Leary, Ted, "Time For A Catfish Fry in KC," *Sports Illustrated*, August 6, 1973.

Articles from unidentified publications in Amos Otis File, provided by National Baseball Hall of Fame and Museum.

# Bobby Pfeil

by Mark Simon

| Season | Age | G | AB | R | H | 2B | 3B | HR | RBI | BB | SO | SB | CS | BA | OPB | SLG |
|---|---|---|---|---|---|---|---|---|---|---|---|---|---|---|---|---|
| 1969 Mets | 25 | 62 | 211 | 20 | 49 | 9 | 0 | 0 | 10 | 7 | 27 | 0 | 1 | .232 | .260 | .275 |
| Career 2 Years | – | 106 | 281 | 25 | 68 | 12 | 0 | 2 | 19 | 13 | 36 | 1 | 1 | .242 | .278 | .306 |

Bobby Pfeil's role on the 1969 Mets may have been small, but it was significant, and it's one that he has cherished for the last four decades.

Robert Raymond Pfeil (pronounced "file") was born on November 13, 1943 in Passaic, New Jersey, but he only lived there for two years. At age two, Pfeil's mom died, and his father, A.C., and grandmother moved to California, where his father settled in as a personnel manager for aircraft companies.

"I felt very fortunate to have had a father who put the time in to play baseball with me, and encouraged my playing," Pfeil said. "He was a good athlete and was very involved in coaching me in Little League and Babe Ruth."

Pfeil was a respectable ballplayer in Little League and Babe Ruth as a shortstop and pitcher, but when he tried out for the Reseda High JV baseball team in 10th grade, he failed to make the cut. Undaunted, he hung around the team as its manager, then made the varsity the following year. He had more success in American Legion competition, where his team won the Southern California American Legion championship.

Pfeil played one year at Pierce Junior College in Woodland Hills, California, as a third baseman and outfielder. He signed with the Cubs in 1961 for a $4,500 bonus. It took Pfeil more than seven seasons of minor league play to reach the majors. The journey began in Palatka, Florida, for $350 a month, with $1.50 a day in meal money.

"That was enough," Pfeil said. "You're doing something that you want to do. That was the great part of being a ballplayer."

His ride through the minors continued in 1963 in St. Cloud, Minnesota and then Fort Worth, Texas in 1964. As a third baseman, Pfeil's path to the majors was blocked by Ron Santo, so the Cubs traded him to St. Louis in 1965. The Cardinals placed Pfeil in Tulsa, Oklahoma, where he won a Texas League championship in 1965. He stayed in Tulsa through the end of the 1967 season, which included a stint playing for new minor league manager, Warren Spahn, whom Pfeil remembered as pitcher-friendly.

"Every pitcher, regardless of how badly they got hit, always got a chance to work out of [a jam], which didn't usually work that well," Pfeil said.

Pfeil had a fun offseason job for four years, working in the art props department for Walt Disney Studios in Burbank, California, storing old animation artwork. It paid well enough to help support his minor league career.

In 1968, Pfeil was traded to the Mets and reported to triple-A Jacksonville. Setting the precedent for what would happen in the majors the next season, the Mets minor leaguers won a championship that year, with Pfeil leading the league in hits. That winter, he expected to be claimed in the expansion draft by either the Padres or Expos, figuring that would be his best and last chance to make the majors. When it didn't happen, he was disappointed. He asked permission to report to the Mets' new Tidewater triple-A team three weeks later than usual, then played respectably when he returned.

In June, Pfeil got his first big league call-up, as Bud Harrelson's required military service opened up a roster spot. "I remember when I introduced myself to Gil Hodges, he asked if I could play second base," Pfeil said. "I had played maybe 10 games at second base my whole life, but I said sure I could. So I was in that night at second base."

Pfeil's first major league game came on June 26 against the Phillies. He popped to second in his first at-bat and flied out in each of his next two trips before recording the first of 68 career major-league hits, a two-out double in the eighth inning against Grant Jackson in a 2–0 loss.

Pfeil's first RBI came a little more than a week later on July 4 against the Pirates, when his ninth-inning single plated a run in an 11–4 victory in the first game of a doubleheader. He added two hits and a run scored in the second game victory, which moved the Mets to within 7½ games of first place.

On July 8, the Mets rallied to beat the Cubs 4–3 in a critical early matchup with the NL's best team. Pfeil started, went 0-for-3, and was pinch-hit for by Donn Clendenon, who had a key double in the Mets three-run ninth inning rally.

The next game was nearly the most significant night in the short and mostly futile history of the Mets to that point. Tom Seaver took a perfect game into the ninth inning. Pfeil drove in New York's first run with a first-inning double, but he played a more significant role later in the contest, as Seaver would write.

> *Jimmy Qualls came up to bat, a rookie hitting .243, facing the New York Mets for the first time in his life. I didn't know much about him, but before the game, Bobby Pfeil, our rookie infielder, told me that he'd played against Qualls in the minors several years earlier. "He can get his bat on the ball," Bobby said. "Give him hard stuff."*[1]

Qualls singled, on a fastball, ending Seaver's bid for perfection. The Mets' stretch of games without a no-hitter, one that would last far longer than anyone

PHOTO COURTESY OF DWAYNE LABAKAS

*Bobby Pfeil*

would have thought at the time, continued.

On July 20, man landed on the moon, but earlier that day against the Expos in Montreal, Pfeil had his best moment as a Met. With Ron Swoboda on third base and two outs in the ninth inning of a tie game, Pfeil bunted on his own, and reached safely when the ball hit the third base bag.

Nearly 40 years later, Pfeil's Mets teammates still remember that play very well. Former Met Rod Gaspar cited it when he referred to Pfeil as "one of the most intelligent players I ever played with." Management took notice too, as Pfeil found a supporter in Gil Hodges, who made sure that Pfeil stuck with the team even when Harrelson returned.

"We were in the airport in Montreal, and I told Gil that my two weeks were up, my wife was still in Tidewater, and what do I do?" Pfeil said.

"[GM Johnny Murphy] may want you to go down, but I want you here," Hodges told Pfeil. "You'll be here the rest of the year."

Pfeil remained on the roster and figured in some key moments over the rest of the season. In an August 30 game in San Francisco, Pfeil was involved in a bizarre play that helped the Mets win. The Giants had a runner on first with one out in the ninth inning of a tie game, with Willie McCovey at the plate. McCovey was known for pulling the ball, but hit this one just fair, down the left-field line.

Gaspar, playing left field, retrieved the ball and fired quickly to the plate, just in time to get Bob Burda trying to score the winning run. However, after applying the tag, Mets catcher Jerry Grote forgot that there were only two outs and rolled the ball to the pitcher's mound. Clendenon saw that happen, raced over, grabbed the ball and threw to third base where Pfeil was covering, doubling up the surprised McCovey to end the inning. The Mets won in the 10th inning on a Clendenon home run. That may have been a sign that it was meant to be their year.

Pfeil also played in the September 12 doubleheader against the Pirates, in which the Mets won each game 1–0 on a pitcher's RBI. Pfeil scored the lone run of the opener, coming home on Jerry Koosman's fifth-inning single.

"I actually remember sliding into home plate," Pfeil said. "Gil Hodges said that the way the catcher blocks the plate, if you hook-slide, you're going noplace. I was more straight legged. My object was to kick out the catchers legs."

Pfeil's last at-bat as a Met was a successful one, as he drove in the only run of a 1–0 victory over the Phillies on September 27, with an eighth-inning single against the pitcher he faced in his debut, Grant Jackson.

Though Pfeil hit only .232, that doesn't tell the whole story of his season. Pfeil was 5-for-9 as a pinch-hitter and was 8-for-24 with two outs and runners in scoring position. He was also the team's most reliable defender at third base, with only three errors there in 49 games. The Mets were 33–17 in Pfeil's 50 starts as compared to 67–45 when he didn't.

"Isn't that something?" he said upon learning about that last stat. "My reputation was that of a guy who understood the game and wasn't going to embarrass you. A guy who could, catch, who could field, and who could advance the runner. I didn't hit as well as I should have, but everybody on the team had a purpose. Everyone played. A slow week for me, I played three games. I have a world of respect for Gil Hodges as a manager. What a great way for someone to manage a team."

Pfeil and his wife made friends with several of the other couples on the team, most notably Tom and Nancy Seaver, and the four were regular dinner partners. "Everyone got along really well," Pfeil said. "I have a lot of respect for him."

Pfeil didn't play for the Mets in the postseason, as he got caught in a roster crunch, but he didn't harbor any bitterness. "We had 26 guys eligible for 25 spots, and I was the odd man out," Pfeil said. "But they got permission from baseball for me to suit up."

He remained useful though. When then-Vice President Richard Nixon attended a World Series game, he was given Pfeil's glove to wear while sitting in his box seat. "I never thought to have him sign my glove," Pfeil said.

Pfeil's first wife, Melanie, garnered some attention as well, joining the wives of Seaver, Nolan Ryan, and Duffy Dyer in parading through Baltimore's Memorial Stadium with a "Lets Go Mets" banner. Fans threw peanut shells at the wives in Baltimore, but that didn't stop the Mets from getting an important win in Game Two.[2]

"I kind of wish she didn't do that," Pfeil said, noting that he still had a picture of that moment. "I thought it was a little showboat-ish to do that in [Baltimore's] park."

Pfeil enjoyed his time in the Fall Classic though and can often be seen in shots of the Mets dugout during the World Series.

"That's fun to look back at now," Pfeil said. "The way the last 45 days went, with our pitching being so dominant, we knew we had a chance. The truth in baseball is that good pitching takes you a long ways. Everything seemed to snowball. Everything went our way."

Returning to the Mets for spring training in 1970, Pfeil knew he'd have a tough time making the team, as the Mets obtained third baseman Joe Foy from the Royals, which made the infield rather crowded. Hodges asked Pfeil if he would try to catch. "That was a difficult spring," Pfeil said. "My glove hand wound up being two times the size of a normal hand, because they beat me up every day."

PHOTO COURTESY OF METSILVERMAN.COM

*The logo for Major League Baseball, modeled on the left sleeve by Bobby Pfeil the year it was unveiled in 1969, remains the logo for the majors some four decades later.*

The lessons would come in handy, but not for a couple of years. Pfeil didn't make it back to the majors until 1971 with the Phillies. He was traded to Philadelphia in May 1970, spent the rest of the year in the minors, but won a utility role in spring 1971. On July 27, in the first game of a doubleheader against the Astros, Pfeil was asked to start at catcher for the first time in his career. It would be one of his all-time playing highlights.

"I had never hit a home run before, and that day, I hit two off Larry Dierker," Pfeil said. "Larry grew up on the next block from where I did, in California. I also threw Jimmy Wynn out trying to steal and tagged Dennis Menke out at the plate."

Pfeil hit .271 in 70 at-bats, playing at least one inning at every position except pitcher. Yet his efforts were not enough to make it back to Philadelphia. He was traded to the Brewers, then the Red Sox in the spring of 1972. He played in the Red Sox organization briefly, than retired for good, moving back to California in 1976. He married his second wife, Chrissie, and had a son, Spencer. They now live in Stockton, California.

Pfeil went into the apartment building business, partnering with three friends to form RPM Company, a successful enterprise, which built properties in 14 states. He also assisted coaching high school baseball for seven years, pitching batting practice four days a week, though he has since retired from that position.

"If I resented anything from when I tried out for high school baseball, it was that you only got five swings and five grounders," Pfeil said. "When I was coaching, we looked at every kid for a month. I was the one who would say that we didn't have to cut a guy, that if you worked hard and would be a good teammate, we'd be happy to have you."

Pfeil's Mets teammates were always happy to have him around at oldtimers days and reunions. On the bus after one event, Donn Clendenon noted that he heard Pfeil talk more then than he had at any point in 1969. At another, Pfeil took batting practice and couldn't get the ball out of the batting cage. "Some things never change," kidded Tommie Agee.

"There's a special bond we have with the guys now," Pfeil said. "We're all old men now, but we shared something that was really special."

**Notes and Sources**

1. Seaver, Tom with Schaap, Dick, *The Perfect Game: Tom Seaver and the Mets,* New York: EP Dutton and Co, 1970
2. Isaacs, Stan, "The 1969 Chronicles, A Sportswriters Notes," available on the internet at *http://www.izix.com.* Chapter 2, column 10

Interviews with Bobby Pfeil, January 27, 2008, and February 24, 2008

Interview with Rod Gaspar, February 17, 2008

Isaacs, Stan, "The 1969 Chronicles, A Sportswriters Notes," available on the internet at *http://www.izix.com*

Seaver, Tom with Schaap, Dick, *The Perfect Game: Tom Seaver and the Mets,* New York: EP Dutton and Co, 1970.

*New York Times*

*www.retrosheet.org*

*www.baseball-reference.com*

## Baseball Turns 100

One way you can always tell if a photo of major leaguers was taken in 1969 or subsequent years is if you see a uniform sleeve with a silhouette of a ballplayer peeking out as he waits on a pitch. That patch commemorated the 100th anniversary of baseball as a truly professional pursuit. The '69 patch differed greatly from the crude 1939 patch all players had worn to mark the fanciful century of baseball since Abner Doubleday stumbled across the game—while Cooperstown is an idyllic place for a museum commemorating the game's history, even the Hall of Fame now admits that the evidence regarding the claims that General Abner Doubleday had anything to do it are baseless, if not baseball-less.

The 1969 anniversary commemorated the Cincinnati Red Stockings as the first openly professional team. And they were good. The Red Stockings pounded amateur nines throughout the country during their legendary 1869 season, featuring the likes of future Hall of Fame brothers Harry and George Wright. That club ended all foolhardy notions that good exercise and discipline by well-intentioned—or well-heeled—amateurs could outplay men doing it for money. The Red Stockings won every game of a 21-game eastern swing in 1869 and won 89 straight games in all before finally losing to the Brooklyn Atlantics in 11 innings on June 14, 1870 in front of a crowd in excess of 10,000. In 1871, the first professional league was formed, the National Association, precursor to the National League. The best Red Stockings moved on to Boston in the NA, but Cincinnati was later part of the first eight-team NL in 1876—finishing last that year—and getting bounced from the league in 1880 for serving beer and whiskey asx well as for renting out their park on Sundays. The Reds helped found the rival American Association in 1882 and rejoined the NL for good in 1890. Cincinnati's pro baseball pioneers were honored throughout baseball in 1969.

There have long been rumors that the batter silhouetted in white against a blue and red background in the logo was modeled after Harmon Killebrew. Artist Jerry Dior, credited with creating the image, told Paul Lukas at *uniwatch.com* that it was a composite and not based on any one individual, while Killebrew maintained that it was based on a photo from a Twins yearbook earlier in the 1960s. Whoever is batting in the design, he's been waiting for that pitch to come for a long time and has adorned countless official MLB items.

In 1969, all teams wore the patch on their left sleeve. It took the place of the Mets logo patch that had been worn on the same sleeve of the team's road uniforms since the franchise's first game in 1962 and on their home uniforms from 1966 to 1968. The Mets played remarkably well in '69 without their accustomed team patch. Credit for their success goes to the manager, the pitching staff, the timely hitting, or maybe the little MLB man in red, white, and blue on their left sleeve had something to do with it. When the Mets made it to the '69 World Series, they defied fashion and edicts and banished the MLB logo to their right sleeve and went back to the Mets logo on their left. Aces high again.

# Les Rohr

by Jon Springer

| Season | Age | W | L | Pct | G | GS | SV | IP | H | BB | SO | WHIP | ERA |
|---|---|---|---|---|---|---|---|---|---|---|---|---|---|
| 1969 Mets | 23 | 0 | 0 | – | 1 | 0 | 0 | 1.3 | 5 | 1 | 0 | 4.500 | 20.25 |
| Career 3 Years | – | 2 | 3 | .400 | 6 | 4 | 0 | 24.3 | 27 | 17 | 20 | 1.808 | 3.70 |

Amidst the wealth of pitching talent developed by the Mets in the 1960s, few hurlers arrived in the organization with as much promise as Les Rohr. But the big left-hander—the second player ever selected in baseball's amateur draft—would have only fleeting success in the big leagues.

Leslie Norvin Rohr was born on March 5, 1946 in Lowestoft, England, where his parents had met. His father, Norvin, was finishing a tour of duty with the US Air Force and his mother Lilian, was a local girl. The family settled later that year in Billings, Montana. Norvin worked in Billings as a truck driver.

Les Rohr grew into a dominant amateur athlete, leading the Billings American Legion club to state championships and national appearances throughout the early 1960s. And as a senior at West High, Rohr compiled a 23–0 record and a 0.64 ERA. Scouts raved about his power arm and 6-foot-5, 200-pound frame. Following Rohr's selection in the amateur draft, Mets officials acknowledged having scouted him for four years.

Still hungry for talent and possessing a financial advantage over most of their competitors for amateur ballplayers, the Mets were strongly opposed to the implementation of the amateur draft, which baseball launched to put a drag on bonuses in 1965. But New York was more than satisfied to have come away with the 19-year-old Rohr with the second overall choice. Arizona State outfielder Rick Monday, the consensus top available amateur that year, went to the Kansas City Athletics with the first overall pick.

John "Red" Murff, the Mets' scout who 10 rounds after gathering in Rohr would sign Nolan Ryan, did not hold back his regard for his top choice. "He is as impressive as Ray Sadecki when the Cardinals signed him," Murff told Leonard Shecter of the *New York Post* following the draft, which took place in New York on June 7, 1965. Sadecki by then was a 24-year-old lefty coming off his first—and as it turned out, his only—20-win season.

"[Rohr] strikes out everyone," Murff continued, "and his own catcher is in danger of being injured. He should be a 20-game winner in the big leagues in a few years."

Mets assistant general manager Bing Devine described Rohr as having an overpowering fastball, rare poise for teenager, and an excellent move to first base. With negotiating help from his father, Rohr signed for about $55,000, including bonuses and was assigned to Class AA Williamsport, where despite a 4–6 record he posted an ERA of 1.84 over 12 starts.

Rohr spent part of 1966 at Williamsport again but this time was 0–6 with a 4.32 ERA. In Class A Auburn, he showed he could dominate hitters—striking out 91 in 82 innings—but also struggled with control, walking 53. "All he needs is to learn to move the ball around and improve [his] curve," according to a scouting report published in *Baseball Digest* in 1967. "[His] fastball is alive. If he continues improvement he has good future, even in the majors."

Military service commitments delayed Rohr's 1967 debut until July of that season. And after 33 innings at Class A Durham (during which he struck out 41 and fashioned a 2.45 ERA) Rohr was recalled to the Mets when rosters expanded in September. In his big league debut—a start on September 19 at Shea Stadium—Rohr threw six innings, struck out six, and earned the victory as the Mets defeated the Dodgers, 6–3.

Rohr beat the Dodgers again less than two weeks later in Los Angeles, outdueling Don Drysdale in a 5–0 Mets victory. He finished his first stint in the majors with a 2–1 record, a 2.12 ERA and 15 strikeouts in 17 innings. "That was something else, to pitch against someone like Drysdale and have a great game like that," Rohr was quoted as saying by *mlb.com* in a 2006 article. "I thought I was on my way after that."

But it wasn't to be. Although he made the Opening Day roster in 1968, an injury that Rohr suspects was sustained during a bizarre 24-inning affair on April 15 hastened a trip to the disabled list.

That game, which began as a battle between respective aces Tom Seaver and Don Wilson, would eventually go down as the longest night game and longest shutout in baseball history (breaking the record of 23 innings set by the Mets in a 1964 loss; they later broke it in a 25-inning loss in 1974). Rohr, who had expected an off-day after throwing 20 minutes of batting practice that afternoon, was New York's eighth pitcher, entering the scoreless game in the bottom of the 22nd inning. He wound up as the loser in the 24th after Norm Miller led off with a single, was balked to second base and later—at 2:37 a.m. to be precise—he scored on an error by shortstop Al Weis. The bad hop on that play led to a change where ground crews would drag the infield every seven innings, regardless of how long the game lasted.

Rohr believes his strenuous day led to an elbow injury. "My arm swelled up real bad," after the game, Rohr later told *mlb.com*. In his next appearance, six days later, he couldn't get out of the fourth inning in a start against the Dodgers. He was summarily optioned to Class AAA Jacksonville and spent the summer rehabbing his arm over 10 games split between Jacksonville, Class AA Memphis, and Class A Durham.

Rohr spent the 1969 season primarily with Memphis, helping the Blues win the Texas League championship. In 21 starts, Rohr went 9–7 with a 3.18 ERA, striking out 116, and walking 52 in 150 innings. He was recalled to the Mets following the Texas League playoffs and got into one game, being charged with four runs in relief in an 8–2 loss to Pittsburgh at Shea Stadium on September 19. The Mets clinched their first division title five days later.

Rohr struggled in 1970 at AAA Tidewater, posting a 5.65 ERA over 15 appearances. He also spent time with Class AA Memphis. (4–3, 2.89 ERA)

That October, the Mets traded Rohr to Milwaukee on a conditional deal but a physical by the Brewers revealed Rohr was suffering from a ruptured disc in his back. They returned Rohr to New York, and the Mets subsequently released him. Rohr reportedly had spinal fusion surgery and never played professionally again.

Rohr took on several manual labor jobs to support his family in Billings, which included his wife Jean and children Jason and Angela. He coached for many years for the same Billings American Legion team he'd played for as a teen, and in 2003 was inducted into the Billings American Legion Hall of Fame, named after its coach Ed Bayne. Orioles great Dave McNally was in the inaugural Ed Bayne Hall of Fame class a year before Rohr.

Rohr's major league record shows a 2–3 mark and a 3.70 ERA over six appearances and 24⅓ innings. He won 27 and lost 37 over six seasons in the minor leagues. Rohr never achieved the greatness predicted of him because of injury, but he does have his place in history as the first player drafted in Mets history—and the second ever chosen overall.

**Sources**

Girandola, Chris. "Injuries Curtailed Rohr's Big-League Stint," *mlb.com*.

Leone, Jack. "Baseball's Gone Autograph Hunting." *Newsday*, June 9, 1965.

Shecter, Leonard. "Mets, Yanks Pick Pitchers" and "The Drafters," *New York Post*, June 8, 1965.

"Billings American Legion Post 4 Baseball History" (*billingsbaseball.org*).

"Gaspar of Mets Sent to Padres," *New York Times*. October 21, 1970.

"Mets Lose in 24th, Longest Night Game," *New York Times*, April 16, 1968.

"Ultimate Mets Database" (*ultimatemets.com*)

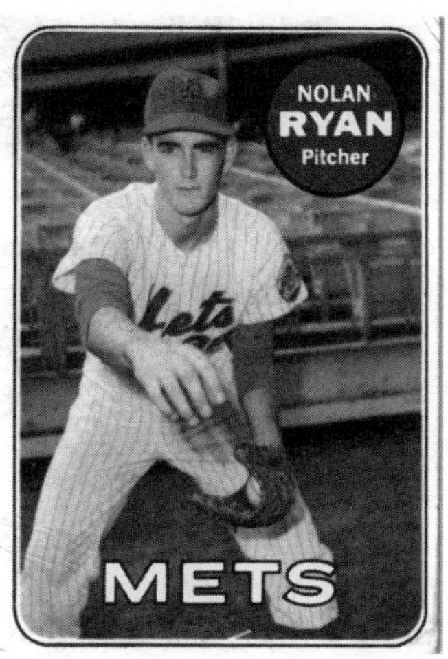


# Nolan Ryan

by Talmage Boston

| Season | Age | W | L | PCT | G | GS | SV | IP | H | BB | SO | WHIP | ERA |
|---|---|---|---|---|---|---|---|---|---|---|---|---|---|
| 1969 Mets | 22 | 6 | 3 | .667 | 25 | 10 | 1 | 89.3 | 60 | 53 | 92 | 1.265 | 3.53 |
| Career 27 Years | – | 324 | 292 | .526 | 807 | 773 | 3 | 5386 | 3923 | 2795 | 5714 | 1.247 | 3.19 |

Nolan Ryan has more strikeouts and no-hitters than any other pitcher in history. Despite never winning a Cy Young Award, he started more games than anyone except Cy Young. Though he played mostly for mediocre teams, his 324 wins are as many as contemporary Don Sutton, who pitched for four pennant winners and just missed a fifth. Yet Ryan was one of the most dominatnt pitchers ever. His 5,714 strikeouts were 2,000 more than Sutton and 1,500 better than Steve Carlton, whom he once trailed in the all-time K race—puts The Ryan Express head and shoulders above almost any other pitcher since 1970. His longevity—winning a strikeout crown and throwing a no-hitter while being the oldest player in the game at the age of 43—makes him the stuff of legend. And in one day in 1971, Ryan's change of coasts became the best trade the California Angels ever made and the worst deal in New York Mets history. He may have walked more batters and thrown more wild pitches than anyone else in the game's history, but that just proved he was human.

Born on January 31, 1947, in Refugio, Texas, Lynn Nolan Ryan was the son of Robert Ryan and Martha Lee Hancock Ryan (a descendant of John Hancock, first signer of the Declaration of Independence). The youngest of six children, he had a brother and four sisters. The Ryans moved from Refugio to Alvin, Texas, when Nolan was six weeks old because his father was transferred to the Alvin area. His father was plant supervisor at Hastings plant for Stanton Oil Company, which became Pan American Petroleum.

Nolan began playing baseball at seven with his father in their front yard. From there, the boy decided on his own that he loved playing the game and he started playing on a nearby vacant lot, where neighborhood kids built a diamond. Little League baseball had only recently come to Alvin, and it soon provided the official start to Nolan Ryan's career at Schroeder Field, where he became an all-star for the first time.

Between the ages of 8 and 18, Nolan spent every morning between 1 and 4 a.m. with his father delivering the *Houston Post* to homes in the Alvin area (his father was the distributor for the paper in town). Nolan rolled the newspapers into tight cylinders and delivered them to residents long before the sun rose. The paper route instilled a sense of personal responsibility and maturity that would lead to his becoming a team leader in high school and a professional ballplayer immediately thereafter. It also didn't hurt his arm. Nolan Ryan's ability to throw hard and throw often was a gift, but one honed by a strong work ethic both in the quiet predawn hours in Alvin and before the dropped jaws of midday onlookers on the playing fields in town.

By the time he reached junior high, Ryan had

the arm strength to stand on the goal line of a football field and throw a softball over 100 yards—30 yards farther than any other boy in the area. In the ninth grade, he became even more focused on baseball after abandoning his short-lived football career in the aftermath of a head-on collision with future NFL running back Norm Bulaich; the impact produced a dazed and embarrassed Alvin cornerback and a La Marque Junior High touchdown.

Ryan pitched for the Alvin High School varsity as a sophomore in 1963. He started attracting major league scouts in his junior year by averaging two strikeouts per inning, including 21 in a nine-inning game against LaPorte.

Because of Alvin's close proximity to Houston, where the Colt 45s had recently joined the National League, scouts frequented Ryan's Alvin starts and in the pre-radar gun days tried to gauge how fast the kid threw. New York Mets scout Red Murff remembered the first game he saw Ryan pitch: "The night before, I had seen the two fastest pitchers in the National League at that time, Jim Maloney and Turk Farrell. Nolan Ryan was already faster than both of them by far."

The arrival of the major leagues in Houston helped Ryan in another way: it gave him the opportunity to observe first-hand the pitching performances of his baseball hero, Sandy Koufax, whose strikeout and no-hit records the Alvin teenager would later break. While watching Koufax, Ryan became so mesmerized that he would not speak to Ruth, his girlfriend, who later became his wife.

During his senior year, Ryan dominated Gulf Coast baseball, posting a 19–3 record and pitching the Alvin Yellow Jackets into the Texas high school state finals in Austin. During that 32-game season in the spring of 1965, Ryan pitched in 27 games, starting 20, and finished with 12 complete games, 211 strikeouts, and only 61 walks.

Alvin head coach Jim Watson and the other players on the '65 team described Ryan's senior year performance with the same term: "wheel horse." That meant the horse closest to the wagon who pulls the heaviest share of the load—and Ryan's statistics proved it. On March 25, 1965, Ryan pitched a seven-inning, complete-game shutout. The next day, in a doubleheader, he appeared as a reliever in the opener and threw three innings, giving up one run and striking out five. In the nightcap, he started the game, pitched five innings, gave up one hit, and struck out 10 in a 9–2 victory. On April 1 and 3, in a space of 48 hours, Ryan pitched back-to-back complete-game victories. Then he kicked it up a notch.

To reach the state playoffs, Ryan pitched a no-hitter against Brenham on June 10, striking out 12. His inside fastballs caused opposing hitters' bats to break with such frequency that fans complained, genuinely believing his pitches had razor blades attached to them. Five days later, in the state semifinals, Ryan threw a two-hit shutout against Snyder, striking out nine.

The stories behind Nolan Ryan's senior year exceeded his statistics. In the first inning of a March 20 game against Deer Park, after he cracked the batting helmet of the leadoff hitter, then hit and broke the next batter's arm, the third hitter decided he had seen enough, and refused to enter the batter's box until his coach finally shamed him into an at-bat that produced the season's quickest three-pitch strikeout.

As the 1965 season progressed, Alvin catcher Jerry Spinks observed a tear that soon developed into a sizeable hole in his mitt caused by the force of receiving Ryan's fastball. The sound of ball, glove, and Ryan force led scout Red Murff to compare it to a "muffled rifle shot." The bullet-holed mitt produced a side effect—Spinks's underwhelming batting average during his senior year. "No matter how much padding I put in my glove, as each game wore on, I had fewer fingers on my left hand capable of gripping a bat," he recalled.

The only blemish on Nolan Ryan's senior year proved to be costly. New York Mets scouting director Bing Devine finally responded to Red Murff's pleas by making an unexpected appearance to see Ryan pitch against Channelview on May 20, 1965. Murff's top prospect reluctantly took the mound that afternoon, less than a day after Coach Watson had death-marched the Yellow Jacket team through endless windsprints over a perceived lack of concentration in practice. With his strength depleted, Ryan simply could not perform with distinction in front of his most important audience, causing his stock to plunge on the eve of the baseball draft.

In the spring of 1965, at the insistence of scout

Murff, the Mets selected 18-year-old Nolan Ryan in the 12th round, the 295th player in baseball's first major league amateur draft. Ryan left Alvin that summer, taking the first airplane trip of his life, on the way to Marion, Virginia, where he began his professional career in the Appalachian League. Ryan fanned 313 at three stops in 1966, including his debut at Shea Stadium on September 11. He made his first major league start a week later in front of his hometown folks at the Astrodome on September 18. He struck out the side in the first, but he also allowed four runs and four hits, plus two walks, in the only inning of his first decision in the big leagues, a 9–2 loss.

He was a little green for the majors, but as per Murff's prediction, Ryan's fastball overpowered minor league hitters as if they were Texas high schoolers. In 291 innings, he struck out 445 batters from 1965 through 1967, an average of 14 per nine innings.

Aside from his staggering power numbers, Ryan demonstrated unusual maturity during his brief time in the minors. In 1967, he suffered an arm injury. Though the team doctor recommended surgery, Ryan refused, preferring to rehabilitate the arm on his own. The 20-year-old pitcher already knew enough to realize that no one should cut prematurely on what Murff had already described in his Mets scouting report as "the BEST arm I ever saw ANYWHERE in my life!"

By 1968, the Mets could no longer hold Nolan Ryan down on the farm. In spring training, his fastball earned him a spot in new manager Gil Hodges's starting rotation. In Ryan's first start of the year, on April 14, 1968—again in Houston—the young right-hander got his first major league win by holding the Astros hitless for the first five innings. He left the game because of a blister on his pitching hand in the seventh inning.

In the first six weeks of the 1968 season, Ryan pitched a shutout for seven innings against the Philadelphia Phillies, threw his first complete game to beat the world champion St. Louis Cardinals, and hurled a four-hitter while striking out 14 Cincinnati Reds. The national news media took immediate notice of the rookie sensation, highlighted by *Life* magazine's feature on him in its May 31, 1968 issue. The National League's best hitters already rated Ryan ahead of Sandy Koufax in the speed of his fastball, and 1967 MVP Orlando Cepeda observed, "Nolan Ryan is the best young pitcher I've ever seen in the major leagues."

Injuries, finger blisters, and a continuing military obligation prevented Ryan from maintaining his dominant pace for the remainder of 1968 and most of 1969. The 1969 season was the only time until his final year in the major leagues—in 1993—that he failed to reach 100 strikeouts. And he still had 92 in 89⅓ innings, along with his first winning season at 6–3.

The '69 season, of course, ended on a happy note for both Ryan and his club. Ryan got the win to clinch the first National League Championship Series with seven innings of relief in Game Three against the Atlanta Braves at Shea Stadium. Fellow Texan Jerry Grote, whom Ryan would later name as a key influence in his Hall of Fame speech, rushed into Ryan's arms as the Mets became the first expansion team to ever win a pennant. Ryan followed that with what would prove to be the only World Series appearance of his career, helping the Amazin' Mets win a championship over the heavily favored Baltimore Orioles by saving Game Three with 2⅓ innings of shutout relief pitching. The first batter he faced, Paul Blair, blasted a drive to right-center with the bases loaded that turned into Tommie Agee's second remarkable catch of the game.

Ryan made some strides in 1970 with a 7–11 record and a 3.42 ERA. The next year, despite reaching 10 wins for the first of what would be 16 straight seasons, his walk numbers—always high—reached 116, compared with 137 strikeouts in 152 innings. There was plenty of frustration to go around.

By the end of the 1971 season, Ryan had fulfilled his early career goal of pitching long enough in the majors to earn a pension, but he had not fulfilled the many predictions of greatness due largely to inconsistent control. After four years with the Mets, his career record stood at 29–38, and he had struck out almost a batter an inning for over 500 innings, but had also averaged six walks per game.

Three factors hindered Nolan Ryan's development in New York:

1. His Army Reserve commitment disrupted each season, sometimes causing him to go more

than a week between starts. Manager Hodges exacerbated the situation by refusing to adjust his pitching rotation to accommodate Ryan's schedule.

2. Despite throwing the National League's hardest fastball, Ryan got no special treatment from Hodges because the Mets had several pitchers who were more effective. Tom Seaver, Jerry Koosman, and Gary Gentry were already complete pitchers with good control and a more versatile repertoire of pitches. Seaver and Gentry, coming from top college programs, had benefited from sound college coaching. Ryan, on the other hand, received no significant pitching help before reaching the major leagues at the age of 19.

3. Ryan received no meaningful instruction from the Mets coaching staff. Pitching coach Rube Walker described his simple (unsuccessful) strategy for working with Ryan: "We tell him to throw as hard as he can for as long as he can." This combination of circumstances appeared to be leading toward a dead end to a once promising baseball career. The young pitcher told his wife, Ruth, after the close of the 1971 season that if the Mets failed to trade him over the winter, he would quit the game.

On December 10, 1971, in what would prove to be one of the most lopsided deals in baseball history, the Mets traded Ryan and three marginal players (Don Rose, Leroy Stanton, and Frank Estrada) to the California Angels for former All-Star shortstop Jim Fregosi. The trade did nothing to help the club's continued fruitless search for a third baseman—Fregosi, who'd never played the position in the majors before becoming a Met, was out of New York by July 1973—but it allowed baseball's most awesome thrower to grow into a consistently dominating pitcher. Nolan Ryan wouldn't be quitting the game for quite some time.

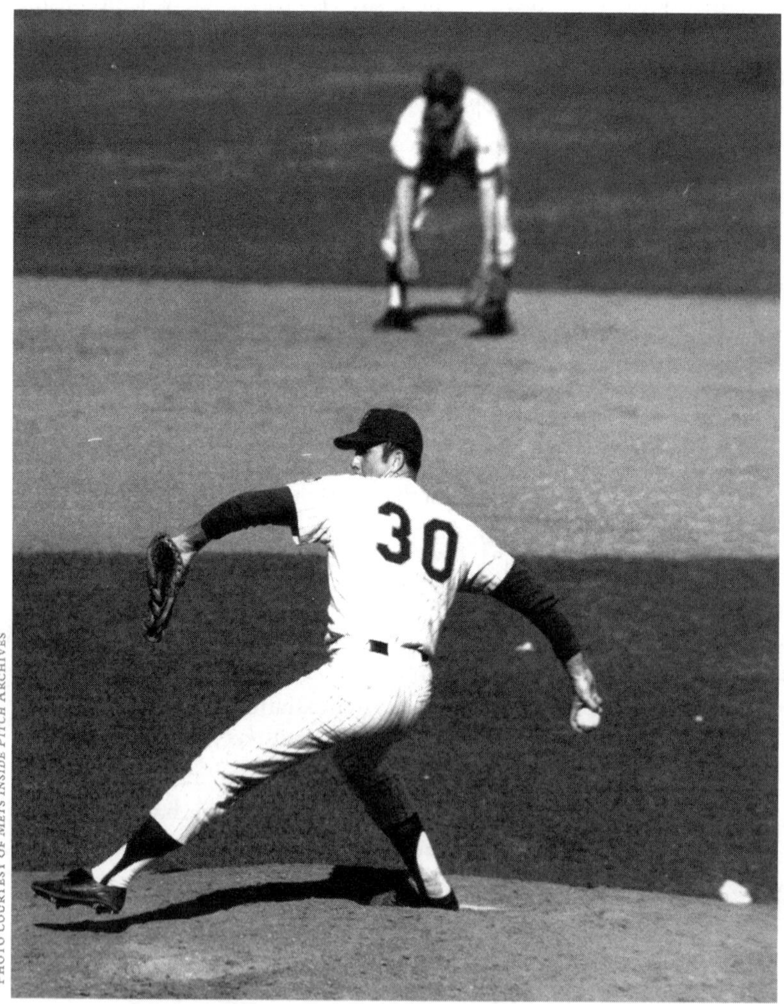


Photo courtesy of *Mets Inside Pitch* Archives

*Though Nolan Ryan was a member of the 1969 Mets, helping secure wins in both the NLCS and World Series, one of the greatest disappointments in franchise history is that his great accomplishments in baseball were achieved with other teams.*

Ryan spent the most productive eight seasons of his career with the Angels. In Anaheim, all obstacles that had prevented his achieving greatness in New York seemingly disappeared. With his Army Reserve duty completed, Ryan could develop a better rhythm by getting to pitch every four days. He eliminated the blister problem on his pitching hand—failed attempts to do so in New York had included bathing his fingers in pickle brine—by using a surgeon's scalpel to remove scar tissue and calluses on his fingers before every start. *Sports*

*Illustrated* compared the process to "peeling grapes, causing the baseball clutched in his right hand to feel as smooth as a bullet."

More important, Ryan got his first exposure to a coach who could actually teach him how to be a complete pitcher. Angels pitching coach Tom Morgan broke down and overhauled Ryan's delivery, taught him how to throw a sharp breaking curveball, and provided the moral support the young right-hander had never received with the Mets.

Inclined initially as a young pitcher toward the use of homespun remedies, Ryan tried treating a sore right elbow in his first year as an Angel by rubbing rattlesnake oil on the joint. What proved to be more successful than the snake oil, however, was the weight conditioning program he started in California to build up his arm and entire body. Before 1972, baseball "experts" had concluded that weight training made a player too muscle bound, causing him to lose the smooth movement necessary for arm speed in a pitcher and bat speed in a hitter. Nolan Ryan became the first big league pitcher to enhance his performance through the use of weights. "It's weight *conditioning*, not weight lifting," he later explained. "I was not trying to see how much weight I could lift. I was trying to lift the right weights in the right way."

As an Angel, Ryan threw four no-hitters to tie Sandy Koufax's career record, broke Koufax's single-season mark with 383 strikeouts in 1973, had four other 300-strikeout seasons, led the league in strikeouts in all but one season as an Angel (teammate Frank Tanana won the crown the one year Ryan didn't, in 1975), established the world record for a timed fastball at 100.9 miles per hour, averaged 7⅓ innings per start with an ERA slightly above 3.00 in his 288 California starts, won 20 or more games twice, and had 19 victories two other times.

Ryan never won the Cy Young Award as an Angel, though a strong argument can be made for his entitlement to it in the 1972, 1973, 1974, or 1977 seasons. What prevented him from having the sensational won-loss record in any one year necessary to win baseball's most prestigious pitching award was the Angels' inability to score runs. (Though his friend Tom Seaver suffered the same lack of support with the Mets, Seaver did win three Cy Youngs with Ryan's former team.)

In Ryan's first five years with the Angels, they finished last in the American League in runs scored four times and next-to-last the other year. Billy Martin said of those California teams, "They could take batting practice in a hotel lobby and never break anything."

Ryan once described the difficulty of pitching for the weak-hitting Angels: "I feel like I have to pitch a shutout every night or lose. If I throw one bad pitch, I'll be beaten." Ryan's first year with the Angels proved the point. Six times in 1972 he pitched games allowing two runs or less and still lost because California could not score a single run.

California's inability to score did help Ryan break Koufax's modern strikeout mark in 1973. Through seven innings of what would be last start of 1973, Ryan fanned 14 Minnesota Twins and stood one strikeout shy of Koufax's 382 of 1965, set when Ryan was still in high school and avidly following the Dodgers ace. In the eighth inning in the '73 finale, he fanned Steve Brye to tie Koufax. The Angels got the leadoff man on base in both the eighth and ninth and failed to score. Meanwhile, Ryan endured severe leg cramps requiring almost constant massages when not on the mound. He did not fan a Twin in the ninth or 10th, pitching out of jams with the winning run in scoring position in each of his last two innings of work. He finally fanned Rich Reese, who'd earlier replaced slugger Harmon Killebrew in the lineup, to set the record and strand Rod Carew at second base in the 11th. Angel Richie Scheinblum doubled home the deciding run in the bottom of the inning to give Ryan his 21st win.

Though Cy Young voters failed to recognize Ryan's greatness, hitters knew which pitcher they least wanted to face. When Ryan's night to pitch arrived, the opposing team's regulars often came down with a disease known as "Ryanitis," a one-day malady that prevented them from playing. One victim of the epidemic commented, "A good night against Nolan Ryan is going 0-for-4 and you don't get hit in the head." Oakland catcher Dave Duncan, who'd later spend more than three decades as a pitching coach in the major leagues, put it this way: "Ryan doesn't just get you out. He embarrasses you."

Nolan Ryan's confidence grew to the point where he would advise league MVPs Dick Allen and Reggie Jackson that in his next start against them, he would throw only fastballs, daring them to match his power. Neither managed a hit in those confrontations.

Jackson gave his own unique account of facing Ryan: "I love to bat against Nolan Ryan and I hate to bat against Nolan Ryan. It's like ice cream. You may love it, but you don't want it shoveled down your throat by the gallon. I've never been afraid at the plate but Mr. Ryan makes me uncomfortable. He's the only pitcher who's ever made me consider wearing a helmet with an ear flap."

The ultimate in-game tribute was made by Detroit's Norm Cash at Tiger Stadium in the ninth inning of Ryan's second no-hitter, on July 15, 1973. (Ryan had completed his first no-hitter exactly two months earlier in Kansas City.) Cash, who'd already struck out twice, came up with two outs in the ninth wielding a piano leg at the plate. Umpire Ron Luciano, laughing hysterically, made him go back for a regulation bat. Cash did make contact: a popup to shortstop.

Ryan's other two no-hitters for the Angels both came in Anaheim. He beat the Twins, 4–0, on September 28, 1974. It was his career-high 22nd win of the season, despite eight walks. He fanned 15. Ryan's fourth no-hitter came against the Baltimore Orioles, winners of five division titles in the previous six years, in a 1–0 win on June 1, 1975. And '75 was Ryan's down year. It's worth noting that those four no-hitters came after the advent of the designated hitter, so he threw the four no-hitters in less than a 100-start span against teams that did not send a pitcher to bat. Pitcher batting or no, Ryan made plenty of hitters look like easy outs.

In 1976, Ryan went from 186 strikeouts to 327. He increased that number to 341 in '77, though he also surpassed the 200-walk plateau for the second time. His 204 walks—in 299 innings—gave him the highest total since Bob Feller in 1938.

After a lackluster 1978 season, Ryan roared back in 1979, posting a record of 12–6 in the first half of the year, leading to his being named the American League's starting pitcher in the All-Star Game. In early August, however, he strained a muscle near his right elbow, causing him to finish that year with an underwhelming 16–14 record. Still, he started the first postseason game in Angels history, throwing seven innings against Baltimore's Jim Palmer in the ALCS opener. The eventual AL champion Orioles won in 10 innings.

When the 1979 season ended, the Angels decided to abandon their top star, as California general manager Buzzie Bavasi justified his decision by saying, "Nolan Ryan can be replaced by two 8–7 pitchers." California figured Ryan's effectiveness as a power pitcher had to be in its final stages at the age of 32. Like the Mets before them, the Angels soon came to regret their decision. History would show that when he left the Angels, Nolan Ryan had not yet reached the halfway point in his career.

In the early years of free agency, Ryan fulfilled a lifelong dream in November 1979 by signing to pitch for his hometown team, the Houston Astros. Many years before, he had remarked, "I'd buy my own bus ticket to get to Houston if I could pitch for the Astros." New owner John McMullen provided his new pitcher with a lot more than a bus ticket, signing Ryan to a three-year contract that allowed him to become the first athlete on a professional sports team to be paid $1 million per year.

Initially, the biggest part of the Ryan media story in Houston was the money. In his first two years with the Astros, he made more than he had in his 12 seasons with the Mets and Angels combined. As more major league stars became millionaires in baseball's lucrative free-agent market during the early 1980s, attention finally focused on the mound performance of the game's premier power pitcher.

Ryan's nine years in Houston became a time for achieving career milestones. On July 4, 1980, he recorded career strikeout number 3,000. On September 26, 1981, on a Saturday *Game of the Week,* he no-hit the Los Angeles Dodgers, the eventual World Series champions. That established the major league record with five no-hitters, breaking another Koufax mark—and doing it against Koufax's old team to boot. At the time, Ryan called it his favorite no-hitter because his family was all there and it came in the heat of a division race. He finished the year with a 1.69 ERA, nearly half a run per game better than runner-up and teammate Bob Knepper. Likewise, his mark of 5.98 hits per game was 0.51 better than runner-up and old friend Tom Seaver.

On April 27, 1983, Ryan broke Walter Johnson's career strikeout record of 3,509, which had stood since 1927. Number 4,000 came on July 11, 1985, against the Mets, of all teams. Ryan and Steve Carlton went back and forth for the all-time strikeout mark before Ryan outlasted Lefty. Ryan outlasted everybody.

In 1987, Ryan became the first pitcher in major league history to lead his league in both strikeouts and ERA and not receive the still elusive Cy Young Award. His 8–16 record, clearly the result of no run support, was the worst mark of his career. It ruined an otherwise brilliant season and relegated him to fifth in the Cy Young voting. In 1987, and again in 1988, Ryan became the oldest pitcher ever to lead his league in strikeouts.

More important than the records in Houston, Nolan Ryan came into his own as a complete pitcher. Though he put up amazing numbers as an Angel, Ryan was every bit as effective during his nine years with the Astros. His Houston ERA was almost identical to what it had been in California, and his strikeout-to-walk ratio was far better. His increased control culminated in his winning the 1987 National League Control Pitcher of the Year Award, in recognition of having the league's lowest ERA, giving up the fewest hits, and recording the most strikeouts and the least walks per nine innings.

Having surpassed 40, Ryan lost essentially no velocity on his fastball and still had the big breaking curve he had learned from Tom Morgan in California. In addition, as an Astro he added to his repertoire a more effective changeup taught him by former Cincinnati pitcher Joe Nuxhall; Ryan later put a circle change learned from scout Red Murff into the mix.

Unlike the hapless Angels, the Astros were a first-division team in the Ryan years, getting into postseason play in 1980, 1981, and 1986. The best start of his postseason career came in Game Five of the 1986 National League Championship Series. Though he had lost to the Mets at the Astrodome in Game Two, he was superb in his first postseason game at Shea Stadium since 1969. He had a no-hitter into the fifth inning, when Darryl Strawberry hit a line drive that just cleared the fence. Ryan was dominant, fanning 12, walking one, and allowing just one other hit in nine innings, although the Mets won in 12. And Ryan did it all with a sore elbow and a stress fracture in his right foot.

As Ryan had conquered the American League's best hitters in the 1970s, he did the same to the top National League stars in the 1980s. Two-time MVP Dale Murphy commented on Ryan's dominance: "He is the only pitcher you start thinking about two days before you face him." Going into Ryan's final season in Houston, Pete Rose made a stronger statement: "At the age of 41, Nolan Ryan is the top power pitcher in the league. You can talk about Dwight Gooden, you can talk about Mike Scott, you can talk about whoever you want, but none of them throw as consistently hard as Ryan does."

Ryan continued smoking pitches past hitters years after his contemporaries had retired thanks to a training regimen developed by Gene Coleman, Houston's strength and conditioning adviser. Adhering to the doctor's weightlifting, running, exercise, and stationary bicycling program, Ryan maintained the body of a man 20 years younger.

After the 1988 season, Houston owner John McMullen ignored the facts that Ryan had come within two outs of throwing a no-hitter that year and had also led the league in strikeouts the previous two years, and decided a pay cut was in order for his theoretically aging pitcher. Knowing his value, Ryan left his hometown team, but he didn't go far. Arlington, to be precise.

Texas Rangers ownership welcomed Ryan with open arms and a sizeable raise. Veteran Houston sportswriter Mickey Herskowitz accurately expressed his city's sorrow after Ryan left the Astros: "In Houston, the fans had mixed feelings about Nolan. Some miss him every day of their lives, and some just miss him every fifth day."

After spending a career being ultimately rejected by the Mets, Angels, and Astros, Nolan Ryan finally found a team that wanted to embrace him on a permanent basis. The Rangers had long been a floundering organization, having relocated from Washington, playing in an expanded minor league ball park, and never participating in postseason play.

With the signing of Ryan on December 7, 1988, the Rangers gained something they never had before: national credibility. Texas general manager Tom Grieve put it in perspective: "To get a player of his caliber, all those statistics, and the kind of guy he is, well, you don't want to get up on a podium and start bubbling over, but that's how we felt."

Motivated by the challenge of continuing to succeed on a power level with younger competition, Ryan proceeded to have three full-blown years of greatness with Texas, from 1989 to 1991. In those years, he compiled a record of 41–25 with a 3.16 ERA, struck out more batters than anyone else in the American League (736), had a strikeout-to-walk ratio of better than 3-to-1, and pitched through the fifth inning in 54 of his 59 starts.

As a Ranger, Ryan's continual racking up of milestones overshadowed his contributions every fifth day in the rotation. On August 22, 1989, he achieved career strikeout number 5,000. That same year, at the age of 42, he had his sixth 300-K season. Only former Astros teammates J.R. Richard and Mike Scott had managed the feat since Ryan had last done it in 1977. But he was just warming up.

On June 11, 1990, Ryan pitched his sixth no-hitter, beating the defending world champion Athletics at Oakland. He suffered for most of the game with constant pain in his lower back (later discovered to be a stress fracture), the significance of which he tried to minimize after the game. "It wasn't all that bad," he said. "It only hurt when I threw the ball."

On July 31, 1990, he won his 300th game in the major leagues, beating the Brewers in Milwaukee. On May 1, 1991, Ryan shut down Toronto, the league's best hitting team, to record his seventh no-hitter. He fanned 16 that night with a sore Achilles tendon, constant back pain, and a cracked-skinned, bloody right middle finger, all of which went with the territory of power pitching into his mid-forties. Earlier that day in Oakland, Rickey Henderson had shattered Lou Brock's all-time stolen-base record, but that legendary feat was pushed down on nearly every front sports page in the country in honor of the Ryan Express. He made the front page of plenty of news sections, too. But nowhere was he bigger news than in Texas.

In his first season as a Ranger, the team drew over 2 million fans for the first time in franchise history. When he pitched, average attendance was 8,000 more than on other nights. Texas continued to top the 2 million mark every year after 1989, making the ownership's decision to build The Ballpark in Arlington—and the opportunity for public funding—as easy as a 1-2-3 inning from Ryan. Construction commenced in 1991.

Fans knew that every time Nolan Ryan took the mound, it might be a no-hitter. In his first three years with the Rangers, on top of the two no-hitters, Ryan also pitched six one-hitters, eight two-hitters, and 12 three-hitters.

The most enduring memory of Texas Rangers fans who witnessed the Ryan Express during his five glorious years in Arlington, from 1989 to 1993, was not a statistic but a sound. Every time the 40-something power pitcher delivered his heat, he threw the ball with such total passion that a bellowing grunt could be heard throughout the ballpark. When he wasn't pitching, he was pushing it as well. The game's oldest player devised daily offseason workouts that lasted up to five hours. During the season, on nights he pitched, Ryan rode a stationary bicycle for at least 45 minutes after the game. Between starts, baseball's bionic man spent more than two hours every day lifting weights, running, and biking. Rangers pitching coach Tom House said of his star pupil, "He's still throwing hard because he does what it takes to prepare himself. He's like the mailman. Nothing keeps him from making his rounds in the weight room."

Ryan completed his final season as a Ranger in 1993 hampered by injuries to his knee, rib cage, and elbow. Pitching in between stays on the disabled list, he gave Texas fans one final lasting memory. On August 4, 1993, in the third inning of a game against Chicago, a Ryan fastball hit Robin Ventura in the arm. The young White Sox third baseman stormed the mound and tried to attack a man 20 years his senior. Ryan had been in this situation once before when Dave Winfield charged him at Houston. In that incident, Ryan followed his coaches' instructions and simply ducked Winfield's punches, and coiled up to protect his pitching arm.

Rejecting the Winfield defensive strategy that had bothered him for 13 years, Ryan responded to Ventura's attack with force of his own—putting the

Chicago third baseman in a headlock, and punching the top of his head, making the batter pay for his overaggressive tactics. Ryan said later that night, "All you can do is react. You don't have time to figure your options." After the fight, the umpires ejected Ventura and allowed Ryan to stay in the game. Unfazed by the altercation, he lasted seven innings, allowing three hits and retiring 12 of the last 13 men he faced to get the victory. It spurred a three-game winning streak. But the Ryan Express, believe it or not, was finally pulling into the station.

The end came on September 22, 1993, at Seattle. In his last career start, while throwing a fastball in the first inning, Ryan tore the ulnar collateral ligament in his right elbow. Later that night in the clubhouse, he described his final game. "I heard the ligament pop like a rubber band. There's no way I'll ever be able to throw again. My body is telling me it's time to move on and do something else."

The Rangers years established that Nolan Ryan was more than a major league superstar. In Texas, he became a baseball legend whose final career records were light years ahead of those of his nearest rivals. In the words of 1993 World Series hero Joe Carter, "There's always one guy who defies the odds. In baseball, Nolan Ryan is that guy."

To the surprise of no one, Ryan became a first-ballot inductee into the National Baseball Hall of Fame. He was joined in Cooperstown on July 25, 1999, by George Brett, Robin Yount, and Orlando Cepeda. Their respective fan clubs generated the biggest attendance for a Hall of Fame induction ceremony that the village had ever witnessed until July 29, 2007, when Cal Ripken and Tony Gwynn were initiated into the game's most hallowed fraternity.

To the surprise of many, in his acceptance speech, Ryan paid tribute to Marvin Miller, leader of the players union in its early years, who caused player salaries to increase exponentially by getting arbitration, free agency, and a strong pension plan into the compensation mix, allowing the ballplayers of Ryan's era to obtain lifetime financial security before their playing days ended.

Missing the thrill of pitching competitive baseball, Nolan Ryan kept finding ways to stay active in the game. While sons Reid and Reese pitched in college in the mid-1990s for Texas Christian University, their dad served as volunteer pitching coach for the Horned Frogs and donned a uniform for games.

After the boys graduated, Nolan Ryan joined with longtime colleague Don Sanders to form Ryan-Sanders Baseball, and purchased the Jackson Generals, the Houston Astros' double-A farm team in the Texas League. They decided the team needed to move from Mississippi to Texas, and with the

PHOTO COURTESY OF *METS INSIDE PITCH* ARCHIVES

*Nolan Ryan (left) with catcher and fellow Texan Jerry Grote.*

help of chief executive officer Reid Ryan and chief financial officer Reese Ryan, the baseball enterprise started its search for the best possible location in the Lone Star State.

Knowing North Texas already had the Rangers and the Gulf Coast had the Astros, Ryan approached Austin about bringing his ballclub there. City leaders rejected his proposal, not wanting competition with Texas Longhorns baseball. Then Ryan had another idea. He called the mayor of Round Rock, north of Austin, to explore the possibility of locating his Jackson team there. The mayor instantly thought of an available piece of land with frontage on Highway 79 that for years had been a cornfield, and invited Ryan to take a look. A few weeks later, the deal was made, and the city of Round Rock held a groundbreaking ceremony. There, in the middle of the field, after walking over a path cut through rows of stalks, Nolan Ryan smiled, and giving his best Kevin Costner imitation, announced to the crowd, "If we build it, they will come."

Dell Diamond hosted its first game on Opening Day of the 2000 Texas League season… and the people came. Over the Round Rock Express's first four seasons, they shattered all league attendance records, and their success motivated the Ryan-Sanders ownership group to purchase the Triple-A Edmonton Trappers in the Pacific Coast League, move the Edmonton franchise to Round Rock in time for the 2005 season (where it became the Astros' triple-A team), and transfer the Houston's Double-A franchise from Round Rock to Corpus Christi. The Corpus Christi Hooks proceeded to maintain a Round Rock pace of record-breaking Texas League attendance, averaging a higher level of game ticket sales than the team's new Whataburger Field had seats, due to a grassy berm in left field that attracted hundreds of fans every game. Overall, Round Rock and Corpus Christi attracted more than 6 million fans in their first seven years.

In February 2008, Ryan was named president of the Texas Rangers, becoming the first Hall of Fame player to be the top executive at a major league franchise since Christy Mathewson with the Boston Braves some 85 years earlier. Ryan was not content to have a title and do things as other had done them. Taking over a team in a hitter's ballpark with thin pitching in past years, he decided to try to take the young pitchers the Rangers had and try to make them throw deeper into games. "I haven't been pleased with the direction baseball's taken pitching over the last 15 or 20 years, and I felt like we needed to regain some of what we had lost," Ryan told the *New York Times* in 2009. "I felt like we had a lot of pitchers that have been on pitch limits ever since Little League, and we don't know what their genetic potential is as far as the number of pitches and workload they can handle."

Ryan's career as an executive is yet to be determined, but his legacy as a pitcher is etched in stone. Though several pitchers were considered better in their prime, no pitcher's prime ever lasted as long as Ryan's. What helped him break so many baseball records was the application of old-fashioned common sense to his daily regimen. He never risked wearing out his arm by pitching in winter ball. The offseason physical activities Ryan pursued did not include bowling, volleyball, skiing, or any other sport that might result in a hand or leg injury. Adding to his prudent exercise decisions, he maintained a calm lifestyle sustained by a balanced moderate diet, no smoking, and no excessive drinking, celebrating his no-hitters drinking orange juice instead of the traditional champagne.

The science behind the artistry of Nolan Ryan involved the full utilization of his body and mind, knowing when to accept instruction and when to follow his own instincts. The late *Newsweek* sportswriter Pete Axthelm summarized the total commitment to pitching that drove Ryan's unprecedented career. "Other pitchers are satisfied in getting a win after a routine outing," Axthelm wrote. "Nolan Ryan spent over two decades using everything he had to be Picasso."

**Sources**

Boston, Talmage. *Baseball and the Baby Boomer: A History, Commentary, and Memoir* with a foreword by Frank Deford (Houston: Bright Sky Press, 2009). The Nolan Ryan biography is excerpted from this book.

Kepner, Tyler. "Ryan Instills His Toughness in the Rangers, *New York Times*, May 27, 2009.

Ryan, Nolan, with Frommer, Harvey, *Throwing Heat* (New York: Doubleday, 1988).

*Sports Illustrated*, selected issues.

# Tom Seaver

by Maxwell Kates

| Season | Age | W | L | Pct | G | GS | SV | IP | H | BB | SO | WHIP | ERA |
|---|---|---|---|---|---|---|---|---|---|---|---|---|---|
| 1969 Mets | 24 | 25 | 7 | .781 | 36 | 35 | 0 | 273.3 | 202 | 82 | 208 | 1.039 | 2.21 |
| Career 20 years | – | 311 | 205 | .603 | 656 | 647 | 1 | 4782.7 | 3971 | 1390 | 3640 | 1.121 | 2.86 |

As baseball has often been described as a game of numbers, fans, reporters, and students of the game would most certainly recognize these significant digits: 4,256; 755; 5,714; 511; and .366. They are career accomplishments linked to the respective immortals Pete Rose, Hank Aaron, Nolan Ryan, Cy Young, and Ty Cobb. To that list, another number should be added to commemorate longevity in hits, home runs, strikeouts, wins, and batting average. The number? 98.8.

On January 7, 1992, that was the percentage by which Tom Seaver was elected to the Baseball Hall of Fame. No player has ever received a higher approval rating by the Baseball Writers Association of America, not even Ty Cobb. Few players were ever more connected as a "franchise" player than Tom Terrific with the New York Mets. No member of the team was as intricately associated with their meteoric rise from cellar dwellers to world champions. Seaver was an immediate success upon arriving in New York in 1967. His miracle season of 1969 was highlighted by the game of his career against the division rival Chicago Cubs. He continued to pitch brilliantly in the 1970s, fanning 10 consecutive Padres in a game, collecting 200 strikeouts for nine straight seasons, and becoming the first right-hander to win three Cy Young Awards. In 1977, an ugly contract squabble led to what became known as the Midnight Massacre, a trade to the Cincinnati Reds that devastated the Mets and drove countless fans away from Shea Stadium. After more than five years of exile in the Queen City, Seaver returned to Queens in 1983. Although he wore sox of a different color scheme toward the end of his career, he saved his final crowning achievement for the New York fans to enjoy.

George Thomas Seaver was born on November 17, 1944, in Fresno, California. His mother, Betty, was a homemaker and his father, Charles, was an executive with the Bonner Packing Company, which harvested and shipped raisins to all corners of the country. The Seavers were an athletically minded family. Charles had been a Walker Cup golfer in his youth, while swimming, volleyball, and surfing were also represented in the family.

Seaver joined the North Rotary team in the Fresno Little League at the age of nine as a pitcher and outfielder. Within three years, he had pitched a perfect game while batting a robust .540. Later, Seaver pitched for Fresno High, a school that had already graduated pitching luminaries Jim Maloney, Dick Ellsworth, and Dick Selma.

"Even in high school, Tom was a thinking pitcher," remembered Selma, later a teammate of Seaver's on the Mets. "He knew how to set up a hitter by working the corners of the plate and the batter would usually pop the ball ... for an easy out."[1]

After graduating from high school in 1962, Seaver registered at Fresno City College while working in the raisin trade. (While a student, he also put in training time in the Marines.) Scouts had begun to notice his pitching repertoire after his second year, when he won 11 consecutive games while setting numerous school strikeout records. So did Rod Dedeaux, the legendary baseball coach who led the University of Southern California to 11 College World Series titles. Dedeaux asked Seaver to join the Trojans for his junior year. To prove his reputation and earn his scholarship, Seaver went to Alaska to pitch for the semiprofessional Goldpanners.

At USC in 1965, Seaver went 10–2, striking out 100 batters in 100 innings. Although only one organization scouted Seaver in 1965, the Atlanta Braves wasted no time the following year, drafting him in January and signing him a month later. The Braves had been Seaver's team of choice growing up in Fresno. Hank Aaron was his hero, and as he told interviewer Marty Appel, "I loved their uniforms, and I loved their hitters . . . Aaron, Mathews, Adcock."[2]

But as much as he loved the tomahawk, Seaver never wore it for an inning of his professional career. Major league rules prevented any organization from signing a college player while his season was in progress. Although Seaver had yet to pitch in 1966, the USC baseball season had already started when the Braves signed their right-handed prospect. Commissioner William Eckert voided Seaver's contract with the Braves on March 2. If other teams matched Atlanta's offer of $51,500, they would participate in a lottery for Seaver's services. Three teams—the Indians, the Phillies, and the Mets—stepped forward with contractual offers. The lottery was conducted on April 3 as each organization had its name thrown into a hat. Would Seaver join Sam McDowell and Sonny Siebert in Cleveland's rotation? Would he emerge as Philadelphia's third starter behind Jim Bunning and Chris Short? Neither. The winning paper selected belonged to the losingest team in baseball, the Mets.

Seaver earned a bonus contract worth $10,000 more than the Braves' offer, and began his professional career with Jacksonville. Pitching for the Mets' top farm club, Seaver went 12–12, throwing four shutouts and fanning 188 International League hitters. He married his high-school sweetheart, the former Nancy Lynn McIntyre, on June 6. Jacksonville manager Solly Hemus was overwhelmed by his pupil's talent and poise, insisting that his "35-year-old head attached to a 21-year-old body" was ready for prime time.[3] Earl Weaver, then managing the Orioles affiliate at Rochester, agreed with Hemus from the visiting dugout: "It was apparent in Tom Seaver's pro debut that he was ready for the majors. He had an excellent fastball and slider and he put them precisely where he wanted to, in and out on the black of the plate, mostly knee-high. After Jacksonville beat us, I phoned [general manager] Harry Dalton and said that Seaver was going to be sensational and the Orioles could give up a piece of the franchise and do well to get him."

Having never won more than 66 games or finished higher than in ninth place since coming into existence in 1962, the New York Mets underwent a 19-player overhaul under new general manager Bing Devine. One of the new faces in New York in 1967, true to Hemus's prediction, was Tom Seaver.

His baptism into the major leagues for manager Wes Westrum occurred on the second day of the season, April 13, as he yielded six hits to the Pittsburgh Pirates in 5⅓ innings with eight strikeouts and four walks. Seaver gave up just two runs as the Mets won, 3–2, but Chuck Estrada was the winning pitcher. By July, Seaver had amassed a record of 6–4 with a 2.60 ERA, commanding sufficient respect to merit a spot on the National League All-Star team. This midsummer classic, played at Anaheim Stadium, was deadlocked after 14 innings. After Tony Perez homered to give the senior circuit a 2–1 lead, manager Walter Alston summoned Seaver to face the American League in the bottom of the 15th. On that night, a nationally televised audience was introduced to a rookie with a 35-year-old head; Seaver got Tony Conigliaro to fly out before walking eventual Triple Crown winner Carl Yastrzemski. After Bill Freehan flied out, Seaver ended the game by striking out Ken Berry on a high fastball. Tom Terrific was bound for greatness.

Seaver rewrote the Mets' pitching record book in 1967. It wasn't hard given the team he was on (10th and last in the National League with 60 victories and 101 defeats), but in the four decades since, he has held his grip in most categories. His 16 victories,

tories, 18 complete games, 170 strikeouts, and 2.76 ERA in 1967 set new marks for the club. He also became the first Met in history to earn the National League Rookie of the Year Award. Even the normally reticent Hank Aaron expressed his admiration for Seaver. "You've got a nice pitch, kid," he told Seaver. "Good fastball, nice curve."[5] As for Bill Bartholomay, whose Braves were 0–4 against Seaver in 1967, all he could muster in light of the contract nullification was "I get sick every time I watch him pitch."

As Mets broadcaster Howie Rose later reminisced to author Bruce Markusen, Seaver brought a sense of hope that was absent from previous Mets teams. Before he joined the Mets, Rose said, "There was this inescapable culture of losing, and at least among their fans, a growing sense of losing was going to be something permanent." He added, "People who watched [Seaver] as a rookie got the sense that they had finally developed a player who was capable of doing special things, and therefore capable of helping the Mets achieve some pretty good thing of their own along the way."[7]

Seaver did not fall prey to the sophomore jinx in 1968, winning 14, fanning 205, and committing only one error all season. He could sense that greatness was around the corner for the Mets:

"We pass over 1968 too quickly," Rose said. "That was the season the executives were getting the pieces together ... getting Agee to play center field, getting Grote along as the catcher, getting the pitching staff together. They could see there was a Seaver, Ryan, Koosman, Grote, Harrelson, and getting Gil Hodges."[8]

If the Mets were destined for immortality in 1969, it was certainly not evident from their Opening Day performance on April 8. Broadcaster Ralph Kiner remembered Seaver "getting knocked out of the box" by the expansion Montreal Expos, who defeated the Mets, 11–10. The ensuing weeks were no kinder to the Mets. Injuries, slumps, erratic defensive play, and a lack of experience all prevented them from advancing beyond the second division of the National League East. In May, Hodges even told reporter Jack Lang that his hitters "looked like wooden soldiers."[9]

On May 21 in Atlanta, Seaver shut out the Braves to improve his record to 6–2. The Mets, meanwhile, evened their record at 18–18. To Seaver, the milestone was no cause for celebration. He defined the .500 mark as "neither here nor there" and said that his teammates' embrace of mediocrity "isn't going to get us very close to a pennant." To Ralph Kiner, Seaver's role as a motivator was crucial for the Mets' renaissance in 1969.

"Tom Seaver was the driving force behind the players, always pushing the team to be better than they were, never letting them settle," Kiner reminisced.[10] He might not have remembered the legacy he imprinted on Seaver at a far younger age. At the Bing Crosby Pro-Am Golf Tournament, Charles Seaver approached Kiner and said he would appreciate an autograph for his son, who aspired to become a baseball player. The retired Pirates outfielder gladly signed a school photograph: "To Tom, work hard and good luck, Ralph Kiner."

Diligence and luck, along with talent, were essential ingredients in the Mets' 11-game winning streak in late May and early June. For every player, there was a different highlight that augmented their confidence, but for Seaver, it was an extra-inning clutch hit to win the contest on June 4 in Los Angeles.

"We were in a scoreless game until the 15th inning. Then [Wayne] Garrett hit a ball up the middle with [Agee] on second. There was going to be a close play at the plate. Willie Davis came charging in and the ball was under his glove. The winning run scored. There was real electricity. I remember going into the clubhouse and making eye contact with Grote," Seaver said. He described the experience as "the last ounce that tipped me over into believing we could win."[11]

By now, the Mets were in second place behind the Chicago Cubs. When he defeated the Padres on June 14, Seaver improved his record to 10–3. The Mets' mound excellence behind Seaver, Jerry Koosman, Don Cardwell, and rookie Gary Gentry was renowned throughout the league. Seaver claims that a renewed collective excellence in the field was equally important, "especially up the middle with Grote, Harrelson, and Boswell, and Agee in center field."[12] The Mets upgraded their offense on June 15 when they acquired Donn Clendenon in a trade from Montreal. A veteran first baseman who studied law in the offseason, the sardonic Clendenon complemented the more cheerful Ed Charles across the diamond. In a tense racial period the year after the assassination of Martin Luther King, both clubhouse leaders on the Mets were African Americans. In Seaver's estimation, that hardly seemed to matter to his teammates, black or white. With sterling pitching and defense, solid offense, a hard-nosed manager, clubhouse chemistry, and confident players, the Mets had no reason to look back. Only the Cubs stood in their way of a division title.

All of these factors set the stage for what was arguably the strongest game Seaver ever pitched. It certainly is the best remembered Seaver game, even more than his no-hitter pitched for Cincinnati in 1978.

The Cubs, leading the division by four games, were visiting the Mets at Shea Stadium on July 8, 1969. Among the 59,083 exuberant spectators packed into the stands was Charles Seaver, who had flown from California on business. The younger Seaver had not even been certain he could pitch that evening due to a sore shoulder, but his pitches early on surpassed even his own perfectionist standards. While the Mets amassed a 3–0 lead in the third inning, no Chicago batsman even reached base. At this point, pitching coach Rube Walker broke one of baseball's cardinal rules, turning to Hodges and confiding, "Gil, I see something special out there. He's razor sharp. He's going to throw a no-hitter tonight."[13]

"Emotionally, I was fully aware of what was going on," remembered Seaver. "I came to bat and got this incredible standing ovation [in the sixth inning]. I felt as if I was almost levitating."[14] It mattered not that Seaver struck out. Eighteen Cubs batters had strode to the plate. Eighteen returned disappointed to the dugout. The Flushing faithful were glued to the edges of their seats both at Shea and on WOR-TV as Seaver continued to baffle the Cubs. Don Kessinger led off the seventh inning by flying out to left. Glenn Beckert flied out the opposite way before Billy Williams ended the inning with a groundout to third base. Seaver was equally masterful in the eighth inning. After Ron Santo flied out to center field, Tom Terrific fanned Ernie Banks and Al Spangler for his 10th and 11th strikeouts of the night. Twenty-four up, twenty-four down.

Shea Stadium, courtesy of Jim Bunning in 1964, had been the site of the first National League perfect game since 1888. Now it seemed like the perfect place for a repeat as Seaver took the mound for the top of the ninth. The inning began with a gasp as Randy Hundley led off with a bunt to the pitcher's mound. Seaver trapped it and tossed Hundley out at first base.

Enter Jim Qualls.

Of any Cubs hitter, Qualls had hit "the only hard-hit balls of the night." Seaver had already yielded two sharply hit balls to the obscure rookie outfielder. The pitcher mused that "if anybody gets a hit off me tonight, it would be this guy."[15] Seaver was right. He pitched the left-handed hitter away, and Qualls unleashed a clean base hit to shallow left field. The perfect game was over. The "Imperfect Game" became a part of the Mets lexicon.

A consummate professional, Seaver retired the last two batters and threw the first of his club-record five one-hitters. The Mets won the game, 4–0, defeating the front-running Cubs in the most crucial game of the season to that point. The baseball universe knew that the Mets were for real.

Although the Mets and Seaver faded in late July, the third-place Cardinals could not capitalize on their errors to overtake them in the standings. Then, in August, the Mets were dealt a grueling test of endurance: 20 games in 20 days, including four doubleheaders against three California teams. While some teams would have capitulated to the exhausting schedule and the transcontinental flights, the Mets went 15–5. As the winner of three games during the Golden State marathon, Seaver had improved his record to 19–7. He had not lost since August 5, when he dropped a decision to Cincinnati's Gary Nolan, and would be perfect in his final six decisions. The Mets took sole position of first place on September 10, and captured the division title two weeks later.

As the staff leader with 25 wins, Seaver was given the starting assignment for Game One of the National League Championship Series against the Atlanta Braves. But had the Miracle run its course? The Braves, behind their ace Phil Niekro, jumped Seaver for five runs on eight hits in seven innings. Trailing by one in the eighth, the Mets rallied for five runs to preserve the victory for Seaver. The Mets easily disposed of the heavily favored Braves by winning the next two games, claiming a spot in the World Series against Baltimore.

Despite the best overall record in the National League, the Mets remained the heavy underdog in the World Series against the 109-win Orioles. The O's were an older, more experienced club with most of the same personnel who had won a world championship in 1966, a year when the Mets were still excited over not losing 100 games for the first time. In the minds of many, the success of the Miracle Mets could not erase the image of Jimmy Piersall running backward around the bases or Marv Throneberry's disqualified triple on the grounds that he failed to touch first *or* second base. Earl Weaver, the first-year manager of the Orioles, was not convinced that this would be another four-game sweep for the Birds. "I didn't think for a minute that the so-called 'Miracle' Mets would be easy opponents in the Series," he said in his autobiography. "Their pitching was too good, particularly that of Tom Seaver and Jerry Koosman, whom I managed in the minors."

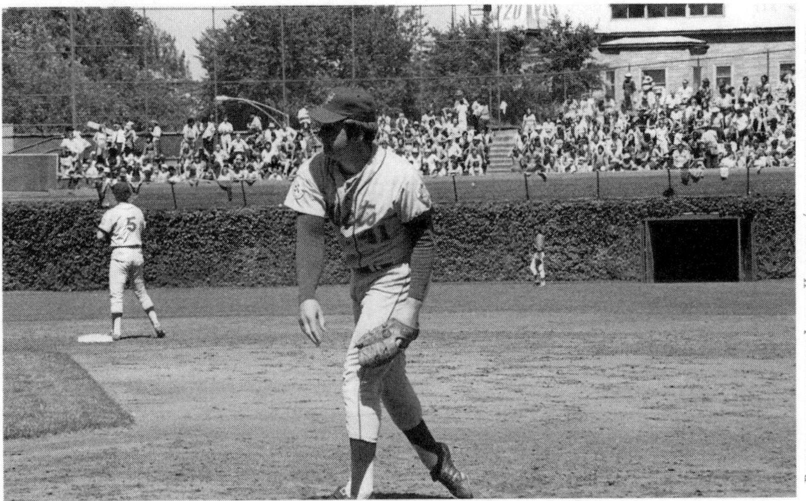
PHOTO COURTESY OF JACOB KANAREK/METSINTHESEVENTIES.COM

*Tom Seaver followed his Cy Young Award in 1969 by winning the award again in 1973 and 1975, making him the first right-hander to win it three times.*

Yet after one batter in Game One, the skeptics appeared correct, as Baltimore's Don Buford unleashed a home run to lead off the bottom of the first against Seaver. The Mets found themselves in worse trouble by the fourth inning, when Seaver allowed four hits, including a double to Buford, to bring in three additional runs. The Mets, meanwhile, managed to produce only one run against Baltimore starter Mike Cuellar. Compounding matters, a journalistic rumor began to circulate that if the Mets won the World Series, Seaver would purchase a full-page advertisement in the *New York Times* urging the United States to withdraw from Vietnam. Though the statement was without an ounce of truth, the baseball establishment was shocked that one of its brightest stars could lend his name to a controversial and divisive cause. Although Seaver could not dodge the bats of Cuellar and his teammates, he circumvented the Vietnam issue by stating that he "did not want to be used for political purposes."[17]

As it happened, Seaver's next turn to pitch in Game One was Moratorium Day, a nationwide day of protest against the conflict in Indochina. Seaver, like countless others entering Shea Stadium, was asked to don a black armband as part of the demonstration. True to his word, he refused. Game Four was a rematch of the opener, with Cuellar and Seaver facing off again. Only now, the Mets had won two straight and Seaver looked almost as good as he had against the Cubs in June. He threw eight shutout innings and held a one-run lead on Clendenon's second-inning home run. The ninth inning was more cumbersome, particularly as Seaver faced Baltimore opponents named Robinson. A Boog Powell single advanced Frank from first to third, and Brooks hit a wicked liner to right that only a stupendous catch by right fielder Ron Swoboda kept as a game-tying sacrifice fly instead of a go-ahead triple. Despite losing the lead, Gil Hodges left Seaver to pitch the 10th inning. In the bottom half of the frame, Grote led off with a double against 39-year-old accountant Dick Hall. Rod Gaspar pinch-ran. Pete Richert was called from the bullpen to face the left-handed J.C. Martin, who batted for Seaver. Martin bunted to the right of the mound, and Richert's throw glanced off Martin's wrist, then bounced into the outfield, allowing Gaspar to score from second base. Seaver got his only career World Series win and the next day the Mets completed one of the most stunning world championships in history.

One month shy of his 25th birthday, Tom Seaver was at the height of his game. He was a leader and motivator on a talented Mets team which, in their eighth National League season, defied all expectations. He led the league with 208 strikeouts while limiting opposing batters to a 2.21 ERA. He won the National League Cy Young Award and the *Sports Illustrated* Sportsman of the Year title, the only Met ever so honored. He finished a close second to Willie McCovey in the MVP voting (265 to 243), after no previous Met had even got near the top 10. Seaver took part in a ticker-tape parade described by the *Wall Street Journal* as a more colossal celebration than V-E Day, Charles Lindbergh's flight, and the return of the Apollo astronauts, all rolled into one.[18] He appeared on *The Ed Sullivan Show*, performed at a Las Vegas supper club, and purchased a Victorian farmhouse in Greenwich, Connecticut. However, if Seaver himself read this list of accomplishments, he probably would have added, "But you forgot one thing. I'm the only Mets pitcher who's lost a ballgame in the World Series."[19]

Seaver would not rest on his laurels. The next season, he led the league with a 2.81 ERA and 283 strikeouts. Nineteen of those whiffs were recorded on April 22 against the Padres, including the last 10 San Diego batsmen he faced, a feat still unmatched. In 1971, he had as good a year as he ever enjoyed in baseball statistically, setting personal marks with 289 strikeouts and a radiant 1.76 ERA to lead the NL in both categories. His 20 wins were four behind Ferguson Jenkins's total and the Cubs hurler took the Cy Young award by 36 votes.

Tragedy overshadowed New York's 1972 season in spring training when Gil Hodges died of a heart attack after a round of golf. Seaver paid an eloquent tribute to his late manager, affirming that "Gil is here inside each man, and he will be here all season. The man made a terrific impact on this ballclub."[20] Under new skipper Yogi Berra, Seaver led the club with 21 wins and 249 strikeouts. In his first six seasons 1967–72, Seaver led all National League pitchers with 116 wins and 1,404 strikeouts. Only Bob Gibson's 2.42 ERA was better than Seaver's 2.44.

In 1973, Seaver became the first pitcher to win the National League Cy Young Award without winning 20 games. As was the case with his first Cy Young, it was evident to anyone associated with the Mets that he was indeed their franchise player. Off to a promising start, the Mets ended April atop their division with a record of 12–8. However, mediocrity soon prevailed, after injuries to key players Jerry Grote, Cleon Jones, Bud Harrelson, and even Willie Mays. By June 25, the Mets languished in the divisional basement, 8½ games behind the Cubs. Still, the second-place Montreal Expos were only two games ahead of the Mets. "It was the kind of year that nobody seemed to want to win," Seaver later remarked.[21]

The Mets entered July with a losing record, but so did four of their opponents in the "NL Least." Gloom prevailed in Flushing as the Mets posted a 32–49 record from May through July. When rumors circulated that Berra would be fired, chairman M. Donald Grant rushed to the manager's rescue,

Photo courtesy of metsilverman.com

*Tom Seaver was the first Hall of Famer depicted with a Mets hat on his plaque and the first to garner 98.8 percent of the vote.*

affirming that Berra would not be fired "unless public opinion demands it."[22] The *New York Post* capitalized on the remark, conducting a poll to ask which Mets executive should be fired, Berra, Grant, or general manager Bob Scheffing. Only 611 of the more than 3,000 ballots cast found Berra culpable for the Mets' futility.

Amid the despair there was one bright hope, embodied in a blue and orange pinstriped uniform emblazoned with the number 41. After defeating the Phillies on Opening Day, Seaver's consistency outshone that of his teammates. When the Mets were 30–35, Seaver was 7–3. In a three-week stretch of late May and early June, Tom Terrific was responsible for the only four wins registered by the Mets. In one of those games, on May 29, he struck out 16 San Francisco Giants and was named National League Player of the Week. When Berra rhetorically asked sportswriter Terry Shore where the Mets would be without Seaver, the writer replied, "In last place with a 17-game losing streak and certainly out of any division race."[23] Seaver was particularly effective after Grote returned from the disabled list in late July.

Although the Mets remained in last place through late August, Grant ignited confidence in a clubhouse meeting in which he reminded his players that they could win their division if they believed in themselves. Tug McGraw's repeated exclamation of "Ya gotta believe!" drove Grant from the locker room and a rallying cry was born. Berra echoed Grant's sentiments in observing the divisional race. He remarked that every team so far had a hot streak except the Mets, adding, "It ain't over 'til it's over."[24]

Berra, Grant, McGraw, and company were right. The Mets surged in September, winning 21 of their last 29. On September 21, Seaver defeated the Pirates to even the club's record at 77–77, which in their mediocre division was good enough for first place. Seaver took the mound again on October 1 and defeated the Cubs, 6–4, to win his 19th and final victory of the regular season and clinch the division title. Until the San Diego Padres won their division in 2005, no National League team finished first with a worse record than the 1973 Mets' 82–79. For his part, Seaver led the league with 251 strikeouts and a 2.08 ERA. He completed 18 games, tying Steve Carlton for the league lead.

Yet there was some concern about Seaver's shoulder and it took a workout at Shea Stadium two days after the clinching for him to be pronounced as fit to start the NLCS opener against the powerhouse Reds, winners of 17 more games than the Mets and with an 8–4 mark against New York during the season. Cincinnati, which had represented the National League in two of the previous three World Series, had a lineup that was a veritable Murderers Row: Even if the Mets succeeded against Pete Rose, Joe Morgan, and rookie Dan Driessen in one inning, they still had Tony Perez, Johnny Bench, and Ken Griffey due up the next inning. Facing Jack Billingham, a distant relative of Christy Mathewson, Seaver fanned 13 and walked none in the NLCS opener; he also benefited his own cause by doubling in a run in the second inning. Nevertheless, the ghost of Big Six smiled upon his cousin and the Big Red Machine in the latter frames of the game. Rose tied it in the eighth with a home run and Bench's ninth-inning blast won the game, 2–1. The Mets came right back from the disappointment and won the next day on Jon Matlack's two-hit shutout. The Mets took Game Three at Shea despite a nasty brouhaha between Rose and Bud Harrelson. Seaver, along with Mays, Berra, Cleon Jones, and Rusty Staub, went out to left field to restore order after fans at Shea pelted Rose in left field with everything from paper cups to a whiskey bottle. The Mets won the game, but Rose exacted some revenge by homering to win Game Four in 12 innings. The stage was set for a Seaver-Billingham rematch in the finale.

In the first inning of Game Five, Ed Kranepool drove in two with a bases-loaded double. The Reds struck back as Driessen brought in Morgan in the third inning, while Rose crossed home plate to tie the game on a single by Perez in the fifth. Then the Mets blew it open with four runs in the home fifth to chase Billingham, and who better to drive in the go-ahead run than the Say-Hey Kid. Having already said "goodbye to America" at his retirement game, the 42-year-old Mays, batting for Kranepool, collected a bases-loaded single to score Felix Millan. Seaver led off the sixth inning with a double and scored on a Cleon Jones single to give the Mets a 7–2 lead. McGraw relieved Seaver and got the last two outs and then ran for his life as fans stormed the field.

Amid banners that proclaimed "Rose is a Weed" and "This Rose Smells," the series marked an acrimonious victory over the otherwise superior Reds. Charlie Hustle compared the Mets and their fans to a flock of zoo animals, while manager Sparky Anderson expressed his dismay at their riotous celebration: "I can't believe this could happen in this country, but then I'm not sure New York is part of this country."[25] In spite of geography, and against all probability, the Mets were returning to the World Series for the second time in five years.

To paraphrase Yogi Berra's rhetoric, the 1973 World Series was indeed "déjà vu all over again" for the Mets. After winning an unexpected division title and then pulling off a stunning upset for the pennant, the underdog Mets faced a proven winner in the World Series: the Oakland A's. The defending world champion A's upset the baseball establishment by uniforming their long-haired, bearded players in green and gold haberdashery while experimenting with orange baseballs, designated runners, and ballgirls. Even their manager, Dick Williams, otherwise a traditionalist, sported long hair and a mustache. The Swingin' A's boasted a rotation featuring Catfish Hunter, Vida Blue, and Ken Holtzman, with Rollie Fingers in the bullpen, while their lineup was punctuated by Bert Campaneris, Joe Rudi, Sal Bando, Reggie Jackson, and Gene Tenace. After the teams split their first two games amid more controversy—Oakland owner Charles O. Finley forced infielder Mike Andrews to sign a waiver that he was unfit to play after he bungled two routine grounders in New York's 12-inning victory in Game Two—Seaver faced Hunter in Game Three. Night games in the World Series were still a novelty and didn't seem like such a great idea when the temperature hovered near 40 degrees for the three games at Shea. The Mets still started out hot, taking a 2–0 lead before Hunter could gain his composure. Bando doubled in the sixth inning and scored on another double by Tenace. Campaneris led off the eighth inning with a single, stole second, and tied the game on an RBI single by Rudi. Seaver exited after eight innings. McGraw, who threw 10 innings in relief in the first three games, left after the 10th. Harry Parker allowed the go-ahead run the following inning. But the Mets managed to win the next two and jetted back to warm, sunny Oakland a win away from a world championship. Berra could have handed the ball in Game Six to George Stone, who became the favorite among second-guessers, but Yogi went with his best and brought back Seaver to face Hunter again.

Seaver later admitted that he lacked his "good hard stuff" as Oakland scored twice early and held on for the 3–1 win that tied the Series. Remarkably, the A's had yet to hit a home run in the Series entering Game Seven, but two third-inning blasts by Campy and Reggie sank the Mets and Matlack, 5–2. A decade would pass before the Mets even competed again to play October baseball.

Despite a bittersweet 1973 season, Seaver converted his stellar performance and second Cy Young into a $172,000 contract. At the time, he was the highest paid pitcher in baseball. However, the pain in Seaver's shoulder and hip that impeded his performance down the stretch continued to plague him in 1974. Facing Steve Carlton and the Phillies on Opening Day for the second consecutive year, Seaver twice failed to hold leads before Tug McGraw surrendered the winning home run to rising star Mike Schmidt. Seaver's fastball was even less effective in his second start, prompting pitching coach Rube Walker to ask if he was injured. Only after five starts did Seaver finally register a win; by Memorial Day, he was 2–5. Atlanta's Johnny Oates called his fastball "a lame duck." Meanwhile, Seaver was being described as surly in the clubhouse and in dealings with the media. In his column in the *New York Daily News*, Dick Young wrote that Seaver was an agent of discontent among his teammates. In a summer of headlines dominated by Watergate, this curmudgeonly Dick made it perfectly clear that Seaver had made an enemy in him; it would not be the final war of words between the two.

For the first time in his star-studded career, Seaver had an ERA above 3.00 and failed to make the All-Star team. But 1974 was not a complete washout. Through September, he managed to strike out 187 batters while pitching through pain. Late in the month, he attended two osteopathic sessions with Dr. Kenneth Riland. The doctor diagnosed him with a sciatic nerve problem and a dislocated pelvic structure, both legacies from years of hard throwing. Seaver later estimated that Riland worked on him for less than 10 minutes. After previously announcing that his season was over, he requested one final start. Facing Philadelphia in the next to last game of the 1974 campaign, Seaver still had a remote chance of becoming the first National League pitcher to strike out 200 batters in seven consecutive seasons. Despite an early two-run double by Willie Montanez that proved to be the deciding hit in an inevitable 2–1 loss, Seaver was masterful. He fanned eight Phillies through six innings and struck out the side in the seventh. The Phillies put the ball in play in the eighth and he entered the final inning still two strikeouts shy of the elusive 200 mark. After punching out Mike Schmidt with fastballs to lead off the ninth inning, Seaver fanned Montanez to achieve 200 strikeouts in seven straight seasons. The Mets had the cover image ready for their 1975 yearbook, a photo of Seaver posed with baseballs forming the number 7. For good measure, Seaver ended his season by striking out Mike Anderson. The Mets went down meekly to ensure Seaver's first nonwinning season at 11–11.

With a rejuvenated arm and a new pelvic structure, the Seaver of old re-emerged at Shea in 1975. The pinnacle of his season occurred on September 1 when he reached two statistical milestones in midst of a shutout against Pittsburgh. When Seaver struck out Manny Sanguillen in the seventh inning, he reached a plateau that even Walter Johnson and Rube Waddell never attained. He became the first pitcher to strike out 200 batters in eight consecutive seasons. (Earlier in the season, Dan Driessen became his 2,000th career strikeout victim.) The victory for interim manager Roy McMillan—Yogi had been fired in August—would be Seaver's 20th of the season, and he added two more to finish at 22–9 and earn his third Cy Young Award. He would be denied another victory despite taking a no-hitter two outs into the ninth inning at Wrigley Field on September 24. Joe Wallis singled to break up the bid, but even if he'd gotten Wallis, it wouldn't have been a no-hitter because the Mets did not score. Seaver left after 10 shutout innings and the Mets lost on a bases-loaded walk in the 11th inning, 1–0.

PHOTO COURTESY OF METSILVERMAN.COM

*Tom Seaver displays his Hall of Fame form in an exhibit in Cooperstown.*

Seaver edged out San Diego's Randy Jones to earn his third Cy Young, becoming the second pitcher, after Sandy Koufax, to win the award three times. Contract negotiations, on the other hand, would prove to be a whole different ballgame.

Two National League pitchers, Los Angeles' Andy Messersmith and Montreal's Dave McNally, had played the entire 1975 season without contracts. On December 23, arbitrator Peter Seitz ruled that both players were free to negotiate new contracts to the highest bidding team on the open market. The reserve clause, which had bound a player to his employer for life, was obsolete, and the replacing system that granted free agency to players was met with vociferous opposition by the baseball establishment. As the Mets' union representative, Seaver worked to create an equitable negotiating environment for his fellow players. Now he wanted to experience the rewards.

Seaver demanded a three-year, $825,000 contract. Team president M. Donald Grant grew incensed and threatened to trade him to the Dodgers for Don Sutton. One pitch into the 1976 season, Seaver would become a "10-and-5 man." In another coup for the players in a previous round of labor negotiations, any player with ten years' experience, five

Photo courtesy of metsilverman.com

*That ball's not going anywhere... Tom Seaver watches a pop fly against the Cubs in 1969.*

with the same team, could reject any prospective trade, leaving the Mets only a few months to arrange a deal for Sutton. Rather than risk a public relations nightmare from trading their franchise player, the Mets agreed to renegotiate with Seaver, offering an incentive-based contract with a base annual salary of $225,000 through 1978. Though Seaver reluctantly agreed, it cost him any professional rapport he had with Grant.

Though Seaver's record in 1976 was a disappointing 14–11, his offensive support produced only 15 runs in his aggregate losses. Registering seven consecutive fruitless starts (0–4 with three no-decisions) between July 13 and August 24, he still managed to limit the opposition with a 2.13 ERA. Seaver's ERA for the year was 2.59 (third in the league), and his 235 strikeouts earned him his fifth NL strikeout crown. He also extended his record to 200 whiffs in nine consecutive seasons. As impressive as Seaver's 1976 numbers might have been, they represented his last hurrah in a Mets uniform.

The Mets reacted to baseball's new economic reality by failing to initiate any intention to sign any of the 24 potential free agents. After they had finished a pedestrian third place in each of the previous two seasons, the environment was ideal for the Mets to improve their offense by signing a free agent. In sportswriter Bill Madden's eyes, Gary Matthews would have been "a perfect fit" to play center field. Yet, as Seaver decried to a barrage of reporters in spring training, he was dismayed by his club's refusal to adapt to changing economic times.[28] The contract squabble of the year before still fresh in his mind, Seaver watched as other teams signed players of star caliber. Across town in the Bronx, the six-year, $2 million contract the Yankees gave Don Gullett to sign him away from Cincinnati suddenly rendered Seaver's contract outmoded. Observant of the ordeal teammate Dave Kingman endured in his own negotiations, Seaver wondered if he would have been better off not signing a 1976 contract and filing for free agency. Grant's reaction was predictable, deprecating Seaver as "an ingrate" and blasting the economic system his union had brought forth.

"We will try to run our business in a sensible way," Grant said. "Nobody is going to plan to spend a lot of money for players and lose money at the park."[30] He understood the economics of the game, that free-agent contracts would inflate ticket prices, thereby pricing his product out of the reach of thousands of Mets fans. An acrimonious relationship between Seaver and Grant became even more pronounced. Most of the New York writers sided with Tom Terrific, including Maury Allen of the *New York Post.*

"When you have the best pitcher in the world, you sign him," Allen wrote. "You don't humiliate him. Grant can't stand opposition from Seaver or anybody." In assessing Grant's stance on contract negotiations, Allen charged that "he'd sooner lose a pennant" than cede to the demands of his players and their agents. [31]

There was one notable holdout in the press. On the Seaver front, Grant soon formed an axis with one of the city's most powerful voices, Dick Young of the *Daily News*. A maverick Republican in a city of Democrats, Young reacted to Seaver's free agency regret by labeling him "a troublemaker," insistent that no team would be interested in signing him.[32] The sports section at the *Daily News* was rendered into "the battle page," as Young and the pro-Seaver Jack Lang sparred using pens rather than foils. Seaver appeared unfazed by the diversions off the field, posting a record of 4–0 by the end of April and tossing his fifth one-hitter as a Met, against the Cubs. Seaver's performance did not prevent Young, however, from continuing his offensive:

"Tom Tewwific," he wrote, "[is] a pouting, griping, morale-breaking clubhouse lawyer poisoning the team."[33] Young was correct about the Mets' position in the standings. By the end of May, the team was already 13 games out of first place. The Mets had hired their fourth manager in two years, replacing Joe Frazier with the untested Joe Torre. Meanwhile, the trading deadline was only two weeks away.

Rumors began to circulate that general manager Joe McDonald was arranging a deal with Bob Howsam, his counterpart in Cincinnati, to send Seaver to the Reds. On June 7, Seaver struck out 13 Reds in an 8–0 shutout at Shea to improve his record to 6–3. Sparky Anderson remembered the game: "For years, I had been naming Tom, whenever I was asked, as baseball's best pitcher. I never saw him better than he was [that night] when he whipped us. It was an artistic effort. I drooled when I thought of what a pitcher of Seaver's class could do for us."[34]

After Seaver won in Houston on June 12, the Mets offered to extend his contract so that it would be comparable to a free-agent offering elsewhere. He would receive a three year extension which included a pay raise to $300,000 in 1979 and then to $400,000 in 1980 and 1981. On June 14, one day before the trading deadline, Seaver contacted McDonald to halt trade negotiations with the Reds. He planned to remain a Met.

Conventional wisdom suggests that if something sounds too good to be true, it often is. After he agreed in principle to a three-year contract extension with the Mets, the ordeal appeared over for Seaver. However, as he read the *Daily News* on the road in Atlanta, he became appalled by the latest offensive launched from Dick Young's typewriter:

"Nolan Ryan is getting more now than Seaver, and that galls Tom because Nancy Seaver and Ruth Ryan are very friendly and Tom Seaver long has treated Nolan Ryan like a little brother."[35] As Seaver told Bruce Markusen years later, his welcome mat with M. Donald Grant had finally run out. Incensed that Young would pull a false punch aimed at his family, Seaver bolted in search of public relations director Arthur Richman. "Get me out of here!" he ordered Richman, "and tell Joe McDonald everything I said last night is forgotten."[36]

McDonald had no leverage to pull the trigger on a deal he regretted to make. On June 15, Tom Seaver was traded to the Cincinnati Reds for a package of players, none older than 26: pitcher Pat Zachry, infielder Doug Flynn, and outfielders Steve Henderson and Dan Norman. Not only would New Yorkers endure the turbulence of the .44 caliber killer, a crippling blackout followed by massive looting and rioting, and a bitter four-candidate campaign for mayor of a near-bankrupt city—for Mets fans, the summer of 1977 would also live in infamy for a trade known as the Midnight Massacre.

After an emotional press conference in the Shea Stadium clubhouse, Seaver was ready to move on, joining his new teammates in Montreal. Disappointed by the situation he was leaving in New York, at least he would no longer have Johnny Bench, Pete Rose, or Joe Morgan to face. Though victorious in the previous two World Series, the Reds trailed Los Angeles in the 1977 National League West standings. Tony Perez was gone, but George Foster emerged as a power source; his 52 home runs were the most by any major-league slugger in a dozen years. Despite a 14–3 mark with a 2.34 ERA for Cincinnati—including a victory over old pal Jerry Koosman at Shea Stadium in August—Seaver did not re-ignite his teammates to overtake the Dodgers in the standings. While he earned his fifth and final 20-win season, he fell short of his ninth straight 200-K season by four strikeouts.

He brought out scores of fans to Riverfront on days he pitched, and he also conveyed a presence to the locker room that was felt even among the two-time world champions. "Seaver was a joy to have around. He is such a bright young guy that his weird sense of humor almost seems out of character," recalled Sparky Anderson on Tom Terrific's immediate impact. "His personality fit right in with the veterans. They accepted him and he accepted them. Moreover, Tom was of tremendous help to our young pitchers who frequently sought his advice."[38]

Seaver, who hadn't really bonded with a manager since the death of Gil Hodges, worked well with one of the game's top dugout minds. "Sparky communicates well. He's intelligent. He has the 'smarts.' He believes in his convictions. He'll argue to the death when he thinks he's right. And he often is right."[39] Expectations were high for the 1978 Reds to re-establish themselves as the pre-eminent club in their division. Seaver did his part, posting a record of 16–14 with 226 strikeouts and a 2.88 ERA. On June 16, he reached an achievement never accomplished as a Met: he pitched a no-hitter against the St. Louis Cardinals. The Reds, however, fell short in the standings to the Dodgers and with Dick Wagner now operating as Reds' general manager, he wanted his own man in the dugout. Anderson was let go.

Although injuries impeded Seaver's performance early in the 1979 season, he recovered to win 14 of his last 15 games. After two bridesmaid finishes, the Reds won their division once again under new manager John McNamara. The Pittsburgh Pirates, clad in their stovepipe hats emblazoned with stars from Willie "Pops" Stargell, emerged victorious from a white-knuckle divisional race with the Expos. It would be the fourth League Championship Series of the decade between Pittsburgh and Cincinnati, with the first three won by the Reds. This time, however, Cincinnati was without Rose, who'd signed as a free agent with Philadelphia the year before. Though Seaver limited the Pirates to two runs and five hits in Game One, Pittsburgh starter John Candelaria was equally effective. Tom Terrific had long since exited the game when Stargell snapped the tie in dramatic fashion, hitting a three-run homer off reliever Tom Hume in the top of the 11th inning. The Pirates went on to sweep the Reds before defeating the Baltimore Orioles in the 1979 World Series.

Seaver's 10–8 season in 1980 was marred by disappointment. The Reds finished third and he suffered from arm trouble for the first time in his career. The following season was equally disappointing, but for vastly different reasons.

Although the Reds posted the best record in baseball, a midseason players' strike resulted in a unique split-season format. As the Reds finished second in both halves, they had little recourse in the postseason besides watching the Dodgers' divisional playoff against the Astros on television. Moreover, Seaver's record of 14–2 represented the highest winning percentage in either league. Unfortunately, his comeback season coincided with Fernandomania, the pandemonium that surrounded the Dodgers' unhittable rookie phenom Fernando Valenzuela. Seaver lost the Cy Young Award to Valenzuela by one vote. The 1981 season was not without personal acclaim for Seaver. He reached the 3,000-strikeout plateau when he fanned Cardinal Keith Hernandez on April 8.

As the decade of the 1980s progressed, so did the frustration for Seaver. Defections continued as Ken Griffey and George Foster were traded, while Dave Collins was lost to free agency. Consequently, the Reds plunged to the divisional cellar in 1982, recording an abysmal record of 61–101 (even worse than the last-place Mets). Not even Seaver was immune, going just 5–13 with an unsightly ERA of 5.50. Emerging from the worst record in franchise history, the Reds were eager to part with their 38-year-old pitcher with the suspect shoulder. At least one team was equally enthusiastic in trading for Seaver.

In 1980, the New York Mets were sold to a consortium led by publisher Nelson Doubleday and developer Fred Wilpon. Rebranding the Mets as "the People's Team," Doubleday and Wilpon vowed to field a winning team at Shea Stadium, and allowed general manager Frank Cashen the pursestrings to field a contender. The resurrection of the Mets was a struggle at first. Not even George Foster, brought to the Mets with great fanfare, and new manager George Bamberger could lift the Mets in 1982. Cashen turned his sights to a third George, trading pitcher Charlie Puleo and two minor-league players to reacquire Seaver from the Reds on December 16. As M. Donald Grant had retired and Dick Young was reduced to journalistic obscurity, the coast was clear for Seaver's return to New York.

Over 48,000 fans flocked to Shea Stadium for Mets nostalgia on April 5, watching Tom Terrific throw six shutout innings against the Phillies in his return. Rookie Doug Sisk, who got the win in relief against Steve Carlton, observed that he "didn't know [Seaver] could still throw that hard." It was his 14th Opening Day assignment, tying another Walter Johnson pitching record. Seaver was the most durable pitcher on the 1983 Mets, tying Mike Torrez with 34 starts and leading the staff with 135 strikeouts in 231 innings. However, not even Seaver, rookie Darryl Strawberry, nor midseason acquisition Keith Hernandez could save the Mets. Seaver went 9–14 in New York's seventh consecutive losing season. Though that long streak was about to end, Seaver would not experience it.

The resolution of the 1981 players' strike established an annual pool of players from which teams could select players as compensation for free-agent losses. With several young prospects they were anxious to keep, the Mets did not envision that any team would want Seaver, now 39, whose value was higher in New York because of his appeal as an attendance draw. The 68–94 Mets kept their young players but lost their Franchise. Again.

The Chicago White Sox lost pitcher Dennis Lamp to the Toronto Blue Jays as a free agent and were eligible to take an unprotected player from any other club as compensation. On January 20, 1984, they selected Seaver. On the heels of winning 99 games before losing the American League Championship Series to the Orioles, the White Sox were excited to bring in a pitcher of Seaver's craft and experience.

"Tom's a competitor. I think he's going to be happy here," said White Sox president Eddie Einhorn. "This is the best place for him for the rest of his career. It's an excellent way to end it. It's possible he'll get back into the World Series. He'll certainly reach 300 wins with us. And the atmosphere is great."[41]

Einhorn's predictions were not entirely wrong. Seaver did achieve his 300th win with the White Sox on August 4, 1985, crashing Phil Rizzuto Day at Yankee Stadium to defeat the Bronx Bombers at home. (Tom Terrific joined the Scooter in the Yankees' broadcast booth after retiring as a player.) Though he ended his career with a World Series entrant, it would not be in a Chicago White Sox uniform.

The White Sox capitalized on weak American League West opponents in 1983, winning the division by 20 games over second place Kansas City. However, their style of "winning ugly" proved to be a one-year wonder. Though he won a respectable 15 games in 1984 and 16 in 1985, the White Sox had returned to mediocrity. Seaver did enter the record books by being the pitcher of record on May 9, 1984. When Harold Baines won the game with a home run in the 25th inning, Seaver won the first eight-hour game in major league history. It had been stopped after 17 innings and resumed the next afternoon. As the scheduled starter later that day, he became the first White Sox pitcher since Wilbur Wood to win two games played in the same day. In 1968, Seaver had started and thrown 10 shutout innings in what turned into a 24-inning game at the Astrodome. Now he entered a game after 24 innings and picked up the win in his first relief appearance since 1976.

As the 1986 season approached, Seaver could see the terminus of his professional baseball career. After his mother passed away that spring, he wanted to spend more time with his family, which now in-

Photo by Dan Carubia

*Tom Seaver came back in 1983 to a team almost as bad as the one he first joined in 1967, but like the club he led his rookie year, the senior Seaver's Mets weren't as far from turning everything around as it first seemed.*

cluded two young daughters. Seaver asked to be traded to a New York team or to Boston to be closer to his Connecticut home. On June 29, the White Sox granted him his wish, dealing him to the Red Sox for utilityman Steve Lyons. A change of Sox reunited Seaver with manager John McNamara in Boston. Led by perennial batting champion Wade Boggs, dependable outfielders Jim Rice and Dwight Evans, and pitching sensation Roger Clemens, these Sox were poised for their first World Series appearance since 1975. After a tight pennant race with the Yankees and an exciting Championship Series victory over the Angels, the Red Sox did indeed return to the October classic. As for Seaver, after posting a 7–13 record in an injury-plagued season, he was left off the postseason roster. He was unavailable in Game Six when Johnny Mac required a right-hander in the 10th inning, a frame that ended when a groundball passed through Bill Buckner's weathered ankles. The Red Sox went on to lose Game Seven and the World Series. The winners? The New York Mets.

Seaver he did try to put on uniform number 41 for the Mets one last time. His attempted comeback with the 1987 Mets proved fruitless and Seaver announced his retirement on June 22. A year later, he joined Casey Stengel and Gil Hodges on the short list of Mets notables to have their numbers retired. Two decades later, he remained the only Met to have his number retired for his achievements as a player. And they were many. Most of his Mets records may never be broken, including wins (198), complete games (171), shutouts (44), starts (395), innings (3,045), strikeouts (2,541), and ERA (2.57).

Besides broadcasting Yankees games for five seasons, Seaver worked as a public-relations representative for the Chase Manhattan Bank. He spent seven years as a Mets broadcaster before leaving after the 2005 season. Inducted in the Baseball Hall of Fame in 1992 by an unprecedented margin, Seaver attracted a then-record 10,000 pilgrims to witness his induction speech. Among them, Rudy Gafur, who chronicled the milestone in his baseball diary entitled *Cooperstown is My Mecca:*

> *Seaver finished his career with 311 wins and 205 losses. Among his numerous awards and honors are Rookie of the Year, National League Pitcher of the Year, and Cy Young Award. He also shares or holds many National League records such as the lowest earned run average (2.73) for a pitcher with 200 or more wins and most consecutive seasons with 200 or more strikeouts. In a speech filled with emotion, Tom Terrific spoke of his deep love and respect for the game which meant so much to him. He thanked his family and friends for support.*[42]

Now, after living most of his adult life in Connecticut, Seaver returned to his native California, establishing a winery with his wife, Nancy, near Calistoga. Seaver always has been a man of his times. Born into a middle-class family and raised during America's period of postwar prosperity, Seaver represented a new breed of player: independent, cerebral, educated. As the New York Mets' "franchise player," he was the spokesman for thousands of suburbanites, blue-collar workers, and immigrants united by their team's emergence as World Series champions in 1969. A man of profound opinions, he preferred not to disclose his personal opinions. Though he worked tirelessly on behalf of the Major League Baseball Players' Association, he never filed for free agency. Decades from now, fans will continue to visit his Cooperstown plaque, the only one in the Hall of Fame as of 2009 bearing a Mets insignia. In spite of Seaver's many complexities, to them, he will always be Tom Terrific.

**Notes and Sources**

1. Schoor, Gene. *Seaver.* Chicago: Contemporary Books Inc., 1986: 32.
2. Schoor: 58.
3. Schoor: 58.
4. Weaver, Earl, and Berry Stainback. *It's What You Learn After You Know It*

*All That Counts: The Autobiography of Earl Weaver.* Garden City, New York: Doubleday & Co. Inc., 1982: 171.

5. Bock, Duncan, and John Jordan. *The Complete Year-By-Year N. Y. Mets*

*Fan's Almanac.* New York: Crown Publishers Inc., 1992: 50.

6. Bock: 110.
7. Lang, Jack, and Peter Simon. *The New York Mets: Twenty-Five Years of Baseball Magic* New York: Henry Holt and Company, Inc., 1986: 133.
8. Allen, Maury. *After the Miracle: The Amazin' Mets – Two Decades Later.* New York: St. Martin's Press, 1989: 233.
9. Markusen, Bruce. *Tales from the Mets Dugout.* Champaign, Illinois: Sports Publishing LLC, 2005: 22.

10. Kiner, Ralph, and Danny Peary. *Baseball Forever*. Chicago: Triumph Books,
2004: 198.
11. Allen: 236.
12. Allen: 235.
13. Schoor: 125.
14. Allen: 237.
15. Allen: 237.
16. Weaver and Stainback: 171.
17. Bock: 75.
18. Schoor: 162.
19. www.imdb.com
20. Bock: 94.
21. Hamilton, Tim, ed. "That Championship Season 1973," in *Now The Fun Starts! The New York Mets Official 1983 Yearbook*. Flushing, New York: Doubleday Sports Inc., 1983: 6S.
22. Bock: 106.
23. Schoor: 194.
24. Schoor: 195.
25. Bock: 111.
26. Bock: 120.
27. Bock: 117.
28. Madden, Bill. "The True Story of the Midnight Massacre: How Tom Seaver Was Run Out of Town 30 Years ago." *New York Daily News*, June 17, 2007: par 9; [journal online]; Available from *www.dailynews.com*; Internet; accessed October 5, 2007.
29. Schoor: 235.
30. Bock: 138.
31. Schoor: 238.
32. Schoor: 238.
33. Schoor: 238.
34. Anderson, Sparky, and Si Burick. *The Main Spark: Sparky Anderson and the Cincinnati Reds*. Garden City, New York: Doubleday & Company, 1978: 224.
35. Madden: par 24.
37. Markusen: 88.
38. Anderson, op. cit.: 226.
39. Anderson, op. cit.: 281
40. Bock: 175.
41. Jensen, Paul, and Ken Valdiserri, eds. *Chicago White Sox 1984 Yearbook*. Chicago: White Sox Public Relations Department, 1984: 21.
42. Gafur, Rudy A.S. *Cooperstown Is My Mecca*. Toronto: Rudy A.S. Gafur, 1995: 100-101.

*www.baseball-reference.com*
*www.IMDB.com*
*www.retrosheet.org*
Allen, Maury. *After the Miracle: The Amazin' Mets – Two Decades Later.* New York: St. Martin's Press, 1989.
Anderson, Sparky, and Si Burick. *The Main Spark: Sparky Anderson and the Cincinnati Reds.* Garden City, New York: Doubleday & Company, 1978.
Appel, Martin. *Yesterday's Heroes: Revisiting the Old-Time Baseball Stars.* New York: Wm. Morrow & Co., 1988.
Aron, Eric. "Dick Williams," in *The 1967 Impossible Dream Red Sox: Pandemonium on the Field*, Bill Nowlin and Dan Desrochers, eds. Burlington, Massachusetts: Rounder Books, 2007.
Bock, Duncan, and John Jordan. *The Complete Year-By-Year N. Y. Mets Fan's Almanac.* New York: Crown Publishers Inc., 1992.
Gafur, Rudy A.S. *Cooperstown Is My Mecca.* Toronto: Rudy A.S. Gafur, 1995.
Hamilton, Tim, ed. "That Championship Season 1973," in *Now the Fun Starts! The New York Mets Official 1983 Yearbook.* Flushing, New York: Doubleday Sports Inc., 1983.
Jensen, Paul, and Ken Valdiserri, eds. *Chicago White Sox 1984 Yearbook.* Chicago: White Sox Public Relations Department, 1984.
Kiner, Ralph, and Danny Peary. *Baseball Forever.* Chicago: Triumph Books, 2004.
Lang, Jack, and Peter Simon, *The New York Mets: Twenty-Five Years of Baseball Magic.* New York: Henry Holt and Company, Inc., 1986.
Lyons, Douglas B. *The Baseball Geek's Bible: All The Facts and Stats You'll Ever Need.* London: MQ Publications Ltd., 2006.
Madden, Bill. "The True Story of the Midnight Massacre: How Tom Seaver Was Run
Out of Town 30 Years Ago," on the *New York Daily News* (June 17, 2007): 35 pars. [Journal Online]. Available from www.dailynews.com. Internet. Accessed October 5, 2007.
Manuel, John. "Coaching Legend Dedeaux Dies at 91," on *Baseball America* (January 6, 2006): 13 pars. [Journal Online]. Available from http://www.baseballamerica.com/today/news/060106dedeaux.html. Internet. Accessed February 2, 2008.
Markusen, Bruce. *Tales from the Mets Dugout.* Champaign, Illinois: Sports Publishing LLC, 2005.
Miller, Marvin. *A Whole Different Ballgame: The Sport and Business of Baseball.* New York: Carol Publishing Group, 1991.
Ranier, Bill, and David Finoli. *The 1979 World Champion Pittsburgh Pirates: When the Bucs Won It All.* Jefferson, North Carolina: McFarland & Company Inc., 2005.
Schoor, Gene. *Seaver.* Chicago: Contemporary Books Inc., 1986.
Weaver, Earl, and Berry Stainback. *It's What You Learn After You Know It All That Counts: The Autobiography of Earl Weaver.* Garden City, New York: Doubleday & Co. Inc., 1982.
Weissman, Harold, ed. *New York Mets Official 1975 Yearbook.* Flushing, New York: The New York Mets, 1975.

## And the Winner Is...

While the Mets embraced the championship trophy in October 1969, the individual hardware that was doled out later that year went to Tom Seaver. He won took home *The Sporting News* Pitcher of the Year Award, Cy Young Award, and the title of Sportsman of the Year by *Sports Illustrated* in December. While Dwight Gooden also won a Cy Young, no other Met has been named Sportsman of the Year. Seaver earned 23 of 24 votes cast—only first-place votes were given then—with Atlanta's Phil Niekro getting the lone other vote. Seaver woud go on to won two more Cy Youngs.

In 1969 there weren't as many awards as there are today. There was no Manager of the Year, which clearly would have gone to Gil Hodges (he did claim top manager honors from *The Sporting News*), and there was no MVP awarded for the brand-new NLCS, which might have been won by Art Shamsky (.538) or Cleon Jones (.427, 1 HR, 4 RBIs, 2 SBs). There was also no award for relievers. An often overlooked award that did go to a Met in January 1970 was the Babe Ruth Award, given by the New York Baseball Writers at their annual dinner to the best player of the World Series. It went to Al Weis, while the more acknowledged Series MVP—at the time given by *Sport* magazine and a relative newcomer compared to the Ruth Award—had gone to Donn Clendenon the day the World Series was decided.

The Gold Glove, which surprisingly no Met won despite the team's superior defense in 1969, does not publish voting results. Nor does the World Series MVP. No Met received votes for Rookie of the Year, but four Mets earned MVP votes. Seaver was the first Met to be runner up in the league MVP balloting—an award no Met won in the franchise's first 47 seasons. Here's how the top 10 voting for that award went in '69, plus Jerry Koosman's spot on the list, which tied future Met Joe Torre; another future Met, Rusty Staub, was the lone Expo on the list...with one vote:

| NL MVP | Team | Points |
|---|---|---|
| 1. Willie McCovey | Giants | 265 |
| 2. Tom Seaver | Mets | 243 |
| 3. Hank Aaron | Braves | 188 |
| 4. Pete Rose | Reds | 127 |
| 5. Ron Santo | Cubs | 124 |
| 6. Tommie Agee | Mets | 89 |
| 7. Cleon Jones | Mets | 82 |
| 8. Roberto Celemente | Pirates | 51 |
| 9. Phil Niekro | Braves | 47 |
| 10. Tony Perez | Reds | 28 |
| 23. Jerry Koosman | Mets | 6 |

# Art Shamsky

by Eric Aron

| Season | Age | G | AB | R | H | 2B | 3B | HR | RBI | BB | SO | SB | CS | BA | OBP | SLG |
|---|---|---|---|---|---|---|---|---|---|---|---|---|---|---|---|---|
| 1969 Mets | 27 | 100 | 303 | 42 | 91 | 9 | 3 | 14 | 47 | 36 | 32 | 1 | 2 | .300 | .375 | .488 |
| Career 8 Years | – | 665 | 1686 | 194 | 426 | 60 | 15 | 68 | 233 | 188 | 254 | 5 | 7 | .253 | .330 | .447 |

In the locker room celebration after the Mets won the 1969 National League pennant, he was quoted by the *New York Daily News* as saying, "I'll walk down the street in New York now and people will say, 'There's Art Shamsky of the Mets.' People used to laugh. They won't anymore."[1] Indeed, after his performance in the 1969 National League Championship Series, a three-game sweep over the Atlanta Braves, nobody would laugh. His seven hits in the NLCS led both teams, and, had the honor been bestowed, Shamsky might well have been named Most Valuable Player. He hit .300 during that Miracle Mets season and became a fan favorite, particularly among the area's large Jewish population.

Art Shamsky played professional baseball for 13 seasons, between 1960 and 1972, eight in the major leagues. Nicknamed Sham and Smasher, the lanky left-handed outfielder/first baseman began his career with the Cincinnati Reds organization and later became a key part of the 1969 New York Mets world championship offense. In addition to his contributions to the Mets, Shamsky is best known for his four consecutive home runs spread over two games in August 1966 while he was with Cincinnati. He is the only major leaguer to hit three home runs in a game without being in the starting lineup.

Arthur Louis Shamsky was born in St. Louis on October 14, 1941. He grew up in a predominantly middle-class Jewish area of University City. His father ran a small scrap-iron business. Art was the only son, and had an older sister. "We were Jewish but we weren't very religious," he told an interviewer. "We observed the holidays but we didn't make a big thing out of religion. About all I did as a player in recognizing the religion was to take off the major Jewish holidays."[2]

"As a young boy growing up, my life was basically two things, following the St. Louis Cardinals or playing baseball with my friends," Shamsky said.[3] He told another interviewer, "We used to put a quarter in the light machine at tennis courts just to hit some fungoes at night. We played every day, we played in the rain, we played every chance we got."[4] He listened to Harry Caray call Cardinals games on the radio and his biggest hero was Stan Musial.

Shamsky was an outstanding basketball and baseball player at University City High. Famous alumni of the school include playwright Tennessee Williams, 1960s Cubs southpaw Ken Holtzman, and one-time Mets outfielder Bernard Gilkey. Shamsky didn't try out for baseball until his senior year in high school. He played two games at Busch Stadium during the state high school playoffs, getting hits in both, but University City lost in the championship game.

"I wasn't spectacular," Shamsky said, "I hit only

about .300, and I didn't consider pro ball right away. I was only 16 when I graduated from high school."[5] After graduating in 1958, Shamsky attended the University of Missouri for a year, where he played college ball. He then decided to leave school to play professionally.

Shamsky got offers from many teams, and signed with the Cincinnati Reds on September 9, 1959. "My father would have preferred that I had gone into business, but he was into baseball and I think he was thrilled when I signed," Shamsky has said. "My mother certainly wanted me to go to college and become a doctor, of course. What else is a Jewish boy supposed to do?"[6]

Shamsky hit a home run in his first professional at-bat, for the Geneva Redlegs in the New York-Penn League. He was a teammate of Tony Perez and Pete Rose, whom he also roomed with while with Geneva in 1960. For the season, playing in 119 games, he hit .271, with 18 homers, and 86 RBIs, making the league all-star team. He led the league's outfielders in assists, with 24. Despite the presence of the two baseball superstar teammates, Shamsky said, "That Class D team was so bad that we got our manager fired with a third of the season left."[7] In a move Shamsky considered somewhat ironic, he was promoted to Class B Topeka while his teammates Rose and Perez remained in Class D. In a piece for the *New York Times* in 1986, Shamsky wrote, "I guess, though, when you stop to think about it, somebody knew something because they're still playing and making a lot of money and I'm watching."[8]

Shamsky hit .288 with 15 home runs and 66 RBIs in 116 games for the Topeka Reds of the Three-I League in 1961. Dave Bristol, who managed him in the minor leagues in 1961 and 1962 and later with the Reds, remembered the left-handed hitter's power. "It's Artie's wrists," said Bristol. "Watch Artie's wrists when he whips a bat and you won't be surprised by the long balls he hits.... They had a big barn behind the fence in right-center at Topeka. Artie's the only player I ever saw bounce a homer off the roof of that barn."[9]

His 1962 season was spent with the Macon Peaches in the Class A Sally League. He started out strong, hitting six homers in the first 13 games, but went on the shelf for seven weeks with a hand injury. He ended up on the disabled list when he had surgery to remove calluses from his left hand. In 81 games, he hit .284 with 16 home runs and 61 RBIs. Shamsky was promoted to the Reds triple-A affiliate San Diego Padres, where he spent two seasons in the Pacific Coast League. In 1963, he played in 150 games, batting .267 with 18 home runs and 68 RBIs. In 1964, the Padres, including Shamsky and teammates Tommy Helms, Don Pavelitch, Tony Perez, and other future major leaguers, won the PCL championship. Shamsky hit .272, slammed 25 home runs, and drove in 69, setting the record for the longest home run hit in the Padres' park, a tape-measure shot of 500 feet.[10]

Shamsky was now ready for the major leagues. "Art Shamsky has great potential," said San Diego general manager Eddie Leishman, who was named Minor League Executive of the Year after Shamsky and Co. took the '64 league title. "He certainly has the tools to make the grade and go far in baseball. He has the swing and actions of the Yankees' Joe Pepitone."[11]

Shamsky made his major league debut on April 17, 1965, against the very team he loved growing up as a child, the St. Louis Cardinals. In front of family and friends at Busch Stadium, he batted for pitcher Gerry Arrigo in the seventh inning of a game the Cardinals won, 8–0. Shamsky had no easy task for a debut, as he was called upon to hit against one of the greatest pitchers of all time. "I had to pinch-hit against Bob Gibson, a great pitcher, and I was really nervous. I ended up striking out and I was very upset. However, I got over it, and the next time I faced him I pinch-hit a home run."[12]

Shamsky's first hit came five days later at Wrigley Field against the Chicago Cubs, when he lined a pinch-hit single to right in the ninth inning off Ted Abernathy. It was during his rookie season that Shamsky got to face fellow Universal City High alum Ken Holtzman, four years his junior and also a rookie in the big leagues. Shamsky walked and sacrificed in his only two career plate appearances against the Cubs southpaw, an example of the strict platooning that Shamsky endured during his career (he hit .223 with three home runs in 112 career at-bats against lefties and .255 with 65 homers in 1,574 at-bats against righties).

Shamsky did not end up as a regular outfielder in 1965, but instead became the top pinch hitter on a team boasting a lineup of All-Stars and future Hall of Famers. Pete Rose played in all 162 games and was the National League's starting second baseman in the All-Star Game; Frank Robinson belted 33 home runs in his final season as a Red, and Tony Perez hit .260 in his rookie year. Cincinnati had two 20-game winners, Sammy Ellis and Jim Maloney. The 1965 Reds finished in fourth place at 89–73, eight games behind the Los Angeles Dodgers.

After playing for Santurce in the Puerto Rican Winter League in the winter of '65, Shamsky returned to Cincinnati the following spring. He appeared in 96 games for the Reds, again serving primarily as a Pinch hitter and reserve outfielder. His team finished in seventh place in the National League with a record of 76–84, falling to 18 games behind the Dodgers.

During the 1966 season, Shamsky made history on August 12 and 14. Over the span of two games at Crosley Field in Cincinnati, he homered in four consecutive at-bats. On the 12th, the Reds and the Pittsburgh Pirates played an extra-inning affair in which 11 home runs were hit. The Pirates were ahead six times and the Reds three. With the Pirates ahead 7–6 in the eighth inning, Shamsky came into the game to play left field.

In the bottom of the inning, with a runner on base, Shamsky homered off Al McBean to give Cincinnati an 8–7 lead. The Pirates tied the game in the ninth and took the lead in the 10th on a Willie Stargell home run. In the bottom of the frame, facing pitcher Roy Face, Shamsky hit another shot into the right-field seats to tie the game again. Finally, in the home 11th, with Pittsburgh up 11–9, Shamsky faced pitcher Billy O'Dell. On a 3-and-1 count, he homered a third time, another two-run blast to tie the game at 11–11. Teammate Pete Rose called it "One of the greatest clutch-hitting exhibitions ever seen."[14]

In the end, however, despite Shamsky's heroics, the Pirates came away with a 14–11 victory in 13 innings. After the game, he took the loss hard and declined an opportunity to go on a Cincinnati post-game radio show, *Star of the Game*. "How can you be a star when your team loses?" he commented.[15]

Despite becoming the first player to homer three times after not starting, Cincinnati manager Dave Bristol sat out Shamsky for the second game of the series against Pittsburgh lefty Woodie Fryman. He then sat out the next game against right-hander Vernon Law. When Bristol sent him up to bat for catcher Johnny Edwards in the seventh, he connected on a two-run shot against Law that gave the Reds a brief 2–1 advantage. After the game, a 4-2 loss to the Bucs, the wild speculation and media circus began. Could he do it again? Could he make it five in a row?[16]

Shamsky said he wasn't even aware he had tied a major-league record. "I didn't know a thing about it until the Cincinnati public address announcer made mention of it after my fourth homer. I can't say I tried to hit any of them.... It's a funny thing. They come pretty easy when I don't try."[17]

Shamsky's teammates made light of the event. "Just think," kidded Sammy Ellis, "a few days ago Artie was just an average bench warmer. Today he's a national hero."[18] Outfielder Tommy Harper said, "Artie's act sure is a tough one to follow. I struck out after three [actually, two] of those four homers. No one noticed it, though, they were still cheering Artie."[19] Shamsky himself said, "If I do hit the fifth straight one, there will be champagne for everyone—on me."[20]

After the Pirates series, the Reds moved on the Los Angeles to play the Dodgers. He sat against Dodgers lefty Claude Osteen on the night of August 15, but Shamsky stepped up to the plate to bat for Tony Perez against righty reliever Bob Miller with no outs and nobody on base, and lined a single to right field. "If I was going to hit one out of the park that would have been the pitch."[21] Sportswriter Jack Disney wrote the next day, "By lining a base hit to right in the eighth inning at Dodger Stadium, the Cincinnati outfielder was stopped three bases short of immortality."[22] The *Los Angeles Herald-Examiner* ran a parody of *Casey at the Bat* that concluded, "But there is no joy in any town—just tears and sadness mingled; After four straight homers, mighty Shamsky only singled.[23]

Shamsky's four consecutive home runs put him in impressive company. Other players to hit four successive home runs over two games: Jimmie Foxx,

Mickey Mantle, Hank Greenberg, Ralph Kiner, and his hero Stan Musial. That season, Shamsky hit 21 home runs in just 234 at-bats, finishing second on the team behind Deron Johnson's 24 in more than 500 at-bats. Despite his slugging, Shamsky finished the season batting only .231 with just 47 RBIs.

The next season, 1967, was Shamsky's last with the Reds. He had had an injury-riddled year, struggling primarily with back issues that plagued his entire career. He hit only .197 with 13 RBIs in '67 and hit as many home runs all season (three) as he did the previous year in a game he entered in the eighth inning. Shamsky was traded to the Mets on November 8 for utility infielder Bob Johnson.

Initially, Shamsky was not happy about the trade. He learned the news while recovering from surgery in St. Louis to remove a cyst from his tailbone. Reds general manager Bob Howsam called him at home, and Art expected to be asked how he was feeling. He immediately said he felt great and was looking forward to next season. "That's good," said Howsam, "because we just traded you to the Mets."[24]

Shamsky was leaving an organization and teammates he had been with for his entire career to the team with the worst record in baseball—in five of its six years of existence. After Howsam called, Mets GM Bing Devine phoned to reassure Shamsky about coming to New York. Devine was previously general manager of the Cardinals and had known Shamsky growing up. Things were different, he told Art, and the fans were great. "Two days later I picked up the St. Louis newspaper and read that Bing Devine was just named general manager of the Cardinals. ... Two days earlier he had told me how good the Met organization was and how great New York City was, and now he left to come back home. It was the longest winter of my life."[25]

Still in 1968, things were looking brighter for both Shamsky and the Mets. Three weeks after Shamsky was traded to New York, the Mets acquired manager Gil Hodges in a trade with Washington. Johnny Murphy, who helped negotiate the Hodges deal, succeeded Bing Devine as general manager and brought up young talent from the minors that—combined with Hodges at the helm—brought a winning atmosphere to a team that had only known misery in its brief existence. Upon arriving in New York, Art joked that, like Sandy Koufax in 1965, he would miss any World Series game that fell on a major Jewish holiday. Everybody laughed; no one could have predicted the miracle to come one year later.

The 1968 New York Mets were the youngest team in the major leagues, with an average age of 26. Shortstop Bud Harrelson and outfielder Ron Swoboda were the only two everyday players in the Opening Day lineup who had opened the season with the club in '67. The team now had young players like Tommie Agee and Al Weis, both brought over in a trade with the Chicago White Sox, and Ken Boswell made the club for the first time out of spring training. Boswell, like Shamsky, the part of a left-handed platoon, became Art's close friend and roommate.

It was pitching, however, that would carry the team to a world championship. Flamethrower Nolan Ryan won the job as a starter in spring training, and rookie Jerry Koosman, the greatest southpaw in Mets history, made the team despite a mediocre September call-up in 1967. Koosman finished second in Rookie of the Year voting to the Reds' Johnny Bench in 1968. Then, of course, there was Tom Seaver, who himself had won the Rookie of the Year award the previous season. Though the Mets barely avoided the basement in the final season with a 10-team National League, the 1968 Mets had a different look and feel than their predecessors

Despite only a .238 average, Shamsky hit 12 home runs with 48 RBIs. "While we weren't breaking any records in 1968, we were competitive," Shamsky said. "We were a little less than a .500 ball club through the middle of the season. The one thing we did have, though, was harmony. It was a clubhouse filled with people who generally liked each other. We had a few 'characters' and some loners, but, all in all, the 1968 Mets were a team that pulled for each other."[26]

Shamsky, a bachelor, also spent his first offseason in New York. "The city had put its claws on me. I learned that New York City is really one of a kind," he said. "The city energizes you. There is never a dull moment in New York City. After a few months I fell in love with the city. And I got used to 'Auttie.' It's Artie in New York City lingo. I was okay with it now."[27]

The next season, 1969, was the first year of divisional play and new National League teams were added in Montreal and San Diego. Gil Hodges, who had suffered a heart attack right before the end of the 1968 season, predicted that the Mets would win 85 games. His club won 100.

Yet the season could not have started any worse for Shamsky. After playing in only three spring-training games, his back went out. "I was about to play first base that afternoon [March 15, 1969], and we were taking batting practice on the other field. When we finished our swings, I said to Kenny [Boswell], 'C'mon down in the right-field corner and throw me some grounders.' He did, and about the 15th one, I bent over and felt something snap in my back. It was like somebody had taken a gun and shot me. I felt this pain shoot all the way down my left leg."[28] After what was initially thought to be back spasms, Shamsky was diagnosed with a slipped disk that was pressing against the sciatic nerve. Doctors told him to get plenty of bed rest, take pain medications, and even wear a protective corset. He was unable to get out of bed for a week. One doctor even told him he might never play again. His condition began to improve, however, and he soon felt strong enough to pick up a bat.

After three weeks, Shamsky was given permission by the medical staff to work out, but he played the entire 1969 season in pain, even taking pain medications throughout the playoffs and World Series.[29] Just before the Mets were to leave St. Petersburg and head north in April, Shamsky was informed by Hodges and GM Johnny Murphy that he was going on the disabled list. After three weeks on the DL, rehab games at triple-A Tidewater would follow.

Shamsky did not take the news well. The last thing he wanted was to get sent down by a ninth-place team. He even considered retirement. He didn't know if he would ever be recalled to the Mets and was given no guarantees by Hodges. He was placed on the disabled list on April 8 and came off on April 29. He was optioned to Tidewater and flew to Syracuse for a game against the Chiefs. In his first game he got three hits, including a grand slam, to highlight a 10-run first inning in a 13–2 Tidewater victory. Mets farm director Whitey Herzog saw him hit the grand slam and said, "What the hell are you doing here?"[30]

After batting .289 with five doubles, four homers, and 12 RBIs in 11 games with the Tides, Shamsky was recalled by the Mets on May 13. In his first game back, he hit a pinch-hit RBI single against the Atlanta Braves at Shea. From his time rehabbing, he had learned how to become a better hitter, using a heavier bat and hitting to all fields. He adjusted his swing to make better contact and cut down on his strikeouts. In 1969, he struck out only 32 times in 302 at-bats

With the Mets, Shamsky became part of a crowded outfield with Ron Swoboda, Tommie Agee, Cleon Jones, and Rod Gaspar, who'd come north with the club after Shamsky went down. Gil Hodges liked to platoon his players, using as many of them as possible. For the left-right combo in right field, Shamsky shared time with Swoboda, and he made the most of it. He began swinging the bat with power and was hitting nearly .350 in August.

Photo courtesy of mestilverman.com

*Art Shamsky*

Shamsky got the game-winning RBI five times that season. None came bigger than on June 6. He lined an eighth-inning pinch-hit single off pitcher Gary Ross to break a 3–3 tie in San Diego. The Mets won, 5–3, setting a franchise-record eighth in a row. They wound up winning 11 in a row. After trailing the Cubs by 10 games on August 13, New York took over first place for good on September 10 and clinched the National League East title on September 24. Shamsky played in 100 games and for only time in his professional career, he hit .300—exactly that figure—to place second on the team to Cleon Jones's .340. He was also second on the team in home runs with 14, behind Tommie Agee's 26.

Shamsky indeed sat out Rosh Hashanah with the Mets battling for first place late in the season. In typically miraculous fashion of the final push that month, the Mets won both ends of a September 12 doubleheader by identical 1–0 scores with the pitchers driving in the only run in each game. The Mets won again the next day with Shamsky still sitting it out in the hotel. Back on the field on Sunday and batting cleanup...the Mets lost. In 11 games after sitting out the Jewish holiday, Shamsky batted .306 with a homer and six RBIs—with the Mets losing just three times with him in the lineup (and one of those defeats came after the Mets clinched the division).

In the National League Championship Series against the Atlanta Braves, Hodges continued his platoon system and Shamsky was in the starting lineup to face right-handed pitching—batting cleanup—for all three games of the best-of-five series. He went 7-for-13 at the plate (.538), but had only one RBI.

After the three-game sweep of Atlanta, the Mets faced the heavily favored Baltimore Orioles in the World Series, winner of 109 regular season games. With left-handers Mike Cuellar and Dave McNally making four appearances for the Orioles, Shamsky sat for four of the five games. In Game Three, against right-hander Jim Palmer, he started and batted fourth. He entered Gamed One as a pinch hitter with two outs in the ninth inning. The Mets trailed 4–1 and had runners on first and second. "I would be lying if I didn't say my heart was beating as fast as it could," he said. "Even though I had hit over .500 in the playoffs and was swinging the bat well, I was nervous."[31] Shamsky grounded out to second baseman Davey Johnson to end the game. The Mets won the next four games to win the Series, but Shamsky had no hits in six at-bats.

While the 1970 Mets were unable to repeat as NL East champs, Shamsky was almost as solid as 1969. Splitting time between first base and right field, he led the team in hitting with a .293 batting average, with 11 home runs and 49 runs batted in. His 122 games played and 49 RBIs were career highs as a major leaguer. But 1971 was another injury-plagued season, as he lost his platoon positions at first base and right field to left-handed hitters Dave Marshall and Ed Kranepool. Playing in 68 games, Shamsky hit only .185 with five home runs and 18 RBIs. On October 18, 1971, the Mets traded Shamsky along with three minor-league pitchers to the Cardinals for four players, including Harry Parker and Jim Beauchamp.

Shamsky did not survive spring training, however, and was unconditionally released by the Cardinals on April 9, 1972. He signed as a free agent with the Cubs but played in only 15 games, hitting .125 with no home runs and one RBI. The Oakland A's purchased his contract in June but released him on July 19 after he had appeared in eight games with no hits in seven at-bats. "This time I decided to quit," he told an interviewer. "Three teams didn't want me. That was enough."[32]

While still with the Mets, Shamsky had opened restaurants with former Yankee and Met Phil Linz, and later became a real estate consultant. He was a play-by-play and color broadcaster for the Mets in 1980 and 1981. In 1980, he worked alongside Bob Goldsholl for cable, and in '81, he did radio and cable TV with Ralph Kiner, Bob Murphy, and Steve Albert. In a 1999 episode of the sitcom *Everybody Loves Raymond,* Shamsky appeared as himself along other 1969 teammates. (The dog on the show was named Shamsky and others, including comedian Jon Stewart, have followed suit in their pet naming.) In 2004, Shamsky wrote a book with Barry Zeman called *The Magnificent Seasons.* It is the story of the three championship sports teams in New York in 1969 and 1970, the Mets, Jets, and Knicks.

In 2007, it was announced that Shamsky, Ken Holtzman, and Ron Blomberg would manage in the new Israel Baseball League. "I decided to get involved in the new Israeli Baseball League because I like the challenge of starting something at the very beginning... particularly in a country that is just beginning to develop the game of baseball," Shamsky was quoted as saying in *Mets Inside Pitch*. "Managing is something I thought I would never be interested in, but this situation is different. There are many transplanted New Yorkers in Israel, and many New York Mets fans. I'm hoping that my credibility will help the new league get off on the right track."[33] Shamsky's team, the Modi'in Miracle finished in third place in the six-team league. The league halted operations after one season.

For his eight-year major-league career, Shamsky hit .253 with 68 home runs and 233 RBIs. He has been married twice and has two daughters and, as of 2009, five grandchildren. As of 2009, he was still a New York resident. Shamsky is a member of the New York Jewish Sports Hall of Fame and was inducted into the National Jewish Sports Hall of Fame in 1994.

Shamsky expressed pride in what the 1969 Mets accomplished. "History will show that a team that was a 100-to-1 long shot at the beginning of the season became the toast of the sports world seven months later," he said "I have always said that the 1969 New York Mets probably weren't the greatest baseball team to win the World Series, but they were certainly one of the most memorable."[34]

**Notes and Sources**

1. Shamsky, Art, with Barry Zeman. *The Magnificent Seasons.* New York: Thomas Dunne Books, 2004: 142.
2. Allen, Maury. *After the Miracle: The 1969 Mets Twenty Years Later.* New York: Franklin Watts, 1989: 198.
3. Shamsky and Zeman: 255.
4. Allen: 199.
5. "Art Shamsky's Long Drive for Majors May Be Over," *St. Louis Post Dispatch,* April 16, 1965.
6. Allen: 199.
7. Shamsky, Art. "Rose and Perez Can Do It, So Why Not Me, Too?" *New York Times,* April 6, 1986.
8. Ibid.
9. Lawson, Earl. "Shamsky Looks Like Comedian—N.L. Pitchers Wish He Were." *Cincinnati Post,* May 28, 1966.
10. Ibid.
11. "Art Shamsky's Long Drive for Majors May Be Over," *St. Louis Post Dispatch,* April 16, 1965.
12. Art Shamsky clipping, National Baseball Hall of Fame.
13. Epstein, Andy. "Out of Left Field: With a Miracle Met." *Mets Inside Pitch,* May 2007: 20.
14. Lawson, Earl. "Shamsky Equals Record, Hitting 4 HRs In Row." *Cincinnati Post,* August 27, 1966.
15. Burick, Si. "Shamsky lets his stick do the Swaggering." *Dayton Daily News,* August 15, 1966.
16. Disney, Jack. "End of Shamsky Era." *Los Angeles Herald Examiner,* August 16, 1966.
17. "Shamsky Bat to Fame Hall," *Cincinnati Post and Times-Star,* August 16, 1966.
18. Ibid.
19. Ibid.
20. Ibid.
21. Disney, "End of Shamsky Era."
22. Ibid.
23. Ibid.
24. Shamsky and Zeman, p. 96.
25. Ibid.
26. Shamsky and Zeman: 99.
27. Shamsky and Zeman: 102.
28. Young, Dick. "Disabled and Displaced... Art Swings Back." *New York Daily News,* July 19, 1969.
29. Young, Dick. "Shamsky Plays With Pain." *New York Daily News,* March 2, 1970.
30. Allen: 204.
31. Shamsky and Zeman: 155.
32. Allen: 201.
33. Epstein: 21.
34. Shamsky and Zeman: 186.


Allen, Maury. *After the Miracle: The 1969 Mets Twenty Years Later.* (New York: Franklin Watts, 1989.)

Burick, Si. "Shamsky lets his stick do the Swaggering." *Dayton Daily News,* August 15, 1966.

Disney, Jack. "End of Shamsky Era." *Los Angeles Herald Examiner,* August 16, 1966.

Epstein, Andy. "Out of Left Field: With a Miracle Met," *Mets Inside Pitch,* May 2007.

Lawson, Earl. "Shamsky Equals Record, Hitting 4 HRs In Row." *Cincinnati Post,* August 27, 1966.

Lawson, Earl. "Shamsky Looks Like Comedian—N.L. Pitchers Wish He Were." *Cincinnati Post,* May 28, 1966.

Shamsky, Art. "Rose and Perez Can Do It, So Why Not Me, Too?" *New York Times,* April 6, 1986.

Shamsky, Art, with Barry Zeman. *The Magnificent Seasons.* (New York: Thomas Dunne Books, 2004.)

Young, Dick. "Disabled and Displaced... Art Swings Back." *New York Daily News,* July 19, 1969.

Young, Dick. "Shamsky Plays With Pain." *New York Daily News,* March 2, 1970.

"Art Shamsky's Long Drive for Majors May Be Over," *St. Louis Post Dispatch,* April 16, 1965.

"Shamsky Bat to Fame Hall," *Cincinnati Post and Times-Star,* August 16, 1966.

Art Shamsky clip file, National Baseball Hall of Fame.

## They Shoot Baskets, Don't They?

After the New York Jets shocked the world by upsetting the Baltimore Colts in Super Bowl III in January 1969, and the New York Mets further stunned the globe by beating the heavily-favored Baltimore Orioles in the World Series that fall, the planet was seemingly getting used to New York teams winning in unlikely fashion against Baltimore-based clubs. In the spring of 1970, the sport was basketball, the heroes were the New York Knicks and the surprised Crab City nemesis the Baltimore Bullets. By March 1970, though, the script was getting a little worn, so the Baltimore club was only a first-round opponent in the National Basketball Association playoffs, though in truth the Bullets proved scrappier than either the Colts or the Orioles in their battles against New York.

The Knicks, who had swept the Bullets in the playoffs a year earlier, won the 1969–70 playoff opener at Madison Square Garden in double overtime. They went to Baltimore and won the second game, 106–99. The Bullets, however, captured the next two games to even the series. After the Knicks took Game Five, the Bullets won the next contest to force a seventh game—something the Orioles didn't even approach the previous October against the Mets. The Bullets got 32 points from Earl "The Pearl" Monroe, but he was outdone by a balanced Knicks attack that featured the fearsome shooting of Dick Barnett and Dave DeBusschere (28 points each), the grace of Walt "Clyde" Frazier, the leadership of Willis Reed, the feistiness of Cazzie Russell, and the defense of "Dollar" Bill Bradley. New York had prevailed over Baltimore once more, 127–114.

The Milwaukee Bucks, by comparison, seemed a veritable pushover in the next round, but the five-game victory for Red Holtzman's club tasted sweet after having lost to the Boston Celtics in the conference finals the previous year. The Los Angeles Lakers—and the championship—awaited. The Lakers had been to the NBA finals seven times—and lost seven times—since 1959, when the team was still located in Minneapolis.

Lakers legends Elgin Baylor, Jerry West, and Wilt Chamberlain went head to head with the determined Knicks. With the series tied, Reed went down with a painful hip injury in Game Five, but New York rallied from 13 down at the half to win at the Garden. Without their captain in Game Six, Chamberlain scored 45 points as L.A. romped. The Knicks feared Chamberlain would run wild again in the deciding game. With the entire Garden anxiously watching the player's entrance, Reed emerged slowly but surely after enduring a cortisone shot. Playing with a noticeable limp, he hit his first two shots. Reed played roughly half the game, but the Knicks defense was inspired and held the Lakers under 100 for the only time that series to take the title, the team's first championship...and the city's third.

The Knicks were the only one of the three New York clubs to continue the momentum after the city's magical 18 months of sport. (For those thinking about a quartet, the New York Rangers lost in the National Hockey League quarterfinals in the spring of 1969 and again in 1970.) The Knicks went to the finals again in 1972, losing a rematch with the Lakers, who ended their skid in the finals on the ninth try. The Knicks won another championship in 1973, a precursor to the "Ya Gotta Believe" Mets of that autumn, though the Mets fell a game short of their own second title.

Art Shamsky, a '69 Mets outfielder, later wrote a book (with Barry Zeman) about the three convergent championship runs. In *The Magnificent Seasons,* Knicks great Walt Frazier said, "The Jets and Mets put a lot of pressure on us. We had to keep it up." They did.

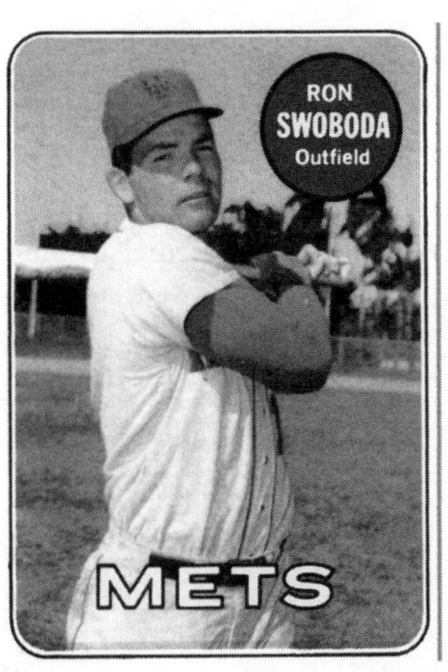


# Ron Swoboda

by Len Pasculli

| Season | Age | G | AB | R | H | 2B | 3B | HR | RBI | BB | SO | SB | CS | BA | OBP | SLG |
|---|---|---|---|---|---|---|---|---|---|---|---|---|---|---|---|---|
| 1969 Mets | 25 | 109 | 327 | 38 | 77 | 10 | 2 | 9 | 52 | 43 | 90 | 1 | 1 | .235 | .326 | .361 |
| Career 9 Years | – | 928 | 2581 | 285 | 624 | 87 | 24 | 73 | 344 | 299 | 647 | 20 | 14 | .242 | .324 | .379 |

The casual fan of the game might know Ron Swoboda for "The Catch" in the 1969 World Series, or for his home run heroics in a game against Hall of Famer Steve Carlton, or for Casey Stengel's early summation: "He will be great, super, even wonderful. Now if he can only learn to catch a fly ball." The true fan of the man will also know Ron Swoboda for his wit, heart and humility, and for his drive to become the best outfielder he could be.

Ronald Alan Swoboda was born in Baltimore on June 30, 1944 to John and Delores Swoboda. His father was a waist gunner in World War II and then a mechanic, salesman, and teacher. His mother was a secretary, case manager, and supervisor in social services. At Sparrows Point High School, he played three sports. Ron's baseball coach was Andy McDonald. Swoboda also helped his Sparrows Point basketball team to the state title, and he was the goalkeeper and captain of his soccer team. He played goalkeeper for the freshmen soccer team at the University of Maryland as well.

But of course baseball was his game, and Ron started playing at age nine. He played 15-to-17-year-old amateur baseball for Sterling "Sheriff" Fowble, acclaimed Baltimore City coach and scout for the Cincinnati Reds and New York Mets. When he was 18, Swoboda played on the Dolphin Club. At 19 he played on Leone's Boys Club, where his coach was Walter Youse, a scout for the Baltimore Orioles. But somehow, Youse let Swoboda get away. In 1963, the summer following his first year at the University of Maryland, he played in the AAABA tournament in Johnstown, Pennsylvania. Following a wonderful performance in that tournament, Swoboda was offered a $35,000 contract to sign with the Mets by scout Pete Gebrian. He signed as a Met on September 5, 1963.

Swoboda was invited to major league spring training in 1964 and made a fine showing with a home run outburst. He was assigned to the Mets triple-A club, the Buffalo Bisons in the International League. In his first professional game, Swoboda had three hits including a home run in five at bats. In his second game, he struck out four times. When he reflected on that somewhat inauspicious start to his professional baseball career, Ron would say, "That's about how my career went. That was it in a microcosm."[1] Later on in the summer of 1964, he played for the Williamsport Mets in the Eastern League, the Mets double-A club, but returned to Buffalo for the playoffs later that summer.

On April 12, 1965, he made his debut with the New York Mets. He wore uniform number 14 that year. (The next year the Mets traded for Ken Boyer who took number 14, and Swoboda switched his uniform number to 4. He remained in that number throughout his Mets career—manager Gil Hodges took 14 in 1968 and it was later retired in his honor—though Swoboda switched back to 14 in his subsequent major league stops.)

Ron's first major league manager was Casey Stengel. Swoboda was fascinated by Stengel, who called him "Saboda," among other things. Here was a boy of 20 with so much to learn being managed by a man of 75 with so much to teach. Ron remembers Casey's teaching style. While Casey appeared to be talking to the reporters—he of course loved to talk to the reporters—he would often deliver a message to his ballplayers by directing an instructive or critical remark about that player to the reporter when he knew the player was within earshot.

And then there was a less fondly remembered lesson Casey taught Ron. On May 23, 1965, in a game against the Cardinals in St. Louis, the Mets took a 7–2 lead into the ninth inning, with Mets reliever Larry Bearnarth on the mound. The bases were soon loaded and the Mets clinging to a three-run lead with two outs. Dal Maxvill lifted a fly ball

Photo courtesy of Dwayne Labakas Collection

*Ron Swoboda started his Mets career wearing 14, a number manager Gil Hodges reclaimed for all time.*

out to right field, but Ron lost it in the sun. The ball got by him, and three Cardinals scored. When Ron batted in the 10th, he did not get on base. As the Mets took the field in the bottom of the 10th, Swoboda's pent-up frustration seemed to burst. When he reached the top of the dugout steps, he angrily stomped on a batting helmet with the intent of smashing it. Instead, his foot stuck in the helmet, and he continued to kick at it to shake it off while taking the field. Casey rushed over to him, grabbed him by the shirt and hollered, "When you missed that fly ball, I didn't go looking for your watch to break it. So quit busting up the team's equipment. You're done for today." In the locker room, Swoboda thought he just blew his major league chance. He sat there, alone, and cried.

Ron Swoboda was one of the "Youth of America," Stengel's expression for the corps of young players who would take the Mets from worst to first in four short years—players like Cleon Jones, Bud Harrelson, Tug McGraw, and Swoboda, who all made their debut in 1965; Nolan Ryan, who came aboard in 1966; Tom Seaver, Jerry Koosman, and Ken Boswell in 1967; Jim McAndrew and Duffy Dyer in 1968; and Gary Gentry and Wayne Garrett in 1969. Casey Stengel said the Mets were "amazin', amazin', amazin'." Swoboda knows simply—and humbly—that he was part of something special in 1969: "If you're lucky enough to get into the World Series, that's a privilege. All I was trying to do was play baseball."[2]

Swoboda was pictured on the May 6, 1968 cover of *Sports Illustrated* with the caption "Slugger Ron Swoboda." Indeed he was. So many of his 73 career home runs were memorable. As a rookie in 1965, in only his second major league at-bat, the right-handed slugger hit a long, pinch-hit home run over the back wall of the bullpen at Shea Stadium against Turk Farrell of the Houston Astros. "The longest ball I ever hit," says Swoboda.[3]

He hit four home runs in his first 16 at-bats and 10 in his first 90 at-bats. Swoboda hit a career-high 19 home runs that year, which led the Mets, and was the most home runs by a Mets rookie until Daryl Strawberry hit 26 in 1983.

Swoboda's rookie home run record was actually victimized by an umpiring error. On April 30, 1965, at a game in Cincinnati, he came to bat in the first

PHOTO COURTESY OF METSILVERMAN.COM

*Ron Swoboda was always good for a quote as a player and after his career ended he was just as comfortable holding the microphone as a broadcaster in several cities.*

inning with the bases loaded and one out against right-handed pitcher John Tsitouris. Crosley Field had a concrete outfield wall with a bright yellow line at the top. However, above that home run line and set back about four inches from the concrete wall in center field was a plywood wall installed to prevent batters from having to look into the headlights of the cars on the nearby elevated highway. Swoboda hit a grand slam home run off the plywood wall—except second base umpire Frank Secory never signaled that the ball left the playing field. When center fielder Vada Pinson threw the ball back to the infield, one run scored but the other runners held, and all Swoboda got was a long single. Mets coach Yogi Berra was ejected from the game for arguing the call. Ron recalls Yogi's famous quote: "Anybody who couldn't hear that ball hit the wood is blind." Swoboda hit two grand slams in his career. And then there was this one that got away.[4]

On July 4, 1966, he hit a ball onto the left-field roof in Connie Mack Stadium in Philadelphia. On August 4 that season, he hit a three-run, pinch-hit, walk-off home run to beat the Giants 8–6 at Shea Stadium against Bill Henry. (Swoboda remembers, "Every time he threw it, I hit it hard somewhere.") He hit home runs in four consecutive games for the Mets in April 1968. Later that month, on April 30, he homered off Philadelphia's Chris Short to give the Mets a 1–0 victory. On September 13, 1969, with the Miracle Mets on their way to their first championship season, Swoboda hit a grand slam home run, his first, in the eighth inning to beat the Pittsburgh Pirates, 5–2.

Even more memorable was his performance two days later. On September 15, 1969, a night when the Cardinals southpaw Steve Carlton struck out 19 batters, setting a new major league record, Swoboda hit two two-run home runs off Carlton at Busch Stadium. In his other two at bats, Swoboda struck out to aid Carlton's record, but his two-run homer in the fourth, with two strikes on him, put the Mets up 2–1, and his two-run homer in the eighth, again with two strikes, gave the Mets the 4–3 victory.

Swoboda hit a home run for every 36 at-bats while playing for the Mets. However, perhaps his most satisfying hit was not a homer, but rather his double in the eighth inning of the fifth and final game of the 1969 World Series that broke a tie and helped New York defeat those Orioles from his hometown of Baltimore. Another significant hit in Ron's career was a single off Mike Kekich of the Dodgers on August 4, 1968. That hit was the only one Kekich allowed that day.

Fielding did not come as easily to Swoboda as hitting—hence the nickname "Rocky"—but Swoboda had a strong and accurate arm and always worked hard at improving his fielding technique. He had 53 outfield assists in his career and a lifetime .972 fielding percentage. He was the Mets left fielder in 1965 and 1966 but slid over to right when Tommy Davis joined the Mets in 1967, while Cleon Jones covered center. When the Mets traded for center fielder Tommie Agee from the Chicago White Sox in 1968, the Mets were now able to play Cleon in left, and Swoboda and newly-acquired Art Shamsky in right. Ron also played 20 games at first base for the Mets under manager Wes Westrum in 1967, including Opening Day.

After escaping the cellar in 1966, the Mets slipped back to last place in 1967 and the beleaguered Westrum resigned on September 20. Gil Hodges became the Mets manager beginning with the 1968 season. Although he played for both Gene Mauch and Ralph Houk later in his career, Hodges was Swoboda's most influential manager. "Gil was so on top of the game," says Swoboda. "There was no one better than Hodges. He was interesting, and creative, but in a way a player could understand." Swoboda enjoyed perhaps his best season under Hodges in 1968, batting .242 with 450 at-bats (a career high) in 132 games, and he led the team in RBIs with 59, triples with six, and walks with 52, all personal bests. He played 125 games in right field in 1968 with career highs in total chances (231), putouts (217), and assists (14). However, with the flashy fielding and switch-hitting rookie outfielder Rod Gaspar joining Swoboda and left-handed hitting Shamsky in 1969, Hodges's strategy of platooning batters reduced Swoboda's playing time to 109 games and 327 at-bats in that championship year. In fact, Swoboda did not get a single at-bat in the 1969 National League Championship Series, in which the Mets swept Atlanta in three games, because the Braves started three right-handed pitchers—Phil Niekro, Ron Reed, and Pat Jarvis. Hodges was consistent and stayed with his platoon plan, even in crunch time. Right-handed hitters Ed Charles and Donn Clendenon, who would be MVP in the World Series against Baltimore, did not bat against the Braves either; righty-swinging Al Weis, whose two crucial late-inning hits helped sink the Orioles in the World Series, batted only once against the Braves.

In the 1969 World Series, Ron and the other Mets righties got their chance when the Orioles started Mike Cuellar and Dave McNally, two lefties, in four of the five games. In that Series, one of the more famous upsets in baseball history, Swoboda batted 15 times and collected six hits, the most by any player from either team, with three coming in Game Four and two in Game Five. His eighth-inning double in Game Five off Eddie Watt—a right-handed reliever—knocked in Cleon Jones from second base with the go-ahead run and helped seal the championship for the Miracle Mets. Yet, this is not the moment in the 1969 Series for which Swoboda is most remembered.

Despite a less than stellar defensive reputation, the single event for which he is best known was made in the field, in the fourth game. With the Mets holding onto a 1–0 lead in the ninth, courtesy of Donn Clendenon's second inning home run off Mike Cuellar, Frank Robinson and Boog Powell each singled to put runners on first and third with one out for the Orioles. Brooks Robinson then hit a smash toward right-center that Swoboda raced for and caught backhanded as he dove flat out to his right. Frank Robinson tagged and scored but Swoboda's grab surely prevented the go-ahead run from

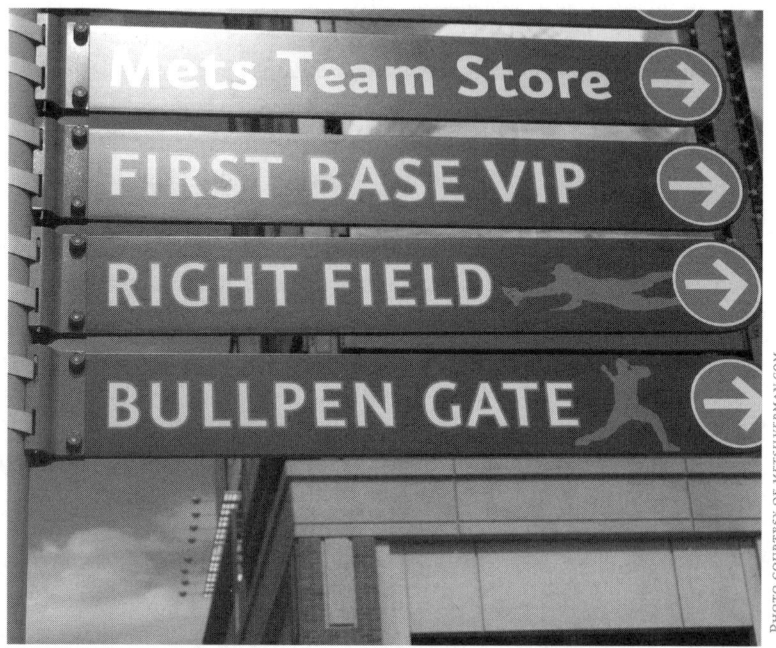


PHOTO COURTESY OF *METSILVERMAN.COM*

*The patch of Shea Stadium ground in right field that Ron Swoboda so famously protected in Game 4 of the 1969 World Series is now paved over, but his catch lives on in the minds of Mets fans and as a silhouette marker at Citi Field.*

coming home and potentially evening the Series. The Mets won the game in the 10th inning when pitcher Pete Richert cleanly fielded J.C. Martin's sacrifice bunt but then hit Martin with the throw to first base, allowing the winning run to score. *Baseball Weekly* later ranked Swoboda's catch as one of the "10 Most Amazing Plays of All-Time."[5]

Rocky Swoboda, Mets hero, had numbers somewhat similar to his 1969 campaign in the year that followed the championship, but it wound up being his final year with the club. On March 31, 1971, Ron Swoboda and infielder Rich Hacker were traded to the Montreal Expos for outfielder Don Hahn. Swoboda appeared in just 39 games for the Expos, and on June 25 he was traded to the New York Yankees for Ron Woods.

"I remember putting on the Yankee uniform and walking out onto the field in the old Yankee Stadium," Ron says. "I was not prepared to be awed...but I was." Swoboda played 152 games for the Yankees, during which he collected 69 hits with four home runs. Swoboda's last game in the majors turned out to also be the final game at original Yankee Stadium before it was closed for two years during reconstruction. On September 30, 1973, Swoboda was the last Yankee to man the fabled patch in center field where Joe DiMaggio and Mickey Mantle had stood with the monuments still in play nearby.

Ron had also flirted with a place in history at the start of the 1973 season as well. The last year of his playing career was the first year of the designated hitter rule in the American League. On April 6, 1973, Opening Day, the Yankees' Ron Blomberg appeared in the game against the Boston Red Sox at Fenway Park as the first "designated pinch hitter" in major league history. But had the Red Sox started a left-handed pitcher that day instead of right-hander Luis Tiant, Swoboda would have been the first. Swoboda did DH against lefty John Curtis in the third game of that season-opening series.

Swoboda was released by the Yankees on December 11, 1973. He was signed as a free agent by the Atlanta Braves on January 3, 1974, but he was released before the 1974 season began. Swoboda finished his nine-year playing career with a lifetime batting average of .242 in 928 games (his career high was .281 in 1967). He hit 73 home runs and knocked in 344 runs. His lifetime slugging average was .379 and his on-base percentage .324.

Ron and his wife Cecilia, whom he met at the University of Maryland, were married on October 9, 1965. ("I admire everything she does," says Ron.) They have two sons, Ron, Jr. and Brian Christopher. After baseball, Swoboda turned to writing and TV and radio broadcasting, holding jobs in New York, Milwaukee, Phoenix, and New Orleans.

He once ran a restaurant with Ed Kranepool, his former Mets teammate and roommate. On March 1, 1999, he appeared on the popular TV show *Everybody Loves Raymond* with other members of the 1969 New York Mets, including Agee and Kranepool. Ron's hobbies and interests include studying impressionist art and New Orleans history. In his adopted hometown of New Orleans, he served as broadcaster and unofficial Mets ambassador when the franchise had its Class AAA team there in 2007–08. He remained in the broadcast booth with the Zephyrs when the franchise was taken over by the Florida Marlins in 2009.

**Notes and Sources**

1. Golenbock, Peter, *Amazin': The Miraculous History of New York's Most Beloved Baseball Team*, New York: St. Martin's Press, 2002: 165
2. Freeman, Kevin, "Ron Swoboda, October star of the Miracle Mets, savors his good fortune," *Intelligencer Journal*, July 16, 2004, p. D-1.
3. Gergen, Joe, "Shea's Amazin' Grace," New York *Newsday*, July 25, 2004.
4. Leonard Koppett, "3 Home Runs Hit Off Spahn in 6th; Swoboda's 'Grand Slam' Is Ruled a Single--Rose Goes 5 for 5 at Bat," *New York Times*, May 1, 1965: 22.
5. *Baseball Weekly* Cover Report, July 24, 2002.

Much of the information contained in this article came from an interview by the author with Ron Swoboda on July 15, 2004, in Landisburg, Pennsylvania. The author also consulted several baseball-related websites. In addition, he made use of the following:

Adell, Ross and Samelson, Ken, *Amazing Mets Trivia*, (Lanham, Maryland: Taylor Trade Publishing, 2004).

Cohen, Stanley, *A Magic Summer: The '69 Mets*, (New York: Harcourt Brace Jovanovich, 1988).

Freeman, Kevin, "Ron Swoboda, October Star of the Miracle Mets, Savors His Good Fortune," *Intelligencer Journal*, July 16, 2004.

Gergen, Joe, "Shea's Amazin' Grace," *New York Newsday*, July 25, 2004.

Golenbock, Peter, *Amazin': The Miraculous History of New York's Most Beloved Baseball Team*, (New York: St. Martin's Press, 2002).

## Rocky vs. Lefty

After his playing days were over, Ron Swoboda often joked that he was grateful to at least have compiled a few seconds of highlight material throughout his nine-year career. He was referring, of course, to his game-saving catch in Game 4 of the 1969 World Series, a moment forever immortalized as one of the greatest plays in Series—and Mets—history.

But Swoboda's otherwise ordinary, some might even say disappointing, baseball legacy is not completely absent of additional glimpses at the superstar potential many believed he possessed. His performance against Steve Carlton in another 1969 game in St. Louis would have merited more than enough highlight-reel consideration had Swoboda not eclipsed the feat with "The Catch" less than a month later.

With the Mets having passed the Cubs in the standings only five days before, and surging to an improbable four-game lead behind 10 straight September wins, they faced future Hall of Famer Carlton in a key Eastern Division matchup with the third-place Cardinals on September 15. Lefty brought a 16–9 record into the game, enjoying the best success of his young career thus far after posting 27 wins in his first two full seasons in the big leagues.

The lanky 24-year-old southpaw appeared poised to at least temporarily derail the Mets' late-summer miracle, as it was apparent early on that he had complete command of his dominating fastball and lethal hard slider. The game's historic implications began to grow with each passing strikeout, and Swoboda would account for two of Carlton's record-setting 19 Ks on the evening.

Swoboda, known as Rocky to his loyal followers, had played in 95 of New York's 146 games so far that season, compiling a less-than-imposing .237 batting average with seven home runs and driving in 45. New York's 10-game tear had been halted the previous day in Pittsburgh, and the course of a beleaguered young franchise seemed to hang in the balance as Carlton's mastery evoked more miserable Mets memories than pennant promises.

But Swoboda changed all of that with two swings of the bat, the first coming with two strikes and a man on in the top of the fourth to take a 2–1 lead. St. Louis countered with two more in the fifth off starter Gary Gentry, and the Mets trailed 3–2 when Swoboda stepped to the plate for his final at-bat in the top of the eighth. Carlton got two strikes on the No. 5 hitter for the fourth time in as many at-bats, but Swoboda connected for his second two-run homer of the game and an emphatic 4–3 victory during the crucial stretch run. Carlton's single-game strikeout record was matched the next season by none other than New York's Tom Seaver, and later surpassed by Roger Clemens, Kerry Wood, and Randy Johnson. But while Carlton went on to fill endless reels of celluloid with his 24-year career highlights, it was the less likely Swoboda who earned top billing on September 15, 1969.

—Linc Wonham

# Ron Taylor

by Maxwell Kates

| Season | Age | W | L | Pct | G | GS | SV | IP | H | BB | SO | WHIP | ERA |
|---|---|---|---|---|---|---|---|---|---|---|---|---|---|
| 1969 Mets | 31 | 9 | 4 | .692 | 59 | 0 | 13 | 76 | 61 | 24 | 42 | 1.118 | 2.72 |
| Career 11 Years | – | 45 | 43 | .511 | 491 | 17 | 72 | 800 | 794 | 209 | 464 | 1.254 | 3.93 |

A biography may be defined as a "remarkable odyssey through life and the lessons learned." This description could have suited virtually anyone, but Bart Mindszenthy adapted it to introduce Ron Taylor before the Empire Club of Canada. Taylor's odyssey ranged from the University of Toronto (the only alumnus to play major-league baseball), to the Ontario Society of Professional Engineers, the Major League Baseball Players Association, and the Ontario Medical Association. His dry, self-deprecating sense of humor pervaded his multifaceted, half-century-plus career. When approached to deliver a 20-minute autobiographical speech before the Empire Club in October 2004, Taylor replied, "Well, we've got the first five minutes covered."

Ronald Wesley Taylor was not the first member of his family to lend numerous talents to a career that crossed geographical and interdisciplinary borders. His paternal grandfather worked in a variety of professions in urban and rural environments on both sides of the Atlantic. Walter Taylor and his wife, Elizabeth, immigrated to Canada from Ireland, settling in Flesherton, Ontario, as pioneer farmers. The Taylors eventually moved to Toronto, where Walter established a confectionery in the east end of the city. He took a second job as a streetcar driver for the Toronto Transit Commission in order to feed a family that grew to include five children. Tragedy struck the Taylor household in 1919 when Walter became one of millions to fall victim to the global influenza epidemic. Their son Wesley, at the age of 13, left school to support his family, accepting a job at Dunlop Tire and Rubber. Although his employer endured financial difficulties during the Great Depression, Wesley never lost his employment. Consequently, he remained at Dunlop out of loyalty for better than 50 years. Wesley married Maude Evans, a Welsh immigrant with a noteworthy family legacy of her own. Her father, William, was a cavalry soldier during the Boer War who fought the Battle of Mafeking under Colonel Robert Baden-Powell. After he died, his widow, Emily, led the family to immigrate to Canada—"their intended destination was Australia but they missed the ship."

Ron Taylor was born on December 13, 1937, a brother to older sister Carole.[1] He was raised in the north end of Toronto, joining the Leaside Baseball Association at the age of eight.[2] Although he was a natural left-hander, his mother feared that young Ron would suffer cardiovascular ailments from extensive use of his left arm, and insisted that he learn to pitch right-handed—"Insist? She tied my left hand behind my back!" He played at Talbot Park, a facility of unusual configurations. As only 275 feet separated home plate from the left-field fence, commuter traffic on Eglinton Avenue often saw windows fall prey to home run balls. Meanwhile, a baseball could travel 400 feet to right field and remain in fair territory. Worse yet, there were two light standards in play. As Howie Birnie, longtime president of the Leaside Baseball Association, once remarked, "You have to be part mountain goat to play here."[3] To play there, candidates were required to either live in Leaside or be enrolled at St. Anselm Catholic School. Under ordinary circumstances, Taylor would have been disqualified. Had the school's recreational director, Phil Stein, not made an exception for Taylor, he might never have developed into a professional baseball player.

By 1954, Taylor had graduated to the Metropolitan Motors Club, where at 16 he managed to baffle 21-year-old hitters.[4] Often attending Taylor's games was Chester Dies, a sheet-metal worker and part-time scout for the Cleveland Indians. Despite Dies's rave reviews over Taylor's performances, his telephone calls to the Indians' area scout remained unanswered. Consequently, Dies took Taylor to Cleveland for an uninvited tryout at Municipal Stadium, even paying for the young pitcher's train ticket.[5] Although initially admonished for bringing a prospect without an invitation, Dies ultimately received permission for Taylor to throw in the bullpen.[6] Pitching coach Mel Harder, impressed by what he saw, invited Taylor to return the following day.[7] This time, he pitched to Al Lopez, the Indians manager, who had begun his career catching Walter Johnson some three decades earlier.[8] Impressed, Lopez and minor league director Laddie Placek offered Taylor a contract on the spot, signing the pitcher for $4,000, the maximum bonus allowed at that time without roster restrictions.[9] An airman with the Royal Canadian Air Force (Auxiliary 411) fighter squadron, Taylor had considered training to become a pilot until receiving his offer from the Indians.

Now 18, Taylor attended his first training camp with the Indians in 1956. Out of 250 players, he was assigned uniform number 247.[10] Bewildered, he later remarked that "I knew that 'T' was low in the alphabet, but not that low." Taylor was befriended by a Cleveland farmhand who wore number 9, outfielder Roger Maris. Reporting to Daytona Beach of the Florida State League for the 1956 season, he went 17–11 with a 3.13 ERA in 227 innings. After the season, Taylor decided he wanted to return to school to pursue his education. Although Placek offered to register him at the Case Institute in Cleveland, Taylor decided that he would rather return to Canada to finish Grade 13 before enrolling as an engineering student at the University of Toronto. According to his plan, Taylor would pitch only during the summer, missing spring training for the duration of his education. Placek, though reluctant to accept, agreed to Taylor's conditions.[11]

By 1961, Taylor had risen through Cleveland's farm system, pitching for Fargo-Moorhead, Minot, Reading, and Salt Lake City. Pitching for Minot, he was one of the Northern League's three premier pitchers, along with Gaylord Perry and Bo Belinsky. Perhaps more importantly, he graduated from the University of Toronto in 1961 at the top in his class of engineers.[13] After the season, Taylor asked Walter "Hoot" Evers, Cleveland's farm director, to guarantee him a spot on the rotation at Salt Lake City along with an invitation to the major league training camp. Evers agreed and at spring training in Tucson, Taylor pitched 23 scoreless innings to earn a spot in the major-league rotation.[14]

Starting the second game of the 1962 season, Taylor faced Boston's Bill Monbouquette at Fenway Park on April 11.[15] Through 11 innings, spectators saw nothing but zeroes on the Green Monster scoreboard as both pitchers were hurling extra-inning shutouts. However, Taylor surrendered a leadoff triple to Carl Yastrzemski in the bottom of the 12th. After two intentional walks, he surrendered a grand slam to Carroll Hardy. Despite the loss, the *Cleveland Plain Dealer* called Taylor's performance "one of the most remarkable pitching performances in all baseball history."[16] He beat Dean Chance of the Los Angeles Angels, 3–2, on April 24 but was demoted to Jacksonville a month later. Tim McCarver, who caught for the Atlanta Crackers that season, described Taylor as "lights out that year." Pitching every three days, he won 12 and lost 4 with an ERA of 2.62 as Jacksonville won the International League pennant.[17] Little did either Taylor or McCarver realize that both would return to the major leagues in 1963—as teammates.

After the 1962 season, Taylor pitched for the San Juan Senadores of the Puerto Rican Winter League.

When St. Louis Cardinals manager Johnny Keane saw him pitch, he immediately telephoned general manager Bing Devine. On the grounds that the Canadian hurler was "not afraid of the bat," Keane insisted on arranging a deal for him.[18] On December 15, 1962, Taylor was traded with infielder Jack Kubiszyn to the Cardinals for first baseman Fred Whitfield.[19] Developing a sinker-slider to complement his fastball, Taylor won nine games and saved 11 with a 2.84 ERA in Stan Musial's farewell tour of the major leagues.[20] His first save of the 1963 season was at the expense of the eventual world champion Los Angeles Dodgers on April 28. He struck out Frank Howard and got Ron Fairly to fly out to right before giving up a single to John Roseboro and fanning Moose Skowron to end the game.[21] Meanwhile, Taylor returned to Toronto in the winter to pursue work as an electrical engineer.

Taylor remained productive in 1964, winning eight games in 63 appearances as the Cardinals won their first National League pennant in 18 years. His quiet and reserved personality made him a contrast from a clubhouse full of future broadcasters. However, he was a fierce competitor on the mound as the situation warranted—as he demonstrated in Game Four of the 1964 World Series. Already trailing the New York Yankees two games to one, the Cardinals appeared headed for another defeat when starter Ray Sadecki surrendered three runs in one-third of an inning. After Roger Craig pitched solidly in relief, the Cardinals claimed the lead in the sixth inning on a grand slam by Ken Boyer.[22] Now leading by one run, manager Keane summoned Taylor from the bullpen.[23] Taylor held the lead by pitching four no-hit innings against the Yankees, whose lineup included former minor league teammate Roger Maris. The walk Taylor surrendered to Mickey Mantle in the eighth inning represented the only baserunner he allowed.[24] A loss would have given the Yankees a 3–1 Series lead, but instead the Cardinals forced a tie. Mike Shannon, one of the future broadcasters on the Cardinals, later said, "We shut down that powerful Yankee club. If we don't win that game, I don't even know if we're going back to St. Louis."[25] Back to St. Louis the Series went, where Bob Gibson pitched his legendary complete-game win in Game seven to secure the championship.

The defending world champions disappointed in 1965, languishing in seventh place at the June 15 trading deadline.[26] Satisfying the need for a left-handed reliever, general manager Bob Howsam acquired Hal Woodeshick from the Houston Astros at a cost of Taylor and pitcher Mike Cuellar.[27] Immediately, Taylor knew it was "a bad deal for both clubs." Unhappy in Houston, he saw his ERA soar to an astronomical 5.71 in 1966.[28] After the season, his contract was sent outright to Oklahoma City. As he told Maury Allen of the *New York Post* years later, he became frustrated by the direction of his baseball career.

"I felt I wasn't used properly. I never had a chance to pitch, and in order to be effective, I needed to pitch a lot," Taylor said. Meanwhile, Bing Devine had left the Cardinals to become general manager of the New York Mets. "Bing... asked me if I could pitch. I told him I was sound—'Get me out of here!' He said that he thought he could make a deal."[29] The following day, February 10, 1967, Taylor's contract was purchased by the Mets triple-A affiliate at Jacksonville.[30] A change of scenery may have been just what the doctor ordered for Taylor. He earned a spot on the Opening Day roster for the Mets in 1967, leading the team with eight saves in 50 games while setting a personal mark with a 2.34 earned run average.[31] He allowed only one home run all season, to Pittsburgh's Manny Jimenez on April 17.[32] (Taylor's homerless streak lasted 92 innings, well into the 1968 season, when he allowed a ninth-inning blast by the Dodgers' Ted Savage on June 23.)[33]

"In New York, I really found a home. I worked hard and I pitched well," Taylor said. The Mets, meanwhile, were ensconced as the doormat of the National League. The team lost 101 games in 1967 to finish in last place for the fifth time in its six-year history, "When there was a rainout, half the team held a victory party," Taylor said. The Mets bade the cellar farewell in 1968 when they signed Gil Hodges as their manager. Although a record of 73–89 typically goes unnoticed, for the Mets in 1968, it was one small step in the right direction. Taylor contributed by tying Jack Hamilton's club saves record with 13 and finished fourth among senior circuit hurlers with 58 appearances.[34]

After the 1968 season, Taylor joined several major leaguers on a tour of military hospitals in

Guam, the Philippines, and Okinawa.[35] The following year, he traveled to Saigon to visit soldiers in war-ravaged South Vietnam after the Tet Offensive. This second tour offered him "the chance to meet doctors and talk to them about what they were doing."[36]

As the Mets prepared to entertain the expansion Montreal Expos on Opening Day of 1969, the franchise had never finished higher than ninth place or won more than 73 games. Moreover, Taylor's two appearances in the 1964 World Series with the Cardinals marked the extent of postseason play among his teammates.[37] Bookmakers in Las Vegas gave the Mets 100-to-1 odds to win the pennant, while in the Shea Stadium clubhouse, only Jerry Grote foresaw his team as contenders.[38] Ignoring the disbelievers, Gil Hodges assigned specific roles to his entire roster. Through a combination of natural talent and proper communication, Hodges foresaw his players contending in 1969.

"Everybody knew what their role was," Taylor remembered. "Everybody was quite happy with their role—even more so when we started to win."[39] Taylor was consistent once again, pitching in 59 games out of the bullpen. In a dozen appearances from May 30 to June 24, he worked 15 scoreless innings.[40] By this point, the Mets were surprising even baseball experts as they stood in second place with a 38–28 record, five games behind the division-leading Chicago Cubs.[41] While his 2.72 earned run average was virtually identical to his 1968 record, Taylor went 9–4 for a team that won 100 games to earn a National League East division title.[42]

Taylor pitched two scoreless innings in Game One of the NLCS, preserving Tom Seaver's 9–5 victory over the Braves and earning the first save in League Championship Series history.[43] He came on the next day to get the last out in the fifth inning and also threw a scoreless sixth to earn the win. Taylor was familiar with the Atlanta lineup, and offered the following anecdote from the regular season which featured two of their Hall of Fame sluggers.

"Orlando Cepeda's in the on-deck circle and Henry's up. So Hodges comes up to me and says, 'I want you to put Henry on and face Cepeda.'"

Taylor, who had a history of trouble facing Cepeda, insisted, "No, I want Aaron."

"Hodges said 'You *what*?' I knew he was angry. When he got angry, that jugular vein popped out of his neck. He said, 'You want to pitch to Aaron. You better get him out.'"[44]

Aaron grounded out to the infield.

After sweeping the Braves in the Championship Series, the Mets faced the Baltimore Orioles in the World Series. Taylor pitched in relief of Tom Seaver once again in Game One, limiting Baltimore to one baserunner—a walk to Paul Blair—in two innings.[45] Although the Mets were defeated by Mike Cuellar, Taylor's former St. Louis and Houston teammate, in the opener, they took a 2–1 lead in the second game. After retiring the first two Orioles in the bottom of the ninth, Jerry Koosman walked Frank Robinson and Boog Powell. With the tying run on second and Brooks Robinson at the plate, Hodges called Taylor from the bullpen to save the game and tie the Series at a game apiece.[46]

"I got to 3-and-2 on him and they were off and running on the pitch; it was the worst possible situation for me," Taylor said. In a classic case of role reversal, Robinson hit a grounder to third baseman Ed Charles, who threw the ball to Donn Clendenon at first for the final out of the game.[47]

Taylor was sitting in the dugout at Shea Stadium four days later, on October 16, when Davey Johnson flied out to Cleon Jones in left field for the last out of the deciding Game Five. The Mets were world champions. For Taylor, the experience was both exhilarating and humbling:

"After we won … we were riding down Broadway in that ticker-tape parade and the crowds were cheering and the paper was floating down from high above from those office buildings. I couldn't stop thinking that this was the path that MacArthur, Eisenhower, and Kennedy had ridden. I never felt so euphoric," Taylor said.[48]

Taylor remained a mainstay in Hodges's bullpen for two more seasons, becoming the Mets' first-ever Opening Day winner, over the Pirates at Forbes Field in 1970.[49] The Canadian's contract was sold to Montreal on October 20, 1971, but rather than wearing the Expos' tricolor cap, Taylor found himself dressed in the all-yellow double-knits of the San Diego Padres.[50]

The Expos released him on April 20, 1972, five days into the season, without having appeared in a game, he signed with San Diego on the same day.[51] Taylor surrendered five home runs in four relief appearances, pitching for the last time on May 14 in relief of Clay Kirby at Montreal's Jarry Park.[52] The final batter he faced was a Mets teammate only one season earlier—Ken Singleton.[53] At 34, Taylor knew it was time to call it a career.

If there were a chance of Taylor spending any more time in a major league clubhouse, it would be more likely as a doctor than as a baseball player. During that road trip to Montreal, Taylor took a sojourn to his hometown for an interview with the dean of student affairs at the University of Toronto medical school. Hank Aaron and Orlando Cepeda now paled by comparison as Taylor faced the dean in an interview.

"You graduated in engineering in 1961. What have you been doing for the past 11 years?"

"Playing major league baseball."

"What's *that?*"

Taylor knew he was in trouble. After providing a response, the associate dean explained what the odds were against the former world champion.

"We very rarely accept people over 30. We don't want people changing careers."

"My career died a natural death," Taylor pleaded. "My arm went dead."

The dean then asked to see his transcript. Scanning the grades, he turned to Taylor and asked, "Are these *yours*? With these grades, if you were 25, you'd be in. What I suggest to you is to go back and enroll in an honors course in all the pre-med courses—organic chemistry, microbiology. If you get the same grades, we'll consider you."

Taylor asked, "What are the odds?"

"Depends on the personality of the registrar. About 50-50."

"Those sound like good odds to me."

"I moved back into my old bedroom. I was single at the time and didn't have any responsibilities," Taylor said.[54] His daily routine would appear draconian even to a Rhodes scholar. He attended classes daily from 8 a.m. to 5 p.m., slept for four hours, and studied until 7 the next morning.[55] Asked to produce references, Taylor offered a glowing letter of recommendation from Mets president and Montreal native M. Donald Grant.[56] Excelling academically as expected, Taylor overcame all probabilities as his candidacy was accepted. He spent the summer of 1973 managing the Lethbridge Lakers of the semi-professional Alberta Major League.[57] Under Taylor's tutelage, the Lakers advanced to represent Alberta at the national finals held in New Brunswick. Taylor also returned to Shea Stadium that summer to make an appearance at Old Timers Day.[58]

He remembered the astonishment of his classmates that a middle-aged student was in their midst. As he told members of a baseball class at Seneca College in Toronto, "They just assumed I was the maintenance man. They were looking for my tool kit."

Hardly a janitor or a volunteer patient, Taylor persisted for four years and graduated from medical school in 1977. He was appointed team physician to the Toronto Blue Jays in 1979, and also pitched batting practice for several years at Exhibition Sta-

Photo courtesy of metsilverman.com

*Ron Taylor*

dium. Taylor began a general practice in midtown Toronto, working six days a week, often exceeding 12 hours a day at the office. Two evenings a week, he operated the S.C. Cooper Sports Medicine Clinic at Toronto's Mount Sinai Hospital.

Mount Sinai was significant for Taylor on several counts. Not only did he practice there during his residency, but it was also where he met the mother of his children. Rona Douglas was a nurse when she met Taylor, and they married on September 26, 1981.[59] Their oldest son, Drew, was born in August 1982, while younger son Matthew was born in April 1984. Matthew pursued studies in history and film while Drew decided to follow in his father's footsteps. Which footsteps? Baseball or medicine? After graduating from the University of Michigan, Drew was signed by the Blue Jays in 2006. He pitched at the Rookie League level for two seasons. He pitched in the independent Frontier League in 2008.

Although Ron Taylor's schedule left no room for hobbies, he amassed an impressive collection of rings over the years. They include his wedding ring, two for his world championships as a player, two earned as team doctor for the world champion Blue Jays in 1992 and 1993, and another to commemorate the All-Star Game held at SkyDome in 1991. However, pointing to the engineering ring on his left hand, Taylor said, "It's the only one you see." He was inducted into the Canadian Baseball Hall of Fame in 1985, and into Canada's Sports Hall of Fame eight years later. In 2006 he was inducted into the Order of Ontario by Lieutenant Governor James K. Bartleman for his work in medicine.

Into his 70s, he showed little inclination toward retirement. John Koopman of the Empire Club of Canada described Taylor's life as "a power of will." Before the era of free agency, Taylor served as his own agent. Without the deal with Laddie Placek, he would never have attended spring training. In the absence of a subsequent deal with Hoot Evers, his major league career may have ended before it began. Finally, if his negotiations to enter the University of Toronto medical school had not succeeded, he would not have practiced medicine. His baseball career remained an important component of his career, which he explained as follows:

"I might be able to name ten doctors in my graduating class and perhaps fifteen engineers. But I can name all my World Series teammates, both with the Mets and the Cardinals. The pressures we went through ... when you win championships like those, you're like brothers for life. That how we are, we're all brothers."

**Acknowledgements**

Wanda Chirnside, Eric Cousineau, Scott Crawford, Alan Gans, Bill Humber, Anthony Kalamut, Ben Kates, Nanda Lwin, Kelly McNamee, T. Kent Morgan, Ron Taylor, Rona Taylor, Dan Turner, Tom Valcke, Max Weder, Eric Zweig

**Notes and Sources**

1. "Ron Taylor" Brooklyn: Topps Chewing Gum Inc., 1964: 183.
2. Dan Turner, *Heroes, Bums, and Ordinary Men.* (Toronto: Lester & Orpen Dennys, 1988), 104.
3. Bob Elliott, *The Northern Game: Baseball The Canadian Way.* (Toronto: SportClassic Books, 2005), 137.
4. Elliott, 136.
5. Turner, 104.
6. Elliott, 138.
7. Elliott, 138.
8. Arthur Daley, "The Two Managers," *New York Times*, September 26, 1954, 39.
9. Elliott, 138.
10. Elliott, 138.
11. Elliott, 138.
12. Elliott, 139.
13. Turner, 105.
14. Elliott, 139.
15. *www.retrosheet.org*
16. Turner, 106.
17. Elliott, 139.
18. Turner, 106.
19. *www.baseball-reference.com*
20. Turner, 106.
21. *www.retrosheet.org*
22. Turner, 107.
23. Elliott, 141
24. Turner, 107.
25. Elliott, 141.
26. Elliott, 142.
27. *www.baseball-reference.com*
28. Turner, 107.
29. Maury Allen, *After the Miracle: The Amazin' Mets—Two Decades Later.* (New York: St. Martin's Press, 1989), 42.
30. Harold Weissman, *The Mets Official 1967 Year Book.* (Flushing, New York: The Metropolitan Baseball Club, Inc., 1967), 41.
31. Duncan Bock and John Jordan, *The Complete Year-by-Year N.Y. Mets Fan's Almanac.*, (New York: Crown Publishers Inc., 1992), 54.

32. Harold Weissman, *The Mets Official 1968 Year Book.* (Flushing, New York: The Metropolitan Baseball Club, Inc., 1968), 43.
33. Harold Weissman, *The Mets Official 1969 Year Book,* (Flushing, New York: The Metropolitan Baseball Club, Inc., 1969), 21.
34. Bock, 63.
35. Elliott, 144.
36. Elliott, 144.
37. Bock, 78.
38. Bock, 65.
39. Bruce Markusen, *Tales from the Mets Dugout,* (Champaign, Illinois: Sports Publishing LLC, 2005), 44.
40. Harold Weissman, *The Mets Official 1970 Year Book.* (Flushing, New York: The Metropolitan Baseball Club, Inc., 1970), 17.
41. *www.retrosheet.org*
42. Weissman (1970), 17.
43. Turner, 107.
44. Markusen, 44-45.
45. Turner, 108.
46. *www.retrosheet.org*
47. Elliott, 143.
48. Allen, 45.
49. Harold Weissman, *The Mets Official 1971 Year Book,* (Flushing, New York: The Metropolitan Baseball Club, Inc., 1971), 22.
50. *www.baseball-reference.com*
51. Elliott, 143.
52. *www.baseball-reference.com*
53. Elliott, 144.
54. Allen, 44.
55. Elliott, 145.
56. Elliott, 144.
57. Allen, 44.
58. Turner, 111.
59. Harold Weissman, *The Mets Official 1974 Year Book.* (Flushing, New York: The Metropolitan Baseball Club, Inc., 1974), 59.
60. Elliott, 146.

*www.baseball-reference.com*
*www.retrosheet.org*
"Ron Taylor" Brooklyn: Topps Chewing Gum Inc., 1964: 183.
Allen, Maury. *After the Miracle: The Amazin' Mets—Two Decades Later.* (New York: St. Martin's Press, 1989.)
Bock, Duncan, and John Jordan. *The Complete Year-By-Year N. Y. Mets Fan's Almanac.* (New York: Crown Publishing Inc., 1992.)
Daley, Arthur. "The Two Managers," *New York Times,* September 26, 1954.
Elliott, Bob. *The Northern Game: Baseball The Canadian Way.* (Toronto: Sport Classic Books, 2005.
Markusen, Bruce. *Tales from the Mets Dugout.* (Champaign, Illinois: Sports Publishing LLC, 2005.)
Turner, Dan. *Heroes, Bums, and Ordinary Men.* (Toronto: Lester & Orpen
Dennys, 1988.)
Weissman, Harold. *The Mets Official 1967 Year Book.* Flushing, New York: The Metropolitan Baseball Club, Inc., 1967.
Weissman, Harold. *The Mets Official 1968 Year Book.* Flushing, New York: The Metropolitan Baseball Club, Inc., 1968.
Weissman, Harold. *The Mets Official 1969 Year Book.* Flushing, New York: The Metropolitan Baseball Club, Inc., 1969.
Weissman, Harold. *The Mets Official 1970 Year Book.* Flushing, New York: The Metropolitan Baseball Club, Inc., 1970.
Weissman, Harold. *The Mets Official 1971 Year Book.* Flushing, New York: The Metropolitan Baseball Club, Inc., 1971.
Weissman, Harold. *The Mets Official 1974 Year Book.* Flushing, New York: The Metropolitan Baseball Club, Inc., 1974.

## Leading Man/Men

The name Ed Kranepool has long graced the top of many of the categories in the all-time leader charts for Mets offense, and with good reason: No one has played as long as Kranepool. He debuted as a Met at the Polo Grounds barely two months after graduating James Monroe High School in the Bronx in 1962 and played at least a portion of each of the club's first 18 seasons, appearing in his final game in 1979. He was the last Original, Amazin', and "Ya Gotta Believe" Met who never left the team.

Going back to 1969, though, Kranepool had been a sporadic starter and spent parts of several seasons in the minors. How did he stand on the all-time lists back then? Since *ultimatemets.com* and *baseball-reference.com* has this information available for both offense and pitching, it seems silly not to investigate Tom Seaver's legacy at the same time we dip into Steady Eddie's. Keep in mind, however, that in '69, Seaver had pitched exactly three years in the major leagues. They say the cream rises to the top—The Franchise rose above the franchise almost immediately.

Saves became an official statistic in 1969, but we're crediting Ron Taylor—the club's saves leader

*continued on next page*

*continued*

through '69—with the 21 saves he had for the club before it became kosher plus the 13 he had as an Amazin' Met. Rate stats for batters are based on 1,000 at-bats and ERA is based on 300 innings. Winning percentage is based on 40 decisions. Note that while Seaver (.640) surpassed Jerry Koosman (.610) after the 1969 season, the two were light years ahead of the field; teammate Don Cardwell was third with a career Mets winning percentage of .385 through 1969.

The name on the left side of each stat features the Mets career leader through 1969, while the person on the right side is the all-time leader through the 2009 season.

**OFFENSE**

| Career through 1969 | All-Time |
|---|---|
| GAMES | |
| Ed Kranepool 887 | Ed Kranepool 1,853 |
| AT-BATS | |
| Ed Kranepool 2,883 | Ed Kranepool 5,436 |
| RUNS | |
| Cleon Jones 278 | Darryl Strawberry 662 |
| HITS | |
| Ed Kranepool 713 | Ed Kranepool 1,418 |
| DOUBLES | |
| Ed Kranepool 110 | Ed Kranepool 225 |
| TRIPLES | |
| Ron Swoboda/Bud Harrelson 18 | Jose Reyes 73 |
| HOME Runs | |
| Ed Kranepool 62 | Darryl Strawberry 252 |
| RBIS | |
| Ed Kranepool 292 | Darryl Strawberry 733 |
| STOLEN BASES | |
| Cleon Jones 68 | Jose Reyes 301 |
| WALKS | |
| Ed Kranepool 223 | Darryl Strawberry 580 |
| STRIKEOUTS | |
| Ron Swoboda 477 | Darryl Strawberry 960 |
| TOTAL BASES | |
| Ed Kranepool 1,041 | Ed Kranepool 2,047 |
| BATTING AVERAGE | |
| Cleon Jones .284 | John Olerud .315 |
| ON-BASE PERCENTAGE | |
| Ron Hunt .344 | John Olerud .425 |
| SLUGGING PERCENTAGE | |
| Frank Thomas .434 | Mike Piazza .542 |

**PITCHING**

| Career through 1969 | All-Time |
|---|---|
| GAMES | |
| Al Jackson 184 | John Franco 695 |
| INNINGS | |
| Al Jackson 980.7 | Tom Seaver 3,045 |
| WINS | |
| Tom Seaver 57 | Seaver 198 |
| LOSSES | |
| Al Jackson 80 | Jerry Koosman 137 |
| RUNS/EARNED RUNS | |
| Al Jackson 541/464 | Jerry Koosman 994/875 |
| STRIKEOUTS | |
| Tom Seaver 583 | Seaver 2,541 |
| WALKS | |
| Al Jackson 304 | Tom Seaver 847 |
| STARTS | |
| Al Jackson 138 | Tom Seaver 395 |
| COMPLETE GAMES | |
| Tom Seaver 50 | Seaver 171 |
| SHUTOUTS | |
| Jerry Koosman 13 | Tom Seaver 44 |
| SAVES | |
| Ron Taylor 34 | John Franco 276 |
| ERA | |
| Jerry Koosman 2.34 | Tom Seaver 2.57 |
| WINNING PERCENTAGE | |
| Tom Seaver .640 | Dwight Gooden .649 |

# Al Weis

by Michael P. Cahill

| Season | Age | G | AB | R | H | 2B | 3B | HR | RBI | BB | SO | SB | CS | BA | OBP | SLG |
|---|---|---|---|---|---|---|---|---|---|---|---|---|---|---|---|---|
| 1969 Mets | 31 | 103 | 247 | 20 | 53 | 9 | 2 | 2 | 23 | 15 | 51 | 3 | 3 | .215 | .259 | .291 |
| Career 10 Years | – | 800 | 1578 | 195 | 346 | 45 | 11 | 7 | 115 | 117 | 299 | 55 | 22 | .219 | .278 | .275 |

"There is a tide in the affairs of men. Which, taken at the flood, leads on to fortune; Omitted, all the voyage of their life is bound in shallows and in miseries," wrote William Shakespeare in *Julius Caesar*. The line, spoken by Brutus, might well have been spoken about Al Weis. The self-described "journeyman ballplayer" took the tide at the flood and became a hero of one of the most fabled World Series championship teams of all time.

Albert John Weis was born on April 2, 1938, in Franklin Square, New York, and grew up in Bethpage, graduating from Farmingdale High School. He joined the Navy at the age of 17 and played for the baseball team in at the Norfolk Navy base. There, the Chicago White Sox offered him a contract.

Twenty-one-year-old Al Weis—known to his teammates as Weasel—broke into pro baseball with Holdrege of the Class D Nebraska State League in 1959, batting .275 in 62 games in the short-season circuit. Over the next three seasons, he progressed through the minor leagues: 1960 in Lincoln (Three-I League, Class B), 1961 in Charleston (South Atlantic League, Class A), and 1962 in Indianapolis (American Association, Triple A). For Indy he slapped 13 triples and batted .296. During his four-year apprenticeship, he hit .266, with 15 home runs.

The White Sox called up the 24-year-old Weis at the end of the 1962 season. He had 12 at-bats and got his first hit but mainly soaked up the atmosphere playing behind the double-play combo of Luis Aparicio and Nellie Fox. At season's end, Aparicio was traded to Baltimore in a six-player deal that brought back Ron Hansen, who had a stranglehold on Chicago's shortstop for the next three seasons.

In 1963, Weis backed up Fox and Hansen, also filling in once at third base. During his career, the thin switch-hitter with the de rigueur early 1960s crew cut demonstrated his utility bona fides by playing 488 games at second and 204 at short. (He also filled in nine times at third and played four games in center field.) Appearing in 99 games in his first full season in the majors, he led the team in stolen bases with 15, a category he led the club in again the next season with 22.

Though still productive, Nellie Fox was past his prime and Weis's progress allowed the White Sox to trade Fox away at the end of 1963 and turn the second-base job over to Weis. He played in a career-high 133 games in 1964, 116 of them at second, contributing materially to the second of three consecutive Chicago second-place finishes, this time one game behind the Yankees. He followed that by hitting a career-high .296 in 1965 though his playing time at second was decreased to 74 games (103 in all) as Don Buford took over the position. Under new White Sox manager Eddie Stanky in 1966,

Weis saw more action at second (96 games) as Buford was moved to third and Hansen was injured, but Weis's offensive productivity fell off dramatically. He batted just .155 in 187 at-bats.

His hitting improved in 1967, the year of the epic American League pennant race between Boston, Detroit, Minnesota, and Chicago. His season, however, ended on June 27 when he broke his leg in a collision with Baltimore's Frank Robinson at second base. He played in just 50 games and had only 53 at-bats. Not surprisingly, Weis was available when the season ended.

Over in the National League, the New York Mets had endured five 10th-place finishes in their six years of existence. The Mets brought in manager Gil Hodges, who had spent the past five seasons directing the Washington Senators to five straight second-division finishes. The Mets had the nucleus of a good young pitching staff with Tom Seaver, Jerry Koosman, and Nolan Ryan, but the club was in need of steady defense up the middle and would take any offense they could find as well. On December 15, 1967, the Mets sent four players to the White Sox for outfielder Tommie Agee and—in what seemed to many like an afterthought—Al Weis.

Weis, 29, had been working for the White Sox public-relations department in the offseason and was pleasantly settled with his wife, Barbara, and family in the Chicago suburb of Hillside. Arriving home from work that day, he got the call from the Mets. "My reaction was, 'Oh, no.' After all these years with a contending team, I was going to a last-place club," Weis said later. "It's the ambition of every player to play in a World Series; now I figured that was the end of that dream." Still, he took the tide that led to fortune.

Weis was not merely a throw-in in the swap. Hodges had seen him play for the past five years and the deal with the White Sox was one of the first things he worked on after joining the Mets. The manager told Weis he would not have made the deal if the White Sox had not included him. "Things like that give you confidence," Weis said. "All through the season he let me hit in a lot of situations where other managers would have taken me out."

The Mets were unsettled at second. Phil Linz had little left and prospect Ken Boswell was unproven. The team was set at short with the light-hitting Bud Harrelson, an aggressive team leader. Harrelson, however, had military obligations that required his occasional absence from the team and he would need backup.

Weis's Mets debut was memorable, though hardly auspicious. Five games into the season, Hodges inserted him at shortstop in the leadoff slot against Houston in the Astrodome. As the game stretched on to 24 innings, Weis went 1-for-9 with a walk—starting the season with an immediate slump—and then allowed a grounder to roll through his legs, an error that gave the Astros the only run in the longest 1–0 game in history—and at the time it was the longest night game ever played. Two days later, in his Shea Stadium debut, there were some boos but Weis had a 2-for-4 afternoon with an RBI that helped lift the Mets over the Giants, 3–0. He was accepted.

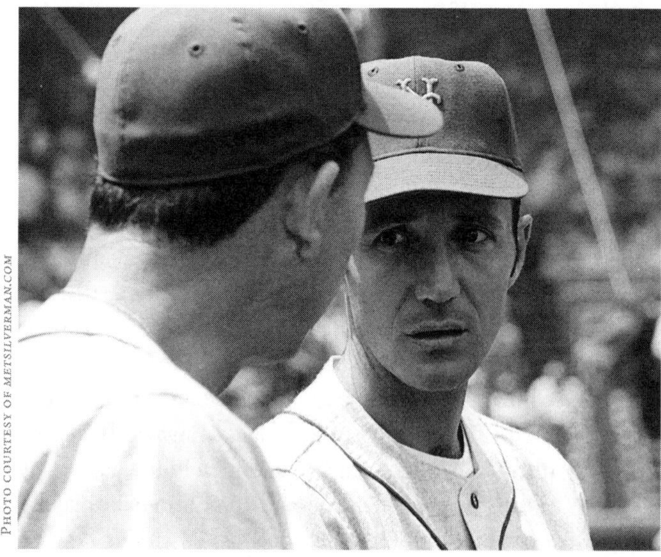

PHOTO COURTESY OF METSILVERMAN.COM

*Al Weis talks with Gil Hodges during the series at Wrigley Field where he became the unlikeliest of home run heroes in 1969.*

With Boswell hampered by a broken finger and Harrelson performing his patriotic duty, Weis appeared in 29 games at second and 59 at short, and his .172 batting average helped "power" the Mets to a 73–89 ninth-place finish, 24 games behind the St. Louis Cardinals. Weis did manage one home run during the "Year of the Pitcher," collected off Cecil Upshaw in Atlanta. It was his first career home run batting left-handed, his fourth homer in seven seasons in the majors, and his first since 1965, when he'd homered off Minnesota's Dick Stigman. His first career home run had come off Cleveland's Tommy John in 1964 and his second came later that year against Baltimore's Dave McNally, which is worth noting.

By 1969, Weis's career was at a crossroads. He was a 31-year-old utility player coming off a .172 season with a club one game out of last place. One factor in his favor was the condition of Harrelson, who had undergone knee surgery and still had military obligations.

Ever adaptable, Weis took steps to increase his value to his team. His playing weight was usually given as 160 on a 6-foot frame but was likely even less than that. The sportswriters' preferred adjective for him was skinny. So, in the offseason, his wife, Barbara, loaded him up with pasta and beer and his weight edged up to 170. By July, however, he would be worn back down to 160.

Weis's fielding remained steady, but improvement was clearly called for in his offensive statistics. He was a switch-hitter, which should have made him appealing to Hodges, who believed firmly in the platoon system, but he wasn't pulling his weight at the plate from either side. With Boswell and rookie infielder Wayne Garrett both left-handed batters, Weis decided to only bat right-handed—his natural inclination—and remained a right-hander for the rest of his career.

Divisional play commenced in 1969. In the National League's Eastern Division, the Cardinals, pennant winners three of the previous five seasons, collapsed as Leo Durocher's Cubs, who had suffered the ignominy of finishing last behind the Mets as recently as 1966, surged into first. After an 11-game winning streak, the Mets were solidly in second place, 5½ games behind the Cubs, in early July.

On July 8, the Mets began the first crucial test in the franchise's history. They were scheduled to face the Cubs for three games at Shea Stadium, then the expansion Montreal Expos for four games at Shea, followed by a three-game foray into the Cubs' lair at Wrigley Field.

Sergeant Bud Harrelson was in the midst of his two-week summer training with the Army Reserve. Hodges penciled Al Weis into the starting lineup at shortstop, batting eighth. With a three-run ninth-inning rally, the Mets took the first game against the Cubs, 4–3. The next night, before a crowd of 59,083, Tom Seaver pitched his legendary one-hit, 4–0 shutout as Weis had a 1-for-4 night with a run scored. The Mets dropped the third game, and then the Expos came to town and beat the Mets 11–4, Weis again having a 1-for-4 game. The next game was rained out.

In the meantime, Harrelson rejoined the squad. In his absence, the team had gone 9–7 with Weis doing a fine job, playing every day, including both games of doubleheaders. The clubhouse man had even placed a sign reading "Iron Man" over Al's locker. He played both ends of the doubleheader with Montreal necessitated by the rainout, which the Mets swept. Weis went 3-for-8 with a double and an RBI.

The next day, at Wrigley, "the little White Sox has-been," as the Cubs Bleacher Bums referred to him, had one of New York's six hits in a 1–0 loss to drop six games behind the Cubs. On July 15, Weis's name appeared in the Mets' lineup again. Asked if he had given any thought to supplanting Weis with Harrelson, the taciturn Hodges responded, "None."

"Gil's saving me for the World Series," Harrelson joked.

Weis led off the third inning with a single and came home on an Agee triple to put the Mets ahead, 1–0. He came up again in the fourth with two out, the score tied, 1–1, Art Shamsky on third and Ed Kranepool on first. On the mound for the Cubs was right-hander Dick Selma, a member of the Mets for the previous four seasons. Three breaking pitches got the count to 1–2. As Weis choked up on his 35-ounce bat, Selma came in with a fastball.

Weis swung, connected, and—to the stupefaction of Cubs and Mets players and fans—the ball sailed over the left-field bleachers and out onto Waveland Avenue, putting New York up, 4–1. It was such a rare occurrence that Weis had to remind himself, "Be sure and touch every base."

The attention was all on Weis in the clubhouse following the 5–4 win. The three-run homer, only his fifth home run in eight years, had come at an opportune moment. "Once, when I hit a homer for the White Sox, I came into the dugout and all the guys were lying on the floor like they were dead or passed out from shock," Weis told reporters.

Asked if he was surprised when the ball went out, Weis admitted, "I'm always surprised."

"With two strikes on me, I choke up on the bat and just try to make contact," he said. "Let's face it. I'm no home-run hitter. I'm not even a hitter. I know my place on this club. I'm a fill-in man. I'm a substitute." Or, as some called him, Supersub.

Weis was back in the lineup the next day and Hodges received no leading questions about putting him in there this time. With the Mets holding on to a 6–5 lead, he led off the fifth by driving a Rich Nye hanging curve into the bleachers. In two days, he had hit half as many as many home runs as he had in the previous 4½ years. The Mets won, 9–5. Afterwards, an exultant Tom Seaver declared, "I have a press release. Al Weis is only 483 years behind Babe Ruth."

In these "crucial" nine days, the Mets won six of nine games and had closed the Cubs' lead to four games. Weis started all nine games at shortstop, played every inning in the field, helped turn nine double plays, and went 9-for-34 (.265) at the plate with five RBIs, a double, and those two home runs.

After the All-Star break, however, the Mets slumped. They slipped to 10 games behind the Cubs by the middle of August... and then the Mets were unstoppable. The Mets went 38–10 the rest of the way, claiming first place on September 10 and clinching the division two weeks later—with Weis's pivot on a game-ending double play setting off a raucous celebration at Shea. Having gained 18 games on the Cubs in seven weeks, the Mets beat them on the next-to-last day of the season at Wrigley and closed at 100–62.

Al Weis was one of a roster of heroes whose contribution to the success of the team was not fully told by his numbers: .215 batting average in 103 games with 53 hits, 23 RBIs, 20 runs, nine doubles, two triples, three steals, and those two home runs.

In the National League Championship Series, the league's first, the Mets swept the favored Atlanta Braves in three games. Weis appeared in all three games as a defensive replacement and went hitless in his lone at-bat.

It appeared as though his contribution to the Mets' success might have run its course as the team headed to the World Series against the favored Baltimore Orioles (109–53). The Orioles pitchers were well aware of Weis's batting tendencies from his days in the American League. Yet the little second baseman turned into their tormentor.

Even in the Series opener, won by the Orioles, 4–1, Weis drove in New York's only run with a sacrifice fly. In Game Two, with the score 1–1 in the top of the ninth, Ed Charles and Jerry Grote singled and Weis came up to face the 20-winner Dave McNally with two outs and Mets pitcher Jerry Koosman on deck. Weis drilled the first pitch into left field to drive Charles home for a 2–1 lead that held up to give the Mets their first World Series win and tie the Series going home to Shea Stadium.

The Mets took Game Three with a 5–0 combined shutout by Gary Gentry and Nolan Ryan—the game best remembered for Agee's brilliant catches and the one game in the Series started by a Baltimore right-hander. In Game Four, Ron Swoboda made a miracle catch of a ninth-inning drive, holding the Orioles to one run. Seaver retired the side in the 10th and in the bottom of the inning, Grote led off with a sun-aided double. Rod Gaspar was sent in to run. Weis was due up, but he was walked intentionally. When J.C. Martin followed with a bunt, the throw to first hit him on the wrist and bounded away, allowing Gaspar to score the winning run. The Mets were a game away from an unfathomable world championship.

It looked like Mets dreams would have to wait as the Orioles built a 3–0 lead in Game Five on home runs by Dave McNally and Frank Robinson in the third inning. In the sixth, the Mets won an argument that Cleon Jones's well-polished shoe was hit by a pitch and Donn Clendenon followed with a home run to make it a one-run game. In the seventh, batting against McNally—shades of their 1964 confrontation—Weis hit a fly ball over the head of ex-teammate Don Buford that cleared the 371-foot sign for the first home run he'd ever hit—or would ever hit—at Shea. It was also the only home run he ever hit at a home park. Talk about timing!

The game tied, Jones doubled leading off the eighth inning and Swoboda laced another double to drive him home. For good measure, Swoboda scored on an error to make the score 5–3. Weis went down looking to end the inning, but few people noticed as fans started thinking about the ninth inning. After a leadoff walk by Koosman, Weis fielded a grounder for a force play and then two fly outs made the Mets world champions and the Shea Stadium turf—and everything that wasn't nailed down—was fair game to the ecstatic throng.

Among the Miracle Mets there was none more miraculous than Al Weis. He led both teams' regulars in the Series with a batting average of .455, more than double his regular-season average. He had a 5-for-11 Series with a home run, four singles, four walks, and three RBIs—one of which won Game Two and another tied Game Five. His slugging percentage was .727 and his on-base average was .563.

PHOTO COURTESY OF METSILVERMAN.COM

*Long Island's own Al Weis hung out at Shea Stadium—on a mural—decades after his greatest moment as a Mets World Series hero.*

Donn Clendenon, with three home runs, received the Series MVP Award. Weis's achievement did not go unnoticed, however. The New York chapter of the Baseball Writers Association of America voted him their Series MVP Award, known as the Babe Ruth Award. It marked only the fourth time that the Babe Ruth Award, given out annually since 1949 (compared with the Series MVP that had been doled out since 1955), had not gone to the same man who won the MVP.

The Mets put up a good fight in 1970 and went into September in the midst of a tight race with Pittsburgh and Chicago. They faded, however, and finished in third place at 83–79, six games behind the Pirates.

Harrelson was a fixture at shortstop and Boswell and Garrett saw more action than Weis, who appeared in 75 games (44 at second and 15 at short) and batted .207 (25-for-121) with one final home run (against future Hall of Famer Steve Carlton). Weis, by then 33 years old, began his 10th major league season and fourth with the Mets in 1971. Harrelson was still ensconced at short, Boswell filled the bill at second, and a prospect named Tim Foli was coming up.

Less than two years since leading all World Series batters, Weis had trouble getting untracked. He had appeared in only 11 games through June 23, starting just once and going 0-for-11. The handwriting was on the wall. On July 1, the Mets released Weis. Hodges told him it was one of the toughest decisions he'd ever had to make.

Weis's totals were 800 games played, 346 hits in 1,578 at-bats for a .219 average, 45 doubles, 11 triples, 115 RBIs, 195 runs scored, 117 walks, 55 stolen bases, and seven home runs—eight, if you want to count his second home run off McNally.

Weis quietly left the world of baseball. He and Barbara continued to raise their family in Elmhurst, Illinois, their home for decades. His avocation became golf and, though he declined to dwell upon his past, the family basement became a shrine full of baseball photographs, his old mitt, and his hot '69 bat.

"I started four of the five World Series games, and I got into the fifth game as a defensive replacement," he recalled. "I would have considered myself lucky to have played in even one game. Think of all the really great players who never got into a World Series, guys like Ernie Banks and Billy Williams. I was lucky just to get the chance, and then I was fortunate enough to perform well."

**Sources**

Allen, Maury. *The Incredible Mets.* New York: Paperback Library, 1969.

Cohen, Stanley. *A Magic Summer: The '69 Mets.* (New York: Harcourt, Brace, Jovanovich, 1988.)

Neft, David S., Richard M. Cohen and Michael L. Neft. *The Sports Encyclopedia: Baseball.* 24th edition. (New York: St. Martin's Griffin, 2004.)

*The Baseball Encyclopedia, 9th ed.,* (New York: Macmillan Publishing Company, 1993.)

Topps Baseball Card #313: Al Weis, 1968.

The Ultimate Mets Database.

# 1969 Mets Trivia Answers

[Continued from Ken Boswell bio, page16]

1. Astros outfielder Jimmy Wynn had six homers against the '69 Mets, one more than Tony Perez, Hank Aaron, and Ron Santo.

2. Heel-clicking Cubs third baseman Ron Santo drove in 17 runs against the Mets, two more than Astros first baseman Curt Blefary.

3. Astros shortstop Denis Menke hit .419 against the Mets, followed by Giants first baseman—and '69 MVP—Willie McCovey at .395.

4. Larry Dierker of the Astros beat the Mets four times in 1969.

5. Don Sutton of the Dodgers and Phil Niekro of the Braves each went winless against the Mets in three 1969 decisions.

6. Tommie Agee had at least four hits in a game six times in 1969. Art Shamsky and Wayne Garrett also had four-hit games. Cleon Jones, who hit .340, didn't have any.

7. Jerry Koosman fanned 15 Padres on May 28, 1969. Kooz went 10 shutout innings but Tug McGraw got the win in 11.

8. The Astros recorded a 16–3 win at Shea on July 30.

9. Hal Lanier had five hits against Tom Seaver in 1969.

10. Giants outfielder Bobby Bonds homered twice against Tom Seaver in 1969. Both came on August 21 in New York.

—Courtesy of *metswalkoffs.blogspot.com*

# Manager and Coaches

Photo courtesy National Baseball Hall of Fame Library, Cooperstown, NY

# Gil Hodges

by John Saccoman

*"Epitomizes the courage, sportsmanship and integrity of America's favorite pastime."*—back of a 1966 Topps baseball card

*"Gil Hodges is a Hall of Fame man."*—Roy Campanella

*"If you had a son, it would be a great thing to have him grow up to be just like Gil Hodges."*—Pee Wee Reese

*"Gil Hodges is a Hall of Famer; he deserves it, and it's a shame his family and friends have had to wait so long."*—Duke Snider

*"[Hodges] was such a noble character in so many respects that I believe Gil to have been one of the finest men I met in sports or out if it."*—Arthur Daley, *New York Times*

*"Kids could sneak into Ebbets Field if they were inside a player's car. We used to wait outside the gates and ask the players to let us sneak in. [Carl] Furillo would take one, Campy would take a couple, but Gilly would always have a carload. He couldn't say 'no' to a kid..."*—Brooklyn Dodgers fan

The bridge that spans the East Fork of the White River in northern Pike County, Indiana, has been named the Gil Hodges Memorial Bridge. The stone monument dedicating the bridge reads as follows:

> *This bridge is named in honor of Gil Hodges. Born at Princeton, Indiana, April 4, 1924. Graduated from Petersburg High School, 1941. Played Major League Baseball, 1943-1963. Brooklyn Dodgers, 1943-1957. Served in US Marines, 1944-1945. Los Angeles Dodgers, 1957-1961. New York Mets, 1962-1963. Managed Washington Senators, 1964[sic]-1967. Managed New York Mets, 1967[sic]-1971, including World Series Championship, 1969. As a player, Hodges played in seven World Series. Played on eight National League All-Star squads. Hit 14 grand slams. Hit 22 or more home runs in 11 seasons. Had 100 or more RBI in seven seasons. Was sixth player to hit four home runs in one game. Has World Series record for most games by a first baseman. Above all, he was dedicated to God, family, country, and the game of baseball. Died April 2, 1972. Buried in Holy Cross Cemetery, Brooklyn, New York.*

Born Gilbert Ray Hodge in 1924 in Indiana's southwestern corner, just north of Evansville, the origin of the discrepancy between his birth name of Hodge and the name by which he became well known is unclear. His parents were Irene and Big Charlie. When Hodges was seven years old, the family moved from Princeton 30 miles north to Petersburg. Big Charlie did not want his two sons, Gil and Bob, to work in the coal mines as he did. Big Charlie lost an eye and some toes in various mining accidents, and while recovering from a knee injury in the hospital, died of a heart embolism in 1952.

Big Charlie taught his sons how to play sports, and Gil was a four-sport athlete in Petersburg, running track and playing baseball, basketball, and football, earning a combined seven varsity letters. In 1941, like his brother before him, Hodges was offered a Class D contract by the Detroit Tigers, but he declined it and instead enrolled at St. Joseph's College outside Indianapolis on an athletic scholarship. St. Joseph's had a fairly well regarded physical education program, and Hodges had designs on a college coaching career.

After two years, he found himself a full-time drill press operator and playing on the company team. He was bird-dogged by local sporting goods storeowner and part-time Dodgers scout Stanley Feezle, who also would later sign hurler Carl Erskine (from the small Indiana city of Anderson) for the Dodgers. Although Hodges was originally scouted as a shortstop, general manager Branch Rickey noticed a hitch in Hodges's throw from short and suggested he try catching.

Hodges had the proverbial "cup of coffee" with the 1943 team, making his debut on August 23, playing third base instead of first and wearing uniform number 4 instead of the 14 he would wear for the rest of his career. He went hitless in his debut, striking out twice, drawing a walk, stealing a base, and making two errors. He did not appear at third base in another major league game until 1957.

A member of the Marines ROTC, he was drafted into the Marine Corps and spent close to three years stationed on Pearl Harbor, Tinian, and Okinawa as a gunner in the 16th Anti-Aircraft Battalion. Discharged as a sergeant in early 1946, Hodges was a recipient of the Bronze Star for his deeds in the South Pacific. Don Hoak, a future Dodgers teammate, said, "We kept hearing stories about this big guy from Indiana who killed [Japanese soldiers] with his bare hands." Hodges finished his college degree in the winters at Oakland City College in Indiana on the GI Bill.

Hodges was a solidly built at 6-foot-1½, 200 pounds, and was considered large for baseball players of the era. Hodges, however, was a gentle giant, often playing the role of peacemaker during the frequent on-field brawls of the time. His hands were so large that teammate Pee Wee Reese once remarked that he could have played first base barehanded but wore a mitt because it was fashionable.

But catcher looked like his ticket to the major leagues when he returned from the war and resumed his baseball career. Rickey had him learn catching in Class B Newport News, Virginia. He spent part of 1947 as the third-string catcher for the Brooklyn club, but with Roy Campanella on the way and soon to be ensconced at the position by the middle of 1948, a position change for Hodges was in order. Dodgers manager Leo Durocher recalled that coach Clyde Sukeforth told him, "This Campanella...is the best catcher in baseball right now." So, Durocher "put a first baseman's glove on our other rookie catcher, Gil Hodges...Three days later, I'm looking at the best first baseman I'd seen since Dolf Camilli."

Hodges played 96 games at first base during his first full year with the Dodgers in 1948. With 13 errors, his fielding percentage was .986, the only year he played regularly that he fielded under .990. In addition, he contributed 11 home runs and 70 RBIs to Brooklyn's 84-win, third-place season. He would not drive in fewer than 100 runs over the next seven seasons, nor would the Dodgers finish lower than second place over the next eight.

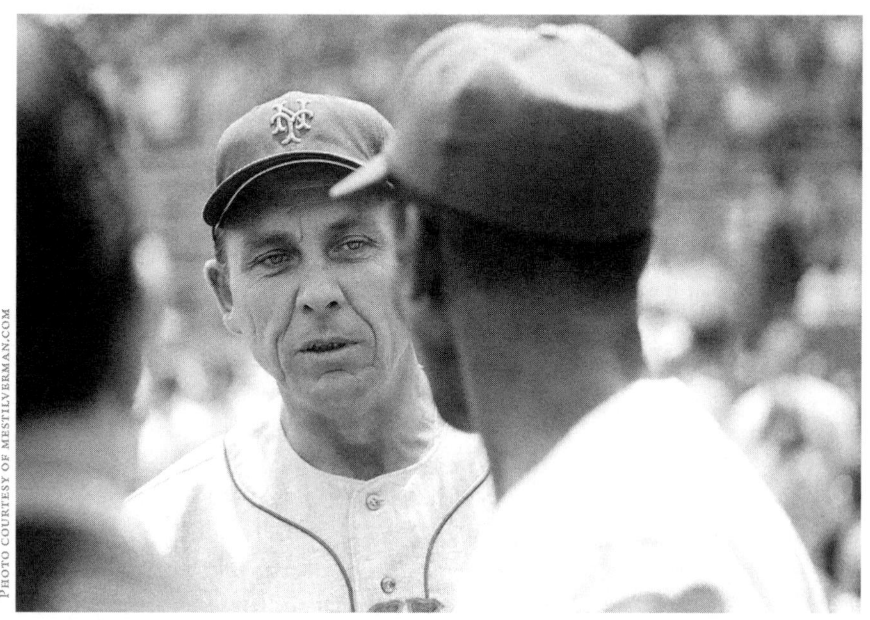

Photo courtesy of mestilverman.com

*Gil Hodges shares a moment with Cubs great Ernie Banks before one of the highly-charged affairs between Chicago and New York in 1969.*

That same year, Hodges met and married the former Joan Lombardi, a Brooklyn girl from the Bay Ridge section. The couple made a permanent home in Brooklyn, one of the few Dodgers to do so, and raised four children, Gil Jr. (who would spend some time as a player in the New York Mets minor league system), Irene, Cynthia, and Barbara. This no doubt made Gil "one of them" in the eyes of the fans. Dodgers owner Walter O'Malley stated, "If I had sold or traded Hodges, the Brooklyn fans would hang me, burn me, and tear me to pieces." (Brooklyn fans had to curb that impulse in 1957 when O'Malley engineered the club's move to Los Angeles.)

By 1949, the Brooklyn Dodgers were poised for the most productive period in the franchise's history. The fabled lineup was in place: Roy Campanella at catcher, Hodges at first, Jackie Robinson at second, Pee Wee Reese at short, Billy Cox at third, Duke Snider in center, and Carl Furillo in right, plus a rotating cast of characters in left. The team finished first with 97 wins, edging the St. Louis Cardinals by one game. Hodges appeared in his first All-Star game and went 1-for-3 with a run scored. He tied with Snider for the team lead in home runs with 23, and his 115 RBIs were second on the team to Robinson, the eventual league MVP. However, the Dodgers lost the World Series to the New York Yankees in five games. Hodges drove in the only run in the Dodgers' only win in Game Two and drove in four of the team's 14 runs in the Series.

The next two years brought consecutive second-place finishes, with the 1951 season burnished in history by the three-game playoff series with the New York Giants that culminated in Bobby Thomson's "Shot Heard 'Round the World." Hodges's power numbers continued to improve, as he averaged 36 home runs and 108 RBIs for the two seasons while batting .276. He established his career high in runs scored in 1951 with 118, one of three seasons in his career in which he topped 100. Defensively, he exceeded 100 assists each year, one indication of exceptional fielding ability at first base. In the 1951 All-Star Game, Hodges went 2 for 5, including a two-run homer.

His biggest day, however, came on August 31, 1950, when he became the sixth player to hit four home runs in a single game. In fact, he went 5 for 6 and drove in nine runs that day, hitting the home runs off four different Boston Braves pitchers, including future Hall of Famer Warren Spahn.

The Dodgers won the first consecutive pennants in franchise history, only to fall to the Yankees in the Series again each time. In 1952, Hodges hit 32 home runs and drove in 102, slugging .500, while in 1953, his numbers he hit 32 homers again and knocked in 122 with a .550 slugging percentage—and that after having a .187 average in May. The slump with which he began the 1953 season actually carried over from the 1952 World Series and, incredibly, cemented the legendary bond between Hodges and the Brooklyn fans. In the seven-game series, he went 0 for 21 with five walks, and this slump continued into the 1953 season. Instead of booing their first baseman, the Ebbets Field faithful embraced him, cheering him warmly, sometimes with standing ovations, before each at bat.

In his classic *The Boys of Summer*, Roger Kahn wrote:

> *The fans of Brooklyn warmed to the first baseman as he suffered his slump. A movement to save him rose from cement sidewalks and the roots of trampled Flatbush grass. More than thirty people a day wrote to Hodges. Packages arrived with rosary beads, rabbits' feet, mezuzahs, scapulars.*

In his book, *The Game of Baseball*, Hodges recalled that slump in his typical humble fashion:

> *The thing that most people hear about that one is that a priest [Father Herbert Redmond of St. Francis Roman Catholic Church] stood in a Brooklyn pulpit that Sunday and said, "It's too hot for a sermon. Just go home and say a prayer for Gil Hodges." Well, I know that I'll never forget that, but also I won't forget the hundreds of people who sent me letters, telegrams, and postcards during that World Series. There wasn't a single nasty message. Everybody tried to say something nice. It had a tremendous effect on my morale, if not my batting average. Remember that in 1952, the Dodgers had never won a World Series. A couple of base hits by me in the right spot might have changed all that.*

Five decades after the fabled slump, political columnist and Brooklyn native Thomas Oliphant published a memoir of his youth entitled *Praying for Gil Hodges*. Oliphant called Hodges, "The person parents wanted their kids to emulate. He was not just quiet and well-mannered; he also worked ceaselessly, hustled like a rookie, and never complained." Hodges's support in Brooklyn coupled with the experience of his renowned slump undoubtedly helped him later in his managerial career, when he took over struggling expansion teams.

*Gil Hodges continued to be honored long after he led the Mets to greatness with pins and plates.*

Photos courtesy of metsilverman.com

The 1954 season saw the Dodgers finish in second place and Hodges post career highs in home runs (42), RBIs (130), and slugging (.579). Twenty-five of those homers came at Ebbets Field, establishing a new club mark. On August 8, he tripled and homered in the eighth inning as the Dodgers scored 13 runs on their way to a 20–8 rout of the Cincinnati Reds.

The 1955 season is the one most fondly remembered by Brooklyn fans. Hodges, now 31, contributed 27 homers, 102 RBIs and a .500 slugging percentage to the Dodgers' 98-win campaign. For the fifth time in nine years, they met the Yankees in the World Series. Hodges drove in the only two runs scored in the seventh and deciding game of the Series, and recorded the final clinching out on a throw from Reese.

Hodges would play in two more World Series, 1956 and 1959, and the Dodgers would win in 1959. He continued to play as a regular over the span of these years, averaging more than 26 home runs and 82 runs batted in each season. Hodges homered once in each Series; in the 1956 seven-game series loss to the Yankees, he had a hand in 12 of the Dodgers' 25 runs, and he batted .391 as the 1959 Los Angeles Dodgers defeated the Chicago White Sox in six games for the franchise's second world championship. In the '59 Series, Hodges hit a solo homer in the bottom of the eighth to snap a 4–4 tie in front of more than 92,000 fans at Los Angeles Coliseum.

Hodges played for parts of four more seasons, but knee and other injuries slowed him down; he hit only .198 in 197 at-bats in 1960. Despite the Dodgers' move to Los Angeles, the Hodges family maintained the home in Brooklyn, and in 1961, the newly formed Mets selected Hodges in the first National League expansion draft. The rules of the expansion draft were much less liberal than those of recent baseball expansions. In the expansion from eight to ten teams in each league, the new clubs were allowed to select from a very small pool of players. These rules would affect Hodges in both cities he wound up in over the next decade.

Hodges played in the first Mets game ever and hit the first home run in Mets history, but his injury paved the way for the brief yet treacherous Marv Throneberry era at first base in 1962. Though Hodges began 1963 as an active player, he retired after his trade to the Washington Senators of the American League (for outfielder Jimmy Piersall) to become manager. At the time of his retirement, Hodges's 370 career home runs were the most by a right-handed hitter in NL history, breaking the mark set by Mets announcer Ralph Kiner.

Each year after Hodges's arrival, the expansion Senators improved on their record from the previous year, peaking with a 76–85 mark in 1967. Among their top players were four the Senators had pirated from the Dodgers in a 1964 trade: Hodges's former teammate, fellow gentle giant and slugging outfielder Frank Howard, third baseman Ken McMullen, and pitchers Phil Ortega and Pete Richert.

Yet while the Senators had improved in the previous five seasons, the Mets continued to backslide. Wes Westrum, the replacement for Casey Stengel after he broke his hip in 1965, quit in the final week of the '67 season before his imminent firing. The Mets set their sights on Washington for their managerial search. When Hodges confirmed that the feeling was mutual, the two clubs worked out an agreement to bring him back to New York for $100,000 and pitcher Bill Denehy.

Hodges's reputation preceded him. In Paul D. Zimmerman and Dick Schaap's book, *The Year the Mets Lost Last Place*, published while the 1969 Mets were still fighting for the title, the authors said that "because of his image—he has been the quiet hero, the humble, gentle giant ever since his Dodger days—he is secure as a losing manager can be."

Despite that job security, he suffered a "mild" heart attack during a game in Atlanta on September 24, 1968, at the age of 44. Besides the stress, which he seems to have always kept bottled up, he also had developed a smoking habit on Okinawa, two contributing factors for such an attack so early in life. It was unknown for many weeks whether Hodges would be able to manage the club in 1969, but he was in his office in St. Petersburg when spring training began.

His first winning season as manager, of course, came that year, a team that went 100–62, or 27 wins over the previous year (and 15 games better than their manager's seemingly bold spring training prediction of 85 wins). The Mets were led by rising star pitchers Tom Seaver and Jerry Koosman, rookie Gary Gentry, and a promising fireballer named Nolan Ryan, plus veteran Ron Taylor and excitable lefty Tug McGraw in the bullpen. Hodges demanded superior defense. Though he favored platoons, he played catcher Jerry Grote and shortstop Bud Harrelson against both lefties and righties. The Mets also had superb seasons from home-grown everyday left fielder Cleon Jones and center fielder Tommie Agee, whom Hodges knew from the American League and had pushed to acquire—along with Al Weis—from the White Sox shortly after he took over the Mets. Hodges platooned at three infield positions and right field. That included the club's chief power source: midseason acquisition Donn Clendenon, whom Hodges had worked with at first base years earlier during the offseason. Though the team had 19 players age 26 or younger, Hodges got contributions from his whole roster by making sure youngsters and veterans alike received enough playing time—unlike his former skipper Leo Durocher, whose Cubs he had his sights on.

After winning two series from the front-running Cubs in July and suffering a slight swoon after the All-Star break, New York rallied from 10 games out in mid-August to take the first National

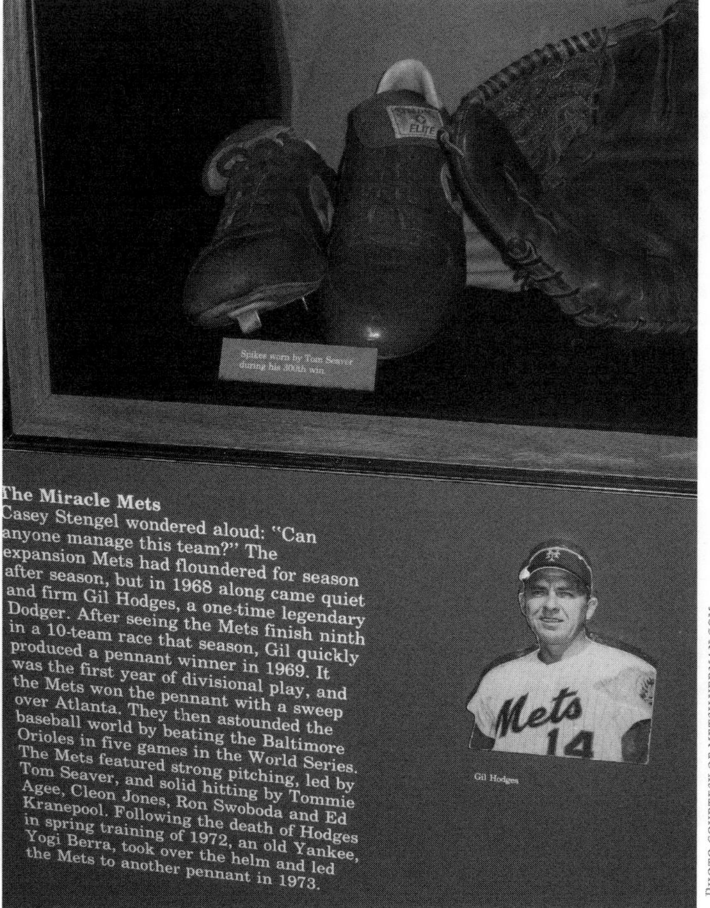

he Miracle Mets
asey Stengel wondered aloud: "Can
anyone manage this team?" The
expansion Mets had floundered for season
after season, but in 1968 along came quiet
and firm Gil Hodges, a one-time legendary
Dodger. After seeing the Mets finish ninth
in a 10-team race that season, Gil quickly
produced a pennant winner in 1969. It
was the first year of divisional play, and
the Mets won the pennant with a sweep
over Atlanta. They then astounded the
baseball world by beating the Baltimore
Orioles in five games in the World Series.
The Mets featured strong pitching, led by
Tom Seaver, and solid hitting by Tommie
Agee, Cleon Jones, Ron Swoboda and Ed
Kranepool. Following the death of Hodges
in spring training of 1972, an old Yankee,
Yogi Berra, took over the helm and led
the Mets to another pennant in 1973.
Mets
14
Gil Hodges


Photo courtesy of metsilverman.com

*Though a Hall of Fame plaque can't be seen with his name on it in Cooperstown, an image of Gil Hodges can be found at the Hall of Fame at the feet of a Tom Seaver tribute.*

League East title, becoming the first expansion team to ever reach the postseason. The Mets swept the Atlanta Braves in three straight games in the inaugural National League Championship Series and defeated the heavily favored Baltimore Orioles in five games in the World Series. His quick thinking in Game Five on a pitch near the foot of Cleon Jones resulted in him producing a ball with shoe polish and umpire Lou DiMuro immediately reversed his call. Two home runs, an eighth-inning rally, and a Jerry Koosman pitch skied to Cleon Jones in left put the Mets on top of the world. While ever the quiet and patient disciplinarian, Hodges let the champagne pour over his head as the Mets celebrated one of the great upsets in the game's history.

Hodges was voted *The Sporting News* Manager of the Year while earning his third—and most unlikely—World Series ring, but trying to repeat that magic proved elusive. The Mets finished with identical 83–79 records in each of the next two seasons. For Hodges, there would be no more championships.

The spring of 1972 saw the first modern players strike. On April 2, Easter Sunday, Hodges played golf at the Palm Beach Lakes Golf Course in Florida with coaches Joe Pignatano, Rube Walker, and Eddie Yost. The first two were old Brooklyn Dodger pals, while Yost had been with Hodges since the Senators days.

As they walked off the final hole of their 27-hole day toward their rooms at the Ramada Inn, Pignatano asked Hodges what time they were to meet for dinner. Hodges answered him, "7:30," and then he fell to the pavement. He was pronounced dead of a coronary at 5:45 p.m. The Mets were scheduled to open the season in Pittsburgh on April 7, the day of the funeral, but the players agreed to forfeit the game to attend. The game was not played anyway because of the lingering strike.

Coach Yogi Berra took over the stunned Mets as Hodges's replacement and led the Mets back to the World Series in 1973. Berra's star hitter was Rusty Staub, whose acquisition Hodges had signed off on shortly before his untimely death.

In the years since, some attention has been given to Hodges's absence from the Hall of Fame. He has received more votes than anybody else, elected or not. Hodges was eligible for the Baseball Writers Association of America vote from 1969 until 1983.

PHOTOS COURTESY OF METSILVERMAN.COM

*The order of the retired numbers changed and they were in play in left field when Citi Field opened for real on April 13, 2009. Tom Seaver threw out the first pitch at the new yard to start the 40th anniversary season of the 1969 world champion Mets. The number 14, worn by Gil Hodges, was retired in his honor at Shea and Citi Field.*

In each year, he received more votes than at least four and as many as ten men who would ultimately be elected to the Hall. The Veterans Committee has failed to elect him in the years since. The Hall of Fame requires that a candidate be enshrined in Cooperstown based on either his record as a player or as a manager (660–753, including a 339–309 mark with the Mets—still the third-most wins in franchise history).

In an op-ed piece in the *New York Times* on Christmas Day, 1977, Bishop Francis Mugavero of the Diocese of Brooklyn, the main celebrant at Hodges's funeral mass, made a case for Hodges's enshrinement. He discussed his on-field playing and managerial feats, and then cited his character. "There was never a more religious man in sports.... From his first day in the major leagues, he recited a 'Hail Mary' and an 'Our Father' during the playing of the National Anthem." Mugavero continued, "He would never accept a fee [for speaking at public functions]."

One time, when his team was flying on a Friday, the in-flight meal was a steak. Hodges refused to eat it. When reminded there was a dispensation for such circumstances, Hodges said, "I know, but we're a little too close to headquarters up here."

Hodges led all first basemen of the 1950s in the following categories: home runs (310), games (1,477), at-bats (5,313), runs (890), hits (1,491), runs batted in (1,001), total bases (2,733) and extra-base hits (585). He made the All-Star team eight times, every year from 1949–55 and again in 1957, the most of any first baseman of the time. In addition, Hodges won the first three Gold Gloves at his position and was considered the finest defensive first baseman of the era as well. Also, he was second among all players in the 1950s in home runs and runs batted in, third in total bases and eighth in runs.

Hodges's funeral Mass could have been held at St. Patrick's Cathedral in Manhattan, but that would have not been in keeping with his unassuming ways. During his funeral Mass, held at his Flatbush parish church, Our Lady Help of Christians, the Reverend Charles Curley said, "Gil was an ornament to his parish, and we are justly proud that in death he lies here in our little church." Repeating the story of Father Herbert Redmond's concern for Hodges's slump, Father Curley said, "This morning, in a far different setting, I repeat that suggestion of long ago: Let's all say a prayer for Gil Hodges."

His number 14 was retired by the Mets in 1973, the second number in team history to be so honored. He was enshrined in the Mets Hall of Fame in 1982, the year after it opened.

A space was left at the bottom of the monument at the Gil Hodges Memorial Bridge in Indiana to include the wording of Hodges' Cooperstown plaque. Perhaps it is time to fill in the rest of the monument.

**Gil Hodges Managing**

| Season | Age | G* | W | L | Pct |
|---|---|---|---|---|---|
| 1969 Mets | 45 | 162 | 100 | 62 | .617 |
| Career 9 Years | – | 1414 | 660 | 753 | .467 |

*The wins and losses do not add up to the games managerd because of a tie. (The Mets had one tie in 1968.) Hodges's record with the Mets was 339–309 (.523) in 649 games over four seasons.

**Sources**

Joe D'Agostin, personal communication.
Rob Edelman, personal communication.
*New York Times*, April 3-8, 1972
Amoruso, Marino. *Gil Hodges: The Quiet Man.* (Forest Dale, Vermont: Paul S. Eriksson, 1991.)
Durocher, Leo and Ed Linn. *Nice Guys Finish Last.* (New York: Simon & Schuster, 1976.)
Kahn, Roger *The Boys of Summer,.* (New York: Signet, 1971.)
Hodges, Gil. *The Game of Baseball.* (New York: Crown, 1970.)
Zimmerman and Dick Schapp, *The Year the Mets Lost Last Place.* (New York: Signet, 1969.)

## The Prote-Shea

When one compares the two managers in the first—and still perhaps most memorable—NL East race, the pair could not seem more different. Gil Hodges of the Mets was quiet, disciplined, went about his business without much fuss, and liked to move his players around the lineup and the diamond. Leo Durocher, a Hall of Fame caliber manager before he even came to the Cubs in 1966, was loud, opinionated, liked to hob-nob with celebrities, and put the same players on the field every day. Durocher was 19 years Hodges's senior and was playing in the major leagues when Gil was in diapers.

One thing that is rarely mentioned is that Hodges came to the major leagues in Brooklyn under the tutelage of Leo the Lip, who managed the Dodgers between 1939 and 1948. Hodges appeared in one game for the 1943 Dodgers at third base—a position he did not play again in the major leagues until 1957—and he subsequently became a sergeant in the Marines, serving with distinction in the South Pacific. When Hodges returned to the majors in 1947, Durocher was in the midst of a year-long suspension by commissioner Happy Chandler for consorting with known gamblers. Hodges was a catcher, but he would be converted to first baseman the following year by none other than his manager. Durocher's decision to move Hodges was a smart move all around with future Hall of Fame catcher Roy Campanella coming up that year in Brooklyn.

The fiery Durocher famously jumped to the New York Giants in midseason 1948. Several Dodgers developed during Durocher's reign would help Brooklyn dominate the National League from 1949 to 1956, winning six pennants with the only breaks in that chain coming from the Phillies in 1950 and by Durocher's own Giants in 1951 and 1954.

Durocher and Hodges reunited in 1961 when Leo returned to the Dodgers—this time in Los Angeles—as a coach. Hodges went to the Mets in that fall's expansion draft and started his own managerial career in 1963 in Washington. Looking at their overlapping careers (and throwing out the '47 flag because of Durocher's suspension and Hodges's minor role with the Dodgers), the pennant count would be Hodges 7, Durocher 2. But give Leo the Lip a little credit for Gil's Gold Gloves at first base the first three years the award was given (1957–59).

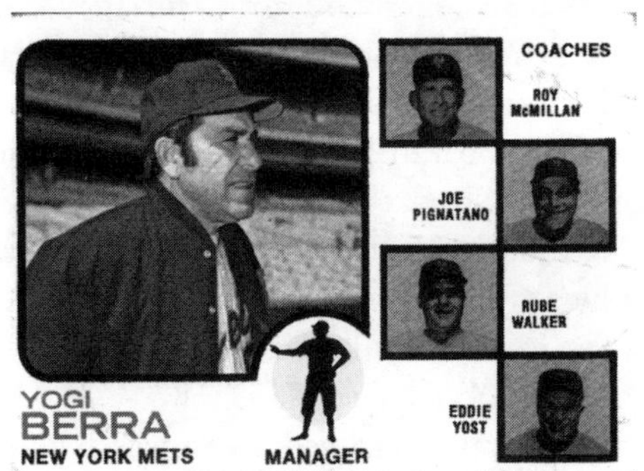

COACHES
ROY McMILLAN
JOE PIGNATANO
RUBE WALKER
EDDIE YOST
YOGI BERRA
NEW YORK METS
MANAGER


# Yogi Berra

by Dave Williams

There are many things that come to mind when one hears the name Yogi Berra. One of the more obvious images the name conjures is that of a winner. He appeared in 14 World Series as a player and another five as a manager or a coach, winning a total of 13 championship rings. His name is littered all over the World Series record books and he won three American League Most Valuable Player awards. That Yogi was one of the winningest players not only in baseball but in all of sport is a testament to his drive and determination. He met with some roadblocks along his journey to fame but with grit and dedication he overcame and went on to become one of the more beloved figures in American sports history.

Pietro Berra arrived on Ellis Island, in New York Harbor, on September 28, 1912, at the age of 17 from Malvaglio, Italy, a town just south of Milan, where he was a tenant farmer. Pietro, who stood only 5-foot-3, left behind a young girl named Paulina whom he planned to marry after earning enough money to pay her way to the United States. Once Paulina arrived, they settle in a largely Italian section of St. Louis called The Hill. Their first child, Anthony, was born in 1914. The second child was born back in Malvaglio as Paulina, pregnant and homesick, went back to Italy for a visit. While she was there, World War I broke out and mother and child were stranded and could not return to St. Louis for several years. They had a third son, John, in 1922, and on May 12, 1925, Lorenzo Pietro came into the world. His parents' desire to assimilate in their new homeland led them to the English translation of Lawrence Peter, which, due to their accent, they pronounced Lawdie.

Lawdie Berra and his family lived on 5447 Elizabeth Avenue, across the street from Giovanni Garagiola and his family; they had a boy named Joe who was Lawdie's age. The two youngsters spent most of their time playing games with the other neighborhood boys and it is no surprise that their favorite sport was baseball. One of the boys was Bobby Hofman, the nephew of Solly Hofman, who once played center field for the Chicago Cubs, a position he was playing in September 1908 in a game at the Polo Grounds in which New York Giants rookie Fred Merkle committed his infamous—to New York Giants fans, anyway—baserunning boner. Besides sports, the boys loved to go to the movies. One day they watched a feature that had a Hindu fakir, a snake charmer who sat with his legs crossed and wore a turban on his head. When the yogi got up, he waddled and Hofman joked that he walked like Lawdie. From then on Berra was known as Yogi. Even his parents called him by his nickname.

As a youngster Berra displayed a stubbornness and determination that carried over to his playing days. This was no more in evidence than when he decided he was going to quit school after the eighth grade. Yogi had never been a very good student and felt he was wasting his time in school, but naturally Pietro was dead set against the idea. To help his effort to keep his son in school, he enlisted the aid of the school's principal and the local parish priest. Yogi held firm and eventually his father relented and Yogi went to work in a coal yard. He lost the job because he often left work early to play ball with his friends once they got out of school. Pietro, furious that his son would lose a job that paid $25 a week, was able to get Yogi a job working on a Pepsi Cola truck that paid $27 a week. He was fired from this job as well. After much arguing, it was decided that Yogi would find a job that would allow him to play ball in the afternoon.

Yogi and Joe Garagiola were teammates on the same American Legion team and were stars on the squad that made it to the semifinals two consecutive years. Garagiola was tall, athletic, and handsome and by contrast Berra was short and dumpy, and had an awkward swing in which he chopped at the ball. He would also swing at anything near the plate. The man who ran the team, Leo Browne, arranged a tryout with the Cardinals for his star players. Garagiola did well and was offered a contract with a $500 bonus with the order to keep quiet about it until he turned 16 (the boys were 15 at the time.) Despite not having a particularly good tryout, Berra was offered a contract but no bonus. Berra knew he could not go home without the same bonus as Garagiola, so he refused the offer. Cardinals general manager Branch Rickey offered a $250 bonus and again Berra refused. Yogi later had a tryout with the St. Louis Browns and once more was offered a contract without a $500 bonus; once more he turned it down.

Browne wrote to his old friend George Weiss, general manager of the New York Yankees. He said all Yogi wanted was a $500 bonus and whatever he made a month was fine. Berra signed with the Yankees in October 1942 for the $500 bonus he so adamantly desired, plus a monthly salary of $90. Rickey, now with the Dodgers, sent Berra a telegram offering him a chance to sign with Brooklyn but Yogi never responded because he was the property of the Yankees. So Yogi Berra was off to Norfolk, Virginia, to begin his professional baseball career...not as a Cardinal, a Brown, or a Dodger, but as a Yankee.

Yogi batted only .253 for Norfolk in 1943 but had two outstanding games. On August 1, he had six hits and knocked in 13 runs against Roanoke; the next game he had six more hits and had 10 RBIs. In the other 109 games he played, he had four home runs and 33 RBIs. After the season, with the US in World War II, Yogi volunteered to join the Navy. He became a machine gunner and saw action on D-Day aboard a rocket boat that was deployed just off the Normandy coast before the soldiers assaulted the beach. He thought all the rockets and gunfire reminded him of the Fourth of July. Berra spent 10 days on the 36-foot boat before he finally returned to his ship, the USS Bayfield, P833.

Before he was discharged, Berra was shipped to the submarine base at Groton, Connecticut. He played for the base's baseball team, managed by Lieutenant James "Gee Gee" Gleeson, who before entering the service was a big-league outfielder for the Indians, Cubs, and Reds. Gleeson had a difficult time believing the squat, awkward-looking seaman was a professional ballplayer, much less property of the Yankees. But in a game between the sailors and the New York Giants, Berra went 3-for-4 and impressed Giants manager Mel Ott so much that he called the Yankees and offered $50,000 for Berra. Yankees president Larry MacPhail turned Ott down. Years later, MacPhail confessed that he had never heard of Yogi, but that if Ott thought he was worth that kind of money, then the Yankees should keep him.

Upon leaving the service, Berra was assigned to Newark of the International League, then managed by former Yankees All-Star George Selkirk. Just like Gleeson before him, Selkirk was skeptical that this squat young man was a ballplayer or a Yankee. He forced Yogi to show him the telegram from MacPhail ordering him to report to Newark. Berra played in 77 games and batted .314 with 15 home runs and 59 RBIs but displayed an erratic arm behind the plate. In the regular-season finale, Berra tied the game with a ninth-inning homer, a game that Newark eventually won. The victory put Newark in the playoffs for the 14th consecutive season, though the Bears lost to a Montreal Royals squad that included Jackie Robinson, Johnny Jorgensen, and Al Campanis.

After the loss to Montreal, Berra was called up to the Yankees and made his major-league debut on September 22, 1946, against the Philadelphia Athletics. He went 2-for-4, homering off Jesse Flores

*Gil Hodges, left, and Mets general manager Johnny Murphy, center, meet with Yogi Berra after Hodges was named Mets manager is late 1967. Berra, who had been passed over as Mets manager following Casey Stengel's injury-induced retirement in 1965, was briefly considered for the post two years later. Berra would become Mets manager in 1972 after the untimely death of Hodges.*

in his second at-bat. His second home run came the next day. Berra had a terrific spring training the following year and saw considerable time in right field, where he showed little skill. He was, however, earning a reputation as a hitter and one who would often hit pitches well out of the strike zone; the Yanks were seeking ways to get his bat in the lineup. Because of Berra's erratic outfield play, he saw more time at catcher once the season began; this seemed to be the safest place for him to play. On June 16, he made an unassisted double play in a game against St. Louis. A week later he hit his first grand slam in a win over Detroit and when he homered again the next day, he had registered six RBIs in two games. Later that year, a group from The Hill organized Yogi Berra Night in St. Louis to honor their native son. He came down with strep throat in Cleveland just before the series in St. Louis and had to be hospitalized. When he arrived in town for his night, Yogi was very nervous about making an acceptance speech. That was the night he uttered the famous line, "I want to thank everyone for making this night necessary."

Berra finished his rookie campaign with a .280 average with 11 home runs and 54 RBIs in 83 games. The Yankees faced Brooklyn in the World Series, the first fall classic to be televised. He went 0-for-7 in the first two games and then came off the bench in Game Three to hit the first pinch-hit home run in Series history. New York won in seven games and Yogi went 3-for-19 at the plate. He spent the off-season in St. Louis and that winter he met a pretty waitress named Carmen Short working at a restaurant co-owned by Stan Musial. Yogi and Carmen hit it off and six months later were engaged. They were married on January 26, 1949, and old pal Joe Garagiola served as best man.

The 1948 All Star Game was played in St. Louis and Berra made the squad but did not play. He did, however, have a strong year at the plate, batting .305 with 14 home runs and 98 RBIs while appearing in 125 games (71 of those as a catcher). The Yanks finished third behind Cleveland and Boston and entered the offseason in the market for a better defensive catcher. This changed when the Yankees surprised the baseball world by picking 59-year-old Casey Stengel as their manager; Stengel nixed any thought of replacing Berra behind the plate. Casey took a liking to Berra immediately and referred to him as "my assistant manager." Stengel had an idea that Yogi was much more sensitive than he let on and decided to act as a buffer against those who criticized or just made fun of his young catcher—a group that included members of his own team. Stengel was fearful that the needling would get out of control and hinder Berra's development. He also assigned Bill Dickey to act as Berra's personal tutor. The old catcher, later elected to the Hall of Fame, spent hours working with his student to improve his mechanics behind the plate and his ability to think ahead of time.

Despite the improvement in his defensive play, Berra had some trouble with Yankees pitchers, in particular Vic Raschi and Allie Reynolds, who thought he smothered curveballs and stabbed at fastballs, and thus made it difficult to get close calls from umpires. For his part, Stengel did not trust Berra yet either. In some critical situations the manager would call the pitches from the dugout, infuriating the veteran pitchers. Finally, one day in a game against the Athletics, Reynolds had enough. Stengel began waving to Yogi to get his attention so that he could call a pitch and Allie warned his young catcher that if he looked into the dugout he would cross him up intentionally. Berra knew that this was not an idle threat and ignored his manager at the risk of being fined. This proved to be a real turning point in his relationship with the pitching staff; they now felt that they could trust Berra. The season ended with the Bronx Bombers sweeping a two-game series against the Red Sox to end the season and claim the pennant. Yogi was a disappointing 1 for 16 in the World Series, though the Yanks beat Brooklyn in five games.

By now Berra had established himself not only as a big league catcher but also a rising star in the American League. He had a stellar season in 1950 and drove in 124 runs, banged out 28 home runs, and batted .322 as the Yanks won their second straight world championship by sweeping the Philadelphia Phillies. Berra won his first Most Valuable Player award in 1951, when he batted .294 with 27 homers and 88 RBIs in leading New York to yet another World Series title, this time at the expense of the Giants.

The next two seasons were more of the same as the Yanks won their fourth and fifth consecutive titles with wins over Brooklyn. Berra continued to develop his reputation as a clutch hitter, driving home 98 runs in '52 and 108 in '53. He batted a robust .429 in the six-game World Series victory in '53. A second MVP came in 1954 despite the Cleveland Indians temporarily interrupting the Yankees dynasty. That year Berra batted .307 to go with 22 homers and 125 RBIs.

Berra entered the 1955 season as the highest-paid Yankee; he earned his $48,000 by winning his second consecutive MVP and third overall. That year he batted across 108 runs and had 27 home runs. The season ended in disappointment as the Dodgers were finally able to take a Series from the Yankees, in a seven-game thriller. Jackie Robinson stole home in Game One and Berra argued vociferously while jumping up and down. He never stopped insisting Robinson was out and he even signed photos of the play, "He was out." In the decisive seventh game Yogi came to the plate in the sixth inning with two men aboard and hit a shot that was headed for the left-field corner. But Sandy Amoros tracked it down with a spectacular catch and turned it into a double play.

The Yankees regained the world championship in 1956—against the Dodgers—and Berra had a big Series with three home runs, including two off Don Newcombe in the decisive seventh game. Berra batted in 10 runs. However, for Yogi the highlight of the Series was catching Don Larsen's perfect game in Game Five. Larsen said he did not shake off Yogi once during his masterpiece. When it was over, Larsen caught his catcher when Yogi famously leaped into the pitcher's arms. For more than a half-century running, no other battery ever pulled off a postseason no-hitter.

Berra slumped to a .251 average in 1957 but was still productive with 24 home runs and 82 RBIs. He followed that with a similarly productive 1958 with 22 homers and 90 RBIs with a batting average of .266. In those two seasons the Yanks and Milwaukee Braves split the World Series with New York winning in '58 by erasing a three-games-to-one deficit. Berra batted .320 in the 1957 fall classic and in Lew Burdette's stellar Game Seven shutout, his only walk was an intentional pass to Berra in the first inning. He had batted .429, .417, and .360 in the three previous World Series, further solidifying his reputation as a clutch hitter and a winning ballplayer.

There was a game in 1958 when the Yanks played Detroit with Hall of Famer Jim Bunning on the mound. Yankees pitcher Bob Turley was stealing the signs from the catcher and whistling to the hitter if the pitch was to be a curveball. Hank Bauer came up first, heard Turley whistle and promptly singled to right field. The same thing happened with the next hitter and Bunning had enough. Mickey Mantle came to the plate and Bunning warned Turley that if he whistled that he was going to drill Mantle, which he did. The next hitter due up was Berra and once again Turley whistled. Yogi stepped out of the box, cupped his hands and yelled to Bunning, "Jim, he's whistling but I ain't listening."

Berra reached some milestones in 1959, including his 300th career home run. He also set records for the most consecutive chances by a catcher without an error, 950, and most consecutive games without an error with 148. The erratic catcher of the early years was now a distant memory.

As if he hadn't feasted off Dodgers pitching enough in the World Series when they were in Brooklyn, Berra spoiled the first West Coast All-Star Game for the home fans by hitting a two-run homer off Los Angeles Dodger Don Drysdale at the Los Angeles Coliseum. Though the Yankees didn't win the World Series in 1959—the Dodgers did, over the White Sox—the Yankees recovered and took another pennant in 1960, the 10th and final one under Casey Stengel. Yogi began to put more time in the outfield, appearing in only 63 games as a catcher. In the thrilling Game Seven against Pittsburgh he hit a three-run homer in the sixth inning that only served as backdrop to Bill Mazeroski's Series-ending home run in the ninth inning. That fabled shot sailed over left fielder Berra's head.

It was now apparent that Berra was in the twilight of a magnificent career as his playing time diminished the next three years. He retired after the '63 World Series, batting only once in a sweep at the hands of the Dodgers. Even with that loss, he retired with a 10–4 record in the World Series, a championship ring for every finger. He was named an All-Star 18 times between 1948 and 1962 (including three years when two All-Star Games were played each summer). He started behind the plate for the American League All-Stars 11 times. In the regular season, he batted .285 with 358 home runs. As a Yankee he drew 704 walks against just 411 strikeouts—proof that this legendary bad-ball hitter indeed hit what he chased.

On October 24, 1963, Berra was named the Yankees manager to replace Ralph Houk, who moved upstairs to become general manager. Surprisingly, this scenario had been in the making for a year. General manager Roy Hamey was in ill health and informed owner Dan Topping that he would resign after the '63 season. It was decided that Houk would replace Hamey and Berra, who was a player-coach in '63, would take over as manager. Amazingly, news of this never leaked. Yogi did not even tell Carmen, in what has to be one of the best-kept secrets in baseball history. Another unusual aspect of this was that the Yankees offered Berra a two-year contract but he insisted on a one-year deal as he was not sure he could manage. This he would later regret.

Berra had intended on keeping pitching coach Johnny Sain on his staff but Sain could not agree on a contract and Berra turned to old friend Whitey Ford to be player-coach. He always believed Ford was one of the more intelligent pitchers and he thought he would be outstanding in handling young pitchers.

The Yankees came out of the gate sluggish in 1964 and as June rolled around they were 21–16. That group of players was not a particularly easy bunch to manage. Veterans Mantle and Ford were famous for their off-the-field drinking and carousing, and the young players wanted to follow along. Players like Jim Bouton and Joe Pepitone were brash and the clubhouse was out of control. Berra somehow had the club back in first place in early August, yet they spent the rest of the month playing uninspired and inconsistent ball, climaxing with a four-game sweep at the hands of the White Sox that dropped the third-place Yankees 4½ games behind Chicago. After the series concluded, the team bus was stuck in traffic on the way to the airport and everyone was feeling impatient. One of the most famous incidents in Yankees history took place as Phil Linz pulled out his harmonica and began to play "Mary Had a Little Lamb." Berra angrily yelled from the front of the bus for him to stop. Here there are different accounts of what happened next. According to Mantle, Linz asked him what Berra said. Mantle responded, "Play louder." Linz obliged. When Yogi heard the harmonica again he stormed to the back of the bus, smacked the instrument away, and a heated argument ensued. When news of the confrontation came out, Houk told reporters he had no intention of speaking to Berra about the incident. With Berra's job security already in danger, this appeared to make his firing a fait accompli.

The club lost the next two games to Boston immediately after the incident to fall six games out, but then the Yankees poured it on. New York finished August strong and went 22–6 in September to win the pennant. Their opponent in the World Series was the St. Louis Cardinals, who had also rallied to claim a thrilling National League race. It was a back-and-forth Series that came down to a seventh-game matchup of Bob Gibson and young Mel Stottlemyre. St. Louis broke through for three runs in the fourth inning with the aid of some sloppy New York defense and Gibson held on to clinch the Series. Overall, Berra had done a good job with an aging team on its last legs. Ford had a sore arm and Mantle's bad legs were making it increasingly difficult for him to cover center field. It was Berra who pushed for Stottlemyre to be called up and the rookie came through with a 9–3 record. It is unlikely the Yankees would have won the pennant without the young right-hander.

Courtesy of Dr Pepper Snapple Group

*The chocolate soft drink Yoo-Hoo wasn't selling in the 1950s and Yogi Berra changed all that. He did the ads plus personal appearances, eventually becoming a vice president and owning a fair bit of stock before exiting the company.*

They had responded well after the Linz episode and Yogi had every intention of asking for a two-year extension.

In one of the worst-kept secrets in baseball, Cardinals manager Johnny Keane was not going to be back in St. Louis in 1965. The Cards were not playing well in the middle of the season and owner August Busch had denied Keane's request for a contract extension and reached out to Leo Durocher to manage the team in '65. After this leaked, Busch rescinded his offer to Durocher and then offered Keane an extension, but at this point the manager told Busch that he preferred to wait until after the season was over. At some time before the end of the season Houk contacted Keane about managing the Yankees in 1965 and in a strange twist of fate, Keane went into the World Series knowing that he could be leading his opponent the following season. That's exactly what happened. Keane resigned his post the morning after his team won the World Series; Yogi was let go by the Yankees, who then immediately hired Keane. The Yankees offered Berra a job as a scout.

Across town, the New York Mets had finished their third season of play and two former Yankees were running the show; general manager George Weiss and manager Casey Stengel had found employment after being let go by the Yanks. Now it was Yogi's turn. With Carmen advocating that he break with the Yankees after their shabby treatment of him, he took Weiss's offer and joined Stengel's staff as a player-coach. He caught only two games and batted .222, playing his final game three days before his 40th birthday in May. When asked if he and Warren Spahn, the club's other player-coach, were the oldest pitcher and catcher combination in baseball history, Yogi said, "I don't know if we're the oldest battery, but we're certainly the ugliest."

Yogi stayed with the Mets even though he was passed over for manager on three occasions. The first was when Stengel retired after breaking his hip in August 1965 and the Mets—with Stengel's input—chose Wes Westrum as his replacement. Salty Parker was tabbed as Westrum's interim replacement when he resigned in the final week of the 1967 season. In October 1967 the Mets dealt for Senators manager Gil Hodges to replace Parker. Berra knew and respected Hodges and was not upset at being passed over in favor of his old Dodgers rival. But what about being skipped over for Westrum and Parker? In both instances the Mets did consider naming Yogi as their manager but decided not to because they felt that with such a poor team there was no way he could succeed and they were reluctant to put a New York legend in a situation where failure was inevitable. And for his part, Berra preferred to stay in New York rather than pursue a managing job elsewhere.

So Berra stayed on to coach under Hodges and won his 11th World Series ring in 1969 as the Miracle Mets stunned the baseball world by winning the world championship. Berra's opportunity to finally manage the Mets came under tragic circumstances. He replaced Hodges when the Mets manager died of a massive heart attack on April 2, 1972, after playing golf. Berra was the only one of his coaches who wasn't there when Hodges fell over while the foursome was talking in the parking lot. Rube Walker, Eddie Yost, and Joe Pignatano, who had all come from Washington with Hodges, became Yogi's coaches.

Although Berra had coached under Hodges for four years, he was a different type of manager. Hodges was a disciplinarian who took a more hands-on approach with his players. By contrast, Berra treated his players as adults and left the responsibility of being in shape to them, figuring that just being a ballplayer should be motivation enough to take your job seriously and be prepared. Unlike his predecessor, Berra did not platoon and kept the same lineup, a change the veterans found to their liking. Though some felt the Mets were callous in signing Berra to a two-year contract just hours after the death of the beloved Hodges, the team got off to a strong start when the season began. The Mets were 14–7 when they acquired aging superstar Willie Mays from San Francisco. The team continued to surge and improved to 30–11 with solid performances from rookies Jon Matlack and John Milner as well as Rusty Staub, who had been acquired from Montreal, as it happened, three days after Hodges died (Gil knew of the deal and had supported it). The Mets looked every bit like a team headed for the Eastern Division crown when suddenly they were beset by injuries. Staub broke his hand and injuries also befell everyday players Ken Boswell, Tommie Agee, Cleon Jones, and Jim Fregosi (who'd arrived that winter from the Angels in the lamentable deal for Nolan Ryan). The Mets staggered to a third-place finish. On a brighter note for Berra, that summer marked his induction into the Hall of Fame in Cooperstown.

The injuries mounted on the Mets again the following year and there were rumors that Yogi might not make it through the summer. The team stood in last place at the end of August, but as players regained their health, the Mets made a move in an NL East where all six teams were within seven games of one another. After a heart-to-heart talk with left fielder Jones and a resurgence by reliever Tug McGraw, the Mets caught fire. "It ain't over 'til it's over," Yogi had said when the Mets were floundering. It was just beginning.

For the stretch run, Berra went with a four-man rotation of Tom Seaver, Jerry Koosman, Matlack, and George Stone—three lefties plus the eventual Cy Young winner—and McGraw's mantra, mojo, and screwball out of the pen had the city believing. On September 21 the Mets reached .500 and first place at the same time. With a victory over the Cubs in the first game of a makeup doubleheader after the rest of the league had finished the schedule, the Mets completed their remarkable comeback. They won the NL East with the lowest winning percentage of any postseason team to that time (82 victories, 79 defeats, .509). They faced the 99-win Cincinnati Reds, going for their third pennant in four years, in the National League Championship Series. Just as in 1969, the superior Mets pitching bested a heavily favored opponent. Though the series is best remembered for the fight between the Mets' Bud Harrelson and the Reds' Pete Rose, the NLCS win made Yogi only the second manager in history to win a pennant in each league. (Joe McCarthy had done it in 1932.)

Waiting for the Mets in the World Series were the defending world champion Oakland A's. The teams split the first two games and the Mets won two of three at frigid Shea Stadium to head back to Oakland needing to win one game. In a controversial decision, Yogi named Tom Seaver to start Game Six on three days rest. While Seaver's shoulder had been cause for worry at the end of the season, Stone had gone 12–3 for the season, hadn't lost since July, and even got the save in Game Two in Oakland when McGraw tired after six innings of relief. Seaver pitched well but lost a tight game to Catfish Hunter to even the Series. Oakland wrapped up the second of what would be three straight world championships by hammering Matlack in Game Seven in the young lefty's third start of the World Series.

For a third straight year the Mets were hit hard by injuries in 1974, but this time there would be no miraculous late-season charge. They fell to fifth place with a 71–91 record, the club's worst mark since the year before Hodges was hired. Simmering trouble between Berra and Cleon Jones deepened in 1975 and when the left fielder refused to enter a game on July 18, matters came to a head. Yogi refused to let Jones back on the team and demanded that he be released. Chairman of the board M. Donald Grant did not want to cut Jones loose but Berra remained firm and soon thereafter Jones was waived. The team was struggling and when it suffered a five-game losing streak in early August—culminating with a doubleheader shutout at home at the hands of the last-place Expos—Yogi was fired. Coach Roy McMillan was picked to replace him and the next day Berra came into the clubhouse. He made sure there was a photo taken of him wishing McMillan good luck. McMillan was replaced after the season.

After a 12-year absence, Yogi returned to the Yankees when old friend and teammate Billy Martin picked him to be on his staff in 1976. (Martin had replaced Bill Virdon late in 1975 and if he had hired the recently fired Berra then, Yogi would have been in uniform for both the Yankees and Mets at Shea since both clubs played in Flushing that year while Yankee Stadium was being renovated.) With Berra on board at the reopened Yankee Stadium in 1976, the Yanks won their first pennant since the one Yogi had managed them to in 1964. Though they were swept in the '76 Series by the Reds, Berra added two more World Series rings with back-to-back titles in 1977 and 1978. Berra was a constant on the Yankees coaching staff through the 1983 season despite several managerial changes. And he got one more chance to manage when he was named Yankees manager for 1984.

New York struggled early in the season and there was no catching the Detroit Tigers, who ripped off a historic 35–5 start and cruised to the division title. Prior to the '85 season, rumors swirled that owner George M. Steinbrenner wanted to fire his manager, but as spring training came around he declared Berra safe for the year. This was a season that Yogi looked forward to because the Yankees had acquired his son Dale from Pittsburgh. Not only did Berra not survive the season but he was fired before the end of April with a record of 6-10. Upset that Steinbrenner broke his promise to let him manage the entire year, Berra stayed away from Yankee Stadium until a reconciliation in 1999.

While his managing days were now over, his coaching career was not. Houston Astros owner John McMullen offered Berra the Astros manager position just three days after he was fired but he turned it down. At the end of the season, he did accept a coaching job with Houston under rookie manager Hal Lanier. The next year he had the odd distinction of being in uniform for each of the three pennant clinchings by the Mets; Bud Harrelson could say the same thing, though he'd been on hand in a Mets uniform all three times, while Berra watched from the other dugout in the Astrodome after the 16-inning Game Six. Yogi stayed on with the Astros through the 1989 season and called it quits a year after Lanier was fired, thus ending a long and illustrious career in uniform. Including his two stints as a player-coach, Berra spent 19 years as a player, 20 as a coach, and seven as manager.

Berra remained not only a Yankees legend but an American icon as well. A museum dedicated to him opened in Montclair, New Jersey, his and Carmen's hometown for more than half a century. There they raised their three sons: Larry, a former minor league catcher; Tim, who played in the NFL for the Baltimore Colts in 1974; and Dale, who spent the last couple of months of his 11-year career in uniform with his dad after all as a 1987 Astro. He promoted numerous products—most famously Yoo-Hoo, the chocolate soft drink—and a cartoon bear was even named after him. The former catcher's Yogi-isms are known worldwide, especially "When you come to a fork in the road, take it." As one of the oldest and most recognizable Hall of Famers, Yogi Berra maintained a connection back to what many consider the Golden Era of baseball.

Yogi was on hand for both the closing of Yankee and Shea Stadiums in 2008. As homage was paid to Yankees greats who had died, he turned to Whitey Ford and said, "Boy, I hope they're not alive when they do that for me."

**Notes and Sources**

DeVito, Carlo. *Yogi: The Life and Times of an American Original.* (Chicago: Triumph Books, 2008.)

Jack Lang and Peter Simon. *The New York Mets: Twenty-Five Years of Baseball Magic.* (New York: Henry Holt and Co., 1986.)

Hernandez, Keith and Matthew Silverman. *Shea Good-bye: The Untold Story of the Historic 2008 Season.* (Chicago: Triumph Books, 2009.)

Pete Palmer and Gary Gillette (editors), *The 2005 ESPN Baseball Encyclopedia.* (New York: Sterling, 2005.)

Lawrence Peter "Yogi" Berra, http://www.achievement.org/autodoc/page/ber0int-3

Baseball Hall of Fame player file

Interview with Jerry Koosman, December 16, 2008

## The Bronx Is Burning...With Envy

So what were the Yankees doing while the Mets were taking the country by storm and winning the World Series in 1969? The 80–81 Yankees were enduring their fourth losing season in five years and struggling through their first season since 1950 without Mickey Mantle. The Mick's bad knees and ailing body forced him to call it quits on March 1. His 536 career home runs were good for third on the all-time list at the time, behind only Babe Ruth and Hank Aaron. The Yankees retired Mantle's number 7 on June 8 at Yankee Stadium in front of over 60,000.

The Yankees hovered around fifth place, briefly pulling into fourth in mid-August. They were soon displaced again by the Washington Senators, guided by rookie skipper Ted Williams, who would be named American League Manager of the Year. No team threatened the Baltimore Orioles, who took over first place nine games into the season and were never challenged on their way to 109 wins. Likewise, there was no threat of the Yankees winding up in the basement of the newly-configured AL East as the 99-loss Cleveland Indians grabbed sixth place on Opening Day and never let go.

The Yankees, who started the decade with five straight pennants and had dominated the 1950s under manager Casey Stengel and three-time MVP Yogi Berra behind the plate, tumbled to 10th place in 1966—ironically, that was the first year the Mets *did not* finish last. The Mets doubled the Yankees' attendance in 1969 (2,175,373 at Shea; 1,067,966 in the Bronx). The Mets outdrew the Yankees each of the first dozen seasons of Shea Stadium's existence, including 1974–75 when the clubs shared Shea during renovations to Yankee Stadium.

The Mets and Yankees met once during the 1969 season—in the annual Mayor's Trophy Game. At the time, the Mets had four in-season exhibition games on the schedule: at minor league affiliate Memphis and a visit to the new triple-A club in Tidewater (Norfolk), plus closer to home exhibitions at West Point and against the Yankees. Rescheduled from July, the Mayor's Trophy Game was held at Shea the last week of the season. The charity game was the first test of the re-sodded field that had been pillaged by fans six nights earlier in the euphoric celebration following the division clinching. The field held and so did the Mets, winning 7–6 over the Yankees with Art Shamsky driving in five runs.

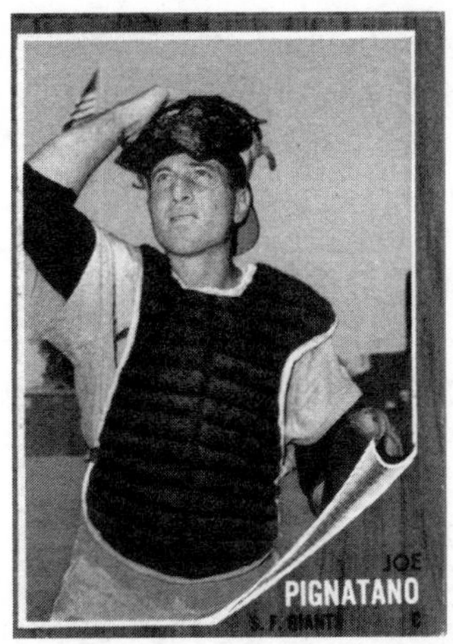


# Joe Pignatano

by Paul Hirsch

Joe Pignatano was almost out of baseball within a month of his debut. Instead, his mother intervened and he enjoyed 38 years in the game, 27 of those in the majors as a player and coach. He was the bullpen coach for the 1969 Miracle Mets, and the backup catcher to John Roseboro on the 1959 Cinderella Dodgers team that upset the Braves in a playoff and knocked off the White Sox in the World Series.

Let's start with his near-early exit from the game that became his life's work. "I signed with the Dodgers in 1948 after a tryout with 50 other players. They signed two of us," he remembered. "I was first sent to Sheboygan, Wisconsin, where I didn't play at all. Then I went to Cairo, Illinois." Pignatano played in three Class D games for Cairo. In those games, he hit .375, scored and drove in two runs, and got "a standing ovation for catching a popup. No other catcher had caught a foul popup for them."

As a reward, Pignatano was released a few days later and was sent back to his home in Brooklyn with a check for $127 and no cash in his pocket. Pignatano traveled 27 hours without food since he could not cash the check. He was sleeping in a train station in Chicago when a cop roused him and told him he couldn't sleep there. "I explained that I had no money and was catching a train in the morning," said Pignatano. The police officer then took Pignatano to a hotel, paid for the room, and made sure he would be awakened in time to make his train.

Once home in Brooklyn, he explained what had happened to his mother, Lucy. Mrs. Pignatano could not believe the way her boy had been treated and immediately called the Dodgers offices and spoke with Fresco Thompson, who was Brooklyn's minor league chief. When she identified herself, Thompson congratulated her on how well Joe was doing. "He couldn't be doing that well," Lucy Pignatano said. "He's sitting right next to me." Mrs. Pignatano related Joe's story to Thompson, who immediately asked Joe to come to Ebbets Field.

At Ebbets Field, Pignatano worked out for some local Dodgers scouts, including head scout and Hall of Famer George Sisler. At the end of the workout, Sisler asked his staff to explain "why we would release this player." No one could, and soon Pignatano was on his way to seven teams in seven leagues: Cambridge, Valdosta, Asheville, Elmira, Fort Worth, St. Paul, Montreal, and eventually Brooklyn.

Joseph Benjamin Pignatano was born in Brooklyn on August 4, 1929, and always kept the borough as his home. He loved sports and was a "pretty good athlete." Growing up in the 1930s and '40s in New York, the only sports he played were baseball, softball, and stickball. He became a catcher because no one else wanted to do it. When the Dodgers offered him a contract he was ecstatic. "Playing for the Dodgers was the pinnacle," he said.

His minor league career, after the hiccup in Cairo, was essentially a straight line up the ladder. His stop in the Texas League in 1955 was notable in that Pignatano hit just .199 but was still promoted to St. Paul in the American Association for 1956. He hit .295 for the Saints, following that up with a .299 performance in 70 games for Montreal in the International League in 1957 before getting his shot in Brooklyn. "The Texas League was a pitchers' league then," Pignatano explained. "Only a few guys hit over .300. I got off to a rough start and didn't recover until I got to St. Paul." Indeed, Maury Wills was Pignatano's teammate at Fort Worth, and the future National League MVP hit just .202 with only 12 steals. Six Texas League players hit .300 with more than 400 at-bats that year, but none spent as much time in the show as Pignatano or Wills.

The highlight of Pignatano's time in Brooklyn was catching the last five innings of a Danny McDevitt shutout in the last game played at Ebbets Field. "I didn't realize we might move until the last week," Pignatano said. "Everyone in Brooklyn blamed [Dodgers owner Walter] O'Malley then, but it was really [City Planning official Robert] Moses. He thought O'Malley was bluffing and wouldn't arrange for him to purchase land at the site he wanted to build a new stadium." Pignatano and McDevitt reenacted the final major league pitch in Brooklyn before a game by the Mets affilate Brooklyn Cyclones at Key Span Park on June 24, 2007.

By the time the Dodgers moved to Los Angeles for the 1958 season, Roy Campanella was paralyzed from an automobile accident, and Pignatano and Roseboro were the front runners to replace him. As it turned out, Roseboro played in about twice as many games as Pignatano over the next two seasons and emerged as the main Dodgers catcher though most of the 1960s. "Johnny [a left-handed hitter] played against the right handers and I played against the lefties," remembered Pignatano. "I never got a real shot [at the number one job]. I never got to catch six or eight games in a row. We sure got the job done in 1959, though."

That was the year the Dodgers rebounded from a seventh-place finish in 1958 to win the World Series. "That year was the highlight," Pignatano said. He replaced Roseboro for the last three innings of the pennant clincher against Milwaukee as Game Two of the best-of-three playoff went into extra innings. In the decisive 12th frame, Pignatano singled with two outs and Gil Hodges on first base, setting up the Carl Furillo hit that, with the help of a throwing error by Felix Mantilla, brought home Hodges with the pennant-winning run. "I can still hear Vin Scully's call, 'We're going to Chicago,'" said Pignatano.

That hit followed a key sequence in San Francisco about two weeks earlier. The Dodgers came to Seals Stadium for a three-game series trailing the Giants by two with nine games left. Behind 1–0 in the seventh inning in the second game of a September 19 doubleheader, Pignatano walked with Don Demeter on second and Wills on first and one out. Chuck Essegian then hit a double play ball to Jim Davenport at third. Pignatano came into second base hard and hit Daryl Spencer, who dropped the ball on the pivot. Demeter scored and everyone else was safe. The Dodgers went on to score four more runs on doubles by Jim Gilliam and Charlie Neal, and won the game 5–3, keying a three-game sweep. The play by Pignatano was highlighted in the next issue of *Sports Illustrated.*

The breakup of that double play, the single in the playoff, plus an inning behind the plate in the Dodgers' Game Five loss in the 1959 World Series were the top moments of his time in Los Angeles. According to then-General Manager Buzzie Bavasi, the team's need for cash to complete Dodger Stadium and the emergence of Norm Sherry as the preferred target for Sandy Koufax led to the sale of Pignatano to the Kansas City A's in January of 1961. A's catching duties were split that season between Pignatano and Haywood Sullivan. "I enjoyed Kansas City. I hit well for awhile and [owner Charlie] Finley took care of us. As long as I had a uniform I really didn't care where I was." It was the only season in which Pignatano played in more than 90 games or had more than 200 at-bats.

Pignatano split 1962 between the Giants and the Mets. He played just seven games for San Francisco before his sale to the Mets on July 13. "Alvin Dark never cared for me," Pignatano said of the time he backed up Ed Bailey and Tom Haller. With the Mets, Pignatano played out the string and hit into a triple play in his last big league at-bat on September 30. By then, he knew the end was near.

"My arm was hurting, the fastball was starting to get by me, and I had a sense that it was about over," he said. Pignatano spent 1963 and 1964 in the International League with Buffalo and Rochester. His 1964 Rochester club won the International League championship, and Pignatano was invited back for 1965, but the accumulating aches and pains led him to walk away.

Pignatano always worked in the offseason, first as a plumber's helper for about 10 years and then 23 years with the A&S Department Store in Brooklyn helping with toys before Christmas and the January White Sale. "I needed to work in the offseason to make ends meet," he said. He got into coaching following a winter 1964 social evening with ex-Dodgers teammate Gil Hodges, who had become manager of the Washington Senators, and their wives. "At the end of the evening Gil said, 'I have a question I want to ask you. Would you like to come to the Senators and be my first base coach next season?' I told him I'd love to."

Pignatano worked for the Senators from 1965 to 1967 before following Hodges to New York. Yogi Berra was established as first base coach on the Mets,

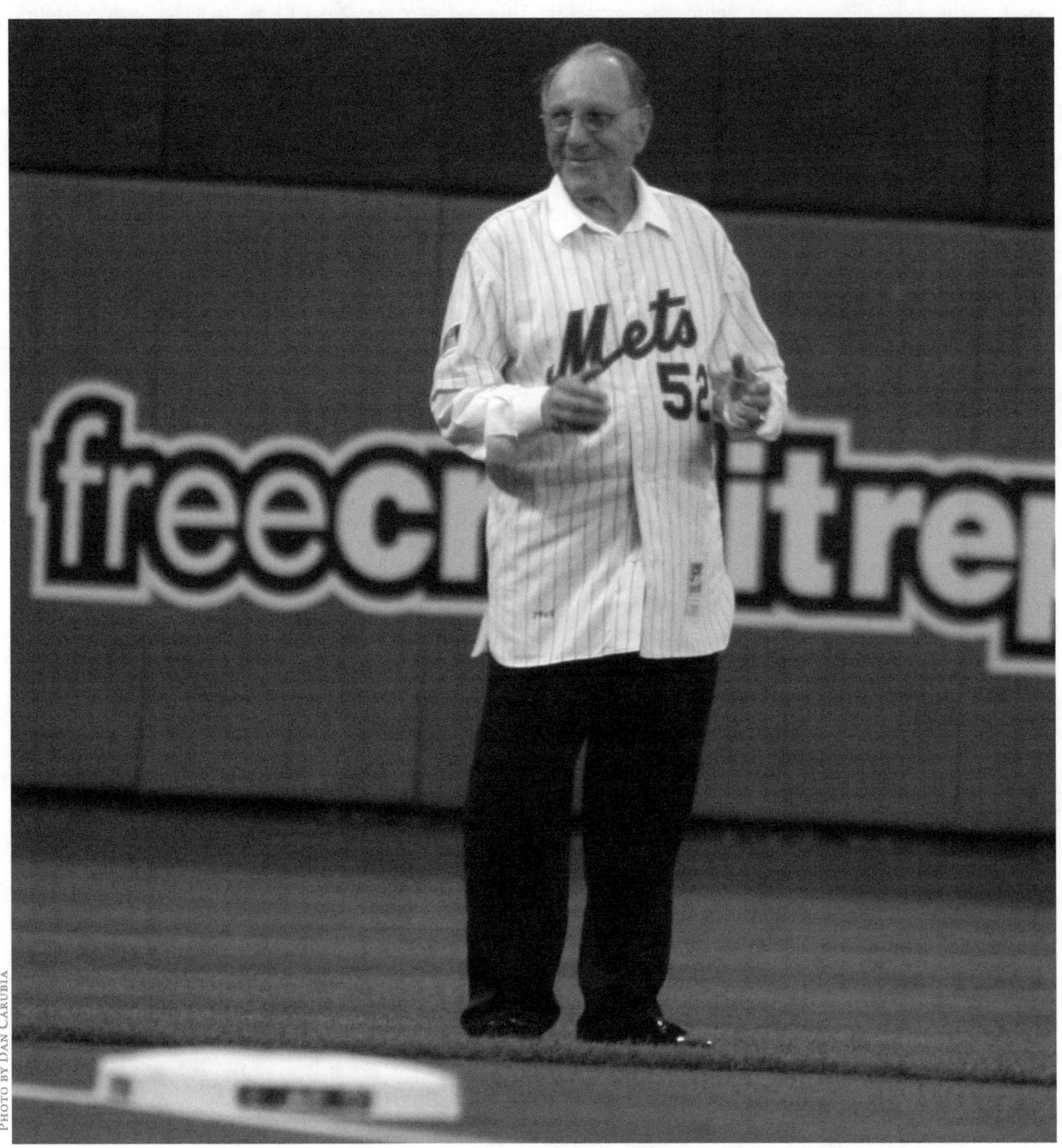


PHOTO BY DAN CARUBIA

*Joe Pignatano was all smiles as the Mets honored the 1969 Mets at Citi Field in 2009.*

so Pignatano moved to the bullpen. "My job was to work with the relievers, make sure they were ready, and advise Gil," he said. Pignatano's most famous contribution may have been the vegetable garden he nurtured in the Mets bullpen.

"In 1969 I discovered a wild tomato plant in the bullpen and nurtured it the rest of the season," he remembered. "We got some tomatoes off it, but most important we won the whole thing. After that, I kept up the garden as long as I was with the Mets as a good luck charm." Pignatano feels the turning point of the 1969 season was a September game at Shea Stadium against the Cubs. Tommie Agee had been knocked down in the first inning, and Jerry Koosman retaliated by drilling Ron Santo on the arm. While Santo continued to play, he was less effective and the Mets passed Chicago to win the division title. "Koosman sent a message, especially to Leo [Durocher, the Cubs manager]. Leo started the whole thing," Pignatano said.

"That season was baseball at its best," he said. "We had a bunch of young kids and a few veterans playing great. [Donn] Clendenon won a lot of games for us with late hits, and Jerry Grote remains the best defensive catcher I have ever seen."

Pignatano continued coaching with the Mets through 1981, and finished with three years as a Braves coach under Joe Torre. He was with the Mets when Hodges died in 1972, but said the death didn't really affect the team. "We lost a good man. Life went on and baseball went on. We all missed Gil, but it was just life."

His top salary as a coach was $43,000, which, he says, was more than his total income in six years as a big league player. Now, he fills his days with golf while enjoying a pension from baseball that is "far greater then any salary I earned as a player or coach." He also makes appearances at Dodgers and Mets Fantasy Camps. Pignatano says he always worked hard, and that all his employers "got their money's worth."

Pignatano married his wife Nancy in 1954. Together, they have two sons and two grandchildren.

**Sources**

Interviews with Joe Pignatano, 2007, 2009
Email correspondence with Buzzie Bavassi
Dodgers Yearbooks, 1957-60

Courtesy of Dwayne Labakas Collection

Courtesy of Dwayne Labakas Collection

*The 1969 Mets had two Hall of Famers: Tom Seaver, top left, and Nolan Ryan, top right. Jim McAndrew, below left, had double the starts and the same number of wins as the wild, young Ryan. Future physician Ron Taylor was dispatched 59 times in '69 when aid was needed.*

Courtesy of Dwayne Labakas Collection

Courtesy of Dwayne Labakas Collection

Courtesy of Mets Inside Pitch Archives

Courtesy Dwayne Labakas Collection

*Lefty-swinging Ken Boswell played second base against right-handers. His .279 average was third-highest on the team.*

*Manager Gil Hodges, above, favored platoons for his 1969 Mets, but the care of his young pitching staff was paramount. Jerry Grote, right, one of the best defensive catchers in the game, caught most days regardless of which arm the opposition's starter used.*

Photo courtesy metsilverman.com

PHOTO COURTESY METSILVERMAN.COM

*The infield for the 1969 Mets fluctuated depending on who was on the mound for the other team. Three of the four positions had platoons. Ed Kranepool, left, who debuted during the club's first season, manned first base against right-handers.*

COURTESY DWAYNE LABAKAS COLLECTION

COURTESY DWAYNE LABAKAS COLLECTION

*Switch-hitting Bud Harrelson, left, was the everyday shortstop, though his spot in the batting order changed if there was a righty or a lefty facing the Mets. Ed Charles spent his final major league season manning third base against southpaws in 1969.*

Courtesy of Dwayne Labakas Collection

Courtesy of Dwayne Labakas Collection

*Part of the New York-Gulf Coast outfield connection, Amos Otis, above left, was miscast as a third baseman. The future Gold Glove center fielder spent his last summer as a Met in the minors and off the postseason roster. Right fielder and 1969 New York hero Ron Swoboda, above right, was from Maryland, but he later became a Mets emissary in New Orleans.*

Courtesy of Dwayne Labakas Collection

*Center fielder Tommie Agee, left, like Amos Otis and childhood friend Cleon Jones, came from Mobile, Alabama. Agee led the 1969 Mets in home runs and RBIs out of the leadoff spot, but he became a legend for what he did with his glove with the world watching in October.*

Photo courtesy of Keith Hernandez

*After the final game at Shea Stadium in 2008, Mets representing every era walked the field for the last time. From left: Dwight Gooden (16), Jerry Koosman (36), Al Leiter (22), John Franco (45), Jesse Orosco (47), and Cleon Jones (21). Below, Darryl Strawberry, center, and Dwight Gooden, right, tower over 1969 Mets coach Yogi Berra, yet Yogi's records stand tallest of all.*

Photo courtesy of Keith Hernandez

PHOTO COURTESY OF METSILVERMAN.COM

*The image of the late Gil Hodges dwarfs emcee Howie Rose during the 40th anniversary festivities for the 1969 Mets at Citi Field on August 22, 2009.*

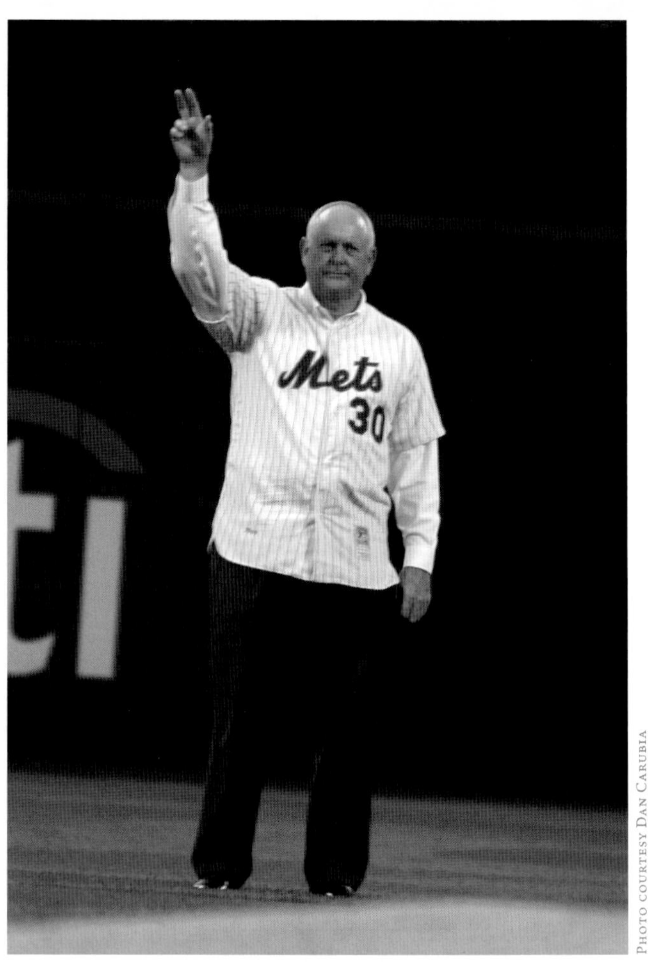


PHOTO COURTESY DAN CARUBIA

PHOTO COURTESY DAN CARUBIA

*Nolan Ryan dons No. 30 as a Met for the first time since 1971 and then throws out the first pitch at Citi Field with 1969 teammates Tom Seaver, center, and Jerry Koosman, right. The catching corps: Yogi Berra (8), Jerry Grote (15), and Duffy Dyer (10).*

# Rube Walker

by Dave Williams

The Miracle Mets of 1969 rode their powerful young pitching to an improbable World Series championship, and the man who developed and nurtured that staff was an easygoing ex-catcher named Rube Walker. Despite not being a pitcher himself, he had an innate sense of the mental side of pitching and he used this to help his young stable of arms mature and get them to pitch with a savvy beyond their years.

Born Albert Bluford Walker on May 16, 1926, in Lenoir, North Carolina, the son of Albert and Beulah Walker, he was the oldest of three boys. He enjoyed a typical middle-class upbringing for the time. His father, a semipro catcher in his younger days, would bring home string every day from his job at the cotton mill to wrap around golf balls until they were the size of baseballs, and, once they were wrapped with black tape, the Walker boys would have homemade baseballs to play with. Young Albert earned the nickname that would stay with him the rest of his life when he was batboy for the Lenoir team of the Class D North Carolina State League and his idol was the star of the team, Rube Robinson. Walker and his brothers had to work at his grandparents' farm to help support the family. Rube learned how to cure meat as well as handle other farm chores. He enjoyed many sports, including football and wrestling, but it was baseball that was his favorite and which he excelled at.

Upon graduation from Lenoir High School in 1944, he signed with Erwin of the Class D Appalachian League, a Chicago Cubs farm team, and batted .264. In 1945 he began the season with Nashville of the Southern Association but hit only .216 before he was sent back to play the rest of the year with Portsmouth of the Class B Piedmont League, where his average was .258. He played with Davenport in the Class B Three-I League in 1946 and enjoyed a spectacular season, leading the circuit in batting at .354 while also clubbing 13 home runs and driving home 85 runs. He was back with Nashville for 1947 and had another tremendous campaign with 22 home runs, 105 RBIs and a .331 batting average, and at one point had hits in 10 consecutive at-bats. The Cubs were impressed with the slugging young catcher and signed to him to a contract for 1948.

In his rookie season, Walker showed promise as he appeared in 79 games for the Cubs and batted .275. But both the games and the batting average were career highs as Rube settled in as a career backup. He appeared in just 56 games in 1949 and 74 in 1950 and had batting averages of .244 and .230 respectively. He began 1951 with the Cubs and on June 15 he was part of an eight-player trade that sent him to Brooklyn along with outfielder Andy Pafko, pitcher Johnny Schmitz, and infielder Wayne Terwilliger for outfielder Gene Hermanski, catcher Bruce Edwards, infielder Eddie Miksis, and pitcher Joe Hatten. In Brooklyn, Walker backed up future Hall of Famer Roy Campanella and, after Campy was injured, Walker was behind the plate for Games Two and Three of the playoff series against the New York Giants. The series ended with the famous Bobby

Thomson home run off Ralph Branca in the bottom of the ninth of the decisive third game, and years later Rube said that pitch was supposed to be a brushback, but "Branca didn't get the ball far enough inside."

Things were looking a little better for Rube in his personal life at the time. On February 13, 1951, he married a local woman named Mildred whom he met in a soda shop. Walker was very devoted to his wife and later his three daughters, spending as much time as he could despite the demands of a baseball season. His first daughter, Debbie, was born in 1952, followed by Barbara in 1955, and Janet in 1963. Just like his father, Rube was more laid back and left the disciplining of the children to Millie.

He played out the rest of his career with the Dodgers as a reserve catcher. There were few highlights on the field as a backup to a future Hall of Famer. On May 21, 1952, he had two hits and scored two runs in an inning, and he hit two of his three lifetime triples off Johnny Sain. What Walker did accumulate were lifetime relationships such as with his roommate, Dodgers captain Pee Wee Reese (he named his first child after Pee Wee's daughter), and, in what proved to be the most important relationship of his professional life, with first baseman Gil Hodges. Hodges and Walker had tremendous respect for each other and the seeds of a great working relationship were planted during the Brooklyn days.

After the Dodgers moved to Los Angeles, tragedy struck with the automobile accident involving catcher Roy Campanella before the 1958 season. Walker was greatly affected by the injuries that ended the playing career of his good friend and found little solace in the first opportunity of his career to be a number one catcher. Rube was a great handler of pitchers but his limited production at the plate kept him from getting more playing time and precipitated his release from the Dodgers. He was waived on June 17, 1958, after batting only .114 in 44 at-bats backing up John Roseboro, who was batting a more robust .296 at the time. There was speculation that Rube would be named manger of the Dodgers minor league affiliate at Spokane, but instead he was kept on as a coach with the big league club. His release was met with consternation by some Dodgers pitchers. Don Drysdale moaned, "Why does it have to be Rube?" Johnny Podres said. "I love to pitch to him....When it comes to setting up the hitter, there were none better."

Rube embarked on a minor-league managing career in 1959 as he was named player-manager of Houston of the American Association. This position proved to be short-lived; he was fired on June 21 with the club mired in last place in the league's West Division. He was picked up as a catcher by St. Paul of the same league and batted a combined .268 in 103 games, with five home runs and 43 RBIs playing for both St. Paul and the Dodgers' Houston farm club. The next season he became manager of Atlanta, the Dodgers affiliate in the Southern Association, which won the league pennant with an 87–67 record. He also appeared in 62 games and batted .252. It was Walker's last season as an active player. Future major-league pitcher Pete Richert, whose costly throwing error would help Rube's Mets win the 1969 World Series, was named Minor League Player of the Year under Walker's tutelage. The club dropped to fourth place in 1961 and Walker moved on to manage Amarillo, a New York Yankees affiliate in the Texas League, in 1962 and finished sixth with a record of 56–84. In 1963 he led the Yankees' Augusta team in the South Atlantic League and finished first with a record of 41–21 in the first half of a split season but dropped off to fifth in the second half. His final season as a minor league manager came in 1964 with Columbus, a Yankees affiliate in the Southern Association, finishing in seventh place.

Walker was slated to manage the Mets affiliate at Greenville of the Western Carolinas League in 1965 when old friend Gil Hodges asked him to become the pitching coach with the Washington Senators. The Mets released Walker from his obligation and Rube was back in the big leagues. When Hodges took over as the Mets manager in 1968, he brought Walker with him and the move could not have been more fortuitous for both. Despite the Mets' history of futility, they did have some fine young pitching on the major league roster and in the farm system.

Walker believed there were only so many pitches in an arm and he watched over his young staff like a mother hen. He instituted "Walker's Law"—no pitcher was allowed to throw without Rube's knowing. There was some criticism that he babied the Mets pitchers and in some sense that may have been true, but to many on the staff Walker was a father figure and he treated the young hurlers like the sons he never had. Maybe because he was a catcher in his day, Walker was not real strong on mechanics but stressed conditioning and the mental aspect of the game. This approach seemed to work. Even with a brilliant rookie season from Tom Seaver, the Mets finished ninth in the National League in team ERA in 1967 and lost 101 games; the club improved to fourth in the same category in 1968, knocking a full run off the team ERA. The Mets finished 1968 with the best record of their brief history at 73–89. Tom Seaver matched his 1967 win total of 16 and rookie Jerry Koosman went 19–12 with a 2.08 ERA and seven shutouts. The hard-throwing staff, which included rookie Nolan Ryan, finished just seven strikeouts behind league-leading Houston—the Mets did manage to finish ahead of the Astros in the standings, the second time the Mets had avoided the basement in their checkered history.

The big change Rube Walker instituted was the five-man rotation. He believed it would keep his pitchers stronger and healthier over the long grind of 162 games. The leader of the staff, Seaver, grumbled about this at first because he had grown accustomed to pitching every four days and wondered if he would lose some of his effectiveness with more time between starts. But Seaver later became one of the biggest advocates of the five-man rotation, which subsequently was adopted by all teams.

In keeping with his philosophy that an arm had only so many pitches in it, Walker set up a strict regimen for all the team's pitchers from the beginning of spring training right through the end of the season. When pitchers reported to St. Petersburg, they ran hard to get their legs in shape. Walker strongly believed that conditioning would make the difference late in a game when a pitcher had to reach back for something extra to get out of a jam. Once the season began, a pitcher did not throw on the day after a start but ran hard. The next day he threw hard for 10 minutes, and the day after that it was back to running without throwing. The day before his next start, the pitcher would throw a little, run a bit more, and then keep the chart on that night's pitcher.

It was pitching that led the comeback from a 10-game deficit in August to the Eastern Division crown in 1969. Was it a case of the Cubs' four-man rotation wearing down in the heat of all those day games in Wrigley Field while the younger Mets had the benefit of an extra day's rest between starts? That is impossible to say, but it is a fact that the New York's pitching excelled over the last third of the regular season while the Cubs faded to second place, eight games out. The Mets set a franchise record with 36 consecutive shutout innings in early September and then broke it two weeks later. The Mets won 23 times that month, throwing 15 complete games, 10 shutouts, and compiling a 2.15 ERA. Even veteran Don Cardwell, the old man of the rotation at 33, had a 28-inning scoreless streak and five straight wins before losing the meaningless final game of the year... against the Cubs.

Though New York's pitching faltered in the first National League Championship Series, registering a 5.00 ERA, the Mets bats picked them up and the club still swept Atlanta. The Mets then silenced the powerful Baltimore Orioles in the World Series, throwing 19 consecutive scoreless innings and allowing just five runs over the last four games. Seaver, who won his last 10 decisions in the regular season and went 10 innings to beat Baltimore in Game Four of the Series; and Koosman, who'd shaken off early season arm woes to win 17 games, won Games Two and Five of the World Series. Rookie Gary Gentry and Nolan Ryan combined to win the third game in the Series, though Tommie Agee's two brilliant catches in center had as much to do with it as anything.

Walker had the respect and trust of his pitchers. Though mechanics may not have been his strong suit, he was able to help pitchers by spotting flaws in their delivery. What he did demand and teach was how to think like a major league pitcher, and this aided in the maturation of the young staff and their ability to manage a game and set up hitters. Jerry Koosman recalled how Rube helped him by insisting that he scrap his slider, and this made his curveball more effective. The pitchers loved their laid-back mentor and enjoyed playing pranks and teasing him. One of their favorite ways of needling Rube was reminding him that he called the pitch that became one of the most famous home runs in history: the Bobby Thomson blast in the 1951 National League playoff.

The Mets did not repeat as champions in 1970 as Seaver grew fatigued down the stretch and Koosman had another bout of shoulder woes. The Mets dropped to 83 wins and repeated that total in 1971. Rube suffered some personal tragedy during this stage of his life as his mother died in April 1969; his brother Verlon, a minor league catcher from 1948 to 1961, and a Cubs coach for a decade, died of leukemia in 1971; his father died in April 1972; and his boss and good friend Gil Hodges died of a heart attack on April 2, 1972, after a round of golf in which Walker was a member of the foursome. Yogi Berra replaced Hodges as manager and he, like Hodges, let Rube run the pitching as he saw fit. The Mets charged out of the gate in 1972 and were at 30-11 when injuries began to mount and they fell to a third straight third-place finish. Two bright spots on the staff were Seaver, who won 21 games, and Jon Matlack, who won 15 and was National League Rookie of the Year.

The next season, 1973, looked like a repeat of the previous year as the Mets were hit hard by injuries. As August came to a close they were in last place, 6½ games behind the St. Louis Cardinals. Then they came to life. Tug McGraw had struggled all year and at one point had an ERA over 6.00. In an attempt to get their ace reliever going, Walker and Berra decided to give him a start against Atlanta and he gave up seven runs in six innings. But he followed that with a start against Montreal in which he allowed only one run. This seemed to work; once he returned to the bullpen, McGraw led a furious September charge to the division title. His last 16 appearances of the season resulted in 4 wins and 11 saves. As in 1969, the strong Mets pitching led them to an upset in the National League Division Series over a heavily favored team, the Big Red Machine of the Cincinnati Reds, winner of 99 games. The Mets nearly completed the miracle in the World Series, falling to defending champion Oakland in seven games.

After the Series, some questioned the Mets starting Game Six with Seaver, who had battled shoulder soreness at the end of the regular season, on short rest. With the Mets up three games to two, Berra and Walker were trying to avoid a seventh game and decided that Seaver, who agreed with their assessment, could handle starting the sixth game. He pitched well but lost, 3–1. When the Mets lost the next day, some critics said the Mets should have used 14–3 George Stone and held Seaver to pitch Game Seven on full rest.

The Mets fell to fifth place in 1974, but Seaver had his last great season as a Met in '75 to claim his third Cy Young Award and Koosman had his only 20-win season the following year. Walker's beloved pitching staff was broken up by management in some questionable moves. Hard-throwing Nolan Ryan was sent to the California Angels after the 1971 season for Jim Fregosi. While Walker was not enamored with the deal, he did understand it as the Mets were near desperate in their search for a third baseman with power. To that point, there had been some doubt that Ryan would ever harness his incredible fastball and be a consistent winner; and the Mets still had Seaver, Koosman, Gentry, and a young Jon Matlack. Gentry was the next to go, after the '72 season, but this move panned out for the Mets as they acquired a quality player in Felix Millan who manned second base for the next five seasons and also got the southpaw Stone.

Seaver, was sent to Cincinnati after a feud with Mets management and newspaper columnist Dick Young ran him out of town. Matlack and Koosman both were gone shortly thereafter and the Mets struggled mightily. Joe Torre was named manager during the 1977 season and Walker remained on board. New ownership and front office management fired Torre and Walker after the 1981 season. Torre was quickly named to manage the Atlanta Braves in 1981 and he took Walker with him to be pitching coach, as well as bullpen coach Joe Pignatano, who'd been a teammate of Walker's with the Dodgers and had coached with him since 1964 in Washington and New York.

The Braves were a surprise winner of the Western Division title in 1982, their first since 1969, but Atlanta lost to St. Louis in the NLCS. The Braves finished second the next two seasons, and Torre and Walker were let go. This ended Rube's nearly 40 years in uniform and he finished his career scouting for the Braves and Cardinals. He was diagnosed with cancer in the summer of 1992, when Seaver was to be inducted into the Hall of Fame. Seaver invited Rube to the ceremony but he was too weak to attend and on December 12 of that year he died. "He was a pitcher's pitching coach," Seaver commented. That quote may sum up best the laid-back character who helped lead the 1969 Mets pitching staff to baseball glory.

## Rube's Five-Man Miracle Innovation

The five-man pitching rotation has been the major league standard for almost four decades. The four-man rotation, however, was once set in stone, with a longman or swingman utilized to start when doubleheaders piled up. Because pitching dominated much of the 1960s—even after increasing the schedule from 154 to 162 games—there seemed little call or need for change. But the pitching coach on a team previously known for its lousy pitching initiated the revolutionary alteration to the standard.

Upon the arrival of Gil Hodges and his new Mets staff to training camp in St. Petersburg in 1968, incoming pitching coach Rube Walker asked *Long Island Press* beat writer Jack Lang to see the notebook the reporter kept on every player—the 1960s equivalent of studying trends on a computer. "When he checked into the Colonial Inn for the first time in spring 1968, he borrowed my book on pitchers and carefully studied how each had worked the year before under [manager Wes] Westrum, especially how they fared after a certain number of days of rest," Lang wrote in *The New York Mets: Twenty-Five Years of Baseball Magic.* "Walker and Hodges were planning to introduce the five-man rotation anyway, but Rube's check of my 1967 statistics, he later admitted, confirmed their decision."

Tom Seaver, a workhorse and a man not afraid to question authority, was at first reluctant to go to four days rest between starts. "Walker, a fatherly figure," Lang wrote, "convinced him that though he might miss a start or two over the course of the year, he would be stronger and last longer in the games he did start because of the extra days of rest."

Seaver turned out to be the big winner, both literally and figuratively. When off days and rainouts occurred, the other pitchers on the staff were usually skipped in

*continued on next page*

*continued*

favor of Seaver. Nolan Ryan, who was shifted back and forth between starting and relieving because of injuries plus military duty—and the young pitcher's inconsistency—wanted more regular work, but the team was in the unaccustomed situation of needing to eke out every win possible.

Gary Gentry, who in seasons to come would grumble about being skipped over for Seaver, had little to complain about in 1969. Seaver and Gentry each had 35 starts to share the club lead, with Seaver logging almost 40 more innings (plus one relief appearance), winning 12 more games, losing five fewer, recording three times as many complete games (18–6), having a far lower ERA (2.21-3.43), and finishing one vote shy of unanimous selection for Cy Young. Granted, Gentry was a rookie—and his failure to garner a single vote for National League Rookie of the Year Award was puzzling in a year without any spectacular freshmen—but the record again favors the astute use of personnel by Walker and Hodges.

The rest of the 1969 starts were apportioned rather fairly. Jerry Koosman's early season arm problems limited him to 32 games and necessitated four starts by Tug McGraw. Jack DiLauro made four fill-in starts during the summer. The rest of the starts went to Jim McAndrew and Don Cardwell (21 each) and Ryan (10). The club's record of 100-62? Bet that wasn't in Jack Lang's notebook.

Team Pitching 1969

| Tm | #Pitch | PitchAge | R/G | W | L | W-L% | ERA | G | GF | CG | SV | IP | H | R | ER | HR | BB | IBB | K | WHIP |
|---|---|---|---|---|---|---|---|---|---|---|---|---|---|---|---|---|---|---|---|---|
| ATL | 18 | 27.5 | 3.9 | 93 | 69 | .574 | 3.53 | 162 | 124 | 38 | 42 | 1445 | 1334 | 631 | 567 | 144 | 438 | 49 | 893 | 1.226 |
| CHC | 17 | 27.6 | 3.75 | 92 | 70 | .568 | 3.34 | 163 | 105 | 58 | 27 | 1454.1 | 1366 | 611 | 540 | 118 | 475 | 72 | 1017 | 1.266 |
| CIN | 17 | 27.3 | 4.71 | 89 | 73 | .549 | 4.13 | 163 | 140 | 23 | 44 | 1465 | 1478 | 768 | 673 | 149 | 611 | 78 | 818 | 1.426 |
| HOU | 18 | 25.6 | 4.12 | 81 | 81 | .500 | 3.60 | 162 | 110 | 52 | 34 | 1435.2 | 1347 | 668 | 574 | 111 | 547 | 65 | 1221 | 1.319 |
| LAD | 14 | 27.3 | 3.46 | 85 | 77 | .525 | 3.09 | 162 | 115 | 47 | 31 | 1457 | 1324 | 561 | 500 | 122 | 420 | 41 | 975 | 1.197 |
| MON | 18 | 26.8 | 4.88 | 52 | 110 | .321 | 4.33 | 162 | 136 | 26 | 21 | 1426 | 1429 | 791 | 686 | 145 | 702 | 76 | 973 | 1.494 |
| NYM | 15 | 25.8 | 3.34 | 100 | 62 | .617 | 2.99 | 162 | 111 | 51 | 35 | 1468.1 | 1217 | 541 | 487 | 119 | 517 | 70 | 1012 | 1.181 |
| PHI | 15 | 26.1 | 4.60 | 63 | 99 | .389 | 4.17 | 162 | 115 | 47 | 21 | 1434 | 1494 | 745 | 664 | 134 | 570 | 57 | 921 | 1.439 |
| PIT | 16 | 28.2 | 4.02 | 88 | 74 | .543 | 3.61 | 162 | 123 | 39 | 33 | 1445.2 | 1348 | 652 | 580 | 96 | 553 | 48 | 1124 | 1.315 |
| SDP | 17 | 24.9 | 4.60 | 52 | 110 | .321 | 4.24 | 162 | 146 | 16 | 25 | 1422.1 | 1454 | 746 | 670 | 113 | 592 | 86 | 764 | 1.438 |
| SFG | 14 | 29.5 | 3.93 | 90 | 72 | .556 | 3.26 | 162 | 91 | 71 | 17 | 1473.2 | 1381 | 636 | 534 | 120 | 461 | 65 | 906 | 1.250 |
| STL | 20 | 27.9 | 3.33 | 87 | 75 | .537 | 2.94 | 162 | 99 | 63 | 26 | 1460.1 | 1289 | 540 | 477 | 99 | 511 | 61 | 1004 | 1.233 |
| **LgAvg** | **15** | **27.0** | **4.05** | **81** | **81** | **.500** | **3.60** | **162** | **118** | **44** | **30** | **1449** | **1372** | **658** | **579** | **123** | **533** | **64** | **969** | **1.315** |

statistics courtesy of *Baseball-Reference.com*

# Eddie Yost

by Andrew Schiff and Matthew Silverman

Eddie Yost was a slick-fielding, high-on-base-percentage third baseman, an athlete who continued to make his name at the hot corner after his playing days were over, as the third base coach for the Washington Senators, New York Mets, and Boston Red Sox. Known as "The Walking Man" for his propensity at getting bases on balls, he played in more games than any third baseman before him, though he was often overlooked because he spent most of his career in cavernous Griffith Stadium playing for the dreadful Senators.

Edward Frederick Joseph Yost was born in Brooklyn, New York, on October 13, 1926. Yost attended John Adams High School in Queens, where he played baseball and basketball. Because of World War II, the rules allowed the freshman Yost to play both sports at New York University—shortstop in baseball, guard for the accomplished basketball team. "We used to fill Madison Square Garden every time," Yost reminisced of the NYU basketball team. "I remember how most of us—Sid Tannenbaum, John Derderian, Frank Mangiapane, Ralph Branca—used to study down at Washington Square, then take the long subway ride up to University Heights just to practice every afternoon. We spent half our lives on the subway." Mangiapane and Tannenbaum wound up playing basketball for the New York Knicks while Branca pitched for the Brooklyn Dodgers. Sam Mele, who preceded Yost on the NYU court and diamond, later played with Yost in Washington.

After his freshman year, Yost, still 17, had a weeklong trial with the Red Sox, staying at a hotel and working out at Fenway Park for the Boston brass. Though manager Joe Cronin reportedly liked what he saw, general manager Eddie Collins did not sign the young infielder. Washington scout Joe Cambria offered Yost a contract for $500—the Phillies offered double that amount but were a day too late. Signing with the Senators, Yost immediately reported to the major league club, making his debut on August 16, 1944. He played in only seven games and batted .143, drawing one walk, the first of his 1,614 bases on balls. After the season, Yost turned 18, and joined the US Navy.

He was placed on the National Defense Service List on January 23, 1945. In a letter to Senators owner Clark Griffith to inform the club of his draft status, Yost wrote, "I didn't expect to leave quite so soon but as you said, they seem to be taking every available man. Thank you for the fine opportunity you gave me in the baseball world.... I hope I can fulfill that contract before long."

During his 18 months in the service, Yost spent the summer months playing baseball at the Naval Training Station in Sampson, New York, on Seneca Lake. That was the closest Yost ever got to the minor leagues. He was still 19 when he was discharged in 1946 and he finished out the year in Washington. The Senators wanted to send him to their farm club in Chattanooga so he could develop his skills and Yost even petitioned the commissioner's office, willing to accept a waiver of the mandate in the GI Bill of Rights that guaranteed returning veterans their jobs—for baseball players their roster position—for two years. Commissioner Happy Chandler refused the request, not willing to set a precedent. Most veterans had the opposite problem that Yost had. Cecil Travis, a star shortstop for the Senators before the war, endured severe frostbite in the Battle of the Bulge and was never the same player. Travis was moved to third base so he wouldn't have to range as far. By 1947, though, the youngster Yost took over regular duty at third and Travis spent time at shortstop and on the bench.

"I didn't think I was ready [for the majors], but Chandler wouldn't let me do it," Yost said. "Then, a month after the season [started] I got into the lineup and played 115 games." He wound up hitting .238 and remained Washington's third baseman for a dozen seasons.

The 5-foot-10 right-handed hitter had a lifetime batting average of only .254, but because of his penchant for drawing walks, his career on-base percentage was .394. Yost's best season with the Senators was 1950, when he hit .295 with 141 walks, and an on-base percentage of .440. One season, which best demonstrated the split between his batting average and his on-base percentage was 1956, when Yost hit only .231 but walked a career-high 151 times. His on-base percentage was a robust .412. Standing close to the plate, he was also hit by pitches 99 times in his career.

During that 1956 season, with Mickey Mantle receiving plenty of publicity for challenging Babe Ruth's home run record of 60—The Mick wound up with 52 en route to the Triple Crown—the Senators issued a release about Yost's challenge to the Babe's 1923 record for walks. In late August, Yost averaged 1.1 walks per game and was on pace to break Ruth's mark of 170. Though he fell short of the mark, Yost broke his own club record for walks and led the league by 39 over Mantle.

Had Yost played several decades later, in the free-agency era, his skills would have been much more valued. As it was, he made the All-Star team only once while playing on a Washington team that never finished better than .500 and ended up in last place five times during his career there. Moreover, Washington's ballpark was cavernous—Griffith Stadium was 405 feet down the line in left field until it was reduced to 350 in 1957. Of the 101 home runs he hit as a Senator, 78 were hit on the road. He homered in every park in 1953—a year that he hit nine all told—and only one of those was hit at home. In his first seven full seasons as a Senator, only three of his 55 home runs were hit at Griffith Stadium.

Yost's power was most prolific at the start of a game. His 28 career home runs leading off a game stood as the record until Bobby Bonds broke it in the 1970s. That mark was later shattered by Rickey Henderson, who also passed Yost, Ruth, and everyone else for most career walks. "Henderson's the best leadoff hitter to ever play the game," Yost said.

Free agency might also have allowed Yost to wind up in a better situation than Washington, where the standing joke went, oft-repeated by Yost: "First in war, first in peace, and last in the American League."

Yost may have languished playing for a perennial loser, but he was indeed appreciated.

Washington owner Clark Griffith, who sent his own son-in-law, Joe Cronin, to the Red Sox in a $225,000 deal in 1934, turned down a $200,000 offer from Boston two decades later for Yost. Griffith called him "the most sought-after .233 hitter in the American League" in 1953. "They look at his batting average and think they can swing a deal for him. I wouldn't swap him for Mickey Mantle straight up, and to prove it, I'm paying him almost twice as much as the Yankees are paying Mantle." Yost asked for, and received, a $5,000 raise that brought his salary to $21,000.

Griffith got his money's worth out of Yost, who played 838 consecutive games from July 6, 1949, until tonsillitis finally knocked him out of the lineup on May 12, 1955. It was the longest such streak since the mark set by Lou Gehrig; like Yost, Gehrig was of German descent and the Iron Horse was his favorite player growing up. Yost had the fourth longest consecutive game streak in history at the time, and it still ranks ninth all-time.

Yost was certainly reliable and durable, but what about that batting eye? Yost retired with more walks than all but Babe Ruth, Ted Williams, and Mel Ott. Even today, with the walk more highly prized than it was in his day—and with more games on the schedule—Yost still ranks

10th in walks (1,614) and ninth in walks percentage (17.59 percent of his plate appearances). Hall of Fame manager Bucky Harris, Washington's skipper during Yost's walking prime, once said, "What I'd like to have is a pair of Yosts: one to lead off and another to drive in some of those runs with the hits he makes."

As manager of the Yankees, Casey Stengel coveted Yost for his New York dynasty, but with no success. Stengel picked Yost for his only All-Star berth when the third baseman was batting .196 in 1952. Stengel defended his choice simply, "Every time I look up, that feller is on base." Umpire Bill McGowan said of Yost, "The kid looks 'em over better than anyone else."

"It's something you can't teach. Just something I was lucky enough to be born with," Yost told *Sports Collector's Digest* four decades after his last game as a player. "First, I had a good eye at the plate and knew the strike zone. Also, I took the time to know the pitchers and how they worked. And I had enough bat control to be able to foul off a lot of pitches." Illustrating that point, Yost fouled off 13 consecutive pitches in one at-bat in 1953; he fouled off seven his next time up.

"I also hit from a slight crouch and during my swing I was able to make my strike zone even smaller by dropping my right shoulder," Yost explained. "Back then a lot of pitchers threw rising fastballs and I found that if I could lay off them and didn't swing, they'd be called balls. And after a while I got a reputation for walking a lot and it seemed like the umpires began to give me the calls on the close ones."

Yost kept also kept an eye out for his fellow players. At a time when owners held all the cards in negotiations with players and took a dim view of anyone looking to change that, Yost served as the American League player representative. Yost, Robin Roberts, and Jerry Coleman even testified before the House antitrust subcommittee regarding the legal status of sports in June 1957. Though he attended college full-time for only one year before signing with the Senators, he did complete his education at NYU. Yost spent eight offseasons during his playing career accruing credits, eventually earning a master's degree in physical education in 1955. He occasionally taught school in New York City, but his main occupation was baseball.

Yost was a bachelor for most of his playing career, sharing his home with his mother in South Ozone Park, Queens. He was ever popular in Washington. His fan club in Chevy Chase, Maryland, even put out a publication about the eligible bachelor's doings. During the 1953 season, when teammate Bob Porterfield was zooming to 22 wins and perennial All-Star Mickey Vernon was winning a batting title, the fans held a night in support of Yost, hitting just .246 at the time. Among the gifts he was showered with was a new car.

Popular though he was, time keeps moving and younger players take the place of their elders. Yost was traded to the Detroit Tigers in December 1958 to make room for up-and-coming third baseman Harmon Killebrew. Calvin Griffith, president of the Senators since the death of his adoptive father Clark Griffith in 1955, traded the third baseman his adopted father wouldn't have swapped for Mickey Mantle to the Tigers for two utility infielders, Reno Bertoia and Ron Samford, plus spare outfielder Jim Delsing (the Senators also sent infielder Rocky Bridges and outfielder Neil Chrisley to Detroit in the deal).

The short porch in Detroit was immediately to Yost's liking. Eddie, who had dropped 10 pounds in the offseason, clubbed a career-best 21 home runs in 1959 and led the league in runs with 115. And after two years without drawing 100 walks—the first time since 1950 he had back-to-back years without reaching triple figures—Yost drew 135 bases on balls, his fifth time leading the American League. And that wasn't an easy title to take with Ted Williams still in Boston. Yost led the league in walks for the sixth and final time in 1960. He also led the league in on-base percentage in both his seasons as a Tiger and was on base more than anyone else in the AL both years as well. As he was in Washington, Yost also served as team captain of the Tigers.

After the 1960 season, the American League expanded by two teams and Detroit did not protect the 34-year-old Yost in the expansion draft. He was taken by the Los Angeles Angels. Yost became the first batter in Angels history when he popped up as the Angels' leadoff man in the first inning in Baltimore on April 11, 1961. His second time up... he walked. It was not a great season for Yost, however, as he batted only .202, his lowest average as an everyday player. His on-base percentage was still .358, the 14th straight year it was .349 or better. He hit his 139th—and what turned out to be his last—home run in his last official at-bat in 1961—against the Senators, no less. His last time up that season... he walked.

In that final season, Yost was a part-time player and batted .240 with a .412 on-base percentage, the best of any Angel who played more than 10 games. Yost hoped he might play longer, but when George Thomas was discharged from the military, the Angels released the 35-year-old Yost to make room for Thomas.

While most people thought of Yost simply as The Walking Man, he was pretty good with the glove at third base. He set American League career records with 2,356 putouts, 3,659 assists, and 6,285 chances. He led the AL in fielding percentage twice, in assists three times, in double plays seven times, and in putouts eight times. Though Brooks Robinson later erased his fielding marks, Yost was the first third baseman in history to appear in more than 2,000 games.

Yost did not stay out of baseball long. The Senators he'd spent so many years with relocated to Minnesota and were rechristened the Twins, yet Yost was hired as a coach for the expansion Senators in 1963 as part of old friend and teammate Mickey Vernon's staff. Yost was to be the first base coach, but he was moved to third base two days into the season. When Vernon was fired early in the season and Gil Hodges came over in a trade from the Mets to be Washington's manager, some of the coaches were fired but Yost stayed on and forged a long friendship with Hodges.

By then married with two daughters and a son, Yost still lived in South Ozone Park when Hodges was dealt to the Mets after the 1967 season. The coaches were not part of the trade, but Hodges brought Rube Walker and Joe Pignatano from Washington along with Yost, who now worked five miles from his home. He was a fixture in the third base coach's box in New York, trying to squeeze as many runs out of the paltry offense as possible through the judicious waving home of runners. Though Yost never came close to the World Series as a player, he earned a World Series ring with the Miracle Mets in 1969 and nearly got another in 1973.

Yost, Walker, and Pignatano were on hand when Hodges died of a heart attack after a round of golf in St. Petersburg just before the start of the 1972 season. Yogi Berra, also a coach under Hodges, was named manager. Yost remained with the Mets through 1976, when manager Joe Frazier changed coaches. The Red Sox hired Yost to take over the third base box for manager Don Zimmer. Yost remained there through the end of the Ralph Houk regime in 1984. In the wake of the 1969 victory, there were rumors of his becoming a manager—especially in Minnesota, still owned by Calvin Griffith—but it never happened. Yost spent 22 seasons waving runners home from third base and 39 consecutive years drawing a paycheck while in a major league uniform.

After years of living near his New York birthplace, the Yost family moved to Wellesley, Massachusetts. Among his newfound hobbies after retirement was working on antique clocks, which started from a class he took while coaching the Mets. Yost's name inadvertently came up in political circles when it was revealed that 2004 Democratic presidential candidate John Kerry had said on a Boston radio program that "my favorite Red Sox player of all time is The Walking Man, Eddie Yost." Yost, you'll note, never played for the Red Sox, though he did serve as coach for eight seasons. A minor gaffe? In some cities maybe, but in Sox-centric Boston, even Eddie Yost himself wouldn't be able to put up the stop sign fast enough.

**Sources**

Bedingfield, Gary, "Baseball During Wartime," Eddie Yost. *http://www.baseballinwartime.com/player_biographies/yost_eddie.htm.*

Bailey, Arnold, "Player Profile: The Walker Man." *Sports Collector's Digest,* January 18, 2002.

Kaus, Mickey, "Is Kerry Toast? No, He's Yost!" *http://www.slate.com/id/2104072/*

McConnell, Bob, and David Vincent, eds., *The Home Run Encyclopedia: The Who, What, and Where of Every Home Run Hit Since 1876.* New York: Macmillan, 1996.

McGovern, Hugh, "The Walking Man," 1977 Boston Red Sox yearbook (second edition).

Povich, Shirley, "Yost Too Good to Bat Leadoff." *The Sporting News*, January 18, 1952.

Povich, Shirley, "Young Ironman Yost Keeps Strolling Along." *The Sporting News*, October 6, 1954.

Rosenthal, Harold, "Yost Ready for First Move in 15 Years." *The Sporting News*, January 15, 1959.

Washington Baseball Club Release, "Eddie Yost's Threat to Babe Ruth's Record Increases." August 24, 1956.

Correspondence from Player File at National Baseball Hall of Fame Library, Cooperstown, New York.

## The Black Cat: September 9, 1969

Durocher figured something drastic had to be done to thwart the New York assault, so he summoned Jenkins on only two days' rest to go toe-to-toe with Seaver the following night. It could be argued that the reason for the move was twofold: Obviously, the team needed to place its best pitcher on the mound in this game, but Leo also saw a chance to reestablish trust and confidence in Jenkins after their spat 48 hours earlier. To make things right in Jenkins's world, all the big right-hander wanted was the ball—and he got it. Dozer pointed out that Jenkins might have some extra motivation in this game, as Seaver had beaten him as the first major leaguer to reach 20-win mark a week earlier. Nonetheless, the bad omens were all around and one in particular of a four-legged variety was looking to place a hex on the visitors.

As the Cubs were getting ready to hit in the first inning, a black cat sneaked onto the field and trotted menacingly toward the Chicago bench. Santo peered nervously over his shoulder at the intruder from the on-deck circle, as the feline appeared to have business with the rest of the Chicago men. The cat stopped at the edge of the dugout, a few feet in front of Durocher, and stared right into the eyes of the manager. It is hard to say who was more spooked; Leo twitched nervously as he got up and moved, and the cat darted across the home plate area toward safety on the Mets' side of the field and disappeared through the wall as quickly as he arrived.

The Mets got to Jenkins right away as Agee led off their first inning with a walk, and a free pass soon followed to Jones, who was back in the lineup after his injury. Boswell then laced a double to right that scored both of them, and Hodges's

*continued on next page*

*continued*

troops were off and running. Clendenon homered in the third to double the margin to 4-0, and the Mets never looked back. After Seaver retired the first 10 batters, Santo singled home Beckert in the fourth to get the Cubs on the board, but the apple of New York's eye once again prevented Jenkins from getting to the 20-win mark. "Tom Terrific" went the distance just as his teammate Koosman had done the night before, beating the Cubs, 7–1, for his sixth straight win and the 53rd in his career with the Mets, which had not yet reached three full years. He performed the feat in front of more than 58,000 cramped fans in Shea Stadium, most of whom had been waving celebratory handkerchiefs at each piece of Mets success during the evening and who sent the Cubs packing with strains of a "Good-bye Leo" song. Even when the Cubs fell further behind in the middle of the game, Jenkins wanted to take matters into his own hands, and he was not afraid to let his manager know it. "Before I went to the plate to hit in the fifth," he would recall, "Leo asked how I felt. I said 'fine' and he said, 'Go ahead.' If there had been anyone on base, he probably would have hit for me, though."

It was the sixth loss in a row for the Cubs, their longest losing streak of the season. Some thought that the cat had indeed caused some mischief for the Cubs, for in an unlucky trifecta, the game was Jenkins's 13th loss of the season, caused in part by the 13th home runs of the season by Clendenon and Mets outfielder Art Shamsky.

The New York players were greeted in the locker room by the team's founder and owner, Joan Payson, who was as excited as any fan could be. She reached out to embrace her field general, Hodges, the son of a coal miner from Princeton, Indiana, who was keeping a lucky stuffed rabbit on his office desk. "I'm so happy, so thrilled I can hardly stand it," she blurted out. "This is just so wonderful. I never dreamed we'd be so good so soon. Can I kiss you???" She made her way around the room, shaking hands with all the happy players.

—Doug Feldmann

# Front Office and Announcers

Official N.Y. Mets Album

THE

MIRA

ME

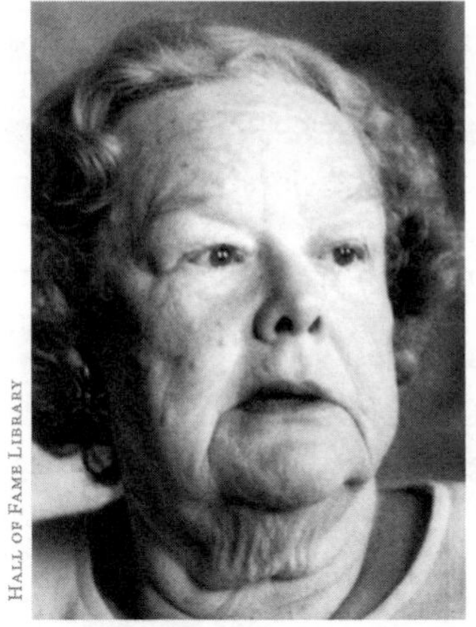
HALL OF FAME LIBRARY

# Joan Whitney Payson

by Joan M. Thomas

Becoming the third woman to own a major league baseball club, Joan Whitney Payson marked history by heavily investing in the expansion New York Mets of 1962. The club's first majority stockholder, she was also the first of her gender to purchase such an enterprise with her own funds. Born into considerable wealth, she used much of her fortune to benefit public hospitals and advance medical research. A famous patron of the arts, she owned some of the world's most valuable paintings. Her very impressive genealogy, coupled with that of her husband's, infers the concept of a snooty high-society matriarch who vaunts her membership in the DAR. However, her character and well-documented passion for horse racing, baseball, and other sports counters that notion. In reality, plump, round-faced Joan Payson's ordinary countenance, jovial disposition, and selfless generosity yielded her such designations as the fairy grandmother, or mother dumpling, of the New York Mets. During an early 2008 phone interview, former Met Ron Hunt said it best: "She was just a nice lady."

More than just a little unique, the annals of that nice lady's life could render her American royalty, or our own queen mother. Born February 5, 1903 in New York, New York, Joan Whitney descended from individuals noteworthy to her country's evolution. Her father Payne Whitney derived his first name from his maternal grandfather, Henry B. Payne, Democratic United States Senator from Ohio 1885–1891. The Paynes trace their ancestral line to William Bradford of the *Mayflower*. Payne Whitney's father, New York streetcar magnate William C. Whitney, was Secretary of the Navy in President Grover Cleveland's Cabinet. His ancestors arrived in this country on the *Arbella*, a ship that arrived 10 years after the *Mayflower*.

Joan's mother, Helen Hay Whitney, was the daughter of distinguished statesman and writer John Hay. Ambassador to Great Britain, and then secretary of state to Presidents William McKinley and Theodore Roosevelt, Hay is best known for his earlier post as assistant private secretary to President Abraham Lincoln. But Joan Payson' s remarkable lineage does not explain her attraction to what some in her class might consider a commoner's amusement, baseball. In fact, both of her parents were sports enthusiasts.

Captain of his rowing crew while attending Yale, Payne Whitney also had a strong interest in horse racing. With his brother Harry Payne Whitney, he owned several Greentree stables, a training base, and a breeding operation. Joan's mother Helen shared her husband's fervor for the track and took over his racing enterprise following his death in 1927. Then, in what may now be considered a preview of her daughter's future legacy, Helen Hay Whitney acquired the title "First Lady of the American Turf." Her Greentree Stables produced such thoroughbreds as Twenty Grand, a 1931 Kentucky Derby winner. Additionally, she adored baseball. She exposed her daughter to the sport early on, taking Joan along on her many trips to the ballpark to see the New York Giants games. Years later in an interview with *New York Times* writer David Dempsey, Joan Whitney Payson notes that for her mom "racing and baseball were social engagements." In view of that statement, it does not seem incongruous that the turf's first lady chose pink and black as her American Jockey Club colors after a favorite tea gown.

Payne and Helen Whitney had two children, Joan and her brother John Hay (Jock) Whitney, who was born August 17, 1904. The family had a number of residences, but the two most often cited are the Greentree estate in Manhasset, Long Island, and an Italian Renaissance-palazzo style mansion in Manhattan. Built as a wedding present from Payne's uncle, Oliver Payne, the Stanford White-designed building at 972 Fifth Avenue housed the Whitney family and some 13 servants.

Joan likely spent much of her youth at the Fifth Avenue house, as she gained her formal education in the city, attending the exclusive all-girls Miss Chapin's School (later called The Chapin School). She then studied at Barnard College for a year, and took a course at Brown's Business College. Aside from that, she learned to ride horses at a very early age, and at Saratoga "was allowed to bet a quarter on each race." She picked up her baseball acumen at the Polo Grounds.

Joan's parents introduced her to New York society by giving a ball for her "at the Plaza" just before her 19th birthday. Two years later, after throwing a black and white costume dinner and dance to celebrate her coming of age, they announced her engagement to Charles Shipman Payson of Portland, Maine. The young blonde debutante met the tall, rusty-haired Yale graduate while on a visit to New Haven with her father. In his final year at Harvard Law School at the time of the betrothal, the son of an investment banker brought to the coupling an ancestry equally significant to American history.

Charles Payson's great-grandfather, clergyman Edward Payson, was at one time celebrated for his posthumously published sermons and memoirs. Charles's maternal grandfather, General John Marshall Brown, served in the Civil War. His maternal great grandmother, Alida Carroll, descended from Daniel Carroll, whose farm became part of what is now the nation's capital.

A major social event in the making, the couple's wedding plans made headlines. The predictably large affair included six bridesmaids and two matrons of honor—one being the bride's cousin, the former Evelyn Wadsworth, wife of United States Senator from Missouri, Stuart Symington. With the maids, matrons, and their escorts, a flower girl, the best man (Joan's brother Jock), and other family members present, Charles Shipman Payson and Joan Whitney wed at Christ Church in Manhasset on July 5, 1924.

While Charles emerged as a business tycoon by investing in such ventures as importing sugar syrups from Cuba and backing Rustless Iron Corporation of America (a producer of stainless steel), Joan bore five heirs to the accumulating fortune. By the time the Paysons held a costume dance at their Long Island spread to celebrate their 13th wedding anniversary, the couple had three daughters and two sons. As the clan grew, it gained as many homes, the one most often mentioned by the media being their Manhasset residence on the Whitney Greentrees estate.

Built in the 1920s on the 110 acres given to the Paysons as a wedding gift by Joan's parents, the William Delano-designed house described as "drop-dead fabulous," boasted a cobblestone front courtyard and iron-filigree portals framing the front door. In addition to that home, the Paysons established retreats at Falmouth Foreside, Maine; Hobe Sound, Florida; Lexington, Kentucky; and Saratoga, New York. Reports of frequent soirees such as that July 3, 1937 anniversary party at Long Island would suggest a free-and-easy lifestyle. However, the Paysons always had a place in Manhattan, close to the action. She found fulfillment in more industrious activities than just hosting social affairs.

A bride of five years in 1929, Joan partnered with a former schoolmate, one of her bridesmaids Josephine Dodge Kimball, in establishing a children's bookstore. Located at 714 Madison Avenue in Manhattan, Young Books opened the day before the infamous stock market crash. Likely, the $50,000 Joan Payson contributed to the Emergency Unemployment Relief Committee during that time did not come from the store's profit. Nonetheless, the business operated at that Upper East Side location for more than a decade. Eventually the two women added more grownup materials such as mystery novels, drawing their patrons' parents. And due to the store's prestige, location, and ownership, at least one highly noteworthy event took place there. In March 1931 at Young Books, an anonymous donor presented to Yale University, "three large sheets of parchment [on which] Dr. Albert Eienstein had written a summary of his relativity theory." There for the presentation, the renowned scientist "forthwith sailed on the *Deutschland* for Germany."

In addition to running a retail business, Joan Payson enjoyed reading plays and film scripts, as did her brother Jock, who by the 1930s served as chairman of Selznick International Pictures. The two Whitney siblings made a bundle investing in such classic productions as Hollywood's *Gone With The Wind*. Notwithstanding, the Paysons and the Whitneys did not survive World War II unscathed.

In 1945, just before his 20th birthday, Joan and Charles's oldest son PFC Daniel Carroll Payson was killed in action in Belgium at the Battle of the Bulge. Like so many American sons, he volunteered for Army service in 1943 and was assigned to the infantry. Significantly, at the time of Daniel's death, his uncle John Hay (Jock) Whitney was a Lieutenant Colonel in the Army Air Force. By then Jock had married Betsey Cushing Roosevelt, former wife of James Roosevelt, FDR's eldest son. While on a mission in France during the summer of 1944, Colonel Whitney and four other officers were captured by the Germans. Eighteen days later they made a daring escape from a moving train. Such stories show that the Whitney family valued its citizenship and, regardless of financial status, had a high degree of integrity. At one time Jock Whitney reportedly refused to have his name listed on a social register, calling such a publication a "travesty of democracy."

Jock's sister Joan also shunned the arrogance of aristocracy. A former Saratoga neighbor of hers once commented that he always liked her, and gave an account of how he once spotted her at the track "lined up in a long queue at one of the cashier's windows, waiting to cash in her $2 ticket just as though she didn't have all those millions."

Also civic minded, Joan took an active role in politics as a member of the Women's National Republican Club, still headquartered on New York City' s Upper West Side today. After the country's 1956 presidential election, a senatorial fact-finding committee reported that she had given the "second largest individual contribution [$65,050] during that campaign—to the Republican Party." But great sums of the Whitney siblings' fortune went to charitable and artistic concerns. Some of that fortune came from the Whitneys' Greentree stables that Joan and Jock inherited and controlled after their mother died in 1944. They were as fond of horse racing as their mom. Additionally, Joan came to invest in another favorite sport—baseball.

During the 1950s, she bought into the ballclub that she had followed all of her life. During a luncheon conversation, stockbroker M. Donald Grant happened to tell Joan that he always wanted to manage a ballclub. She commented that she always wanted to own one, and convinced him to sell her his one share in the Giants. She eventually owned nearly 10 percent of the club. Then, when the owner majority decided to move the franchise out of state, Joan opposed them and tried in vain to buy them out.

The end of the 1957 season left her devastated when it became clear that not only would her beloved Giants relocate to California, but so would the Brooklyn Dodgers. Thus, when New York attorney William Shea took Branch Rickey's advice in creating a third major league, the Continental League, he sought ball fans with deep pockets to finance a New York franchise. The perfect candidate, Joan Payson, wound up owning approximately 80 percent of the new club. Her friends M. Donald Grant and fellow stockbrokers Frederick Trask and G. Herbert Walker (an uncle to George Herbert Walker Bush called "Uncle Herbie") got the remaining shares. After the Continental League fizzled, the New York club was awarded a National League franchise in 1960. The official naming took place at Joan Payson's Manhattan apartment on May 6, 1961. A group of New York sportswriters considered a number of club name ideas including the Meadowlarks, which writer Jack Lang reported as Joan Payson's preference.

Maury Allen, in his book *After The Miracle*, draws an entertaining and telling account of that gathering. Revealing that the team's public relations man "spilled a drink on Mrs. Payson' s fifty thousand-dollar rug," and that the group soaked up plenty of her expensive liquor, he veers to a commentary on the franchise owner's priceless art works displayed at her apartment. The announcement of the official name Mets came the next day. Allen writes that on May 8, 1961, at the Savoy-Hilton Hotel, Joan Payson "broke a bottle of champagne over a bat to symbolize the christening." And who better to christen the new organization than the woman destined to mother a group of ballplayers. In those early times, one might say that they were a team that only a mother could love. Which leads to the thought that perhaps it was Mrs. Payson who unwittingly instigated the inexplicable affection showered on them by the fans.

On October 18, 1960, a biographical sketch of the National League' s new New York franchise owner appeared in the *New York Times*. Interestingly, the piece refers to the lady only as "Mrs. Charles Shipman Payson," and "Mrs. Payson" That custom apparently carried over from nearly 50 years earlier when the St. Louis papers reported the new owner of the St. Louis Cardinals. Instead of giving Helene Hathaway Robison Britton's full name, the media simply called her Mrs. Schuyler Britton. Though at the time the baseball world fretted over a woman taking over the helm, little attention was paid to the fact that Helene Britton was the first woman to own a major league baseball club. Joan Payson was the first to purchase one, and that fact also went unnoticed. Joan's brother Jock's credentials by then, his positions as Ambassador to Britain, and publisher of the *New York Herald Tribune* then took precedence, as that information appeared in the story's lead paragraph. Albeit, the article relays some revealing details about Joan Payson's persona.

Describing her as a woman who "dresses simply and wears little makeup," it discloses several of her habits that got frequent mention during her reign as baseball owner. Various stories throughout the years mention her affection for horses and other animals, making it known that she took two or three of her dachshunds with her on her many travels. In his 1968 piece, Dempsey recounts details of the mode of transportation for some Payson family journeys, a private Pullman car named Adios II. The car had three bedrooms, a bar, and a lounge, and in addition to such artwork as a Matisse painting, one could find children's bicycles and games aboard. A devoted grandmother by the time she bought the Mets, Joan Payson preferred playing card games with the kids to conferring with her stockbroker.

In the manner of a true sports fan, Joan carried a portable radio with her and would tune in baseball or football games while at the racetrack. She would even conceal that radio in her evening bag when she attended society events such as charity balls, or while dining out. And, in the time-honored tradition of baseball fanatics from the beginning, she held to superstitions. For instance, she insisted that when the home team took the lead, one remained wherever one happened to be seated at the time. Numerous portrayals of her at a ballgame describe her crossing her fingers during crucial plays.

Just as Helene Britton took great pleasure in keeping score at the ballgame, so did Joan Payson. In fact, Joan had her own unique method that some compared to cuneiform. Dempsey writes that she taught her chauffeur the technique so that when she was out of town, he could fill out the scorecards and airmail them to her. It's hard to tell when she devised that system, but with her history as a spectator, she most likely had it perfected before she telephoned Casey Stengel to say "we want you to manage our club." Stengel's reflection on that conversation is indicative of the influence she held as club owner. Allen quotes him to say "If such a nice rich lady with all that money was trusting the club... I had to help."

With "parasol at the ready," the enthusiastic majority owner joined Stengel in St. Petersburg for the launching of her New York Mets in 1962. Stengel told reporters, "I expect to win every day." An inveterate baseball person, Mrs. Payson no doubt recognized that as tongue-in-cheek braggadocio, but she could not have anticipated the astounding 120 losses of that maiden season. Regardless, she steadfastly supported the club through thick and thin for the remainder of her life. Ever the optimist, at the beginning of the 1963 season, she said that she couldn't stand 120 losses again. "If we can't get anything," she said, "we are going to cut those losses down—at least to 119."

During those early calamitous years, when one win with nothing more at stake than the final tally in the record books gave rise to fan hysteria, Joan Payson nurtured everyone in the organization. Friendly and approachable to players and fans alike, she would wave happily to anyone in the stands who called her name. Ballplayers felt as much at ease chatting with her as they would with one another. Former Mets second baseman Ron Hunt, who made his major league debut with the club in 1963, recalls, "Her and Casey Stengel took care of me." Hunt's wife Jackie warmly remembers how Joan Payson watched over all of the players and their families. Jackie calls her and Ron's first child Tracy a "Mets baby" and still cherishes the sterling silver Tiffany cup and spoon set that Joan Payson gave them when Tracy was born. "She made you feel like family," Jackie reflects, going on to tell how the generous owner would charter a plane and take the whole team and their families to places like Cooperstown. The owner even sent Ron roses as a reward for a game-winning hit.

Ron Hunt echoes the observations of writers of the times. "Sitting in the stands, she looked like an ordinary ball fan," he says, reiterating that the Mets owner was a good family woman. Yet his memory is bittersweet. He first learned about being traded to the Dodgers from a sports writer. Then, the next time the Mets faced Los Angeles, he went up to Payson's box and told her that the trade disappointed him. She responded, "I was disappointed, too. But you were the only one that was tradable." Such quotes shed some light on Joan Whitney Payson as more than a figurehead. She obviously made savvy business decisions in the best interest of the Mets family.

While keeping tabs on her baseball concern, Joan continued to co-own the Greentree Stable enterprise with her brother Jock. Frequently blending her zeal for her prize thoroughbreds with that of the National Game, she had a proclivity for tagging horses with baseball terms. She even named one of the Whitney thoroughbreds Gashouse Gang. Said to admit having a penchant for athletes "with two or four feet" in 1963 she became the first woman recipient of the President's Citation of the People-to-People Sports Committee. A prime example of her unpretentiousness came when she posed with two jockeys for a photo shoot. Alluding to her comparative height and girth, she cracked "Why is it… that I always have my picture taken between Eddie Arcaro and Johnny Rotz?"

Joan Payson's good humor never failed her. Despite the team's dreadful first years, and the bizarre circumstance of heavy attendance that prevented her from claiming a tax loss, the birth mother of the Mets kept up a staunch front. Everyone who came in contact with her seemed bound to her by respect. Bing Devine writes in his memoirs that when he decided to give up his position as club president, he walked 20 blocks just to tell her in person. "I felt that I owed that to her because she had been so good to me," he explains. Following his resignation, a February 1968 news story revealed that "six members of the board 'persuaded' Mrs. Payson to accept the title herself." The story adds, "She accepted with one condition: No speeches." Obviously, she sought neither the position nor the limelight.

Maintaining a wait-and-see attitude when the world began to believe that the Mets were for real during the summer of 1969, the club's inveterate owner continued watching the games from her box behind first base—often accompanied by some of her children, growing flock of grandchildren, and sometimes her husband. When not able to see it in person, she caught the game by radio or TV, or got the final tally by mail. Having made earlier plans to visit her daughter in Europe in September of 1969, her innate baseball superstition kept her from canceling the trip when her amazin' bunch miraculously found themselves in first place. As it happened, Mrs. Payson was in London, sick in bed with bronchitis when the club captured the National League East Division title. Her congratulations to manager Gil Hodges, the players, and the rest of the organization arrived by wire.

Fully recovered, and on her first visit to Atlanta since going with Jock to attend the premiere of their financial boon *Gone With The Wind* 30 years earlier, Joan reflected on the Mets miracle while attending the second National League Championship Series game in Atlanta that year. "In the old days, it wasn't funny… it broke your heart," she told a reporter. She added that when they finally took first place, she just sat there crying. As would most proud mothers.

A week later, in Baltimore for the World Series, Joan was so excited, that she covered her eyes with a scarf during the final play of the second game. Her husband Charles, not known as a baseball fan, boasted at having won $40 betting on the contest. That's not the usual image of a multimillionaire couple observing an investment in action. Joan Whitney Payson got more than she hoped for when the Mets actually won the Series in the fifth game on October 16. In an earlier interview, she explained why she spent so much money to organize the club: "All I wanted to do was bring a National League team back to New York."

Three years later, Joan brought back her favorite Giant, Willie Mays. In 1972, the Mets made a deal with San Francisco for Mays at her insistence. Though in the twilight of his career, the future Hall of Famer rewarded Payson for her faith in him by hitting a game-winning homer in his first game as a Met. Even as the Mets stormed to a pennant and came within a game of their second world championship in 1973, in the next few years the ebullient Joan Payson faced the dusk of her life.

Although reportedly incapacitated for some time, she attended a board meeting and a Mets-Braves exhibition game in Florida on March 20, 1975. The Mets, who had lost eight of their first 11 pre-season games, "treated their principal owner to a 3–0 victory." Then, after suffering a stroke in mid-June, Joan Whitney Payson died on October 4 at the age of 72, dying just one week after Casey Stengel succumbed to cancer in California. She took her last breath at New York Hospital. Her great uncle, father, and brother had been instrumental in expanding that institution to a medical complex that includes Cornell Medical Center. In the family tradition, Joan had donated $8.3 million to its support. That was just a minute part of the legacy of the woman many remember at the ballpark munching on hot dogs, or eating chocolate ice cream with a wooden spoon, or clutching a trusty score-keeping pencil between her teeth while clapping her hands joyously.

The funeral took place at Christ Episcopal in Manhasset, the same church where Joan and Charles were married. In the eulogy, the church vicar observed, "There is no way of measuring the impact of Joan Whitney Payson on the world." Friends she accumulated over the years through her wide array of interests packed the small family church to pay tribute, Willie Mays included. Following the service, she was buried at the Payson family cemetery in Falmouth Foreside, Maine. She left behind her husband Charles, brother Jock, daughters Sandra, Payne, and Lorinda (who assumed the title of president of the Mets), son John, 11 grandchildren, and a host of baseball players, managers, executives, and fans. After the Payson family sold the Mets in 1980, the new owners of the club established a Mets Hall of Fame the following year. The first two inductees were, fittingly, Casey Stengel and Joan Payson.

In addition to New York Hospital, Joan Payson's millions benefited St. Mary's Hospital in Long Beach, Florida, the United Hospital Fund, the Lighthouse in Manhattan, and the North Shore Hospital in Manhasset, which she helped found. She was also president of the Helen Hay Whitney Foundation, a medical research organization. A trustee of New York's Museum of Modern Art and Metropolitan Museum of Art, she also owned the Palm Beach Gallery and Country Life Gallery in Locust Valley, Long Island. The Joan Whitney Payson Collection from the Portland, Maine Museum, which includes paintings by notable artists such as Degas, is now regularly on loan to Colby College in Waterville, Maine. An Impressionist devotee, Joan Payson purchased Van Gogh's *Irises* for $80,000 in 1947. Twelve years after her death, her family sold it for a hefty $39.9 million. The proceeds went to charity.

In April 1984, two nationally historic treasures came to light during preparations for an on-site estate sale at the Payson's Long Island home. The priceless items discovered in a compartment of a Georgian table included a manuscript of President Lincoln's last public address, and an autographed photo of famed American poet Walt Whitman along with a copy of his famous work "Captain! My Captain," as well as a letter written to Joan Whitney Payson's grandfather, John Hay—the poem and letter written in Whitman's own hand. One can only guess what kind of elegy Whitman would have penned about our game' s queen mother.

**Sources**

Allen, Maury. *After the Miracle: the 1969 Mets Twenty Years Later* (New York: Franklin Watts, 1989).

Allen, Maury. *Now wait a minute, Casey!* (Garden City, New York: Doubleday & Company, Inc., 1965).

"Amazin' Again." *Time.* June 5, 1972. *www.time.com/time/printout/0,8816,906009,00.html.*

Berry, Heidi L. "Seeking Autographs and Manuscripts of the Mighty." *Washington Post, The (DC)*. May 31, 1984. *Infoweb. newsbank.com. docid+OEB35EB0.*

"C.S. Paysons Hosts At Costume Dance" *New York Times*. July 4, 1937. D4: 6.

"Col. Whitney Is Honored." *New York Times*. March 30, 1945. 4: 3.

"Commentator." *Time. www.time.com/time/magazine/ article/0,9171,770558,00.html.*

Curtis, Charlotte. "Even Truman Capote Is Aware of the New Heroes." *New York Times*. September 26, 1969. 72: 1-4.

"Daughter of Mr. and Mrs. Payne Whitney to Marry Charles S. Payson of Portland, Me." *New York Times*. February 5, 1924. 23: 1.

Dempsey, David. "Says Mrs. Payson of the Mets, 'You Can't Lose Them All'" *New York Times Magazine*. January 23, 1968. 28-31.

Devine, Bing and Tom Wheatley. *The Memoirs of Bing Devine* (Champaign, Illinois: Sports Publishing, 2004)

Durso, Joseph. *Amazing: The Miracle of the Mets*. (Boston: Houghton Mifflin, 1970).

Durso, Joseph. "Joan Whitney Payson, 72, Mets Owner, Dies." *New York Times*. October 5, 1975. Deaths.

Durso, Joseph. "Mrs. Payson Elected President of the Mets, Succeeding Devine." *New York Times*. February 7, 1968. 55: 2-3.

"George Bush: The Unauthorized Biography." *http:// killtown.911revieworg.bushbio/chapter4.html.*

"He Was Killed in Action Before His 20th Birthday." *New York Times*. February 19, 1945. 15:3.

Hunt, Jackie. Telephone interview by Joan M. Thomas. January 27, 2008.

Hunt, Ron. Telephone interview by Joan M. Thomas. January 27, 2008.

"'Irises' Sale Resurrects Price Issue." January 12, 1990. *Chicago Tribune. infoweb.newsbank.com docid=OFF827367.*

"It Ain't What They Do It's the Way That They Do it." *Time. www.time.com/time/printout/0,8816,830205,00.html.*

"J.H. Whitney Captured; Colonel Reported Taken by Germans Somewhere in France." August 30, 1944. p. 13. *nytimes.com.*

Joan (Whitney) Payson (1903-1975) *www.whitney.gen.org/ archives/biography/joan.html.*

"Mets Win One, 3-0 For Mrs. Payson." *New York Times*. March 21, 1975. 40: 1-2.

Montgomery, Paul L. "Diverse Friends of Joan Payson Fill Church for Last Good-bys." *New York Times*. October 8, 1975. 44: 2-3.

"Mrs. Payson Fails to See Final Out." *New York Times*. October 13, 1969. 60: 6-7.

"Mrs. Payson Says Heartbreak Gave Way to Her Tears of Joy." *New York Times*. October 6, 1969. 60: 3-4.

"Mrs. J. Payson wires congratulations" *New York Times*. September 25, 1969. 59: 7

"Names make news." *Time*. March 16, 1931. *www.time.com/ time/magazine/article/0,9171,769528,00.html.*

Payne, Henry B. (1810-1896) *http;//bioguide.congress.gov. scripts.bidisplay.pl?index=P000151.*

"Payson Collection." *www.colby.edu/academics_cs/museum-of-art/exhibitions.*

"People." *Time*. March 2, 1962. *www.time.com/time/magazine/ article/0,9171,939887,00.html.*

"People." *Time*. October 25, 1963. *www.time.com/time/ magazine/article/0,9171,830504,00.html.*

"Plans For Wedding of Miss Whitney." *New York Times*. May 13, 1924. 21:1

Reif, Rita. April 27, 1984. "The Payson' s home on view; *New York Times*. C. 18. ProQuest document ID: 950927041.

"Rustless Victory." *Time*. March 13, 1933. *www.time.com/time/ magazine/article/0,9171,745327,00.html.*

"She Doubles in Clubs." *New York Times*. October 18, 1960. 2: 3-4.

Lang, Jack and Peter Simon. "New York Mets: Twenty-Five Years of Baseball Magic." (New York: Henry Holt & Co. Inc., 1986).

Smith, J. Y. "Publisher, Former Ambassador John Hay Whitney Dies." *Washington Post*. February 9, 1982. *Infoweb.newsbank. com. docid=0EB33)57.*

"Stanford White." 972 Fifth Ave. *nyc-architechture.com.*

Teltsch, Kathleen. "Medical Center Gets $1.5 Million Whitney Gift." *New York Times*. October 24, 1982. A: 40.

"Van Gogh's Irises Is Bought by California's Getty Museum." *Chicago Tribune*. March 22, 1990. *infoweb.newsbank.com. docid=OFF829866.*

Women In World History. "Payson, Joan Whitney." Vol. 12. 418-419.

Women In World History. "Whitney, Helen Hay." Vol. 12. 492-493.

"31 More Writers Will Aid Book Fair." *New York Times*. October 1936. N8.

## There Are Some Words

The 1969 season was full of episodes, incidents, and moments that continued to give Mets fans icons, totems, and memories to which to cling for generations thereafter. One of them was the sight of Karl Ehrhardt, the Sign Man of Shea Stadium, lifting aloft on October 16, 1969 a placard that read—once Cleon Jones caught a deep fly to left with two outs in the bottom of the ninth inning—THERE ARE NO WORDS. Turns out, four decades hence, there are some words. We offer them here.

**Champagne**

Rheingold was in its Mets-sponsoring heyday and Royal Crown had the cola concession cornered, but it was the bubbly whose profile got the biggest boost among Mets-connected beverages in 1969. There were the three champagne-soaked celebrations at Shea to toast all the clinchings, to be sure (with each of them helping to re-elect troubled incumbent mayor John Lindsay, smart enough to insinuate himself into a winning clubhouse). Yet there was also an occasion when the lack of such a party spoke volumes. When the Mets raised their record to a previously unheard of 18-18 in May, one of 1969's early telling legends was born. Reporters raced to the clubhouse to cover a madcap ruckus that was surely ensuing. There was none. These new Mets, Tom Seaver let it be known, were not to going to pop their corks over a .500 record. They'd have plenty of opportunities to get bubbly later. In the meantime, the club's standards were subtly raised. The laughable Mets were done for good.

**Grass**

With Joe Torre's double-play grounder, Harrelson to Weis to Clendenon, on September 24, the Mets became champs. And with that final out, the Shea Stadium grass became fair game. If the world beyond Flushing needed proof that Mets fans were the most enthused fans anywhere—sticking with them through those first seven seasons when they averaged more than 100 losses annually was pretty strong evidence—it was provided when thousands literally took the field. In some cases, they took it home with them. Hands full of grass were scooped, pocketed, and replanted by those who wanted the feeling of that first title growing. Inevitably the grass would die, but not the feeling. Mets fans stormed Shea's lawn twice more in October, once in 1973 and once in 1986 before the mounted patrol was called in to put a halt to the fun (or vandalism, if you want to be a killjoy). Every time you see the Mets in a position to clinch and you see a horse, it dates back to Harrelson to Weis to Clendenon.

**Miracle**

Having given the '69 Mets their due as individuals, let us now hitch our wagons to the conventional wisdom. It was a miracle. Of course it was a miracle. These were the Mets. The Mets did not stand for quality or anything like it before 1969. They won 27 games more than they had the year before. They destroyed the lead and the morale of a team that boasted Ernie Banks, Billy Williams, Ron Santo, and Fergie Jenkins. They made quick work of another that led with Henry Aaron and Phil Niekro. They then treated a juggernaut of Frank Robinson, Brooks Robinson, Jim Palmer, and a lot of extraordinary company like a pickup squad. The Mets earned everything they won. And it was miraculous. Nobody said good baseball and miraculous baseball has to be considered mutually exclusive.

—Greg W. Prince

Excerpted from *Maple Street Press Mets Annual 2009*

HALL OF FAME LIBRARY

# Johnny Murphy

by John Vorperian

Johnny Murphy was an ace relief pitcher for the 1930s New York Yankees who spent 18 years playing professional baseball. Murphy spent even longer in the front office, first with New England's obsession—the Boston Red Sox—serving as a scout and then ran the team's minor league operations. Moving onto New York's National League expansion franchise, Murphy oversaw scouting activities and became the general manager of the '69 Miracle Mets.

John Joseph Murphy was born July 14, 1908 in New York City. He attended Our Lady of Mercy elementary school and Fordham Prep, located in the Bronx. While in high school, Murphy was noticed by legendary New York Yankees scout, Paul Krichell. He followed Murphy at Fordham University and signed Murphy on the eve of his final college baseball game.

Fordham University was Murphy's school of choice and a highly-regarded baseball program that had produced Frankie Frisch a decade earlier. On March 13, 1927, the *Times* opined at outdoor practices in the Bronx, "Johnny Murphy, a sophomore, is one of the best of last year's freshman team and may take a turn on the mound in some of the minor games." On May 5, the third game of Fordham's '27 season, Murphy started and allowed seven hits against the University of Virginia, including a two-run homer that handed him the loss. However, five days later, the right-hander fared better in relief of starter Joe Harrington in a one-sided game against the University of Delaware. Roger Hanlon permitted the Blue Hens their only tally of the day in a 19–1 rout. Among the few hundred spectators to see the conquest was the Fordham Flash himself—Frankie Frisch.

By 1928, Murphy was a key component to coach Jack Coffey's club. The 6-foot-2, 190-pound, lantern-jawed junior's highlight was a three-hit shutout over Georgetown. His senior year would leave a mark on the Fordham record book and push him into professional baseball.

On April 23, 1929, Murphy fanned 16 Columbia batsmen and scored the game winning run on a passed ball to beat the Lions, 1–0. He set the single-season school record with a 1.47 ERA that stood for 56 years until future Mets hurler Pete Harnisch topped it. Murphy had a chance to match the record set by teammate Bob Cooney with three shutouts in a season when he was scheduled to start on May 25, 1929 against Boston College. He never took the hill against the Eagles. Coffey announced to the press that his pitcher was now ineligible as he had inked a professional baseball contract and was now property of the New York Yankees. Murphy was initially sent to their Albany farm club and later on to St. Paul, where he won 16 and threw 256 innings in his second year with the Saints in 1931.

On December 31, 1931, Murphy wed Elizabeth Havern. Their 48-year marriage produced two sons, John Jr. and Tom.

On March 30, 1932, Murphy pitched the final game of that year's Grapefruit League season for the Yankees in St. Petersburg, Florida. His opposition was baseball's storied bearded, religious sect, the barnstorming team of Benton Harbor, Michigan: the House of David. Babe Ruth was not in the Yank lineup, due to a reported stiff neck. Murphy contributed at the plate with a hit and scored a run off Lefty Moose Swaney. Murphy's three hit-hit shutout helped earn him a trip north with the parent club.

Murphy debuted in the major leagues on May 19, finishing up a 12–7 loss to the Washington Senators. He pitched once more before the Yankees sent him to the International League's Newark Bears. When the Yankees voted on how to distribute their World Series shares—that being the year of Ruth's "Called Shot" and a sweep of the Cubs—Murphy was voted $500. He'd earn a larger chunk of the pie later.

After another year in Newark, making 36 of his 40 appearances in relief and having his best ERA to date as professional (2.97), Murphy came north again with the Yankees in 1934. This time he never went back. Murphy started 20 games for New York—completing 10—but tossed another 20 in relief and going 14–10 with a 3.12 ERA. He made only 20 more starts the rest of his career and he never again approached the 207.7 innings he had as a rookie.

Manager Joe McCarthy's decision to put Murphy in the bullpen paid dividends for the finesse pitcher and his club. At the time, relievers were usually pitchers who were past their prime or deemed not good enough to start; if teams needed a reliever at a crucial point late in a game, they often turned to starters who were in between starts. Though Yankees starters still completed the majority of their games, McCarthy utilized the young pitcher's masterful curveball out of the pen in tight situations. Murphy's reliability to finish close games earned him the trust of his manager and teammates. When perennial All-Star Lefty Gomez was asked to predict how many games he would win one season, the wry pinstriper retorted, "Ask Murphy."

The save was years away from becoming an official statistic, but applying it retroactively, Murphy led the American League in that category four times in five seasons. His 19 saves in 1939 were the second highest total in baseball history, trailing only Firpo Marberry's 22 for the 1926 Washington Senators. Two years earlier in 1937, Murphy notched 12 wins in relief; he matched that number again in 1943.

Murphy made the All-Star team three consecutive years from 1937 to 1939. The Fireman was in six World Series, winning them all. (The year the Yankees won the pennant and Murphy did not appear in the World Series, the Yankees lost to the Cardinals, in 1942.) His postseason numbers totaled a 2–0 record, 1.10 ERA, and four saves in eight games. In four separate World Series, Murphy allowed no runs. He pitched once in each World Series from 1936 to 1939, earning three saves and a win.

His best season was 1941 where he posted an 8–3 mark, 1.98 ERA, and 15 saves. On October 5 that year, Murphy entered Game Four of the World Series in Brooklyn in the eighth inning. Murphy wound up getting the win after Dodgers catcher Mickey Owen's missed third strike set the stage for a four-run Yankees ninth. He set down all six Dodgers he faced. He threw six scoreless innings overall in '41 as the Yankees won in five games.

The most popular nickname attached to Johnny was "Grandma." Many tales attribute the moniker to his rocking motion on the hill. A more plausible explanation is given by *A Legend in the Making* author Richard Tofel. Tofel claimed "Grandma" came from 1935–37 Yankees teammate Pat Malone, who had tired of Murphy's "incessant complaining about meals and accommodations."

Murphy had orderly and fastidious traits on the field and off. He enjoyed the better things in life. He liked fine French cooking and wine. As a front-office exec, he sipped vino at lunch in the Mets press room from his own special bottle. At his first press luncheon as Mets general manager there was French wine for all.

Part of the greatest generation, Murphy voluntarily left baseball in 1944 and worked on a special defense project. On March 7, 1946, fans read the curveballer was re-upping with Joe McCarthy and crew. The *Washington Post* reported, "Baseball's Bronx Bombers will have an atomic specialist in their ranks this year…Johnny Murphy had come to terms…on the retired list the past two seasons while he worked on the atomic bomb project at Oak Ridge, Tennessee."

Murphy had one more solid season, garnering a 4–2 mark with a 3.40 ERA and seven saves. The Yankees failed to win the pennant for the third straight year and McCarthy was replaced by Bucky Harris and Murphy's role—and nickname—of "Fireman" was taken over on the Yankees by Joe Page. Three days after Murphy's release, the Red Sox signed him on April 15, 1947.

He pitched 54.7 innings and had a 2.80 ERA for the defending AL champion Red Sox. Murphy had three saves and finished games in 16 of his 32 appearances. That gave him a career mark of 93–53 in 293 games with a 3.50 ERA and 107 unofficial saves in 1,045 innings.

Though Boston released him on October 20, 1947, Joe Cronin, field manager elevated to Red Sox general manager, made one of his first moves the hiring of Murphy as a team scout. Four months later, Murphy's opinion on the business of baseball would echo throughout the State Capitol.

In January 1948, the Massachusetts Legislature was considering a bill to outlaw the reserve clause in contracts between players and clubs. Murphy went on record to say, "The reserve clause is essential for the players' protection as well as the owners' and should be included as an integral part of the contract." Another player who testified to the Bay State solons and felt the same way was Fred "Dixie" Walker of the Pittsburgh Pirates. (Like Murphy, Walker was at the end of his career and soon to enter the management end of the equation.)

Murphy steadily climbed the team's organizational ladder. He was made vice president and director of minor league systems. When Cronin was chosen as American League president in late 1958, Bucky Harris became Boston general manager. Murphy worked under the man who had released him in New York, but 20 months later, both men were sent packing.

Two days after slugging superstar Ted Williams revealed his retirement as an active player in September 1960, Boston owner Tom Yawkey shook up the front office and fired both the GM and farm director. Hub sports writers alluded that possibly Teddy Ballgame would soon put on a business suit for the franchise, but he never served in the Red Sox front office in a daily capacity.

Murphy departed the American League but not baseball. On April 2, 1961, Murphy signed with the New York Baseball Club of the National League as supervisor of scouting activities. The position reunited him with, George Weiss, who had built up the Yankees farm system during Murphy's playing career and later took over as GM. Sent packing by the Yankees after three decades—along with Casey Stengel—Weiss was the president of New York's yet-to-be named NL club. He assigned Murphy's scouting territory as the New York City area and New England, two areas he obviously knew well.

One of the perks of the job was to watch his son play and call it work. At Yale Field, it was reported that Murphy "sat in the stands and watched his son, John Jr., take over in the fifth inning and ease Yale to a 10–1 victory over Connecticut in a manner reminiscent of his old man." The Bulldogs roster, led by former major leaguer Ethan Allen, also featured third baseman/pitcher Ruly Carpenter, son of Philadelphia Phillies owner Bob Carpenter.

On May 8, 1961, the new NL team held its christening party at New York's Savoy Hotel. Forgoing Continentals, Burros, Skyliners, Skyscrapers, Bees, Rebels, NYBS, Avengers, and Jets—the public selected the team's official nickname as the Mets. Of the 23 scouts employed by the fledgling club, Murphy was one of six at the shindig. When asked what he looked for in a young player before offering a bonus or signing him to a contract, answers touched every base: Rogers Hornsby, "Throwing…"; Babe Herman, "The arm…"; Billy Jurges, "The legs…"; Gil McDougald, "Look for everything." Murphy, the lone pitcher among those surveyed, responded, "Batting. The first thing I want to know about a prospect is: 'Can he swing a bat?'"

Murphy's approach in business dealings could be aptly described as "taking the first pitch." He was a cautious, company man. At a time when bonuses for amateur players were hitting six figures, *New York Times* writer Arthur Daley alerted readers about Murphy spotting a talented ballplayer and being told by the athlete's father, "Make your bid in writing. The price starts at $50,000." With Casey Stengel officially named manager shortly before the expansion draft in October 1961, Daley assessed that "the Mets brain trusters—meaning... Weiss… Stengel… and Murphy tried to direct their player procurement toward men whose styles were tailored along certain lines... In the Polo Grounds scheme of things it isn't important that the center fielder be able to hit the long ball as to catch it." New York picked Richie Ashburn from the Cubs. When asked whether the 35-year-old Ashburn had lost his speed, Murphy said, "We know that Ashburn is not as fast as he once was, but he still is faster that most players in the National League. When [Mets coach] Solly Hemus managed the Cardinals last season he got a good look at him and Solly told us that Richie can still play an awful lot of center field."

Murphy was promoted to Eastern Administrative Assistant to Weiss in late 1962. The famed reliever proved a good number two man to Weiss. In the 1962 annual draft of minor league players, the Mets spent a record for $695,000. Expected to select a pitcher Al Worthington of Indianapolis, they surprisingly plucked Ted Schreiber, a .277-hitting second baseman from the Red Sox farm in Seattle. As Boston's minor league director in 1957, Murphy had signed the St. John's University lad from Brooklyn and had continued to monitor the infielder's upward progress.

In fiscal transactions with fledgling Mets players, Murphy did right by ownership. When first baseman Marv Throneberry sought a pay hike from Weiss and Murphy, Marvelous Marv highlighted to the duo his recent Good Guy Award from the baseball writers.

"Don't forget that I brought a lot of people to the ball park," Throneberry said.

"Yes," replied Murphy, "and you also drove a lot away."

In November 1963 the Mets acquired George Altman and Bill Wakefield from the Cardinals for Roger Craig, who had endured 18 straight losses that year and a 15–46 record in two seasons as a Met. Murphy's first words to the veteran hurler: "I have good news for you. You've been traded." Subsequently, Craig commented, "I was relieved and gratified when Murphy told me where I was going... I was praying it wouldn't be to another second division club. I felt I suffered enough." Craig pitched in the World Series the next year, though not before the Mets nearly kept St. Louis from clinching during a tense final weekend.

As personnel director, Murphy represented the Mets at the 1963 minor league convention. The Mets soon elevated him to vice president; former Brooklyn Dodger and New York Giant Eddie Stanky took his place as personal director. Murphy got another former Brooklyn Dodger, Duke Snider, to accept a renewed salary contract at $32,000, a $6,000 pay cut from the previous season—and then sold him to San Francisco on Opening Day (Snider wanted to go to a competitive team). The basement-dwelling Mets drew 1,732,597 to brand-new Shea Stadium in 1964, far better attendance then the AL-flag winning Bronx Bombers.

The 1965 Grapefruit League sports news buzz focused on outfielder Joe Christopher's pay haggle with Murphy. The battle was termed by Joe Durso in the *New York Times* as the team's "biggest financial headache of the season." Wanting a bigger share of that '64 cash flow, Christopher who batted .300, with 16 home runs and led the Mets in doubles, triples, total bases, slugging percentage, walks, and RBIs, argued with Murphy for days upon days. The two sides finally settled, but Christopher did not match his former year's numbers. He was traded to Boston after the season, then dispatched to Detroit, and then out of the big leagues all together.

Murphy handled the negotiations that wound up changing the future of the franchise. He was sent to Washington to try to bring back Gil Hodges to manage the Mets. The Senators had him under a long-term contract and weren't presupposed to let him go, but Mets board chairman M. Donald Grant was adamant that Hodges manage the Mets. Murphy had been a teammate and one-time roommate of Senators GM George Selkirk and the two old friends eventually worked out the deal: pitcher Bill Denehey and $100,000 for the Hodges. The Mets had a manager but soon lost their general manager when Bing Devine left the Mets to take the same post in his native St. Louis. On December 27, 1967, Johnny Murphy was named the third general manager in Mets history.

At spring training in 1968, the former Yankees fireman and the long-time Brooklyn first baseman made Mets activities uniform and established priorities. Practice sessions were regimented. The team ceased repeatedly rotating players between the farm system and the parent club. GM Murphy worked closely with director of player development Whitey Herzog. The main objective was pitching... something the Mets so happened to have a bumper crop of in 1968.

These organizational maneuvers perpetuated by Murphy came to fruition in the storied 1969 season. The Miracle Mets pitching staff, a significant key to the pennant and World Series was primarily comprised of club developed talent, namely Tom Seaver, Jerry Koosman, Gary Gentry, Nolan Ryan, Jim McAndrew, and Tug McGraw. The team needed hitting, an area the 1969 Mets did not excel in outside of homegrown Cleon Jones and his .340 average, but Murphy grabbed young third baseman Wayne Garrett from the Braves in the Rule V draft and when the Mets were surprisingly in contention in June, he acquired veteran slugger Donn Clendenon from Montreal. Though many of the players who starred for the 1969 team had been signed and developed by others in the organization, it was Murphy who worked out the trade for the manager who made it happen and acquired the veteran big bat in Clendenon without sacrificing the club's top prospects: Amos Otis and Nolan Ryan, both of whom the Braves had asked for in a proposed swap for Joe Torre during spring training.

Murphy did trade Otis—and pitcher Bob Johnson—in December in a regrettable trade with the expansion Kansas City Royals for troubled third baseman Joe Foy. Murphy had his reasons, though. Veteran third baseman Ed Charles had been released and the Mets didn't think Garrett could play the position regularly. Many gave Murphy the benefit of the doubt when the trade was made. He had, after all, helped turn the game's biggest loser into world champions—the first expansion team to ever win the World Series. Would he get them to repeat? The answer, tragically, was no.

On December 30, 1969, Murphy was felled by a heart attack at his home in Yonkers, New York. He was taken to New York's Roosevelt Hospital, where he died on January 14, 1970, following another massive heart attack. He was buried at Woodlawn Cemetery in the Bronx. He was 61.

The Mets still honor their former GM by annually handing out the Johnny Murphy Award to the top rookie in spring training, a tradition that dates to 1972. The Mets inducted Murphy into the team's Hall of Fame in 1983. Though George Weiss was inducted by the Mets before him, no GM since Murphy—including his successor, Bob Scheffing—has been so honored by the team.

**Sources**


Lang, Jack, and Peter Simon. *The New York Mets: Twenty-Five Years of Baseball Magic.* (New York: Henry Holt, 1986.)

Pietrusza, David, Matthew Silverman, and Michael Gershman. *Baseball: The Biographical Encyclopedia.* (Kingston, New York: Total Sports Illustrated, 2000.)

Thorn, John, Pete Palmer, Michael Gershman, and David Pietrusza. *Total Baseball,* sixth edition. (Kingston, New York: Total Sports Publishing, 1999.)

Tofel, Richard J. *A Legend in the Making: The New York Yankees in 1939.* (Chicago: Ivan R. Dee, 2004.)

Tuite, James (ed.). *Sports of the Times: The Arthur Daley Years.* (New York: Quadrangle/New York Times Book Co., 1975.)

National Baseball Hall of Fame

Hall of Fame Questionnaire #718/(1959)

*baseballlibrary.com*

*baseball-reference.com*

*en.wikipedia.org*

## Mets Transactions 1969

The transactions listed were made by the Mets between November 1, 1968 through April 1, 1970. Only players selected in the major league draft who eventually reached the big league level are included. Players involved in transactions are listed as "minors" if that is the highest level attained in their careers.

**December 1968:** Traded Jerry Buchek to the St. Louis Cardinals. Received Jim Cosman.

**December 2, 1968:** Drafted Wayne Garrett from the Atlanta Braves in the 1968 Rule 5 draft.
Tommie Reynolds drafted by the Oakland A's in the 1968 Rule V draft.
Juan Rios drafted by the Montreal Expos in the 1968 Rule V draft.
Bill Short drafted by the Cincinnati Reds in the 1968 Rule V draft.

**December 4, 1968**: Traded Hector Valle to the Detroit Tigers. Received Jack DiLauro.

**February 5, 1969:** Sold Greg Goossen to the Seattle Pilots.

**June 5, 1969:** Drafted Randy Sterling in the first round (fourth pick) of the 1969 amateur draft.
Drafted Joe Nolan in the second round of the 1969 amateur draft.
Drafted Larry Fritz in the third round of the 1969 amateur draft (Secondary Phase). Player signed June 13, 1969.
Drafted John Andrews in the seventh round of the 1969 amateur draft (Secondary Phase), but did not sign the player.
Drafted Lute Barnes in the 21st round of the 1969 amateur draft.
Drafted Vic Harris in the 25th round of the 1969 amateur draft, but did not sign the player.
Drafted Buzz Capra in the 27th round of the 1969 amateur draft.
Drafted George Theodore in the 31st round of the 1969 amateur draft.

**June 13, 1969:** Sold Al Jackson to the Cincinnati Reds.

**June 15, 1969:** Traded Steve Renko, Kevin Collins, Bill Carden (minors), and Dave Colon (minors) to the Montreal Expos. Received Donn Clendenon.

**August 12, 1969:** Sold Bill Sorrell to the Kansas City Royals.

**September 9, 1969:** Purchased Jim Gosger from the Seattle Pilots.

**October 28, 1969:** Released Ed Charles.

**December 1, 1969:** Jim Cosman drafted by the Chicago Cubs in the 1969 Rule V draft.
Drafted Bill Denehy from the Cleveland Indians in the 1969 minor league draft.
Jack Di Lauro drafted by the Houston Astros in the 1969 Rule V draft.
Roy Foster drafted by the Milwaukee Brewers in the 1969 Rule V draft.

**December 2, 1969:** Traded Bernie Smith to the Seattle Pilots. Received Gary Upton (minors).

**December 3, 1969:** Traded Amos Otis and Bob Johnson to the Kansas City Royals. Received Joe Foy.

**December 12, 1969:** Traded Bob Heise and Jim Gosger to the San Francisco Giants. Received Ray Sadecki and Dave Marshall.

**January 1970:** Signed Greg Harts as an amateur free agent.
Signed Brian Ostrosser as an amateur free agent.

**January 17, 1970:** Drafted Roy Staiger in the first round (24th pick) of the 1970 amateur draft (Secondary Phase).

**March 29, 1970:** Traded J.C. Martin to the Chicago Cubs. Received Randy Bobb.

The transaction information used here was obtained free of charge from and is copyrighted by RetroSheet (www.retrosheet.org)

HALL OF FAME LIBRARY

# M. Donald Grant

by Rob Edelman

June 15, 1977 is a black day in the history of the New York Mets.

On that date, in what came to be known as The Midnight Massacre, M. Donald Grant, the team's chairman of the board, traded away Tom Seaver, AKA "The Franchise," to the Cincinnati Reds for Pat Zachry, Doug Flynn, Dan Norman, and Steve Henderson. Later that night, he also unloaded slugger Dave Kingman, who, like Seaver, was involved in a contract dispute.

Imagine how New York Yankees fans might have responded in 1955 had general manager George Weiss dealt Mickey Mantle to the Boston Red Sox for Norm Zauchin, Ted Lepcio, Ike Delock, and $10,000. Or...if, four decades later, the Yanks traded Bernie Williams to the cross-town Mets for Rico Brogna, Ryan Thompson, Bill Pulsipher, and a pack of baseball cards.

Thirty years after the Midnight Massacre, *New York Daily News* sportswriter Bill Madden described Grant as "the buttoned-down, authoritarian Wall Street stockbroker whose tight-fisted fiscal policies had contributed mightily to the Mets' decline and evoked widespread criticism from players and the media." Madden also quoted Tom Terrific: "There are two things Grant said to me that I'll never forget, but illustrate the kind of person he was and the total 'plantation' mentality he had. During the labor negotiations [Seaver was the team's player representative], he came up to me in the clubhouse once and said: 'What are you, some sort of Communist?' Another time, and I've never told anyone this, he said to me: 'Who do you think you are, joining the Greenwich [Connecticut] Country Club?' It was incomprehensible to him if you didn't understand his feelings about your station in life."

Given Grant's value system and Seaver's punch-the-clock standing as a Mets employee, such questions were entirely predictable.

One might assume then that Grant was a child of America's aristocracy. But this was not the case. Michael Donald Grant was born on May 1, 1904 in Montreal. He came from a sporting family. His father, Michael "Mike" Grant, was a star hockey player, winning fame as a defenseman and captain of the five-time Stanley Cup champion Montreal Victorias between 1893 and 1900. In 1950, Mike Grant was inducted into the Hockey Hall of Fame. M. Donald's second cousin was David Mulligan, a Montreal (and, later, New York) hotel manager and golf aficionado for whom the term "mulligan" was coined. However, his paternal grandfather was a Montreal blacksmith.

In his youth, Grant was an avid golfer and squash player, and starred in amateur hockey. Because of the stiff competition and meager salaries then earned by athletes, his family discouraged him from pursuing a professional sports career. Instead, Grant quit school at age 15, never to return, and took an entry-level job at the Bank of Montreal. At age 20, the Montreal Canadiens offered him a professional contract, but by then he had committed himself to a business career. "I told them I didn't want a contract to play hockey," Grant recalled. "I told them, 'Instead of money just give me the program concession at the Forum.'" They didn't—and, that same year, 1924, Mulligan convinced Grant to come to New York. He arrived with less that $100 in his pocket, determined to achieve success. He was hired as a night clerk at the Commodore Hotel and refereed hockey games on the side.

Grant also married well. In 1932, he wed Alice Waters, the daughter of Thomas J. Waters, a high-profile civil engineer whose company, Thomas J. Waters & Sons, constructed churches, libraries, schools, and armories. Through his connection to his wife's family, Grant's name began appearing on newspaper society pages. The September 16, 1932 *New York Times* reported, "Mrs. John P. Hennessy gave a luncheon yesterday in the white and gold room of the Plaza for Miss Mona Ryan, daughter of Dr. George J. Ryan, president of the Board of Education, and Mrs. Ryan." Among the guests: "Mrs. M. Donald Grant." At the end of the month, Mona Ryan wed Alice's brother, James Joseph Waters.

On October 20, 1941, the *Times* duly reported, "Mrs. M. Donald Grant of Hewlett [Long Island] gave a luncheon yesterday at her home after the informal tennis matches at the Rockaway Hunting Club in Cedarhurst." On December 8, 1941, the *Times* reported that the club "gave a buffet luncheon yesterday for the visiting players in the gold squash racquets tournaments, which ended last night. Among the hosts were...Mr. and Mrs. M. Donald Grant." Interesting to note that this was the day of the Pearl Harbor attack, but perhaps the gold squash racquet tournaments had to go on.

By that time, Grant had eased into the investment business, and was a rising star on Wall Street. He first was affiliated with Billings, Olcott & Co. and E.B. Smith & Co. In 1936, he became manager of the stock department of Redmond & Co., overseeing customers' money. Two years later, he was named a general partner of Fahnestock & Company, a brokerage house that catered to the elite. Recalled Fahnestock's Sherburn Becker, "One of the partners at the time said, 'Here's a young man with something on the ball.'" A one-sentence item in the August 13 *New York Times* announced, "M. Donald Grant to be admitted to Fahnestock Co." His specialty was administration, rather than stock trading. In 1977, the *New York Times* quoted an unidentified broker, who tellingly noted, "He runs a tight ship at Fahenstock. He keeps his costs down. He's been smart this way. He gets the most he can out of his old equipment, and he pays the young guys the least he can get away with." Grant became a managing partner at Fahnestock in 1945.

In November 1941, Grant was on a nominating committee whose mission was to determine the slate of governors for the reconstituted Association of Stock Exchange Firms. Among the nominees was George Herbert Walker, Jr., the uncle of George W. Bush and, like Grant, a future minority owner of the New York Mets. So the 43rd President of the United States was not the first member of his family to enjoy ownership of a major league baseball team.

Despite his burgeoning career, Grant's participation in athletics did not wane. From the late 1920s through 1950s, he partook in sporting competitions, mostly in the New York City area. Occasionally, he suffered defeat. In 1935, Grant and J. F. Billings lost to Robert W. Ryle and Edward S. Knapp, Jr., in an annual invitational golf tournament at the Piping Rock Country Club in Locust Valley. A decade later, he and John J. Smith were defeated by Hunter Lott and William Slack, national amateur squash racquet doubles champions, in the semifinals in the Gold Racquets Squash Invitational at Cedarhurst. But he occasionally prevailed. In 1942, he and William T. Ketcham, Jr. were doubles champions in the Gold Racquets Squash Invitational. In 1944, he and Smith won the Metropolitan (New York) Doubles and Canadian Doubles squash championships. That same year, he and Carl Timpson were victors in the Arthur Man Memorial golf tournament at the Sewane Harbor Club in Hewlett Harbor. In 1948, he and Mark Stuart emerged victorious in the Meadow Brook invitational golf tournament in Westbury. Then in 1954, he was teamed with Cary Middlecoff in a pro-celebrity round robin golf tournament at the Meadow Brook club. Other participants were golfers (Tommy Bolt, Jimmy Demaret, Gene Littler) and movers-and-shakers and celebrities (John Hay Whitney, Carroll Rosenbloom, Perry Como).

For years, Grant resided in Hewlett with his family, and was a member of the Rockaway Hunt Club in Cedarhurst and a life member of the United States Squash Racquets Association. Meanwhile, he basked in his position as a New York civic leader, and for decades was a regular at high-society charitable events. At fundraising affairs, he often would be called to the dais where he would entertain the audience with dialect jokes.

Grant preferred the name Donald to Michael and his friends referred to him as Don or Donnie, but his patrician demeanor resulted in his being dubbed "M. Donald Grant." He reportedly abhorred the name, but was referred to as "M. Donald" in official Mets publications.

One of those who called him Donnie was Joan Whitney Payson, heiress to the vast Whitney fortune and the original majority owner of the Mets. They first met in the early 1940s. While visiting a private club in Florida, Grant and a number of individuals became immersed in a diversion in which each participant declared how they might spend all the wealth in the world. Grant stated that he would purchase the New York Giants baseball team; at the time, he owned five shares in the club. The person who followed him was Joan Payson, a diehard Giants supporter who added that she, too, desired to own the team—and a friendship and business relationship was born. He became her trusted financial advisor, but they also enjoyed each other's company. Payson savored listening to and singing old songs, and often requested that Grant perform one of her favorites, "Jimmy Crack Corn." Grant happily complied, and sang all its verses.

By the 1950s, through Grant, Payson owned almost 10 percent of the club, and he became her representative on the Giants board of directors. As the Giants contemplated the abandonment of New York for San Francisco, Grant was the lone board member not in favor or relocation. He voted against the move on August 19, 1957. "It just tears my heart to see them go," he observed. "I've been a Giant rooter all my life. Then, too, as a businessman, I think they would do better staying here. I would rather have a National League franchise here than any other city."

After the Giants forsook New York, Grant was among the leaders of an effort to establish the Continental League, a fledgling enterprise that would challenge the baseball establishment. Though the league never played a game, New York lawyer William Shea put the Continental League in a position where Major League Baseball thought it a potential threat and major league owners reluctantly decided to add expansion teams. One team was the New York Mets.

In 1962, upon the inception of the Mets, Payson became the team's founding principal owner while Grant was her chief advisor and chairman of the team's board of directors. Additionally, he and George Herbert Walker, Jr. each owned approximately 10 percent of the team, while Payson controlled 78 percent. Grant was not merely a figurehead who presided over board meetings, but he was directly involved in the team's decision making—even though a general manager handled the ballclub's day-to-day operations. It was Grant's insistence that led to the Mets working out a trade for manager Gil Hodges after the 1967 season.

The Mets were not Grant's lone business enterprise, as he remained a managing partner at Fahnestock & Company. After the Mets completed their 1969 miracle, Grant beamed, "Our team finally caught up with our fans."

As a baseball executive, Grant was strictly old guard. He was fabled for inviting Mets stockholders and dignitaries to the team clubhouse, where he would introduce the ballplayers as "boys." He believed that ballplayers should smile on cue, accept whatever deals management offered them, sign their contracts, and play ball; he supported the notion that ballplayer salaries should be comparable to that of the average American working person, rather than similar to the remuneration of a stockbroker or CEO. It was as if he was presiding over a deadball-era team, rather than one whose ballplayers soon would be demanding higher salaries, contract renegotiations, and free agency.

Grant's tenure with the Mets was crammed with lowlights. While the Tom Seaver affair is the best-known incident, he grossly mishandled the Cleon Jones situation—at the time, the club leader in most career offensive categories—and Grant was roundly criticized in the press. Grant publicly chastised Jones in May of 1975 when the popular outfielder, an African American, was arrested for indecent exposure while in the company of a white woman during extended spring training. The charge eventually was dropped, but Grant fined Jones $2,000, suspended him, and ordered him to offer a public apology in the company of his wife. Afterward, Grant told what *Newsweek*'s Pete Axthelm described as "an off-color joke about a man who wanted 11 women in one night" and cluelessly added, "I hope [Jones] will not be persecuted here by anyone." Dave Kindred, writing in the *Washington Post*, lambasted the board chairman for presenting himself as "righteousness incarnate" and transforming Jones into "Hester Prynne in spikes." Axthelm dubbed Grant a "sanctimonious, insensitive baseball executive" for staging "his own public trial and humiliation." Grant's firing of popular manager Yogi Berra in August earned the board chairman additional jeers.

By 1977, Payson had died, and the Mets were floundering—and Tom Seaver was publicly criticizing Grant for failing to improve the team and renegotiate his contract. Maury Allen, then a *New York Post* columnist, recalled that, at the time, Grant "was growing weary and jealous of Seaver's connection with the team and the town." The estimable Red Smith, writing in the *New York Times*, observed, "For a decade, Tom Seaver has been one of the finest pitchers in the game. More than that, he is his own man, thoughtful, perceptive, unafraid to speak his mind. Because of this, M. Donald Grant and his sycophants put Seaver away as a troublemaker. They mistake dignity for arrogance." Added Jack Lang, writing in *The Sporting News*, "Donald Grant envisions his Mets as one big happy family. Forget it. They are not. Hardly a day passes that there is not some new conflict."

For the 1977 and 1978 seasons, the 98- and 96-loss Mets were mired in last place. The franchise had been run into the ground, and the board chairman was viewed as the chief culprit. Not surprisingly, attendance plummeted, with detractors increasingly referring to Shea Stadium as "Grant's Tomb." Indeed, M. Donald Grant had become a public laughingstock. At the New York baseball writers' dinner, a ditty was performed—in Grant's presence—whose lyrics were:

"Don, you're driving me crazy.
Your fans are all gone but me.
I wish you'd push up a daisy.
The Mets are sad to see."

In November 1978, the eight-person Mets board of directors convened at the team's corporate headquarters in Manhattan and relieved Grant of his duties as the team's board chairman. Grant had attended every Mets home opener since the club's inception. In 1979, however, the *New York Times* reported that it "was uncertain if he would attend this one" because he feared the reception he would receive from fans. Grant did come, but "his entrance was a discreet one. He did not take his seat in his accustomed box—the one to the left of the Mets dugout, where visiting dignitaries used to sit—until the official ceremonies were over." The paper added that Grant "has become a nonperson. His name appears only among the board of directors in the club's press guide." He declared, "I'm here as a spectator. I'm not consulted. I'll try to come to as many games as I can." The Mets drew a record-low 788,905, even if it was no longer—technically—Grant's Tomb.

Grant stayed on as a Mets director and stockholder through January 1980, when the team was purchased by Doubleday & Co. and Fred Wilpon. Even though he no longer was a piece in the New York sporting pie, his name remained synonymous with stubbornness, frugality, and poor decision making. In 1983, the football New York Jets abandoned Shea Stadium for the Meadowlands in New Jersey. New York City officials and Leon Hess, the team's owner, partially blamed Grant for the action. The Mets were the stadium's principal tenants, and Hess believed that Grant had been the prime culprit in forcing his team to play all its early-season games on the road. Shea only would be open to them after the end of the baseball season, although by 1978, the Jets had begun to play some September games at Shea after taking the issue to court.

Grant remained a senior partner at Fahnestock & Company until his retirement in 1988, at which point he permanently settled in Hobe Sound, Florida, his longtime winter residence. For years, he was a director of the Hobe Sound Company, which controlled 4,000 acres of Florida investment property. His name occasionally popped up in the *New York Times*, upon an announcement of the wedding of one of his grandchildren.

The media sporadically referenced his affiliation with the Mets. Upon the passing of Joan

Payson in 1975, Lorinda de Roulet, Payson's daughter, had taken over the team's stewardship. In 1996, *New York Times* columnist Murray Chass described the de Roulet family's operation of the team as "misguided"—and labeled Grant the clan's "Rasputin."

M. Donald Grant died on November 28, 1998 at his home in Hobe Sound after a long illness. He was 94 years old, and was survived by his wife, Alice, to whom he was wed for 66 years, two sons (Michael, Jr. and Tim), one daughter (Patsy Warner), and 10 grandchildren. A daughter, Sheila, predeceased him.

Murray Chass, who covered the Mets during the Grant's Tomb era, wrote in Grant's obituary that the Mets president:

> *Shunned free agents because of the cost, maintaining that his style of conducting baseball business would put the Mets ahead of teams that spent lavishly to lure players from other teams. He adopted that stance at the same time that the Yankees aggressively sought top free agents. While the Yankees won the World Series in 1977 and 1978, the Mets finished in last place with a total of 130 victories compared with 200 for the Yankees.*

Asked in February 1978 when the Mets would become contenders, Mr. Grant said, "We are contenders right now."

The gutted franchise still did not climb above fifth place until 1984.

**Sources**


Axthelm, Pete. "The Lousy Losers." *Newsweek.* June 2, 1975.

Barkow, Al. "Don't Like It? Hit Another." *New York Times.* August 10, 1997.

Chass, Murray. "Game's Big Problem: Futile Tigers." *New York Times.* May 21, 1996.

"Grant, in Quieter Fashion, Joins Applause for Seaver." *New York Times.* July 21, 1977.

"M. Donald Grant, 94, Dies; Executive Angered Mets Fans." *New York Times.* November 30, 1998.

Costello, Brian. "Summer of Seaver: 30 Years ago, Mets fans suffered through

'Midnight Massacre.'" *New York Post.* June 10, 2007.

Eskenazi, Gerald. "M. Donald Grant: Taking the Heat." *New York Times.* July 24, 1977

"Mets' Grant: Forgotten but Not Gone." *New York Times.* April 11, 1979.

Hockey Hall of Fame, *http://www.hhof.com/*

Kahn, Roger. "'I'm a Good Guy.'" *New York Times.* February 27, 1978.

Kindred, Dave. "When a Man Is Holy, Solutions Come Easily; The Mets' Messiah."

*Washington Post.* June 18, 1977.

Lang, Jack. "Dissension? It's Name of Game on Sinking Mets." *The Sporting News.* June 11, 1977.

"Met Brass Gives Itself Pat on Back." *The Sporting News.* May 28, 1977.

"'The Time Had Come' as Mets Ease Out Grant." *The Sporting News.* November 25, 1978.

Madden, Bill. "M. Donald Infamy Grant, trader of Tom Seaver, dies at 94." *New York Daily News.* November 29, 1998.

"The true story of The Midnight Massacre; How Tom Seaver was run out of town 30 years ago." *New York Daily News.* June 17, 2007.

Werden, Lincoln. "Bolt and Hutton Deadlock for Pro-Celebrity Golf Honors." *New York Times.* May 13, 1954.

Young, Dick. "Young Ideas." *The Sporting News.* May 14, 1977.

"Young Ideas." *The Sporting News.* November 18, 1978.

Zug, James. *Squash: A History of the Game* (New York: Scribner, 2003)

"Admitted to Partnership in Stock Exchange House." *New York Times.* September 2, 1938.

"Exchange Firms to Vote Nov. 17." *New York Times.* November 7, 1941

"Financial Notes." *New York Times.* May 1, 1936.

"Grant and Stuart Take Links Honors." *New York Times.* September 27, 1948.

"Grant and Timpson Triumph on Links." *New York Times.* August 7, 1944.

"How the Franchise Went West." *Time.* June 27, 1977.

"John H. Smith Dies; Ex-Squash Player and Broker was 75." *New York Times.* September 25, 1988.

"Lott-Slack Annex Finals in Racquets." *New York Times.* December 10, 1945.

"Luncheon for Miss Logan." *New York Times.* September 16, 1932.

"Miss Ryan Bride of J.J. Waters." *New York Times.* September 30, 1932.

"Ryle and Knapp Take Golf Final." *New York Times.* June 17, 1935.

"Social Activities in New York and Elsewhere." *New York Times.* October 20, 1941.

"Social Activities in New York and Elsewhere." *New York Times.* December 8, 1941.

"Stock Exchange Notes." *New York Times.* August 13, 1938.

## Miracle Rat

Between the end of Whitey Herzog's so-so playing career and his superb managing career, he had a hand—a very big hand—in the Miracle Mets. White-haired lefty outfielder Dorrel Norman Elvert Herzog originally signed as a Yankee at age 17, playing for five American League organizations and batting .257 over eight seasons before appearing in his final game in 1963. "The White Rat" scouted for the Kansas City A's and served as a coach there before joining the Mets as third base coach in 1966. Herzog had a superior baseball mind and an eye for talent, plus he was far more engaging with reporters than Mets manager Wes Westrum; so Westrum hinted that maybe Herzog was better suited for the front office—lest he wind up behind the desk in Westrum's office. That decision had more lasting impact than anything Westrum did with the Mets.

The Mets needed all the help they could get to locate talent. Herzog served as a "special assignment" scout in 1967 before taking over as farm director. Jon Matlack, Gary Gentry, and John Milner were the most successful Mets drafted during his tenure. Herzog was responsible for evaluating the talent within the organization, balancing it against their sizeable needs, and helping find available players from other organizations. One such find, Amos Otis (drafted from the Red Sox), was traded against Herzog's wishes, as was Nolan Ryan; Ken Singleton went to Montreal in the Rusty Staub deal, a deal Herzog thought would strip the farm system. Staub gave the Mets a much-needed power bat (with the Expos receiving three everyday players in Singleton, Tim Foli, and Mike Jorgensen), but the Otis and Ryan trades are often regarded as the two worst deals in Mets history. Another horrendous move was letting Whitey leave.

Herzog spoke plainly and sometimes abrasively, and it didn't matter who was on the other end. He repeatedly told Mets board chairman M. Donald Grant not to interfere with baseball operations. "Whitey snickered at Grant's appraisals of players and was not opposed to arguing with the chairman of the board when he disagreed with him," former Mets beatman Jack Lang wrote in *The New York Mets: Twenty-Five Years of Baseball Magic*. "More than once, Herzog told Grant he didn't know a hill of beans about baseball." As a result, after the shocking deaths of general manager Johnny Murphy in 1970 and manager Gil Hodges in 1972, Herzog was passed over for both vacant posts.

He left the Mets after the 1972 season to manage the Texas Rangers. Though Herzog didn't last there long—and he served as coach and interim manager of the Angels in 1974—he landed on his feet in Kansas City during the '75 season. He transformed a six-year-old franchise into a three-time division champion by building the club around pitching, defense, and speed in a spacious Astroturf ballpark. He used the same formula—known as "Whiteyball"—in St. Louis in the 1980s. He served as both manager and GM when the Cardinals won a world championship in 1982. His Cards beat out the Mets for NL East titles in 1985 and 1987, though St. Louis fell in the seventh game of the World Series both times. Arguably, his greatest blunder in evaluating talent was trading Keith Hernandez in the prime of his career to the Mets for Neil Allen and Rick Ownbey in 1983. That was one major deal he signed off on that greatly benefitted the Mets.

PHOTO BY DAN CARUBIA

# The Three Amigos
## Lindsey Nelson, Bob Murphy, and Ralph Kiner

by Curt Smith

The New York Mets were born in sin, cleansed by pain, and saved in 1969. Sin: the National League's 1957 *adieu* to New York City. Pain: Marvelous Marv, Roger Craig, and Casey Stengel's other expansion '62ers. Salvation: In the year men first walked on the moon, the Amazin's walked on air: miracle and metaphysical, climbing a stairway to baseball heaven.

"The Mets may last a thousand years, as Churchill would say," mused Lindsey Nelson, their grand radio/TV stylist. "They may win a dozen championships. But they can only do it the first time once, and the first time was incomparable."

The 1969 Mets—Casey's "Metsies"—took a fractured time and briefly made it whole: then and now, crying *gotcha* to the soul. Let us retrieve perhaps The Greatest Baseball Story Ever Told, and the Magi which superbly told it.

"That was some sad year, that 1957," Lindsey described the Mets' genesis. The August 19 page 1 of the *New York World-Telegram* read: "It's Official: Giants to Frisco." On October 7, once baying, "My roots are in Brooklyn," Dodgers don Walter O'Malley decamped for Los Angeles, confirming the other elephant in the room. For New York, Moving Day had truly come.

Having baseball do unto him, Mayor Robert Wagner forged a five-man committee led by lawyer William A. Shea to do unto others. Ill-wind: The Reds, Pirates, and Phillies scorned re-location in the Apple. Whirlwind: In 1959, the threat of a proposed third major league—the Continental League—made the National League reconsider expansion; ergo, the New York Metropolitans.

New York's new NL club began with castoff Yankees management: George Weiss became general manager and Casey Stengel unretired to manage. The New York State Senate approved $55 million for a new park to open in 1963 in Queens. Job One was the 1961 expansion draft, age trumping beauty. "Weiss picked old Dodgers and Giants," mused Nelson. "[Roger] Craig, Gil Hodges, Charlie Neal." They looked great on paper, "but paper doesn't play." Unsolved: Who would announce them? For a time, it depended on whom you read.

That October, the *Los Angeles Times* rumored that "[Vin] Scully is secretly planning to shed his Dodger microphone and steel back to New York to report... the Mets." Actually, Weiss phoned another New Yorker, the Minnesota Twins' Bob Wolff, who missed the East. The *New York Daily News* pealed: "Wolff Coming." Problem: no station/sponsor. Time passed. "Weiss couldn't make a commitment," said Bob, "so I reupped with the Twins."

Weiss soon signed WABC Radio and WOR-TV, and the Tennessee phoneticist who at age eight heard Graham McNamee call a fight so near that he could "reach out and touch the canvas." To Nelson, the box speaker—an Arbiphone—"looked like a question mark." His answer began at the University of Tennessee, airing football on legendary WSM. Later, Lindsey became a World War II Army publicist. In 1945, US and Soviet troops drank captured German champagne at the Elbe. A photo showed Nelson with Russian officers: "To Lindsey Nelson, a very busy man the day this picture was taken. Dwight Eisenhower."

PHOTO COURTESY OF METSILVERMAN.COM

*Lindsey Nelson donated one of his patented gaudy sports coats to the Hall of Fame. Even in black and white, it's still tough to look at.*

Lindsey returned to print, radio, and 1952 NBC-TV, airing golf, basketball, college football, and weekly *Major League Baseball*: by 1961, a two-time National Sportscaster of the Year. How could he trade that for The Metropolitan Baseball Club of New York, Inc.? Easily, as it occurred. Nelson thought daily baseball broadcasting's king of the hill. NBC's 1957 to 1961 *Major League Baseball* had been blacked out in New York. "Many people that, not knowing, said, 'Why are they hiring this *football* guy?'" If this were Broadway, he replied, the tryout had run five years.

For *seven* straight years (1946–52), Ralph Kiner led the National League in homers, saying, "Home run hitters drive Cadillacs. Singles hitters drive Fords." At age four, Kiner's father died. Soon mom and son left New Mexico for California, where a neighbor and semipro baseball manager "let me tag along and shag." Ralph's last Pirates team (1952) was 42–112. That fall he asked for a raise. "I know you hit all those homers," general manager Branch Rickey said, "but we could have finished last without you." Kiner retired with 369 home runs: only Ruth had more per at-bat. How to top the topper? It took until 1969, but Ralph found a way.

"Nelson gave Weiss a household name," Bob Murphy mused. Hired in late 1961, Kiner lent an ex-jock's cachet. The third man should leaven them, Bob said: "Be a steady professional." Born in Oklahoma, he made the Marines, graduated from the University of Tulsa, and drifted into radio: Class C-Muskogee and Texas League's Oklahoma City before graduating to the big leagues and Fenway Park, then 1960 Baltimore. A year later Jack Fisher faced Roger Maris. "It's number 60!" Murphy bayed on WBAL Radio. "He's tied the Babe!" Next month the Orioles dumped sponsor Theo. Hamm Brewery. Admitting to being "lost in the shuffle," Bob sent the Maris tape to Weiss in New York. George found his man. "He had a distinctive voice that filled the air," Nelson said of Murphy. The Amazins' were distinctive, if nothing else.

"The '62 Mets played for fun," Lindsey conspired with memory, "not being able to play for anything else." In March, they convened in Florida. "We got to work on the little finesses," said Casey. "Runners at first and second, and the first baseman holding a runner, breaking in and back to take a pickoff throw." New York lost, 17–1. The Perfessor saw the light, not liking what he saw. "The little finesses aren't gonna' be our problem." Yarns stitched what were. "They were gruesome," Nelson mused. "Only attitude made it tolerable": love "at first laugh."

The first game was truly Metsian, losing, 11–4, to St. Louis two days before the Friday, April 13 home opener at their temporary den, the Polo Grounds. Hobie Landrith caught: Casey's first expansion pick. "If you ain't got no catcher," he explained, "you get all passed balls." The question is whether New York would pass.

Instead, the rookies drew 922,530—"amazing," Nelson gaped, "given our [40–120] atrocity." The "New Breed" scribbled on bed sheets. Placards waved at the roving camera eye. "The most amazing fans that we've seen in baseball," said Casey. "They stick by ya," even when their two-headed progenitor returned home On May 30, the Dodgers packed (55,704) the Polo Grounds. "We are frauds—frauds for this attendance," the Perfessor said. "But if we can make losing popular, I'm all for it."

Stengel never asked "how we lost 120. I asked how we won 40." He told a barber, "Don't cut my throat. I'm saving that for myself." Craig was 10–24. Al Jackson finished 8–20. An umpire called Marvelous Marv—Marvin Eugene Throneberry (MET)—out for missing first base on a triple. Coach Cookie Lavagetto told Stengel, "Don't argue too long, skipper—he missed second, too."

The 1962 season ended with Joe Pignatano hitting into a triple play in the 120th loss in what was his final major league at-bat. Richie Ashburn, a .306 hitter for a club with a .250 winning percentage, was voted team Most Valuable Player. He took the prize, a boat, out on the Delaware River, where it sank.

Not surprisingly, the Mets' Three Amigos tried whenever possible to divert attention from anything germane to score. WOR's post-game *Kiner's Korner* was a black and white period piece: "The best bad show," the *New York Post*'s Phil Mushnick said, "in TV history." Then it seemed revolutionary: "Interviews with stars—few of whom were Mets." To Kiner, it felt like 1952 again. The Mets could have finished last without him.

Murphy worried about the first-place Yanks. "I thought we'd have to struggle." For a time *Bob* did. "Lindsey didn't like my conversational style. He was a straight-ahead announcer, eyes on baseball." One day Nelson eyed a men's clothing store on Broadway. "Show me jackets that you can't sell," he told the owner, buying seven "gaudy, awful" coats. Next month a cabbie said, "You're the guy who wears all those wild jackets!" Nelson told a friend, "See, he doesn't know my name, but he knows what I do. Against the Yankees, it pays to advertise."

Journalist and *Sixty Minutes* commentator Andy Rooney served with Nelson in World War II. "Of all my old buddies," he said, "only Lindsey dressed better then." Murphy and Kiner scavenged on the road. "If we saw a wild enough jacket, we'd tell him." Nelson's daughter Nancy bought a jacket in Ireland. Both were stopped at customs. The inspector, a Mets fan, joked, "*Nobody* would wear a jacket like this."

"My daddy will," she beamed. In time, he owned 350.

By 1963, Mets radio/TV topped the Bombers—akin, said Murphy, to a mule lapping Man O' War. The Polo Grounds closed. *E Pluribus Unum*. The Mets' new abode, Shea Stadium, named for Bill, was christened April 16, 1964, with Dodgers Holy Water from Brooklyn's Gowanus Canal and Giants Holy Water at the Harlem River at the point it passed the Polo Grounds. Seats formed a four-tiered circle from one line to another. "The lower boxes were on rails that moved in into position for football," wrote the *Daily News*' Dick Young. Upper decks rose almost vertically. Few complained, glad merely to have baseball back—plus the first new stadium in New York in four decades.

A 1964 *The New Yorker* cartoon showed several Mets near the dugout. A bystander said, "Cheer up. You can't lose 'em all." One game took a record 7 hours, 22 minutes. "Pitch to Cepeda. Runners go," said Lindsey in the 14th inning. "And it's lined to McMillan. And a double play! And maybe a triple play! A triple play!" Incrementally, "hapless has-beens," he mused, "became hopeless maybes." Five times in their first seven seasons, the Mets hit last. They crawled out in 1966 only to fall back in. When they left the cellar again in 1968, the question was: for how long?

By 1969, the less United than Divided States blared hawk *v.* dove; hard hat *v.* hippie; Silent Majority *v.* hip, camp, and pop art intelligentsia. Vietnam was a horror house. Said H. Rap Brown: "[Urban] violence is as American as cherry pie." By contrast, the Miracle Mets rivaled Father Christmas. "Who can explain it? Who can tell you why?" Ezio Pinza sang in *South Pacific*. Later, Casey told us *how*: "They came on slow," he said, "but *fast*."

On April 8, their road began roughly: first-year and first game Expos, 11–10. In Chicago, Willie Smith pinch-homered a first-day, 7–6 Cubs victory. All year the teams intertwined like vines around a trellis. Tommie Agee became first to reach Shea's upper deck. Second-year skipper Gil Hodges devised a four-man outfield *v.* Richie Allen. The Mets forged an 11-game winning streak as May merged into June. Donn Clendenon arrived from Montreal five days after the streak ended. On July 9, Tom Seaver retired the first 25 Cubbies. "Here's the pitch on the way," Murphy said. "Line drive hit hard into left-center field! A clean base hit for Jimmy Qualls. And the roar goes up from the big [Shea record

59,083] crowd! A roar of disappointment." Seaver recouped, winning, 4–0.

Yin: Next week banjo hitter Al Weis zinged the Cubs. "Swung on, a high drive well hit toward left field!" said Bob. "A three-run homer!" The next day Weis would hit his second home run of the season to spark another New York win. Yang: The Mets fell to third, 10 games behind in August. Chicago's Billy Williams' 895th straight game set an NL record. while the entire Cubs infield—Ernie Banks (106 RBIs), Ron Santo (123 RBIs), Glenn Beckert (.291), and Don Kessinger (.273)—played in the All-Star Game, as did Randy Hundley (151 games caught). Santo clicked his heels upon each victory. Towel-waving reliever—and ex-Met—Dick Selma conducted Wrigley's Bleacher Bums. Rarely had the Friendly Confines seemed friendlier.

At this point, "sixty-nine" was not a term, like Watergate or Waterloo, that now stands alone. "*Pennant race*?" Nelson smiled. "We were given up for dead." The Metsies first swept San Diego at Shea and had a 9–1 homestand to creep within 5½ games. A Western road trip then went 6–4. At Candlestick Park, Willie McCovey slashed an August 30 apparent game-ending hit. "The throw coming in by Rod Gaspar!" said Murphy. "And he is *out* at the plate!" Thinking it the final out, Mets catcher Jerry Grote rolled the ball to the mound, where Clendenon nabbed it, threw to third, and got McCovey! Extra innings: Amazin's, 3–2. Planets realigned.

PHOTO COURTESY OF METSILVERMAN.COM

*Lindsey Nelson and Bob Murphy are together on the wall in Cooperstown that honors all recipients of the Ford C. Frick Award for broadcasting greatness. Between Murphy and Nelson is Bob Wolff, who was considered for the inaugural Mets booth.*

On September 8, Chicago invaded Shea 2½ games ahead. Like Canute, hoping to reverse the tide, Bill Hands almost beaned Tommie Agee in the opener. "[The next pitch] is hit to deep left-center field!" said Kiner. "Going, going, it's gone!" Agee later doubled, scoring the decisive run. A day later, appearing out of nowhere, a black cat hissed at the Cubs skipper. The crowd sang, "Good night, Leo [Durocher]," Seaver romping, 7–1. The next night, Ken Boswell's overtime hit edged Montreal, 3–2 in the first game of a doubleheader. "So, for the first time," Ralph said, "the Mets have gone into first place! The New York Mets, seven years and four months, for the first time n their history, have gone into first place in the National League race!" The crowd heaved, "We're Number One!" The Mets won the second game that night on a Nolan Ryan three-hitter. The moon was in the seventh house.

The Mets swept a 1–0 twinbill against Pittsburgh. Amazin' pitchers Jerry Koosman and Don Cardwell knocked in each run. The Cardinals' Steve Carlton K'ed a record 19 men—and *lost*, 4–3. On September 23, the magic number fell to one: "Line drive, hit sharply into left-center field for a base hit!" said Murphy. "Ron Swoboda gets the green light from Eddie Yost... and he'll score!" A 3–2 win in 11. A day later the East River flowed upstream. "Ground ball hit to shortstop!" Bob sang in the one-out ninth. "Harrelson to Weis! There's one! First base!" Double play! The Mets win! [6–0] It's all over! Oh, the roar going up from this crowd! Oh, the scene on the field! Fans are pouring out on the field!"

WOR-TV's off-season documentary on the '69 team proclaimed *To The Mets With Love*. "In a book he wrote, *Joy In Mudville*," Lindsey said, "George Vecsey said he saw more honest and enthusiastic joy in the crowd that night and on that program than he ever saw on television." A reporter asked, "Gil, tell us what this proves." He sat back, spread his hands, and laughed, "Can't be done." The last laugh lay ahead

"No way anyone could believe that the butt of everybody's jokes was finally going to win," said Nelson, until it did. Seaver was 25–7. Koosman went 17–9. Jones hit .340. Agee had 26 homers. New York drew an Apple NL regular-season record 2,175,373. The 100-to-1-ers proceeded to meet Atlanta in the first best-of-five League Championship Series—the new gateway to the World Series. Cleon Jones batted in the eighth inning of the opener. "There's a swing and drive into center field!" said Nelson. "It will score [Wayne] Garrett, I believe!" The game was tied at 5. Next: "There's a [Ken Boswell] swing and a ground ball topped to first. Taken by Cepeda. Play at the plate, and he's safe!" Final, 9–5.

New York encored, 11–6, then repaired to Shea. Atlanta knocked out Gary Gentry early in favor of Nolan Ryan and led Game Three, 4–3. "A high drive *deep* to right!" Murphy gaped. "A [two-run Garrett] homer!" The ninth commenced, 7–4. "So the Mets are one out away from their impossible dream. And the batter coming up is Tony Gonzalez," said Kiner. "The pitch, a curve, chopped out to third. Garrett has the ball! The throw to first! And the Mets are the National League champions! A wild, wild scramble as the Mets celebrating their National League championship!" Growing up in Queens, future voice Gary Cohen left Section 48, "in left field, five rows from the top," to maneuver toward the field. "Had to get my little piece of turf."

Heaven rarely looked so green. The American League champion Orioles eyed the fall classic, unimpressed. "We are here," Brooks Robinson said, "to prove there is no Santa Claus." Don Buford dinged Seaver's first-set second pitch: home run, 4–1, Baltimore. Koosman, pitching, and Weis, singling, countered, 2–1. Elves awoke. Pre-1981's Series forebade even local radio. NBC's Jim Simpson thus aired Game Three's fourth-inning heist. "Hit high and deep to center field! Agee, who was pulled around to right, goes over with his speed... He's got it!" Baltimore's Bill O'Donnell manned the seventh. "Fly ball to right-center field! Deep in right center! Shamsky with Agee! Agee dives—and he makes the catch!": Mets, 5–0. The North Pole warmed.

Photo courtesy National Baseball Hall of Fame Library, Cooperstown, NY

*Commissioner Bowie Kuhn right, stands with Ralph Kiner after the slugger was inducted into the Hall of Fame in 1975.*

Next day Seaver led, 1–0: one out, ninth inning, tying run on third. Brooks Robinson's line out scored it but Swoboda's diving catch kept Baltimore from scoring more. In the 10th, J.C. Martin bunted "down the first base line," said O'Donnell, with no out and two Mets on. "[Pitcher Pete] Richert fields, throws, and it hits the runner!" on the wrist, bouncing wildly. "Here's the runner coming on from third base! Gaspar! And the Mets win the ballgame by a score of 2 to 1!" The Orioles protested Martin's circuitous path to first. Plate umpire Shag Crawford cried humbug. Santa readied for Christmas Eve.

Game Five, sixth inning, O's, 3–0: Jones claims to be hit by a pitch on the foot. Spying shoe polish, Hodges retrieves the ball; at which point Lou DiMuro explores it; whereupon Cleon takes first. "Fly ball deep left field!" O'Donnell followed. "To the warning track! It is in and up for a home run by Donn Clendenon!" Weis had never gone yard at Shea and hadn't circled the bases since his Wrigley blasts in July. Dave McNally threw him seventh-inning heat. "A fly ball out into deep left-center field! Buford going back!... It is over the fence for a home run!"

Swoboda batted in a one-out, one-on, three-all eighth. "A fly ball, deep left field, headed for the fence, and it's on the warning track, picked up by Buford!" said O'Donnell. "On comes Jones to the plate! He throws it late." Mets, 4–3. A double O's error doubled their deficit. At inning's end, Lindsey left the NBC TV booth. "By pre-arrangement, I headed for the elevator to get to the clubhouse for the victory celebration. That's when it hit me—the whole enormity of the thing."

The Chinese discovered the 365½ day solar year in 2300 B.C. The Mets discovered Canaan October 16, 1969. At 3:16 p.m., Dave Johnson swung at Koosman's 2–1 pitch. "There's a fly ball out to left!" said NBC's Curt Gowdy. "Waiting is Jones! The Mets are the world champions! Jerry Koosman is being mobbed! Look at this scene!" We still are, reliving Nelson's "incomparable" year. Go ahead. Pinch yourself. You still do not believe it.

Nelson aired the post-game bash, then crossed into Manhattan. "'If we don't go into town, we'll have missed the celebration,' I told my wife and kids. So we did and it was marvelous. Dancing in the streets, throwing confetti. Once in a while a cop would recognize me and go wild." Santa cleared the chimney. A ticker-tape parade snaked through Manhattan. Said Mets chairman of the board M. Donald Grant. "Our team finally caught up with our fans."

Karl Marx called religion the people's opiate. For a time the Mets remained New York's.

The 1970 Amazins' drew 2,697,479, more than they had, or would till 1985. The '73ers waved another flag, Nelson again airing Series video.

Each year the Amigos aired 162 radio and 130–137 TV games. In 1975, Kiner entered the Hall of Fame for his exploits as a slugger; Nelson and Murphy were honored in Cooperstown in 1988 and 1994, respectively for their work at the microphone. The early Mets had trouble turning two. "Here we are, three for three," Bob laughed.

In the booth, the trio remained together a record 17 years. But on the field, having swung from bottom to top, the Mets swung back.

Lindsey resigned in January 1979, outlasting the Polo Grounds, seven Mets managers, and 238 players from A (Tommie Agee) to Z (Don Zimmer). He called San Francisco Giants games, taught broadcasting, did CBS Radio baseball, and aired a 26th Cotton Bowl. Upon the ceremony for Nelson, he removed his coat and gave it to the Hall. A visitor can still see its 12 colors randomly jiggered into squares.

In June 1995, Lindsey died, at 76, of Parkinson's Disease. *Sans* senior partner, Murphy increasingly seemed "the voice of all things Mets," wrote Marty Noble—at the beach, aboard the Staten Island ferry, home rabbit ears ferrying WOR Channel 9, and later exclusively on radio. "The Happy Recap" became a life, not a game. "I remember thinking it was corny, dropping it, then mail on its behalf" brought his moniker back where it belonged after every Mets win. The ex-Marine had a baritone that rose an octave, home phone number with last four digits 6-3-8-7 (METS), and team radio booth named after him. Retiring, he died in 2006, having "tried to bring friendliness to the game."

Only Kiner endured from 1969, its glow perceptible, inexhaustible. "Today is Father's Day," he began. "To all of you fathers in the audience, happy birthday." American Cynamid Co. became a TV sponsor. "We'll be right back," Ralph said, "after this word from American Cyanide." Some lines were planned. "Statistics are like bikinis. They show a lot but not everything." Some were not. "The Mets got their leadoff batter on only once this inning." In 1995, WOR canceled *Kiner's Korner*. He left the air, beat Bell's Palsy, and rejoined Mets TV, *its* booth named after him, imbedded in our DNA.

Each day, sitting there, Gary Cohen recalled learning to see with his ears. "Lindsey and company, with those great word-pictures. [Today] I scream when I *can't* see what's happening. The one thing I knew I wanted in radio was not to have preconceived phrases." Perhaps only God could conceive the Amazin's, their plot so otherworldly it must have hatched on another planet.

In 1988, Cohen froze airing a test game. Reaching over, Murphy patted Gary's hand. "He started talking, reassured me. It was my greatest memory." Our greatest memory is a year. In *Casablanca*, Bogart tells Bergman, "We'll always have Paris." We'll always have '69.

# Ralph Kiner 1969 Q&A

by Matthew Silverman

Ralph Kiner was in his eighth season as a Mets announcer in 1969. Kiner, along with Bob Murphy and Lindsey Nelson, broadcast the Mets their first day as a franchise in 1962. The broadcasters remained together for 17 seasons—a record for a trio with one team—until Nelson moved on to the San Francisco Giants after the 1978 season. Murphy remained with the club, switching to radio full-time in 1982, until he retired following the 2003 season. Kiner still broadcast a few selected Mets games per season in his late 80s (he was born on October 27, 1922, in Santa Rita, New Mexico—the only man elected to Cooperstown as a native of that state). Though Kiner never played for the Mets—he retired at age 32 in 1955 because of a chronic bad back—he is one of the most revered men in franchise history. His beloved postgame show was a staple among Mets fans for two generations. The show was dubbed *Kiner's Korner* for the porch in left field at Forbes Field, where he won an unprecedented seven consecutive National League home run titles (including ties in 1947 and 1952). He hit 369 home runs in just a 10-season career with the Pirates, Cubs, and Indians. He was elected to National Baseball Hall of Fame in 1975 and to the Mets Hall of Fame in 1984.

He took time in September 2007, two months after Ralph Kiner Night at Shea Stadium, to talk about the 1969 Mets and how things were handled in the booth.

**Maple Street Press:** *In 1968 did you feel there was something changing about the team, or was it something you didn't really see until 1969?*

**Ralph Kiner:** They had acquired both Koosman and Seaver by then. Ironically, they got them by happenstance. Seaver was originally signed by the Atlanta Braves and he was signed through a technicality. [It was done] illegally and they would not honor the signing. They put his name in a hat and there were three teams trying to get Seaver [in the special lottery set up by commissioner William Eckert in 1966]. One was Philadelphia, the other was Cleveland, and the Mets. And the Mets drew his name out of the hat.

Koosman was also going to be released by the Mets [in the minor leagues], but he owed them some money for a used car and Joe McDonald, who was running the farm system, said, "Let's keep him around for another month and get our money and then let him go." He ended up having a good month in the minors, so they didn't let him go and he stayed with the Mets and of course he was part of that real good pitching staff they had and at that time.

Their idea was that pitching was the way to build a club and that's basically how they came to have such good pitching. In '68 they had quite a few shutouts [25, second in the major leagues]. It was an abnormal amount of shutouts for a team that wasn't winning, but they pitched very well. Then in '69, they had never been at .500, and in the early part of the year they got to .500 for the first time in their history and they, the writers, celebrated it, but Seaver was quoted as saying, "We're only .500. They were 10 back on August 13 and the Cubs were dominating the league at the time, but all the things were going right for the Mets. The Mets wound up beating the Cubs and winning 100 games. They were getting all the breaks you need to get to be a winner. Everything has to go right all the way around for a team to win.

**MSP:** *The double shutout, when both pitchers drove in the only runs in 1–0 games in Pittsburgh, was that the strangest doubleheader you've ever seen, at least the strangest that didn't go 30-plus innings?*

**RK:** Cardwell [had one of the RBI hits] and the other was Koosman. Koosman was a hell of a pitcher. He certainly was one of the best competitors the Mets have ever had. He was really an outstanding pitcher along with Tom Seaver. That team also had some really good pitching along with Ron Taylor. Those guys had a real solid ballclub and all those guys had their career years in that year that they won. They beat a really good team in Baltimore. Frank Cashen was GM of Baltimore.

**MSP:** *Do you think that the five-man rotation the Mets developed in 1969 was good for the game or was that something that has led to teams rarely allowing starting pitchers to throw complete games, even when the outcome is crucial?*

**RK:** That became the rule of baseball and I don't really understand it. I don't know why you have to go to five-man rotation and not pitch complete games. And Seaver feels the same way. Seaver and Koosman that year, they didn't take them out automatically when they got to a certain number of pitches.

**MSP:** *Between August 13 and the end of 1969 the Mets had 25 complete games in that span.*

**RK:** Over the years, the Atlanta Braves with Glavine and Smoltz, they pitched all through the game. And Seaver, his pitch count would be up around 150 or whatever. To me, that theory that you don't throw more than 110 or 120 pitches, I don't understand that myself. I think the more you use your arm the stronger it gets. Of course that was the way they all pitched at one time in major league baseball. The starters would relieve in between starts on top of that.

**MSP:** *The platoon system, is there something about the way the Mets used that? Gil Hodges used it religiously. Donn Clendenon was the team's best slugger and he didn't play at all in the Championship Series in his very strict platoon. Do you think that helped keep the players rested, as opposed to the Cubs, who played the same guys every game?*

**RK:** Credit Stengel with the platoon system. He used it a lot when he managed the Yankees and he himself was platooned a lot when he played for John McGraw [for the 1920s New York Giants]. That system was not brought in by Hodges. He just continued using it when he took over. Might have been passed over from Stengel to him.

I think the platoon system that they use now with the middle relief and the closer is a cop out for the manager. That way at the end of the ballgame if they lose it they can say, "I did it like everyone else and I went to my middleman and he didn't do the job." Or it might have been the closer. I don't really understand the advantage. When I played, we were so happy to get the starting pitcher out of the ballgame because every club had maybe three outstanding pitchers and when you had to go to the bullpen for a pitcher who didn't have that kind of stuff. The closer does have the ability to throw hard for one or possibly two innings. That could be an advantage, but other than that I know whenever we were hitting against someone like [Warren] Spahn, who had so many complete games it was unbelievable, or good pitchers like that, we were happy to see them get out of the lineup.

**MSP:** *Getting back to 1969, when Agee hit that home run in the upper deck, it was the only one hit there at Shea. You probably had the best view of anyone of that ball.*

**RK:** Agee hit that ball up there. He had outstanding power. He wasn't that consistent, but he could hit the ball well.

The key to that '69 team was getting Donn Clendenon on that team. It gave them the right-handed bat that they really needed to score enough runs for that real good pitching staff. All those guys had really good years. You get down to Al Weis, Grote, and all those background guys—they had career years that year.

**MSP:** *In the World Series, especially. Al Weis, who had never hit a home run at Shea Stadium, hits a game-tying home run. Ron Swoboda, under the Hodges platoon, would have normally come out for Art Shamsky, who actually hit more home runs in fewer at bats than Swoboda. But in that particular spot with Eddie Watt on* *the mound in Game Five, Hodges let Swoboda bat in the eighth inning and he ended up getting the winning hit.*

**RK:** They had one of those years that was unreal. They had everything go their way the second half of that season.

**MSP:** *So during the postseason did you do the broadcast on the radio?*

**RK:** I did the radio broadcast for the network [NBC]. That's how they did it then. They had the local guys do it for the network. Lindsey did the TV and I did the radio.

**MSP:** *Now the way they would do it, the team's station broadcasts on the radio with their regular announcers and then there's a separate national broadcast. But instead of doing that, you guys would just do one broadcast to go all across the country.*

**RK:** Yes.

**MSP:** *Did you, Lindsey, and Bob Murphy have a set rotation during the season where one would do TV, the other do radio, and the third would be off?*

**RK:** We would alternate. All three of us would do TV and radio every single game. I don't remember how it would break down, but it was something close to that. I would do TV with Bob or Lindsey, then I'd do radio alone.

I know when we originally started, [Mets president] George Weiss said no one is going to be the number one announcer. We were going to be a team of three announcers. There were only three of us and we did all the games on radio and almost all of them on TV.

**MSP:** *That was one thing he told you early on and that was something that really was the case, because you guys really were really quite the team. When Lindsey would go do football and he wouldn't come back on Sundays, what would you guys do?*

**RK:** I'd do half TV and half radio and Bob would do half TV and half radio. We both worked alone. There was no other announcer involved.

**MSP:** *Did they have it arranged in general so that you'd be available at the end of the game for* Kiner's Korner *or would you go right from the booth to the studio?*

**RK:** At the end of the game I'd go right down to the studio and do *Kiner's Korner.*

**MSP:** *There was one story of one of the 20-inning games where you had gone down to the studio to get ready for* Kiner's Korner *because it looked like the game was going to end, and then it didn't, so you wound up sitting down in the studio for something like 10 innings.*

**RK:** That was in 1964 when we had the doubleheader that went 7 hours, and 23 minutes. I went down for the second game of the doubleheader that went 23 innings. I went down in the eighth inning and it looked like it was going to be over after nine and it was tied. I started to come back up to relieve either Bob or Lindsey and I never really got back up. There was a triple play in that game and things like that, so I never got back up. I was down there for all the extra innings of the second game of that doubleheader that went 23 innings.

**MSP:** *Was the* Kiner's Korner *set big? Sometimes those sets on TV look huge and then when you're there they're not much bigger than a broom closet.*

**RK:** It wasn't bad. [*Kiner's Korner*] had two cameras that we used for the interviews and everything and also the working part of the thing was the producer's room right next to it. But they didn't use the *Kiner's Korner* room for anything but *Kiner's Korner*.

One of the things you might want to note is the replays. Originally, and this goes back to 1962, the replays were done in the downtown studios. Those were new to television and the tape machines that they used to do the replays came from downtown. I would indicate what I wanted to be replayed and downtown they would play it back through. Quite a few times they would get the wrong replay up and then we had to ad lib and make the excuses or whatever it was. It was very Mickey Mouse in the very early days of our broadcasts. They really didn't do replays in those days.

**MSP:** *And what about the graphics?*

**RK:** They were done in production. They did the graphics ahead of time.

**MSP:** *When they do occasionally have a game from a while back on SNY or something like that, one of the first things you notice is how spare the graphics are. They're not giving you a lot of information. They're giving you home runs, runs batted in, batting average, and it's up to the people to pay attention to find out how many outs there are or what the score is. Was that something you noticed over time that changed?*

**RK:** The equipment got much better. They added a lot more cameras. We only used about five cameras, and now they use about 10 or 11. They can set up their graphics on a camera that would not be in use. Because of a lack of cameras, we weren't able to set up the items you see now that are done and well done.

**MSP:** *One of the things you don't see so much is the behind the catcher view. That used to be one of the predominant views.*

**RK:** That's really the director. He might say, "Let's use the center field camera." That's determined by the director and the producer.

**MSP:** *Did you have the same producers throughout?*

**RK:** We had about five different producers. Maybe more. But we had the guy that did the Dodgers games, I think his name was Griffin. The producer was a studio guy. It was too long ago. Bill Webb came out as an assistant and he went on to great fame. He's still doing the games for us. We had real good production, there's no question about that.

**MSP:** *Going back to 1969 is there a game you remember the most, or one where you said at the time, "Oh, my Gosh, this is a whole different ballgame from what I've been watching"?*

**RK:** We had eight years, really, of tough times with the game. One game I really remember was the game where Seaver pitched the one-hitter where Jimmy Qualls had the only hit of the game. Of course, no one has ever pitched a no-hit game for the Mets.

**MSP:** *One last thing, when you were doing the interviews on* Kiner's Korner, *going back to 1969, was there anyone who was especially good interview or especially tough? How about Gil Hodges?*

**RK:** He never gave you a lot of information. But he was a terrific guy, a great guy to be around. I had a good relationship, but he was not a gregarious type guy.

**MSP:** *You got to call the home run that broke your record for home runs by a right-handed batter in the National League when Gil Hodges was playing for the Mets. You had 369 and his last home run was 370. That had to be interesting because you played against him so long.*

**RK:** I played against him his whole career. I probably kept him out of the Hall of Fame because he never led the league in home runs. And if he'd have done that maybe two or three times, he might be in the Hall of Fame.

**MSP:** *Do you think Gil Hodges will ever get in the Hall of Fame?*

**RK:** It's going to be real tough for him to get in now with the Veteran's Committee, I'm talking about the Old-Timers.

**MSP:** *You have a vote on that, do you not?*

**RK:** I vote for him. No question about it. I vote for him for the Hall of Fame.

# The Miracle Has Landed

SHEA STADIUM

Use Roosevelt Avenue Entrance Only

ENTRY TO THE RESERVED PARKING AREA IS RESTRICTED TO THE TOLL BOOTHS LOCATED ON ROOSEVELT AVENUE.

PLEASE USE THIS ENTRANCE

No. 0444

ATTENDANT

RESERVED PARKING AREA

RESERVED PARKING

RETAIN THIS STUB

SHEA STADIUM

Use Roosevelt Avenue Entrance Only

No. 0444

The automobile for which this check is issued is accepted for parking purposes only, and under the following conditions to which the holder hereof assents by receiving this check.

No responsibility is assumed by the Metropolitan Baseball Club, Inc., for loss from fire, damage, or theft of car or articles left in car or for any damage whatsoever. No employee has any authority to vary any of the above terms.

1969 WORLD SERIES

RESERVED PARKING

# Meet the Mets
## From Birth to Rebirth

by Matthew Silverman

The New York Mets and Houston Colt 45s were the first new franchises in the National League in 70 years. The last time the league had expanded was 1892, after the folding of the American Association led to the NL absorbing four AA clubs. The two new teams in 1962 had come from another league as well—though it was a league that never played a game.

The departure of the Brooklyn Dodgers and New York Giants for sunnier shores after the 1957 season marked the first time since 1883 that New York was without National League baseball. In 1959, after unsuccessful attempts to lure existing teams to New York—and having the idea of expansion rebuffed by the eight-team NL—New York lawyer William A. Shea turned his eyes toward starting a new league. The Continental League had a big-name president in Branch Rickey and big dreams as well. The league had commitments from well-heeled investors in several cities, including New York and Houston.

The Continental League disbanded after a year without ever playing a game, but it fulfilled its purpose: It made the major leagues blink. The National League agreed to expansion in New York and Houston, though it would hold off on adding teams until 1962. The American League voted to expand in 1961 with the Los Angeles Angels and Washington Senators (a team that would take the place of the old Senators—an AL franchise since 1901—that was relocating to Minnesota to be heretofore known as the Twins). Everything in baseball seemed to be growing—the schedule even expanded from 154 to 162 games in '61.

Joan Payson, who had owned 10 percent of the Giants and had been the lone dissenting vote in their move to San Francisco, had been part of the Continental League dream, owning equal shares with Dwight Davis and Dorothy Killian. With Killian departing after the Continental League folded and Davis eventually giving up his shares when it became clear that M. Donald Grant would be running things, Payson wound up owning 80 percent of New York's NL franchise. With her Whitney family pedigree and interests in the worlds of art and horse racing, Payson's wealth was estimated at between $100 and $200 million. The Mets were a business investment as well as a cause. She favored the name Meadowlarks for the team, but she acquiesced to "Mets"—the same name as an American Association championship club in the 1880s—when it proved to be the public's choice in a fan poll.

George Weiss had put together the New York Yankees team that won 10 pennants between 1949 and 1960, and continued winning after he left. All of those pennants had been won by manager Casey Stengel, who, like Weiss, had been let go in the Bronx after the team was stunned by the Pittsburgh Pirates in the 1960 World Series. Weiss hired Stengel as the first manager of the fledgling Mets—and it seemed a natural choice. Stengel had played for the Giants in the 1920s under John McGraw, managed Brooklyn in the 1930s, and guided the Yankees to dominance in the 1950s, so it only seemed fitting that he take over a fourth New York club in his 70s. Yet unlike his other stops in the city, Stengel would be the star of this show. It was easy to see why.

An equitable amateur player draft wouldn't be instituted for almost another four years, so the Mets had to sign available talent wherever they could find someone willing. The Mets could also make deals with other clubs, but that was hard because the Mets had little to offer in return other than Payson's cash. So Weiss and the Mets banked on history and recognizable names nearing the end of their careers, especially former Giants and Dodgers. The rest of the NL chipped in a few names as well at the expansion draft on October 10, 1961 at the Netherland-Hilton Hotel in Cincinnati. The expansion clubs felt pick pocketed when it was over.

The Mets paid the eight existing National League teams a total of $1.8 million for 22 players, many of whom probably would have been released or buried in the minors had expansion not come calling. It was hardly a who's who of great NL players.

Looking over the names that would comprise his new club, Stengel deadpanned, "I want to thank all these generous owners for giving us those great players they did not want. Those lovely, generous owners."

The astute Stengel was sure of one thing: His team would be at the bottom of the league. So he worked tirelessly to overshadow his team by applying ever greater doses of Stengelese (his own language that New York sportswriters were already fluent in) and trying to sell the team to the public as entertainment as opposed to competition. It worked. The press covering this new team was a young, hard-working crew seemingly up to the challenge of taking on something new in an old city. "The New Breed" made the Mets front-page news, even if what they achieved on the field should have doomed them to obscurity. While the '62 Mets were a horrendous club, they were new, they were fun, and in a decade when the staid ways of the older generation had started to change, the Mets were something that the young and disenfranchised could latch onto and call their own. Though playing at the ancient Polo Grounds, abandoned by its previous tenants, the Mets still drew 922,530 fans in their inaugural year. That may not sound like a lot today, but that still put the Mets ahead of four teams in the league. The Mets would not be so fortunate in the standings.

The Mets lost the first nine games of their existence and they followed that with double-digit losing streaks of 17, 11, and 13 games. The team did see a few players enjoy solid years with the bat: 34 home runs and 94 RBIs from Frank Thomas, an All-Star performance from Richie Ashburn (.306 bat-

**National League Expansion Draft—October 10, 1961**

| Price | Position | Player (Team) | Years as Mets | W-L, ERA/BA-HR-RBI as Mets |
|---|---|---|---|---|
| $125,000 each | Pitchers | Jay Hook (Reds) | 1962–64 | 12–34, 5.22 |
| | | Bob L. Miller (Cardinals) | 1962, 1973–74 | 3–14, 4.41 |
| | Infielder | Don Zimmer (Cubs) | 1962 | .077-0-1 |
| | Outfielder | Lee Walls (Phillies) | None | – |
| $75,000 each | Pitchers | Craig Anderson (Cardinals) | 1962–64 | 3–20, 5.56 |
| | | Roger Craig (Dodgers) | 1962–63 | 15–46, 4.14 |
| | | Ray Daviault (Giants) | 1962 | 1–5, 6.22 |
| | | Al Jackson (Pirates) | 1962–65, 1968–69 | 43–80, 4.26 |
| | Catchers | Chris Cannizzaro (Cardinals) | 1962–65 | .236-0-30 |
| | | Choo Choo Coleman (Phillies) | 1962–63, 1966 | .206-9-26 |
| | | Hobie Landrith (Giants) | 1962 | .289-1-7 |
| | Infielders | Ed Bouchee (Cubs) | 1962 | .161-3-10 |
| | | Elio Chacon (Reds) | 1962 | .236-2-27 |
| | | Sammy Drake (Cubs) | 1962 | .192-0-7 |
| | | Gil Hodges (Dodgers) | 1962–63 | .248-9-20 |
| | | Felix Mantilla (Braves) | 1962 | .275-11-59 |
| | Outfielders | Gus Bell (Reds) | 1962 | .149-1-6 |
| | | Joe Christopher (Pirates) | 1962–65 | .265-28-156 |
| | | John DeMerit (Braves) | 1962 | .188-1-1 |
| | | Bobby Gene Smith (Phillies) | 1962 | .136-0-2 |
| $50,000 each | Pitcher | Sherman Jones (Reds) | 1962 | 0–4, 7.71 |
| | Outfielder | Jim Hickman (Cardinals) | 1962–66 | .241-60-210 |

ting/.424 on-base/.393 slugging), solid play at third base from Felix Mantilla (.275-11-59), and the club drew more walks than any team in the league. The pitching and defense, however, were entirely different matters. The Mets had a 5.05 ERA—a half run higher than any other team—and that does not count the astounding 147 unearned runs that crossed the plate. The Mets led the majors with 210 errors and made horrendous fielding into an art form. The shortcomings of the team seemed to be encompassed by Marv Throneberry. The defensively-challenged and slow-footed first baseman was celebrated as "Marvelous Marv," even though he was anything but.

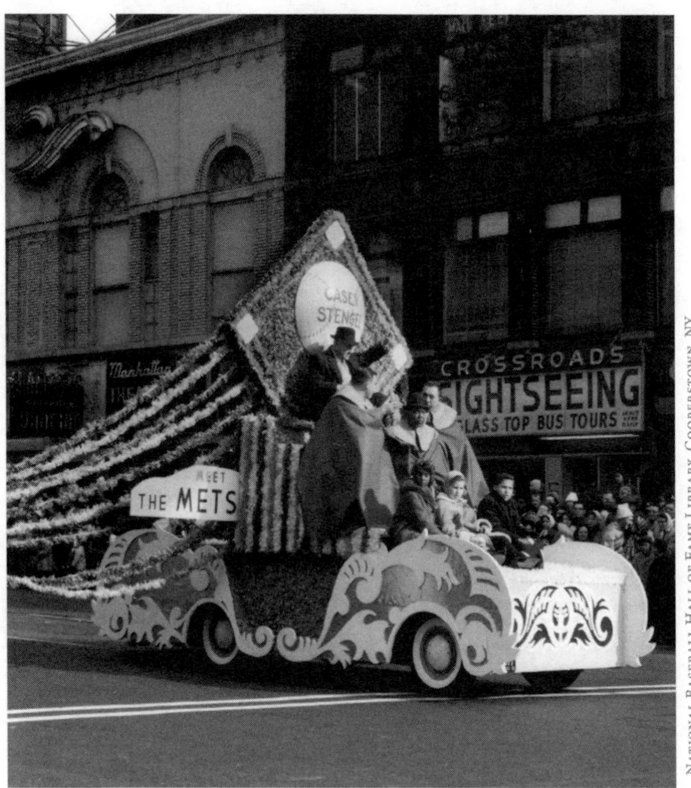

National Baseball Hall of Fame Library, Cooperstown, NY

*Floating to their new home and freezing cold to boot, Casey Stengel and his brand-new Mets—with Gil Hodges and Charley Neal—make their way to the Polo Grounds in 1962.*

The Mets were 40 games behind first place by July, reached 100 losses with August still on the calendar, and were 61½ games out heading into the last weekend of the season. They managed to win one of those last three games against the worst team in the Cubs' 90-year history—a 103-loss Windy City debacle under owner Philip K. Wrigley's "College of Coaches." Thanks to two merciful rainouts during the season, the Mets' legendary line of losing came out at an even 40–120, a full 60 games out in the NL. True, the Cleveland Spiders had gone 20–134 in 1899 (an unrivaled 84 games out), but that club had been plagued by syndicate ownership, had divested itself of every decent player, drew crowds so miniscule that they transferred almost every home game to the road after June, and was on its way to being dissolved after the season (along with three other clubs). The '62 Mets, on the other hand, were in the "just born" category. Stengel, who'd turned nine years old during the Spiders' milestone final year, had the final say on losing and the Mets: "They have shown me ways to lose I never knew existed."

The Mets were better in 1963. It would have been impossible not to be. The Mets lost "only" 111 and finished a mere 48 games out of first. It was a season of landmarks, however.

As a result of the outpouring of emotion and bedsheets sprawled with homemade sayings about the club—"placards," Stengel liked to call them—the Mets held their first Banner Day in 1963, an annual event that allowed fans to parade on the field; it would remain a Mets tradition into the mid-1990s. The Mets played their first "Mayor's Trophy Game" against the Yankees—and won—with Stengel using his best pitchers for the exhibition game and Mets fans invading Yankee Stadium with their homemade signs. (The Mets would go 8–7–1 through 1981 vs. the Yankees in the charity exhibition in New York.) The team's laughable exploits in 1962 made for entertaining reading in 1963—and beyond—in Jimmy Breslin's still classic book, *Can't Anybody Here Play This Game.* And those who didn't know whether to laugh or cry at the team could always sing—a catchy little ditty called "Meet the Mets" was sold in 45s at the Polo Grounds—the record cost a buck and had a cute new character with a giant head on the dust jacket: Mr. Met.

Beloved Brooklyn icon Gil Hodges ended his playing career after a trade in May of '63 sent him from the Mets to the Washington Senators, where he was named manager. Another old-time Dodgers favorite, Duke Snider, hit his 400th career home run on June 14, one of his few highlights in a Mets uniform. The Mets won that night against the defending NL champions in Cincinnati, and won again the next day to creep to within one game of ninth place... and then the Mets began an assault on the 20th century mark for consecutive road losses in the National League. The Mets dropped 22 straight away from New York, a period of seven weeks between road victories. The losing, though, continued wherever the Mets played. Roger Craig suffered 18 straight losses; not to be outdone, teammate Craig Anderson, who had won three times in a week for the '62 Mets, would go nearly three seasons without winning, ending his career on 1964 with a 19-game losing streak (that mark would be broken by another Met, Anthony Young, with 27 straight defeats in 1992–93). One of Anderson's defeats came on September 18, the final major league game at the Polo Grounds. Though the team was shut out 30 times in '63, the Mets managed to plate one run off Chris Short of the Phillies that day; Philadelphia scored five off Anderson and Craig. The Mets' tenure in Manhattan ended fittingly, with a double play grounder by Ted Schreiber.

Shea Stadium, named after the lawyer who had helped land NL baseball back in New York—and who had worked with politicians to get the state to fund the new stadium—opened for business on April 17, 1964. The World's Fair next door kept the neighborhood hopping for two years. The dual attractions helped the 1964 Mets draw 1,732,597, second only to the Dodgers. The shining state-of-the-art stadium, which would host the American Football League's rechristened New York Jets, was a sight to behold, but the Mets simply remained a sight. The team's progress seemed incremental, though Shea saw its share of spectacle: a 23-inning loss to the Giants in May (in the second game of a doubleheader), a Father's Day perfect game by Jim Bunning, and a thrilling All-Star Game with Johnny Callison sending NL backers back home happy with a three-run home run in the ninth.

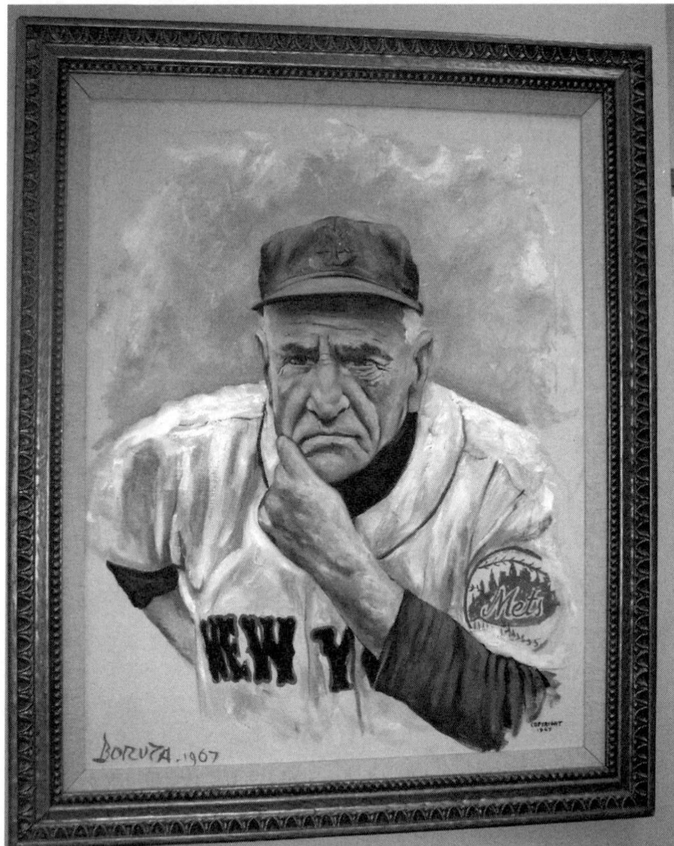


*Casey Stengel's perplexed visage in Mets cap greets visitors to the National Baseball Hall of Fame Library.*

The Mets lost 109 games and finished 40 games back, but that last loss was actually hard to come by and almost cost the Cardinals dearly. Al Jackson outdueled Bob Gibson in the opener of the season-ending series in St. Louis, 1–0. A 15–5 pounding of the Cards the next day gave the collapsing Phillies and gurgling Reds a shot at a three-way tie, but Gibson came on in relief on Sunday and the Cardinals rallied against Galen Cisco to take the pennant. St. Louis would go on to beat the Yankees in the World Series.

Warren Spahn and Yogi Berra signed as player-coaches in 1965, but Spahn left to finish his esteemed pitching career in San Francisco; Berra, dismissed as Yankees manager after winning a pennant as a rookie manager, retired as a player after nine at-bats and remained in a Mets uniform for the next decade. Stengel was also still in a Mets uniform, though even as he prepared to celebrate his 75th birthday with a lavish gathering, there were grumblings that the team needed a new leader. The argument was legitimate. The Mets continued to be fodder for every team, though occasionally showing signs of vitality that seemed uniquely Metsian, such as on June 14, when the Mets were no-hit for 10 innings by Cincinnati's Jim Maloney and won in the 11th on a home run by Johnny Lewis. Just as that was the only hit of the game, it was also the only win by the Mets over a 16-game span. The Mets stood at 31–64 on July 24 in 10th place, 24 games out and twice as far back as the ninth-place Cubs. With Stengel celebrating the diamond anniversary of his birth, he slipped and fell in the bathroom at Toot Shor's Restaurant and wound up with a broken hip. After a 175–404 beginning as a franchise, Wes Westrum took the reigns. Though infinitely less colorful than Stengel, the Mets picked right up where they left off with their new manager. They finished at 19–48 under Westrum, a .284 percentage that was actually 40 percentage points worse than they'd done under Stengel in '65.

The Mets did show improvement in 1966, avoiding 100 losses and last place for the first time. The Mets enjoyed rarefied air indeed, getting within one game of .500 in mid-May and climbing as high as sixth place. They made forays at the rechristened Astros for eighth place as late as August 23 before settling into ninth place for good. The 66–96 Mets were never threatened on their lofty perch by the basement-dwelling, 103-loss Cubs, who were starting from scratch under manager Leo Durocher after five season of letting coaches run the show.

The biggest win for the Mets in 1966 did not come on the field, but rather in the lottery. The Dodgers had selected Tom Seaver in the 10th round in the inaugural draft in 1965 (two rounds before the Mets took Nolan Ryan), but Seaver did not sign and went to the University of Southern California. The next winter he was taken by the Braves in a special phase of the draft. The Braves signed Seaver a couple of days after USC had started its season. Even though the Trojans were only playing exhibition games against a Marine Corps team, it still violated the league rules and commissioner William D. Eckert called for a special drawing with every team except the Braves allowed to take part. Only the Phillies, Indians, and Mets entered and the Mets were the lucky winners. Seaver was in New York the following spring as the team's number two starter.

Seaver went 16–13 for an awful 1967 Mets club. Though the team had lucked into an obvious ace, the Mets as a whole regressed. General manager Bing Devine, who had replaced the retired George Weiss after the 1966 season, kept busy in what turned out to be his only year in that job. Many of the faces he brought in were not worth looking at twice, but he did acquire several names that would play key roles in 1969: Don Cardwell, Ron Taylor, Cal Koonce, Ed Charles, and Art Shamsky; Devine also drafted '69 Mets Gary Gentry and Rod Gaspar, plus a couple of players who would become known later: Ken Singleton and Jon Matlack. His best deal, though came after the 61–101 season, when he traded for manager Gil Hodges from the Senators.

Acquiring Hodges—Westrum had resigned during the final week of the '67 season amid rumors of his imminent firing—was actually at the behest of board chairman M. Donald Grant. Assistant GM Johnny Murphy went to Washington to handle the negotiations, which entailed the Mets sending pitcher Bill Denehy and $100,000 to DC. And it was the newly installed Hodges who pushed Murphy, the newly-promoted GM, for three players from the White Sox: Al Weis and Tommie Agee (those two came in a trade involving Tommy Davis), and backup catcher J.C. Martin (the Mets were owed a player in a previous deal with Chicago).

Hodges brought a completely new approach to the team. His spring training camp was compared to a boot camp with Hodges serving as sergeant (he'd been a decorated Marine non-commissioned officer in the Pacific during World War II). Yet he commanded in a quiet manner that still let everyone know who was in charge without a shadow of a doubt. The Mets might not finish that much higher in the standings, but they would be fundamentally sound. It also helped that the pitching was coming along. In addition to the veteran pitchers added over the previous year, the Mets had a young catcher they'd picked up from Houston with an irritable nature but magnificent hands, a strong arm, and stronger game-calling instincts: Jerry Grote. The Mets had endured Grote's hideous .195 batting average in 120 games in 1967 and were rewarded with an All-Star season in '68. Grote hit .282 in a year when NL hitters batted a mere .243. The '68 Mets were the worst-hitting team in the league, but one could also argue that their pitching staff was getting to be as good as anybody's.

Led by rookie southpaw Jerry Koosman (19–12, 2.08), New York's team ERA of 2.72 was fourth behind the NL champion Cardinals, who were shown the way by Bob Gibson and his otherworldly 1.12 mark. The cool and confident Kooz wound up one vote shy of becoming the second straight Mets hurler to win Rookie of the Year (Johnny Bench won the award). Koosman and Seaver gave the Mets two All-Star hurlers at the top of the rotation and rookie right-hander Nolan Ryan, though very wild, threw as hard as anyone in the major leagues ... or the planet. With this arsenal of arms, the Mets allowed fewer hits than any team in the league and only the Cardinals allowed fewer overall runs.

With Hodges stressing defense and fundamentals, the '68 club committed 24 fewer errors than any Mets team in history. Cleon Jones, just 25 and in his first year as an everyday left fielder (Jones had played center before the arrival of his boyhood friend Agee), led the team with a .297 batting mark. Ron Swoboda, Ken Boswell, and Bud Harrelson continued to develop, while Ed Kranepool, just 23, already could claim seven seasons as a Met.

The team was growing up. The young players were eager to learn and were willing to follow their manager anywhere. And the way pitching dominated the game in 1968's "Year of the Pitcher," it wasn't impossible to believe that with a little bit of hitting and a lot more luck, the New York Mets might not be light years away from contention.

**Sources**

Breslin, Jimmy. *Can't Anybody Here Play This Game.* (Chicago: Ivan R. Dee, 2003.)

Lang, Jack, and Peter Simon. *The New York Mets: 25 Years of Baseball Magic.* (New York: Henry Holt, 1986.)

Ultimate Mets Database, *http://www.ultimatemets.com/*

## Pythagoras, Pyshmagoras

What would Pythagoras say? This does not refer to the ancient Greek mathematician's theorum, but to a baseball formula using runs scored and runs allowed to derive how many games a team should have won in a given season. The Pythagoean method, as credited to Bill James, is defined as

$$\text{Win\%} = \frac{\text{Runs Scored}^2}{\text{Runs Scored}^2 + \text{Runs Allowed}^2} = \frac{1}{1 + (\text{Runs Allowed}/\text{Runs Scored})^2}$$

Doing the math, the Cubs should have won the 1969 National League East title with 93 wins to New York's 92. The Cubs outscored the Mets, 720–632. New York, however, ruled the day when it came to pitching, allowing 541 total runs (earned and unearned) to Chicago's 611.

Of course, the game is not played on paper, and the '69 Cubs actually wound up winning 92 games and the Mets 100. Some would attribute the disparity in the Mets' record to luck, others to Mets manager Gil Hodges, while the wisest still would credit both Lady Fortune and Gil of Flatbush.

# Here's Looking Up Our Old Address

by Greg W. Prince

"*Shea Stadium continues to be a fun place, even in triumph.*"

—From Dick Young's script for *Look Who's No. 1*, the 1969 Mets highlight film that reassured fans unhinged by a world championship that Banner Day and Helmet Day weren't going anywhere.

You know you're in Queens when you look up and see that virtually every address in your midst is hyphenated. In a borough full of numbered thoroughfares, it attempts to create order from the chaos you might get when you're dealing with, for example, a 55th Road in Elmhurst that runs a block south of 55th Avenue not all that many blocks east of 55th Street in Woodside. Better a hyphen than those other punctuation marks cartoonists use to express the frustration of getting lost without a sturdy Queens atlas.

For 45 years, there may have been no more famous hyphenated address in Queens or anywhere than the one memorized by generations of New York Mets fans: 123-01 Roosevelt Avenue, indicating the intersection of Roosevelt and 123rd Street. It's where, before you could dot-com it, you wrote to the Mets to send away for tickets, to request an 8 x 10 glossy photo, to pledge undying loyalty to your favorite player until he was traded, demoted, or released. Want the all-new revised edition of the official yearbook, the one with the guy who took your previous hero's place? Write to the New York Mets, 123-01 Roosevelt Avenue, Flushing, New York, 11368.

There are still New York Mets. They still print yearbooks. They don't revise them much. But that address has left town. There is no longer a 123-01 Roosevelt Avenue in Flushing. There is no longer anything on which to inscribe that house number. There is no house and that number's been lost.

There is, however, plenty of parking.

Shea Stadium doesn't live here anymore. The Mets have packed up the plantation and reset it at 120-01 Roosevelt Avenue, a.k.a. Citi Field (until further notice). If you saw a game from Shea Stadium in 2008, you know the two parks were back to back during their brief co-existence and that the Mets didn't move very far across Flushing. In fact, the street that borders Citi Field, 126th Street, was the same one used to mark the approximate location of Shea. Queens cartography being what it is, there was never really a 123rd Street running through Shea. If there had been, it might have caused havoc right around third base.

But there sure was a Shea. There was never more a Shea than there was 40 years ago when the Mets played at 1969-01 Miracle Place and sanctified every blade of grass, every clump of dirt, every fan who passed through the turnstiles, whether via fully paid admission, membership in the Midget Mets, or dairy carton coupon. It may have been built in 1964, but Shea Stadium was made holy in 1969.

Here's looking up our old address.

To view Shea Stadium in its 1969 format is to observe a Shea that is recognizable to the 21st century fan, but not a perfect match. The shape remained a horseshoe and, give or take three feet down the foul lines, the dimensions stayed true. The variations lie, as Vincent Vega put it in *Pulp Fiction*, in the little differences. The Stadium that Shea'd goodbye in 2008 was a Royale with Cheese compared to the comparatively no-frills burger served up in Queens four decades earlier.

Blue fences. DiamondVision. The Home Run Apple. Cow-Bell Man in the stands. Neon men on the exterior. The Pepsi Picnic Area. The scoreboard skyline. The Tommie Agee marker. Plastic orange seats ringing Field Level. Cushy blue chairs behind home plate. A photographer's well of Nikon-branded stools off of first. Billboard advertising on everything that didn't move and maybe a few things that did. Italian sausages grilling. T-shirts flying. Everybody clapping their hands on command. Somebody named Mary, said to be Lazy.

Those were touchstones of Shea Stadium in its final seasons. Those are the memories Mets fans could pack away on September 28, 2008 and bring with them to Citi Field come April 13, 2009. The stuff of the late '00s will be nostalgia for an entire generation. Yet it was way in the future on October 16, 1969.

None of it existed as part of the Shea tableau when Cleon Jones ensured Davey Johnson a lifetime sinecure as a last-out trivia question. Shea Stadium in the 1960s, so often described in real time as a combination carnival and baseball stadium, was staid by comparison to its later incarnation. Real time will do that to a ballpark.

After standing pat on stadium improvements (let alone stadium maintenance) for the balance of the '70s, Shea attempted to add glitz to its persona over its final three decades, albeit in that Wal-Mart manner that Shea had whenever it attempted to shop for glamour. Each would-be high-end innovation—say the addition of TV monitors for fans squeezing past concession lines—was a victim of its essential Metness. Ever try to actually watch one of those televisions? Ever try to have a conversation over that state-of-the-warped sound system? Ever wonder why you couldn't get into those left-field bleachers without a hundred friends or, on lucky Wednesdays, a can of Pepsi? Shea never got any glitzier. It just got grittier.

It was still new in 1969. Six seasons young. To watch it in action on DVD now is to see a fairly Spartan setting (that's William A. Shea *Municipal* Stadium, thank you very much) whose sense of humanity is one part World's Fair whimsy and nine parts Mets fans. The blue and orange speckles, the curved scoreboard with its inevitable failure to get all the bulbs to cooperate on CLENDENON, the Plexiglas-covered bullpens not yet sprouting tomatoes...it was as modern as it needed to be. What the old video picks up is that it was windier at Shea then. They fixed that over the years. The diamond dust kicked up a lot quicker back then. They made improvements there. Oh, and don't forget the puddles you used to see gather on the warning track. Somebody eventually installed drainage that drained.

Yes, in some respects Shea Stadium got better after 1969. In many respects, it grew different. Physically what was fresh in the '60s was deemed hopelessly outdated as early as 1980, when new owners couldn't yet paint over the rot of the roster, so they slapped on new seats and such wherever they could. Jane Jarvis's organ gave way to constant recorded admonitions (albeit, some of them catchy). When watching nothing between innings seemed passé, a ginormous screen was erected over the left-center field fence to produce a stream of distractions. Color schemes were impermanent. The Sign Man Karl Ehrhardt folded up his running commentary. A stadium built to appeal to Long Islanders by loading it with parking spaces invited its guests more and more to visit via mass transit. A whole bunch of those parking spaces beyond right field were disappearing.

Because that was where 120-01 Roosevelt Avenue was going to be.

The 1969 version of Shea Stadium won't necessarily be the Shea Stadium that survives in the first row of the collective consciousness. Relatively fewer images survive. The median age of those who remember attending games there then is Old and Getting Older. That championship season sits squarely between the onset of the Great Depression and the impact of a pretty dismal recession. Who in 1969 was thinking of 1929 as anything but the most ancient of history?

That said, when archaeologists come around to excavate the parking lot that lay due west of that fancy pile of red bricks at 120-01 Roosevelt, which season's soul will they discover embedded below the surface? 1969's. They have to. It was the signature season of Shea Stadium. There was nothing like it at 123-01 Roosevelt. Nothing.

A few years jump out and scream Mets at you if you've followed the franchise forever and a day. Actually, there are years that make you scream and want to jump from the nearest Upper Deck/Promenade, but let's leave that sensible sentiment aside for now. Let's think of some of the years that truly say Shea.

**1964:** Opened.
**1973:** Believed.
**1977:** Traded.
**1986:** Dominated.
**2000:** Frustrated.
**2007:** Collapsed.
**2008:** Closed.

If you're a Mets fan, you get the implications of each of those years on contact. For example, Shea Stadium will forever be linked to 1964, the only 53–109 effort ever pointed to with pride as providing the best record a team ever managed. The '64 Mets outdid their two predecessors at the Polo Grounds by 13 and two wins, respectively. And while their previous home in Manhattan belonged to a previous generation, the '64 Mets established Shea as baseball's premier funhouse: it hosted a doubleheader that went 32 innings, an opposing pitcher who retired 27 consecutive batters, and every All-Star on Earth. And that was just by July.

As important in the telling of Shea was 1973, the Mets' second pennant season and, from August 30 forward, its most improbable. In rapid-fire succession the Met lexicon was irrevocably altered over approximately six weeks' time: You Gotta... It Ain't Over 'Til...The Ball Off The...Willie, Say Goodbye To...Pete [Bleeping]...Mets fans spoke differently from then on out because of what happened at Shea. They could finish each other's sentences.

All that believing and all that fun screeched into silence in 1977. The best Mets player of any position—a pitcher—was traded in June. The lights went out in July. They stayed out for a very long time after Tom Seaver left the room. For those loyal, unlucky, and maybe foolhardy Mets fans who arrived on the scene post-1973, that Shea Stadium became *the* Shea Stadium they would forever point to as their own (the lovable dopes).

The Shea of 2000 represented the culmination of a ton of Mets frustration that defined two eras: the early and mid-'90s when nothing went right and the late '90s when something inevitably went wrong. A Subway Series rumbled through that Shea. Partisans can be forgiven for missing their stop.

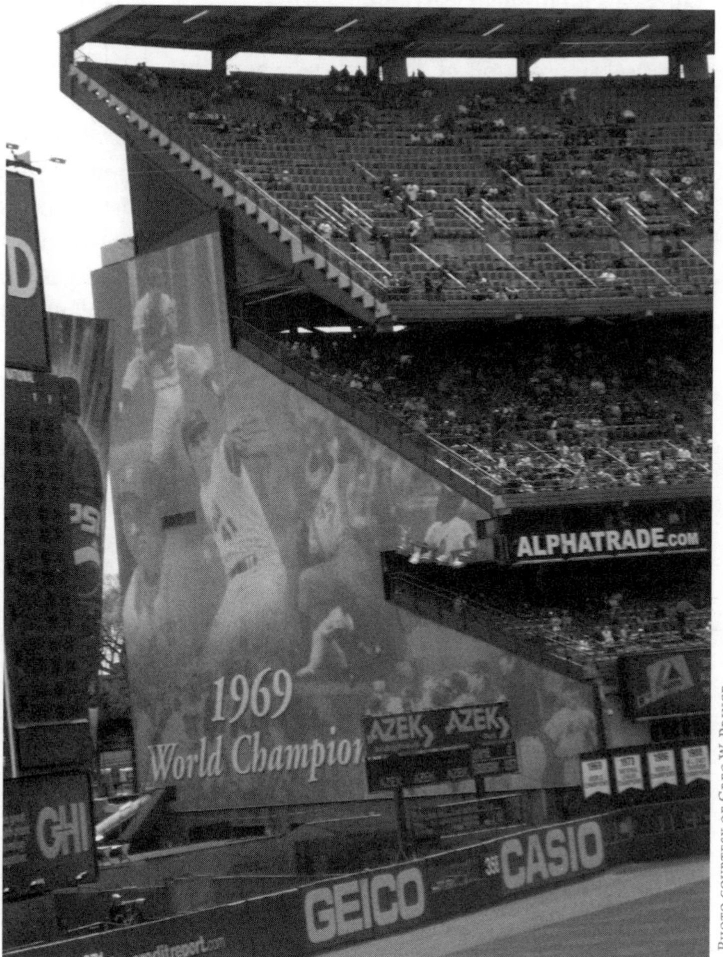

PHOTO COURTESY OF GREG W. PRINCE

*The area adjacent to the bullpen in Shea Stadium's latter years featured a tribute to the '69 team, with heroes who stood literally 80 feet high.*

Someday, perhaps, 2007 will recede in significance. Events have a way of blotting out previous events in a team narrative; 2006's last-game NLCS failure seemed pretty monumental for about 11 months. By the end of 2007 (seven up, 17 to play, you might have tattooed to your frontal lobe), Carlos Beltran standing and staring at strike three seemed like the good old days at Shea. The someday that blots out 2007 has yet to arrive. It didn't even come in 2008, though that being the year Shea shuttered linked it inextricably to 1964. (And isn't it funny how the 53–109 from then seemed a lot sunnier than the nice try of 89–73 in '08 does now?)

Did we leave one of those essential Shea seasons cited on that list earlier out of our analysis? Yes we did. It was not an oversight.

When you get right down to it, you have two contenders for the mythical title of signature season of Shea Stadium, for rights to perform as the hypothetical house band at the address where the postman no longer delivers mail. You have 1969 and its world championship and you have 1986 and its world championship.

The 1986 world champions were more impressive. The 1986 world champions were more talented. The 1986 Mets were the only Mets team to romp through a schedule as the uncontested best team in baseball. And when they were finally contested, they responded magnificently. No team or season unfurled by the Mets in the Shea Stadium era stood taller or proved greater.

But 1969 was better. 1969 was the best. 1969 was everything the Mets had been leading up to from 1964—1962 even. And everything after 1969 would have to live up to 1969—1986 even. At 1986's moments of October doubt, where was the karmic bench strength? Where was the indispensable precedent? What was the one time that you knew the Mets had gone up the hill and successfully fetched a pail of water, thus giving you some comfort that they could do it again?

It was 1969. That was the Miracle. That was the Amazin'. That was the Magic heralded come 1980 as Back (though how they were measuring magic that spring remains a mystery). There was no Believe in '73 without that which boggled belief four seasons earlier. 1977 wouldn't have been so morosely sad had not 1969 been so riotously happy. The frustrations that followed '86 were leavened by the knowledge that somewhere deep in our inner Mr. Met resided that '69 DNA. Bill Buckner—even if Mookie was gonna beat it out—was the other guy's mistake. And we didn't get that 'til October 25 (after midnight on the 26th, actually). 1986 was awesome all year. It was only miraculous when it absolutely had to be. Few years anywhere were like our 1986, but they have occurred in other places.

Photo courtesy of Bill Cotter/worldsfairphoto.com

*The iconic blue and orange steel panels on the side of Shea stadium somehow worked when the place was new in the 1960s.*

Has anybody else ever had a 1969? No, not really. Often imitated, never fully replicated. Teams can climb from worst to first, but who harks back to the 1991 Minnesota Twins outside of WJM's broadcast range? When the 2008 Tampa Bay Rays rose from absolutely nothing, with whom were they historically aligned? They were going for a '69

Photo by Mike McCann/mikemccann.blogspot.com

*Before there was any Miracle there were plenty of Amazin' fans who followed the Mets fervently from the upper deck and the upper reaches of sanity.*

Mets, just as the '77 Broncos attempted in Super Bowl XII ("the Mets of the Mountains," Time called the Broncos in January 1978, and they were talking about the Mets of Gil Hodges, not Ron Hodges). Everybody who doesn't fancy themselves the '69 Orioles aspires to be the '69 Mets.

Yet does any professional team ever really pull it off like the '69 Mets? Has anybody turned the trick of so decisively morphing from The Biggest Loser to The Immortal Winner? You have to look at Olympic hockey or college basketball for echoes of the 1969 Mets and their Oh, God! success that prompted the line far more memorable than the 1977 movie—or 1977 season: "The last miracle I did was the 1969 Mets. Before that, I think you have to go back to the Red Sea."

George Burns was onto something about Biblical-style miracles. They don't come along that often.

The one the Mets pulled off in 1969 happened at Shea...and nowhere else. Seriously, in the common retellings, do the Mets play more than maybe six road games? Al Weis hits a homer at Wrigley; Ron Swoboda foils Steve Carlton in St. Louis; Koosman and Cardwell each drive in the only runs in a doubleheader at Pittsburgh; Don Buford briefly puts Tom Seaver in a hole in Baltimore; maybe there's a West Coast swing. Otherwise, that whole year is Shea, Shea, Shea. It's where a cat filled in as a utilityman and Jimmy Qualls served as a rat. It's where Tommie Agee marked his territory and Karl Ehrhardt recorded every emotion. It's where the ghosts of the Giants and Dodgers were once and for all buried and hankies were waved at Leo Durocher and Montreal first became part of America's national pastime. It's where a left fielder called Cleon was removed for the team's own good and a phenomenal starter named Seaver became an ace for the ages, it's where a leader of men named Gil led men to points previously uncharted. It's where what would surely fall in was caught, where sac bunts wound up sailing down the line, where shoe polish sparkled. It was where everything was clinched and everything was celebrated.

123-01 Roosevelt Avenue has since been plundered, plowed, paved, and parked upon. It's space for cars now. Yet it's the spot for miracles always.

## Show Me a Sign, Sign Man

There were signs about the Mets from the beginning. No matter how bad the Mets got, people could not stop writing down their feelings about the club. But these weren't just "dear diary" entries. Decades before anyone ever heard of a blog, fans wrote their feelings big, bold, and on bedsheets that they brought to the ballgame. Manager Casey Stengel pointed the "placards" out at every turn—better than focusing on the early team's horrid play—but the club was reluctant at first to allow banners because stodgy general manager George Weiss claimed they blocked the view of other patrons. The club wisely relented and embraced the phenomenon. The Mets wound up holding an annual Banner Day that remained a popular promotions for more than 30 years. But in between Banner Days, there was the Sign Man.

Karl Ehrhardt was a commercial artist who attended games at Shea Stadium every Tuesday and Friday from 1965 to 1981 in Section 72 E box seats provided by a typesetter he knew from work. His crushed Mets derby and quick wit made him perhaps the most beloved fan among Mets diehards until Jerry Seinfeld. In one of Ehrhardt's last interviews before his death at age 83 in 2008, with Charlie Vascellaro in *Shea 1964–2008*, the Sign Man said he created about 1,200 signs and brought about 30-40 to each game with him.

His sayings, for all to see at Shea and on WOR cameras, rubbed a few people the wrong way—most notably Ed "Superstiff" Kranepool, Tom "$300,000 for What?" Seaver, and M. Donald Grant; Ehrhardt created the "Grant's Tomb" sign a dozen years before the Mets chairman of the board truly turned the place into a mausoleum following the Seaver trade. Yet the Sign Man had his fans on the field as well as in the stands.

"He was amazing," '69 Met Ron Swoboda told Vascellaro. "He became the official reaction of the crowd. Everybody would see what the official reaction to the play or player. He was always right to the point, direct and clever. He was as much a part of the game as the umpires."

The Sign Man's pinnacle was 1969. His photo was featured in *Life* magazine with the placard reading, "Toothless Cubs Just a Lotta Lip," and when the Mets won the World Series he held up probably his most famous sign, "There Are No Words." The former Brooklyn Dodgers diehard turned uber-Mets fan received the ultimate compliment when, after riding in the final car in the victory parade, he had an audience with the Mets manager and long-time Brooklyn great at Grace Mansion. "Gil Hodges came over to me and said, 'I just want to thank you for all your contributions to the team.'" That would be enough to render any fan speechless.

COURTESY OF ANDY FOGEL

# Spring Ahead

by Matthew Silverman

Spring training in 1969 was one of the most disjointed preseasons in major league history. There was much being seen for the first time. New franchises were added, new divisions created new rivalries, the pitcher's working environment was irretrievably altered, and for the first time a work stoppage threatened training camps. The Mets had to deal with these issues like any other team, but heading into spring training 1969 their chief concern was about the health of their manager.

Gil Hodges was a quiet leader. Beloved as a player in Brooklyn, his slump was the cause of prayers throughout the borough during the early 1950s, and he had returned home to join the fledgling Mets when they took the place of the departed Dodgers and Giants in 1962. Even when Hodges was traded to Washington the following year, fans were happy because he was getting the chance to manage. The Mets traded to get him back after the 1967 season, and the love affair between fans and Gil Hodges, which had never extinguished, burned hot again. He immediately worked with the Mets front office to acquire players he was familiar with from the American League, yet he let his young players learn on the field. He showed patience and stressed hard work. There was no miracle in 1968, but there was marked improvement at Shea Stadium. Besides battling the Astros to stay out of the basement, the Mets had exceeded their manager's preseason goal of 70 wins when they arrived in Atlanta for the last road stop of the year on September 24.

Hodges had thrown batting practice despite suffering from a cold for a few days. Early in that night's game, Hodges left the dugout and told pitching coach Rube Walker that he was going to lie down. Walker, his pitching coach in Washington before coming with him to New York, had never known Hodges to do any such thing during a game. Trainer Gus Mauch called for a doctor and Hodges was soon on his way to Henry Grady Hospital, not a mile from Atlanta-Fulton County Stadium. The hospital confirmed that Hodges had suffered a heart attack and he was placed in the intensive care unit. He missed the rest of the season and was still in the Atlanta hospital a month later. The question whether he would manage the team in 1969, according to Mets beat writer Jack Lang, "went unanswered for months."

Time eventually provided the answer. A three-pack a day smoker, Hodges gave up cigarettes, went on a strict diet, and spent the offseason relaxing and recuperating with his wife, Joan. From the time Hodges went to the hospital until spring training in February, the manager was virtually unseen and unheard as the team kept the press and public in a veil of secrecy that, in Lang's words, "would have made the Kremlin proud." So spring training in St. Petersburg was the first time many reporters got to see the Mets manager since his heart attack. By then, there were a lot of other developments to follow.

The astonishing dominance of pitching in 1968 had been a few years in coming. The 1960s had been a decade of remarkable achievements, but many of them had come from the mound. The major leagues, under pressure for the first time due to the burgeoning popularity of professional football, adopted changes that the powers that be in

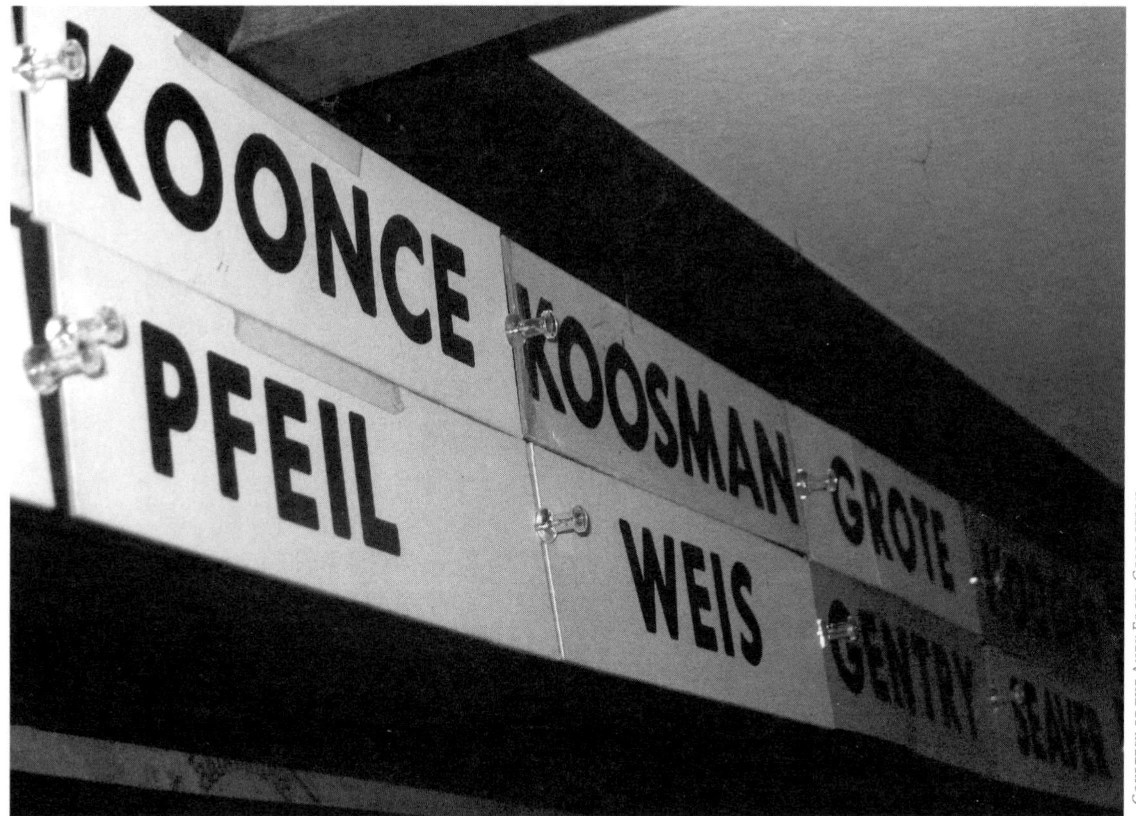


COURTESY OF THE ANDY FOGEL COLLECTION

*The 1969 Mets nameplates spell out a range of names from the well-known to the unknown to the obscure. All would contribute to the whole.*

baseball would have once resisted with every fiber of their being.

The strike zone was changed. Umpires were required to call strikes as they had before the broadening of the zone in 1962. After six seasons with umpires calling strikes all the way to the shoulders, the strike zone returned to the earlier definition as "that space over home plate between the batter's armpits and the top of his knees when he assumes a natural stance." The pitching mound was lowered from 15 to 10 inches to try to bring pitchers down to size and not have a repeat of a 31-game winner in Detroit (Denny McLain of the world champion Tigers) or a .301 batting champion in Boston (Carl Yastrzemski of the Red Sox). It was hoped these changes would also bring Bob Gibson back to the earthly strata after his 1.12 ERA for the National League champion Cardinals, the lowest ERA for a qualifying pitcher since Mordecai "Three Finger" Brown's 1.04 in 1906. In case those changes didn't work, an idea first flouted by Connie Mack in that 1906 season was given a spring trial 63 years later. Both leagues agreed to test out a rule where a "designated pinch hitter" would bat for the pitcher every time up in a game. The NL didn't take as much of a shine to it as the AL, but both leagues shelved the idea at the end of spring training.

Divisional play, approved by owners in July 1968, became a reality for the first time in major league history in 1969. Two teams the Mets considered close rivals and major draws because of history—the Giants and Dodgers—would now be in the Western Division and oppose them only 12 times a year (six home and six away). The Braves, Astros, Reds, and the brand-new San Diego Padres would make up the rest of the division. The geographically-challenged realignment would put the Midwestern Cubs and Cardinals in the East with the Mets. They would be joined by the two Pennsylvania clubs—the Pirates and Phillies—plus Canada's first entry into the major leagues: the Montreal Expos. Division opponents played one another 18 times per season. The American League also split into two divisions, with the expansion Kansas City Royals and Seattle Pilots in the Western Division along with the Angels, Twins, White Sox, and recently relocated Oakland A's—making Chicago the only team in that division not relocated or created since 1961. The AL East had the majority of the old-line junior circuit clubs as well as eight of the last nine pennant winners: the Tigers, Red Sox, Orioles, and Yankees, plus the long-languishing Indians and the Senators, the latter a '61 expansion creation (the 765 Senators games managed by Hodges would remain the franchise record in Washington; Bobby Valentine would surpass it after the club relocated to Texas).

The two division winners in each league would now play a best-of-five postseason series to determine the pennant winner. Season-ending ties for the National League pennant had previously been decided by best-of-three series; any ties for a division title would now be settled by a one-game playoff, as had always been the case in the American League.

Presiding over the two leagues was a new commissioner, Bowie Kuhn. Formerly the attorney for the National League, he had been hired as commissioner to replace the ineffective William Eckert, who did nothing to try to stem the coming labor unrest in the game. Kuhn beat out challenges from Yankees president Mike Burke and Giants head of baseball operations Chub Feeney, the latter was soon named NL president. Kuhn was hired in February for one year at a rate of $100,000, at a time when the average salary was $10,000 and the highest-paid Met, Tom Seaver, made $35,000. Kuhn was thrown right into the fire. The Major League Players Association called for players to not sign their 1969 contracts until a dispute regarding the pension fund and benefits was resolved. Kuhn and MLBPA head Marvin Miller settled the situation with a three-year deal on February 25, exactly three weeks after Kuhn had been elected to office.

Mets players had kept busy during the brief stoppage, working out and joking with the press at "Camp Seaver." Though informal in nature, the player-run camp gave Mets pitchers a leg up on teams that passively waited out the stoppage. With a little over a week between the delayed start of spring training and first exhibition games, Mets pitchers were young and limber. It was the hitting that was the bigger problem.

The Mets still lacked a big bat. Despite the presence of Ed Kranepool—the union rep and last original Met still in the team colors—first base was the obvious spot for an upgrade. With third-year pro Rod Gaspar hitting .333 in his first 36 at-bats in Florida, the temptation was to start the kid in right, move Ron Swoboda to left field and put career outfielder Cleon Jones at first base. Hodges, a three-time Gold Glove winner at the position, opined, "Anybody can play first base."

Joe Torre, a catcher by trade, was poised for a move to first base and Atlanta was looking to deal him. Atlanta general manager Paul Richards talked with the Mets and wanted its top two young players: Nolan Ryan and Amos Otis. Though Torre was just 28 and already a five-time All-Star, the price was too steep for GM Johnny Murphy or the Mets. The Mets had gone to West Palm Beach to face the Braves on St. Patrick's Day hoping to return to St. Petersburg with Torre. Otis was considered a better prospect than Ryan by the Mets, who had drafted "Famous Amos" from the Red Sox and converted him from shortstop to center fielder. (A Hodges spring experiment to convert him to a third baseman did not work.) Ryan would have given the Braves the league's fastest pitcher to go along with the slowest (knuckleballer Phil Niekro). Both Otis and Ryan remained Mets while Torre was indeed sent to the St. Pete training facility on March 17, only it was to the Cardinals' side of the complex. Orlando Cepeda went from the Cardinals to the Braves as compensation.

As spring training started to wind down, the annual prognostications started rolling in. Las Vegas had the Mets at 100-to-1 odds to win the World Series. The sportswriters were going with conventional wisdom as well. After feeding statistics into a computer and coming up with a "Strength Ratio" to determine where a team would finish, Bud Goode of the *New York Daily News* reported the results. "Detroit and St. Louis figure to repeat as [league] champs," he wrote. "The Mets have some great young hurlers. However, the Mets need to score 100 more runs to challenge. The computer pinpoints their inability to win close games as a major factor in their ninth-place finish last year." (The computer turned out to be wrong, the Mets would score 159 more runs in 1969 than the previous year, raising their per game offensive total from 2.90 to 3.90—even in a year of enhanced offense, that was the fourth-highest increase in the NL, and the best in the Eastern division.)

The Mets finished the spring with an exhibition doubleheader against the Twins in New Orleans, a chance for that city to display its major league readiness should any club decide to make the Big Easy the 15th city to land a team since the Braves first shifted locations in 1953. The Mets and Minnesota—two of those aforementioned 14—played an Easter Day doubleheader after the Saturday game was rained out. Each game was to be seven innings, but the Mets won the first and took off with the lead in the fifth inning of the nightcap to catch a plane. The Mets finished the spring at 14–10, tying them with the 1966 Mets for the best percentage in spring training.

The '66 club, under Wes Westrum, had been the first Mets team not to lose 100 games. As the Mets left for New York on April 7, 1969, no one would have imagined that the team could actually match their .583 spring mark in the regular season ... much less better it by 34 points and win 100 games. It was beyond the unthinkable, it was impossible, it was destiny.

**Sources**

*Daily News Legend Series, Amazin' Mets: The Miracle of '69* (Sports Publishing, 1999).

Koppett, Leonard. *The New York Mets* (New York: Macmillan Publishing Co., 1974).

Lang Jack and Simon, Peter. *The New York Mets: Twenty-Five Years of Baseball Magic* (New York: Henry Holt & Co., 1986).

"The Strike Zone: A Historical Timeline" *http://mlb.mlb.com/mlb/official_info/umpires/strike_zone.jsp*

## An Oriole Never Forgets

In 1969, Curt Gowdy called two of the most remarkable upsets in sports history, the New York Jets' win over the Baltimore Colts in Super Bowl III and the New York Mets' triumph in five games over the Baltimore Orioles in the World Series.

"The Orioles had an All-Star at every position and a great pitching staff," Gowdy said. "How the Mets beat them, I'll never know. Those guys made catches that they would never make again. Ten years later I was doing a bird show in Maine with Brooks Robinson. We came in from the field, had dinner, and went up to the hotel room. He starts pacing the floor. I asked him what was the matter and he said , 'Jesus, how did those Mets ever beat us?' He was still upset over that."

—Mark Simon

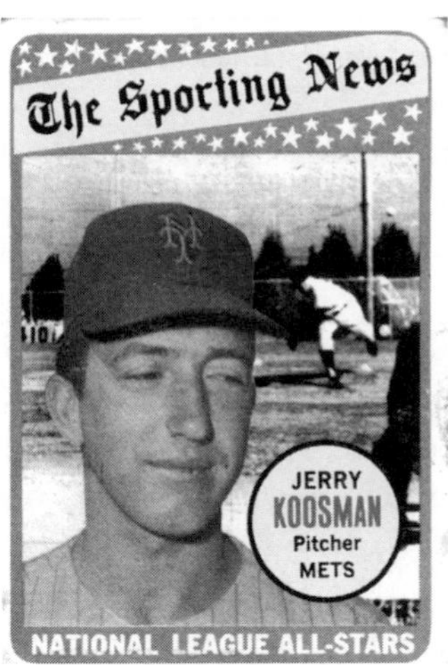


# A Season of Streaks, Shocks, and Shutouts

by Matthew Silverman

One of the key elements of drama for a baseball miracle is that the team in question should walk out on stage for the first time as if nothing has changed, as if nothing ever will change. So the 1969 Mets lost to the brand-new Montreal Expos with their star pitcher on the mound on Opening Day. Duffy Dyer's home run in the ninth made the score 11–10. It also put the Mets into the category of scoring double-digits against a team that had never played before... and losing. The loss made it eight straight Opening Day losses, dating back to the franchise's first game in 1962. The first scene of the play had gone off flawlessly.

Meanwhile, a few subtle hints of impending greatness were sprinkled amidst the mostly empty seats at Shea the next two afternoons. After Jim McAndrew was knocked out in the second inning of the second game, Tug McGraw came in and threw 6⅓ innings of relief—portending his future in the bullpen—while Nolan Ryan got the first save in Mets history (the save became an official statistic in 1969). The next afternoon, rookie Gary Gentry won his first career game and Tommie Agee, coming off a monumentally disappointing first year as a Met in 1968, sent a Larry Jaster pitch into Shea's upper deck for a home run. It was the first ball hit fair into that deck in either left or right field—and the only one that would be hit in the 45 seasons of Shea Stadium's life. The scant fair territory and the height of the deck made the feat practically impossible, yet Agee did it and the Mets went on to win the game and that first series against the Expos.

The Mets could breathe the rarified air of winning. It marked only the second time in club history that the Mets had been on the good side of .500. Just like in 1966, the '69 Mets stood at 2–1. The Mets were just one game behind the Cubs in the newly-christened National League East. The Mets would not get that close to first place again for five months.

New York was swept three straight at Shea Stadium by the two-time defending NL champion Cardinals and wound up dropping six of seven. In the club's first 10 games, rookie Gary Gentry (2–0) was the only starter to have earned a win. The Mets were already six games out, the fastest they'd reached that deficit since they'd called the Polo Grounds home in 1963. Gil Hodges's preseason prediction of 85 wins looked like the stuff of utter nonsense.

Tom Seaver finally won his first game of the year, winning in St. Louis, and the Mets won the next day as Ryan gained his first victory. A packed April schedule that was to have seen the Mets play the first 20 dates on the schedule without rest—with a scheduled doubleheader tossed in—instead saw the Mets get three days off in a week due to rain. No matter how often the tarp was dragged across the field or how many times Gil Hodges tinkered with his lineup, the results seemed the same: All wet.

After dropping three-straight to the fast-starting Cubs at the end of April, the Mets were 6–11. They salvaged the nightcap of the Sunday doubleheader when Cleon Jones broke a scoreless tie with a three-run homer in the bottom of the ninth. The teams had drawn just 16,252 as Bill Hands beat Don Cardwell the previous afternoon—a slightly bigger crowd had come Friday night to see Fergie Jenkins top Seaver—but Sunday brought more than 37,000, the biggest gathering at Shea since Opening Day. Still, the Cubs left town with a six-game lead over the Mets, who were tied for last place. Not much new to see here.

The first venture by the Mets into Canada was not televised, and poor luck continued to plague the Mets—in any language. Though they won the opener on a pair of home runs by Ed Kranepool, the club lost Jerry Koosman for nearly a month with what was termed a dead arm. The Mets looked dead themselves, losing three straight after starting the trip with a pair of wins at Jarry Park. Dropping consecutive games at Wrigley Field gave the Mets a 1–5 record against the Cubs to begin 1969. Chicago held an eight-game lead on the 9–14 Mets in the first weekend in May. The next day, in front of 40,484 looking for the their red-hot Cubs to wring out the same old results from the same old Mets, New York instead rolled out a pair of complete-game, 3–2 wins by Seaver and McGraw, the latter making his first start of the year. The deficit stood at six games, the same as it had been when the Mets arrived in Chicago—and the same as it had been a week earlier when the teams had met at Shea—but the Cubs had won every previous series of three games or more in 1969. The Cubs responded by winning five of the last seven games on their homestand.

The Mets had a 4–4 homestand in their first foray against the clubs now constituting the National League West. It was their best homestand to date in 1969 and produced the only two wins of the year the Mets would manage against the Astros, their brothers in expansion in 1962, who were clearly the more mature sibling to that point. The Mets split two with Cincinnati and lost two of three to the Braves. The Mets took to the road to face the same clubs, winning the first three and reaching .500 for the first time since the opening week of the season. Prompted by the press to celebrate their newfound mediocrity, the Mets shrugged, saying they had bigger goals in mind. Conventional wisdom said the Mets should have made merry when they could, as the club dropped the last four games of the trip, including three straight at the Astrodome. The Mets were 18–22 and nine games behind the Cubs on Memorial Day weekend.

The Mets got their first look at the expansion San Diego Padres, who had just one fewer win than the Mets, though they'd racked up seven more losses because they didn't have to fret about rainouts in sunny San Diego. The Padres got to experience one firsthand as the teams were washed out on Memorial Day. The Padres won the first game ever played between the two franchises, but the Mets won the next day when Bud Harrelson broke a scoreless tie with a single in the 11th inning. The Mets won every remaining game on the homestand and the first four of the ensuing road trip. The 11-game winning streak—all against West Coast teams—was not only unprecedented for the club, it was achieved with pitching and timely hitting. The Mets plated more than five runs only once during the streak—a 9–4 win in San Francisco the night before Gaylord Perry finally stopped them—and twice New York won 1–0 games in extra innings. Six of the wins were by one run and three victories belonged to Seaver (Koosman—his arm now alive and well—along with Gentry and Ron Taylor won twice apiece during the streak). Still, their 29–23 mark kept them a full seven games behind the unblinking Cubs juggernaut—the Mets gained just two games in the standings during the streak while the Cubs went 8–1 in that span and improved to 20 games over .500. The consolation was that the Mets were the only NL East team within double-digits of Chicago.

The Mets dropped three of their last four on the coast after the streak ended (briefly dropping to nine back), but they concluded their 12-game trip by winning three of four in Philadelphia. The last game showed the Mets were made of something stronger than past versions of the club. After Taylor blew a save for Seaver on a two-out, two-run single in the bottom the eighth, the Mets were down to their last out at Connie Mack Stadium in the top of the ninth. Ken Boswell singled in the tying and go-ahead runs against Turk Farrell; McGraw made the lead stand up by setting down the Phils in the bottom of the ninth. The Mets not only returned from an 8–4 road trip as a true contender, they also brought with them the bat they had long craved.

On June 15, general manager Johnny Murphy acquired Donn Clendenon from the Expos. A longtime Pirate, the Expos had selected Clendenon and traded him to the Astros for Rusty Staub. Clendenon retired rather than play in Houston, unretired when Montreal offered more money, and in the end new commissioner Bowie Kuhn made the Expos send two players to the Astros to complete the deal. The trade with the Mets was relatively simple—and one-sided. The Mets sent backup third baseman Kevin Collins, pitcher Steve Renko, and two minor leaguers that never made it, to Montreal in exchange for Clendenon, who had driven in 87 runs the previous year (the Mets hadn't had anyone exceed 76 RBIs since their inaugural year). Because the new acquisition batted right-handed, Ed Kranepool started the majority of the time at first base in Hodges's platoon system, but Clendenon saw right-handers on occasion and was one of the league's biggest threats off the bench when he wasn't starting. It took until July 6 for Clendenon to hit his first home run as a Met. The homer came at his old stomping grounds in Pittsburgh, where the failure to protect him in the expansion draft the previous autumn had precipitated his eight-month, three-state, two-country odyssey. His three-run blast at Forbes Field wiped out a Pirates lead and was the difference in an 8–7 win that culminated a three-game sweep for Clendenon's newest team. That gave Clendenon 11 RBIs in his last five games. The new guy was paying off.

And the Mets were on another streak. An 11-game homestand to end June against St. Louis, Philadelphia, and Pittsburgh had seen the Mets win one, lose one, win four, lose four, and finish on a winning note by beating the Bucs behind Tom Seaver. The Mets were 8½ back after they'd cut the deficit to five games just a few days earlier.

After dropping two of their first three in St. Louis, the Mets won in 14 innings against the Cardinals thanks to Boswell's deciding hit and six scoreless innings of relief from McGraw, whom Hodges leaned on during those rare games when his starters faltered. The Mets followed by winning the next four games on the trip. The Cubs came into Shea with a 5½-game lead, still sizeable to say the least, but the Mets had a chance to cut their deficit to its smallest margin since April 23. And they got there behind two unforgettable ninth innings at rollicking Shea. The first game saw fly balls falling when they should have been caught in the final inning as the Mets rallied to take the opener. The next night's ninth inning had even more tension ... and the score was never in question. An opposite-field single in the ninth by Jimmy Qualls broke up Tom Seaver's perfect game with two outs to go. The Mets had won seven straight and had cut the lead to 3½ games, but the joy was short-lived as the Cubs stymied the Mets the next day, 6–2. When Cubs manager Leo Durocher was asked after the game if "those were the real Cubs," the Lip chimed, "No, those were the real Mets."

After taking two of three from Montreal, the New York-Chicago set-to resumed. Wrigley Field was packed on a Monday afternoon and the Cubs handed Seaver his first loss since May. Seaver, in his first start since his one-hitter, was again brilliant. The game's lone run came on a Don Kessinger bunt single and a two-out, opposite-field hit by Billy Williams in the sixth. The lead was back to six games, more than what it had been before the teams met at Shea a week earlier, but the Mets had a couple of surprises in store. With Bud Harrelson in military duty for close to a month, light-hitting Al Weis became a regular shortstop. He homered in each of the next two games—his only two home runs of the regular season—and the Mets left Chicago trailing by four games, almost the same margin it had been after Seaver's near-perfecto.

In front of big crowds at little Jarry Park, the Mets split four with Montreal—and were lucky to get that. In the second game of the Sunday doubleheader, the Mets blew leads in the eighth and ninth before Bobby Pfeil's bunt brought in the go-ahead run and another unsung hero from the minors, Jack DiLauro, got the last three outs. On the day that man first landed on the moon, the Mets disembarked for the All-Star break with 53 wins, a total they did not surpass in any of their first four seasons of existence. Now these Mets, watching the lunar landing from the Montreal airport, stood five games behind the team with the best record in the National League ... and there were 70 games to play.

CURTAIN

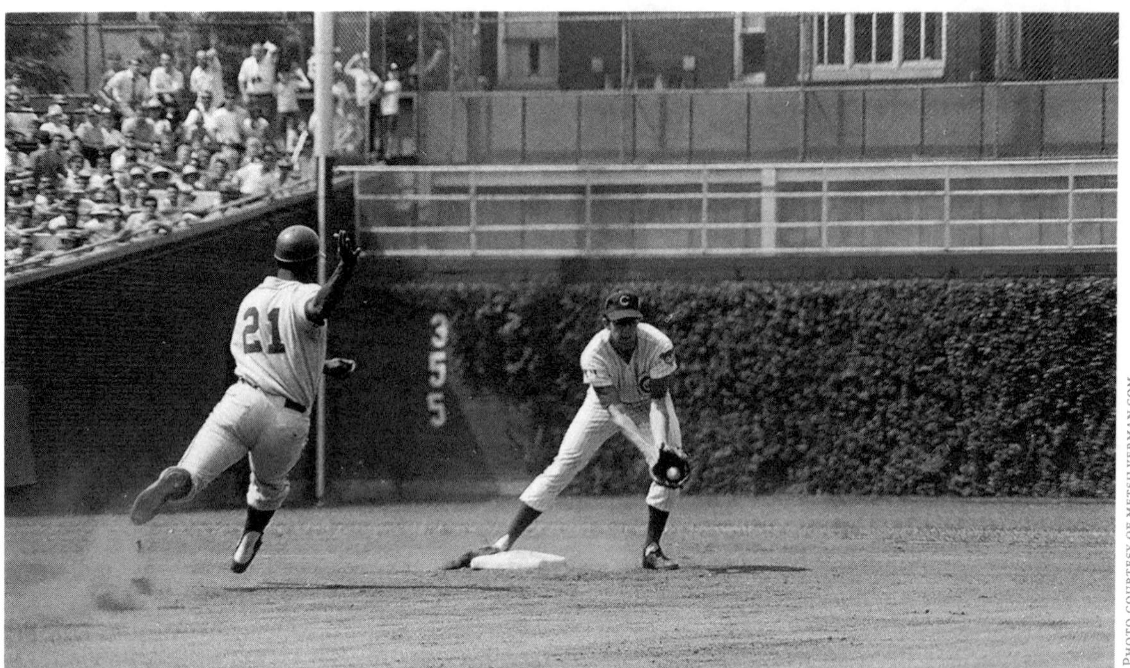


Photo courtesy of metsilverman.com

*Cleon Jones goes in hard at second base as Cubs shortstop Don Kessinger takes the throw.*

Act II opened with the Mets facing their NL West foes again at Shea Stadium. The Reds scored three times to take the lead in the top of an inning—including both the eighth and ninth—only to see the Mets tie it. This pattern was broken in the 12th, when Tony Perez broke the tie with a home run in the top of the inning and Boswell was tagged out at third in the bottom of the inning. The Mets won the next two, but proceeded to drop four straight. A rainout necessitated a doubleheader against the Astros, and a perceived lack of effort chasing a ball by Cleon Jones—the starting left fielder in the All-Star Game and a .346 hitter—necessitated Gil Hodges to pay a visit.

"Everyone expected him to stop at the mound and change pitchers," longtime Mets beat writer Jack Lang wrote. "But Hodges walked past the mound, past the shortstop, and on to left field. There he confronted Jones, inquired of his physical condition, then did a complete turnabout and walked just as slowly back to the dugout. Behind Hodges by a few steps, walking just as slowly and with head hung low, Jones followed.... No other manager had ever walked to the outfield so deliberately to remove a player."

The Mets were outscored in that day's doubleheader by an astonishing 27–8. They were shut out the next day as Jones sat—the "concocted" story was that he had a pulled muscle—but he played sparingly over the next week for a player whose average hovered at .350. The Mets rebounded by sweeping the Braves and they would take three of four in Atlanta on the ensuing road trip, but the Mets again had trouble with the Reds and could not beat the Astros to save their life.

The Cardinals were pushing the Mets in the standings and the Cubs seemed poised to pull away once and for all. St. Louis jumped ahead of the Mets in the standings and stood nine games back on August 13. The Mets were an even 10 behind Chicago. It seemed the Mets had been a nice story, but they were experiencing the classic August fade that many had suffered before them. Divisional play had done strange things to the records and to the teams—only three of a dozen NL teams had losing records (and two of those clubs were brand new). Maybe the Mets were just moving up a little in line, good summer drama, and all that sort.

Leonard Koppett, beat writer for the *New York Times*, looked back on things as they seemed at the time. "On August 15, back from a depressing series at the Astrodome, the Mets had no reason to consider themselves anything special, not being blessed with the gift of foreknowledge." But it was fate, luck, and no doubt skill that propelled the Mets to the top. And the first stroke of fate was that the schedule maker handed the Mets the Padres.

One of the reasons that nine of the NL's now dozen teams were playing winning baseball was the presence of the expansion clubs. Someone had to absorb those losses. The pitiful, porous Padres arrived in New York to kick off the Mets' 10-game homestand. The Mets scored two runs in each game of the Saturday doubleheader and won both. The Mets scored three apiece in the Banner Day twin bill the next day... and again swept a doubleheader. In their next game, the Mets did not score at all for 13 innings against the Giants, and they won in the 14th. In fact, the only game they lost on the 9–1 homestand was an 11-inning defeat to San Francisco, and even then the Mets rallied from 6–2 to force extra innings, with Ron Swoboda's two-out hit tying the game in the ninth. The Mets took three straight from the NL West-leading Dodgers, winning in the ninth on Saturday on Jerry Grote's double and rallying from behind on Sunday behind Swoboda's bases-clearing double as Shea shook. The Mets had drawn more than 300,000 to the last seven dates on the homestand, but more importantly to the people who packed Shea was this: Their team was back to within 5½ games of first place.

The Cubs, meanwhile, were starting to stumble. Coming off a 22–12 stretch, the Cubs—like the Mets earlier in the month—had trouble with the western clubs, going 4–7 against Atlanta, Houston, and Cincinnati. Though one of those games was a Ken Holtzman no-hitter against the Braves, it was a little disquieting in Chicago that the tough patch had come at Wrigley Field. The Mets hit the road and remained hot. They swept in San Diego to pull within 2½ games of the Cubs, but Juan Marichal cooled off New York with a four-hit shutout at Candlestick Park. The Mets bounced back the next day with Donn Clendenon homering off Gaylord Perry in the 10th inning after the Mets had escaped the

NATIONAL BASEBALL HALL OF FAME LIBRARY, COOPERSTOWN, NY

*The Miracle behind the Miracle Mets was the pitching staff. The Mets have had many great seasons by starting staffs since then, but 1969 is the year all are measured against. Five homegrown pitchers, all 26 or younger, made it happen. From left: Tom Seaver, Jerry Koosman, Nolan Ryan, Gary Gentry, and Jim McAndrew.*

bottom of the ninth thanks to a 7-2-3-5 double play that had begun as a seemingly game-winning hit. The clubs split a Sunday twin bill.

The Mets moved on to Los Angeles and lost the series there, giving New York three losses in four games. They trailed by 5½ games, a half-game closer than they'd been when they embarked on the 6–4 trip. The Cubs had seemed to right the ship with five straight wins—four of them on the road—but they lost the final game of the trip to Jim Maloney in Cincinnati and then dropped three straight to the Pirates at Wrigley, with Willie Stargell's two-out home run tying the series finale in the ninth. The Bucs won in 11. The Mets, meanwhile, shook off their California doldrums and won three of four from the Phillies, putting the New York and Chicago just 2½ games apart as the clubs played for the final time at Shea Stadium in 1969.

The battle began with Tommie Agee hitting the deck when Bill Hands came in tight in the bottom of the first. Ron Santo, whose celebratory heel clicks after Wrigley wins had irritated many Mets and other National Leaguers, took a pitch from Jerry Koosman on the arm leading off the second inning. Agee and the Mets got the last laugh. Agee homered his next time up with a man on and the Mets center fielder slid just under Randy Hundley's tag in the sixth inning to snap a 2–2 tie. Hundley snapped as well, jumping high in the air and arguing vehemently with umpire Satch Davidson. After the game, with Santo's arm encased in ace and the third baseman still in discomfort, Kooz admitted, "I threw at him…they threw at Tommie. I had to do it to end it right there. If I don't, they keep doing it, and they keep getting away with it." At this point, the Cubs weren't getting away with anything. The lead was 1½.

The next night is remembered for the appearance of black cat in front of the Cubs dugout, plus fans serenading Leo Durocher with handkerchiefs, but what is often overlooked is the dominating performance by Tom Seaver. Pitching against Cubs ace Fergie Jenkins in the biggest game of his career to that point, Seaver was staked to an early lead on a Ken Boswell double and cruised to his 21st win of the season in front of 58,436 (counting all admissions).

The next night brought a doubleheader with Montreal. Boswell's hit handed the Expos their 12th consecutive extra-inning loss to start their existence and pushed the Mets a percentage point ahead of the Cubs, who'd endured their seventh loss in a row. Nolan Ryan threw a three-hitter in the nightcap and the Mets—hold on to your hat—had a one-game lead. After the Cubs controlled first place for 129 days, the National League East had a new leader. Future vintner Seaver, who'd led the deadpan routine when the press wanted the club to bubble over for being .500 in May, doled out champagne in paper cups for all in the clubhouse.

The party continued. Gary Gentry threw a shutout the next day and the Mets were two games up. Friday brought the third doubleheader in a week for the Mets. Cleon Jones was unable to play with a pulled muscle in his back and Art Shamsky sat out in observance of Rosh Hashanah. All right, the pitchers just had to work harder. Jerry Koosman knocked in the only run of the first game in Pittsburgh and threw a shutout. Don Cardwell followed suit and singled in the only run in the nightcap, though Tug McGraw helped out by tossing the final inning. The twin 1–0 wins with the pitchers doing it all pushed the Mets beyond Amazin'. It was time to go back in history, to the 1914 Boston Braves—a sad sack franchise that had been in last place and 15 games out on July 4—who wound up winning the pennant going away before sweeping the mighty Philadelphia Athletics in the World Series. If the Miracle Braves could do it…

This was uncharted territory for the Mets. And their response was—don't let the other team score. The Mets reeled off 36 consecutive scoreless innings. Even though Seaver allowed a run in the third inning the next day in Pittsburgh, Ron Swoboda crushed a grand slam over the 406-foot sign at Forbes Field in the eighth against right-hander Chuck Hartenstein to give the Mets had their 10th straight win. The Cubs, who'd ended an eight-game losing streak the night before, lost in St. Louis. The Mets were up by 3½.

The Mets finally lost on Sunday in Pittsburgh, but made up for it the next night with another win of the miraculous variety. In St. Louis, where the Cardinals had just taken two of three from the Cubs,

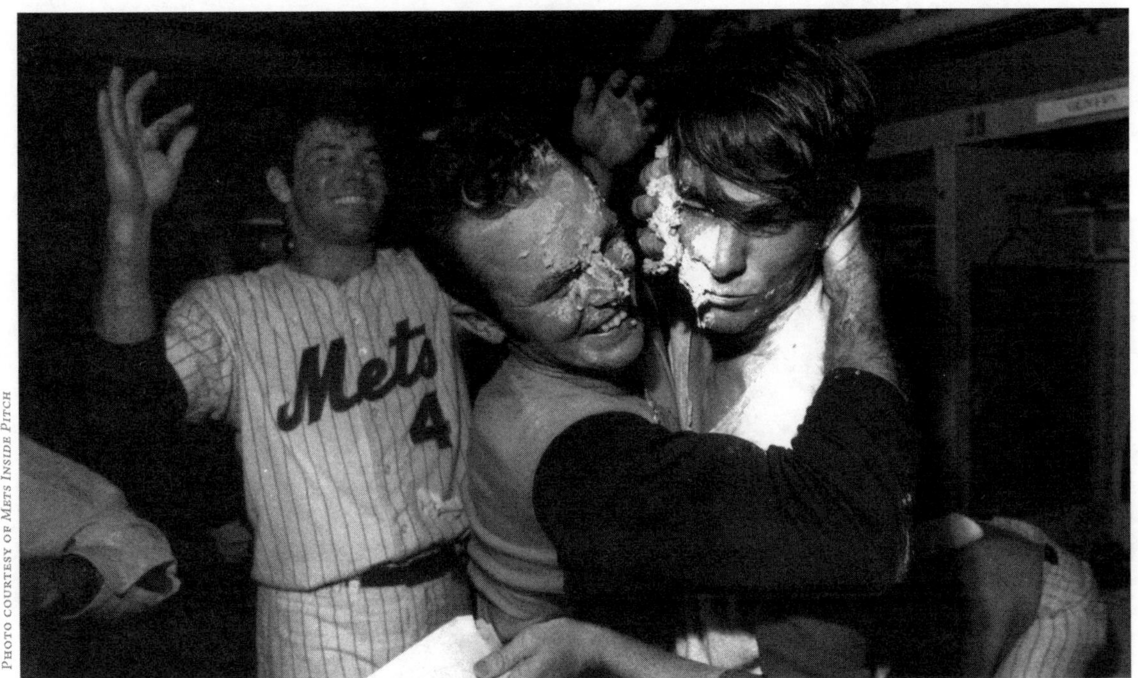


Photo courtesy of Mets Inside Pitch

*Veteran Jerry Grote, center, shows rookie Gary Gentry the many uses of shaving cream as Ron Swoboda beams his approval during one of the many causes for celebration in the 1969 Mets locker room.*

Steve Carlton set the nine-inning major league record with 19 strikeouts in a game. And lost. Rocky Swoboda hit two two-run homers in between striking out his other two times up. After a rainout the next night, Koosman and Seaver went to Montreal and kept the Expos off the scoreboard in a two-game sweep. The Mets had 13 wins in 14 games and a five-game lead.

Back in New York the next day, they had another doubleheader. This time, the Pirates were ready. They pummeled the Mets 8–2 and 8–0. The lead dropped to four, but it could have been more had the Cardinals and Cubs not split their twin bill. The next afternoon, Bob Moose threw a no-hitter against the Mets at Shea—and New York lost no ground as the Cards topped the Cubs again. Chicago won on Sunday to gain a split in St. Louis—and they lost a game. The Mets swept a twin bill from the Pirates. Again, amazingly, the wins went to Koosman and Cardwell. Though this time they went a combined 0-for-7 at the plate, they both went the distance.

The Mets picked up a home game the next day—the rainout in St. Louis was transferred to Shea—and a half game in the standings as Seaver won his 24th. The Mets won in 11 innings the next night as Bud Harrelson's opposite-field single off Bob Gibson brought in Swoboda. The Mets now led by six. The magic number was one.

The suspense was over quickly. Steve Carlton, who'd struck out 19 Mets yet lost two starts earlier, and whose previous start had helped the Mets by beating the Cubs, got the party started early for the Mets. Lefty retired just one batter. He allowed a hit to Harrelson, a walk to Agee, and a home run to Donn Clendenon. He walked Ron Swoboda—a wise move after Carlton's last start against the Mets—and then served up a two-run home run to Ed Charles. That was the last pitch Carlton threw in 1969. Gary Gentry took the lead and ran with it. He allowed only two singles through eight innings before surrendering two hits to start the ninth. Gentry then fanned Vada Pinson. Up stepped Joe Torre, a hitter the Mets had tried to trade for in March (and an eventual manager at Shea). Bob Murphy, who along with Lindsey Nelson and Ralph Kiner had called every season of Mets baseball since their inception was at the mic.

> *The crowd is chanting, "We're number one!' The Mets made up fifteen-and-a-half games since the 13th of*

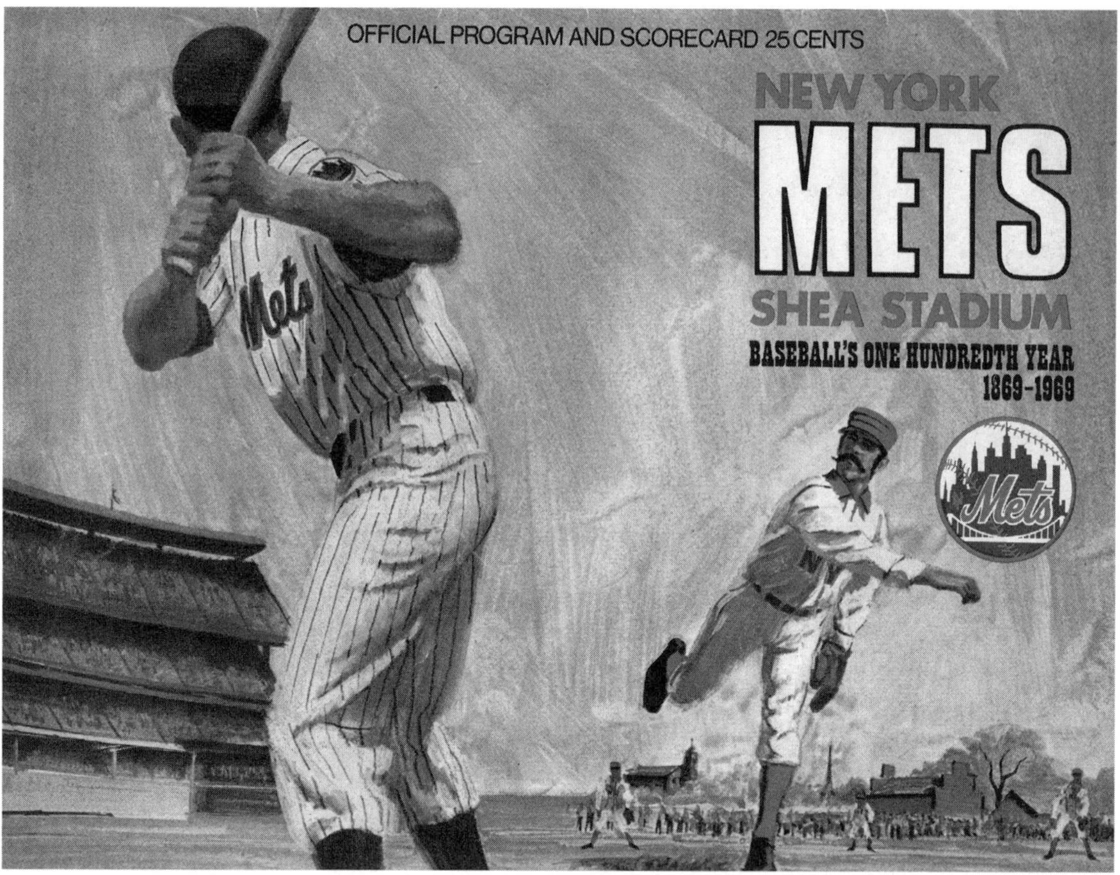


Photo courtesy of Gene Caputo

*August. Lou Brock is on second, and Vic Davalillo, the runner on first with one man out...ninth inning, 6-0, New York. Gentry pitching, working hard here against Joe Torre. Now in the set position, here's the pitch...ground ball hit to shortstop...Harrelson to Weis, there's one, first base...Double play...The Mets win! It's all over! Ohhhh, the roar going up from this crowd! An unbelievable scene on the field... fans are pouring out on the field.*

And they kept on pouring. *New York Times* beat writer Leonard Koppett, who watched the scene from the Shea press box, later wrote. "Just 2,724 days after Stengel exposed his 'Metsies' to the Cardinals in their first National League game. The seven-year famine had ended."

The celebration was long, hard, and wet in the clubhouse, but still the Mets kept on winning. They went to Philadelphia and did not allow a run all weekend—breaking their club record of two weeks earlier with 42 straight scoreless innings. The Mets kept winning even as the games were meaningless: winning the Mayor's Trophy Game against the Yankees and then defeating the Cubs at Wrigley for their ninth straight win and making it an even 100 victories. The team that Las Vegas had as a 100-1 shot in March to reach the World Series was in the postseason as the calendar flipped to October. All bets were off.

**Sources**

1969 Official Mets Yearbook.

*Baseball Reference.com*

*Amazin' Mets: The Miracle of '69, The Daily News Legend Series* (Sports Publishing, 1999)

Koppett, Leonard, *The New York Mets* (Macmillan, 1974)

Lang, Jack, *The New York Mets: Twenty-Five Years of Baseball Magic* (Henry Holt & Co., 1986)

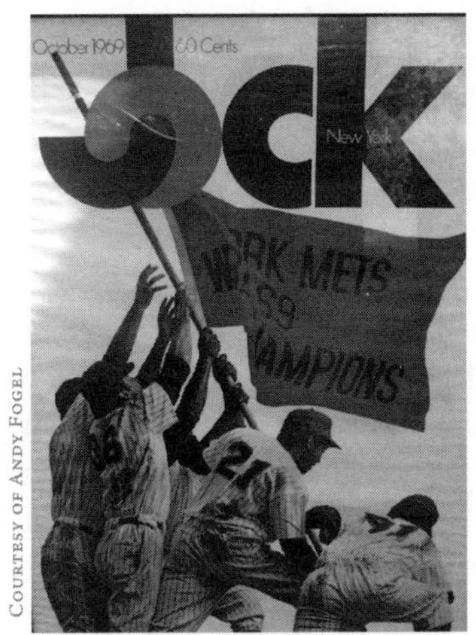


Courtesy of Andy Fogel

# Putting the Miracle in Miracle Mets

by Mets Walk-Offs and Other Minutiae
*(http://metswalkoffs.blogspot.com)*

Even when the Mets were at their most mediocre, dramatic victories were a common occurrence, and that trait carried over to the 1969 regular season. The Mets had their share of unlikely wins that season, including 11 in walk-off fashion. *Mets Walk-Offs and Other Minutiae* offers a closer look at those Amazin' games.

## April 27, 1969: Mets 3, Cubs 0

The first time that the Mets and Cubs convened in 1969 came at the end of April and didn't exactly serve as a foreshadowing for what was to come that season. The Mets opened the weekend four-game series with a pedestrian 6–8 mark, while the Cubs held first place with a surprising 11–5 start.

The Cubs won the first two games of the series as Ferguson Jenkins edged Tom Seaver, 3–1, and Bill Hands followed by going the distance in a 9–3 pasting of Don Cardwell. Chicago made it three straight wins by taking the opener of a Sunday doubleheader, 8–6, thanks to a four-run ninth. The way that things broke, it looked like this was going to be a special year in Chicago. There was no reason to believe that anything special was going to happen for the floundering Mets. Until the nightcap.

Tug McGraw, in relief of Jim McAndrew, danced around jams to keep the score tied into the last of the ninth when the Mets worked a little magic. Hall of Famer Billy Williams muffed Rod Gaspar's line drive to open the inning, giving the Mets a leadoff baserunner in scoring position. After an intentional walk to Ken Boswell, Rich Nye got Ed Charles to pop up for the first out.

This brought up Cleon Jones, whose whiff concluded the first game of the day, but whose torrid start made him a feared hitter at this juncture of the season. He finished off this contest as well, only in a much more positive manner, with a three-run walk-off home run that raised his batting average to .443.

The win gave the Mets a little bit of satisfaction, though the Cubs still left Flushing smiling, with a 14–6 mark. It didn't strike anyone at the time that Chicago had just beaten the rival who would become most important to them within a few short months.

## May 28, 1969: Mets 1, Padres 0 (11)

On April 29, Jerry Koosman suffered a shoulder injury while pitching against the Montreal Expos, noting to reporters afterward that something snapped like a piece of elastic.[1]

The resulting tenderness sidelined Koosman for nearly a full month, but the good news was that he returned as good, if not better, than ever. In his first start back, on May 24, against the Houston Astros, he allowed two runs and three hits over seven innings, in what turned into an eventual 5–1 defeat.

In that era, there was no hesitation, once a pitcher was healed, to throw him fully into the fire. Koosman's next start came on three days' rest, on May 28, against the Padres. The Mets had lost five straight and while there were promising signs of progress, there were also indications that this was going to be a troublesome season.

If there was any concern over whether Koosman could handle the physical and mental pressure, it was erased with this game, perhaps his finest as a Met to that point. Gil Hodges permitted him to work 10 innings, as he yielded only four hits and struck out a club-record and career-high 15.

The Mets squandered their share of opportunities by hitting into three double plays. It took until the 11th inning (and Koosman's subsequent departure for Tug McGraw) for the Mets to plate their first and only run.

Cleon Jones led off, reaching when he beat out a grounder up the middle, judged to be an error on Padres shortstop Tommy Dean. After Ed Kranepool whiffed, Ron Swoboda advanced Jones to third with a single, putting the Mets within 90 feet of triumph. The Padres walked Jerry Grote to load the bases in the hopes that Bud Harrelson would hit into a double play. No such luck. Harrelson singled down the left-field line, scoring Jones with the winning run. It was the first of nine 1-0 wins for the Mets in 1969—and the first of three that came in walk-off fashion.

The win might have been the story of the day, but the real key to come out of this was Koosman's effort on short rest. Now fully healed, Koosman got on a roll that helped propel the Mets to great things the rest of the season. In his first 60 innings back from the DL, Koosman allowed only four earned runs as the Mets went on an 18–7 spurt that turned their season around.

## June 1, 1969: Mets 5, Giants 4

Some batters are masters of the walk-off home run. Ron Swoboda was the master of the walk-off walk. Of the first 15 walk-off walks in Mets history, Swoboda was the only player to have more than one. He had four.

The third of them came on June 1, completing a three-game sweep of the Giants, part of an 11-game win streak in which the Mets went from five games under .500 to six-over at 29–23.

The Giants held early leads of 2–0 and 3–2, but on both occasions, the Mets rallied quickly, and the Giants had to rally from a 4–3 deficit to even the score in the sixth against Don Cardwell, who pitched 6⅓ game innings in relief of Jim McAndrew, who left with a finger blister.

Ron Taylor dodged trouble in the top of the ninth, surviving a Willie McCovey double to escape with the score still even. In the bottom of the frame, the Mets were able to win without hitting the ball out of the infield. Giants reliever Joe Gibbon walked Bud Harrelson, Cleon Jones (intentionally), and Amos Otis, sandwiched around two outs. That brought up Swoboda, who was 2 for 4 with an RBI already and Gibbon couldn't find the plate against him either. Swoboda's walk brought home the winning run.

Alas, being the master of the walk-off walk doesn't quite bring the glory of the other kinds of walk-off scenarios. When we interviewed Swoboda in 2005, he admitted having nary a recollection of any of his "walk"-offs.

"That's odd, isn't it?" said Swoboda, who couldn't come up with a reason for his success in that department. "I was a bit of a free swinger. Sometimes you walk because you're swinging the bat well, and sometimes you'll walk because you'll miss a pitch that you should have hit. Those [walk-offs] aren't the ones you remember."[2]

## June 4, 1969: Mets 1, Dodgers 0 (15)

The Mets and Dodgers played an extra-inning classic, featuring a great pitchers' duel between Bill Singer and Mets rookie Jack DiLauro. The two teams matched zeroes as Singer flirted with a perfect game for six innings and DiLauro escaped a couple of early jams. The contest went into extra-innings and both teams went to their bullpens.

In the top of the 15th, the Dodgers threatened, putting runners at the corners with one out. Willie Davis was the hitter and he hit a grounder off pitcher Ron Taylor that caromed towards second base. Al Weis charged the ball, made a barehand play and threw home just in time for catcher Jerry Grote to get incoming baserunner Billy Grabarkewitz at home plate. On the Mets highlight album that season, *Miracle Mets*, that moment is re-created by Bob Murphy, who states "Oh, what a play by Al Weis! I've never seen a better one by an infielder." (As an aside, the real play took about three seconds to unfold. The recreated version takes about 30 seconds, allowing Murph to provide every detail.)

The Mets stole the game in the bottom of the 15th, when with one out, Tommie Agee scored all the way from first when Davis misplayed Wayne Garrett's single to center. That gave the Mets a sweep of the Dodgers and matched a team record with their seventh straight win.

## July 8, 1969: Mets 4, Cubs 3

The Mets win over the Cubs on July 8 may be a little underappreciated in comparison to Tom Seaver's near-perfect game of the following day, but the impact it had was extremely significant.

Trailing 3–1 in the ninth inning against future Hall of Famer Ferguson Jenkins, the Mets rallied, with the aid of a couple misplays by Cubs center fielder Don Young, who incurred significant wrath from Cubs manager Leo Durocher (plus third baseman Ron Santo).

Cleon Jones followed the miscues by getting the game-tying double, then scored the winning run on a single by Ed Kranepool. This was the biggest win in franchise history, at least for a few hours, as it moved the Mets to within 4½ games of the first-place Cubs. It was the first Mets win to be reported on the front page of the *New York Times* since 1962.

"We've got the momentum now," Jones told the media afterwards. "We beat their big man. Now we've got our big man. We're in command. Now we can relax."[3]

Durocher was anything but relaxed. "That kid in center field. Two little fly balls. He just stands there watching one, and he gives up on the other.... If a man can't catch a fly ball, you don't deserve to win. Look at [Jenkins]. He threw his heart out. You won't see a better-pitched game. And that kid in center field gives it away on him. It's a disgrace."[4]

Is it any surprise that Seaver followed that game up the way that he did, given the moods of the two teams? And is it a surprise that a rookie named Jim Qualls was in center field that night?

## August 3, 1969: Mets 6, Braves 5 (11)

The 1969 Mets had not yet reached their turning point on August 3, 1969, when they faced the Braves in the finale of a three-game series. It was evident that the team was closing in on something special though, having taken two straight one-run affairs from the NL West leaders to stand at 57–44 and in second place in the NL East. The Mets had succeeded in making their opponents nervous, because they were a squad capable of doing anything. This contest was another example.

The Mets were shorthanded, with a couple of pitchers out on military duty, so when the Braves tallied four sixth-inning runs against Gary Gentry, extending their lead to 5–0, the outcome for the day looked rather bleak. The Mets hadn't managed a hit in the previous three innings against veteran hurler Milt Pappas, and with the Braves needing the game to maintain sole possession of the top spot in their division, it seemed like this one was all but in the books.

Or maybe not. Tommie Agee doubled to lead off the sixth inning and scored on a one-out single by Wayne Garrett. Atlanta felt it had gotten enough from Pappas, who was pitching on three days' rest, and replaced him at that juncture with Cecil Upshaw. That move didn't work.

The Mets loaded the bases on singles by pinch hitter Art Shamsky and Rod Gaspar, then caught a break when Jerry Grote reached after Braves second baseman Felix Millan dropped a throw while trying to get a force play. That brought home a run, making it 5–2. Cleon Jones, who was out with an injury (and was only a few days removed from being pulled in mid-game against the Astros for lack of hustle), pinch-hit and drove in two more runs with a single. That made it a 5–4 game.

The Braves went to the pen again, choosing rookie Paul Doyle. Bud Harrelson greeted Doyle by plating the tying run with a sacrifice fly. Doyle got out of the inning without further damage, but the score was now even, 5–5.

Jack DiLauro and Ron Taylor did great work out of the Mets bullpen, combining to shut out the Braves over the next five innings.

This was a game that was looking for a hero and the choice of the moment happened to be the first batter in the 11th inning: Jerry Grote. The catcher had homered off Phil Niekro earlier in the series, his first homer in Flushing that season and only his third round-tripper of the year. Raymond ran the count to 2–0 and made the mistake of grooving his next pitch, right over the heart of the plate. Grote's opposite-field drive cleared the right-field fence for a walk-off home run.

"If it had been anywhere else [but over the middle of the plate], I'd have taken it," Grote told reporters afterward, acknowledging that he was just trying to get on base. [5]

You would have presumed that this was a pretty big win. However, it was not the one that tipped the season in the Mets favor. It would seem logical that this victory set off a big win streak, but it didn't. The Mets lost their next two contests, and within a week, they were in third place, facing a nearly insurmountable deficit of 10 games after getting swept by the Astros. The chances of the Mets and Braves meeting in the postseason that autumn seemed rather bleak. It would take a miracle.

### August 19, 1969: Mets 1, Giants 0 (14)

If you were going to rank the best pitchers' duels in Mets history, this game might go at the top of the list. Rookie Gary Gentry went toe-to-toe with future Hall of Famer Juan Marichal for the first 10 innings, matching zeroes and avoiding damage of any significance. Marichal was 19–2 against the Mets to that point in his career and not surprisingly, he was sensational in this game. Gentry also threw one of his best games. It was a game that lived up to the cliche: "Neither team deserved to loose."

The Mets had one threat in regulation, but their best chance to score came in the 12th when Marichal's throw to nail Tug McGraw on a bunt attempt rolled away from ex-Met Ron Hunt after a collision between the former teammates at first base. Cleon Jones tried to score, but he was thrown out at the plate when Hunt recovered.

Jones redeemed himself in the top of the 13th when the Mets went to a four-man outfield against Willie McCovey. The subsequent smash to left-center was caught by a perfectly positioned Jones, who made a leaping catch at the fence to take away a home run.

The night's only extra-base hit concluded this contest, a home run by Tommie Agee, good for his 500th career major league hit. There were some nights in which the Mets were willing to play forever to win and this was one of them. Whatever it took.

### August 23, 1969: Mets 3, Dodgers 2

Sometimes the 1969 Mets got a little lucky. Their win over the Dodgers on this date was one of those times. Tied in the bottom of the ninth, the Mets pulled out the unusual victory when Jerry Grote's two-out pop fly fell between three Dodgers players, plopping on the grass for a game-ending double.

The Mets had bungled a 2–0 lead in the eighth inning. The Dodgers tied the game on Willie Davis's RBI triple, and a subsequent throwing error by Cleon Jones, who put himself in danger of being the game's goat when then hit into a rally-killing double play in the home eighth.

The Mets picked up for their teammate in the bottom of the ninth, getting a win on a day when the opposing starter was Mets killer Jim Bunning, who

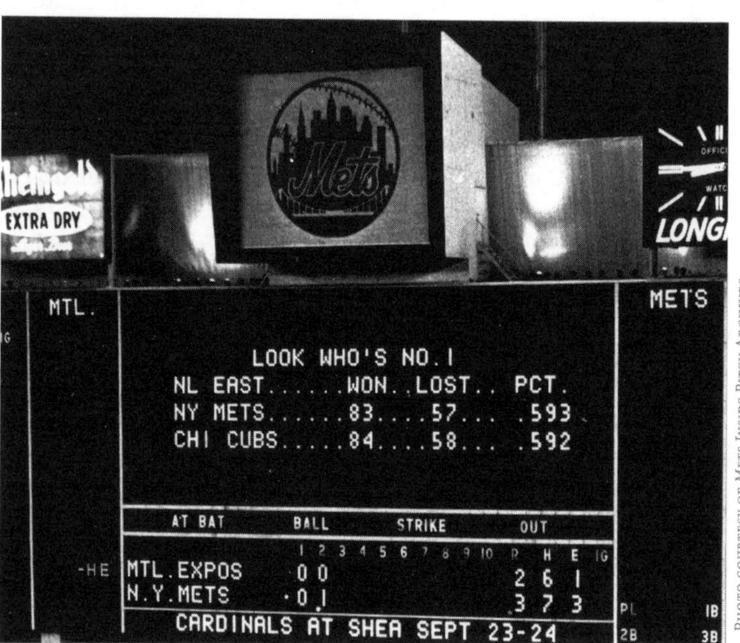


*Look Who's No. 1! The Mets pulled ahead of the Cubs for the first time on September 10, 1969.*

PHOTO COURTESY OF *METS INSIDE PITCH* ARCHIVES

didn't have perfect-game kind of stuff but held the Mets to only two runs in his seven innings.

"That ball has to be caught if we're to win the pennant," Dodgers shortstop Maury Wills said of the game-ending blunder.[6] And it has to drop for the Mets to win it.

### September 10, 1969: Mets 3, Expos 2 (12)

The Mets entered September 10, 1969 on the precipice of great things, just a half game behind after beating the first-place Cubs twice at Shea Stadium. Chicago then traveled to Philadelphia while the Mets caught a scheduling break: a doubleheader against the expansion Expos. The Expos had spoiled Opening Day at Shea by winning in their first game. That seemed like an awfully long time ago. The Expos had lost 97 times since then and would leave New York with an even 100 following the short three-game set.

The first game started in twilight and the Mets, winners of four straight, put Jim McAndrew on the mound against rookie Mike Wegener. Neither a first nor second inning run by the Expos dampened spirits, as the Mets responded with unearned runs in the first and fifth to knot the game at 2–2.

The game evolved into a pitchers' duel. Wegener, who never reached double digits in strikeouts before or again in his two-year career, whiffed 15 and walked seven. McAndrew walked five, but yielded only four hits. Both starters went deep into the contest, deeper than most managers nowadays would allow. Mets manager Gil Hodges stuck with McAndrew, even letting him bat with the score still tied, a man on base and two outs in the ninth. He lasted 11 innings and Expos manager Gene Mauch left Wegener alone for 11 as well.

Hodges finally relented and sent up a pinch hitter for McAndrew with two on and two out in the 11th. Jim Gosger struck out to end the scoring chance.

In the 12th inning, with Ron Taylor pitching, the Expos failed in an effort to take the lead, though they came close. With two outs, Angel Hermoso singled, as did ex-Met Kevin Collins, who was batting for Wegener. Hermoso tried to take third on that hit, and was successful as Tommie Agee's throw got away. However, the fundamentally sound Taylor backed up the plate, and when Hermoso tried to score, Taylor pegged the ball to catcher Jerry Grote for the third out.

Bill Stoneman, who had thrown a no-hitter earlier that year and would no-hit the Mets in 1972, was Mauch's choice to take the ball in the 12th, an odd choice considering Stoneman had pitched a shutout just three days previous (he would toss another two days later). Mauch had a full slate of relievers to choose from yet went with his top starter.

Stoneman got the first two Mets out in the 12th, but then magic struck. A single to center by Cleon Jones was followed by a walk by Rod Gaspar. Ken Boswell had the game-winning single to center despite a desperate dive by Expos second baseman Gary Sutherland (captured in a marvelous photo the next day in the *New York Times*).

The Cubs game against the Phillies was still going, and was close through the middle innings, but the win gave the Mets a piece of first place for the first time in their eight seasons of existence. Philadelphia extended its cooperation, snapping a 2–2 tie with a run in the seventh and three insurance tallies in the eighth, sending the Cubs to a 6–2 defeat, their seventh straight loss. The news came through on the Shea Stadium scoreboard after the third inning of the nightcap, just before 10:15 p.m., with a peek at the standings and the words, "Look who's number one." Nolan Ryan pitched a complete-game win in the nightcap and the Mets were on their way.

The rest of the world noticed. "Mets March to Head of Class" read the *Washington Post* headline the next day. "Hysteria Rocks Shea" said the *Los Angeles Times.* The *New York Times* told a fine story, of how Hodges had received a stuffed rabbit from a fan who "deemed a rabbit's foot not enough." The Mets had won six straight since Hodges put the rabbit on his desk.[7]

### September 23, 1969: Mets 3, Cardinals 2

The Mets have never cinched a division championship in walk-off fashion, though their first such celebration came a day after such an event. The game of September 24, 1969 is well remembered for its conclusion, with Joe Torre hitting into a 6-4-3 double play, assuring the Mets of their first NL East crown (and the first such crown in league history). The contest of the previous day isn't as easily recalled.

The Mets entered September 23 with a magic number of three, and when Bill Stoneman and the Expos topped the Cubs that afternoon, that was sliced to just two. In order to reduce it to one and guarantee at worst, a tie for the title, the Mets would have to topple nemesis Bob Gibson.

Jim McAndrew was up to the challenge and kept the Cardinals off the board for three innings. Wayne Garrett put the Mets ahead with a two-out single in the last of the third. It was not McAndrew's fault that he surrendered the lead in the fifth, as a two-out error by Ken Boswell allowed the tying run to score, and then Torre's RBI single put the Cardinals up, 2–1.

McAndrew held the Cardinals, but he left after seven frames with a one-run deficit. Gibson had ramped up his performance, retiring the Mets in order in the fifth and sixth, then escaping trouble in the seventh. Gibson had a chance to add to his lead in the eighth, but the hard-hitting hurler flew out with the bases loaded against reliever Tug McGraw. This was no ordinary fly out—it required a terrific diving catch by Ron Swoboda, something that Mets fans would see again.

In the home eighth, the Mets evened things up. Tommie Agee started with a single, went to second on Garrett's bunt, and scored on Art Shamsky's game-tying hit. Gil Hodges decided that the Mets fortunes were best served with McGraw pitching. The lefty weaved out of a jam in the top of the 10th, getting Phil Gagliano to ground out with two on. Gibson stayed in, even though he must have been fatigued by the 11th. With one out in that inning, Ron Swoboda and Jerry Grote got aboard on singles with light-hitting Bud Harrelson coming up.

Now normally, this would figure to be a mismatch, but for whatever reason, throughout their careers, Harrelson had Gibson's number. They would face each other many times and Harrelson was extremely successful with 20 hits in 60 at-bats (as well as 14 walks and just three strikeouts).

In this instance, Gibson got ahead two strikes before Harrelson dropped a single into left-center field, plating Swoboda with the winning run and setting the stage for the Metmorable events of the following day.

**Notes and Sources**

1. Durso, Joseph; "Kranepool Hits 2 Homers as Mets Top Expos." *New York Times, April 30, 1969, p. 50.*
2. Interview with Ron Swoboda, June 2005
3. Vecsey, George; "55,096 Watch Mets Shock Cubs With 3-Run Rally in Ninth for 4–3 Triumph." *New York Times*, July 9, 1969: 47.
4. Zimmerman, Paul D. and Dick Schaap. *The Year The Mets Lost Last Place.* (New York: World Publishing, 1929): 30-31.
5. Durso, Joseph "Mets Beat Braves, 6–5, on Grote's HR in 11th," *New York Times.* August 4, 1969: 42.
6. Durso, Joseph "Mets Defeat Dodgers, 3-2. Pop Fly Hit Wins," *New York Times*, August 24, 1969: S1.
7. Author uncredited. "For The Players, No Heady Stuff," *New York Times. September 11, 1969. p. 56*

*The New York Times*
*www.retrosheet.org*
*www.baseball-reference.com*
Blatt, Howard, *Amazin Met Memories.* Albion Press, Tampa Fla. 2002.
Bock Duncan & Jordan, John, *The Complete Year-By-Year N.Y. Mets Fan's Almanac.* (New York: Crown Publishers, NY. 1992.)
Cohen, Stanley, *A Magic Summer: The '69 Mets.* (New York: Harcourt Brace Jovanovich, 1988.)
Koppett, Leonard, *The New York Mets, The Whole Story.* (New York: The Macmillan Company, 1970.)
Zimmerman, Paul D. and Dick Schaap. *The Year The Mets Lost Last Place.* (New York: World Publishing, 1969.)

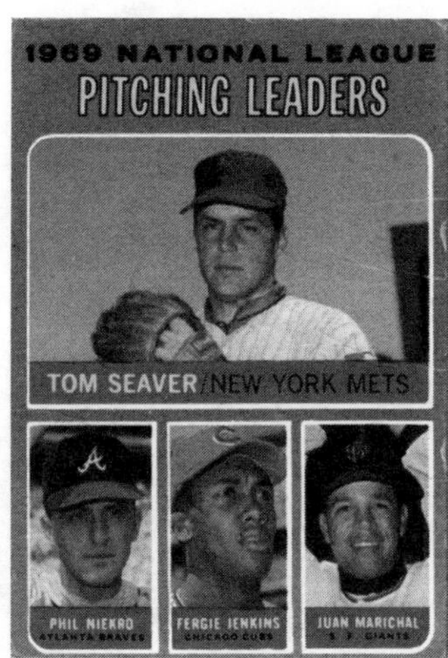


# Terrific Imperfection

by Matthew Silverman

George Thomas Seaver and George Herman Ruth shared the same unused first name and the distinction of being the greatest players in the history of their respective New York teams. Shea Stadium opened while Tom Seaver was still in school, so "The House that Seaver Built" was never a suitable sobriquet—but it could have aptly been called "The House that Seaver Filled."

Even as Shea filled well beyond capacity on the night of July 9, 1969, Seaver was already the greatest Met ever. For a franchise known for its horrible pitching before his debut, Seaver had quickly reversed that view. In 1967, just his second year of professional baseball, Seaver was the first All-Star pitcher in Mets history, the first to win more than 13 games in a season (at a time when starters generally accrued plenty of decisions), and the first National League pitcher in a decade to win the league's Rookie of the Year Award (needless to say, he was the first Met to win that trophy). He was an All-Star and 16-game winner again in 1968, while increasing his innings (to 277⅔), lowering his ERA by half a run (to 2.20), fanning 200 for the first time, and allowing less than a runner per inning (second only to Bob Gibson). Though another outstanding rookie named Jerry Koosman surpassed him in several Mets categories that year, Seaver had a sensational start in 1969. And for the first time, so had the Mets.

Seaver was 13–3 for the 46–34 Mets as he took his warmups in the bullpen on that Wednesday night in July. Manager Gil Hodges, a Brooklyn icon and an original Met, had already led the Mets to more wins in 80 games than the '62 Mets had managed in 160. But that loveable loser tag past them now—and their opponent that night could say the same thing.

The Cubs had not a world championship since 1908 or a pennant since 1945. They had finished last five times since then, lost 100 games for the first (and second) time in franchise history, suffered through the humiliation of the laughable College of Coaches regime, and become—in 1966—the first team to ever finish behind the sad-sack Mets. That was ancient history by July 9, 1966. Though they had cooled some after their best start since 1880, the Cubs came in at 53–31 for their three-game Shea showdown with the upstart Mets. Even after a disheartening ninth-inning loss the day before, Chicago still held a 4½ game lead on the Mets. Everyone else in the first-year National League East—including the two-time defending NL champion St. Louis Cardinals—trailed by double digits; only the Baltimore Orioles, playing at a scalding .699 clip in the American League East, had a bigger lead in baseball's new four-division format.

Leo Durocher, known for running the same players out every day without fail, inserted two left-handed hitters in the outfield against the right-handed Seaver: Al Spangler took over in right field (ex-Met Jim Hickman had started on July 8 against the southpaw Koosman), and rookie Jimmy Qualls took over for Don Young in center. The latter move was not simply a platoon. Young had misplayed two balls in the ninth inning the previous afternoon; both runners wound up scoring on Cleon Jones's double to tie the game and Ed Kranepool followed with a single to beat Fergie Jenkins. Durocher be-

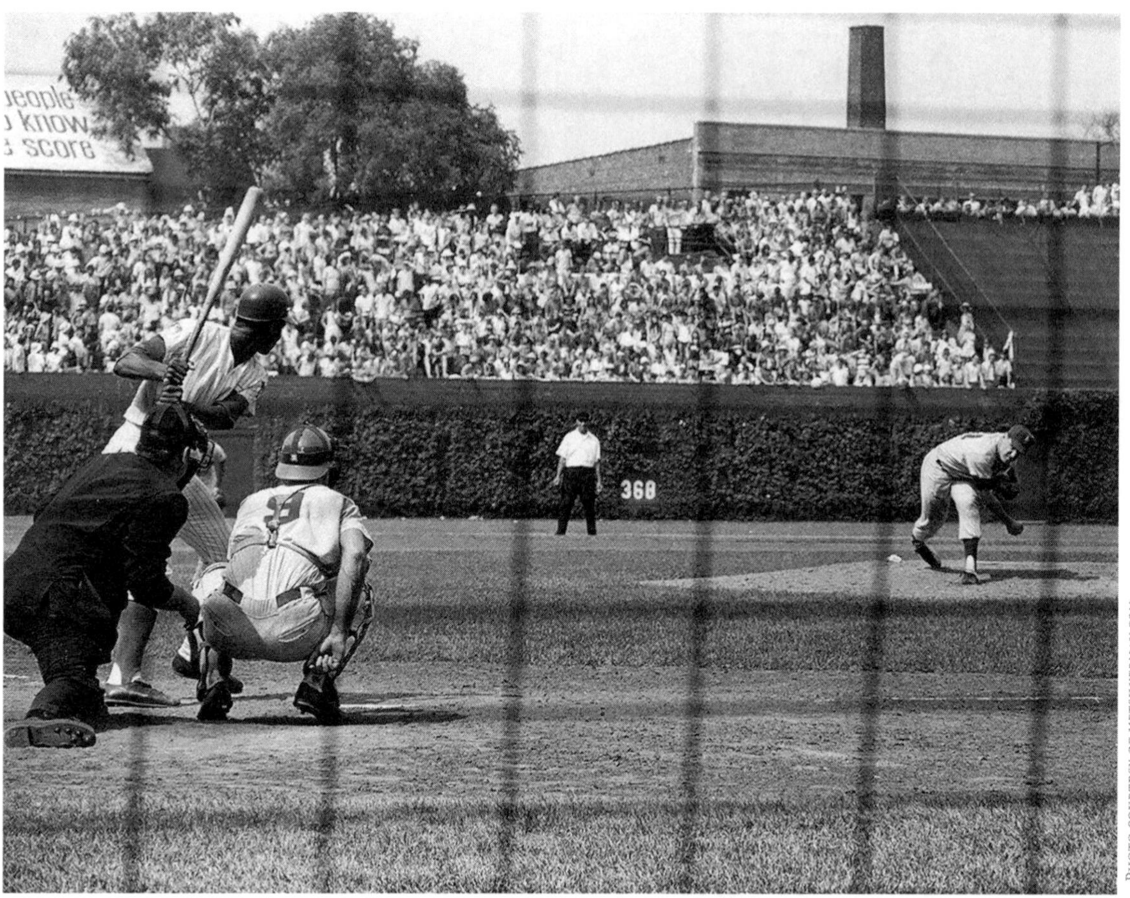


PHOTO COURTESY OF *METSILVERMAN.COM*

*Mets ace Tom Seaver fires to Cubs legend Ernie Banks at Wrigley Field one start after The Franchise was nearly perfect against Chicago during the summer of '69.*

rated the young center fielder in front of the team after the game. Emotional third baseman Ron Santo, who'd already drawn the ire of Hodges and many others around the league for clicking his heels after Cubs wins at Wrigley Field, told the press, "I know the Dodgers won pennants with just pitching, but this Mets club is ridiculous."

July 9, 1969 was indeed ridiculous.

Santo called the press that afternoon in the hotel to apologize about remarks he made about Young—not about the Mets comments—but the Cubs clearly seemed like they were still contemplating the previous day's defeat as the game started. Seaver, 1–1 against the Cubs so far in '69 (plus a relief appearance), struck out five of the first six Chicago batters. Randy Hundley and Qualls each pulled the ball in the air their first times up in the third inning, but both were caught with relative ease. Seaver completed his third perfect frame by fanning Cubs reliever Ted Abernathy. That Abernathy was in there at all told another side of the story. Ken Holtzman, who'd started the year 10–1, was in line for his fourth loss in a row after the Mets reached him for a run in the first and two in the second—one coming in on a Seaver single—to send the Chicago lefty to the showers after just 10 batters.

That 3–0 lead looked like plenty as Seaver fanned Don Kessinger for the second time and retired Glenn Beckert and Billy Williams on grounders in the fourth. Santo hit a ball to deep center to start the fifth, but Tommie Agee hauled it in. Ernie Banks bounced out and Spangler whiffed to end the inning. Hundley grounded out to third and Qualls hit the ball hard but right at first baseman Donn Clendenon. Abernathy became Seaver's ninth strikeout victim.

All three Cubs put the ball in play in the seventh, going the opposite way as Seaver continued throwing almost all fastballs. All three were corralled flawlessly. The jammed in crowd of 59,083 (the paid crowd was 50,709 but many others had used coupons from milk cartons for entry) cheered every time Seaver retired a batter. Those at Shea, watching on WOR-TV, or listening on WJRZ 970 were all thinking no-hitter now, even if no one dared speak it. Gil Hodges made his thoughts known by replacing third baseman Ed Charles with Bobby Pfiel, who'd started the game at second, and inserting rookie Wayne Garrett to play second base. Rod Gaspar took over for Ron Swoboda in right field. It had nothing to do with the manager's myriad platoons because Charles and Swoboda had both batted the previous inning against the righty Abernathy, who had allowed a home run to Cleon Jones during his sixth inning of relief to make it 4–0.

Santo hit the ball well for the second time, but Agee again tracked it down some 400 feet away in center in the eighth. Banks and Spangler both struck out to give Tom Terrific 11 K's. More importantly, Seaver was through eight. The pitcher received an ovation that lasted nearly two minutes when he stepped up in the bottom of the inning with Al Weis on first base. Seaver sacrificed... perfectly.

He took the mound to start the ninth inning with the crowd reacting on every pitch. Fans gasped as Randy Hundley bunted, but Seaver fielded it and threw to first. Up stepped Qualls. Along with Santo, Qualls had probably hit the ball as well as any Cub in the game. Bob Murphy called it on WOR-TV:

> *And it's hit hard to left field...It's going to be a base hit... A base hit by Jimmy Qualls and it breaks up the perfect game...Now the applause for Tom Seaver...Eight and one-third innings of perfect baseball by Seaver.*

First baseman Donn Clendenon came over and spoke with his pitcher for a moment, reminding him he needed to finish the task at hand. Seaver, always the professional—even at 24—set back to work. He got pinch hitter Willie Smith to pop up and Kessinger to fly to left to finish the 4–0 shutout. The Mets had again beaten the best team in the NL, New York had won its seventh game in a row, Seaver had his eighth win in a row, and a packed house had seen the best pitching performance by a Met at Shea Stadium. It was the first one-hitter by a Met at Shea, but surprisingly, it was the third one-hit game in the club's ignominious history. Al Jackson had thrown one at the Polo Grounds against Houston on June 22, 1962, and Jack Hamilton had thrown one in St. Louis on May 4, 1966 (the last shutout thrown at old Busch Stadium, a.k.a. Sportsman's Park). But in both those instances the hits had come the first time through the lineup... and clearly there had been no first-place drama involved in either game.

This game would indelibly be marked in Mets history, a history that would include pitchers like Koosman, Nolan Ryan, Jon Matlack, Dwight Gooden, Ron Darling, Sid Fernandez, Bobby Ojeda, David Cone, Al Leiter, Pedro Martinez, and Johan Santana, yet none of them—nor even a lesser pitcher having the game of his career—would throw a no-hitter in a Mets uniform. Seaver wound up throwing four more one-hitters as a Met and nine years after his flirt with perfection, he would actually complete a no-hitter... while pitching for the Reds. But even that achievement is overshadowed by what became known as the "Imperfect Game," the night Seaver showed once and for all that he—and his team—would no longer be part of anybody's joke.

**Sources**

Feldmann, Doug. Miracle Collapse: The 1969 Chicago Cubs. (Lincoln: University of Nebraska Press, 2006.)

"Murphy's Classic Calls," *http://newyork.mets.mlb.com/news/article.jsp?ymd=20040804&content_id=818742&vkey=news_nym&fext=.jsp&c_id=nym*

Retrosheet, *http://www.retrosheet.org/boxesetc/1969/B07090NYN1969.htm.*

## Ryan vs. Seaver

Tom Seaver, 24, and Nolan Ryan, 22, were on the same pitching staff in 1969, the duo must have dominated the opposition, right? Well, half right.

Seaver (25–7) started 35 times in 1969, while Ryan (6–3) started 10 games and relieved in 15. Were the Mets crazy not to use Ryan more in '69? First of all, Ryan's military obligation required him to report for duty at various times during the season, including a month between appearances when the Mets were getting things together in late spring. Second, he was the valuable swingman, filling in when an extra starter was needed—half his starts came during doubleheaders. And third, he was wild.

The eventual all-time bases on balls leader (2,795) walked 53 in 89.3 innings in 1969, including seven on July 1 after fanning 10 and walking only one in his previous start. He threw as hard as anyone in the National League, but where the ball would wind up was a mystery. Of the record 215 times he fanned 10 or more in his career, only two came in 1969—including the second game of a doubleheader on September 10, when he K'ed 11 Expos the night the Mets went ahead of the Cubs for good.

The important thing is that Ryan did pitch regularly at the end of the season. While he wasn't part of the postseason rotation of Seaver, Jerry Koosman, and Gary Gentry, Ryan won as many games as Seaver or Gentry in the postseason. He came in with no one out in the third inning in Game 3 of the NLCS and went the rest of the way for the pennant-clinching victory. He came out of the pen in Gentry's World Series start and earned the save—with a little help from Tommie Agee's glove—in what turned out to be his lone Fall Classic appearance.

Beyond '69, who's the better pitcher: Tom Terrific or the Ryan Express?

Mets fans don't need much convincing, but beyond the East Coast—and certainly in the Southwest—Ryan is probably better known than Seaver. Even though Ryan started his career earlier and ended it seven years after Tom Terrific's last pitch, their numbers are remarkably similar in terms of wins (324 Ryan, 311 Seaver), complete games (231 Seaver, 222 Ryan), and shutouts (61 apiece). Where they differ greatly is ERA (2.86 Seaver, 3.19 Ryan), winning percentage (.603 Seaver, .526 Ryan)—both played much of their careers for teams with paltry offenses—and of course strike-outs, with all-time leader Ryan having 2,074 more than Seaver, who is sixth all-time (3,640). So even with hindsight in full force, that 40-year-old decision to use Seaver full bore and keep Ryan in reserve seems wise indeed. Wiser still would have been keeping Ryan in New York and never trading him for Jim Fregosi.

# Beware of Moose
## Buc No-Hits '69 Mets

by Bruce Markusen

As great a season as the Mets crafted in 1969, New York's offense sometimes struggled to score runs—or even collect hits. That was never more evident than on September 20 that season, when the Mets faced a promising young right-hander for the rival Pittsburgh Pirates. When healthy, Bob Moose possessed an overpowering repertoire: a moving fastball, an effective curve, and an occasional knuckleball mixed in to throw hitters off balance.

In 1969, Moose was in the midst of his finest season as a major leaguer. After a rough stretch in May and June, Moose had enjoyed a terrific run in July and August, pitching at first in the bullpen before earning a promotion to the starting rotation. He entered the Saturday matinee with a record of 11–3 and an ERA of 3.18, facing Mets rookie Gary Gentry. The Mets had been swept by the Pirates in a doubleheader the previous night after having lost only once over a 14-game span. Things did not get any better for the Mets at Shea Stadium on a cool Saturday afternoon against Pittsburgh's 21-year-old right-hander.

Moose set down the first four Mets in order, all on groundouts. He experienced little trouble through the first five innings, allowing only a pair of walks, one to Ed Kranepool and the other to Ron Swoboda. Then came a watershed moment in the sixth inning. After striking out pinch hitter Jim Gosger (who was batting for Gentry) and retiring Tommie Agee on a groundout, Moose faced rookie third baseman Wayne Garrett. The left-handed hitting Garrett lofted a deep fly ball toward right field. The drive had all the earmarks of a an extra-base hit (a double at the least, and possibly a home run), but right fielder Roberto Clemente tracked the ball down before running into the Shea Stadium wall. It was vintage Clemente, allowing Moose to finish off the sixth inning with his no-hitter intact.

Energized by Clemente's effort and uplifted by a 3–0 lead (the Pirates scored three times in the third inning on one hit, one hit batter, two walks, and two wild pitches), Moose continued sailing. He picked up two more groundouts in the seventh, though he did breathe a sigh of relief when Ken Boswell hit a line drive right at Pirates second baseman Dave Cash. Then came the eighth, when Moose forged his strongest inning. He struck out the side, fanning Swoboda, J.C. Martin, and Bud Harrelson in succession. That gave Moose six strikeouts, his final total for the afternoon.

Thanks to an insurance run in the top of the ninth inning, Moose returned to the mound with a 4–0 lead (the same score Tom Seaver took to the ninth in his "Imperfect Game" at Shea in July). He prepared to face a pinch hitter in the pitcher's spot, followed by the top of the order, still a considerable task at hand needed to finish his masterpiece. Utilityman Rod Gaspar, called on to bat for reliever Tug McGraw, did not cooperate with Moose, drawing a leadoff walk. Having allowed his third base on balls of the afternoon, Moose then stiffened. He overpowered Agee, who popped up meekly to first base. Moose now faced Garrett, who had threatened the no-hitter with his sixth-inning drive that Clemente snagged. Pitching Garrett away, Moose induced a ground ball to third, with Richie Hebner taking the sure out at first base. That brought up Art Shamsky, one of the Mets' toughest outs against right-handed pitching. On his way to a career-best .300 season at the plate, Shamsky managed only a ground ball to second base. Cash flipped the ball to first baseman Al Oliver to finish the game—and the no-hitter.

For the 38,784 fans who had come out on Ladies Day for the chilly Saturday matinee, they had seen history. It would also mark the last no-hitter at Shea Stadium during the final 39 seasons at the pitcher-friendly ballpark. The only other no-hitter pitched there was Jim Bunning's perfect game during Shea's inaugural season, the first game of a Father's Day doubleheader with the Phillies on June 21, 1964. No Met ever pitched one at Shea Stadium or has thrown one any place else, for that matter. They are the longest tenured franchise to not have a no-hitter.

Moose's gem, however, barely paused the Mets on their road to destiny. The Mets swept the Pirates in a doubleheader the next day—returning the favor the Pirates had done in Friday night's twin bill—and starting a nine-game winning streak that included the NL East clincher in New York against St. Louis. The Mets did not lose again at Shea in 1969 after Moose's no-hitter, winning the last five regular-season games there, the NLCS clincher against Atlanta, and all three games against the Orioles in the World Series to cap the Miracle.

The 1969 no-hitter also represented the pinnacle of Moose's career. He would win his final two starts that season, sandwiched around a scoreless three-inning relief stint, to finish with a record of 14–3 and an ERA of 2.91. His .824 winning percentage led the league—43 points ahead of runner-up Seaver.

Seemingly born to be a Pirate, Robert Ralph Moose Jr. grew up just 15 miles from Forbes Field, throwing six no-hitters in high school and American Legion ball. He was drafted by his hometown club in the 18th round of the first major league draft in 1965 and made his pro debut in 1965 at age 17 with a 1.95 ERA that summer in Salem, Virginia. He moved right up the ladder and debuted while still a teen in 1967. While Moose possessed a live repertoire when healthy, he made more of an impression on his teammates with his workmanlike approach. The gritty pitching style of Moose, who never shied from taking the ball—either as a starter or a reliever—drew the admiration of other Pirates pitchers. "Bob came from the old school and was a hard worker," says former Pirates closer Dave Giusti, who played with Moose in Pittsburgh from 1970 until 1976. "When he had a sore arm, you'd never know it, because he still wanted to go out there and pitch."

Moose's willingness to pitch through pain might have cost him. Plagued by arm troubles in his later years with the Pirates, Moose's effectiveness fell into quick decline. He matched his 1969 ERA (2.91) while going 13–10 in 1972, but the everlasting image of him that year was his wild pitch in Cincinnati that ended the NLCS. After struggling through a 1–5 season in 1974 Moose evened his record at 2–2 the next year. After going 3–9 and lowering his ERA for the third straigh year in 1976, Moose's life would end suddenly. He died in a car accident on October 9, just a few days after the conclusion of the 1976 regular season. Moose perished on the day of his 29th birthday.

Giusti remembers hearing the news of Moose's passing. "In fact, we were down at Bill Mazeroski's golf tournament," says Giusti. "It was myself and [Pirates pitcher Jim] Rooker, and a few other guys on the ballclub who were down there. Yeah, I remember that. In fact, I got a call from Rooker. He had found out that Bob Moose was in an accident, so we went down and identified the body. It was an awful time."

Though still a young man, Moose had left a defined impression with the Pirates teammates. "He was a nice guy to be around," Giusti says. "He was kind of a maverick, too. He would be one of those guys that would start some stuff in the clubhouse, also. He had the Afro-type hairdo, and he would curl it, just to get on Dock Ellis's case. He'd try to find ways to get under people's skins, also."

For one day in 1969, Bob Moose found a way to imbed himself deeply in the skins of the eventual world champion Mets.

# Platoon... Halt!

by Matthew Silverman

The platoon system that became legend for the 1969 Mets was not in place when the team broke camp. The team's offense was porous enough—and personnel and needs shifted often enough—that manager Gil Hodges essentially used a different lineup combination every other day.

Rule 5 pick Wayne Garrett was the 25th man on the roster and the fourth option at third base to incumbent Ed Charles. "The Glider," coming off a year in which he led the club with 15 home runs, played every inning of the first seven games of the year at third base and batted .154 before Amos Otis started a couple of games there. Otis's uninspired play at the position inspired Hodges to put him in the outfield where he belonged, though he did not play there regularly. Kevin Collins got the next try at third base, but his batting average was down to .150 in early May when he was sent down (and eventually sent north to Montreal in the Donn Clendenon deal). Garrett made the team mainly because if he were demoted, the Mets would have had to offer him back to the Atlanta, the team they drafted him from (as per the rules of the Rule 5). He did not start at third base until May 4—he had started twice at second and once at shortstop. Red became the 40th Met to man the hot corner in the club's brief existence, a fraternity that would add almost 100 new members over the ensuing 40 years.

Ed Kranepool, on the other hand, was coming off a so-so season, yet he earned increased playing time at first base by hitting well over .300 for the first month. Cleon Jones began the season playing first base against lefties, with Ron Swoboda taking Jones's spot in left field. Rod Gaspar, who made the '69 club after just two years in the minor leagues, saw a lot of playing time in the early going. Art Shamsky's bad back helped Gaspar make the team out of spring training, and 23-year-old switch hitter wound up starting each of the team's first 10 games. Shamsky reclaimed his playing time upon his return in mid-May and platooned in right field with Swoboda. Gaspar remained with the team all season, however, and often entered games in eighth or ninth innings for defense or to pinch run. The acquisition of the much needed power bat of right-handed slugger Donn Clendenon on June 15 made him the first baseman...but only against lefties.

It was a system of trial and error. Though the mound had been lowered in response to the major league wide pitching dominance that crested in 1968, offense was still hard to come by for the Mets. They raised their batting average 14 points from '68, but it was still only .242 (league average was .250) and good for eighth place in a league that added two new teams in '69. Hodges squeezed every drop he could out of the team's offense and relied on the pitching. Mets pitchers held the league to a league-best .227 average and no other team in the league could match their miniscule 1.18 baserunners allowed per inning. The team's 2.99 ERA was second only to the Cardinals' 2.94.

Part of Hodges's lineup tinkering was the result of injuries and part was predicated by Bud Harrelson missing three weeks because of military commitments (during the Vietnam era the major leagues did not want to appear to be shielding players from service and many spent time at stateside bases during both the season and offseason). As a result, Ken Boswell, Bobby Pfeil, Al Weis, and Garrett moved around the infield and lineup as the need arose.

Hodges used 98 different batting orders during the 1969 regular season. Though the lineups were more stable in the postseason, the platoons were still strictly adhered to, and to good effect. The player used most often in the same spot in the batting order during the season was Tommie Agee in the leadoff spot. Hodges wrote his name there 93 times, yet seven other players took shots in the opening spot, including Harrelson 32 times. Though not part of a regular platoon, Pfeil still batted second more often than any other Met (32 times). Jones was the most oft-used hitter in both the third hole (54) and cleanup slot (73) in the batting order. Kranepool was the most frequently used batter in the fifth spot (40). Swoboda hit sixth 59 times, a half-dozen more times than Kranepool. The seventh spot saw more men used (14) than any other spot in the lineup, with Jerry Grote's name written there 81 times. Weis usually found himself in the eighth spot against lefties (69 times), while Harrelson often batted there against right-handers (61).

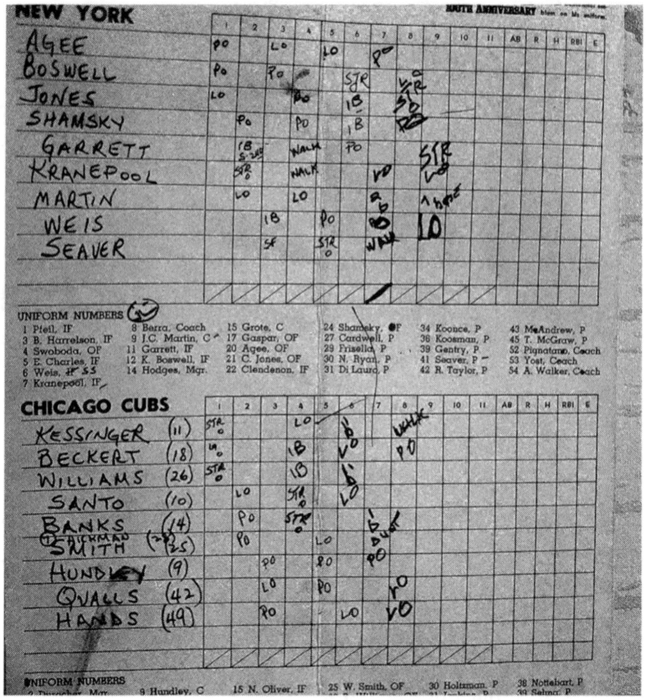

*In this scorecard from July 14, 1969, with Cubs righty Bill Hands on the mound, the Mets use lefty swingers Ken Boswell, Art Shamsky, Wayne Garrett, and Ed Kranepool. With Al Weis filling in at shortstop for Bud Harrelson and J.C. Martin giving Jerry Grote a day off, Tommie Agee and Cleon Jones are the only everyday players starting in support of Tom Seaver, who wound up a 1–0 loser.*

Photo courtesy of metsilverman.com

The pitcher's spot was one place where those scoring at home could find blessed regularity. Only eight pitchers started for the Mets all season. Tom Seaver and Gary Gentry made 35 turns of the rotation apiece, Jerry Koosman had 32 starts, while Don Cardwell and Jim McAndrew had 21 apiece in Rube Walker's novel five-man rotation. Nolan Ryan, who also had to pitch around military commitments that summer, made 10 starts. Tug McGraw and Jack DiLauro started four times each.

Critics of the Cubs—including some of the team's players—blamed Leo Durocher's penchant for running out the same lineup every day for wearing down the club and costing Chicago a lead that had stood at 10 games in mid-August. The Mets did not have the star power the Cubs could provide in an everyday lineup, but the Mets were certainly rested. While Randy Hundley caught the first 68 games of the year for the Cubs—including both games of a doubleheader seven times in that span (he would do double duty a dozen times in '69)—only outfielder Cleon Jones played anywhere close to 60 consecutive games to start the season for the Mets. The most frequently-used Hodges lineup in 1969 (not taking the pitcher into account) was used just five times and included J.C. Martin behind the plate as opposed to regular catcher Jerry Grote:

1. Agee
2. Garrett
3. Boswell
4. Jones
5. Shamsky
6. Kranepool
7. Martin
8. Harrelson
9. Pitcher

Pennant.

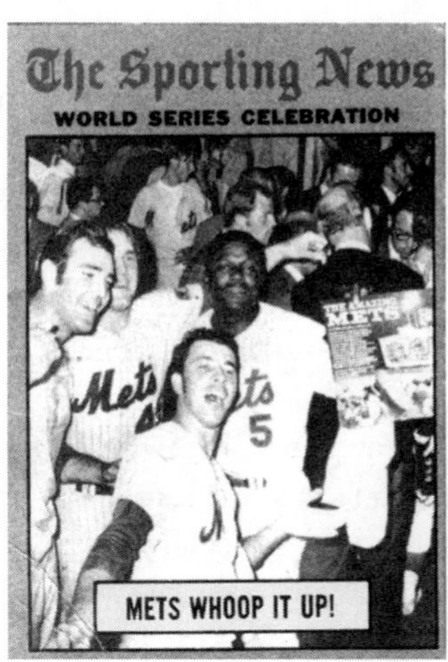


# October '69
## The Miracle at Willets Point

by Ron Kaplan

If you had asked fans prior to the 1969 baseball season which scenario was more likely—man landing on the moon or the New York Mets wining the world championship—they would probably have been hard-pressed to choose, both being equally improbable. Casey Stengel, original Mets manager and overseer of the ugliest launching of a franchise in the 20th century, often made the correlation between a champion in Flushing and a man on the moon. Who would've thought Casey would be right?

When Gil Hodges was named manager in 1968, he made it clear that the team's legendary ineptitude would no longer be acceptable. He then led them to the best season in their short history: 73–89 and a ninth-place finish (although just one game above the last-place Houston Astros). With a cadre of young stars including Tom Seaver, Jerry Koosman, Jerry Grote, Tommie Agee, Cleon Jones, and Bud Harrelson, backed by a strong bench, Mets fans looked forward to a promising future. They just didn't expect it to happen so quickly.

The 1969 season didn't get off to a great start: the Mets lost to the expansion Montreal Expos, 11–10 on Opening Day. (By contrast to the nouveau Expos, it took the Mets 10 tries before they won their first game in their first year as a franchise.) By the end of April, New York was 9–11, good by Mets standards, but not good enough for their skipper. On May 31, they were still below .500, but they had embarked on the 11-game winning streak that turned everything around. The Mets won 19 of 28 games in June, though they were still 7½ games behind Chicago. The Mets won two series against the Cubs in July—including Tom Seaver's "Imperfect Game" at Shea Stadium, but still stood 6½ games out at the end of the month. Though they slipped all the way to 10 games back, the Mets flourished in the dog days of August and on into September, winning 37 of their final 48 games.

Mets pitchers were dominant, but the offense was less potent. Agee led the team with 26 home runs and 76 RBIs while his boyhood friend Cleon Jones finished third in the league with a .340 batting average, the highest to that time in Mets history...by 37 points.

If their remarkable achievement had come a year earlier, the Mets would have advanced directly to the World Series. But the addition of two teams to each league inaugurated a new round of playoffs: the League Championship Series. For the Mets to advance to the fall classic, they would have beat the veteran-filled Atlanta Braves of Hank Aaron, Phil Niekro, Orlando Cepeda, Rico Carty, and company.

Because the focus fell on the Mets' unlikely success, fans tend to forget how well the Braves did in 1969. They had not appeared in the postseason since losing to the Yankees in the 1958 World Series, when they called Milwaukee home. The 93-win Braves were third in the league with 141 home runs (led by Aaron's 44) and fifth in runs per game. Their pitching was also strong, Niekro was second to in the NL to Tom Seaver in wins (23), and Ron Reed, a 6-foot-6 former Detroit Pistons forward, chipped in 18 victories. Pat Jarvis and George Stone won 13 apiece.

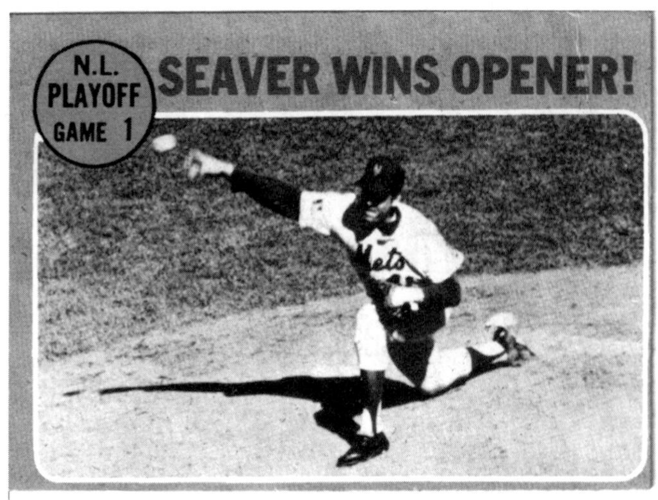


*A 9–5 win over Atlanta starts the postseason.*

Hodges was relatively modest, picking his team to take the playoff to the five-game limit. The oddsmakers didn't even give the Mets that much credit. The Braves were made 13-10 favorites in Las Vegas, despite going 4–8 against the Mets during the regular season. Only Jones and Art Shamsky batted over .300 for the year on a team that only hit .242, a mark the Braves bettered by 16 points. The Braves bettered the Mets in virtually every offensive category and slugger Hank Aaron led the league in total bases and extra-base hits while finishing one behind Willie McCovey for the NL lead with 44 homers. Pitching was the Mets' strong suit: first in shutouts (28) and fewest hits allowed (1,217), second in the league in ERA (2.99), and third in saves (35).

The Braves were to host the first two games of the best-of-five National League Championship Series. Many sports pundits expected the bubble to burst on the Miracle Mets.

### Game One, October 4

*For a Change, the Hitters Cover for Seaver*

If the Mets were nervous, it wasn't evident. In the second inning, Art Shamsky singled off Phil Niekro, who then walked second baseman Ken Boswell. Ed Kranepool, the last of the original Mets from 1962, struck out, but Jerry Grote, the team's All-Star catcher, singled in Shamsky with the first postseason run in Mets history. With Boswell on third, Niekro's knuckler eluded rookie catcher Bob Didier for a passed ball as the Mets took a 2–0 lead.

In Atlanta's half of the inning, Rico Carty, a perennial .300 hitter, doubled to left and moved to third as Boswell misplayed Orlando Cepeda's grounder. Former Yankee Clete Boyer drove in the Braves' first run with a sacrifice fly. Atlanta took a 3–2 lead in the bottom of the third on consecutive doubles by Felix Millan, Tony Gonzalez (a midseason pickup from the San Diego Padres), and Hank Aaron.

But the Mets answered immediately with a single by Kranepool, a Grote walk, and a Bud Harrelson triple to right, putting them back on top, 4–3. Gonzalez led off the bottom of the fifth with a home run to deadlock the contest and Aaron homered two innings later to give Atlanta a 5–4 lead. Their elation was short-lived.

In the top of the eighth, third baseman Wayne Garrett, a "Howdy Doody" look-alike plucked from Atlanta's farm system by the Mets in the Rule 5 draft, doubled to left field. He came in on a single by Cleon Jones. Shamsky's third hit on the afternoon moved Jones to second. After he stole third, Boswell hit a sharp grounder to the veteran Cepeda, who foolishly tried to nab the speedy Jones at the plate, but the throw was wild and Jones scored New York's sixth run. Gil Hodges sent in Al Weis to run for Shamsky, and the slow-footed Kranepool managed to keep out of a double play, setting the stage for an improbable hero.

J.C. Martin, a left-handed hitting catcher, had come over to the Mets from the Chicago White Sox in November 1967 as the player to be named later in the Ken Boyer trade. With Grote firmly in place as the number one backstop—and rookie Duffy Dyer working his way into a backup catching role—Martin started just 44 games in 1969. Hodges sent Martin up to bat for Seaver, who hadn't enjoyed a Cy Young-type day. Martin delivered a bases-clearing hit—abetted by a Gonzalez error—to ice the game, 9–5. Ron Taylor came on in relief for the final two innings, yielding two hits in the bottom of the ninth before getting Cepeda to pop up to second for the final out.

### Game Two, October 5
*Leaving Atlanta and Laughing*

Tommie Agee, who had gone hitless in the NLCS opener, singled against Ron Reed to begin the festivities on day two. He continued his tour of the bases with a walk to Wayne Garrett, taking second on a steal of third, another Reed walk, and a clutch single by Ed Kranepool with two out.

Bud Harrelson lined out to open the second, but Jerry Koosman—who batted an anemic .048 in 84 at-bats—worked out a walk, to the disgust of Braves fans. That came back to haunt Reed as Agee followed with a home run, the first postseason homer in Mets history. After Garrett grounded back to the pitcher, Cleon Jones doubled and Art Shamsky drove him in with a single to right; he ended up on third base after Tony Gonzalez's error in center field. That was it for Reed, who was charged with four earned runs in 1⅔ innings. Reliever Paul Doyle didn't fare much better; the Mets added two more runs off the 30-year-old lefty in the third inning. After Kranepool struck out, Orlando Cepeda booted Jerry Grote's ground ball for another miscue. Harrelson drove in the catcher with a double to left. Koosman followed with a strikeout and the Braves decided to walk Agee intentionally, but the strategy backfired when Garrett singled to center, plating Harrelson. Out with Doyle, in with veteran Milt Pappas. The Mets added two more in the fourth when Shamsky single was followed by Ken Boswell home run.

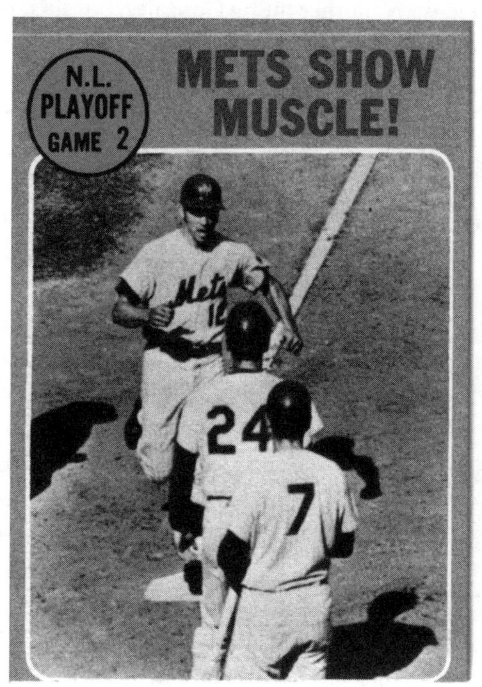

*Runs to spare in an 11–6 win.*

The Braves, however, didn't get this far because they were quitters. They had rallied from fourth place and three games back in early September to win the NL West by that same margin. Rico Carty doubled to right and came in on a Cepeda single against Koosman in the fourth inning for Atlanta's first run of the game. The next inning, after the Mets made it 9–1, the Braves exploded for four tallies, all after two were out. After a Millan single and a walk to Gonzalez, Hank Aaron blasted a three-run home run; Koosman was starting to lose steam. He walked Carty and gave up a double to Cepeda; both came around on Clete Boyer's single. Gil Hodges replaced Koosman with Ron Taylor, the only Met with previous postseason experience (as a member of the St. Louis Cardinals in the 1964 World Series).

The Mets weren't finished either. Facing Cecil Upshaw in the top of the seventh, Agee walked, stole second, and advanced to third on a fly ball by Garrett. Jones came up to the plate now and Agee had the idea of trying to steal home. Unfortunately, no one told the batter, who swung and hit a vicious line drive at the head of the oncoming runner, who miraculously avoided the ball. After a collective sigh of relief, Jones made things much easier a minute later when he hit a home run to put the game on ice, 11–6. Tug McGraw picked up a three-inning save in what would be his only postseason action of 1969. Taylor was credited with the victory.

### Game Three, October 6
*A Pennant in Three Easy Steps*

In his 2004 memoir, *The Magnificent Seasons*, Art Shamsky recalled the emotions he and his teammates felt when they arrived in Atlanta. "It's men against boys," he wrote. Even with the first game in the bag, Shamsky said the Mets were still worried. But once back in New York, amidst the familiar surroundings and loving fans—they relaxed, and when

*Reliever Nolan Ryan pitches the Mets to their first pennant, 7–4.*

they won, "It was pandemonium." Again. The year had begun with the Jets winning a Super Bowl and shocking the establishment almost as much as the Mets would during the baseball season—by the following spring, the Knicks would also be world champions for the first time. All those championships culminating in a short period were important to New York City and a nation still reeling from the assassinations of Robert Kennedy and Martin Luther King, Jr., as well as fiscal difficulties and social unrest of the end of the 1960s.

With no time off in the NCLS in 1969, the series resumed in New York the next day. A Monday afternoon crowd of 54,195 squeezed into Shea Stadium for the third game, which pitted Gary Gentry, the Mets' unheralded rookie third starter, against Pat Jarvis. Both righties had won 13 games for their respective teams, but Jarvis, at 28, already had four major league campaigns under his belt.

Despite being the second-youngest pitcher on the staff after Nolan Ryan, Gentry—who was making the start on his 23rd birthday—was no greenhorn. He had allowed just 192 hits in 234 innings, which would prove to be his career-best. In fact, he had just one more season in which he pitched more than 200 innings; he was out of the majors by 1975, finishing his career with—of all teams—the Atlanta Braves.

Gentry erased Felix Millan on a fly ball to lead off the game, but Tony Gonzalez singled and Hank Aaron followed with his third homer of the NCLS, giving the Braves a 2–0 lead. Gentry made it through the second inning with just a walk, but he didn't retire a batter in the third. That inning started with another hit by Gonzalez, but this time Aaron merely doubled, moving the runner to third. When Rico Carty drove a liner that was just foul of the left-field foul pole, Hodges decided he'd seen enough, lifting Gentry with a one-ball, two-strike count on the batter and calling in the fireballing but erratic Nolan Ryan.

The future Hall of Famer had a 6–3 record in 25 games, 15 of which came as a reliever. He struck out 92 batters in 89 innings, allowing just 60 hits while walking 53. In Peter Golenbock's *Amazin': The Mi-*

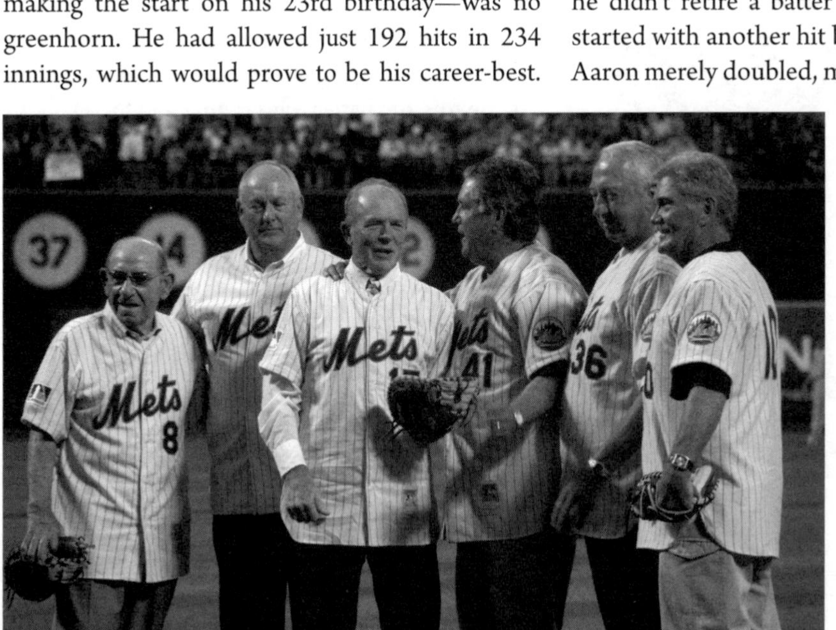


Photo courtesy of Dan Carubia

*Plenty of battery left for the heroes of 1969 in 2009: Yogi Berra, Nolan Ryan, Jerry Grote, Tom Seaver, Jerry Koosman, and Duffy Dyer.*

*raculous History of New York's Most Beloved Baseball Team,* Ron Swoboda recalled the team's surprise at the manager's move. "When he brought him in I thought, 'This is interesting.'" Jerry Koosman went further: "The whole bench said, 'If he's bringing in Ryan, Gil has given up.'"

But, in fact, Ryan was superb. He blew a third strike past Carty, walked Orlando Cepeda intentionally to load the bases, caught Clete Boyer on a called strikeout, and finally retired Bob Didier on a fly ball. Ryan had kept the Braves off the scoreboard in the third and the Mets responded quickly when Tommie Agee hit his second NLCS homer in the bottom of the inning.

Shamsky started a rally in the fourth with his series-high seventh single. He crossed the plate on Ken Boswell's second playoff home run to give the Mets a 3–2 lead. Though the Braves regained the lead on a two-run Cepeda home run in the top of the fifth, Hodges left Ryan in to bat and the pitcher led off the bottom of the inning with a single. He scored on Wayne Garrett's just-fair four-bagger for a 5–4 lead. Jones singled and scored on another hit by Boswell, his third RBI of the game. They added their final run in the sixth on a double by Jerry Grote and a single by Agee.

The Braves never mounted another serious threat. Ryan's third inning heroics had proved the turning point. Gonzalez ended Atlanta's suffering by grounding to third for the final out of the playoffs. In seven innings, Ryan allowed just three hits, walked two, and struck out seven to pick up the victory that propelled the Mets into their first World Series.

In the three-game sweep, the Mets outscored the Braves 27–15, batting an improbable .327, led by Shamsky's .538; Jones, Garrett, Agee, and Boswell all batted .333 or better. Koosman told Golenbock, "The tension of the world was on us. Everybody wanted to be on the bandwagon. [Governor Nelson] Rockefeller and [New York Mayor John V.] Lindsay and numerous big names were suddenly appearing in the clubhouse."

Despite public address pleas, Mets fans stormed the field for the second time in three weeks, threatening to destroy the diamond in their frenzied joy, wanting a fistful or grass or dirt as a souvenir to mark this most amazing season. "The management might just have well have spared the voltage for the speaker system," wrote Norm Miller in the *New York Daily News.* Yet the excitement didn't seem to match that of the NL East pennant-clincher against the St. Louis Cardinals. "The main difference was that the first time we had done something nobody believed we could do," Shamsky said during the locker room celebration. What thrilled him the most were the contributions from players like Boswell and Garrett, who were now receiving overdue recognition for their work. "We've been that way all year," he said. "If one guy didn't [come through], another did."

*The young Mets quickly learned how to win...and how to celebrate.*

### The 66th World Series

While the Mets were marching for their league's pennant, the Baltimore Orioles were doing the same. The Orioles, who had upset the Los Angeles Dodgers by sweeping them in the 1966 fall classic, finished sixth in 1967 and in second place in 1968. They roared back in 1969, winning 109 games and finishing 19 ahead of second-place Detroit in Earl Weaver's first full season as a major league manager.

Baltimore's squad boasted the AL Cy Young Award co-winner, Mike Cuellar, one of three Orioles who finished in the top 10 in AL MVP voting (Boog Powell and Frank Robinson were second and third, respectively, to Minnesota Twin Harmon Killebrew for MVP). Six players—Powell, Frank and Brooks Robinson, Paul Blair, Davey Johnson, and Dave McNally—appeared in the All-Star Game that summer. As a team, they were second only to the Minnesota Twins in batting average and third to the Red Sox in home runs. Yet they were a disciplined lot, striking out a league-low 806 times and working out 634 walks (second most).

Defensively, the Orioles were without peer, finishing first in fielding percentage and committing the fewest errors (101) of any team in the game. The pitching staff—led by McNally, Mike Cuellar, and Jim Palmer—had the only ERA under 3.00 and gave up the fewest home runs (117) and walks (498).

The Orioles faced the American League West champion Twins in the ALCS and, like the Mets, swept the series. The first two games, played in Baltimore, were tight affairs: 4–3 in 12 innings and 1–0 in 11. In the Metropolitan Stadium finale, the brawny Orioles busted loose, with Jim Palmer scattering 10 hits in an 11–2 romp.

So it was no surprise that the Orioles were the favorites in the 66th World Series. Maybe it was a sense of bravado, but some of the Mets and the New York media predicted a sweep for the home team, including Cleon Jones and Casey Stengel, the original Mets skipper, who was penning a guest column. Phil Pepe of the *New York Daily News* wrote, "The Mets are behind. They're behind in hitting, fielding, pitching, running, and betting. But they haven't lost yet. Not yet they haven't."

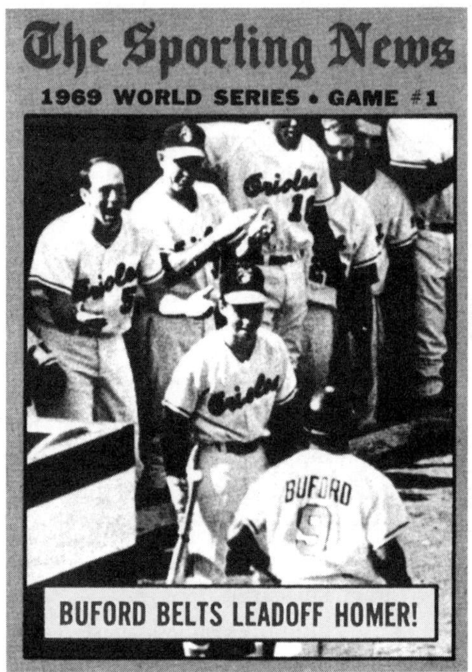


*O's look as good as advertised in 4–1 win.*

Earl Weaver, Baltimore's Napoleonic manager, told reporters the Mets had "two pitchers, some slap hitters, and a little speed. They say the Mets have desire. The Orioles have just as much desire and a lot more talent."

After watching Rod Gaspar, a bench player reveling in the NLCS victory glow, predict a sweep, Frank Robinson challenged, "Bring on Ron Gaspar." A teammate corrected him, "Not Ron, *Rod*, stupid."

"Okay, bring on Ron Stupid," Robinson responded.

He would come to regret that remark.

## Game One, October 11

*Not the Way to Start Things Off*

The two eventual Cy Young winners faced off in the first game at Memorial Stadium in Baltimore on a brilliant fall Saturday afternoon in front of 50,429 fans, shy of a full house. The World Series was indeed a showcase, not just for players, but celebrity fans as well. Commissioner Bowie Kuhn threw out the first two pitches, one to each starting catcher. Several members of the First Family, including Pat Nixon, daughters Julie and Tricia, and Tricia's husband, David Eisenhower, were in attendance.

Tom Seaver had become the first pitcher in National League history to defeat 11 different clubs in a season—a mark made possible by expansion and Chicago's Ferguson Jenkins also beat all 11 clubs in 1969—but Seaver was not his usual polished self in his first game against an American League foe. After the Mets went down in the top of the first, Don Buford, Baltimore's leadoff hitter, took a Seaver pitch over the right-field fence for a home run. That lone tally held up until the fourth inning when Seaver—as he had done in the NLCS opener Atlanta—had an uncharacteristic inning. He retired Boog Powell and Brooks Robinson, but he had trouble finding that third out. Catcher Elrod Hendricks singled to right, followed by a walk to Davey Johnson. Mark Belanger, one of the Orioles unsung heroes, singled to right, driving in Hendricks and moving Johnson to third.

Pitcher Mike Cuellar, who batted .117 with a double and two triples during the season, blooped a single to left-center to score Johnson. With runners now on first and second, Buford came through again, lining a double down the right field line to score Belanger to the Orioles up, 4-0.

In the meantime, Brooks Robinson, one of four Birds who would win a Gold Glove that season, was making his reputation on the national scene with several sparkling plays at third base behind a cruising Cuellar. Seaver set the Orioles down without a hit in the fifth, but he was due to lead off in the sixth. Hodges batted rookie Duffy Dyer for him and the veteran Don Cardwell came in to pitch the bottom of the inning. Cardwell and Ron Taylor kept the Orioles off the scoreboard the rest of the game, but it proved too late.

The Mets had an opportunity to do some damage in the seventh. Donn Clendenon, who came over from the Expos in a June trade, and hit 12 home runs, and drove in 37 as a Met, singled to center and Ron Swoboda walked. After Ed Charles flied out to right, Grote lined a single to left to load the bases. (Clendenon, Swoboda, and Charles had not appeared in a single game of the NLCS because Atlanta had thrown all right-handed pitchers and Hodges adhered to his platoon system.) Al Weis's sacrifice fly to left scored Clendenon but Gaspar, batting for Cardwell, hit a slow roller to third that Robinson turned into one of his patented bare-handed-pickup, throw-on-the-run plays to end the threat.

The Mets had one more chance in the ninth, but with two out and two on, Shamsky grounded out to Johnson to end the game "I had a chance to be a hero, but it didn't work out that way," he told Stanley Cohen in *A Magic Summer*. Shamsky had also made the final out in the September 20 no-hitter by Bob Moose of the Pittsburgh Pirates, one of the few blotches on an otherwise fantastic season.

After the game, Earl Weaver shared his impressions with the media. "They're about what we

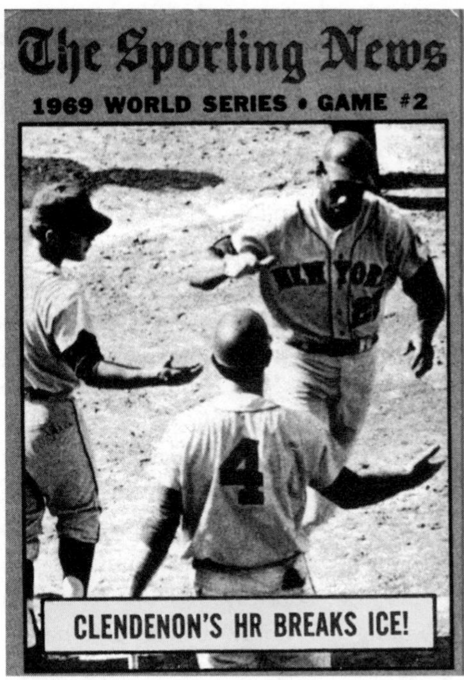


*The Mets even the Series with a 2–1 win.*

expected," he said. "Of course, they have to have more than they showed us today. They must have something because they did win 100 games in that big beautiful National League, didn't they?" Weaver admitted his comments could be construed as sarcastic.

The media played up disparaging remarks made by Weaver, Frank Robinson, and others. Brooks Robinson recalled beating a Los Angeles Dodgers team led by Sandy Koufax and Don Drysdale, "and [Seaver and Koosman] can't be as good as them." He also suggested that "New York ballplayers are built up more than they are."

A scout for the team scoffed, "Team of destiny? I think they're destined to be beaten by the Orioles." But Paul Blair, Baltimore's fleet center fielder (and a former Mets farmhand) had some nice things to say, even as he expressed confidence in his mates. He told reporters he respected Seaver, Koosman, and Gentry, as well as Jones and Agee, "Bad ballclubs don't win 100 games, sweep three from Atlanta, and get to the Series. But we have a better ballclub."

Yes, on paper the Orioles were stronger at just about every position and so were made the "logical favorites" over the Mets. As Leonard Koppett of the

*New York Times* opined, "'Logic' is another name for past performance. But in the four-of-seven game competition that will be watched so intently by millions of television viewers in this country and abroad, history won't count."

### Game Two, October 12
*Kooz's Gem*

Jerry Koosman had a reputation of coming up big in clutch situations. He was the first Met to win a home opener, a 3–0 blanking of the San Francisco Giants in the second start of his rookie year in 1968. The second game of the World Series meant a lot more and Kooz kept the powerful Orioles hitters in check over the first six innings, nursing a one-run lead, courtesy of Donn Clendenon's fourth-inning solo home run. He also hadn't allowed a hit.

In the bottom of the seventh, Paul Blair broke up the no-hit bid with a single to left to start the inning. After outs by Frank Robinson and Boog Powell, Blair stole second and crossed the plate moments later on a single by Brooks Robinson to tie the game.

With two outs in the top of the ninth, Ed Charles, the proclaimed "soul" of the team, singled to left and moved to third on Grote's second hit of the afternoon. With Koosman waiting on deck, McNally pitched to Al Weis. The second baseman's single to left drove in Charles for the slim lead. Rather than put up a pinch hitter, Gil Hodges let Koosman bat for himself, and he made the third out.

The lefty recorded two quick outs in the bottom of the inning before walking Frank Robinson and Powell. Hodges signaled to the bullpen and brought in Ron Taylor, who induced Brooks Robinson to ground out to third for the final out and the first World Series victory in Mets history.

After the game, Mets owner Joan Payson told the press she had covered her eyes when Brooksie hit the final ball. As the media is wont to do, they looked for some angle to spice things up a bit. They found it in a "war of words" between Hodges, the Mets no-nonsense manager, and the equally intense Frank Robinson.

After the game, Robby said he had been surprised by the Mets' low profile on the bench. "I thought it was very strange that they didn't show any enthusiasm when they loaded the bases in the seventh inning [the game before]," he said. Appraised of the ballplayer's remarks, Hodges countered, "I'm glad that Frank is watching our bench, but I'm not concerned with what he says."

So the reporters ran back to Robinson for *his* comments. "Tell Hodges he should manage his club and I'll play right field." But he had one more parting shot at winning pitcher Jerry Koosman. "He didn't exactly dazzle us with his stuff. We hit the ball well 10 or 12 times, but they went right to somebody. If three balls fell in, we could have scored three or four runs."

### Game Three, October 14
*Two for the Price of One*

After a day off, the scene shifted to New York for the third game. The atmosphere, to say the least, was different as the World Series returned to the Big Apple for the first time since 1964, and the first time a National League team had hosted a Series in New York since the Brooklyn Dodgers in 1956.

Gary Gentry, who hadn't made it out of the third inning against the Braves in the NLCS, was

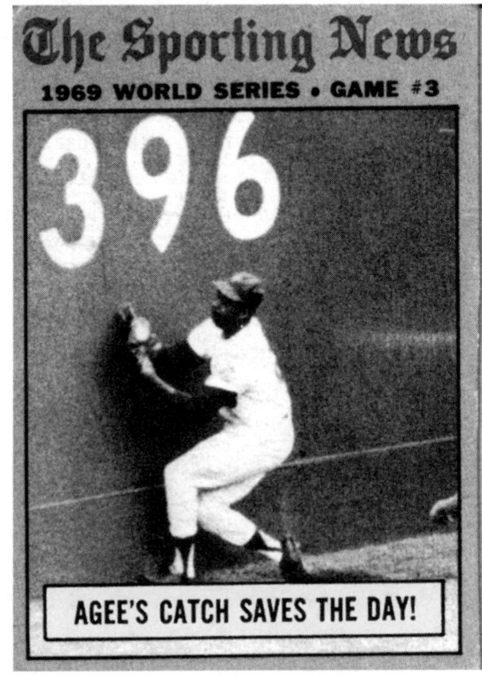


*Tommie Agee 5, Baltimore Orioles 0.*

on the mound for the Mets. Jim Palmer, who threw the AL's only no-hitter that season, an 8–0 gem against the Oakland A's on August 13, took the hill in Game Three of the Series for Baltimore. This time the rookie shut down the opposition, allowing just three hits (but five walks) in 6⅔ innings. Just as happened in the NLCS, he was relieved by Nolan Ryan, who got out of a jam that threatened to change the complexion of the game. Ryan struck out three, walked two, and gave up just one hit for the rest of the game to pick up the save. Unlike his brief NLCS outing, Gentry did more than his share with both his arm and his bat.

In the second inning, with runners on first and second and two outs, Gentry, who had batted .081 during the regular season, doubled over a drawn-in Blair in center field to drive in both runners and give the Mets a 3–0 lead. Palmer said after the game that Baltimore's scouting reports had "underestimated" Gentry's hitting and pitching abilities.

*Another 2–1 win, another amazin' finish.*

The real story, however, was not the sparkling contributions of Gentry or Ryan. In fact, most fans might have a hard time remembering who pitched that day. They would not forget Tommie Agee's contributions. Agee and Al Weis had come to the Mets in a trade with the White Sox in December 1967 for former batting champion Tommy Davis, pitcher "Fat Jack" Fisher, and two other players. Agee was just two years removed from winning the AL Rookie of the Year Award and finishing in the top 10 for MVP, but he hit an anemic .217 with just 17 RBIs in his inaugural season with the Mets. The 1969 season was far better to him... and the Mets.

Just as Don Buford had done against Tom Seaver in the first game in Baltimore, Agee greeted Palmer with a leadoff home run in the home first. Agee's blast to center field was his only offensive contribution, but he did more with soft leather than hard wood.

Sandy Amoros, Al Gionfriddo, Kirby Puckett, Willie Mays. All of these made eye-popping catchers in their World Series. Agee did it twice... and in the same game. The first came in the fourth inning. With one out, Frank Robinson and Boog Powell singled. Brooks Robinson struck out to bring up Elrod Hendricks. Agee shaded the left-handed hitter to pull, but Hendricks lined a shot to the gap in left-center. Agee took off and snow-coned the gapper for the third out at the 396-foot mark. He put his hand up against the wall with the ball to stop himself. The man who hit the ball missed one of the great catches in World Series history. "I didn't see him catch it," Hendricks told reporters. "I look up and I see the white of the ball in his glove and I figured he still might drop it. Then he holds his glove up and I just said, 'Damn.'"

After Jerry Grote doubled to drive in the fourth run for the Mets in the home sixth, Agee came to the rescue once more in the top of the seventh. The Orioles mounted a two-out threat as Gentry walked Belanger, Dave May (pinch-hitting for Palmer), and Buford to load the bases. Hodges brought in Ryan, who was known to walk a batter or two himself.

Blair smacked a Ryan fastball to right-center. Agee sprinted, dove, and came up with the sinking liner on his belly on the warning track. Blair said later that the catch saved four runs, confident that he would have had an inside-the-park homer to tie the game had the ball gotten past Agee. Hodges, who had played in seven Word Series as a member of the Dodgers, assessed Agee's work that afternoon.

"I'd have to say the second [catch] was number one of any World Series I've seen." Agee downplayed his performance, calling the first one the tougher of the two. "It was away from my glove and it almost went through my webbing."

The Mets got their final run in the eighth inning when Ed Kranepool homered off Dave Leonhard. By then the Orioles were a little stunned, having been hit head-on by a Miracle.

## Game Four, October 15

*Victory Most 'Fair'*

Tom Seaver had shaken off the leg injury that hampered him against Atlanta and in the World Series opener. He revealed he had strained a left calf muscle while shagging fly balls during batting practice in Atlanta and that kept him from following his normal workout routine, leaving him more fatigued. But this time Tom Terrific was on top of his game.

In the bottom of the second, with Mike Cuellar once again his opponent, Donn Clendenon hit his second solo shot of the World Series. The Orioles had a good chance to score in the third inning, when Mark Belanger and Cuellar opened the frame with singles. Belanger moved to third on Don Buford's forceout to second. Paul Blair bunted back to Seaver, who threw him out for the second out while holding Belanger at third. Frank Robinson fouled out to Clendenon to end the inning.

The score remained 1–0 until the top of the ninth. After Blair flied out to right, Frank Robinson singled to left and scampered to third on Boog Powell's single to right. Brooks Robinson hit a rocket to right that turned into another Amazin' play by a Mets outfielder. This time it was Ron Swoboda to the rescue. "Rocky" was not known for his smooth defense, but he made a running, flat-out dive to his right on the sinking drive. Frank Robinson tagged up and scored on the play to tie the game, but if Swoboda had missed the ball, it would have given the Orioles the lead and potentially changed the Series. Instead, momentum stayed with the Mets.

New York had an opportunity to finish things off in regulation. With Eddie Watt on the mound for the Orioles, Jones singled with one out. After Clendenon struck out, Swoboda singled to move Jones to third. Gil Hodges called on Art Shamsky, one of the heroes of the NLCS, to pinch-hit for Charles, but Watt got him on a grounder to second to move the contest into extra innings.

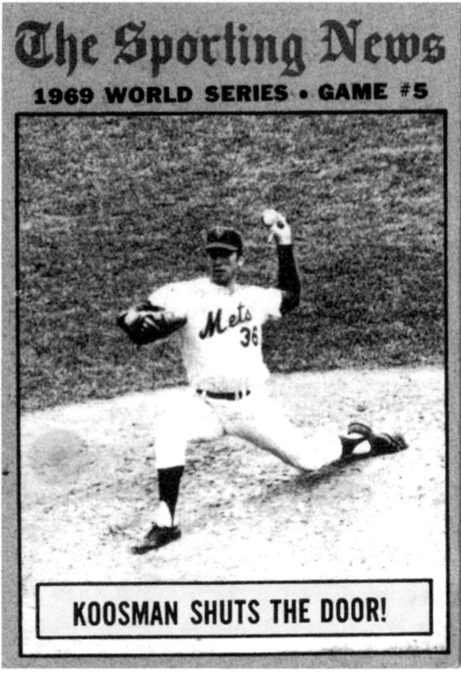


*Mets 5, O's 3. Do you believe in miracles?*

In the top of the 10th with Seaver still on the hill, Johnson reached first on Wayne Garrett's bobble. Belanger fouled out to Grote to bring up Clay Dalrymple to bat for Watt. His single moved Johnson to second and a fly ball out by Buford put him on third base. Seaver ended his afternoon's work by striking out Blair.

In the bottom of the frame, Grote greeted new pitcher Dick Hall with a fly to left that Buford misjudged and turned into a double. After Rod—not Ron—Gaspar came on to run for Grote, the Orioles walked Al Weis—normally a weak batter but he had two hits in the game and had won Game 2 with a late-inning single—to set up the possible double play. With lefty-swinging J.C. Martin out to bat for Seaver, the Orioles went with southpaw Pete Richert. The moves were made by coach Billy Hunter, managing in place of Weaver, who had been ejected by home plate umpire Shag Crawford for arguing balls and strikes. Weaver became the first manager to be so ignominiously treated since Cubs manager Charlie Grimm was booted in the 1935 Series.

What would be Martin's only appearance in a World Series was the latest installment in the Mets' Miracle Motif. Martin laid down a bunt on the first-base side of the mound. Richert and Hendricks converged and the pitcher came up with the ball. Richert turned and fired to first, but the throw hit Martin in the left wrist and caromed away. Gaspar, meanwhile, came all the way around to score, perhaps answering Frank Robinson's earlier jibes.

Photographs later revealed that Martin had been just inside the runner's lane and could have been called out for interference. Richert had witnessed it first hand and continued arguing as the Mets celebrated. The call stood and more than 57,000 at Shea Stadium roared. What else could possibly happen at Shea to top this?

### Game Five, October 16

*Man Steps on the Moon… Leaving a Shoe Polish Mark*

The fifth game featured Jerry Koosman and Dave McNally in a rematch of Game 2. There was a lack of offensive action until the third inning, and it came from an unlikely source. After Mark Belanger, the number eight batter, led off with a single, Koosman committed a cardinal sin: he served up a home run to the opposing pitcher. McNally had batted just .085 in 1969, but one of his eight hits was a home run—and he'd hit three in 1968. Two outs later after McNally's blast, Frank Robinson launched a home run of his own, his only extra base hit of the Series, to make the score 3–0. In one inning the Orioles had scored more runs than they had in three games. Could this be the turnaround of the Series?

The answer came in the bottom of the sixth inning. Cleon Jones led off by dancing away from a pitch in the dirt. It rolled over to the Mets dugout and moments later manager Gil Hodges picked it up and calmly walked out to home plate umpire Lou DiMuro. (See Jerry Koosman biography for his account of what happened during the few seconds after the ball caromed into the dugout.)

Hodges pointed out a dark smudge on the ball from Jones's shoe polish, apparent proof that he had been hit by the pitch. DiMuro waved Jones to first base. Donn Clendenon followed the lucky break with this third home run—a shot over the left-field wall—to bring the Mets to within one.

In the top of that very inning, Frank Robinson thought he had been nicked in the thigh by a Koosman pitch and trotted down to first before he was called back by DiMuro. He argued long and hard, but the umpire denied the claim. To no one's surprise, Earl Weaver popped out for a chat, but since he was still smarting from the previous day's ejection, he kept the conversation accordingly civil. He was more animated after Jones was sent to first in the bottom of the inning, but it just wasn't his day.

The Shoe Polish Incident reminded old-timers of another situation involving a Jones—in this case "Nippy" of the Milwaukee Braves. In Game Four of the 1957 World Series, with the Braves trailing the New York Yankees 5–4 in the bottom of the 10th inning, shoe polish again served as proof that a batter had been hit by a pitch after the home plate umpire had initially ruled differently. Jones was replaced by a pinch runner who scored on a double by Johnny Logan and Eddie Mathews hit a game-winning two-

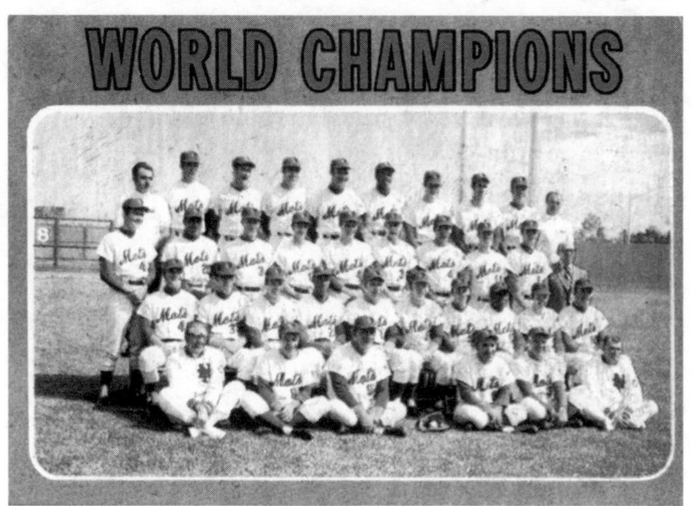


*The Miracle Has Landed.*

run homer. The Braves would go on to beat the Yankees in seven games.

The 1969 Mets were not done with unlikely plot twists. During the regular season, Al Weis had batted a measly .215 with only two home runs, both of which came in consecutive games at Wrigley Field against the Cubs. But on this day, Weis came through big time, to the wonderment of all, with a blast into the left-field seats to tie the game. He had never before homered at Shea Stadium. And he never would again.

His home run not only tied the game, but it also kept Koosman in the game. Eddie Watt, meanwhile, replaced McNally, who had been lifted in the top of the eighth for a pinch hitter. Jones welcomed him with a double off the fence in left-center field. Hodges had been faithful with his platoons to the point that Ed Charles, Ron Swoboda, and Clendenon did not play at all in the NLCS. Now, in a tied World Series, with a chance to take the lead and perhaps end it, he stayed with the right-handed bats against the right-handed pitcher. Though Clendenon grounded out to third, Swoboda followed with a double down the left-field line to give the Mets the lead. After Charles filed out, Grote hit a grounder to first. Powell had difficulty corralling the ball and Watt dropped the throw as he covered first base—each received an error on the play—as Swoboda never stopped running and crossed home plate to make it a 5–3 game.

Koosman faced the heart of the Baltimore lineup for the top of the ninth. Frank Robinson led off with a walk, but Powell forced him at second and left for a pinch runner. Brooks Robinson flied out to Swoboda in right which left it up to future Mets manager Davey Johnson. He gave Mets fans a thrill of a lifetime as his fly ball descended gently into the waiting glove of Cleon Jones. He almost bent to a knee to catch it and when he got up, the Mets were world champions.

The celebration at Shea and through the city was instantaneous and unbridled. The Mets, listed as 100-1 odds to win the World Series back in the spring, did just that in the fall. Clendenon, who batted .357 with three home runs, a double, and four runs batted in, was named the Series MVP. The Babe Ruth Award, voted after the Series by sportswriters, went to the Mets' Bambino of the World Series: Al Weis.

The postseason winner's share for the Mets were just over $18,300 for each player. In contrast to today's marathons, none of the five games lasted longer than a snappy two hours and thirty-three minutes—including the 10-inning classic Game 4.

The Amazin' Mets had cast off the mantle of lovable losers. "This is the summit," said Ed Charles, who retired after the World Series. "We're number one in the world and just can't get any bigger than this."

"Some people still might not believe in us," said Jones. "But then, some people still believe the world is flat."

# Perspectives and Conclusions

Amtrak.com
Gulf

# Cubs Eye View

by Al Yellon

I didn't even know that it would be so at the time, but looking back recently at my extensive 2,000-plus Cubs game scorecard collection, the very first one (it wasn't my first game, but it's the oldest surviving card) is from one of the saddest games in Cubs history.

Not quite 13 years old and not yet beaten down by the ways of the world or baseball, I was taken to Wrigley Field by my dad on Sunday, September 7, 1969, the year the heroes of my childhood were supposed to, going to, absolutely had to, break the Cubs' pennantless drought which at the time, stretched "only" 24 years—long, but not to the absurd extremes it now reaches, 40 years later.

It was nearing the end of what had been, and what was supposed to continue to be, a special season. The Cubs ran out to an 11–1 start after an incredible Opening Day in which they'd blown a 5–2 lead and trailed 6–5 in the 11th inning, only to see Willie Smith hit a two-run walkoff home run (even though we had never heard the term "walkoff" back then). The party continued for five months; on June 29, the Cubs honored Billy Williams with a "day" between games of a doubleheader, in which he tied and then broke Stan Musial's record of 895 consecutive games played. Billy got a car, a boat, various appliances, and the adulation of 41,060 fans, the place packed to the rafters and tens of thousands turned away. He went 5-for-9 in the twinbill and drove in three runs as the Cubs swept their hated rivals, the defending NL champion Cardinals, and extended their record to 50–26 and their lead to 8½ games.

By mid-August, the lead had been stretched to nine games over St. Louis—the Cubs led by 10 over the Mets—and postseason play seemed inevitable. My dad promised he'd find me playoff tickets.

There had been fun early on, too: Pitcher Dick Selma, acquired from the Padres in May, started and relieved and when in the bullpen, led cheers with yellow-helmeted fans who dubbed themselves the "Bleacher Bums." As George Langford described the scene in the *Chicago Tribune*, Selma would stand in the Cubs bullpen next to the left-field stands and...

> *jab his right hand in the air and spin it around like an airport ground crewman giving the signal for the pilot to rev up his engines. Taking their cue, the left field bleacher bums follow Selma's lead, all circling their arms in the air. Then the Cubs pitcher jumps straight up and down, and slams his arm toward the ground and the irrepressible bleacherites burst into song. "Don't keep kicking my dog around," they sing.*

Fun was tempered in July when the Cubs, in front of a raucous Shea Stadium crowd, blew a 3–1 ninth-inning lead and lost, 4–3, because Chicago's rookie center fielder Don Young mishandled two easily catchable fly balls. Third baseman Ron Santo ripped him in public and was forced to apologize the next day; Young, having lost manager Leo Durocher's confidence, was benched. Young's replacement the next night, Jim Qualls, got the ninth-inning hit that spoiled Tom Seaver's bid for a perfect game. Seaver won anyway, but the Cubs won the next day and were 4½ games up in the standings.

On August 28, a Thursday afternoon throng of 29,092—a very large weekday crowd for that era—attended a 3–1 win over Cincinnati; that crowd brought the season attendance to 1,502,222, breaking a record that had stood since 1929. Four wins later, the Cubs' record stood at 84-52, 32 games over .500—the most it had been over .500 since the last pennant season in 1945 (and it wouldn't get that far over .500 again until 2008).

Still, even with the Mets getting hot and the Cubs cooling off, the lead remained at 4½ games as August turned into September. I can recall playing in my back yard, bouncing a ball off the brick wall of my house, the day the Cubs lost 2–0 to the Reds in Cincinnati (September 3), thinking, "Well, they lost—but they're still up five games, it's OK!"

When Sunday, September 7 dawned—the day my father took me to Wrigley and I got (and kept) the scorecard—the Cubs had dropped three straight and the lead was down to 3½ games. It was nervous time. They lost the first two games of a series against the Pirates, and gingerly took a 5–4 lead into the ninth inning of the Sunday finale, having overcome 2–1 and 4–2 deficits. Ace reliever (they weren't modern "closers" yet) Phil Regan was in the game to nail down the win—he had pitched the eighth, too, so he was in line for the victory, as the Cubs had taken the lead in the last of the eighth.

PHOTO COURTESY OF METSILVERMAN.COM

*Phil Regan, known as "The Vulture" for blowing saves and picking up the win later, let a lead go on September 15, 1969, and neither he nor the Cubs got the win.*

The first two batters went out on a popup and a groundout, and Regan got two strikes on the dangerous Willie Stargell. One more strike…

It never happened. Stargell sent a 1–2 pitch onto Sheffield Avenue, tying the game. A funereal silence dropped onto Wrigley Field. Even this 12-year-old felt the gloom. Still, the game was only tied, right? Sure, but when you blow a lead like that, jitters take over. An 11th-inning error by the usually sure-handed Don Kessinger led to two unearned runs, and the 7–5 loss sent the Cubs on a nine-game road trip only 2½ games ahead.

PHOTO COURTESY OF METSILVERMAN.COM

*Beloved Billy Williams set the National League record for consecutive games in 1969, but a year to savor turned sour for Cubs fans as summer headed toward fall.*

The first two games of the trip were in New York, where the Mets fans could sense something good coming for their team. They were right. In the first game, with the score tied in the sixth, Tommie Agee doubled and, on a Wayne Garrett single, tried to score ahead of Jim Hickman's frantic throw.

Catcher Randy Hundley and tens of thousands of Cubs fans, this 12-year-old included, will tell you to this day that Agee was out. But plate umpire Satch Davidson didn't see it that way. He ruled Agee safe; the normally mild-mannered Hundley jumped what seemed like a dozen feet in the air in anger, but to no avail. The call stood, and the Mets won, 3–2.

*The 1969 season was as close as Ernie Banks and most of his Cubs teammates would ever get to the postseason.*

Photo courtesy of metsilverman.com

We didn't know it then, but it was over. The Mets—and that damned black cat—jumped all over Fergie Jenkins the next night, and although the Cubs left New York still clinging to first place by half a game, we knew the fall was going to get worse.

It did. The losing streak reached eight. The last of these was lost to the awful Phillies in Philadelphia when Selma tried to pick a runner off third base—only there was no fielder there. Ron Santo hadn't gotten the message, and the ball wound up in the left-field corner.

The Cubs, who once led the Mets by double digits, finished eight games out of first place. Give the Mets credit: they went 38–11 to finish the year, and… well, I don't want to use that "A" word that Mets fans use to describe that year's team, but it was an incredible run. The Cubs finished the year at home with a 5–3 win over the eventual world champions (otherwise, the Cubs would have finished 10 games out instead of eight) in front of 9,981, extending the attendance record to 1,674,993, a mark that would stand till the Cubs won the NL East in yet another star-crossed year, 1984. Although that year, it was the Cubs who passed the Mets in August and cruised to the NL East title.

But in 1969, the dreams of kids like me—and Cubs fans of every age—were crushed. We kept hoping our heroes, Jenkins, Kessinger, Beckert, Santo, Hundley, and Williams, among others who came and went, would somehow "put it together" over the next few years, but it never happened. Eventually, all of them were shipped to other baseball destinations, while we were left with bittersweet memories of the team that never won anything.

Today, those Cubs are revered, perversely, perhaps *because* they didn't win anything. And, of course, 40 years later, no Cubs team has won it all.

The 12-year-old in me still yearns for that. Someday…

*Normally sure-handed Don Kessinger committed a key error that enabled the Pirates to sweep the Cubs just before Chicago's September showdown at Shea Stadium.*

Photo courtesy of metsilverman.com

## Tom Seaver Game-by-Game 1969

| Date | Opponent | Result | IP | H | R/ER | BB | SO | ERA | W/L | Rec. |
|---|---|---|---|---|---|---|---|---|---|---|
| April 8 | MON | 10-11 | 5 | 6 | 4/2 | 2 | 3 | 3.60 | – | 0-0 |
| April 13 | STL | 1-3 | 8 | 6 | 3/3 | 3 | 6 | 3.46 | L | 0-1 |
| April 19 | @STL | 2-1 | 9 | 9 | 1/1 | 1 | 3 | 2.45 | W | 1-1 |
| April 25 | CHI | 1-3 | 7 | 5 | 3/3 | 2 | 7 | 2.79 | L | 1-2 |
| April 27 (1)* | @CHI | 6-8 | 0.3 | 0 | 0 | 1 | 1 | 2.76 | -- | 1-2 |
| April 30 | @MON | 2-1 | 9 | 5 | 1/1 | 3 | 6 | 2.35 | W | 2-2 |
| May 4 (1) | @CHI | 3-2 | 9 | 9 | 2/2 | 2 | 7 | 2.28 | W | 3-2 |
| May 10 | HOU | 3-1 | 9 | 4 | 1/1 | 6 | 4 | 2.08 | W | 4-2 |
| May 14 | ATL | 9-3 | 8 | 10 | 3/3 | 1 | 3 | 2.24 | W | 5-2 |
| May 21 | @ATL | 5-0 | 9 | 3 | 0 | 2 | 2 | 1.96 | W | 6-2 |
| May 25 | @HOU | 3-6 | 4 | 8 | 5/5 | 1 | 1 | 2.44 | L | 6-3 |
| May 30 | SF | 4-3 | 8 | 4 | 3/3 | 1 | 8 | 2.53 | W | 7-3 |
| June 3 | LA | 5-2 | 8 | 3 | 2/2 | 2 | 9 | 2.51 | W | 8-3 |
| June 8 | @SD | 3-2 | 7 | 8 | 2/2 | 1 | 14 | 2.51 | W | 9-3 |
| June 14 | @LA | 3-1 | 8 | 6 | 1/1 | 2 | 3 | 2.41 | W | 10-3 |
| June 19 | @PHI | 6-5 | 7 | 10 | 5/5 | 5 | 8 | 2.65 | W | 11-3 |
| June 24 (1) | PHI | 2-1 | 9 | 7 | 1/1 | 1 | 9 | 2.53 | W | 11-3 |
| June 29 | PIT | 7-3 | 9 | 6 | 3/3 | 4 | 10 | 2.56 | W | 12-3 |
| July 4 (1) | @PIT | 11-6 | 7.7 | 7 | 4/3 | 4 | 7 | 2.62 | W | 13-3 |
| July 9 | CHI | 4-0 | 9 | 1 | 0 | 0 | 11 | 2.46 | W | 14-3 |
| July 14 | @CHI | 0-1 | 8 | 5 | 1/1 | 1 | 4 | 2.39 | L | 14-4 |
| July 19 | @MON | 4-5 | 2 | 7 | 4/4 | 1 | 3 | 2.59 | L | 14-5 |
| July 26 | CIN | 3-2 | 9 | 8 | 2/2 | 2 | 8 | 2.56 | W | 15-5 |
| July 31 | HOU | 0-2 | 7 | 5 | 2/1 | 1 | 6 | 2.51 | L | 15-6 |
| August 5 (1) | @CIN | 5-8 | 3 | 5 | 4/4 | 2 | 1 | 2.66 | L | 15-7 |
| August 9 | @ATL | 5-3 | 7.3 | 6 | 3/2 | 5 | 3 | 2.66 | W | 16-7 |
| August 16 (1) | SD | 2-0 | 8 | 4 | 0 | 2 | 4 | 2.55 | W | 17-7 |
| August 21 | SF | 6-7 | 7 | 6 | 6/4 | 7 | 5 | 2.64 | – | 17-7 |
| August 26 (1) | @SD | 8-4 | 9 | 4 | 4/3 | 1 | 6 | 2.65 | W | 18-7 |
| August 31 | @SF | 8-0 | 9 | 7 | 0 | 3 | 11 | 2.54 | W | 19-7 |
| September 5 (1) | PHI | 5-1 | 9 | 5 | 1/1 | 1 | 7 | 2.48 | W | 20-7 |
| September 9 | CHI | 7-1 | 9 | 5 | 1/1 | 1 | 5 | 2.43 | W | 21-7 |
| September 13 | @PIT | 5-2 | 9 | 6 | 2/2 | 5 | 4 | 2.41 | W | 22-7 |
| September 18 | @MON | 2-0 | 9 | 5 | 0 | 3 | 9 | 2.33 | W | 23-7 |
| September 22 | STL | 3-1 | 9 | 4 | 1/1 | 4 | 1 | 2.28 | W | 24-7 |
| September 27 | @PHI | 1-0 | 9 | 3 | 0 | 2 | 4 | 2.21 | W | 25-7 |
| **Totals** | **36 Games** | **35 Starts** | **273.3** | **202** | **75/67** | **82** | **208** | **2.28** | **25-7** | |

*Relief appearance
(1) denotes first game of a doubleheader

# Everyone Comes Home in October

by Glen Vasey

A passion for baseball, like all passions, is a webwork of connections. It is a network comprised of moments and memories, of personalities, situations and serendipity. It is a pattern of connections and of circuits completed. If our reactions to and interactions with events help to refine our definitions of ourselves, our reflections on such events help to deepen such convictions. Through theses processes we learn who we are, who we have been, who we yet may be.

Two events, one in the fall of 1969 and the other in the spring of 1970, have served such purpose for me. I have revisited (and likely revised) these memories often.

Two days before my 13th birthday I found myself with my mother and father in the upper deck of Memorial Stadium awaiting the start of the second game of the 1969 World Series. I had been born in Baltimore just after the summer that saw both Brooks and Frank Robinson complete their rookie seasons (one in Baltimore and one in Cincinnati), though neither of them was on my radar for a few years. I do remember with perfect clarity the moment that they did flash onto my screen. It was an early April afternoon in 1966 when I opened a local paper (we had been living for six years in South Jersey by then) and saw a photo of a ballplayer sliding into third base. The photo was captioned: "Frank Robinson of the Baltimore Orioles slides into third with a triple. Robinson later scored the winning run in Baltimore's 3–2 victory over the Cleveland Indians."

Serendipity. I decided on the spot that Baltimore would be my favorite team and that Frank Robinson would be my favorite player. Few choices in my life have ever been more timely or more fortuitous. Frank went on to win the Triple Crown and an MVP. The Orioles went on to a World Series sweep against a heavily favored Los Angeles club that included both Don Drysdale and Sandy Koufax. And I had the good fortune of watching a young right-hander named Jim Palmer become, at 20, the youngest pitcher to ever throw a shutout in the World Series at the outset of what was to be a stellar career. My fate was sealed.

What a delicious fate it seemed on the afternoon of October 12, 1969. That summer my family had moved back to Baltimore, the Orioles had won 109 regular season games and topped it off with a three-game sweep of a strong Minnesota club in the first ever American League Championship Series. That was followed by winning the opening game of the World Series against the New York Mets and their outstanding ace Tom Seaver. The stage was set for an easy Series victory and another world championship. Heck, the Series might not even make it back to Baltimore for Game Six. The atmosphere was positively electric. Then came Jerry Koosman.

The 25-year-old lefty had just won 17 games in his second season—following a 19-win season as a rookie in '68—and he proceeded to show everyone how he had done it. After six innings he was pitching no-hit ball and looked as if he might be able to make Donn Clendenon's fourth inning home run hold up for a 1–0 victory. In the seventh, however, the O's reached him for two hits and tied the score. I thought that we were back in the game, but he shut us down again and when three of his teammates singled with two out in the top of the ninth, the Mets again had a one-run lead, and Koosman was back on the mound needing just three outs.

One thing you need to know about Orioles fans of that particular era is that we were raised on the radio and television broadcasts of Chuck Thompson and Bill O'Donnell. Neither of these men were "homers." They were true fans of the game. Listening to them helped one appreciate the fine play of the opponents as well as that of the hometown heroes. We searched for and applauded excellence when we saw it on either side, because we had been taught to recognize it as such. A gutsy pitch selection by the opposing battery might be responsible for one of our heroes striking out in the clutch. A fine defensive play might retire our side without a run. They did not look to blame our own when they failed, unless they truly deserved such blame. Truth be told, there were not a lot of flaws to point out on the 1969 O's. Usually when we lost it was due to superior performance by our opponents. Chuck and Bill had recognized this fact, and had taught all Orioles fans to be alert to just such possibilities.

After the Mets took a 2–1 lead in the top of the ninth, Koosman retired the first two batters in the bottom of the inning. I honestly don't remember if the O's had managed to get someone on base, or even who was due to bat next, but I do remember Gil Hodges, the New York manager, stepping out of the dugout and walking slowly toward the mound. I remember watching Jerry Koosman awaiting him, head bowed, spikes scraping along the dirt of the mound.

More than 50,000 people waited with a hushed expectancy. No one was certain what the manager would do. No one was even certain what they wanted him to do. Koosman had been magnificent. Was he tiring? Would we have a better chance against their bullpen?

Hodges reached the mound and it began to seem that even he wasn't sure what he was going to do. They talked. We watched and waited. Finally Hodges reached his hand out for the ball. Head downcast, Koosman handed it to him respectfully, and then began his own long slow march back to the New York dugout. He looked, for all the world, like a man who'd just been fired from his job. It started then.

It seemed to build gradually, but it came to fullness rapidly enough that Koosman was only half way back to the dugout by the time that 50,850 fans had risen to give him a rousing standing ovation.

Koosman's stride faltered a little. He raised his eyes from the ground and looked up into the seats above the Mets dugout. He stopped completely. He looked higher. He turned his head to the right very

National Baseball Hall of Fame Library, Cooperstown, NY

*Jerry Koosman is all smiles with expectant wife Lavonne as the Mets head on the bus to the airport after Kooz's win in Game Two of the 1969 World Series.*

COURTESY OF JON SPRINGER

Suffolk Sun *cartoonist Frank Springer was on to something with this cartoon following Game Two of the 1969 World Series.*

slowly. He kept on turning his head until he had to shuffle his feet and turn his body. Now he took in the seats behind home plate. Now he took in the seats in the upper deck above the plate. Now the seats along the third base line and above.

His eyes swept back, taking in the scene again. His posture evinced his disbelief at the suddenness and incongruity of receiving such an ovation in the opposition's ballpark.

When his face came back again so that he was looking in my direction... well, maybe it was some trick of distance and light, maybe it was the sheen of sweat from his exertions on a warm October day, and maybe it is just the way my memory has overwritten the truth over nearly 40 years of telling and retelling of the moment; but it seemed to me that his cheeks were wet with tears.

Koosman raised a hand in acknowledgment, as respectfully and emotionally as he had moved when handing the game ball to his manager, and continued his walk to the dugout. His stride seemed more confident. His pace was quicker, his posture more proud.

It was one of the finest moments that I have ever experienced in a ballpark. I was aware of its import even as it occurred. I think all 50,850 of us were proud to be there.

Some months later my father asked if I wanted to attend the Baltimore premier of the Official Major League Baseball World Series film for 1969. I was, of course, elated, though I had no hope that the Series would turn out any differently than it had the first time.

The film was shown in the auditorium of Eastern High School, right across the street from Memorial Stadium. As I had feared, the Mets still won in five.

After the film there was a panel discussion with three or four Orioles and a like number of Mets available to take questions from the audience. Jerry Koosman was one of the Mets who had taken the time to be with us on that day. You must remember that by now I had passed my 13th birthday and so was worldly wise and knowledgeable in all things, even if I was too shy to raise my hand and offer my own questions.

I was thrilled, however, when Jerry Koosman stepped up to the microphone. I desperately hoped that someone would ask him a question that would get him to talk about that intimate moment that he and I had shared with nearly 51,000 other people that previous October.

I winced when I heard the first question he was asked: "Mr. Koosman, could you tell us what your

Photo courtesy of metsilverman.com

*Jerry Koosman's Game Two win in Baltimore reversed the momentum in the 1969 World Series. He then finished the job in Game Five.*

worst moment ever was on a ballfield, and what was your best?"

Stupid question, I thought, the guy is barely 26 years old and has only played two full seasons. It was a question best asked of a grizzled veteran, or a wily manager who had a long-playing career before stepping up. What a wasted opportunity. But Kooz, once again, came through.

"That's easy," he said, "because they happened almost simultaneously. Right across the street from here, not too long ago.

"I never felt worse on a ballfield than I did when Gil Hodges asked me to give him the ball when I was one out away from completing my first World Series start. I wanted to keep pitching. I felt that I'd let the team down. I didn't want to come out. I've never felt lower.

"Half way back to the dugout I heard a noise. I didn't know what it was. I looked up and realized that the Baltimore fans were giving me a standing ovation. I couldn't believe it. It really lifted me up. It was the best feeling that I've ever had on a ballfield."

Grand slam answer. I swear I cried. A circuit had been completed for me. I'm sure I tried not to let my tears show, but my father wasn't a man who missed much. He kept looking up at the stage. He wasn't a man who would easily breach such a confidence either.

I guess this little essay is about him too. About what I learned from him as much as what I learned while at his side. My father was never a baseball fan until I was, so my fondness for the game and for the Orioles was never inherited. Once I became a fan he was eager to take me to games and events that met and increased my growing fascination with the sport.

Because of him, and Kooz, and Chuck Thompson, and more than 50,000 other attendees who also rose to a particular occasion, my memory of that World Series doesn't key on the disappointment of loss.

That memory is not articulated by the incredible acrobatics of Swoboda and Agee, the heroic offense of Donn Clendenon, a blown interference call or a pair of shady hit-batsmen calls each going the way of the Mets in Game Five.

For me, that Series has always been defined by the circuit completed. Pole one was Jerry Koosman deserving and receiving our ovation with style and grace. Pole two was when he recognized and thanked us for it.

Such moments are rare in any endeavor. Such moments are why I love this silly little game of ball and bat and glove and guile.

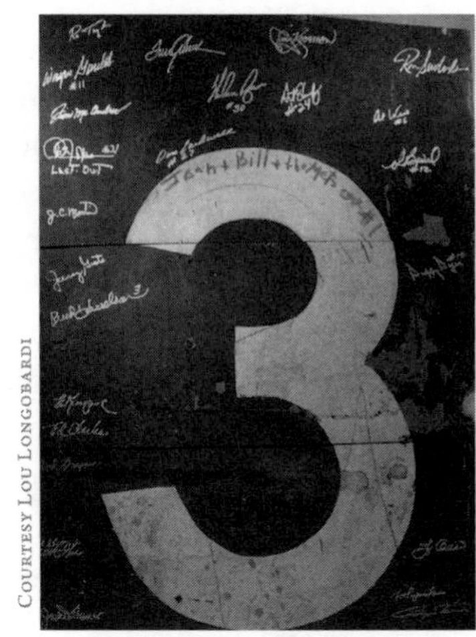
COURTESY LOU LONGOBARDI

# The Wall
## A '69 Mets Quest

by Lou Longobardi

In early 1970, when I was a freshman at St. John's University, I went to Shea Stadium to purchase tickets for Opening Day. As I walked toward the ticket office, I noticed a lot of refuse strewn around the parking lot, including one large piece of green plywood sheeting lying face down on the ground. It was pretty dirty and stained and appeared to have been lying there for quite some time. Since the color had a familiar look, I decided to lift it up and look at the underside. As I suspected, it was a section of Shea Stadium's outfield wall. I knew this for certain because this wall fragment had a white numeral "3" on it, indicating that it had once been part of either the 396 or 371 distance markers from either left-center or right-center field.

Upon closer examination, I noticed graffiti written in both ballpoint pen and magic marker on the white background of the numeral "3." One inscription said "Joan & Bill and the Mets are #1." Another marking read, "*Joe, Byron and Rich,*" and below it said, "10/16/69." That was the very date the Mets won their first world championship! I broke the large sheet into a small enough piece to fit into my friend's car, all the while keeping the numeral "3" intact. I brought it home and stored it in my parents' garage in Queens.

A few years ago, I decided that I would finally give that piece its rightful treatment by having it mounted and framed. When I found it in the garage, I noticed it had inexplicably been cut into four pieces. No one was around to explain. Fortunately, the pieces fit together neatly, leaving the numeral "3" intact. I'd always been almost certain that it was a piece of the Shea wall and time had not dimmed my belief. While doing some research, I found proof beyond a shadow of a doubt.

I stumbled across a photograph taken an hour or so after the last out of the 1969 World Series. The photo portrayed Tom Seaver and Gary Gentry, walking around the pitching mound, surrounded by huge divots of grassy turf liberally lying all over the field. When I looked beyond the main subjects, in the background, I could clearly see that where the right-field wall stood 371 feet from home plate, but only the numerals "71" were visible. As I looked closer…the section of the wall bearing the numeral "3" was clearly missing. After all this time, I finally knew exactly from where and when that piece of wall came from. It actually was, and still is, a tangible link back to that magical moment in Mets history.

From that point, came the next step, getting the participants to sign my little—or maybe not so little—piece of the Miracle Mets. It has been a labor of love acquiring autographs on the Wall from as many of the surviving '69 Mets as I could get. Soon after rediscovering the Wall in March 2006, I realized the first chance I would get to have it autographed would be the following December, when a *Mets Mania* autograph show was to take place in New Jersey.

The experience of meeting each of those '69 Mets was filled with all kinds of emotion: Al Weis had some funny stories to relate about still living in the Chicago area, where the word "Mets" remains a four-letter because the Miracle ruined what had been a dream season for the Cubs. Jerry Koosman, one of the greatest Mets pitchers, used the Wall to make fun of his well-known lack of hitting prowess. Jim McAndrew seemed to just to have a huge smile on his face throughout his entire appearance time, and I'll never forget the warm country gentleman presence of Don Cardwell. Ed Kranepool, Swoboda, The Glider—Ed Charles, Wayne Garrett, Cleon Jones, Bud Harrelson and all the rest were equally friendly, spirited, humorous, and approachable and seemed just as genuinely appreciative of our continued interest in them, as we are for the thrills that they gave us. What an Amazin' event it was for me.

By the time that New Jersey show ended, I had secured all of the autographs that now appear on the Wall, except for Tom Seaver, Yogi Berra, and Nolan Ryan, Hall of Famers, all!

Yogi was scheduled to appear at a Yankees-themed show in February 2007. Despite what I knew would be an "adversarial" Yankees atmosphere at that event, I decided I could not pass up the opportunity to personally meet Yogi, a coach on the '69 team and the manager of the "Ya Gotta Believe" Mets that took the pennant in '73. So with a single-minded purpose, I purchased my tickets to the show, had Yogi sign the Wall, and took the requisite photos. I left that event immediately after getting his signature, dutifully ignoring the sullying effect which that Yankees-themed atmosphere evoked. It was my intent to leave with an image of Yogi as a 1969 *Mets* coach…not as a Yankee. Fortunately, I made it work.

Two weeks earlier, it had been Seaver time. Tom had a scheduled appearance in Baltimore. My wife and I took the 200-mile trek down I-95 on Friday night. Saturday morning, we went to the convention center, bought our tickets and soon after, saw Tom enter the building a bit earlier than his scheduled appearance time. As I waited my turn, things seemed under control. But then rumors began to circulate that Seaver had finished early and was actually on his way out of the building. That's when the panic set in. I grabbed the Wall and rushed down to the area where I had seen him arrive, hoping that I could at least get him to stop and quickly sign the Wall on his way out. All that expenditure of emotion and energy turned out to be unnecessary, as the rumors of a premature exit were not quite accurate. Tom had merely left the first room he was in to move down the corridor to another signing room. We breathed a heavy sigh of relief.

When we finally got up to Tom, not only did he sign the top segment of the Wall which I had reserved for him, but he marveled at the entire two-by-three foot section, showing the entire numeral "3." He repeatedly referred to it as "a great piece of history" and offered to help me get in touch with

Photographs courtesy of Lou Longobardi

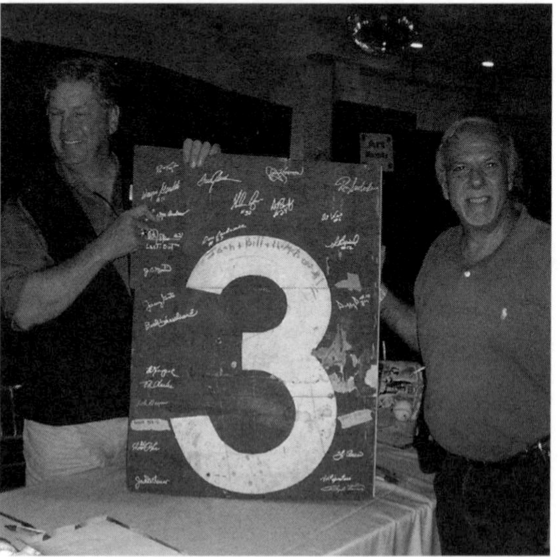

*Everywhere a sign. Nolan Ryan, left, and Tom Seaver, right pose with a piece of the 1969 Shea Stadium wall and Lou Longobardi, finder and keeper of the Miracle Mets relic.*

people in the Mets organization if I were so inclined. I thanked him and exchanged contact information. We said our goodbyes and left the building with the autograph that, with all due respect to any and all of the others on that Wall, most fittingly belonged: Tom Seaver, the Franchise.

Ironically, on that very morning, it had been reported that Nolan Ryan had been hospitalized for some "tests." Fortunately, as was reported a few days later, all turned out to be okay. Nolan Ryan spent most of his long and remarkable career in uniforms that did not say "Mets," but he will forever be remembered by Mets fans of that era as the fireballing hurler who won the clinching game of the 1969 NLCS and whose lone career World Series appearance resulted in a save in Game Three of the '69 Series against Baltimore, that magical afternoon where Tommie Agee made his two miraculous catches. True, Ryan's infamous 1971 trade to the Angels still lives in the annals of Mets history, but also, it was his brief arrival on the scene in the summer of 1966—a year before Seaver's debut—that was the harbinger of things to come, pitching-wise, in the summers that followed. And it was power pitching from extraordinary young arms that would finally cause the worm to turn in 1969.

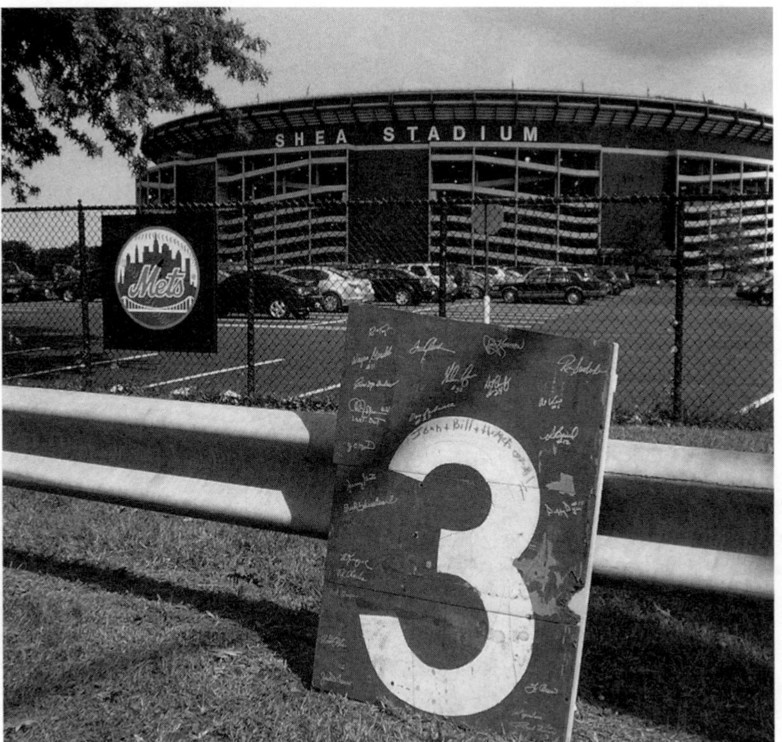

*A piece of the 1969 world championship wall visits where it came from one last time in 2008.*

PHOTOGRAPH COURTESY OF LOU LONGOBARDI

Nolan Ryan does not do many public autograph shows. I contacted his foundation, and while they said he would sign my "artifact" if I mailed it to them, I wasn't of a mind to entrust this, in the words of Tom Seaver, "great piece of history" to the mail or any other delivery service. His foundation appreciated my willingness to fly to Houston personally whenever he would be in, but they said they rarely received much advanced notice of his office visits. I had noticed a private signing he was scheduled to do with a Houston-based memorabilia dealer in early July. So I contacted that outfit and said I'd be willing to fly down if I could get the Wall signed without letting it far from my possession. They suggested I wait, indicating that he might do a public signing in the upcoming fall. I thanked them for the information and resolved to contact them in a few months.

In early September, I noticed Ryan's name on an autograph-signing website. I clicked on it only to find a scheduled *public* signing scheduled for Sunday, September 30, 2007, at 1 p.m. I assumed it was going to be in Texas, but when I clicked further, I saw it was scheduled to occur on Long Island, in Deer Park, not a 20-minute drive from my home! I couldn't believe it! I immediately bought tickets for the event and waited with keen anticipation. It was a long, long couple of weeks building up to that Sunday. Sadly, every Mets fan should remember September 30, 2007. For those who need a hint: last game of the regular season, the Mets needing a win to force a one-game playoff, Tom Glavine on the mound, seven-run first inning...you know how that

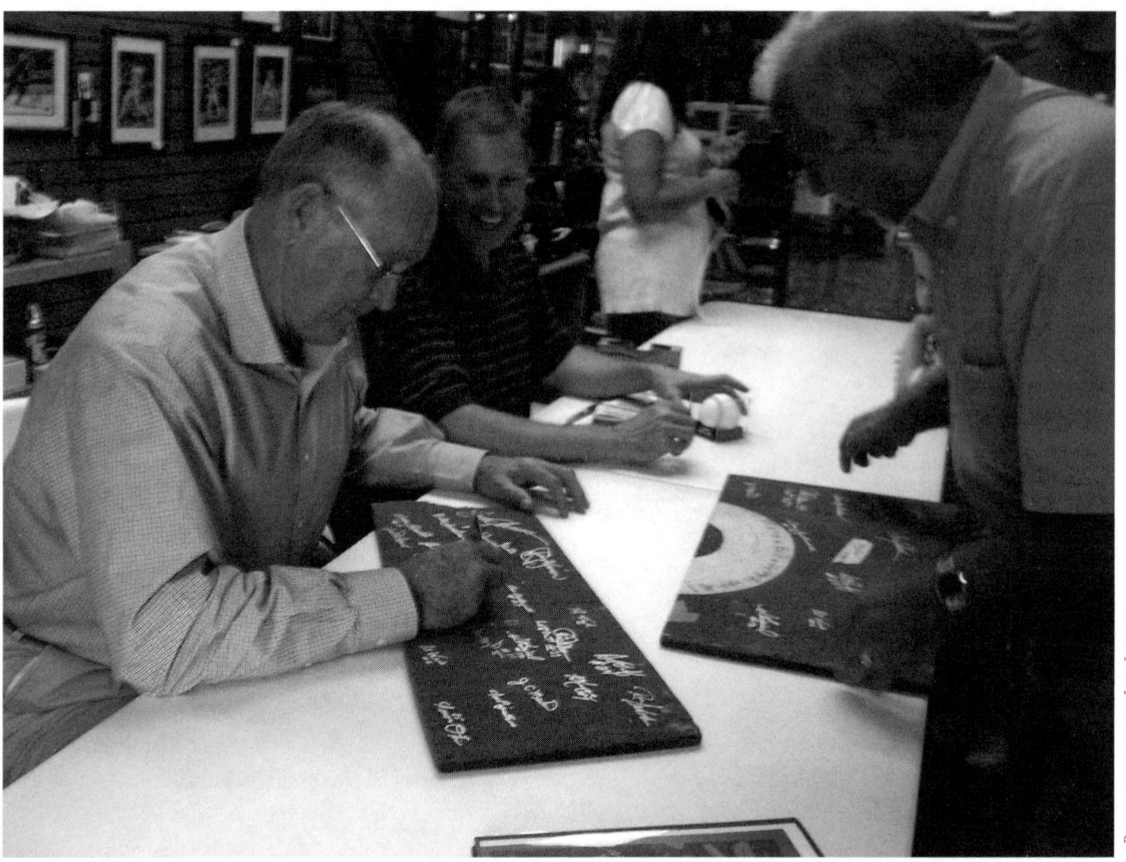

PHOTO COURTESY OF LOU LONGOBARDI

*Hall of Famer and 1969 Met Nolan Ryan puts pen to wall to sign one fan's "great piece of Mets history" as a tribute to the first expansion team to win a world championship.*

came out. Well, I spent those minutes during that first inning on line, listening to the game, waiting to meet Nolan Ryan. By the time I got up to him, those seven runs had crossed the plate. Meeting him was as good an antidote to that first inning as I could ever imagine. He was wonderful. And, getting back to my car, I said there was still time for a comeback, right? No Miracle that day.

In any event, I was thrilled meeting Nolan Ryan and he was fascinated not only by the Wall, but by the album of photos I had brought of his former teammates signing it, nostalgically smiling as he perused each photo. Nolan Ryan was a Met. He always will be a Met to me.

The author of seven no-hitters (none as a Met, of course) he has completed the Wall, my Wall. And he joined a pretty select company missing only Tommie Agee, Donn Clendenon, Tug McGraw, Rube Walker, Cal Koonce, and Gil Hodges, among the deceased.

On August 23, 2009, the day after the Citi Field celebration of the 1969 Mets, I got the last three signatures I needed on the wall: Eddie Yost, Bobby Pfeil, and Gary Gentry. The roll call for the Wall, my piece of the '69 Mets reads as follows:

| | |
|---|---|
| Ed Kranepool | Ken Boswell |
| Al Weis | Bud Harrelson |
| Ed Charles | Wayne Garrett |
| Jerry Grote | Duffy Dyer |
| J.C. Martin | Cleon Jones |
| Rod Gaspar | Art Shamsky |
| Ron Swoboda | Amos Otis |
| Jack DiLauro | Yogi Berra |
| Joe Pignatano | Ron Taylor |
| Jim McAndrew | Don Cardwell |
| Jerry Koosman | Nolan Ryan |
| Tom Seaver | Ralph Kiner |
| Bobby Pfeil | Eddie Yost |
| Gary Gentry | |

# Red Murff: Scouting a Miracle

by Michael J. Bielawa

Just prior to the start of the 1969 World Series, Orioles third baseman Brooks Robinson was said to have uttered the rather Grinch-like statement, "We are here to prove there is no Santa Claus." Such unabashed, un-American hubris could only naturally result in a rude October awakening for Baltimore. No presents under the Orange Birds' postseason tree. Just a lump of coal wrapped in pine tar.

Surprisingly, one individual who contributed mightily to the Miracle Mets that year was a jolly Texan who never swung a bat or fielded a ball at Shea Stadium: Red Murff. It was this super scout's particular insight and dogged persistence that led to the signing of some of the most beloved players ever to doff a royal blue and orange cap. As a Mets scout Red was credited with delivering a core of gifted players to Flushing, thus making the 1969 sugarplum dream a clay and cleat reality. Jerry Koosman, Ken Boswell, and Jerry Grote all came to New York due to Murff's efforts. Red was also credited with discovering a fellow Texan, a lean high school student the majority of scouts ignored. The only way this pitcher could have gotten into the Hall of Fame, so they thought, was if he bought a ticket. Murff proved his genius when he signed this fire-baller from Alvin: Nolan Ryan.

John Robert "Red" Murff was born in Burlington, Texas on April 1, 1921 and came to the game late. There was no baseball program at Red's high school in Rosebud, Texas; he only began playing regularly during World War II while a member of an Army Air Corps team. After the war and a stint at a factory job, he signed on, at the age of 29, with the Baton Rouge Red Sticks of the Class C Evangeline League. Pitching for the 1950 Sticks, Murff went 17–4 while toting a respectable 2.96 ERA. When he wasn't on the mound, Red played the outfield, batting .331 while knocking in 65 runs. Looking back on his Evangeline League Rookie of the Year Award, Murff reflects, "The nicest thing was the recognition that helped get me to the big leagues. The award made it known that I was a good player. And I was a rookie nearly 30 years old!"

The following year, in the process of amassing 19 wins, Red tossed a no-hitter for the Texas City Texans. He won 23 games for the Tyler East Texans in 1952 and led the Texas League with 17 victories the following year for the Double-A Dallas Eagles. Still an Eagle in 1955, he posted a 1.99 ERA, went 27–11, and logged more than 300 innings. *The Sporting News* named him Minor League Player of the Year. Red joined the Milwaukee Braves in 1956 and pitched in 14 games (one start) and had a 4.44 ERA. Sadly, the 34-year-old rookie injured his arm in the third inning of that first start for the Braves. Murff, who'd also suffered back problems, lamented that there was no real rehabilitation practiced in those days. He never graduated beyond being a bullpen pitcher in Milwaukee. His final game in the major leagues came just 13 months after his debut. He started just twice in 26 career games, though he was retroactively credited with three saves.

Murff remained with the Braves over the course of two seasons, going 2–2 for Milwaukee in 1957, but he did not pitch for the Braves after Memorial Day the year they went on to win the World Series. Murff lingered in the minors through 1959, pitching in Wichita and Louisville. He also hurled in the Puerto Rican League, where he later managed as well.

"Injury only stopped my baseball career as a player," Red philosophically noted. "Baseball was still a part of my life. Baseball was my vocation." Red became player-manager of the South Atlantic League Jacksonville Braves. That same year he helped a young pitcher named Phil Niekro, who was struggling with his knuckleball. More than three decades later, the 318-game winner said during his induction speech at the Hall of Fame: "When I played in Jacksonville, Florida, my manager by the name of Red Murff... walked to me and said, 'Son,' he said, 'if you can get that knuckleball over the plate, you can pitch in the big leagues.' And I believed him. I've had a lot of respect for Red and I still do. He's here today and I just want to say thank you for finding someone at that age telling me that I could pitch in the big leagues with that knuckleball."

It was merely Red Murff's first instance of helping a player on the path to stardom.

After scouting for the Houston Colt 45s, Murff joined the expansion team that really needed help. He went to work for the Mets organization in 1963, touring a huge territory that embraced Texas, Louisiana, Oklahoma, and New Mexico. In an attempt to lift the fledgling Mets farm system, Red instituted the first-ever tryouts for young men enrolled in job training programs and helped establish winter instructional camps in Mexico. All the while the scout continued to cultivate a keen, almost prescient, ability to judge those players being overlooked.

Following up on a lead regarding a lefty hurler at Fort Bliss in El Paso, Red was shocked to find a "very fat" Jerry Koosman roaming the outfield. Weight was not the only reason the men in plaid were discouraged about this plump fellow from Minnesota; his lackadaisical approach caused scouts' clipboards to remain blank. Red convinced the pitcher, who proved his craft on the mound, to drop the weight. He signed Jerry shortly after his military discharge. Murff gave a helping hand to Sam Houston State student Ken Boswell, tutoring the infielder how to approach the commissioner's office and enter the major league draft as a special exception. (The Mets took him in the fourth round of the first major league draft in 1965.) Jerry Grote, who would become a lifelong friend of Red's, was inked by Murff while he was scouting for the Colt 45s. When Houston lost interest in the catcher, Red's word convinced the Mets brass to acquire the backstop.

Ryan provides a special example of Red's foresight and determination. Not even Nolan's blossoming fastball attracted scouts. The skinny kid's wild delivery did not resemble anything close to big league potential. It was Red Murff who stood by the young pitcher, seeing what no one else could. During Ryan's 1999 Hall of Fame induction speech, the man who hurled seven no-hitters praised Murff for making his baseball career possible. "Red is a friend and Red took more of an interest in me at an early age," Ryan said. "He thought when he saw me at 6-foot-2 and 140, he wasn't discouraged by my build and by the way I threw the baseball as many other scouts were. And I appreciate the fact that Red spent so much time with me and worked to help me become a better pitcher."

While Koosman, Ryan, Grote, and Boswell propelled the Miracle Mets into a ticker-tape blizzard along the Canyon of Heroes, one should remember it was Red who helped bring these gifted players to the Shea faithful. It is no fairytale for fans and statisticians to look at the contributions of these four '69 Mets and honestly credit Red Murff with winning 23 regular season games while collecting 272 strikeouts during that magic season. By bringing Boswell and Grote to the Mets, Murff can also be credited with uncovering 72 RBIs for that club. Red's postseason numbers for 1969 are even more impressive: two World Series victories and a save, not to mention the clinching victory in the NLCS.

Ironically, by the time the Mets won the Series, Murff was with another club. Murff again joined another expansion club that really needed his help: the Montreal Expos. He joined the Expos in September 1968, before the expansion draft was even held and he helped the club start a major league franchise from scratch. He was named Montreal's Scout of the Year in 1975. Murff also started the baseball program at the University of Mary Hardin-Baylor College near his home in Belton, Texas, and came up with the innovative method of allowing released professional ballplayers to get an education and still be able to play college ball (games against ex-professionals were deemed exhibitions). The school's baseball ballpark was named Red Murff Field in 1994.

Murff, who was also credited for finding John Bateman (Oklahoma), Mike Stanton (Texas), and Norm Charlton (Louisiana), retired from scouting in 1991 after 34 years on the job. He was inducted into the Texas Baseball Hall of Fame in 1989 and the Texas Scouts Association Hall of Fame in 1999. He tried his hand at writing, penning a children's book called *Little Whiskers Fin* after telling his grandson a story. With that under his belt, wrote his own story, *The Scout: Searching for the Best in Baseball* (with Mike Capps).

He remained close to the game even in his 80s. He moved in 2003 and quickly took an interest in the University of Texas at Tyler. "Red loved baseball and I loved it as well and we hit it off," athletic director James Vilade said. "Early on in our program, Red was the only person who supported our team and our players. He was instrumental with having a scouting day and getting our players ready for professional ball and it really helped them out." He was given a Lifetime Achievement Award from the school by Villade.

Even when Parkinson's disease, along with heart problems, forced a move into a Tyler nursing home, he still talked baseball and went with Villade to area games on occasion. One of his prize pupils, Nolan Ryan, even paid a visit. Murff died on November 28, 2008 at the age of 87.

**Sources**

Red Murff interviews conducted by Michael J. Bielawa, 2005.

National Baseball Hall of Fame File of Red Murff, Cooperstown, New York.

Cotham, Jeremy, "'Red' Murff: The Legend of Baseball Legends," *The Patriot Talon* (University of Texas at Tyler), December 8, 2008.

Murff, John "Red" with Mike Capps. *The Scout: Searching for the Best in Baseball.* (Dallas: Word Publishing, 1996.)

*The Sporting News*, 1965–68, 1973.

## Third Chances

For the first eight seasons of their existence, the Mets seemed to go through a new third baseman every month—and with 41 third basemen through the '69 season, the math is just about right: 1.2 third sackers every 30 days. Even on the world championship 1969 club the Mets had no less than nine players on the roster at some point who had manned the hot corner during their Mets careers (listed below in bold).

The retirement of Ed Charles after the '69 World Series left the Mets with a void they felt that rookie Wayne Garrett couldn't fill, which started the club on a slippery slope that saw the trading of Amos Otis and later Nolan Ryan in a vain search for the perfect third sacker. The '69 vet Garrett still wound up at third until he too was traded in 1976. It wasn't until Hubie Brooks (No. 68 in the chain) debuted in 1980 that the position started to find some franchise stability: Ray Knight (No. 76), Howard Johnson (No. 78), Edgardo Alfonzo (No. 100), and Robin Ventura (No. 115). The success of David Wright (No. 129) has enabled the Mets—139 strong at the hot corner through 2009—to turn their angst toward some other positions on the diamond.

| Third Baseman | Mets 3B Debut |
|---|---|
| 1. Don Zimmer | April 11, 1962 |
| 2. Rod Kanehl | April 21, 1962 |
| 3. Felix Mantilla | April 23, 1962 |
| 4. Elio Chacon | May 5, 1962+ |
| 5. Cliff Cook | May 8, 1962 |
| 6. Frank Thomas | June 17, 1962 |
| 7. Rick Herrscher | August 2, 1962* |
| 8. Sammy Drake | August 10, 1962 |
| 9. Charlie Neal | August 29, 1962 |
| 10. Ted Schreiber | April 14, 1963* |
| 11. Chico Fernandez | May 12, 1963 (1st game) |
| 12. Al Moran | May 12, 1963 (2nd game) |
| 13. Larry Burright | May 12, 1963 (2nd game)+ |
| 14. Ron Hunt | May 13, 1963 |
| 15. Jim Hickman | June 19, 1963 |
| 16. Pumpsie Green | September 5, 1963 |
| 17. John Stephenson | April 26, 1964* |
| 18. Amado Samuel | May 8, 1964 |
| 19. Charley Smith | May 24, 1964 |
| 20. Wayne Graham | August 8, 1964 |
| 21. Bobby Klaus | August 15, 1964 |
| 22. Dan Napoleon | April 24, 1965* |
| 23. Chuck Hiller | August 22, 1965 |
| 24. Gary Kolb | September 1, 1965 (2nd game) |
| **25. Kevin Collins** | **September 11, 1965** |
| 26. Ken Boyer | April 15, 1966 |
| 27. Eddie Bressoud | May 14, 1966 |
| **28. Jerry Grote** | **August 3, 1966** |
| 29. Sandy Alomar, Sr. | April 15, 1967 |
| 30. Jerry Bucheck | April 23, 1967 (2nd game) |
| 31. Tom Reynolds | April 29, 1967 |
| **32. Ed Charles** | **May 12, 1967** |
| 33. Bob W. Johnson | June 4, 1967 (1st game) |
| 34. Phil Linz | July 19, 1967 (1st game) |
| 35. Joe Moock | September 1, 1967 (1st game)* |
| **36. Amos Otis** | **September 7, 1967*** |
| **37. Ken Boswell** | **September 18, 1967*** |
| **38. Bob Heise** | **September 25, 1967** |
| **39. Al Weis** | **May 1, 1968** |
| **40. Wayne Garrett** | **May 4, 1969 (2nd game)** |
| **41. Bobby Pfeil** | **June 26, 1969*** |

* Major league debut in the field
\+ Only career appearance at 3B

—*Mets by the Numbers* (New York: Skyhorse Publishing, 2008)

JACOB KANAREK/METSINTHESEVENTIES.COM

# The Miracle's Aftermath
## Mets in the 1970s

by Jacob Kanarek

The Mets entered the decade of the 1970s on top of the baseball world. The first expansion team to ever win a world championship had the best young pitchers in the game, a no-nonsense manager, a state-of-the-art facility, and a rabid fan base. The 1970s promised great hope for the Mets and their loyal followers. And while the team was competitive in the first half of the decade, coming within one game of winning another world championship in 1973, in a very subtle manner the seams started to come apart right after the 1969 World Series.

With third baseman Ed Charles retiring after the '69 season and the Mets looking for a power hitting third baseman, the Mets sent young outfielder Amos Otis (plus pitcher Bob Johnson) to the Kansas City Royals for Joy Foy. In early January, the very capable general manager, Johnny Murphy, died of a heart attack. He was replaced by Bob Scheffing.

Because of the colossal failure of the Foy deal, the elusive search for a third baseman continued. In the winter of 1971, the Mets sent wild but highly-touted Nolan Ryan—plus three other prospects—to the California Angels in exchange for Jim Fregosi, a talented shortstop coming off a bad year. He would be moved to third base in New York, but that was an accident waiting to happen—literally. In Fregosi's first chance handling a ball in spring training 1972, Fregosi broke his thumb. That set the tone for his tenure as a Met, which ended with his release in the middle of the 1973 season.

The most tragic event to touch the team, however, occurred during spring training in 1972. The soft-spoken yet forceful manager Gil Hodges—a father figure to many players and leader to all—was felled by a fatal heart attack. In his stead the Mets named Yogi Berra as his replacement. Berra, the eternal optimist but a lax disciplinarian, had been a Mets coach since 1965 and had been considered to replace both Casey Stengel in late '65 and Wes Westrum after the '67 season. The third time proved the charm for Berra, but many believed that Whitey Herzog, the director of player development at the time, would have been the ideal replacement—and some felt Herzog should have been named GM instead of Scheffing in 1970. Board chairman M. Donald Grant felt threatened by Herzog, who believed Grant was a meddler and should stick to the stock market. Grant passed over Herzog and Berra was offered a contract just hours after Hodges's shocking death.

On the day of Hodges's funeral, April 6, 1972, the Mets announced Berra's signing and a blockbuster trade that brought Rusty Staub to the Mets from the Montreal Expos. In return the Mets sent three promising young players to the Expos: Ken Singleton, Mike Jorgensen, and Tim Foli. While the trade was widely hailed by reporters and fans alike, Herzog was one man who spoke out against it, not believing it was wise to deplete the farm system. Herzog soon left New York and the minor leagues he helped build. He replaced Ted Williams as manager of the Texas Rangers after the '72 season. Much of the Mets' ability to produce talent left with him.

The 1972 Mets got out of the gate very quickly and by mid-June the possibility of the Mets running away with the division seemed quite real. And in what appeared to be more a public relations move more than anything else, the Mets sent pitcher Charlie Williams to the San Francisco Giants—plus $50,000—in return for Willie Mays. Though well past his prime, the just turned 41-year-old Mays had long been coveted by Mets owner Joan Payson, a one-time member of the Giants board and lone dissenter for the club's move from New York to San Francisco after the 1957 season. Ironically enough, the first game Mays started as a Met came against his former team—and Mays rose to the task, hitting a home run that turned out to be the deciding run in a 5–4 win over the Giants. In short order, however, the Mets were suddenly beleaguered by injuries, most notably to Rusty Staub, who was forced to the sidelines after being hit by a Carl Morton pitch. The team slowly faded out of contention.

In the spring of 1973, the Mets made what many felt was the best trade of the decade when they dealt Gary Gentry and Danny Frisella to the Atlanta Braves in return for Felix Millan and George Stone. That season was undoubtedly the highlight of the 1970s—and the first part of the 1980s. The Mets, beset by injuries all season and floundering in last place as late as the end of August, rallied to the battle cry of "Ya Gotta Believe" from energetic reliever Tug McGraw and "It Ain't Over Till It's Over" from skipper Yogi Berra. The Mets swiped the division title from the Pittsburgh Pirates thanks to a fortuitous bounce off the wall, stunned the Cincinnati Reds in a rock 'em, sock 'em NLCS, and took the Oakland A's dynasty to the seven-game limit, falling one game short of repeating the Miracle of 1969.

Despite being desperate for a center fielder after the 1973 season, Mets management was lulled into a false sense of security, electing to focus more on the surprising National League championship rather than the fact that the team's won-lost record was only three games over the .500 mark (the worst ever for a league champion). As a result, the Mets bypassed an opportunity to acquire Jimmy Wynn from the Houston Astros. All the Astros were requesting in return was a package of George Stone and Craig Swan. The overconfident and laid back front office did nothing over the winter and the team was once again decimated by injuries in 1974. This time there was no comeback, only a dismal fifth-place finish. With the conclusion of the '74 season, general manager Bob Scheffing retired and the Mets named farm director Joe McDonald as the new GM.

With it all the more obvious that the Mets were in desperate need of a center fielder, McDonald shipped McGraw, a fan favorite and hero of the 1973 pennant drive, to the Philadelphia Phillies for center fielder Del Unser and top catching prospect John Stearns. (Don Hahn, the center fielder on the '73 champs, and young outfielder Dave Schneck also went to Philadelphia; the Mets received lefty

JACOB KANAREK/METSINTHESEVENTIES.COM

*Felix Millan had one of the most distinctive batting stances in the game. He hit .333 against the Mets in the 1969 NLCS and came to New York from Atlanta in one of the team's few successful trades of the 1970s.*

relliever Mac Scarce, who was hardly a substitute for Tug—the only batter Scarce faced as a Met, Richie Hebner, delivered a game-ending hit in Pittsburgh.)

McDonald also followed his predecessors in the GM chair by bringing home a popular player whose better days were behind him. This time it was Brooklyn-born Joe Torre, whom the Mets had tried to acquire before the 1969 season, but the club decided against it when both Amos Otis and Nolan Ryan were asked for in return. Five years and a NL MVP Award later, all Torre cost was Ray Sadecki and Tommy Moore. McDonald's best move of the offseason came at the end of February, when he purchased slugger Dave Kingman from San Francisco for a reported $150,000.

*Though the "Midnight Massacre" cost the Mets Tom Seaver and Dave Kingman, it did bring Bobby Valentine to New York. He was near the end of his playing career, but he became a coach and later a pennant-winning manager with the Mets.*

Jacob Kanarek/Metsintheseventies.com

While the 1975 team stayed in the race until mid-September, the season was not without turmoil and distraction. Cleon Jones, first injured and then embarrassed by having to publicly apologize for having an affair, rebelled against his manager by refusing to play the field when asked. Jones was suspended and subsequently released, while Yogi Berra was unceremoniously fired just a few short weeks later and replaced by longtime coach Roy McMillan. The day after the season ended, Casey Stengel, the first face of the franchise, died at age 85. That was followed that same week by the death of 72-year-old principal owner Joan Payson, giving M. Donald Grant unbridled powers. With free agency in the air and players salaries becoming more of an issue, Grant ordered McDonald to trade Rusty Staub, who was about to become a 10-and-5 man (thus receiving the power to veto any trade). McDonald could do no better than get Detroit's Mickey Lolich, a once great but clearly over-the-hill and overweight 37-year-old left-hander, in exchange for the popular outfielder who that year had become the first Met to drive in 100 runs in a season.

Once again the team was lulled into a false sense of security, this time by the late-season production of rookie Mike Vail. He had impressed everyone with a 23-game hitting streak in September of '75 and was immediately crowned as Staub's successor in right field. Vail sprained his ankle in a pickup basketball game during the offseason and never came close to showing the success of his first month as a major leaguer. Staub was voted to the American League All-Star team the season after the deal and wound up with 2,716 hits over a long and very productive career that eventually ended back with the Mets.

Another mistake was picking Joe Frazier to manage the team. Though the Mets still had enough talent to win 85 games in 1976—the second-best mark to that point in franchise history—the Phillies ran away with the division early on and the Mets were never in contention. The highlights of the season were Dave Kingman chasing Hack Wilson's National League record for home runs, which came to a crashing halt when he ripped ligaments in his thumb and was out of the lineup for six weeks, and Jerry Koosman winning 20 games for the first time in his career. The lowlight was the senseless trade with Montreal involving Del Unser and Wayne Garrett, the Mets third baseman throughout the club's constant attempts to do better at the position, for Pepe Manguel and Jim Dwyer, neither of whom played in New York beyond that season.

Free agency became a reality after the 1976 season. While the Mets remained desperate for a power bat in the lineup to go with the feast-or-famine Kingman, their tepid pursuit of free agent Gary Matthews was laughable. By contrast, the American League champion Yankees, who had shared Shea for the 1974 and '75 seasons while Yankee Stadium was rebuilt, boldly dove into the free agent pool and came up with Reggie Jackson. The Mets wound up making no major acquisitions and essentially ran out the same team that had ended the previous season. This did not sit well with the players in general and Tom Seaver in particular. Seaver was also annoyed that the new contracts free agents were signing made him grossly underpaid by comparison at $225,000 per year. He wanted to renegotiate his contract—and management adamantly refused. Additionally, Dave Kingman was also looking to sign a contract comparative to the five-year, $2.7 million deal inked by Reggie Jackson in the Bronx. Once again, the Mets refused.

With the team in turmoil, the Mets got off to a slow start in 1977. By May 30, the Mets were 15 games under .500, 14 games out, and ready to change managers. Frazier was let go, replaced by Joe Torre, who actually appeared in two games as a player-manager. He ended his playing career in the middle of June, but Torre remained as manager of the club through 1981.

While Torre added life to the demoralized team in his first weeks on the job in '77, the Mets and Seaver tried one last time to reconcile their differences, and apparently thought that they had. With the Mets in Atlanta on the June 15 trading deadline, longtime *Daily News* columnist Dick Young wrote that Seaver's wife was jealous of Nolan Ryan's wife because the Angels ace made more money. An enraged Seaver called off the agreement and demanded to be traded immediately. Shortly before the midnight trading deadline, the Mets sent Seaver to the Reds in return for Pat Zachry, Doug Flynn, Steve Henderson, and Dan Norman. At the same time, Kingman was exiled to San Diego for Bobby Valentine and Paul Siebert. It was called the "Midnight Massacre" and with it ended any hopes for another Miracle anytime soon at Shea Stadium.

With the team now devoid of stars, the fortunes of the franchise dipped to an all time low. The team finished in the cellar for the first time since 1967. A year after his triumphant 20-win season, Koosman lost 20 games, including Seaver's return to Shea in August. That game provided the last 45,000-plus crowd at Shea Stadium for the rest of the decade.

JACOB KANAREK/METSINTHESEVENTIES.COM

*Jon Matlack took Nolan Ryan's spot in the rotation after the lamentable 1971 trade. Matlack won the 1972 Rookie of the Year Award and combined with Tom Seaver and Jerry Koosman to give the Mets as good a power trio as any team in the league… if only the Mets could score.*

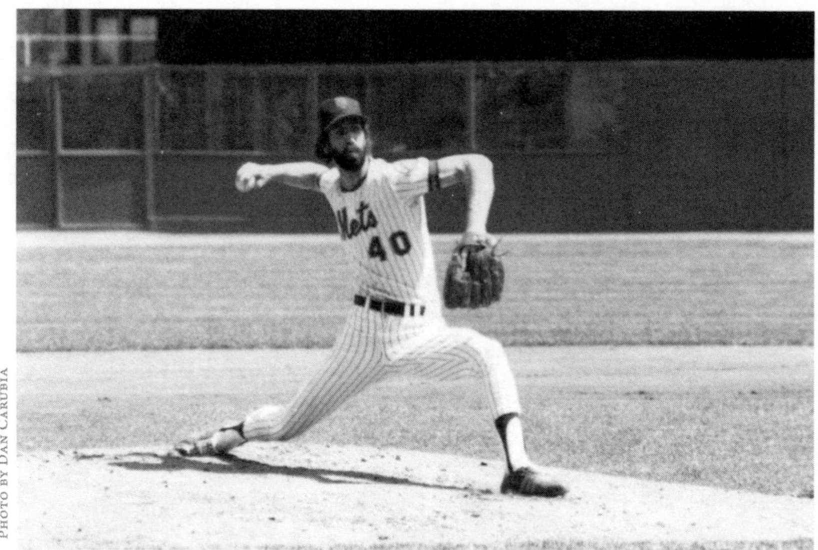


PHOTO BY DAN CARUBIA

*Pat Zachry lasted longer on the Mets than any of the other three players acquired in the 1977 Tom Seaver trade. Coincidentally, Zachry won 41 games as a Met—he lost 46. Number 41, Seaver, also lost 46 over the same period, but he won 75 times for Cincinnati.*

With the team now in rebuilding mode, the Mets sent Jon Matlack and John Milner to the Texas Rangers as part of a blockbuster four-team, 12-player trade that brought Willie Montanez to the Mets. This and the other few moves made by the Mets that winter resulted in little change to the team's record in 1978 (the Mets lost 96 games, as opposed to 98 from the previous year). Koosman, who along with Ed Kranepool was the only holdover from the 1969 team, decided that an 11–35 record over the past two seasons did not compute with his league average 3.62 ERA. He demanded to be traded to his native Minnesota. Management acquiesced and dealt Koosman to the Twins for Greg Field and a young left-handed reliever named Jesse Orosco.

By the time the decade ended, the Mets were in total disarray. Three consecutive last place finishes and the lowest attendance in team history made ownership realize it was time to sell the team. Despite the Mets being at their lowest point, the New York franchise still commanded a record sum of $21.1 million. Nelson Doubleday took over as chairman of the board, Fred Wilpon became team president, and Frank Cashen was hired as general manager. Just as had been the case when the team first took the field in 1962, the Mets had nowhere to go but up.

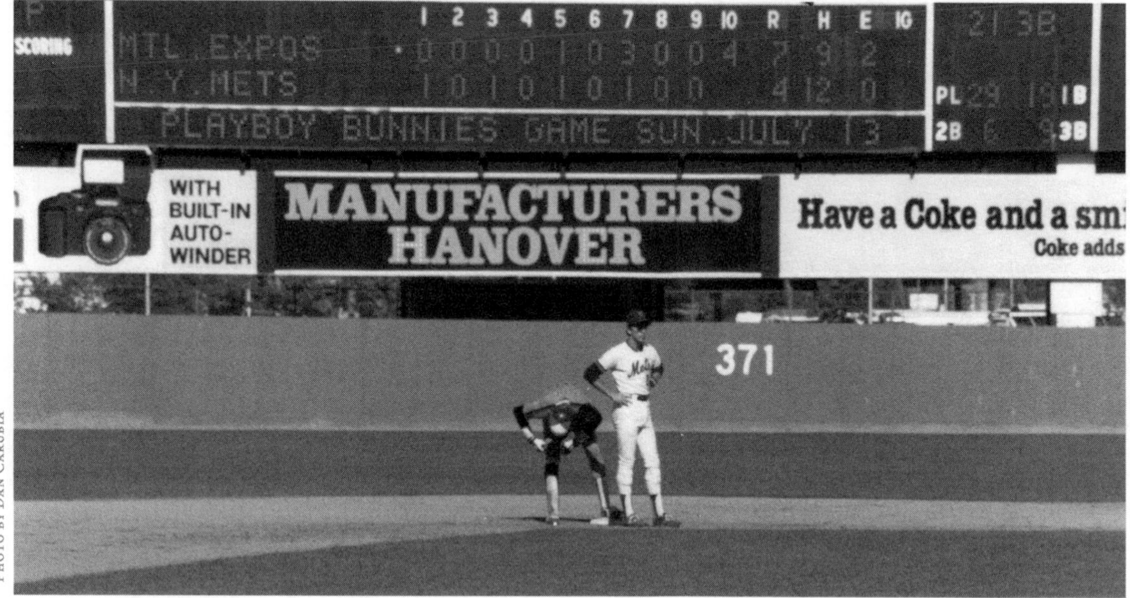


PHOTO BY DAN CARUBIA

*By the time the decade of the 1970s was over, new entertainment was clearly needed at Shea Stadium.*

# Appendix

# STATISTICS FOR REGULAR SEASON 1969

## BATTING

| | Age | Pos | G | PA | AB | R | H | 2B | 3B | HR | RBI | SB | CS | BB | K | BA | OBP | SLG | OPS | OPS+ | TB | GDP | HBP | IBB |
|---|---|---|---|---|---|---|---|---|---|---|---|---|---|---|---|---|---|---|---|---|---|---|---|---|
| Jerry Grote | 26 | C | 113 | 406 | 365 | 38 | 92 | 12 | 3 | 6 | 40 | 2 | 1 | 32 | 59 | .252 | .313 | .351 | .663 | 84 | 128 | 10 | 1 | 5 |
| Ed Kranepool* | 24 | 1B | 112 | 396 | 353 | 36 | 84 | 9 | 2 | 11 | 49 | 3 | 2 | 37 | 32 | .238 | .307 | .368 | .675 | 87 | 130 | 10 | 0 | 7 |
| Ken Boswell* | 23 | 2B | 102 | 405 | 362 | 48 | 101 | 14 | 7 | 3 | 32 | 7 | 3 | 36 | 47 | .279 | .347 | .381 | .728 | 103 | 138 | 13 | 2 | 3 |
| Bud Harrelson# | 25 | SS | 123 | 457 | 395 | 42 | 98 | 11 | 6 | 0 | 24 | 1 | 3 | 54 | 54 | .248 | .341 | .306 | .647 | 82 | 121 | 5 | 2 | 7 |
| Wayne Garrett* | 21 | 3B | 124 | 454 | 400 | 38 | 87 | 11 | 3 | 1 | 39 | 4 | 2 | 40 | 75 | .218 | .29 | .268 | .558 | 56 | 107 | 5 | 3 | 3 |
| Cleon Jones | 26 | LF | 137 | 558 | 483 | 92 | 164 | 25 | 4 | 12 | 75 | 16 | 8 | 64 | 60 | .340 | .422 | .482 | .904 | 151 | 233 | 11 | 7 | 10 |
| Tommie Agee | 26 | CF | 149 | 635 | 565 | 97 | 153 | 23 | 4 | 26 | 76 | 12 | 9 | 59 | 137 | .271 | .342 | .464 | .806 | 122 | 262 | 5 | 3 | 2 |
| Ron Swoboda | 25 | RF | 109 | 375 | 327 | 38 | 77 | 10 | 2 | 9 | 52 | 1 | 1 | 43 | 90 | .235 | .326 | .361 | .687 | 91 | 118 | 10 | 2 | 4 |
| Art Shamsky* | 27 | RF | 100 | 349 | 303 | 42 | 91 | 9 | 3 | 14 | 47 | 1 | 2 | 36 | 32 | .300 | .375 | .488 | .863 | 139 | 148 | 5 | 3 | 2 |
| Al Weis# | 31 | MI | 103 | 269 | 247 | 20 | 53 | 9 | 2 | 2 | 23 | 3 | 3 | 15 | 51 | .215 | .259 | .291 | .550 | 53 | 72 | 3 | 0 | 1 |
| Rod Gaspar# | 23 | RF | 118 | 250 | 215 | 26 | 49 | 6 | 1 | 1 | 14 | 7 | 3 | 25 | 19 | .228 | .313 | .279 | .592 | 66 | 60 | 1 | 2 | 2 |
| Donn Clendenon | 33 | 1B | 72 | 226 | 202 | 31 | 51 | 5 | 0 | 12 | 37 | 3 | 2 | 19 | 62 | .252 | .321 | .455 | .777 | 114 | 92 | 3 | 2 | 4 |
| Bobby Pfeil | 25 | 3B | 62 | 223 | 211 | 20 | 49 | 9 | 0 | 0 | 10 | 0 | 1 | 7 | 27 | .232 | .26 | .275 | .535 | 49 | 58 | 5 | 1 | 0 |
| J.C. Martin* | 32 | C | 66 | 192 | 177 | 12 | 37 | 5 | 1 | 4 | 21 | 0 | 0 | 12 | 32 | .209 | .257 | .316 | .573 | 59 | 56 | 6 | 0 | 1 |
| Ed Charles | 36 | 3B | 61 | 189 | 169 | 21 | 35 | 8 | 1 | 3 | 18 | 4 | 2 | 18 | 31 | .207 | .286 | .32 | .605 | 68 | 54 | 6 | 1 | 3 |
| Amos Otis | 22 | OF | 48 | 102 | 93 | 6 | 14 | 3 | 1 | 0 | 4 | 1 | 0 | 6 | 27 | .151 | .202 | .204 | .406 | 13 | 19 | 0 | 0 | 1 |
| Duffy Dyer | 23 | C | 29 | 79 | 74 | 5 | 19 | 3 | 1 | 3 | 12 | 0 | 0 | 4 | 22 | .257 | .295 | .446 | .741 | 104 | 33 | 3 | 0 | 0 |
| Kevin Collins* | 22 | 3B | 16 | 43 | 40 | 1 | 6 | 3 | 0 | 1 | 2 | 0 | 0 | 3 | 10 | .150 | .209 | .300 | .509 | 40 | 12 | 0 | 0 | 1 |
| Jim Gosger* | 26 | OF | 10 | 16 | 15 | 0 | 2 | 2 | 0 | 0 | 1 | 0 | 0 | 1 | 6 | .133 | .188 | .267 | .454 | 25 | 4 | 0 | 0 | 1 |
| Bob Heise | 22 | SS | 4 | 13 | 10 | 1 | 3 | 1 | 0 | 0 | 0 | 0 | 0 | 3 | 2 | .300 | .462 | .400 | .862 | 142 | 4 | 1 | 0 | 1 |
| Tom Seaver | 24 | P | 39 | 104 | 91 | 7 | 11 | 3 | 0 | 0 | 6 | 1 | 0 | 7 | 34 | .121 | .200 | .154 | .354 | 0 | 14 | 0 | 2 | 0 |
| Jerry Koosman | 26 | P | 32 | 89 | 84 | 1 | 4 | 0 | 0 | 0 | 1 | 0 | 0 | 1 | 46 | .048 | .059 | .048 | .106 | -70 | 4 | 2 | 0 | 0 |
| Gary Gentry | 22 | P | 35 | 84 | 74 | 2 | 6 | 1 | 0 | 0 | 1 | 0 | 0 | 1 | 52 | .081 | .104 | .095 | .198 | -44 | 7 | 0 | 1 | 0 |
| Don Cardwell | 33 | P | 30 | 51 | 47 | 3 | 8 | 0 | 0 | 1 | 5 | 0 | 0 | 0 | 26 | .170 | .184 | .234 | .418 | 16 | 11 | 0 | 1 | 0 |
| Jim McAndrew | 25 | P | 27 | 45 | 37 | 0 | 5 | 1 | 0 | 0 | 3 | 0 | 1 | 3 | 18 | .135 | .200 | .162 | .362 | 2 | 6 | 0 | 0 | 0 |
| Nolan Ryan | 22 | P | 25 | 32 | 29 | 3 | 3 | 0 | 0 | 0 | 2 | 0 | 0 | 0 | 14 | .103 | .103 | .103 | .207 | -42 | 3 | 1 | 0 | 0 |
| Tug McGraw | 24 | P | 43 | 25 | 24 | 1 | 4 | 1 | 0 | 0 | 3 | 0 | 0 | 1 | 6 | .167 | .200 | .208 | .408 | 14 | 5 | 0 | 0 | 0 |
| Cal Koonce | 28 | P | 40 | 17 | 17 | 1 | 4 | 0 | 0 | 0 | 1 | 0 | 0 | 0 | 7 | .235 | .235 | .235 | .471 | 31 | 4 | 0 | 0 | 0 |
| Jack DiLauro# | 26 | P | 23 | 12 | 12 | 0 | 0 | 0 | 0 | 0 | 0 | 0 | 0 | 0 | 9 | .000 | .000 | .000 | .000 | -100 | 0 | 0 | 0 | 0 |
| Ron Taylor | 31 | P | 59 | 4 | 4 | 0 | 1 | 0 | 0 | 0 | 0 | 0 | 0 | 0 | 2 | .250 | .250 | .250 | .500 | 40 | 1 | 0 | 0 | 0 |
| Al Jackson* | 33 | P | 9 | 1 | 1 | 0 | 0 | 0 | 0 | 0 | 0 | 0 | 0 | 0 | 0 | .000 | .000 | .000 | .000 | -100 | 0 | 0 | 0 | 0 |
| Danny Frisella* | 23 | P | 3 | 1 | 1 | 0 | 0 | 0 | 0 | 0 | 0 | 0 | 0 | 0 | 0 | .000 | .000 | .000 | .000 | -100 | 0 | 0 | 0 | 0 |
| Les Rohr* | 23 | P | 1 | 0 | 0 | 0 | 0 | 0 | 0 | 0 | 0 | 0 | 0 | 0 | 0 | - | - | - | - | - | 0 | 0 | 0 | 0 |
| Jesse Hudson* | 20 | P | 1 | 0 | 0 | 0 | 0 | 0 | 0 | 0 | 0 | 0 | 0 | 0 | 0 | - | - | - | - | - | 0 | 0 | 0 | 0 |
| Bob Johnson* | 26 | P | 2 | 0 | 0 | 0 | 0 | 0 | 0 | 0 | 0 | 0 | 0 | 0 | 0 | - | - | - | - | - | 0 | 0 | 0 | 0 |
| **Team Totals** | | | **162** | **6102** | **5427** | **632** | **1311** | **184** | **41** | **109** | **598** | **66** | **43** | **527** | **1089** | **.242** | **.311** | **.351** | **.662** | **84** | **1904** | **105** | **33** | **58** |
| **Rank in 12 NL teams** | | | | | **8** | **9** | **8** | **11** | **6** | **8** | **7** | **8** | **9** | **6** | **3** | **7** | **10** | **11** | **11** | | **10** | | | |

* - bats left-handed, # - bats both, else - bats right; league OPS for OPS+ does not include pitchers.

## PITCHING

| | Age | Pos | W | L | ERA | G | GS | GF | CG | SHO | SV | IP | H | R | ER | HR | BB | IBB | K | BF | ERA+ | WHIP | H/9 | HR/9 | BB/9 | K/9 | K/BB |
|---|---|---|---|---|---|---|---|---|---|---|---|---|---|---|---|---|---|---|---|---|---|---|---|---|---|---|---|
| Tom Seaver | 24 | SP | 25 | 7 | 2.21 | 36 | 35 | 1 | 18 | 5 | 0 | 273.1 | 202 | 75 | 67 | 24 | 82 | 9 | 208 | 1089 | 165 | 1.039 | 6.7 | 0.8 | 2.7 | 6.8 | 2.5 |
| Jerry Koosman* | 26 | SP | 17 | 9 | 2.28 | 32 | 32 | 0 | 16 | 6 | 0 | 241 | 187 | 66 | 61 | 14 | 68 | 11 | 180 | 957 | 160 | 1.058 | 7.0 | 0.5 | 2.5 | 6.7 | 2.7 |
| Gary Gentry | 22 | SP | 13 | 12 | 3.43 | 35 | 35 | 0 | 6 | 3 | 0 | 233.2 | 192 | 94 | 89 | 24 | 81 | 5 | 154 | 962 | 106 | 1.168 | 7.4 | 0.9 | 3.1 | 5.9 | 1.9 |
| Don Cardwell | 33 | SP | 8 | 10 | 3.01 | 30 | 21 | 2 | 4 | 0 | 0 | 152.1 | 145 | 63 | 51 | 15 | 47 | 10 | 60 | 635 | 121 | 1.260 | 8.6 | 0.9 | 2.8 | 3.5 | 1.3 |
| Jim McAndrew | 25 | SP | 6 | 7 | 3.47 | 27 | 21 | 3 | 4 | 2 | 0 | 135 | 112 | 57 | 52 | 12 | 44 | 6 | 90 | 553 | 105 | 1.156 | 7.5 | 0.8 | 2.9 | 6.0 | 2.1 |
| Ron Taylor | 31 | CL | 9 | 4 | 2.72 | 59 | 0 | 44 | 0 | 0 | 13 | 76 | 61 | 23 | 23 | 7 | 24 | 6 | 42 | 300 | 133 | 1.118 | 7.2 | 0.8 | 2.8 | 5.0 | 1.8 |
| Tug McGraw* | 24 | RP | 9 | 3 | 2.24 | 42 | 4 | 26 | 1 | 0 | 12 | 100.1 | 89 | 31 | 25 | 6 | 47 | 7 | 92 | 424 | 162 | 1.355 | 8.0 | 0.5 | 4.2 | 8.3 | 2.0 |
| Nolan Ryan | 22 | RP | 6 | 3 | 3.53 | 25 | 10 | 4 | 2 | 0 | 1 | 89.1 | 60 | 38 | 35 | 3 | 53 | 3 | 92 | 375 | 103 | 1.265 | 6.0 | 0.3 | 5.3 | 9.3 | 1.7 |
| Cal Koonce | 28 | RP | 6 | 3 | 4.99 | 40 | 0 | 19 | 0 | 0 | 7 | 83 | 85 | 53 | 46 | 8 | 42 | 8 | 48 | 367 | 73 | 1.530 | 9.2 | 0.9 | 4.6 | 5.2 | 1.1 |
| Jack DiLauro* | 26 | RP | 1 | 4 | 2.40 | 23 | 4 | 8 | 0 | 0 | 1 | 63.2 | 50 | 19 | 17 | 4 | 18 | 5 | 27 | 256 | 151 | 1.068 | 7.1 | 0.6 | 2.5 | 3.8 | 1.5 |
| Al Jackson* | 33 | RP | 0 | 0 | 10.64 | 9 | 0 | 1 | 0 | 0 | 0 | 11 | 18 | 13 | 13 | 1 | 4 | 0 | 10 | 58 | 34 | 2.000 | 14.7 | 0.8 | 3.3 | 8.2 | 2.5 |
| Danny Frisella | 23 | RP | 0 | 0 | 7.71 | 3 | 0 | 0 | 0 | 0 | 0 | 4.2 | 8 | 4 | 4 | 1 | 3 | 0 | 5 | 24 | 47 | 2.357 | 15.4 | 1.9 | 5.8 | 9.6 | 1.7 |
| Jesse Hudson* | 20 | RP | 0 | 0 | 4.50 | 1 | 0 | 1 | 0 | 0 | 0 | 2 | 2 | 1 | 1 | 0 | 2 | 0 | 3 | 10 | 81 | 2.000 | 9.0 | 0.0 | 9.0 | 13.5 | 1.5 |
| Bob Johnson | 26 | RP | 0 | 0 | 0.00 | 2 | 0 | 2 | 0 | 0 | 1 | 1.2 | 1 | 0 | 0 | 0 | 1 | 0 | 1 | 7 | - | 1.200 | 5.4 | 0.0 | 5.4 | 5.4 | 1.0 |
| Les Rohr* | 23 | RP | 0 | 0 | 20.25 | 1 | 0 | 0 | 0 | 0 | 0 | 1.1 | 5 | 4 | 3 | 0 | 1 | 0 | 0 | 10 | 18 | 4.500 | 33.8 | 0.0 | 6.8 | 0.0 | 0.0 |
| **Team Totals** | | | **100** | **62** | **2.99** | **162** | **162** | **111** | **51** | **16** | **35** | **1468.1** | **1217** | **541** | **487** | **119** | **517** | **70** | **1012** | **6027** | **122** | **1.181** | **7.5** | **0.7** | **3.2** | **6.2** | **1.96** |
| **Rank in 12 NL teams** | | | **1** | **12** | **2** | | | | **5** | **1** | **3** | **2** | **1** | **2** | **2** | **6** | **6** | | **4** | | | **1** | **1** | **3** | **6** | **4** | **8** |

* - throws left-handed

## FIELDING

| | Age | G | GS | Inn | Ch | PO | A | E | DP | Fld% | PB | WP | SB | CS | CS% | Pos. Summary |
|---|---|---|---|---|---|---|---|---|---|---|---|---|---|---|---|---|
| Tommie Agee | 26 | 151 | 141 | 1265 | 351 | 339 | 7 | 5 | 0 | .986 | - | - | - | - | - | CF-RF |
| Ken Boswell | 23 | 96 | 91 | 793 | 437 | 190 | 229 | 18 | 51 | .959 | - | - | - | - | - | 2B |
| Don Cardwell | 33 | 30 | 21 | 152.1 | 53 | 9 | 41 | 3 | 0 | .943 | - | - | - | - | - | P |
| Ed Charles | 36 | 52 | 45 | 387 | 130 | 37 | 86 | 7 | 9 | .946 | - | - | - | - | - | 3B |
| Donn Clendenon | 33 | 59 | 46 | 438 | 450 | 418 | 25 | 7 | 46 | .984 | - | - | - | - | - | 1B-LF |
| Kevin Collins | 22 | 14 | 11 | 98.2 | 40 | 11 | 26 | 3 | 2 | .925 | - | - | - | - | - | 3B |
| Jack DiLauro | 26 | 23 | 4 | 63.2 | 16 | 6 | 10 | 0 | 0 | 1.000 | - | - | - | - | - | P |
| Duffy Dyer | 23 | 19 | 18 | 165.1 | 116 | 105 | 10 | 1 | 0 | .991 | 0 | 3 | 8 | 3 | 27% | C |
| Danny Frisella | 23 | 3 | 0 | 4.2 | 0 | 0 | 0 | 0 | 0 | - | - | - | - | - | - | P |
| Wayne Garrett | 21 | 128 | 98 | 937.1 | 376 | 147 | 218 | 11 | 37 | .971 | - | - | - | - | - | 3B-2B-SS |
| Rod Gaspar | 23 | 103 | 44 | 492 | 117 | 105 | 10 | 2 | 6 | .983 | - | - | - | - | - | RF-CF-LF |
| Gary Gentry | 22 | 35 | 35 | 233.2 | 54 | 13 | 41 | 0 | 4 | 1.000 | - | - | - | - | - | P |
| Jim Gosger | 26 | 5 | 3 | 30 | 5 | 5 | 0 | 0 | 0 | 1.000 | - | - | - | - | - | LF-CF |
| Jerry Grote | 26 | 112 | 100 | 918.2 | 788 | 718 | 63 | 7 | 11 | .991 | 4 | 36 | 31 | 40 | 56% | C |
| Bud Harrelson | 25 | 119 | 115 | 1033 | 609 | 243 | 347 | 19 | 70 | .969 | - | - | - | - | - | SS |
| Bob Heise | 22 | 3 | 3 | 27 | 9 | 4 | 5 | 0 | 0 | 1.000 | - | - | - | - | - | SS |
| Jesse Hudson | 20 | 1 | 0 | 2 | 1 | 0 | 1 | 0 | 0 | 1.000 | - | - | - | - | - | P |
| Al Jackson | 33 | 9 | 0 | 11 | 4 | 2 | 2 | 0 | 0 | 1.000 | - | - | - | - | - | P |
| Bob Johnson | 26 | 2 | 0 | 1.2 | 0 | 0 | 0 | 0 | 0 | - | - | - | - | - | - | P |
| Cleon Jones | 26 | 137 | 131 | 1125.2 | 338 | 325 | 11 | 2 | 3 | .994 | - | - | - | - | - | LF-1B |
| Cal Koonce | 28 | 40 | 0 | 83 | 25 | 7 | 18 | 0 | 2 | 1.000 | - | - | - | - | - | P |
| Jerry Koosman | 26 | 32 | 32 | 241 | 42 | 4 | 37 | 1 | 3 | .976 | - | - | - | - | - | P |
| Ed Kranepool | 24 | 108 | 97 | 867 | 880 | 810 | 64 | 6 | 76 | .993 | - | - | - | - | - | 1B-LF |
| J.C. Martin | 32 | 50 | 44 | 388.1 | 289 | 279 | 9 | 1 | 2 | .997 | 3 | 17 | 15 | 4 | 21% | C-1B |
| Jim McAndrew | 25 | 27 | 21 | 135 | 24 | 10 | 14 | 0 | 1 | 1.000 | - | - | - | - | - | P |
| Tug McGraw | 24 | 42 | 4 | 100.1 | 29 | 6 | 19 | 4 | 2 | .862 | - | - | - | - | - | P |
| Amos Otis | 22 | 38 | 20 | 211 | 54 | 49 | 4 | 1 | 0 | .981 | - | - | - | - | - | CF-LF-3B |
| Bobby Pfeil | 25 | 60 | 50 | 452.1 | 162 | 53 | 105 | 4 | 12 | .975 | - | - | - | - | - | 3B-2B |
| Les Rohr | 23 | 1 | 0 | 1.1 | 0 | 0 | 0 | 0 | 0 | - | - | - | - | - | - | P |
| Nolan Ryan | 22 | 25 | 10 | 89.1 | 5 | 0 | 4 | 1 | 0 | .800 | - | - | - | - | - | P |
| Tom Seaver | 24 | 36 | 35 | 273.1 | 68 | 18 | 48 | 2 | 7 | .971 | - | - | - | - | - | P |
| Art Shamsky | 27 | 88 | 83 | 661.1 | 194 | 190 | 2 | 2 | 7 | .990 | - | - | - | - | - | RF-LF-1B |
| Ron Swoboda | 25 | 101 | 86 | 801.1 | 166 | 159 | 5 | 2 | 0 | .988 | - | - | - | - | - | RF-LF |
| Ron Taylor | 31 | 59 | 0 | 76 | 19 | 6 | 13 | 0 | 1 | 1.000 | - | - | - | - | - | P |
| Al Weis | 31 | 96 | 70 | 654.2 | 369 | 138 | 218 | 13 | 50 | .965 | - | - | - | - | - | SS-2B-3B |
| **Team Totals** | | **162** | **1458** | **13215** | **6223** | **4405** | **1696** | **122** | **402** | **.980** | **7** | **56** | **54** | **47** | **47%** | |

# 1969 METS GAME-BY-GAME

| Date | Opp | | R | RA | W-L | Rk | GB | Win | Loss |
|---|---|---|---|---|---|---|---|---|---|
| 8-Apr | MON | L | 10 | 11 | 0-1 | 4 | 1 | Shaw | Koonce |
| 9-Apr | MON | W | 9 | 5 | 1-1 | 3 | 1 | McGraw | Stoneman |
| 10-Apr | MON | W | 4 | 2 | 2-1 | 3 | 1 | Gentry | Jaster |
| 11-Apr | STL | L | 5 | 6 | 2-2 | 3 | 2 | Carlton | Koosman |
| 12-Apr | STL | L | 0 | 1 | 2-3 | 3 | 2 | Giusti | Cardwell |
| 13-Apr | STL | L | 1 | 3 | 2-4 | 4 | 3 | Gibson | Seaver |
| 14-Apr | @ PHI | L | 1 | 5 | 2-5 | 5 | 4 | Fryman | McAndrew |
| 15-Apr | @ PHI | W | 6 | 3 | 3-5 | 4 | 4 | Gentry | Wagner |
| 16-Apr | @ PIT | L | 3 | 11 | 3-6 | 5 | 5 | Moose | Koosman |
| 17-Apr | @ PIT | L | 0 | 4 | 3-7 | 5 | 6 | Bunning | Cardwell |
| 19-Apr | @ STL | W | 2 | 1 | 4-7 | 4 | 6 | Seaver | Gibson |
| 20-Apr | @ STL | W | 11 | 3 | 5-7 | 3 | 5.5 | Ryan | Briles |
| 21-Apr | PHI | L | 1 | 2 | 5-8 | 3 | 6 | Fryman | Taylor |
| 23-Apr | PIT | W | 2 | 0 | 6-8 | 3 | 4.5 | Koosman | Bunning |
| 25-Apr | CHC | L | 1 | 3 | 6-9 | 4 | 5 | Jenkins | Seaver |
| 26-Apr | CHC | L | 3 | 9 | 6-10 | 5 | 6 | Hands | Cardwell |
| 27-Apr | CHC | L | 6 | 8 | 6-11 | 4 | 6 | Regan | Koonce |
| 27-Apr | CHC | W | 3 | 0 | 7-11 | 4 | 6 | McGraw | Nye |
| 29-Apr | @ MON | W | 2 | 0 | 8-11 | 3 | 6.5 | Ryan | Grant |
| 30-Apr | @ MON | W | 2 | 1 | 9-11 | 3 | 5.5 | Seaver | Wegener |
| 1-May | @ MON | L | 2 | 3 | 9-12 | 4 | 6 | Face | Cardwell |
| 2-May | @ CHC | L | 4 | 6 | 9-13 | 5 | 7 | Holtzman | Gentry |
| 3-May | @ CHC | L | 2 | 3 | 9-14 | 5 | 8 | Regan | Koonce |
| 4-May | @ CHC | W | 3 | 2 | 10-14 | 4 | 6 | Seaver | Hands |
| 4-May | @ CHC | W | 3 | 2 | 11-14 | 4 | 6 | McGraw | Selma |
| 6-May | CIN | W | 8 | 1 | 12-14 | 4 | 6 | Cardwell | Nolan |
| 7-May | CIN | L | 0 | 3 | 12-15 | 4 | 6 | Merritt | Gentry |
| 10-May | HOU | W | 3 | 1 | 13-15 | 3 | 5 | Seaver | Lemaster |
| 11-May | HOU | L | 1 | 4 | 13-16 | 3 | 5.5 | Dierker | Cardwell |
| 11-May | HOU | W | 11 | 7 | 14-16 | 3 | 5.5 | Koonce | Wilson |
| 13-May | ATL | L | 3 | 4 | 14-17 | 3 | 7 | Reed | Gentry |
| 14-May | ATL | W | 9 | 3 | 15-17 | 3 | 7 | Seaver | Niekro |
| 15-May | ATL | L | 5 | 6 | 15-18 | 3 | 7.5 | Jarvis | Cardwell |
| 16-May | @ CIN | W | 10 | 9 | 16-18 | 3 | 7.5 | Koonce | Culver |
| 17-May | @ CIN | W | 11 | 3 | 17-18 | 3 | 6.5 | Gentry | Maloney |
| 21-May | @ ATL | W | 5 | 0 | 18-18 | 3 | 5.5 | Seaver | Niekro |
| 22-May | @ ATL | L | 3 | 15 | 18-19 | 3 | 6.5 | Jarvis | McGraw |
| 23-May | @ HOU | L | 0 | 7 | 18-20 | 4 | 7.5 | Griffin | Gentry |
| 24-May | @ HOU | L | 1 | 5 | 18-21 | 4 | 8.5 | Dierker | Koosman |
| 25-May | @ HOU | L | 3 | 6 | 18-22 | 4 | 9 | Lemaster | Seaver |
| 27-May | SDP | L | 2 | 3 | 18-23 | 4 | 9 | Santorini | McAndrew |
| 28-May | SDP | W | 1 | 0 | 19-23 | 4 | 9 | McGraw | McCool |
| 30-May | SFG | W | 4 | 3 | 20-23 | 3 | 9 | Seaver | Linzy |
| 31-May | SFG | W | 4 | 2 | 21-23 | 3 | 9 | Gentry | Perry |
| 1-Jun | SFG | W | 5 | 4 | 22-23 | 3 | 9 | Taylor | Gibbon |
| 2-Jun | LAD | W | 2 | 1 | 23-23 | 3 | 8.5 | Koosman | Osteen |
| 3-Jun | LAD | W | 5 | 2 | 24-23 | 2 | 8.5 | Seaver | Foster |
| 4-Jun | LAD | W | 1 | 0 | 25-23 | 2 | 8.5 | Taylor | Mikkelsen |
| 6-Jun | @ SDP | W | 5 | 3 | 26-23 | 2 | 8.5 | Gentry | Ross |
| 7-Jun | @ SDP | W | 4 | 1 | 27-23 | 2 | 8 | Koosman | Podres |
| 8-Jun | @ SDP | W | 3 | 2 | 28-23 | 2 | 7.5 | Seaver | Santorini |
| 10-Jun | @ SFG | W | 9 | 4 | 29-23 | 2 | 7 | Cardwell | McCormick |
| 11-Jun | @ SFG | L | 2 | 7 | 29-24 | 2 | 7 | Perry | Gentry |
| 13-Jun | @ LAD | L | 0 | 1 | 29-25 | 2 | 8.5 | Foster | Koosman |
| 14-Jun | @ LAD | W | 3 | 1 | 30-25 | 2 | 8.5 | Seaver | Sutton |
| 15-Jun | @ LAD | L | 2 | 3 | 30-26 | 2 | 9 | Drysdale | DiLauro |
| 17-Jun | @ PHI | W | 1 | 0 | 31-26 | 2 | 7.5 | Gentry | Champion |
| 17-Jun | @ PHI | L | 3 | 7 | 31-27 | 2 | 7.5 | Jackson | Cardwell |
| 18-Jun | @ PHI | W | 2 | 0 | 32-27 | 2 | 6.5 | Koosman | Wise |
| 19-Jun | @ PHI | W | 6 | 5 | 33-27 | 2 | 6 | Taylor | Raffo |
| 20-Jun | STL | W | 4 | 3 | 34-27 | 2 | 6 | Ryan | Gibson |
| 21-Jun | STL | L | 3 | 5 | 34-28 | 2 | 6 | Briles | DiLauro |
| 22-Jun | STL | W | 5 | 1 | 35-28 | 2 | 5 | Gentry | Carlton |
| 22-Jun | STL | W | 1 | 0 | 36-28 | 2 | 5 | Koosman | Torrez |
| 24-Jun | PHI | W | 2 | 1 | 37-28 | 2 | 5 | Seaver | Fryman |
| 24-Jun | PHI | W | 5 | 0 | 38-28 | 2 | 5 | McAndrew | Johnson |
| 25-Jun | PHI | L | 5 | 6 | 38-29 | 2 | 6 | Wilson | Taylor |
| 26-Jun | PHI | L | 0 | 2 | 38-30 | 2 | 7 | Jackson | Cardwell |
| 27-Jun | PIT | L | 1 | 3 | 38-31 | 2 | 7 | Blass | Koosman |
| 28-Jun | PIT | L | 4 | 7 | 38-32 | 2 | 8 | Bunning | Gentry |
| 29-Jun | PIT | W | 7 | 3 | 39-32 | 2 | 8.5 | Seaver | Veale |
| 30-Jun | @ STL | W | 10 | 2 | 40-32 | 2 | 7.5 | McAndrew | Briles |
| 1-Jul | @ STL | L | 1 | 4 | 40-33 | 2 | 8 | Carlton | Ryan |
| 1-Jul | @ STL | L | 5 | 8 | 40-34 | 2 | 8 | Torrez | DiLauro |
| 2-Jul | @ STL | W | 6 | 4 | 41-34 | 2 | 8 | McGraw | Willis |
| 3-Jul | @ STL | W | 8 | 1 | 42-34 | 2 | 8 | Gentry | Grant |
| 4-Jul | @ PIT | W | 11 | 6 | 43-34 | 2 | 7.5 | Seaver | Veale |
| 4-Jul | @ PIT | W | 9 | 2 | 44-34 | 2 | 7.5 | Cardwell | Ellis |
| 6-Jul | @ PIT | W | 8 | 7 | 45-34 | 2 | 5.5 | Taylor | Hartenstein |
| 8-Jul | CHC | W | 4 | 3 | 46-34 | 2 | 4.5 | Koosman | Jenkins |
| 9-Jul | CHC | W | 4 | 0 | 47-34 | 2 | 3.5 | Seaver | Holtzman |
| 10-Jul | CHC | L | 2 | 6 | 47-35 | 2 | 4.5 | Hands | Gentry |
| 11-Jul | MON | L | 4 | 11 | 47-36 | 2 | 4.5 | Wegener | McAndrew |
| 13-Jul | MON | W | 4 | 3 | 48-36 | 2 | 5 | Koosman | Robertson |
| 13-Jul | MON | W | 9 | 7 | 49-36 | 2 | 5 | Koonce | McGinn |
| 14-Jul | @ CHC | L | 0 | 1 | 49-37 | 2 | 6 | Hands | Seaver |
| 15-Jul | @ CHC | W | 5 | 4 | 50-37 | 2 | 5 | Gentry | Selma |
| 16-Jul | @ CHC | W | 9 | 5 | 51-37 | 2 | 4 | Koonce | Jenkins |
| 18-Jul | @ MON | W | 5 | 2 | 52-37 | 2 | 4 | Koosman | Robertson |
| 19-Jul | @ MON | L | 4 | 5 | 52-38 | 2 | 4 | Stoneman | Seaver |
| 20-Jul | @ MON | L | 2 | 3 | 52-39 | 2 | 5 | Waslewski | Gentry |
| 20-Jul | @ MON | W | 4 | 3 | 53-39 | 2 | 5 | DiLauro | Face |
| 24-Jul | CIN | L | 3 | 4 | 53-40 | 2 | 6 | Ramos | McGraw |
| 25-Jul | CIN | W | 4 | 3 | 54-40 | 2 | 5 | Taylor | Carroll |
| 26-Jul | CIN | W | 3 | 2 | 55-40 | 2 | 5 | Seaver | Cloninger |
| 27-Jul | CIN | L | 3 | 6 | 55-41 | 2 | 5 | Arrigo | Cardwell |
| 30-Jul | HOU | L | 3 | 16 | 55-42 | 2 | 5.5 | Wilson | Koosman |
| 30-Jul | HOU | L | 5 | 11 | 55-43 | 2 | 5.5 | Dierker | Gentry |
| 31-Jul | HOU | L | 0 | 2 | 55-44 | 2 | 6.5 | Griffin | Seaver |
| 1-Aug | ATL | W | 5 | 4 | 56-44 | 2 | 6.5 | Koonce | Niekro |
| 2-Aug | ATL | W | 1 | 0 | 57-44 | 2 | 6.5 | McAndrew | Reed |
| 3-Aug | ATL | W | 6 | 5 | 58-44 | 2 | 6.5 | Taylor | Raymond |
| 4-Aug | @ CIN | L | 0 | 1 | 58-45 | 2 | 7.5 | Maloney | Koosman |
| 5-Aug | @ CIN | L | 5 | 8 | 58-46 | 2 | 8 | Nolan | Seaver |
| 5-Aug | @ CIN | W | 10 | 1 | 59-46 | 2 | 8 | Ryan | Arrigo |
| 6-Aug | @ CIN | L | 2 | 3 | 59-47 | 2 | 9 | Merritt | McAndrew |
| 8-Aug | @ ATL | W | 4 | 1 | 60-47 | 2 | 8.5 | Koosman | Pappas |
| 8-Aug | @ ATL | L | 0 | 1 | 60-48 | 2 | 8.5 | Reed | Taylor |
| 9-Aug | @ ATL | W | 5 | 3 | 61-48 | 2 | 8.5 | Seaver | Stone |
| 10-Aug | @ ATL | W | 3 | 0 | 62-48 | 2 | 7.5 | Cardwell | Britton |
| 11-Aug | @ HOU | L | 0 | 3 | 62-49 | 2 | 8 | Griffin | McAndrew |
| 12-Aug | @ HOU | L | 7 | 8 | 62-50 | 2 | 9 | Wilson | Koosman |
| 13-Aug | @ HOU | L | 2 | 8 | 62-51 | 3 | 10 | Dierker | Gentry |
| 16-Aug | SDP | W | 2 | 0 | 63-51 | 2 | 9 | Seaver | Sisk |
| 16-Aug | SDP | W | 2 | 1 | 64-51 | 2 | 9 | McAndrew | Ross |
| 17-Aug | SDP | W | 3 | 2 | 65-51 | 2 | 8 | Koosman | Niekro |
| 17-Aug | SDP | W | 3 | 2 | 66-51 | 2 | 8 | Cardwell | Kirby |
| 19-Aug | SFG | W | 1 | 0 | 67-51 | 2 | 8 | McGraw | Marichal |
| 20-Aug | SFG | W | 6 | 0 | 68-51 | 2 | 7 | McAndrew | Perry |
| 21-Aug | SFG | L | 6 | 7 | 68-52 | 2 | 7 | McMahon | Taylor |
| 22-Aug | LAD | W | 5 | 3 | 69-52 | 2 | 6 | Koosman | Singer |
| 23-Aug | LAD | W | 3 | 2 | 70-52 | 2 | 6 | Taylor | Brewer |
| 24-Aug | LAD | W | 7 | 4 | 71-52 | 2 | 5.5 | Koonce | Sutton |
| 26-Aug | @ SDP | W | 8 | 4 | 72-52 | 2 | 3.5 | Seaver | Sisk |
| 26-Aug | @ SDP | W | 3 | 0 | 73-52 | 2 | 3.5 | McAndrew | Niekro |
| 27-Aug | @ SDP | W | 4 | 1 | 74-52 | 2 | 2.5 | Koosman | Kirby |
| 29-Aug | @ SFG | L | 0 | 5 | 74-53 | 2 | 4 | Marichal | Gentry |
| 30-Aug | @ SFG | W | 3 | 2 | 75-53 | 2 | 4 | McGraw | Perry |
| 31-Aug | @ SFG | W | 8 | 0 | 76-53 | 2 | 4.5 | Seaver | McCormick |
| 31-Aug | @ SFG | L | 2 | 3 | 76-54 | 2 | 4.5 | Linzy | McGraw |
| 1-Sep | @ LAD | L | 6 | 10 | 76-55 | 2 | 5 | Bunning | Koosman |
| 2-Sep | @ LAD | W | 5 | 4 | 77-55 | 2 | 5 | Gentry | Sutton |
| 3-Sep | @ LAD | L | 4 | 5 | 77-56 | 2 | 5 | Mikkelsen | DiLauro |
| 5-Sep | PHI | W | 5 | 1 | 78-56 | 2 | 4.5 | Seaver | Jackson |
| 5-Sep | PHI | L | 2 | 4 | 78-57 | 2 | 4.5 | Wise | McAndrew |
| 6-Sep | PHI | W | 3 | 0 | 79-57 | 2 | 3.5 | Cardwell | Johnson |
| 7-Sep | PHI | W | 9 | 3 | 80-57 | 2 | 2.5 | Ryan | Champion |
| 8-Sep | CHC | W | 3 | 2 | 81-57 | 2 | 1.5 | Koosman | Hands |
| 9-Sep | CHC | W | 7 | 1 | 82-57 | 2 | 0.5 | Seaver | Jenkins |
| 10-Sep | MON | W | 3 | 2 | 83-57 | 1 | up 1.0 | Taylor | Stoneman |
| 10-Sep | MON | W | 7 | 1 | 84-57 | 1 | up 1.0 | Ryan | Reed |
| 11-Sep | MON | W | 4 | 0 | 85-57 | 1 | up 2.0 | Gentry | Robertson |
| 12-Sep | @ PIT | W | 1 | 0 | 86-57 | 1 | up 2.5 | Koosman | Moose |
| 12-Sep | @ PIT | W | 1 | 0 | 87-57 | 1 | up 2.5 | Cardwell | Ellis |
| 13-Sep | @ PIT | W | 5 | 2 | 88-57 | 1 | up 3.5 | Seaver | Walker |
| 14-Sep | @ PIT | L | 3 | 5 | 88-58 | 1 | up 3.5 | Blass | Ryan |
| 15-Sep | @ STL | W | 4 | 3 | 89-58 | 1 | up 4.5 | McGraw | Carlton |
| 17-Sep | @ MON | W | 5 | 0 | 90-58 | 1 | up 4.0 | Koosman | Waslewski |
| 18-Sep | @ MON | W | 2 | 0 | 91-58 | 1 | up 5.0 | Seaver | Stoneman |
| 19-Sep | PIT | L | 2 | 8 | 91-59 | 1 | up 4.0 | Veale | Ryan |
| 19-Sep | PIT | L | 0 | 8 | 91-60 | 1 | up 4.0 | Walker | McAndrew |
| 20-Sep | PIT | L | 0 | 4 | 91-61 | 1 | up 4.0 | Moose | Gentry |
| 21-Sep | PIT | W | 5 | 3 | 92-61 | 1 | up 4.5 | Koosman | Ellis |
| 21-Sep | PIT | W | 6 | 1 | 93-61 | 1 | up 4.5 | Cardwell | Blass |
| 22-Sep | STL | W | 3 | 1 | 94-61 | 1 | up 5.0 | Seaver | Briles |
| 23-Sep | STL | W | 3 | 2 | 95-61 | 1 | up 6.0 | McGraw | Gibson |
| 24-Sep | STL | W | 6 | 0 | 96-61 | 1 | up 6.0 | Gentry | Carlton |
| 26-Sep | @ PHI | W | 5 | 0 | 97-61 | 1 | up 7.0 | Koosman | Fryman |
| 27-Sep | @ PHI | W | 1 | 0 | 98-61 | 1 | up 8.0 | Seaver | Jackson |
| 28-Sep | @ PHI | W | 2 | 0 | 99-61 | 1 | up 8.0 | Gentry | Johnson |
| 1-Oct | @ CHC | W | 6 | 5 | 100-61 | 1 | up 9.0 | Taylor | Selma |
| 2-Oct | @ CHC | L | 3 | 5 | 100-62 | 1 | up 8.0 | Decker | Cardwell |

# STATISTICS FOR POSTSEASON 1969

## 1969 NLCS — METS vs. BRAVES

**Game 1: Saturday, October 4, 1969 at Atlanta Fulton County Stadium (Atlanta Braves)**

| | 1 | 2 | 3 | 4 | 5 | 6 | 7 | 8 | 9 | R | H | E |
|---|---|---|---|---|---|---|---|---|---|---|---|---|
| New York Mets | 0 | 2 | 0 | 2 | 0 | 0 | 0 | 5 | 0 | 9 | 10 | 1 |
| Atlanta Braves | 0 | 1 | 2 | 0 | 1 | 0 | 1 | 0 | 0 | 5 | 10 | 2 |

**PITCHERS:** NYM - Seaver, Taylor (8)
ATL - Niekro, Upshaw (9)
**WP:** Tom Seaver
**LP:** Phil Niekro
**SAVE:** Ron Taylor
**HOME RUNS:** NYM - none
ATL - Aaron, Gonzalez
ATTENDANCE: 50,122

**Game 2: Sunday, October 5, 1969 at Atlanta Fulton County Stadium (Atlanta Braves)**

| | 1 | 2 | 3 | 4 | 5 | 6 | 7 | 8 | 9 | R | H | E |
|---|---|---|---|---|---|---|---|---|---|---|---|---|
| New York Mets | 1 | 3 | 2 | 2 | 1 | 0 | 2 | 0 | 0 | 11 | 13 | 1 |
| Atlanta Braves | 0 | 0 | 0 | 1 | 5 | 0 | 0 | 0 | 0 | 6 | 9 | 3 |

**PITCHERS:** NYM - Koosman, Taylor (5), McGraw (7)
ATL - Reed, Doyle (2), Pappas (3), Britton (6), Upshaw (6), Neibauer (9)
**WP:** Ron Taylor
**LP:** Ron Reed
**SAVE:** Tug McGraw
**HOME RUNS:** NYM - none
ATL - Aaron, Gonzalez
ATTENDANCE: 50,270

**Game 3: Monday, October 6, 1969 at Shea Stadium (New York Mets)**

| | 1 | 2 | 3 | 4 | 5 | 6 | 7 | 8 | 9 | R | H | E |
|---|---|---|---|---|---|---|---|---|---|---|---|---|
| Atlanta Braves | 2 | 0 | 0 | 0 | 2 | 0 | 0 | 0 | 0 | 4 | 8 | 1 |
| New York Mets | 0 | 0 | 1 | 2 | 3 | 1 | 0 | 0 | x | 7 | 14 | 0 |

**PITCHERS:** ATL - Jarvis, Stone (5), Upshaw (6)
NYM - Gentry, Ryan (3)
**WP** - Nolan Ryan
**LP** - Pat Jarvis
**SAVE** - none
**HOME RUNS:** ATL - Aaron, Cepeda
NYM - Agee, Boswell, Garrett
ATTENDANCE: 54,195

**NLCS METS BATTING**

| | G | AB | R | H | 2B | 3B | HR | RBI | BB | SO | BA | OBP | SLG | OPS | SB | CS |
|---|---|---|---|---|---|---|---|---|---|---|---|---|---|---|---|---|
| Tommie Agee | 3 | 14 | 4 | 5 | 1 | 0 | 2 | 4 | 2 | 5 | .357 | .438 | .857 | 1.295 | 2 | 0 |
| Ken Boswell | 3 | 12 | 3 | 4 | 0 | 0 | 2 | 5 | 1 | 2 | .333 | .385 | .833 | 1.218 | 0 | 0 |
| Wayne Garrett | 3 | 13 | 3 | 5 | 2 | 0 | 1 | 3 | 2 | 2 | .385 | .467 | .769 | 1.236 | 1 | 0 |
| Rod Gaspar | 3 | 0 | 0 | 0 | 0 | 0 | 0 | 0 | 0 | 0 | - | - | - | - | 0 | 0 |
| Gary Gentry | 1 | 0 | 0 | 0 | 0 | 0 | 0 | 0 | 0 | 0 | - | - | - | - | 0 | 0 |
| Jerry Grote | 3 | 12 | 3 | 2 | 1 | 0 | 0 | 1 | 1 | 4 | .167 | .231 | .250 | .481 | 0 | 0 |
| Bud Harrelson | 3 | 11 | 2 | 2 | 1 | 1 | 0 | 3 | 1 | 2 | .182 | .250 | .455 | .705 | 0 | 0 |
| Cleon Jones | 3 | 14 | 4 | 6 | 2 | 0 | 1 | 4 | 1 | 2 | .429 | .467 | .786 | 1.252 | 2 | 0 |
| Jerry Koosman | 1 | 2 | 1 | 0 | 0 | 0 | 0 | 0 | 1 | 2 | .000 | .333 | .000 | .333 | 0 | 0 |
| Ed Kranepool | 3 | 12 | 2 | 3 | 1 | 0 | 0 | 1 | 1 | 2 | .250 | .308 | .333 | .641 | 0 | 1 |
| J.C. Martin | 2 | 2 | 0 | 1 | 0 | 0 | 0 | 2 | 0 | 0 | .500 | .500 | .500 | 1.000 | 0 | 0 |
| Tug McGraw | 1 | 0 | 0 | 0 | 0 | 0 | 0 | 0 | 0 | 0 | - | - | - | - | 0 | 0 |
| Nolan Ryan | 1 | 4 | 1 | 2 | 0 | 0 | 0 | 0 | 0 | 1 | .500 | .500 | .500 | 1.000 | 0 | 0 |
| Tom Seaver | 1 | 3 | 0 | 0 | 0 | 0 | 0 | 0 | 0 | 0 | .000 | .000 | .000 | .000 | 0 | 0 |
| Art Shamsky | 3 | 13 | 3 | 7 | 0 | 0 | 0 | 1 | 0 | 3 | .538 | .538 | .538 | 1.077 | 0 | 0 |
| Ron Taylor | 2 | 0 | 0 | 0 | 0 | 0 | 0 | 0 | 0 | 0 | - | - | - | - | 0 | 0 |
| Al Weis | 3 | 1 | 1 | 0 | 0 | 0 | 0 | 0 | 0 | 0 | .000 | .000 | .000 | .000 | 0 | 0 |
| **Totals** | **39** | **113** | **27** | **37** | **8** | **1** | **6** | **24** | **10** | **25** | **.327** | **.382** | **.575** | **.957** | **5** | **1** |

**NLCS BRAVES BATTING**

| | G | AB | R | H | 2B | 3B | HR | RBI | BB | SO | BA | OBP | SLG | OPS | SB | CS |
|---|---|---|---|---|---|---|---|---|---|---|---|---|---|---|---|---|
| Hank Aaron | 3 | 14 | 3 | 5 | 2 | 0 | 3 | 7 | 0 | 1 | .357 | .357 | 1.143 | 1.500 | 0 | 0 |
| Tommie Aaron | 1 | 1 | 0 | 0 | 0 | 0 | 0 | 0 | 0 | 0 | .000 | .000 | .000 | .000 | 0 | 0 |
| Felipe Alou | 1 | 1 | 0 | 0 | 0 | 0 | 0 | 0 | 0 | 0 | .000 | .000 | .000 | .000 | 0 | 0 |
| Bob Aspromonte | 3 | 3 | 0 | 0 | 0 | 0 | 0 | 0 | 0 | 0 | .000 | .000 | .000 | .000 | 0 | 0 |
| Clete Boyer | 3 | 9 | 0 | 1 | 0 | 0 | 0 | 3 | 2 | 3 | .111 | .25 | .111 | .361 | 0 | 0 |
| Jim Britton | 1 | 0 | 0 | 0 | 0 | 0 | 0 | 0 | 0 | 0 | - | - | - | - | 0 | 0 |
| Rico Carty | 3 | 10 | 4 | 3 | 2 | 0 | 0 | 0 | 3 | 1 | .300 | .462 | .500 | .962 | 0 | 0 |
| Orlando Cepeda | 3 | 11 | 2 | 5 | 2 | 0 | 1 | 3 | 1 | 2 | .455 | .538 | .909 | 1.448 | 1 | 0 |
| Bob Didier | 3 | 11 | 0 | 0 | 0 | 0 | 0 | 0 | 0 | 2 | .000 | .000 | .000 | .000 | 0 | 0 |
| Paul Doyle | 1 | 0 | 0 | 0 | 0 | 0 | 0 | 0 | 0 | 0 | - | - | - | - | 0 | 0 |
| Gil Garrido | 3 | 10 | 0 | 2 | 0 | 0 | 0 | 0 | 1 | 1 | .200 | .273 | .200 | .473 | 0 | 0 |
| Tony Gonzalez | 3 | 14 | 4 | 5 | 1 | 0 | 1 | 2 | 1 | 4 | .357 | .4 | .643 | 1.043 | 0 | 0 |
| Sonny Jackson | 1 | 0 | 0 | 0 | 0 | 0 | 0 | 0 | 0 | 0 | - | - | - | - | 0 | 0 |
| Pat Jarvis | 1 | 2 | 0 | 0 | 0 | 0 | 0 | 0 | 0 | 2 | .000 | .000 | .000 | .000 | 0 | 0 |
| Mike Lum | 2 | 2 | 0 | 2 | 1 | 0 | 0 | 0 | 0 | 0 | 1.000 | 1.000 | 1.500 | 2.500 | 0 | 0 |
| Felix Millan | 3 | 12 | 2 | 4 | 1 | 0 | 0 | 0 | 3 | 0 | .333 | .467 | .417 | .883 | 0 | 0 |
| Gary Neibauer | 1 | 0 | 0 | 0 | 0 | 0 | 0 | 0 | 0 | 0 | - | - | - | - | 0 | 0 |
| Phil Niekro | 1 | 3 | 0 | 0 | 0 | 0 | 0 | 0 | 0 | 1 | .000 | .000 | .000 | .000 | 0 | 0 |
| Milt Pappas | 1 | 1 | 0 | 0 | 0 | 0 | 0 | 0 | 0 | 1 | .000 | .000 | .000 | .000 | 0 | 0 |
| Ron Reed | 1 | 0 | 0 | 0 | 0 | 0 | 0 | 0 | 0 | 0 | - | - | - | - | 0 | 0 |
| George Stone | 1 | 1 | 0 | 0 | 0 | 0 | 0 | 0 | 0 | 1 | .000 | .000 | .000 | .000 | 0 | 0 |
| Bob Tillman | 1 | 0 | 0 | 0 | 0 | 0 | 0 | 0 | 0 | 0 | - | - | - | - | 0 | 0 |
| Cecil Upshaw | 3 | 1 | 0 | 0 | 0 | 0 | 0 | 0 | 0 | 1 | .000 | .000 | .000 | .000 | 0 | 0 |
| **Totals** | **44** | **106** | **15** | **27** | **9** | **0** | **5** | **15** | **11** | **20** | **.255** | **.328** | **.481** | **.809** | **1** | **0** |

**NLCS METS PITCHING**

| | G | GS | ERA | W | L | SV | CG | IP | H | ER | BB | SO | WHIP |
|---|---|---|---|---|---|---|---|---|---|---|---|---|---|
| Gary Gentry | 1 | 1 | 9.00 | 0 | 0 | 0 | 0 | 2 | 5 | 2 | 1 | 1 | 3.000 |
| Jerry Koosman | 1 | 1 | 11.57 | 0 | 0 | 0 | 0 | 4.2 | 7 | 6 | 4 | 5 | 2.357 |
| Tug McGraw | 1 | 0 | 0.00 | 0 | 0 | 1 | 0 | 3 | 1 | 0 | 1 | 1 | 0.667 |
| Nolan Ryan | 1 | 0 | 2.57 | 1 | 0 | 0 | 0 | 7 | 3 | 2 | 2 | 7 | 0.714 |
| Tom Seaver | 1 | 1 | 6.43 | 1 | 0 | 0 | 0 | 7 | 8 | 5 | 3 | 2 | 1.571 |
| Ron Taylor | 2 | 0 | 0.00 | 1 | 0 | 1 | 0 | 3.1 | 3 | 0 | 0 | 4 | 0.900 |
| **Totals** | **7** | **3** | **5.00** | **3** | **0** | **2** | **0** | **27** | **27** | **15** | **11** | **20** | **1.407** |

**NLCS BRAVES PITCHING**

| | G | GS | ERA | W | L | SV | CG | IP | H | ER | BB | SO | WHIP |
|---|---|---|---|---|---|---|---|---|---|---|---|---|---|
| Jim Britton | 1 | 0 | 0.00 | 0 | 0 | 0 | 0 | 0.1 | 0 | 0 | 1 | 0 | 3.000 |
| Paul Doyle | 1 | 0 | 0.00 | 0 | 0 | 0 | 0 | 1 | 2 | 0 | 1 | 3 | 3.000 |
| Pat Jarvis | 1 | 1 | 12.46 | 0 | 1 | 0 | 0 | 4.1 | 10 | 6 | 0 | 6 | 2.308 |
| Gary Neibauer | 1 | 0 | 0.00 | 0 | 0 | 0 | 0 | 1 | 0 | 0 | 0 | 1 | 0.000 |
| Phil Niekro | 1 | 1 | 4.50 | 0 | 1 | 0 | 0 | 8 | 9 | 4 | 4 | 4 | 1.625 |
| Milt Pappas | 1 | 0 | 11.57 | 0 | 0 | 0 | 0 | 2.1 | 4 | 3 | 0 | 4 | 1.714 |
| Ron Reed | 1 | 1 | 21.60 | 0 | 1 | 0 | 0 | 1.2 | 5 | 4 | 3 | 3 | 4.800 |
| George Stone | 1 | 0 | 9.00 | 0 | 0 | 0 | 0 | 1 | 2 | 1 | 0 | 0 | 2.000 |
| Cecil Upshaw | 3 | 0 | 2.84 | 0 | 0 | 0 | 0 | 6.1 | 5 | 2 | 1 | 4 | 0.947 |
| **Totals** | **11** | **3** | **6.92** | **0** | **3** | **0** | **0** | **26** | **37** | **20** | **10** | **25** | **1.808** |

*Statisics reprinted courtesy of* baseball-reference.com

# 1969 WORLD SERIES — METS vs. ORIOLES

**Game 1: Saturday, October 11, 1969 at Memorial Stadium (Baltimore Orioles)**

| | 1 | 2 | 3 | 4 | 5 | 6 | 7 | 8 | 9 | R | H | E |
|---|---|---|---|---|---|---|---|---|---|---|---|---|
| New York Mets | 0 | 0 | 0 | 0 | 0 | 0 | 1 | 0 | 0 | 1 | 6 | 1 |
| Baltimore Orioles | 1 | 0 | 0 | 3 | 0 | 0 | 0 | 0 | x | 4 | 6 | 0 |

**PITCHERS:** NYM - Seaver, Cardwell (6), Taylor (7)
BAL - Cuellar
**WP** - Mike Cuellar
**LP** - Tom Seaver
**SAVE** - none
**HOME RUNS:** NYM - none
BAL - Buford
ATTENDANCE: 50,429

**Game 2: Sunday, October 12, 1969 at Memorial Stadium (Baltimore Orioles)**

| | 1 | 2 | 3 | 4 | 5 | 6 | 7 | 8 | 9 | R | H | E |
|---|---|---|---|---|---|---|---|---|---|---|---|---|
| New York Mets | 0 | 0 | 0 | 1 | 0 | 0 | 0 | 0 | 1 | 2 | 6 | 0 |
| Baltimore Orioles | 0 | 0 | 0 | 0 | 0 | 0 | 1 | 0 | 0 | 1 | 2 | 0 |

**PITCHERS:** NYM - Koosman, Taylor (9)
BAL - McNally
**WP** - Jerry Koosman
**LP** - Dave McNally
**SAVE** - Ron Taylor
**HOME RUNS:** NYM - Clendenon
BAL - none
ATTENDANCE: 50,850

**Game 3: Tuesday, October 14, 1969 at Shea Stadium (New York Mets)**

| | 1 | 2 | 3 | 4 | 5 | 6 | 7 | 8 | 9 | R | H | E |
|---|---|---|---|---|---|---|---|---|---|---|---|---|
| Baltimore Orioles | 0 | 0 | 0 | 0 | 0 | 0 | 0 | 0 | 0 | 0 | 4 | 1 |
| New York Mets | 1 | 2 | 0 | 0 | 0 | 1 | 0 | 1 | x | 5 | 6 | 0 |

**PITCHERS:** BAL - Palmer, Leonhard (7)
NYM - Gentry, Ryan (7)
**WP** - Gary Gentry
**LP** - Jim Palmer
**SAVE** - Nolan Ryan
**HOME RUNS:** BAL - none
NYM - Agee, Kranepool
ATTENDANCE: 56,335

**Game 4: Wednesday, October 15, 1969 at Shea Stadium (New York Mets)**

| | 1 | 2 | 3 | 4 | 5 | 6 | 7 | 8 | 9 | 10 | R | H | E |
|---|---|---|---|---|---|---|---|---|---|---|---|---|---|
| Baltimore Orioles | 0 | 0 | 0 | 0 | 0 | 0 | 0 | 0 | 1 | 0 | 1 | 6 | 1 |
| New York Mets | 0 | 1 | 0 | 0 | 0 | 0 | 0 | 0 | 0 | 1 | 2 | 10 | 1 |

**PITCHERS:** BAL - Cuellar, Watt (8), Hall (10), Richert (10)
NYM - Seaver
**WP** - Tom Seaver
**LP** - Dick Hall
**SAVE** - none
**HOME RUNS:** BAL - none
NYM - Clendenon
ATTENDANCE: 57,367

**Game 5: Thursday, October 16, 1969 at Shea Stadium (New York Mets)**

| | 1 | 2 | 3 | 4 | 5 | 6 | 7 | 8 | 9 | R | H | E |
|---|---|---|---|---|---|---|---|---|---|---|---|---|
| Baltimore Orioles | 0 | 0 | 3 | 0 | 0 | 0 | 0 | 0 | 0 | 3 | 5 | 2 |
| New York Mets | 0 | 0 | 0 | 0 | 0 | 2 | 1 | 2 | x | 5 | 7 | 0 |

**PITCHERS:** BAL - McNally, Watt (8)
NYM - Koosman
**WP** - Jerry Koosman
**LP** - Eddie Watt
**SAVE** - none
**HOME RUNS:** BAL - McNally, F. Robinson
NYM - Clendenon, Weis
ATTENDANCE: 57,397

**WORLD SERIES METS BATTING**

| | G | AB | R | H | 2B | 3B | HR | RBI | BB | SO | BA | OBP | SLG | OPS | SB | CS |
|---|---|---|---|---|---|---|---|---|---|---|---|---|---|---|---|---|
| Tommie Agee | 5 | 18 | 1 | 3 | 0 | 0 | 1 | 1 | 2 | 5 | .167 | .250 | .333 | .583 | 1 | 0 |
| Ken Boswell | 1 | 3 | 1 | 1 | 0 | 0 | 0 | 0 | 0 | 0 | .333 | .333 | .333 | .667 | 0 | 0 |
| Don Cardwell | 1 | 0 | 0 | 0 | 0 | 0 | 0 | 0 | 0 | 0 | - | - | - | - | 0 | 0 |
| Ed Charles | 4 | 15 | 1 | 2 | 1 | 0 | 0 | 0 | 0 | 2 | .133 | .133 | .200 | .333 | 0 | 0 |
| Donn Clendenon | 4 | 14 | 4 | 5 | 1 | 0 | 3 | 4 | 2 | 6 | .357 | .438 | 1.071 | 1.509 | 0 | 0 |
| Duffy Dyer | 1 | 1 | 0 | 0 | 0 | 0 | 0 | 0 | 0 | 0 | .000 | .000 | .000 | .000 | 0 | 0 |
| Wayne Garrett | 2 | 1 | 0 | 0 | 0 | 0 | 0 | 0 | 2 | 1 | .000 | .667 | .000 | .667 | 0 | 0 |
| Rod Gaspar | 3 | 2 | 1 | 0 | 0 | 0 | 0 | 0 | 0 | 0 | .000 | .000 | .000 | .000 | 0 | 0 |
| Gary Gentry | 1 | 3 | 0 | 1 | 1 | 0 | 0 | 2 | 0 | 2 | .333 | .333 | .667 | 1.000 | 0 | 0 |
| Jerry Grote | 5 | 19 | 1 | 4 | 2 | 0 | 0 | 1 | 1 | 3 | .211 | .250 | .316 | .566 | 0 | 0 |
| Bud Harrelson | 5 | 17 | 1 | 3 | 0 | 0 | 0 | 0 | 3 | 4 | .176 | .300 | .176 | .476 | 0 | 0 |
| Cleon Jones | 5 | 19 | 2 | 3 | 1 | 0 | 0 | 0 | 0 | 1 | .158 | .200 | .211 | .411 | 0 | 0 |
| Jerry Koosman | 2 | 7 | 0 | 1 | 1 | 0 | 0 | 0 | 0 | 4 | .143 | .143 | .286 | .429 | 0 | 0 |
| Ed Kranepool | 1 | 4 | 1 | 1 | 0 | 0 | 1 | 1 | 0 | 0 | .250 | .250 | 1.000 | 1.250 | 0 | 0 |
| J.C. Martin | 1 | 0 | 0 | 0 | 0 | 0 | 0 | 0 | 0 | 0 | - | - | - | - | 0 | 0 |
| Nolan Ryan | 1 | 0 | 0 | 0 | 0 | 0 | 0 | 0 | 0 | 0 | - | - | - | - | 0 | 0 |
| Tom Seaver | 2 | 4 | 0 | 0 | 0 | 0 | 0 | 0 | 0 | 2 | .000 | .000 | .000 | .000 | 0 | 0 |
| Art Shamsky | 3 | 6 | 0 | 0 | 0 | 0 | 0 | 0 | 0 | 0 | .000 | .000 | .000 | .000 | 0 | 0 |
| Ron Swoboda | 4 | 15 | 1 | 6 | 1 | 0 | 0 | 1 | 1 | 3 | .400 | .438 | .467 | .904 | 0 | 1 |
| Ron Taylor | 2 | 0 | 0 | 0 | 0 | 0 | 0 | 0 | 0 | 0 | - | - | - | - | 0 | 0 |
| Al Weis | 5 | 11 | 1 | 5 | 0 | 0 | 1 | 3 | 4 | 2 | .455 | .563 | .727 | 1.290 | 0 | 0 |
| **Totals** | **58** | **159** | **15** | **35** | **8** | **0** | **6** | **13** | **15** | **35** | **.220** | **.290** | **.384** | **.673** | **1** | **1** |

**WORLD SERIES ORIOLES BATTING**

| | G | AB | R | H | 2B | 3B | HR | RBI | BB | SO | BA | OBP | SLG | OPS | SB | CS |
|---|---|---|---|---|---|---|---|---|---|---|---|---|---|---|---|---|
| Mark Belanger | 5 | 15 | 2 | 3 | 0 | 0 | 0 | 1 | 2 | 1 | .200 | .294 | .200 | .494 | 0 | 0 |
| Paul Blair | 5 | 20 | 1 | 2 | 0 | 0 | 0 | 0 | 2 | 5 | .100 | .182 | .100 | .282 | 1 | 0 |
| Don Buford | 5 | 20 | 1 | 2 | 1 | 0 | 1 | 2 | 2 | 4 | .100 | .182 | .300 | .482 | 0 | 0 |
| Mike Cuellar | 2 | 5 | 0 | 2 | 0 | 0 | 0 | 1 | 0 | 3 | .400 | .400 | .400 | .800 | 0 | 0 |
| Clay Dalrymple | 2 | 2 | 0 | 2 | 0 | 0 | 0 | 0 | 0 | 0 | 1.000 | 1.000 | 1.000 | 2.000 | 0 | 0 |
| Andy Etchebarren | 2 | 6 | 0 | 0 | 0 | 0 | 0 | 0 | 0 | 1 | .000 | .000 | .000 | .000 | 0 | 0 |
| Dick Hall | 1 | 0 | 0 | 0 | 0 | 0 | 0 | 0 | 0 | 0 | - | - | - | - | 0 | 0 |
| Ellie Hendricks | 3 | 10 | 1 | 1 | 0 | 0 | 0 | 0 | 1 | 0 | .100 | .182 | .100 | .282 | 0 | 0 |
| Davey Johnson | 5 | 16 | 1 | 1 | 0 | 0 | 0 | 0 | 2 | 1 | .063 | .167 | .063 | .229 | 0 | 1 |
| Dave Leonhard | 1 | 0 | 0 | 0 | 0 | 0 | 0 | 0 | 0 | 0 | - | - | - | - | 0 | 0 |
| Dave May | 2 | 1 | 0 | 0 | 0 | 0 | 0 | 0 | 1 | 1 | .000 | .500 | .000 | .500 | 0 | 0 |
| Dave McNally | 2 | 5 | 1 | 1 | 0 | 0 | 1 | 2 | 0 | 2 | .200 | .200 | .800 | 1.000 | 0 | 0 |
| Curt Motton | 1 | 1 | 0 | 0 | 0 | 0 | 0 | 0 | 0 | 0 | .000 | .000 | .000 | .000 | 0 | 0 |
| Jim Palmer | 1 | 2 | 0 | 0 | 0 | 0 | 0 | 0 | 0 | 0 | .000 | .000 | .000 | .000 | 0 | 0 |
| Boog Powell | 5 | 19 | 0 | 5 | 0 | 0 | 0 | 0 | 1 | 4 | .263 | .300 | .263 | .563 | 0 | 0 |
| Merv Rettenmund | 1 | 0 | 0 | 0 | 0 | 0 | 0 | 0 | 0 | 0 | - | - | - | - | 0 | 0 |
| Pete Richert | 1 | 0 | 0 | 0 | 0 | 0 | 0 | 0 | 0 | 0 | - | - | - | - | 0 | 0 |
| Brooks Robinson | 5 | 19 | 0 | 1 | 0 | 0 | 0 | 2 | 0 | 3 | .053 | .050 | .053 | .103 | 0 | 0 |
| Frank Robinson | 5 | 16 | 2 | 3 | 0 | 0 | 1 | 1 | 4 | 3 | .188 | .350 | .375 | .725 | 0 | 0 |
| Chico Salmon | 2 | 0 | 0 | 0 | 0 | 0 | 0 | 0 | 0 | 0 | - | - | - | - | 0 | 0 |
| Eddie Watt | 2 | 0 | 0 | 0 | 0 | 0 | 0 | 0 | 0 | 0 | - | - | - | - | 0 | 0 |
| **Totals** | **58** | **157** | **9** | **23** | **1** | **0** | **3** | **9** | **15** | **28** | **.146** | **.220** | **.210** | **.430** | **1** | **1** |

**WORLD SERIES METS PITCHING**

| | G | GS | ERA | W | L | SV | CG | IP | H | ER | BB | SO | WHIP |
|---|---|---|---|---|---|---|---|---|---|---|---|---|---|
| Don Cardwell | 1 | 0 | 0.00 | 0 | 0 | 0 | 0 | 1 | 0 | 0 | 0 | 0 | 0.000 |
| Gary Gentry | 1 | 1 | 0.00 | 1 | 0 | 0 | 0 | 6.2 | 3 | 0 | 5 | 4 | 1.200 |
| Jerry Koosman | 2 | 2 | 2.04 | 2 | 0 | 0 | 1 | 17.2 | 7 | 4 | 4 | 9 | 0.623 |
| Nolan Ryan | 1 | 0 | 0.00 | 0 | 0 | 1 | 0 | 2.1 | 1 | 0 | 2 | 3 | 1.286 |
| Tom Seaver | 2 | 2 | 3.00 | 1 | 1 | 0 | 1 | 15 | 12 | 5 | 3 | 9 | 1.000 |
| Ron Taylor | 2 | 0 | 0.00 | 0 | 0 | 1 | 0 | 2.1 | 0 | 0 | 1 | 3 | 0.429 |
| **Totals** | **9** | **5** | **1.80** | **4** | **1** | **2** | **2** | **45** | **23** | **9** | **15** | **28** | **0.844** |

**WORLD SERIES ORIOLES PITCHING**

| | G | GS | ERA | W | L | SV | CG | IP | H | ER | BB | SO | WHIP |
|---|---|---|---|---|---|---|---|---|---|---|---|---|---|
| Mike Cuellar | 2 | 2 | 1.12 | 1 | 0 | 0 | 1 | 16 | 13 | 2 | 4 | 13 | 1.063 |
| Dick Hall | 1 | 0 | - | 0 | 1 | 0 | 0 | 0 | 1 | 0 | 1 | 0 | - |
| Dave Leonhard | 1 | 0 | 4.50 | 0 | 0 | 0 | 0 | 2 | 1 | 1 | 1 | 1 | 1.000 |
| Dave McNally | 2 | 2 | 2.81 | 0 | 1 | 0 | 1 | 16 | 11 | 5 | 5 | 13 | 1.000 |
| Jim Palmer | 1 | 1 | 6.00 | 0 | 1 | 0 | 0 | 6 | 5 | 4 | 4 | 5 | 1.500 |
| Pete Richert | 1 | 0 | - | 0 | 0 | 0 | 0 | 0 | 0 | 0 | 0 | 0 | - |
| Eddie Watt | 2 | 0 | 3.00 | 0 | 1 | 0 | 0 | 3 | 4 | 1 | 0 | 3 | 1.333 |
| **Totals** | **10** | **5** | **2.72** | **1** | **4** | **0** | **2** | **43** | **35** | **13** | **15** | **35** | **1.163** |

## CONTRIBUTORS

**Mark Armour** (Jim Gosger) is a writer living in Corvallis, Oregon. He is currently finishing up a book on Joe Cronin.

**Eric Aron** (Bud Harrelson, Art Shamsky) is a longtime Mets fan who grew up in Rye, New York, in Westchester County. College brought him to Massachusetts, where he obtained a BA in history from Clark University in Worcester. He then received a master's degree in public/applied history from Northeastern in Boston. Eric has been a SABR member since 2002 and has contributed to other SABR team publications with biographies on Dick Williams, Cecil Cooper, and Alvin Dark. Currently, he is writing a biography of Bob Uecker.

**Mike Bender** (Ken Boswell) was introduced to the joys of baseball at Shea Stadium in the mid-1970s. A native Long Islander—and lifelong Mets fan—he currently resides in Cranston, Rhode Island, with his wife, Amy, and daughters Sarah and Meredith. He received a bachelor's degree in history from Binghamton University, and is currently a senior account executive with United Healthcare. His all-time favorite Met is Mookie Wilson.

**Sam Bernstein** (Jack DiLauro) is a lifelong Mets fan who attended his first game at the Polo Grounds in 1962. Professionally, Sam is a social worker for the Elizabeth, New Jersey public schools. He has contributed articles and biographies for *The National Pastime*, *Deadball Stars of the National League*, *Deadball Stars of the American League*, the Bio-Project, and *Forbes Field Forever*. From 2004 to 2008 he wrote a monthly column on sports history for the *Boston Sports Review*. He graduated from the American University with a BA in history and received a masters in social work from Adelphi University. He resides in West Orange, New Jersey.

**Michael J. Bielawa** ("Red Murff: Scouting a Miracle") has authored baseball histories celebrating New England and Louisiana, and his poetry is permanently housed in the National Baseball Hall of Fame Library. He contributed two pieces in the *Maple Street Press 2009 Mets Annual*. Known as "Bead Man" to the Mets faithful, make sure to say "Let's Go Mets" when you see Mike and his wife Janice at Citi Field.

**Talmage Boston** (Nolan Ryan) is the author of *Baseball and the Baby Boomer: A History, Commentary, and Memoir*, with a foreword by Frank Deford, and preface by Lou Brock (Houston: Bright Sky Press, 2009), from which his chapter on Nolan Ryan for *The Miracle Has Landed* is excerpted. He is also author of *1939: Baseball's Tipping Point*, with a foreword by John Grisham (Houston: Bright Sky Press, 2005); the book was originally published in 1995. He has been a civil litigator in Dallas for more than 30 years, including a term as chair of both the State Bar of Texas' Litigation Section and the Dallas Bar Association's Business Litigation Section. He works in the Dallas office of Winstead PC. He is a Media Member of the Texas Baseball Hall of Fame, and his articles on baseball have appeared in the *Dallas Morning News*, *Fort Worth Star Telegram*, SABR's *Baseball Research Journal*, and the National Baseball Hall of Fame's magazine, *Memories and Dreams*.

**Michael P. Cahill** (Al Weis) was born in New Orleans and graduated from Loyola University there. For Beefield Productions, he has produced and appeared in *The Beauty Queen Of Leenane*, *Long Days Journey Into Night*, *The Playboy Of The Western World*, and *The Lonesome West*. His films include *The Badge*, *Elvis: The Mini-Series*, *Welcome To Academia*, and *Open Road*. He has written *Just Who Is Stocker Fontelieu Anyway?*, the play *Dorothy And Alan*, collaborated on *Miz Caraway and the Kingfish* and *Celtic Christmas*, and curates "The Cahill Archives" at *www.stageclick.com*. Michael's partner in art and life is the actress Janet Shea. He also played for the '69 Mets… in the 10- and 11-year-old league at Lakeshore Playground.

**Rob Edelman** (M. Donald Grant) is the author of *Great Baseball Films* and *Baseball on the Web*. His byline has appeared in many publications, including *Base Ball: A Journal of the Early Game*, *Total Baseball*, and *Baseball and American Culture: Across the Diamond*. He authored the box liner notes and an essay on early baseball films for the Kino on Video DVD *Reel Baseball*, and is the co-author of the biographies *Matthau: A Life* and *Meet the Mertzes*. He is a longtime contributing editor of Leonard Maltin's *Movie Guide*, offers film commentary on WAMC (Northeast) Public Radio, and teaches film history at the University at Albany.

**Doug Feldmann** ("The Black Cat: September 9, 1969") is a professor in the College of Education at Northern Kentucky University and a part-time scout for the Cincinnati Reds. He completed his PhD in curriculum studies at Indiana University, his master's degree in Secondary education at Rockford College, and his bachelor's degree in english and history at Northern Illinois University (where he played baseball and football). He is the author of eight books, including *The 1976 Cincinnati Reds: Last Hurrah for the Big Red Machine*, *St. Louis Cardinals Past and Present*, and *Miracle Collapse: The 1969 Chicago Cubs*, from which this entry was excerpted with permission from the University of Nebraska Press. He has been a multiple-time nominee for the Seymour Medal from the Society for American Baseball Research. A former coach of baseball and football at the high school and college levels, Feldmann is married and lives in Cincinnati, Ohio.

**Irv Goldfarb** (Jerry Koosman) attended his first Mets game at the Polo Grounds on June 26, 1963 and swore that if the Mets won, they'd become his favorite team. Long after he left, Tim Harkness hit a grand slam in the 14th inning and Irv was a Mets fan for life. His first game at Shea Stadium was a doubleheader on May 31, 1964, and long after he left, the Giants won the second game in the 23rd inning, but it didn't change his mind. Irv is currently a unit manager for ABC Television and his articles have appeared in various baseball magazines and SABR publications. He is engaged to a more insane Mets fan than he is.

**Paul Hirsch** (Joe Pignatano) is owner of Paul Hirsch Professional Communications, a marketing and public relations firm in Danville, California. A SABR member since 1983, he was the leader of the Lefty O'Doul Chapter in San Francisco, was a member of the 1998 Convention Committee, helped originate the SABR Donor Program, and currently serves as a director on the SABR Board. Paul and his wife Debbie were married in 1988. Their daughter Rebecca is studying to become an interpreter for the deaf at Cal State Northridge and their son Mark is a left-handed pitcher for a local travel ball team.

**Edward Hoyt** (Ed Charles, Donn Clendenon) is the editor of publications for the National Association of Independent Schools and the founder of the Cranepool Forum (*www.cranepoolforum.net*). He is a lifelong Mets fan.

**William H. Johnson** (Jesse Hudson), an avid A's fan since 1979, is a military analyst and retired Naval Flight Officer. He has contributed several biographies to the SABR Bio-Project, focusing on players from Iowa, as well as an article on the Crybaby Indians of 1940 for the SABR '38 convention program. He lives in Chesapeake, Virginia, with his wife Chris, daughter Marissa, and son Tim.

**Jacob Kanarek** ("A Miracle's Aftermath") is the author of *From First to Worst: The New York Mets, 1973–1977*, with a foreword by Jerry Koosman (McFarland & Company, 2008). His web site is *metsintheseventies.com*. He is an accountant and a member of the Society of Baseball Research. He lives in Lakewood, New Jersey.

**Ron Kaplan** ("Postseason 1969: The Miracle at Willets Point") is the sports and features editor for the *New Jersey Jewish News*.

He also hosts a blog on baseball literature and other media at *www.RKsBaseballBookShelf.wordpress.com* and another on Jews and sports at *www.njjewishnews.com/kaplanskorner.*

**Maxwell Kates** (Rod Gaspar, Tom Seaver, Ron Taylor) works for a boutique accounting firm in Concord, Ontario, a suburb of Toronto. He has lectured at the Limmud Conference at York University and at the SABR annual convention held in Seattle in 2006. His writing has appeared in the journals *The Northern Game and Beyond,* and *The National Pastime,* and in the books *Sock It To 'Em, Tigers* and *Go-Go to Glory*. At age 15, he produced a banner for an ecology project at summer camp which read "Save Water—Don't Send Mets Pitchers to the Showers." The placard was rejected—the camp director was a Mets fan!

**Tara Krieger** (Ed Kranepool) is an editorial producer for *MLB.com.* A lifelong baseball fanatic, she has spent time on staff with *Newsday* and the *Poughkeepsie Journal,* and has contributed to both the Mets and Yankees editions of the *Maple Street Press Annuals.* She lives in New York City and is a member of the Society for American Baseball Research (SABR).

**Bill Lamberty** (Amos Otis), sports information director at Montana State University since 1990, has been a SABR member since 1983, and has served as vice chair of the Deadball Era Committee. Lamberty grew up in Fremont, Nebraska, graduating from the University of Wyoming in 1986. He lives in Bozeman, Montana, with his wife Lynn, and enjoys coaching his son Nate (baseball) and daughter Ellie (basketball).

**Len Levin** (copy editor) is confident that his editing for this book helped him to erase the pain of the 1986 World Series in which the Mets upended his beloved Red Sox. A resident of Providence, Rhode Island, and a lifelong journalist, Len is retired from full-time work but keeps busy editing baseball books. He is happy to report that his wife and two daughters are all baseball fans (to one degree or another).

**Lou Longobardi** ("The Wall: A '69 Mets Quest") is an accountant from Long Island. Besides owning a piece of the original Shea Stadium wall, he is a Beatles aficionado and once sang for Johnny Carson on *The Tonight Show.*

**Bruce Markusen** (Bob Johnson, "Beware of Moose: Buc No-Hits '69 Mets") is the author of seven books on baseball, including the award-winning *A Baseball Dynasty: Charlie Finley's Swingin' A's,* the recipient of the Seymour Medal from the Society for American Baseball Research. He has also written *The Team That Changed Baseball: Roberto Clemente and the 1971 Pittsburgh Pirates, Tales From The Mets Dugout,* and *The Orlando Cepeda Story.* He currently works as a museum teacher at the National Baseball Hall of Fame, the Farmers' Museum, and the Fenimore Art Museum, all located in Cooperstown, New York. In addition to writing for *The Hardball Times* website, he also contributes articles to *Bronx Banter.* Bruce, his wife Sue, and their daughter Madeline reside in Cooperstown.

**Les Masterson** (Wayne Garrett) lives in Malden, Massachusetts, with his wife Danielle and black Lab Jake. He is a New York Mets fan despite having been born and raised in Red Sox Nation. He is a senior editor with HealthLeaders Media and has contributed player profiles to four other SABR books.

***Mets Walk-Offs and Other Minutiae*** ("Putting the Miracle in Miracle Mets," Sidebars) began in 2005 as a blog devoted to chronicling Mets history, with an emphasis on their walk-off wins. It can be found at *http://metswalkoffs.blogspot.com.*

**Bill Nowlin** (Bob Heise, copy editor) is a lifelong Red Sox fan, glad to finally see a certain fielding mishap from the 1986 World Series getting less airtime since 2004. A native Bostonian, he's been vice president of SABR the past five years and is the author or editor of over 20 Red Sox-related books, including the forthcoming *Red Sox by the Numbers* (with Matthew Silverman). In his spare time, he works at his real job as one of the founders of Rounder Records, one of America's largest independent record labels.

**Len Pasculli** (Ron Swoboda), a lifelong New Jersey resident, has been a member of SABR since 2001. He is a lawyer, an adjunct professor, and a father of three. He married Jan, his college sweetheart (Penn State), in 1977. Besides playing at Mets Dream Camp at the Doubleday Farms Baseball Dream Camp (in Carlisle, Pennsylvania), writing for SABR's BioProject, and pulling out his remaining curly hair while managing his Rotisserie League baseball team, his interests include basketball, travel, and theater (watching, not performing).

**Neal Poloncarz** (J.C. Martin) was born and raised in the Philadelphia suburbs. His initial passion for baseball began when his family attended countless games at Veterans Stadium to watch the Philadelphia Phillies. Cupid slung an arrow through his heart (or George Steinbrenner threw money into his wallet, take your pick!) when he attended his first Yankees game at age 16 at the Stadium. A SABR member since 1997, he hosted a sports talk radio show at WVOX 1460-AM, in New Rochelle, New York. An in-studio guest was fellow SABR member and fellow Westchester broadcaster John Vorperian, ardent Red Sox fan. He has also interviewed Arnold Hano, author of *A Day In The Bleachers,* Andy Musser, a retired Philadelphia Phillies play-by-play announcer, and the legendary Detroit Tigers play-by-play announcer and fellow SABR member Mr. Ernie Harwell. Neal's essay is dedicated to Ross Addell who recommended he do some writing for SABR.

**Greg W. Prince** (Al Jackson, "Here's Looking Up Our Old Address," sidebar) is the author of *Faith and Fear in Flushing: An Intense Personal History of the New York Mets* (Skyhorse Publishing, 2009), a book based on the blog of the same name, which Prince has co-written with Jason Fry since 2005; *Faith and Fear* is Prince's first book. He is a regular contributor to the *Maple Street Press Mets Annual* and SNY's *Mets Weekly*; has published baseball essays in the *New York Times,* the *Wall Street Journal* online edition, and on *MLB.com*; consulted on the Billy Joel concert film and documentary *Last Play at Shea*; and is a proud member of the New York Baseball Giants Nostalgia Society. When not following the Mets, Prince works as a communications consultant. He is married to Stephanie Prince and they live on Long Island with their two adorable cats, Hozzie and Avery.

**C. Paul Rogers III** (Jim McAndrew) is president of the Hall-Ruggles (Dallas-Ft. Worth) SABR chapter and the co-author of four baseball books, including *The Whiz Kids and the 1950 Pennant,* written with boyhood hero Robin Roberts, and *Memories of a Ballplayer: Bill Werber and Baseball in the 1930s,* with Bill Werber. His real job is as a law professor at Southern Methodist University in Dallas, Texas, where he served as dean of the law school for nine years.

**John T. Saccoman** (Gil Hodges) is a professor of mathematics and computer science at Seton Hall University in New Jersey. He team-teaches one of the earliest known Sabermetrics courses there with its founder, Rev. Gabe Costa. They, along with Mike Huber, have co-authored two books published by McFarland: *Understanding Sabermetrics* (2008) and *Practicing Sabermetrics* (late 2009). A charter member of the Elysian Fields Chapter of SABR, he resides in northern New Jersey with his son and fellow Mets fan Ryan and BoSox-loving wife Mary.

**Ken Samelson** (coordinating proofreader) is a freelance book editor and writer who grew up in the Bronx the son of a Giants fan mom and Yankees fan dad. He was a regular contributor to New York Mets *Inside Pitch* for 11 years and also served as an associate producer for *Mets Extra* on WFAN Radio from 1987 to 1990. The co-author of *Amazing Mets Trivia, The Great All-Time Baseball Record Book, The Macmillan Baseball Encyclopedia Quiz Book,* and *The Baseball Encyclopedia* (Macmillan), he lives in Larchmont, New York. His two children, Spencer and Lena, are not surprisingly both huge Mets fans.

**Andrew Schiff** (Gary Gentry, Ed Yost) has a master's degree in history from SUNY Albany and is the author of *The Father of Baseball: A Biography of Henry Chadwick.* Schiff is a lifelong Mets fan, attending his first Shea game back in 1976. He misses the old stadium, but he's moved forward to Citi Field.

**Matthew Silverman** (project editor) has written several books on the Mets, including *100 Things Mets Fans Should Know and Do Before They Die, Mets Essential, Shea Goodbye* (with Keith Hernandez), and *Mets by the Numbers* (with Jon Springer). He works as editor with Greg Spira on the *Maple Street Press Mets Annual.* He served as managing editor for *Total Baseball, Total Football, The ESPN Football Encyclopedia,* and as associate editor for *The ESPN Baseball Encyclopedia.* A former associate publisher at Total Sports Publishing, he was lead editor for *Baseball: The Biographical Encyclopedia.* He lives in High Falls, New York.

**Mark Simon** (Bobby Pfeil) grew up in Manhattan and began following the Mets in 1981. He is a researcher for ESPN, working on *Baseball Tonight* and *ESPN.com,* having formerly worked as a sportswriter at the *Trenton Times,* and for one summer as a tour guide at Shea Stadium.

**Curt Smith** ("The Trio: Lindsey Nelson, Bob Murphy, and Ralph Kiner"), dubbed "the voice of authority on baseball broadcasting" by Gannett News Service, is the author of 12 books. A review he prizes was Lindsey Nelson's of the classic *Voices of The Game:* "Absolutely marvelous." Smith wrote more speeches than anyone for former President George H.W. Bush. He is a Gatehouse Media columnist, XM Satellite, and NPR Radio affiliate host, and senior lecturer of English at the University of Rochester.

**Greg Spira** (Danny Frisella) is a writer, editor, and researcher of sports books and other titles. He served as the managing editor of *The ESPN Baseball Encyclopedia* and as an associate editor of *The ESPN Pro Football Encyclopedia.* Born and bred a Mets fan during his childhood in Whitestone, New York, he then attended Harvard College in order to root for the Red Sox against the Yankees. He currently resides in the hostile territory of Philadelphia.

**Jon Springer** (Kevin Collins, Les Rohr) is a New York business writer and former journalist. He is founder of *Mets by the Numbers (www.mbtn.net)* and co-author of the book by that name. He was a contributor to *Armchair Reader: Grand Slam Baseball* and has been a SABR member since 2002. He lives in Brooklyn with wife Heidi and son Ivan.

**Joan M. Thomas** (Joan Payson) is a freelance writer whose baseball essays have appeared in the books *Mudville Diaries, Baseball Stories for the Soul,* and three editions of *Baseball/Literature/Culture.* She is the author of two books, *St. Louis 1875–1940,* and *St. Louis' Big League Ballparks.* She has written a number of biographies for SABR-sponsored publications.

**Adam J. Ulrey** (Duffy Dyer) is a lifetime Los Angeles Dodger fan, working at Sacred Heart Hospital in Eugene, Oregon; contributing writer to the 2006 book *Deadball Stars of the American League.* He enjoys spending much time fly fishing on his creek and the lakes and rivers of Oregon. He lives in Dexter, Oregon with wife Jhody, son Camran, and his two dogs, Behr and Montana.

**Glen Vasey** ("Everyone Comes Home in October") grew up rooting for the incredible Oriole teams of the 1960s through the early 1980s, became fascinated with the history and personalities in the game, and is currently working on an alternative history novel that examines a different road to the integration of baseball than the one Robinson and Rickey took. By day he is a mild-mannered parking meter technician and town friendly guy in Lancaster, Pennsylvania.

**John Vorperian** (Tommie Agee, Johnny Murphy) is host and producer of *Beyond the Game,* a sports history television program (*www.rbpa.tv*). He is also the sports law professor and director of Concordia College Sports Institute in New York. Thanks to Strat-O-Matic, he also piloted the 1962 Metropolitans—that traumatic childhood experience dashed any big league skipper dreams and set him for a team less likely to frustrate his hopes: the Boston Red Sox. He fulfilled a baseball fantasy and played Shea's hot corner in a charity game for Ron Hunt's Foundation. In his first visit to Shea, Vorperian saw Len Dawson's Chiefs outpoint Joe Namath's Jets, but he did get to meet Lindsey Nelson. The year 1969 will always be memorable because of an upstate New York concert, two gents walking the Sea of Tranquility, and a world championship by some Amazin' guys in Queens.

**Joseph Wancho** (Jerry Grote) lives in Westlake, Ohio, and is a lifelong Cleveland Indians fan. Working at AT&T since 1994 as a Process/Development Manager, he has been a SABR member since 2005. He has contributed to three other biography book projects and has written several biographies on the SABR Bio-Project website.

**Dave Williams** (Yogi Berra, Rube Walker) resides in Glastonbury, Connecticut with his wife Julia and daughter Clara. Their unwavering support of him is something he cherishes more than they know. He was six years old in 1969 when the Amazin' Mets embarked on their miracle ride and made him a fan for life. Dave has been a territory manager with Wilson Sporting Goods since 1998 and a SABR member since 2001. He has also contributed to other SABR biography projects, including bios of Tim McCarver, Mike Ryan, and Jim Russell.

**Linc Wonham** ("Rocky Vs. Lefty") is a freelance writer living in Eugene, Oregon. He has been contributing to baseball books and publications for 20 years, and his earliest—and still fondest—memories are as a four-year-old fan watching the 1969 Mets season unfold on a 12-inch, black-and-white television screen in his family's New York City apartment.

**Dr. Fred Worth** (Cleon Jones) has earned a BS (Evangel College in Springfield, Missouri), MS, and PhD (University of Missouri-Rolla) in mathematics. He is a mathematics professor at Henderson State University in Arkadelphia, Arkansas. He is associate pastor at Twin Rivers Church of the Nazarene. Fred and his wife, Beth, have one son, Mark, who lives in Wichita, Kansas with his wife, Debra. Fred is active in homeschooling, having spoken at numerous conventions across the country. He has been an avid Mets fan since the mid-1960s. His main baseball research interest is visiting graves of ballplayers.

**Al Yellon** ("Cubs Eye View") began his life as a Cubs fan in what could have, should have, been a golden era for his team—watching Hall of Famers Ernie Banks, Billy Williams, Fergie Jenkins, and the guy who should be in the Hall, Ron Santo. He's seen many thrills over the years, but not the ultimate one, winning a championship. A television director at ABC-7 in Chicago by day, he is also the editor of the *Maple Street Press Cubs Annual* and co-author of *Cubs By The Numbers* from Skyhorse Publishing: stories of every Cub who has worn a uniform number since the Cubs first donned digits in 1932. He lives two and a half miles from Wrigley Field and can be found in the left-field bleachers for virtually every home game.